Cultural Property in War: Improvement in Protection

CULTURAL PROPERTY IN WAR: IMPROVEMENT IN PROTECTION

COMMENTARY ON THE 1999 SECOND PROTOCOL TO THE HAGUE CONVENTION OF 1954 FOR THE PROTECTION OF CULTURAL PROPERTY IN THE EVENT OF ARMED CONFLICT

Jiří Toman

Ethics series

UNESCO Publishing

Published in 2009 by the United Nations Educational,
Scientific and Cultural Organization
7, place de Fontenoy, 75352 Paris 07 SP, France

ISBN 978-92-3-104142-6

Cover design by Jacqueline Gensollen-Bloch for UNESCO Publishing
Typeset by Oriata Création for UNESCO Publishing
Printed by Imprimerie Laballery, Clamecy

Printed in France

CONTENTS

PREFACE

In 1996 my article-by-article commentary on the 1954 *Hague Convention for the Protection of Cultural Property in the Event of Armed Conflict* was published. That book traced the historical development of international law concerning the protection of cultural property in the event of armed conflict, including an analysis of the 1863 Lieber Code, the 1899 and 1907 Hague Conventions, the 1935 Washington Pact, the relevant provisions of the two 1977 Additional Protocols, and Protocols II and III to the 1980 Convention on Conventional Weapons.

Since 1996 international law concerning the protection of cultural property in the event of armed conflict has continued to develop. Following an eight-year review of the Hague Convention, initiated by the Secretariat of UNESCO and a number of interested States, the March 1999 Hague Diplomatic Conference elaborated and adopted the *Second Protocol to the Hague Convention*. The Second Protocol entered into force on 9 March 2004. At the time of the writing of this commentary, 55 States were party to the Second Protocol and others were considering becoming party to it. The international community now has an additional instrument to reinforce the administrative, legal, military and technical aspects of the protection of cultural property.

When I was approached by the Secretariat of UNESCO to prepare an article-by-article commentary on the Second Protocol, I readily accepted. I decided not only to comment on each article of the Second Protocol but also to compare each of its articles with the relevant provisions of the Convention because the two are often intertwined. This was necessary because we have recently witnessed a number of important events in the development of international law: case-law developments by the International Criminal Tribunal for the former Yugoslavia related to the protection of cultural property in the event of armed conflict, and the adoption of the Rome Statute with its two provisions exclusively focused on such protection.

I hope that my work will contribute to a better understanding of the Second Protocol and, above all, to the better protection of cultural property both in peacetime and during war.

ACKNOWLEDGEMENTS

I would like to express my deep gratitude to Mr Jan Hladík of UNESCO. I would also like to extend my thanks to the Kingdom of the Netherlands authorities, whose generous support made the publication of this work possible. I am also grateful to the Santa Clara University and its school of law for providing me with facilities for the realization of this study.

The ideas and opinions expressed in this book are mine and do not necessarily represent the views of the Kingdom of the Netherlands, UNESCO or any other institution with which the author is associated.

ABBREVIATIONS

AJIL *American Journal of International Law*
BYIL *British Yearbook of International Law*
CDDH Diplomatic Conference on the Reaffirmation and Development of International Humanitarian Law Applicable in Armed Conflicts (1974–1977)
Convention (*also* Hague Convention) *Convention for the Protection of Cultural Property in the Event of Armed Conflict*, adopted at The Hague on 14 May 1954.
1980 Convention *Convention on Prohibition or Restriction on the Use of Certain Conventional Weapons which may be deemed to be excessively injurious or to have indiscriminate effects*. Adopted in Geneva, 10 October 1980 and its Protocols I–III. Protocol II as amended on 3 May 1996. Protocol IV adopted on 13 October 1995.
Diplomatic Conference 1974–1977 Diplomatic Conference on the Reaffirmation and Development of International Humanitarian Law Applicable in Armed Conflicts (1974–1977).
Draft Second Protocol, 1999 *Draft Second Protocol to the 1954 Hague Convention for the Protection of Cultural Property in the Event of Armed Conflict*. UNESCO document HC/1999/1/rev.1, February 1999.
Hague Convention (*also* Convention) *Convention for the Protection of Cultural Property in the Event of Armed Conflict, adopted at The Hague on 14 May 1954.*
ICA International Council on Archives
ICC International Criminal Court
ICCROM International Centre for the Study of the Preservation and Restoration of Cultural Property
ICJ International Court of Justice
ICOMOS International Council on Monuments and Sites
ICRC International Committee of the Red Cross
ICTR International Criminal Tribunal for Rwanda
ICTY International Criminal Tribunal for the former Yugoslavia
IGO Intergovernmental organization
Informal session, 1993 *UNESCO Informal open-ended information session*, Paris, 9 February 1993
IRRC *International Review of the Red Cross* (Geneva)

[IUCN]   International Union for Conservation of Nature and Natural Resources. [Use of the name 'World Conservation Union' began in 1990, but the full name and acronym are often used together since many people still know the Union as IUCN.]

Meeting of Experts, The Hague, 1993   *Report Meeting of Experts on the application and effectiveness of the Convention for the Protection of Cultural Property in the Event of Armed Conflict (The Hague, 14 May 1954).* The Hague, 5–7 July 1993. UNESCO document 142 EX/15.

Meeting of Experts (Second), Lauswolt, 1994   *The Second Expert meeting on the 1954 Hague Convention for the Protection of Cultural Property in the Event of Armed Conflict.* Lauswolt, The Netherlands, 9–11 February 1994. CLT/95/CONF/009/2, 11 p.

Meeting of Experts, The Hague, 1993   *Report Meeting of Experts on the application and effectiveness of the Convention for the Protection of Cultural Property in the Event of Armed Conflict (The Hague, 14 May 1954).* The Hague, 5–7 July 1993. UNESCO document 142 EX/15.

Meeting of Experts (Third), UNESCO, Paris, 1994   *Expert meeting on the Review of the 1954 Hague Convention for the Protection of Cultural Property in the Event of Armed Conflict. Paris, 28 November–2 December 1994.* UNESCO document CLT/CH/94/608/2.

Meeting of Governmental Experts, Paris, 1997   *UNESCO, Meeting of Governmental Experts on the Review of the 1954 Hague Convention for the Protection of Cultural Property in the Event of Armed Conflict. Paris, 24–27 March 1997.* UNESCO document CLT-96/CONF.603/5, Paris, 30 April 1997.

Meeting of Governmental Experts, Vienna, 1998   *Meeting of Governmental Experts on the revision of the Hague Convention for the Protection of Cultural Property in the Event of Armed Conflict of 1954. Vienna, 11–13 May 1998.*

Meeting of the High Contracting Parties (Third), 1997   *UNESCO, Third Meeting of the High Contracting Parties to the Convention for the Protection of Cultural Property in the Event of Armed Conflict (The Hague, 1954). UNESCO House, Paris, 13 November 1997.* UNESCO document CLT-97/CONF.208/3.

NGO   Non-governmental organization

PCIJ   Permanent Court of International Justice

Preliminary Draft Convention of 1938   Preliminary Draft of the International Convention for the Protection of Historic Buildings and Works of Art in Time of War. *International Museum Office, 1938* (League of Nations Official Journal, XIXth year, No. 11, November 1938).

Preliminary Draft Second Protocol 1998   *Preliminary Draft Second Protocol to the 1954 Hague Convention.* UNESCO document HC/1999/1, October 1998.

Records 1954   Intergovernmental Conference on the Protection of Cultural Property in the Event of Armed Conflict. *Records of the Conference convened by the United Nations Educational, Scientific and Cultural Organization and held at The Hague from 21 April to 14 May 1954, published by the Government of The Netherlands.* The Hague: Staatsdrukkerij en Uitgeverijbedrijf, 1961, 452 p.

Regulations for execution   Regulations for the execution of the 1954 Convention for the Protection of Cultural Property in the Event of Armed Conflict.

1996 Summary of comments   UNESCO, Meeting of Governmental Experts. *Summary of comments received from States Parties to the Hague Convention and from International Council on Archives.* UNESCO document CLT-96/CONF.603/INF.4, Paris, December 1996.

1999 Summary of comments   UNESCO, *Summary of comments on Preliminary Draft Second Protocol to the 1954 Hague Convention received from the High Contracting Parties to the Hague Convention for the Protection of Cultural Property in the Event of Armed Conflict 1954, other UNESCO Member States and international organizations.* Paris, 15 January 1999.

UK   United Kingdom

UN   United Nations

UNDP   United Nations Development Programme

UNESCO   United Nations Educational, Scientific and Cultural Organization

UNESCO Draft, 1954   CBC/3 – Text of the Draft Convention, the Regulations for its Execution and the Protocol which formed the basis of the discussions at the Hague Conference. See *Records of the Conference convened by the United Nations Educational, Scientific and Cultural Organization and held at The Hague from 21 April to 14 May 1954 published by the Government of The Netherlands.* The Hague: Staatsdrukkerij en Uitgeverijbedrijf, 1961.

US   United States of America

PART I

COMMENTARY ON THE *SECOND PROTOCOL TO THE HAGUE CONVENTION OF 1954 FOR THE PROTECTION OF CULTURAL PROPERTY IN THE EVENT OF ARMED CONFLICT* (1999)

GENERAL INTRODUCTION:
THE ROAD TO THE SECOND PROTOCOL

IMPLEMENTATION MEASURES AFTER SIGNATURE OF THE CONVENTION

First implementation measures

During the years following the adoption of the 1954 Hague Convention, UNESCO's bodies and its Secretariat made an effort to improve implementation of the Convention and the participation of States in its application.

The first joint effort of the States Parties to the Convention and UNESCO was the *First Meeting of the High Contracting Parties*, held at UNESCO from 16 to 25 July 1962.[1] Thirty-nine States Parties participated in this meeting together with 18 States non-Parties to the Convention which sent observers. If for no other reason than the broad participation of both Parties and non-Parties to the Convention, this meeting may be deemed a success.

No amendments were proposed at this meeting, which confined its proceedings to the examination of problems concerning the application of the Convention. It considered that in order 'to encourage other States to become Parties to the Convention and to facilitate its application, it ought also to make some suggestions for future action'.

The Netherlands Government raised the question of the interpretation of Article 8 of the Convention. The problem concerned, in particular, the interpretation of the expressions 'adequate distance', 'centres containing monuments' and 'other immovable cultural property of very great importance'. The participants were unable to arrive at a more precise definition of those terms and instead proposed the establishment of an advisory committee responsible for certain tasks, such as the study of a specific problem.[2] The participants also agreed that the Convention and the measures taken in

---

1   Report of the meeting, document UNESCO/CUA/120 of 3 September 1962.
2   For further details concerning the committee, see CUA/120, p. 3 et seq. See also Toman (1983), p. 78 et seq.

conformity with its provisions were 'an effective means of protecting cultural property against the dangers to which it is exposed even in time of peace'.

During the discussion the Polish Delegation drew attention to potential issues arising from the application of the text of the Convention:

1) Should difficulties in interpreting the Convention emerge and should the procedure it laid down for its application prove inadequate, the Committee, which was established by its own recommendation, may prove useful.

2) In the case of clauses likely to weaken the effectiveness of the Convention, such as the possibility of waiving special protection in the event of unavoidable military necessity, there would be no other means of remedying the matter than to contemplate a review of the Convention, in the manner provided for by the Convention itself.[3]

The meeting set up a group of experts to examine certain problems concerning application of the Convention, and their report was annexed to the report of the meeting.

At the conclusion of the general discussion, the following points were stressed:

a) the desirability of ensuring that as many States as possible become Parties to the Convention;

b) the importance of taking action at the national level for implementation of the Convention, such as preparation of inventories and exchange of information; and

c) the part that should be played, in compliance with Resolution II adopted by the Hague Conference, by the National Committees set up to advise on the implementation of the Convention.

In 1970, at the request of the Executive Board, the Director-General of UNESCO consulted the States Parties to the Convention on the advisability of convening a new meeting of the High Contracting Parties. Twenty-three States replied, 19 of which were in favour, with various qualifications, and four against. The results of this consultation could not be interpreted as an express request on the part of at least one-fifth of the High Contracting Parties as required by Article 27 of the Convention. After examining the replies received and taking budget resources into account, the Executive Board endorsed the Director-General's view and decided that it would be advisable not to convene a meeting 'in the present circumstances'.[4]

---

3   Report of the meeting, document UNESCO/CUA/120 of 3 September 1962, p. 5, para. 19.
4   Document 87 EX/32 Draft, item 4.4.1.

The 1983 Vienna legal experts meeting

In an effort to improve implementation of the Convention, UNESCO convened a meeting of legal experts, who met in Vienna from 17 to 19 October 1983. In their conclusions, the experts recognized the importance of the Convention but criticized it for being insufficiently effective; they also recommended the organization of a conference of all Member States of the Organization. Special care was given to the preparation of the conference, which was accompanied by a wide-ranging campaign to raise public awareness in which the National Commissions for UNESCO, and many other national and international organizations, participated. The aforementioned institutions encouraged the establishment of national advisory committees, as envisaged in Resolution II of the 1954 Hague Conference, as well as the creation of private associations whose help could prove essential. A long-term programme covering the development of teaching and research should form part of overall UNESCO efforts in the field of culture. Legal experts considered it useful to examine important developments affecting the practical application of the Convention, new developments in the nature of conflicts, the results of the reaffirmation and development of humanitarian international law from 1974 to 1977, and, above all, the adoption of two articles concerning the protection of cultural property by the 1977 Additional Protocols to the Geneva Conventions.

The advisability of convening a meeting of the High Contracting Parties was ruled out:

> On the one hand, if such a meeting were convened, this would risk giving the impression that amendments were necessary to make the Convention more effective. In the present context and, in particular, given the arms reduction talks, any amendment process risked leading to inconclusive results. In these circumstances, the experts considered that it was preferable to direct efforts towards a better application of the Convention in its present form. On the other hand, the interest of States, which were not parties to the Convention could more appropriately be encouraged by convening a conference of all the Member States of UNESCO.[5]

---

5   Meeting of Legal Experts on the Convention for the Protection of Cultural Property in the Event of Armed Conflict (The Hague, 1954), Vienna, 17–19 October 1983, *Final Report* (Paris: UNESCO, 1983), p. 10, para. 31 (CLT-83/CONF.641/1).

It was also considered useful to start by endeavouring to raise the level of awareness of States with respect to the application of the Convention and to promote the ratification of and accession to this important instrument. Furthermore, it was also considered necessary to make an assessment of the current situation and to encourage States to prepare for such a meeting before one was actually convened[6] so as to ensure its success.

In 1988 the Permanent Delegate of the Islamic Republic of Iran, Mr Reza Feiz, informed the Executive Board of UNESCO that he had requested the Director-General to convene a meeting of the High Contracting Parties to the Hague Convention. This information did not elicit a response from the members of the Board.

In the years that followed, the UNESCO Secretariat continued to deal with the legal norms concerning cultural property. It closely followed the implementation of the 1954 Convention, establishing close cooperation with countries that had expressed an interest, in particular, Austria, Germany, Italy, the Netherlands, and Switzerland. The Secretariat also used external consultants to establish a plan of action to improve dissemination and knowledge of the Convention, and began organizing training sessions on a regional basis.

PREPARATORY WORK, 1991–1999

A fundamentally new approach was undertaken in the beginning of the 1990's. It was influenced by new ethnic conflicts that resulted in the destruction of cultural property, particularly in the former Yugoslavia, and, as a consequence, by the willingness of the international community to address this issue by contemplating new amendments or even modifications to the 1954 Hague Convention. This new approach required additional consultative work and a series of expert meetings and preparatory conferences. The result of the long preparatory work was the adoption of the 1999 Second Protocol. Let us now look at the preparatory work.

Table 1.   Review of the 1954 Hague Convention: meetings

UNESCO General Conference, 26th Session (October–November 1991)
Executive Board, 139th Session (May 1992)
Executive Board, 140th Session (October 1992)

---

6   See Toman (1984), pp. 60–62.

Informal, open-ended information session in Paris (9 February 1993)
Executive Board, 141st Session (May 1993)
The Hague Meeting of experts on the application and effectiveness of the Convention for the Protection of Cultural Property in the Event of Armed Conflict (The Hague, 14 May 1954). The Hague, 5–7 July 1993.
Executive Board, 143rd Session (November 1993)
27th session of the General Conference, 27th session (October–November 1993)
Lauswolt Meeting of Experts. Lauswolt, 9–11 February 1994.
Executive Board, 145th Session (November 1994)
Paris Expert Meeting on the review of the 1954 Hague Convention for the Protection of Cultural Property in the Event of Armed Conflict. Paris, UNESCO Headquarters, 28 November–2 December 1994.
Second Meeting of the High Contracting Parties to the Convention for the Protection of Cultural Property in the Event of Armed Conflict (The Hague, 14 May 1954). Paris, UNESCO House, 13 November 1995.
Governmental Experts Meeting on the review of the Convention for the Protection of Cultural Property in the Event of Armed Conflict (The Hague, 14 May 1954). Paris, UNESCO Headquarters, 24–27 March 1997.
Third Meeting of the High Contracting Parties to the Convention for the Protection of Cultural Property in the Event of Armed Conflict (The Hague, 14 May 1954). Paris, UNESCO House, 13 November 1997.
Vienna Governmental Experts Meeting on the revision of the Hague Convention for the Protection of Cultural Property in the Event of Armed Conflict of 1954. Vienna, 11–13 May 1998.
Diplomatic Conference on a Draft Second Protocol to the 1954 Hague Convention for the Protection of Cultural Property in the Event of Armed Conflict. The Hague, 15–26 March 1999.

New efforts in the early 1990s

The *UNESCO General Conference, at its 26th Session in 1991*, reaffirmed its conviction 'that the preservation of the world cultural and natural heritage is of the utmost importance to all humankind' and called 'on all States to increase their effort [in that area] to achieve better implementation of existing instruments and to reinforce UNESCO's action'.[7]

Subsequently, the *Executive Board, at its 139th Session (May 1992)*, endorsed a draft resolution, submitted by Italy, calling for a consultative group of experts. In document 139 EX/29, Italy proposed a possible review of the Convention concerning the Protection of the World Cultural and Natural Heritage (1972) and suggested improvement in the 'co-ordination

---

7   Resolution 26C/3.9, adopted on 6 November 1991.

between the "World Heritage Convention" and the 1954 Hague Convention, in support of UNESCO's action in respect of threats to cultural sites in cases of armed conflicts'.

In his report to the *1992 Executive Board 140th Session*,[8] the Director-General indicated that the 1954 Hague Convention no longer met current requirements, citing slow ratification and unsatisfactory geographical distribution, the small number of entries in the International Register of Cultural Property under Special Protection, cumbersome procedures, a lack of attention to the current state of 'military science', complex procedures for the appointment of Commissioners-General, and weak UNESCO assistance. Three possible courses of action were proposed: a review of the Convention, adoption of a protocol, and the undertaking of practical measures. Consultations took place with the Netherlands with a view to undertaking a study on, *inter alia*, a possible review of the Convention. These and other points were developed in the document presented by the Netherlands.[9] The document referred to recent conflicts in the Middle East, the Gulf Wars and the conflict in the former Yugoslavia. It also indicated that the review of the Convention could form part of the United Nations Decade of International Law (1990–1999), which has just started. The document facilitated a first round of discussions at the Executive Board and presented points for debate by an informal group of experts.

Professor Patrick Boylan was asked by the UNESCO Secretariat and the Netherlands Government to prepare an in-depth analysis of the issues and to present a set of recommendations to the members of the Executive Board.[10] His study recounted the objectives and results of the operations of the Hague Convention and its Protocol. It examined ways to improve the application and effectiveness of the Convention and the Protocol, and explored whether a review of the Convention was necessary.

The Netherlands Government, in close cooperation with the UNESCO Secretariat, organized an *informal, open-ended information session in Paris (9 February 1993)*, where Professor Boylan presented his preliminary views on certain fundamental issues related to future improvements in the implementation of the 1954 Convention.

---

8   Report by the Director-General on the reinforcement of UNESCO's action for the Protection of the World Cultural and Natural Heritage, 140 EX/13 and Corr.

9   Review of the application of the Convention for the Protection of Cultural Property in the Event of Armed Conflict (The Hague, 14 May 1954), 140 EX/26.

10 Boylan (1993).

The *141st Session of the Executive Board* adopted Decision 5.5.1, which acknowledged, *inter alia*, the opinion expressed by the Director-General that the 1954 Convention no longer met current requirements and that its effectiveness should be improved. In addition, it encouraged States to consider appropriate follow-up initiatives and invited the Director-General to convene an open-ended UNESCO meeting to exchange information on the results and recommendations of Professor Boylan's study, to be considered at the 142nd Session of the Executive Board in October 1993. The decision invited States Parties to the Convention to set up national systems of implementation for their obligations under the Convention in order to reinforce measures at the national level. Furthermore, the decision encouraged States Parties to the 1954 and 1972 Conventions to examine the possibility of nominating their sites for inclusion on the World Heritage List for the Register of Special Protection.[11]

The Executive Board decided that its 142nd Session should include this item on its agenda in order to make recommendations to the 27th Session of the General Conference (October–November 1993) on, *inter alia*: 'a) the strengthening and possible revision of the 1954 Hague Convention' and 'b) the coordination of all existing UNESCO instruments for the protection of cultural heritage.'

To prepare the decision of the Executive Board and to provide guidance for discussions on this item, the Netherlands Government, in close consultation with the Director-General of UNESCO, convened a meeting of experts from 5 to 7 July 1993 in The Hague. The issues discussed at the meeting were included in the discussion paper.[12]

---

11 UNESCO contacted the States Parties to the 1954 and 1972 Conventions and asked them to consider the possibility of nominating their cultural sites for inclusion on the World Heritage List for the International Register of Cultural Property under Special Protection. By June 1995, 'seven States have replied positively but have not yet provided the Secretariat with sufficient details to proceed with the inscription'. Information note to the Second Meeting of the States Parties to the 1954 Hague Convention, CLT-95/CONF.009/INF.1, p. 1.

12 *Convention on the Protection of Cultural Property in the Event of Armed Conflict (The Hague, 1954).* Discussion paper, prepared for the Expert Meeting on the Application and Effectiveness of the 1954 Convention, The Hague, 29 June 1993. The following issues were to be discussed: a) scope of the Convention, to be enlarged to include the protection of natural heritage; b) (special) protection regime; c) relation to other (multilateral) cultural protection instruments, mentioning in particular the 1970 Convention; d) the destruction of cultural property in times of armed conflict of a non-international character; e) institutional issues (in particular, the lack of institutional mechanism, possible relationship UNESCO-UN in this field – including UN peacekeeping activities, and possible role of NGOs) – it was suggested that an organ could be modelled on the World Heritage Committee; f) Commissioners-General/Protecting Powers; g) dissemination, including assistance to developing countries; and h) procedural approaches, including the following: i) drafting of a new legally binding instrument, ii) formal amendment or revision, iii) recommendations/guidelines, and iv) a combination of (i) and (ii).

The 1993 Hague Meeting of Experts on the application and effectiveness of the Convention for the Protection of Cultural Property in the Event of Armed Conflict, [13] The Hague, 5–7 July 1993

Experts from 19 countries and two NGOs participated in the meeting. The UNESCO representative gave an account of the events leading up to this meeting and stressed, in conclusion, 'that the issue of the Protocol, additional to the 1954 Convention and its relations to the 1970 Convention, needs further discussion.'

The following essential points were mentioned in the final report:

1) The meeting acknowledged the need for universal acceptance of the Convention, drew attention to the fact that the destruction of cultural property sometimes appeared to be an objective of armed conflict, and underlined the role of regional organizations in encouraging new ratifications.

2) Preventive measures were considered as a condition for the Convention's effectiveness, but no provision was made for essential steps, such as the preparation and availability of accurate and up-to-date documentation on protected cultural property.

3) Following the agenda established in the discussion paper, the experts decided that the scope of the Convention should not be extended to include natural heritage. The protection regime of the Convention did not meet the necessary requirements for natural heritage, which was dealt with elsewhere in other forums.

4) The definition of cultural property as provided in Article 1 of the Convention was considered largely acceptable and sufficiently broad.

5) Some experts expressed doubts about the usefulness of the special protection regime and the complicated procedure for entry on the International Register of Cultural Property under Special Protection. If the regime were to be maintained, it should be simplified, namely by revising its conditions and making them more objective. Furthermore, they contended that certain institutional arrangements similar to the 1972 Convention should be made.

---

13 Report by the Director-General on the Reinforcement of UNESCO's action for the Protection of the World Cultural and Natural Heritage. UNESCO document 142 EX/15, Annex: The Hague Meeting of Experts on the application and effectiveness of the Convention for the Protection of Cultural Property in the Event of Armed Conflict (The Hague, 14 May 1954), *Final Report.* http://unesdoc.unesco.org/images/0009/000958/095820Eo.pdf

6) There was general agreement that it is necessary to strengthen the enforcement of the Convention and that the regime of sanctions deserved further attention. It was suggested that attacks on cultural property should also be described as war crimes through the formulation of an additional instrument, such as a Protocol to the Convention.

7) Ideally, the protection afforded in internal conflicts should not differ from that given in international conflicts, but several experts in attendance felt that this question should be linked to respect for national sovereignty.

8) An organ modelled on the World Heritage Committee could contribute to more effective application of the Convention. Its duties would include evaluating requests for (new) entries in the International Register of Cultural Property under Special Protection, and a reporting system. In addition, it would raise awareness among States and its citizens of the Convention's objectives and purpose. While acknowledging the appropriateness and urgency of establishing some sort of institutional mechanism, some participants noted the need for administrative and secretarial support.

9) The expertise of NGOs was discussed on both a practical and an educational level.

10) The meeting discussed, in fairly general terms, the establishment of a possible relationship between UN peacekeeping activities/ forces and UNESCO, mentioning the appropriateness of having permanent observers, be they representatives of NGOs, ICCROM or UNESCO.

11) The experts recognized the failure of the Commissioner-General and the Protecting Powers system but were hesitant to propose their abolition and the deletion of the relevant provisions. It was observed that their failure was partly the result of the benign neglect of the 1954 Convention; however, States were also extremely hesitant to admit their involvement in any armed conflict. The roles of the ICRC and the International Fact-Finding Commission (art. 90 of the 1977 Additional Protocol I) were discussed. In addition, the report stressed the importance of developing a flexible and simplified regime involving UNESCO representatives and NGOs with respect to operational and preventive activities. Some delegations referred to the possibility of adding a provision to the 1954 Convention along the lines of the common Articles 9–10 (activities of ICRC or any other impartial

humanitarian organization) and 10–11 (substitutes for Protecting Powers) of the Geneva Conventions.

12) The need to disseminate the Convention to the general public and the military, and to develop training schemes, was accentuated.

13) Finally, the meeting expressed the hope that the report would facilitate further discussions and decision-making in UNESCO on this matter.

The *142nd Session of the Executive Board* adopted Decision 5.5.2 on 15 October 1993, which welcomed the report of The Hague Meeting of Experts and expressed, *inter alia*, the opinion that the scope of the 1954 Convention should be maintained. The Board made a series of recommendations to the *27th Session of the General Conference*, which met in Paris in October and November 1993. In Resolution 3.5, concerning the report of Commission IV and adopted at the 28th Plenary Meeting on 13 November 1993, the General Conference endorsed the proposals of the Executive Board and reaffirmed that 'the fundamental principles of protecting and preserving cultural property in the event of armed conflict could be considered part of international customary law'. It invited the High Contracting Parties to the 1954 Hague Convention to consider:

(a) entering into further consultations on the validity of the distinction between the general and special protection regimes in the Convention and, in this regard, on the procedure for entering cultural property in the International Register of Cultural Property under Special Protection;

(b) the need for an institutional mechanism under the 1954 Hague Convention that could perform both advisory and operational functions, taking into account the functions performed by the existing organs established under other UNESCO instruments for the protection of cultural property.

The Conference also addressed the States that were not Parties to the Hague Convention but were Parties to the 1972 World Cultural and Natural Heritage Convention, and asked them to reflect on the fact that the Hague Convention 'offers protection of cultural property that is of national and local importance as well as to sites of outstanding universal importance.' In addition, the Director-General invited States Parties to both of these conventions 'to nominate these sites [of the 1972 Convention] for the International Register of the Hague Convention.'[14]

Furthermore, the Conference also endorsed the request made to the Director-General by the Executive Board, at its 142nd Session, to begin consultations with the Secretary-General of the UN on the possibility of establishing a link between UN peacekeeping activities and the implementation of the Hague Convention, with a focus on the role the UN might play in this regard.[15]

The 1994 Lauswolt Meeting of Experts, held at Lauswolt (9–11 February 1994): Second meeting of experts

Another meeting of experts was held in Lauswolt from 9 to 11 February 1994 at the invitation of the Netherlands Government. The drafting of this legal instrument constituted the beginning of the process of codification which led ultimately to the adoption of the 1999 Second Protocol. This document is known as the 'Lauswolt document'.[16]

The meeting drafted a legal instrument in the form of a Protocol to the Hague Convention which included the following parts:

Preamble
Chapter 1: Protection of cultural property
    Article 1 Protection of cultural property
    Article 2 Precautionary measures
    Article 3 Special Protection
    Article 4 Immunity of cultural property under Special Protection
    Article 5 Cancellation of Special Protection
Chapter 2: Jurisdiction and responsibility
    Article 6 Jurisdiction
    Article 7 Responsibility of States

---

14 UNESCO Executive Board, 145th Session. Report by the Director-General on the review of the Convention for the Protection of Cultural Property in the Event of Armed Conflict, 145 EX/21, 20 July 1994, para. 3, p. 2.

15 The Director-General 'has also undertaken discussions with the Secretary-General of the United Nations concerning the possibility of sending a UNESCO liaison officer with specific responsibility for reporting on the protection of cultural property to accompany United Nations peace-keeping forces, wherever they may be stationed'. UNESCO Executive Board, 145th Session. Report by the Director-General on the review of the Convention for the Protection of Cultural Property in the Event of Armed Conflict, 145 EX/21, 20 July 1994, para. 4, p. 2.

16 The Second Expert meeting on the 1954 Hague Convention for the Protection of Cultural Property in the Event of Armed Conflict. Lauswolt, The Netherlands, 9–11 February 1994.

Article 8 Individual criminal responsibility
Article 9 Grave breaches
Article 10 Other violations
Article 11 Mutual assistance in criminal matters
Chapter 3: The Protection of cultural property in times of armed conflicts of a non-international character
    Article 12 Non-international armed conflicts
Chapter 4: Commissioners-General/Protecting Powers
    Article 13 Substitute for the organization of control
Chapter 5: Institutional issues
    Article 14 Committee
    Article 15 Terms of office
    Article 16 Rules of procedure
    Article 17 Functions
    Article 18 Secretariat
Chapter 6: Dissemination of information/international assistance
    Article 19 Dissemination
    Article 20 Cooperation
    Article 21 International assistance
PM. Final clauses

As this table of contents demonstrates, the draft elaborated in Lauswolt included several new elements, which had not previously been discussed. These issues are analyzed below in the commentary on the individual articles. At this point, we provide only a brief introduction to the Lauswolt document.

The Lauswolt meeting did not consider it necessary to alter the definition of 'cultural property'. Inspired by the provisions of the 1977 Additional Protocol I, it introduced an article on precautionary measures and suggested a new approach to special protection by simplifying the criteria for the International Register of Cultural Property under Special Protection and by according the function to a new body, the Intergovernmental Committee. The experts also presented detailed provisions for the Committee and described its functions. It also proposed the elimination of the reference to military necessity.

The most developed portion of the Lauswolt proposal can be found in the section entitled 'Responsibility of states and individual criminal responsibility'. These provisions reflected recent developments – in particular, the creation of the International Criminal Tribunal for the former Yugoslavia and the preparatory work for the International Criminal Court.

The Director-General informed the *145th Session of the Executive Board (1994)* of the proposals of the Lauswolt meeting and suggested that they 'need to be further discussed by technical, military and legal experts before any written proposal could be presented to the States Parties to the Convention for their consideration'. He decided to organize at least one meeting of experts before the next session of the General Conference. He also began researching the possibility of increasing the staff of the Secretariat and the financial resources allocated to it. In his report to the Executive Board, the Director-General also expressed his intention to convene a meeting of representatives of States Parties to the Convention, to be held during the 28th Session of the General Conference.[17]

The 1994 Paris Expert Meeting on the review of the 1954 Hague Convention for the Protection of Cultural Property in the Event of Armed Conflict

On the basis of the previous studies and reports and numerous expert meetings, the UNESCO Secretariat prepared an excellent working document for the next expert session to be held in Paris in November–December 1994. This document made use of our 1996 Commentary on the Convention, Patrick Boylan's Report, and the reports of the Hague and the Lauswolt expert meetings, and provided the UNESCO Secretariat's comments on each issue.[18]

The discussion at this expert meeting was divided into two parts. The first took the form of a general debate and addressed basic issues already discussed at the Hague (July 1993) and the Lauswolt meetings (February 1994), but also considered the recommendations of the meeting of experts convened by the Swedish section of ICOMOS in Stockholm (June 1994).[19]

The close cooperation with governmental and non-governmental organizations was also discussed in this general debate. The ICOMOS representatives presented a risk-preparedness scheme. Military experts agreed that States' fears regarding the publication of detailed data on their cultural property, and particularly their inclusion in the International Register of Cultural Property under Special Protection, were no longer justified, as technological advances meant that such information could be readily obtained by other means. Among the subjects discussed were dissemination, the

---

17 UNESCO Executive Board, 145th Session. Report by the Director-General on the review of the Convention for the Protection of Cultural Property in the Event of Armed Conflict, 145 EX/21, 20 July 1994, para. 4–6, p. 2.
18 UNESCO document: A working document prepared by the Secretariat, CLT/94/608/1 of 28 November 1994.
19 ICOMOS Sweden et al. (1994).

appropriateness of maintaining the exemption of military necessity and the question of precautionary measures.

The second part of the discussion was devoted to a study of new legal provisions, specifically the text of the Lauswolt document. One expert felt that the principles of the Hague Convention were more than international customary law; they were in fact *ius cogens*.

The discussion concentrated on a few major issues:

- The responsibility of States, individual criminal responsibility, extradition and the role of international tribunals. The distinction between grave breaches and other violations of the Convention.
- The creation of an advisory or executive body to be given specific functions. The Secretariat considered the various advantages that would derive from the creation of a bureau or an advisory committee composed of representatives of ICOM, ICOMOS and ICCROM: lower costs and rapid action were the main advantages. A comparison was made with the ICRC, noting its large secretariat, and this was also reflected in the report.[20] In addition, the need to reinforce the Secretariat was pointed out.
- A general meeting of all States Parties could be held on a regular (biannual) basis.
- The participants remained divided on the issue of military necessity but agreed that this exception could never be invoked in order to justify violations of the Convention, which amounted to grave breaches of the 1977 Additional Protocol I.
- There was broad agreement on the need to improve the system of special protection by establishing more objective criteria and a simpler procedure of registration.

Second Meeting of the High Contracting Parties to the Convention for the Protection of Cultural Property in the Event of Armed Conflict (The Hague, 1954)[21]

The Second Meeting of the High Contracting Parties to the 1954 Convention was convened by the Director-General at UNESCO Headquarters on

---

20 UNESCO Executive Board, 145th Session. Report by the Director-General on the review of the Convention for the Protection of Cultural Property in the Event of Armed Conflict, 145 EX/21, 20 July 1994, p. 5.

21 UNESCO, Second Meeting of the High Contracting Parties to the Convention for the Protection of Cultural Property in the Event of Armed Conflict (The Hague, 1954), UNESCO House, Paris, 13 November 1995, *Final Report*, CLT-95/CONF.009/5, November 1995. See also Hladík (1996).

Monday, 13 November 1995, during the 28th Session of the General Conference, in conformity with Decision 5.5.5 of the Executive Board adopted at its 145th Session in October–November 1994. In the Information Note of June 1995,[22] the Director-General expressed the desire to learn the views of States Parties as to whether new provisions should be adopted and whether this should be done by way of revision of the existing text or by way of an additional protocol.

The meeting's participants included 69 High Contracting Parties, eight observers, the representative of the UN, and four NGOs. A consensus among participants was reached regarding the necessity to improve implementation of the Convention. A number of participants expressed the need for the creation of a supervisory body in the form of an intergovernmental committee or an advisory body. Other issues discussed concerned the role of UN peacekeeping forces in the implementation of the Convention, the role of NGOs, the protection of documentary heritage, the notion of military necessity, and control systems. A majority of participants was in favour of adopting an additional protocol.

The resolution adopted at the meeting, *inter alia*, invited the Parties to submit to the Secretariat written comments on the substantive proposals by 1 September 1996. The resolution also endorsed the initiative taken by the Director-General to send his personal representatives in times of conflict, encouraged him to improve cooperation with the UN peacekeeping forces, and requested him to provide the means necessary to develop dissemination activities. Furthermore, the participants emphasized the importance of organizing a meeting of a limited number of government experts and invited the Director-General to convene another meeting of the High Contracting Parties during the 29th Session of the UNESCO General Conference.

The 1997 Governmental Experts Meeting on the Review of the Hague Convention for the Protection of Cultural Property in the Event of Armed Conflict 1954[23]

The 149th Session of the Executive Board approved the Director-General's proposal to invite 20 States to each appoint one expert to participate in the

---

22   Information Note, CLT-95/CONF.009/INF.1.
23   UNESCO, Meeting of Governmental Experts on the Review of the 1954 Hague Convention for the Protection of Cultural Property in the Event of Armed Conflict 1954, UNESCO Headquarters, Paris, 24–27 March 1997, *Final Report*, UNESCO document CLT-96/CONF.603/5, Paris, 30 April 1997.

meeting.[24] The Secretariat submitted to the meeting the 1996 Summary of comments received from States Parties to the Hague Convention and from the ICA.[25] The experts also received an Information Note suggesting points on which they might focus their work,[26] a provisional agenda,[27] and provisional rules of procedure.[28]

A total of 18 States from the 20 invited participated in the meeting. In addition, 50 UNESCO Member States and two States with observer status took part in the proceedings, as did the representatives of six international organizations. The discussion was based on the Lauswolt document and attention was paid to the comments presented by the nine States.

The drafting group was composed of representatives from Ghana, Lebanon, the Netherlands and Thailand. The group expanded upon the revised version of the Lauswolt document, which was important for future codification work. Redrafted articles were proposed at the conclusion of the meeting by the Chairperson of the drafting group, Ms Estelle Appiah. The

---

24 Nomination of States Parties to the Hague Convention for the Protection of Cultural Property in the Event of Armed Conflict of 1954 to be invited to the Meeting of twenty Governmental Experts organized to discuss the improvement of the Convention. UNESCO document 150 EX/12 of 16 August 1996. Other States Parties had the possibility of sending observers to the meeting. The experts of the following States were invited to the Meeting: Azerbaijan, Belgium, Croatia, Cuba, Egypt, Ghana, Guinea, India, Iraq, Lebanon, Madagascar, Mexico, the Netherlands, Pakistan, the Russian Federation, Spain, Switzerland, Thailand, Turkey and Ukraine.

25 UNESCO, Meeting of Governmental Experts. Summary of comments received from States Parties to the Hague Convention and from the International Council on Archives. UNESCO document: CLT-96/CONF.603/INF.4, Paris, December 1996. As of 28 November 1996, the Secretariat had received replies from nine States of the total number of 88 States Parties to the Convention.

26 *Information Note*, UNESCO document: CLT-96/CONF.603/INF.3, Paris, November 1996. The following points were suggested: 15. When discussing the improvement of the Convention, the Governmental experts may wish to focus their work on the following points: the reconsideration of the whole concept of Special Protection and of criteria for inscription in the *International Register of Cultural Property under Special Protection* of the Convention and its functioning; the replacement of the existing control system of the Convention by a more flexible and efficient structure, and the form that such an alternative system could take; the notion of 'military necessity'; the reinforcement of sanctions for violation of the Convention; individual and state criminal responsibility; the improvement of the implementation of the Convention in conflicts not of an international character; the desirability of setting up a supervisory body which would monitor the implementation of the Convention and the form that such a body could take (intergovernmental, advisory or expert body) and its functions; the enhancement of the potential role of the United Nations peace-keeping forces in the implementation of the Convention; the growing role of non-governmental organizations in the preservation and protection of cultural heritage in the event of armed conflict and how they could participate in the implementation of the Convention; the opportunity for adopting new international norms reflecting the results and discussions of the above and the procedure to adopt these norms, either by amendments to the Convention, or by the adoption of a Protocol to the Convention, or by a new Convention.

27 UNESCO document CLT-96/CONF.603/1.

28 UNESCO document CLT/96/CONF.603/3.

Secretariat was charged to prepare a working document,[29] known as the 'revised Lauswolt document'.

The main issues discussed at the meeting were the following:

- *Protection of cultural property*, concerning the issue of military necessity and illicit export of cultural property from occupied territories.
- *Precautionary measures* (draft art. 2), identified a need for scrupulous verification of the character of possible targets.
- In the case of *Special Protection* (draft art. 3, 4 and 5), the participants introduced two new elements: the extension of protection to cultural property of great importance to humankind, and the nomination of cultural sites to be submitted to the Committee (the body in charge of the new instrument).
- The meeting dealt extensively with the issues of *grave breaches and other violations* (draft art. 6 and 7), *responsibility of States* (draft art. 8), *individual criminal responsibility* (draft art. 9), *jurisdiction* (draft art. 10) and *mutual assistance in criminal matters* (draft art. 11).
- Not all participants were in favour of draft Article 12 dealing with *Non-international armed conflicts*. Some participants preferred to retain Article 19 of the Convention.
- The *institutional issue* formed a major part of the discussion (draft art. 14–17), but experts could not reach a consensus on the form of such a body – committee or bureau – as discussed above. A proposal was made to set up a Fund that could allocate financial resources. The role of NGOs was also welcomed.
- The necessity for *dissemination* was stressed (draft art. 19).

It was not possible to reach unanimity on the form of the new instrument to be adopted.

---

29 *Draft provisions for the revision of the 1954 Hague Convention and commentary from the UNESCO Secretariat.* CLT-97/CONF.208/2, Paris, October 1997. This document included the text of the 'revised Lauwolt document'. Draft articles were followed by the Secretariat's comments comparing the original provisions of the Lauswolt document with the revised versions resulting from the deliberation of participants. Such comments are entitled 'Reasons for change'. The Secretariat also summarized the main points raised in the discussions in the sections entitled 'Main points of discussion'. Some parts of the revised Lauswolt document were placed within square brackets because the discussion did not reveal unanimity on these issues. These were subject to further negotiation.

THE THIRD MEETING OF THE HIGH CONTRACTING PARTIES TO THE CONVENTION FOR THE PROTECTION OF CULTURAL PROPERTY IN THE EVEN OF ARMED CONFLICT (THE HAGUE, 1954)[30]

The Second Meeting of the High Contracting Parties in 1995 invited the Director-General to convene a further meeting during the 29th Session of the UNESCO General Conference. This third meeting took place at UNESCO Headquarters in Paris on 13 November 1997 with the participation of 65 Parties, six observers and the representatives of six international organizations. The Meeting of the High Contracting Parties was informed of the results of the four previous expert meetings (The Hague 1993, Lauswolt 1994, Paris 1994 and Paris 1997), and of the conclusions of the Second Meeting of the High Contracting Parties (November 1995). The Secretariat underlined the significance of the draft provisions for the revision of the Hague Convention, elaborated at the meeting of governmental experts in March 1997, and forwarded these to the UNESCO Member States before the meeting with a commentary from the Secretariat (information document UNESCO CLT-97/CONF.208/2, Paris, October 1997).

The general debate, which comprised 20 Parties, one observer, and two representatives of international organizations, clarified certain points:

1) The participants were in favour of the adoption of a new instrument, but considered that the draft provisions were not sufficiently developed for adoption by a Diplomatic Conference and that a new meeting of experts was required.

2) The majority of speakers wished to keep the provision on military necessity.

3) There was a general consensus in favour of precautionary measures.

4) Some participants were in favour of elaborating the provision on individual criminal responsibility. Others preferred a link to the work of the International Law Commission relating to the International Criminal Court in order to avoid duplication.

5) A majority of speakers were in favour of creating a permanent Intergovernmental Committee.

---

30 UNESCO, Third Meeting of the High Contracting Parties to the Convention for the Protection of Cultural Property in the Event of Armed Conflict (The Hague, 1954), UNESCO House, Paris, 13 November 1997, *Final Report*, CLT-97/CONF.208/3, Paris, November 1997. See also Hladík (1998b).

6) A few delegates expressed the desire not to proceed with discussion on conflicts not of an international character, stating that this matter was sufficiently regulated by 1977 Protocol II.

7) The drafting of a new instrument independent of the Hague Convention was proposed.

The final resolution invited States Parties to provide comments on the draft provisions by 1 February 1998, and convene a preparatory Meeting of Government Experts in 1998. It also asked the Director-General to convene a fourth meeting of High Contracting Parties during the 30th Session of the General Conference.

The 1998 Vienna Governmental Experts Meeting on the Revision of the Hague Convention for the Protection of Cultural Property in the Event of Armed Conflict of 1954[31]

At the request of the participants to the Third Meeting of the High Contracting Parties, the Governmental Experts met in Vienna on 11–13 May 1998.

The Secretariat submitted to the meeting the 1998 *Summary of comments* received from States Parties to the Hague Convention, the ICRC and the ICA.[32] By 18 March 1998, the Secretariat had received replies from nine States (Argentina, Austria, Croatia, France, Germany, Hungary, Israel, Mexico and Sweden) and from the ICRC and the ICA. Comments from the States Parties represented substantial progress in relation to previous discussions.[33]

Fifty-seven States Parties to the Convention, 24 non-party States and three international organizations participated at the meeting, which dealt with five principal issues: the exception of military necessity, precautionary measures, the system of special protection, individual criminal responsibility and institutional aspects. The discussion was based on two documents: 'Draft provisions for the revision of the 1954 Hague Convention and commentary

---

31 UNESCO, Meeting of Governmental Experts on the Revision of the Hague Convention for the Protection of Cultural Property in the Event of Armed Conflict of 1954. Vienna, 11–13 May 1998. UNESCO document: Paris, May 1998, *Final Report*.

32 UNESCO, Meeting of Governmental Experts. Summary of comments received from States Parties to the Hague Convention, the International Committee of the Red Cross and the International Council on Archives. UNESCO document: Paris, March 1998.

33 The comments dealt with the main issues: definition of cultural property, protection and military necessity, precautionary measures, special protection, jurisdiction and responsibility, grave breaches and other violations, responsibility of States and individual criminal responsibility, jurisdiction, mutual assistance in criminal matters, non-international armed conflict, institutional issues and national implementation.

from the UNESCO Secretariat',[34] and the 1998 *Summary of comments* received from States and organizations.[35]

The majority of experts were in favour of the optional Protocol and an enhanced regime of Special Protection was proposed. The majority also agreed to retain the concept of military necessity with appropriate limitations. However, the view concerning jurisdiction and responsibility (in particular, the responsibility of States) was less than unanimous. Most delegates were in favour of the creation of an intergovernmental committee. The experts asked the UNESCO Secretariat to prepare a comprehensive working document to be distributed well in advance of the Diplomatic Conference, which the Netherlands generously proposed to host in The Hague from 14 to 26 March 1999.

The Director-General presented the report on the Meeting to the 155th Session of the UNESCO Executive Board.[36]

The UNESCO Secretariat prepared the document based on several meetings of government experts and particularly on the discussions that took place at the May 1998 Vienna Meeting: *Preliminary Draft Second Protocol.*[37] The Protocol was sent to the Member States of UNESCO, the UN, and selected international organizations with requests that comments be taken into account in the preparation of a final draft for the Diplomatic Conference.

By 15 January 1999 the Secretariat had received substantive replies from 15 States Parties to the Convention: Australia, Austria, Finland, France, Germany, Israel, Italy, Norway, Qatar, Slovenia, Spain, Sweden, Switzerland, the Syrian Arab Republic and Turkey. Comments were also sent by China, the Federal States of Micronesia, the UK and the US. The ICRC provided the Secretariat with a new partial draft. The Secretariat prepared a *Summary* of the comments received.[38] The UNESCO Secretariat and the Government

---

34 Draft provisions for the revision of the 1954 Hague Convention and commentary from the UNESCO Secretariat. CLT-97/CONF.208/2, Paris, October 1997.

35 UNESCO, Meeting of Governmental Experts. Summary of comments received from States Parties to the Hague Convention, the International Committee of the Red Cross and the International Council on Archives. UNESCO document: Paris, March 1998.

36 Report by the Director-General on the results of the Meeting of Governmental Experts on the revision of the Hague Convention for the Protection of Cultural Property in the Event of Armed Conflict of 1954. Vienna, 11–13 May 1998. UNESCO document 155 EX/51, Paris, 17 August 1998. The *Final Report* was included in this document.

37 *Preliminary Draft Second Protocol to the 1954 Hague Convention.* UNESCO document HC/1999/1, October 1998 (English, French and Russian).

38 UNESCO, Summary of comments on Preliminary Draft Second Protocol to the 1954 Hague Convention received from High Contracting Parties to the Hague Convention for the Protection of Cultural Property in the Event of Armed Conflict 1954, other UNESCO Member States and international organizations, Paris, 15 January 1999.

of the Netherlands then drew up a final draft of the Second Protocol: *Draft Second Protocol to the 1954 Hague Convention for the Protection of Cultural Property in the Event of Armed Conflict* (UNESCO doc. HC/1999/1/Rev.1, February 1999).

THE 1999 HAGUE DIPLOMATIC CONFERENCE

The Diplomatic Conference on the Second Protocol to the Hague Convention of 1954 for the Protection of Cultural Property in the Event of Armed Conflict took place in The Hague from 15 to 26 March 1999.

Outcome of the Conference

On 26 March 1999 the Conference adopted the Second Protocol to the Hague Convention of 1954 for the Protection of Cultural Property in the Event of Armed Conflict without a vote, together with the final resolution.[39] It was opened for signature in The Hague on 17 May 1999 within the framework of the centennial celebrations of the First International Peace Conference and signed by 27 States on that date. It remained open for signature until 31 December 1999. By the conclusion of that day, 38 States were signatories of the Second Protocol.

The Second Protocol is additional and supplementary to the 1954 Hague Convention[40] as indicated in Article 2 of the 1999 Second Protocol.

---

39 Second Protocol to the Hague Convention of 1954 for the Protection of Cultural Property in the Event of Armed Conflict, signed at The Hague, 17 May 1999, UNESCO Doc. HC/1999/7, 26 March 1999.

40 During the expert and High Contracting Parties meetings, the review process for the Hague Convention was discussed. Four different possible options were considered. The first consisted of amending the 1954 Hague Convention; however, any amendments would have required unanimous adoption by all States party to the Convention. Article 39 of the Convention provide the details of such a procedure. Since this was to all practical purposes impossible, this option was abandoned, although some States continued to support it. The second option consisted in adopting a new, separate convention. Such a procedure would have required long and substantial negotiations and have had the disadvantage of creating two separate systems, potentially creating more problems rather than resolving existing ones. This option was not mentioned during the review process. The third option consisted in adopting a protocol aimed at revising the 1954 Convention. Several delegations strongly advocated this option, but because unanimity would again have been required, it was rejected by the majority of delegations. In the end, the fourth option prevailed, namely that the new treaty be an additional protocol, which would in no way amend the 1954 Convention but would supplement it and apply only to the States that ratified it. The 1977 Protocols, additional to the 1949 Geneva Conventions, constituted a good example of this solution. The choice of the best solution was discussed during the process of reaffirmation and development of international

The Hague Convention remains the principal and basic text, and no State can become party to the Second Protocol without already being party to the Hague Convention (art. 41, para. 1 of the Second Protocol).

humanitarian law. Jean Pictet, then Vice-President of the ICRC, was the main initiator of the process; he mentioned that the idea of the Additional Protocol surfaced in a discussion he had with Manfred Lachs, then President of the International Court of Justice.

PREAMBLE

The Parties,[41]

Conscious *of the need to improve the protection of cultural property in the event of armed conflict and to establish an enhanced system of protection for specifically designated cultural property;*

Reaffirming *the importance of the provisions of the Convention for the Protection of Cultural Property in the Event of Armed Conflict, done at the Hague on 14 May 1954, and emphasizing the necessity to supplement these provisions through measures to reinforce their implementation;*

Desiring *to provide the High Contracting Parties to the Convention with a means of being more closely involved in the protection of cultural property in the event of armed conflict by establishing appropriate procedures therefore;*

Considering *that the rules governing the protection of cultural property in the event of armed conflict should reflect developments in international law;*

Affirming *that the rules of customary international law will continue to govern questions not regulated by the provisions of this Protocol;*

Have agreed as follows:

Preparatory works

The Second Expert meeting on the 1954 Hague Convention for the Protection of Cultural Property in the Event of Armed Conflict. Lauswolt, The Netherlands, 9–11 February 1994, p. 1.

Draft Second Protocol to the 1954 Hague Convention for the Protection of Cultural Property in the Event of Armed Conflict. UNESCO document HC/1999/1/rev.1, February 1999, p. 2.

1999 Hague conference document HC/1999/5/Add.9.

1999 Hague Conference, Plenary Session, 25 March 1999, pp. 51–54.

---

41 For the definition of the Parties, see Chapter 1, Article 1 Definitions, p. 53.

Bibliography

Chamberlain, K. 2004. *War and Cultural Heritage*. Leicester: Institute of Art and Law, pp. 173–74.

Introductory note on preparatory works

In the modern Law of Treaties, the preamble is part of the context of the treaty together with the text and annexes.[42] It is important for both the interpretation and the determination of the object and purpose of the treaty.

The preparatory works paid little or no attention to the preamble. The first text of the draft Preamble was elaborated at the Second Expert meeting, held in Lauswolt in February 1994.[43] The draft Preamble was not included in the following drafts of the Protocol, also for the simple reason that the decision that the new instrument would be an additional protocol was taken in the later stages of the preparatory works. Even the Preliminary Drafts of the Second Protocol submitted to the States Parties in October 1998 (HC/1999/1) did not contain the proposal for a preamble. It was only the last document submitted to the Conference – the Draft Second Protocol, which formed a basis of discussion at the Conference (HC/1999/1/rev.1, February 1999) – that included a short proposal.[44]

---

42 1969 Vienna Convention on the Law of Treaties, art. 31, para. 2.

43 The States Parties to this instrument,

Considering the need to strengthen the respect for the protection of cultural property in the event of armed conflict, since the damage to cultural property belonging to any people whatsoever, means damage to the cultural heritage of all humankind;

Noting that grave damage has been caused to cultural property during recent armed conflicts including wilful damage resulting from deliberate attacks and noting further that cultural property has been otherwise exposed to damage or destruction through its deliberate use to shield military objects;

Convinced that urgent action is needed to increase understanding and respect for the cultural heritage of all people, including minority people in the event of armed conflict;

Reaffirming the importance of the 1954 Hague Convention for the Protection of Cultural Property in the Event of Armed Conflict, containing generally accepted rules of international law;

Recognizing that the 1954 Hague Convention for the Protection of Cultural Property in the Event of Armed Conflict needs to be supplemented, in order to increase its effectiveness in the event of armed conflict;

Considering that parts of the cultural property are of great importance and therefore deserve to be specially protected,

Have for these purposes adopted the following provisions.

(The Second Expert meeting on the 1954 Hague Convention for the Protection of Cultural Property in the Event of Armed Conflict. Lauswolt, The Netherlands, 9–11 February 1994, p. 1).

44 The text of the preamble:

The Parties to this instrument,

The discussion at the Plenary Session of the Conference was based on the conference document HC/1999/5/Add.9.[45] The discussion of the text started on 25 March 1999 during the evening session.[46] The proposals and remarks are included in the commentary to each paragraph of the Preamble.

ANALYSIS OF THE TEXT

Paragraph 1

The reason for this paragraph is obvious; it explains why the States began reviewing the 1954 Hague Convention and preparing new provisions in order to improve the protection of cultural property in the event of armed conflict.

The first phrase refers to the need to improve protection, which, as we have seen over the years, has been unsuccessful. The adoption of the Second Protocol was therefore another attempt to improve the situation and to protect cultural values more efficiently.

Conscious of the need to give to High Contracting Parties to the Convention for the Protection of Cultural Property in the Event of Armed Conflict (The Hague, 14 May 1954) an optional improved level of protection of cultural property in the event of armed conflict, and to establish a more effective system of protection for specially designated cultural property;

Desiring to provide the High Contracting Parties to the Convention and its First Protocol a means of being more closely involved in the protection of cultural property in the event of armed conflict by establishing an improved administrative structure;

Considering that contemporary developments in international humanitarian law should be reflected in the rules of safeguarding of and respect for cultural property established by the Convention, its first Protocol and by customary law,

Have agreed to adopt a Second Protocol to the Convention as follows:

(Draft Second Protocol to the 1954 Hague Convention for the Protection of Cultural Property in the Event of Armed Conflict, UNESCO doc. HC/1999/1/Rev.1, February 1999, p. 2.)

45 The Parties,

Conscious of the need to improve the protection of cultural property in the event of armed conflict and to establish a more effective system of protection for specifically designated cultural property;

Believing it necessary to reaffirm and develop the provisions protecting cultural property and to supplement them with measures intended to reinforce their application;

Desiring to provide the Parties to the Convention and its First Protocol a means of being more closely involved in the protection of cultural property in the event of armed conflict by establishing appropriate procedures therefore;

Considering that the rules governing the protection of cultural property in the event of armed conflict should reflect the development of international humanitarian law;

Have agreed as follows:

(1999 Hague Conference document HC/1999/5/Add.9.)

46 The President of the Conference, an experienced diplomat, followed the practice of the international conference by not submitting discussion on the Preamble too early, thereby keeping the attention of the delegates away from the main objective: the adoption of the text of the basic instrument.

In the original draft, the second phrase referred to the establishment of a 'more effective system of protection' and was modified by the proposal of the Argentine and Australian delegates, who considered that the wording of the draft 'implied that the previous system was not effective',[47] a charge that, incidentally, was the main impetus for the adoption of the Second Protocol.

This paragraph of the Preamble stresses one of the aspects of the reform: the need for enhanced protection. In many respects the legislators accomplished the main objective of the new process of reaffirmation and development of the protection of cultural property: the elaboration of a fundamentally new concept of enhanced protection, as developed in Articles 10–14 of the present Protocol.

Paragraph 2

This paragraph of the Preamble was not included in the draft submitted to the Conference but was drawn from two paragraphs formulated previously at the 1994 Lauswolt Expert Meeting.[48]

The first statement is quite obvious. The drafters were reaffirming the importance of the provisions of the 1954 Hague Convention, which – even after the adoption of the Second Protocol – continue to govern the protection of cultural property in the event of armed conflict.

The second phrase proclaims the need for improvement as previously mentioned in the first paragraph, indicating the rationale behind the need to develop the rules of protection of cultural property. The aim was to reinforce the implementation of the Convention. As noted above, this was the *raison d'être* of the whole review process, which was adopted by UNESCO and the States Parties to the Hague Convention.

Different possibilities were discussed by the States Parties with regard to methods for reinforcement. The UNESCO Secretariat began to undertake measures aimed at improving protection of cultural property in the event of armed conflict during the decades preceding the 1999 Conference: issuing constant reminders to UNESCO Member States during Executive Board sessions and General Conferences, undertaking studies and plans of action for better implementation, appointing consultants, mobilizing UNESCO

---

47   1999 Hague Conference, Plenary Session, 25 March 1999: Argentine and Australian delegates, pp. 51–52.
48   All other paragraphs of the Draft Preamble of the Lauswolt Meeting were formulated in a different way.

National Commissions, and convening high-level expert meetings, such as the 1983 Expert meeting in Vienna.[49] The majority of these measures met with limited success however, and as a result, two more radical approaches were suggested. The first called for the complete revision of the Convention itself; the second, for the maintenance of the Convention's provisions and their improvement by the adoption of an additional protocol. The latter option was chosen, undoubtedly following precedents from the process of reaffirmation and development of international humanitarian law.[50]

Paragraph 3

This paragraph was adopted from the draft without any modification at the Plenary Session of the Conference.

Most of the measures undertaken for the improvement of the protection of cultural property in the event of armed conflict were conceived and realized by UNESCO and its Secretariat. The problem was that the States Parties were neither fully participating nor giving the impression that they were entirely engaged in this process.

One of the issues was the establishment of the 12-member Committee for the Protection of Cultural Property in the Event of Armed Conflict, which was vested with considerable powers, essentially with regard to the management of enhanced protection, international assistance, the Fund for the Protection of Cultural Property in the Event of Armed Conflict, and the monitoring and supervision of the implementation of the Second Protocol and, de facto, the Hague Convention for those High Contracting Parties bound by the Second Protocol.

Paragraph 4

The draft of the Preamble discussed at the Conference referred, at the end of this paragraph, to the 'development of international humanitarian law'. The Argentine delegate, however, proposed to amend it by including the words 'and of international criminal law'.[51] In order to avoid overlapping,

---

49 Meeting of Legal Experts on the Convention for the Protection of Cultural Property in the Event of Armed Conflict (The Hague, 1954), Vienna, 17–19 October 1983. *Final Report*, CLT-83/ CONF.641/1 (Paris, UNESCO, 1983).

50 The reasons for the choice of the additional protocol instead of the complete review of the Convention are explained on page 38.

51 1999 Hague Conference, Plenary Session, 25 March 1999: Argentina, p. 52.

the UK considered it more appropriate to refer simply to the 'developments of international law'.[52]

The 1954 Hague Convention was the part of the post-Second World War codification during which many legal instruments were adopted as response to the war. This was the case for the 1948 Universal Declaration of Human Rights and other standard-setting instruments, such as the 1948 Convention on Genocide and the 1966 International Covenants on Human Rights, all reflecting the post-Second World War situation. The 1949 Geneva Conventions for the protection of victims of war and the 1954 Hague Convention also formed part of this progressive development of international law.

But after this initial period, the international community and international law began to undergo extraordinary changes due to the Cold War, the increase in international conflicts (such as the Korean War and the Viet Nam War), the growing number of internal conflicts, and wars of national liberation. All these events were indicative of the increasing need to adapt the legal rules regarding armed conflicts to the new situations. This was undertaken in the field of international humanitarian law through the process of reaffirmation, development and adoption, in 1977, of the two Additional Protocols to the 1949 Geneva Conventions.

The end of the Cold War and the disintegration of the Soviet Union enabled the further development of international humanitarian and criminal law. During the 1990s, two ad hoc international tribunals were created to prosecute, on the one hand, the persons responsible for serious violations of international humanitarian law committed in the territory of the former Yugoslavia since 1991 (see Article 1 of the Statute of the International Tribunal for the Prosecution of Persons Responsible for Serious Violations of International Humanitarian Law Committed in the Territory of the Former Yugoslavia since 1991) and, on the other hand, those responsible for serious violations of international humanitarian law committed in the territory of Rwanda, and Rwandan citizens responsible for such violations committed in the territory of neighbouring States between 1 January and 31 December 1994 (see Article 1 of the Statute of the International Criminal Tribunal for the Prosecution of Persons Responsible for Genocide and Other Serious Violations of International Humanitarian Law Committed in the Territory of Rwanda, and Rwandan Citizens Responsible for Genocide and Other Violations Committed in the Territory of Neighbouring States between 1

---

52 Ibid., UK delegate, p. 54.

January 1994 and 31 December 1994). The end of the decade also saw the creation of the International Criminal Court (ICC).

Progress was not limited to these two fields, however. Many other areas of international law, including both public and private sectors, have recently been developed. In addition, the legal rules concerning the protection of cultural property have led to the adoption of numerous conventions in this field.

Paragraph 5

This paragraph was not included in the original draft of the Preamble discussed at the Conference. It was proposed by the delegate of the Syrian Arab Republic, citing its role in the Law of Treaties and the Law of the Sea.[53] This proposal was adopted by all delegates.

The 'Martens Clause'[54] appears here in its succinct formulation. As we have seen, unlike the 1949 Geneva Conventions,[55] the 1954 Hague Convention did not contain the 'classic' provision on the law of armed conflict. This clause was included for the first time in the Preamble of the 1899 Hague Convention II with respect to the laws and customs of war on land, and repeated in most other instruments concerning the laws of armed conflict. I described the reasons for this gap in my 1996 Commentary on the 1954 Hague Convention:[56]

> Taking the common Article of the Geneva Conventions of 1949 as its model, the UNESCO Draft referred in paragraph 4 of the present Article to the 'Martens clause': the denunciation shall in no way impair the obligations which the Parties to the conflict shall be bound to fulfil by virtue of the principles of the law of nations, as resulting from usages established among civilized peoples.
>
> This provision was rejected by eight votes to seven with 29 abstentions, at the pressing invitation of Mr. Eustathiades, the delegate of Greece, who feared that the paragraph 'might be interpreted as meaning that the Convention, in cases where it might be applied, would be opposed to the general principles of international law. . . . Those

---

53 Ibid., Mr Shukri of Syria, p. 52.
54 Strebel (1997), pp. 326–27.
55 In the 1949 Geneva Conventions, the 'Martens Clause' was included in the common articles 63, 62, 142 and 158 concerning the denunciation of the Convention.
56 Toman (1996), pp. 322–23.

principles will remain valid for all items not specifically regulated by the convention.

In our opinion, the fears of the Greek delegate were not justified, as shown by experience with the Geneva Conventions of 1949. Moreover, the Commentary on the Geneva Conventions stressed the usefulness of this reference which 'reaffirms the value and permanence of the lofty principles underlying the Convention and are not limited to the field where covered by it. The clause shows clearly . . . that a Power which denounced the Convention would nevertheless remain bound by the principles contained in it insofar as they are the expression of inalienable and universal rules of customary international law.'[57]

We can only welcome the fact that the authors of the Second Protocol included the clause in the text of the Protocol.

As in the Additional Protocols of 1977, the clause is important because any codification can be sufficiently complete and cover all possible issues. Thus, the Martens Clause 'prevents the assumption that anything which is not explicitly prohibited by the relevant treaties is therefore permitted'. It should also be seen 'as a dynamic factor proclaiming the applicability of the principles mentioned regardless of subsequent developments of types of situation or technology.'[58]

---

57 Pictet (1952–60), Vol. I, p. 413.
58 Sandoz, Swiniarski and Zimmermann (1987), p. 39, referring to the articles of Strebel (1997), p. 252, and Miyazaki (1984), p. 441.

Chapter 1

INTRODUCTION

INTRODUCTION

Chapter 1 is composed of relatively few introductory articles. In Article 1, the Second Protocol follows the practice established in the codifications prepared by the United Nations International Law Commission. It includes the definition of basic terms used in the Protocol. This practice was not used at the time of codification of the 1949 Geneva Conventions or the 1954 Hague Convention. It was most likely first utilized in the 1961 Vienna Convention on Diplomatic Relations – more specifically, in Article 1, which stated, 'For the purpose of the present Convention, the following expressions shall have the meanings hereunder assigned to them'. Two years later, this practice was used again in the 1963 Vienna Convention on Consular Relations. Its Article 1 was simply entitled 'Definitions'. And finally, this practice of the definition of terms was followed in the 1969 Vienna Convention of the Law of Treaties, in Article 2, entitled 'Use of terms'.

The Vienna Convention on the Law of Treaties became the guide for the drafters of the treaties. The authors of the 1999 Second Protocol followed the example of this practice and introduced the following issues in the first chapter of the Protocol:

- Article 1 Definitions
- Article 2 Relation to the Convention
- Article 3 Scope of application
- Article 4 Relationship between Chapter 3 and other provisions of the Convention and this Protocol.

All these issues are usually included in the general part of treaties according to the present practice in the codification of multilateral treaties.

Article 1
DEFINITIONS[59]

For the purposes of this Protocol:

(a) 'Party' means a State Party to this Protocol;

(b) 'cultural property' means cultural property as defined in Article 1 of the Convention;

(c) 'Convention' means the Convention for the Protection of Cultural Property in the Event of Armed Conflict, done at The Hague on 14 May 1954;

(d) 'High Contracting Party' means a State Party to the Convention;

(e) 'enhanced protection' means the system of enhanced protection established by Articles 10 and 11;

(f) 'military objective' means an object which by its nature, location, purpose, or use makes an effective contribution to military action and whose total or partial destruction, capture or neutralisation, in the circumstances ruling at the time, offers a definite military advantage;

(g) 'illicit' means under compulsion or otherwise in violation of the applicable rules of the domestic law of the occupied territory or of international law;

(h) 'List' means the International List of Cultural Property under Enhanced Protection established in accordance with Article 27, sub-paragraph 1(b);

(i) 'Director-General' means the Director-General of UNESCO;

(j) 'UNESCO' means the United Nations Educational, Scientific and Cultural Organization;

(k) First Protocol' means the Protocol for the Protection of Cultural Property in the Event of Armed Conflict done at The Hague on 14 May 1954;

Preparatory works

The Second Expert meeting on the 1954 Hague Convention for the Protection of Cultural Property in the Event of Armed Conflict. Lauswolt, The Netherlands, 9–11 February 1994, p. 1.

---

59 The delegate of Lebanon considered this title inappropriate but had no alternative proposal. Doubtlessly, the better title would have been the one utilized in the 1969 Vienna Convention on the Law of Treaties, namely 'Use of terms', but nobody made such a proposal at the Plenary Session of the Conference. (1999 Hague Conference, Plenary Session, 25 March 1999, p. 56). This title was proposed by the International Law Commission to the 1968 Vienna Conference. The title previously used by the special rapporteur Sir Humphrey Walodck was 'Terminology and definitions' (Sixth report on the Law of Treaties, A/CN.4/186 and Add. 1–7, 1966).

Draft Second Protocol to the 1954 Hague Convention for the Protection of Cultural Property in the Event of Armed Conflict. UNESCO document HC/1999/1/rev.1, February 1999, p. 2.

1999 Hague conference document HC/1999/5/Add.9.

1999 Hague Conference, Plenary Session, 25 March 1999, pp. 51–54.

Bibliography

Chamberlain, K. 2004. *War and Cultural Heritage*. Leicester: Institute of Art and Law, p. 175.

Sandoz, Y., Swiniarski, C. and Zimmermann, B. (eds.). 1987. *Commentary on the Additional Protocols of 8 June 1977 to the Geneva Conventions of 12 August 1949*. Geneva: ICRC, Martinus Nijhoff, para. 2016, p. 635.

Introductory note on the preparatory work

This Article is intended to provide the meaning of the different expressions used in the Protocol.

At the Plenary Session of the Conference, on 25 March 1999, Article 1 was discussed on the basis of the Draft Second Protocol (HC/1999/1/rev.1). This draft was not discussed in any Working Groups, but reference was made to it during the discussion of other provisions. In particular, the Working Group on Chapter 2 made two suggestions contained in footnotes 2 and 4 of document HC/1999/5/Add.5.[60]

We shall refer to the paragraphs as adopted, and in the final section of these comments we shall also mention some additional suggestions and recommendations made during the discussion but which were not adopted by the Plenary Session of the Conference.

ANALYSIS OF THE TEXT

Paragraph (a)

The 1954 Hague Convention began its text by referring to the 'High Contracting Parties' in the Preamble. This term or similar term is usually used for the designation of States Parties to an international treaty.[61] The term

---

60 These footnotes concerned the terms 'military objective' and 'illicit'.

61 We find the following terms for the designation of the Parties: 'Contracting Parties', 'Contracting States', 'Signatory States', 'Member States', etc.

'High Contracting Parties' is used in the Geneva Conventions, the Additional Protocols, the 1954 Convention and the 1954 Protocol.

The 1999 Hague Conference simplified the text by referring to 'The Parties'. This distinction is also important in terms of clarification. The former term, 'The High Contracting Parties', continues to be used for the States Parties to the 1954 Convention and 1954 Protocol, and the simplified term 'The Parties'[62] refers to the States Parties to the Protocol only.

The content of both terms is the same and means 'a State which has consented to be bound by the treaty, and for which the treaty is in force' (1969 Vienna Convention on the Law of Treaties, art. 2, para. 1(g)). Although identical in meaning, reference to the 'Parties' is clearer and so we do not need to clarify the term by distinguishing it from the term 'Contracting State', which is included in paragraph 1(f) of the same Article. The term 'Contracting Parties' has a broader significance,[63] as it also covers States for which the treaty is not in force.

Paragraph (b)

The Second Protocol maintains the same definition of cultural property as the definition included in Article 1 of the 1954 Convention.

In the Commentary of 1996, we presented details on the discussion of the definition of cultural property,[64] and Patrick Boylan drew attention to the definitions used in other international instruments. He also recommended that in any future review of the Hague Convention, every effort should be made to adopt the new definitions modelled for movable cultural property (based on the 1970 UNESCO Convention), and for immovable cultural property (based on the World Heritage Convention). He also considered that natural sites should be included in the protection.[65]

---

62 The terminology question was raised at the last Plenary Session on 26 March 1999 by the delegate of Israel. The Chairman of the Drafting Committee explained that the Drafting Committee 'as a matter of principle adopted throughout the text, the word "Party" and not "States Party"' (1999 Hague Conference, Plenary Session, 26 March 1999, p. 79).

63 Art. 2, para. 1 (f) of the 1969 Vienna Convention states: '"Contracting State" means a State which has consented to be bound by the treaty, whether or not the treaty has entered into force'. Such a distinction is made, e.g., by the Commentary on the 1977 Additional Protocols, which use the term 'The High Contracting Parties'. See *Commentary on the Additional Protocols of 8 June 1977* (Geneva: ICRC, 1987), p. 25, para. 1338.

64 Toman (1996), pp. 45–56.

65 Boylan (1993), p. 51.

The 1993 Hague Meeting of Experts concluded that the scope of the 1954 Convention – because of its very distinctive character – should not be extended to include natural heritage. It was generally considered that the definition given in Article 1 of the Convention is largely acceptable and broad enough to cover all cultural heritage in need of protection. The Lauswolt meeting made no recommendations.

But, as we shall see, besides the efforts to introduce the new definition of cultural property, the States Parties to the 1999 Diplomatic Conference decided to maintain the definition of cultural property as provided in Article 1 of the Hague Convention.[66] This demonstrates the close, almost inseparable connection between the two instruments and the clear supplementary nature of the Second Protocol.

Paragraph (c)

No comments necessary.

Paragraph (d)

The term was affirmed at the Plenary Session of the Conference by the delegate of Turkey as indicating 'that the Convention applies between States with the exception of Article 19 [of the Convention], which referred to parties in the context of internal conflict'.[67] No more comments are necessary here. See also the remarks under Paragraph (a).

Paragraph (e)

All appropriate explanations are provided in the Introduction to Chapter 3 of this Commentary and in the comments on Articles 10–14 of the Second Protocol.

Paragraph (f)

The definition of 'military objective' was included at the request of the Working Group for Chapter 2 on general provisions regarding protection.[68]

---

66 See also Chamberlain (2004), p. 175.
67 1999 Hague Conference, Plenary Session, 19 March 1999: Turkey, p. 236.
68 Hague Conference document HC/1999/5/Add.5, p. 1.

It is based on the definition in Article 52, paragraph 2 of the 1977 Additional Protocol I to the Geneva Convention. As the ICRC Commentary to the Protocol I indicates:

> The definition of military objectives had been the object of study for a long time, and the solution adopted by the Diplomatic Conference is broadly based on earlier drafts. The text of this paragraph certainly constitutes a valuable guide, but it will not always be easy to interpret, particularly for those who have to decide about an attack and on the means and methods to be used.[69]

For more details, see the commentary on Article 6 of the Second Protocol.[70]

Paragraph (g)

The definition of the term 'illicit' was included at the request of the Working Group for Chapter 2 on general provisions regarding protection.[71] This word was formulated under the influence of Article 11 of the Convention on the Means of Prohibiting and Preventing the Illicit Import, Export and Transfer of Ownership of Cultural Property (Paris, 14 November 1970), which states: 'The export and transfer of ownership of cultural property under compulsion arising directly or indirectly from the occupation of a country by a foreign power shall be regarded as illicit.' See the comments on Article 9 of the Second Protocol.

Paragraph (h)

See comments on Article 27 of the Second Protocol.

Paragraphs (i–k)

No comments necessary.

---

69 Commentary on the Additional Protocols of 8 June 1977, para. 2016, p. 635.
70 See p. 91 ff.
71 HC/1999/5/Add.5, p. 2. See also Chamberlain (2004), p. 175.

ADDITIONAL PROPOSALS NOT ADOPTED BY THE PLENARY SESSION

a) Definition of the International Committee of the Blue Shield (ICBS), proposed by Patrick Boylan.[72] Professor Boylan wished to explain the role of the ICBS as an emergency coordinating committee of UNESCO, which is a recognized world-body for libraries, archives, museums and monuments. The proposal was opposed by other delegates (in particular, those from Australia, Switzerland and Canada).

b) Definition of 'parties' with a small 'p' as proposed by the delegate of Israel[73] to identify the parties to a non-international armed conflict. The Australian delegate agreed, but the delegate of Switzerland considered that the Second Protocol was not a place where the definition of 'party to the conflict' should be made, since it was not made in the instruments of international humanitarian law or in the Statute of the International Criminal Court.[74] The ICRC delegate agreed with the Swiss delegate and further agreed that the use of the small 'p' in the case of non-international armed conflict should be made.[75] After the intervention of the representative of the Secretariat, the issue was transmitted to the Drafting Committee for verification. The ICRC delegate

> stressed that throughout the text where the world 'party' could mean a non-State party, it should be written with a small 'p', especially since the definition of the word 'Party' referred to a State. She said that Article 24 merely indicated that the Protocol also applied to non-international armed conflicts. She emphasized that it was important to have 'party' written with a small 'p' throughout the texts where the obligations of the Protocol could also apply to a non-State Party. As the vast majority of armed conflicts these days were not classical international armed conflicts, it was especially important to make the differentiation.[76]

---

72 1999 Hague Conference, Plenary Session, 25 March 1999, p. 55.
73 Ibid., p. 55.
74 Ibid., p. 58.
75 Ibid., p. 59.
76 Ibid., pp. 62–63.

c) Definition of non-governmental organizations (NGOs), as proposed by India.[77] It was generally considered that it was not the instrument concerning the protection of cultural property that should provide the definition of NGOs. The Austrian delegate proposed that reference could be made to the text of Article 29, paragraph 3 (the current art. 27, para. 3), which stated that 'non-governmental organizations in the sense of the Second Protocol are such organizations having objectives similar to those of the Convention, its first Protocol and this Protocol'.[78]

---

77   Ibid., p. 56.
78   Ibid., p. 58.

Article 2
RELATION TO THE CONVENTION

This Protocol supplements the Convention in relations between the Parties.

Preparatory works

Preliminary Draft Second Protocol to the 1954 Hague Convention. UNESCO
document HC/1999/1, October 1998 (English, French and Russian),
art. 2.

Draft Second Protocol to the 1954 Hague Convention for the Protection of
Cultural Property in the Event of Armed Conflict. UNESCO document
HC/1999/1/rev.1, February 1999, p. 4.

1999 Hague Conference, Plenary Session, 19 March 1999.

Bibliography

Chamberlain, K. 2004. *War and Cultural Heritage.* Leicester: Institute of Art
and Law, p. 175.

Sandoz, Y., Swiniarski, C. and Zimmermann, B. (eds.). 1987. *Commentary on
the Additional Protocols of 8 June 1977 to the Geneva Conventions of 12 August
1949.* Geneva: ICRC, Martinus Nijhoff, para. 2016, pp. 1083–86.

Toman, J. 1996. *The Protection of Cultural Property in the Event of Armed
Conflict: Commentary on the Hague Convention of 14 May 1954.* Aldershot:
Dartmouth/Paris: UNESCO, pp. 318–20.

PREPARATORY WORK AND ANALYSIS OF THE TEXT

The present Article is based on Article 1, paragraph 3 of the 1977 Additional
Protocol I, which also stated: 'This Protocol, which supplements the Geneva
Conventions'. The Second Protocol uses the same approach utilized by the
Diplomatic Conference 1974–1977. The Hague Convention of 1954 between
the High Contracting Parties remains unaltered. It is supplemented only by
the rules of the Protocol, but only among the States who are Parties to this
Second Protocol.

These supplementary rules cover new issues included in the Second
Protocol. This is the case for the following provisions: safeguarding, respect,
precaution in attack and against the effects of hostilities, enhanced protection,
criminal responsibility and jurisdiction, scope of application, institutional

issues, dissemination and international assistance, but also the execution of the Protocol.

In case of an incompatibility between the provisions of the Convention and those of the Second Protocol, the provisions of the Protocol take precedence. This is to conform to the laws of the treaties, and in particular to the principle *lex posterior derogate priori*.

The Second Protocol does not include any other provision on relations with other treaties. As all Parties to the Second Protocol are bound by it and are also Parties to the 1954 Hague Convention, relation to previous conventions and treaties is regulated by Article 36 of the 1954 Hague Convention: 'Relation to previous Conventions'. It was not necessary to include the same provision in this Protocol.

While the wording of Article 1, paragraph 3 of the Additional Protocol I may not have caused any difficulties at the Diplomatic Conference of 1974–77, this was not the case for the adoption of the Second Protocol.

The Preliminary Draft of October 1998 included Article 2, 'Relation to the Convention'. The first paragraph of this draft became the present Article 2 of the Second Protocol.[79] It is important to mention that Article 2 of the Preliminary Draft of October 1998 was divided by the Working Group of the Conference into three separate articles of the Second Protocol: Articles 2, 3 and 4.

The Comments presented by the Governments for the Preliminary Draft of October 1998 show that the States' positions were still profoundly divided. Several States still considered the Draft Protocol to be an amendment to the Convention in conjunction with Article 39, paragraph 5 of the Convention.[80] Other States, such as Sweden, even proposed replacing the word 'supplement' with 'modify'. Only Austria and Italy were in favour of applying Article 41 of the 1969 Vienna Convention on the Law of Treaties

---

79   The second paragraph of Article 2 of the Preliminary Draft was included in Article 3, paragraph 2 of the Second Protocol. *Preliminary Draft Second Protocol to the 1954 Hague Convention.* UNESCO document HC/1999/1, October 1998 (English, French and Russian).

80   France, Israel and the US. Israel even maintained that Article 2 contradicted the provisions of Article 39(5) of the Convention and recommended that the Draft Protocol be explicitly made subject to the same conditions and provisions of the Convention, including those relating to its entry into force. The US felt that the adoption of the Draft Protocol by a non-consensus procedure would undermine the consensus process, which was particularly important when elaborating new rules of armed conflict.

to avoid obligations under the new Protocol modifying obligations of States Parties to the Convention.[81] Finland and Norway voiced concern about the relationship between the new Protocol and the Convention because some provisions of the new Protocol related only partly to the Convention and differences in interpretation might arise. Germany, Italy and the UK shared this concern.[82] Furthermore, the UK delegate proposed that the supplementary character of the instrument be expressed at the very beginning of the draft.[83]

The Draft Second Protocol submitted to the Conference included almost identical provisions to the aforementioned Preliminary Draft, with few stylistic modifications.[84]

At the Plenary Sessions of the Conference, the situation did not improve, and States remained divided between those in favour of the amendment according to Article 39 of the Convention[85] and those wanting to supplement the Convention[86] following the rules of Article 40 and 41 of

---

81 Synoptic report of comments, 15 January 1999, p. 2.

82 Ibid., pp. 1–2.

83 1999 Hague Conference, Plenary Session, 19 March 1999: UK delegate, p. 239.

84 Draft Second Protocol to the 1954 Hague Convention for the Protection of Cultural Property in the Event of Armed Conflict, UNESCO doc. HC/1999/1/rev.1, February 1999. The text of Article 2 reads as follows:
Article 2 Relation to the Convention
1. The present Protocol shall supplement the Convention in relations between the Parties to this Protocol.
2. When one of the parties to the conflict is not bound by the present Protocol, the Parties to this Protocol shall remain bound by it in their mutual relations. They shall furthermore be bound by the present Protocol in relation to each of the parties which are not bound by it, if the latter accepts and applies the provisions of the present Protocol.

85 France. Israel stressed the intention of drafters in 1954 to the unified regime for all Parties. 1999 Hague Conference, Plenary Session, 19 March 1999, pp. 240–41.

86 Australia, Spain, Syrian Arab Republic and the UK. Remaining neutral in the face of this division, the delegate of Thailand nevertheless drew attention to the fact that this question was discussed 'from the very beginning, including the Executive Board of UNESCO in 1991 and also during the Hague Meeting of 1993' (1999 Hague Conference, Plenary Session, 19 March 1999, p. 240). The Australian delegate also mentioned Article 24 of the Convention concerning the special agreements and the fact that the Convention already had an Additional Protocol showing 'that such a process was both possible and had already been undertaken' (Plenary Session of the Conference, 19 March 1999, p. 241).

the 1969 Vienna Convention on the Law of Treaties.[87] This division was also confirmed by the Chairman of the Conference.[88]

The following was the conclusion of the Working Group[89] submitted to the Plenary Session of the Conference:

> There was then an extensive discussion on the relationship of the Protocol to the Convention. The majority of States were of the view that the Protocol would be supplementary to the Convention in the sense that States Parties to the Protocol would assume additional rights and obligations in respect of the protection of cultural property in the event of armed conflict, and that the Protocol could be validly adopted by the Diplomatic Conference. Three States (France, Israel, Turkey) were however strongly of the view that the Protocol should be regarded as amending the Convention and that it could be validly adopted only by the procedure laid down in Article 39(5) of the Convention. At

---

87 Articles 40 and 41 read as follows:
Article 40 Amendment of multilateral treaties
1. Unless the treaty otherwise provides, the amendment of multilateral treaties shall be governed by the following paragraphs.
2. Any proposal to amend a multilateral treaty as between all the parties must be notified to all the contracting States, each one of which shall have the right to take part in:
a) the decision as to the action to be taken in regard to such proposal;
b) the negotiation and conclusion of any agreement for the amendment of the treaty.
3. Every State entitled to become a party to the treaty shall also be entitled to become a party to the treaty as amended.
4. The amending agreement does not bind any State already a party to the treaty which does not become a party to the amending agreement; Article 30, paragraph 4(b), applies in relation to such State.
5. Any State which becomes a party to the treaty after the entry into force of the amending agreement shall, failing an expression of a different intention by that State:
a) be considered as a party to the treaty as amended; and
b) be considered as a party to the unamended treaty in relation to any party to the treaty not bound by the amending agreement.
Article 41 Agreements to modify multilateral treaties between certain of the parties only
1. Two or more of the parties to a multilateral treaty may conclude an agreement to modify the treaty as between themselves alone if:
a) the possibility of such a modification is provided for by the treaty; or
b) the modification in question is not prohibited by the treaty and:
(i) does not affect the enjoyment by the other parties of their rights under the treaty or the performance of their obligations;
(ii) does not relate to a provision, derogation from which is incompatible with the effective execution of the object and purpose of the treaty as a whole.
2. Unless in a case falling under paragraph 1(a) the treaty otherwise provides, the parties in question shall notify the other parties of their intention to conclude the agreement and of the modification to the treaty for which it provides.
88 1999 Hague Conference, Plenary Session, 19 March 1999, pp. 239 and 243.
89 HC/1999/5/Rev.1.

the end of this discussion, it was agreed that the Article would read, 'This Protocol supplements the Convention in relations between the Parties', and that official note should be taken of the understanding that use of the word 'supplements' in Article 2 signified that the Protocol did not affect the rights and obligations of States Parties to the Convention.[90]

The Plenary Session of the Conference adopted this Article without further discussion on 26 March 1999, the last day of the Conference.

---

90 Working Group on Chapters 1 and 5. Chair's Note of Meeting of 25 March 1999, p. 1.

Article 3
SCOPE OF APPLICATION

1. *In addition to the provisions which shall apply in time of peace, this Protocol shall apply in situations referred to in Article 18 paragraphs 1 and 2 of the Convention and in Article 22 paragraph 1.*
2. *When one of the parties to an armed conflict is not bound by this Protocol, the Parties to this Protocol shall remain bound by it in their mutual relations. They shall furthermore be bound by this Protocol in relation to a State party to the conflict which is not bound by it, if the latter accepts the provisions of this Protocol and so long as it applies them.*

Preparatory works

Report by the Director-General on the Reinforcement of UNESCO's action for the Protection of the World Cultural and Natural Heritage. UNESCO document 142 EX/15, Annex: Hague Meeting of Experts on the application and effectiveness of the Convention for the Protection of Cultural Property in the Event of Armed Conflict (The Hague, 14 May 1954), *Final Report.* http://unesdoc.unesco.org/images/0009/000958/095820Eo.pdf
1999 Hague Conference, Plenary Session, 19 March 1999.

Bibliography

Chamberlain, K. 2004. *War and Cultural Heritage.* Leicester: Institute of Art and Law, p. 175.
Sandoz, Y., Swiniarski, C. and Zimmermann, B. (eds.). 1987. *Commentary on the Additional Protocols of 8 June 1977 to the Geneva Conventions of 12 August 1949.* Geneva: ICRC, Martinus Nijhoff, p. 40.
Pictet, J. S. (ed.). 1952–60. *The Geneva Conventions of 12 August 1949: Commentary.* 4 vols. Geneva: ICRC, Vol. I, p. 32.
Toman, J. 1996. *The Protection of Cultural Property in the Event of Armed Conflict: Commentary on the Hague Convention of 14 May 1954.* Aldershot: Dartmouth/Paris: UNESCO, pp. 318–20.

PREPARATORY WORK AND ANALYSIS OF THE TEXT

Even if provision on the scope of application was originally planned to enlarge the definition of cultural property and include not only cultural but also natural heritage, the need for such modifications disappeared in the first stage of the revision process.[91]

In the Hague Convention the scope of application of the treaty was not included at the forefront of the Convention but in Articles 18 and 19. It seems, however, that the authors of the Second Protocol wanted to keep the same scheme and structure as the Geneva Conventions and the Additional Protocols, whereby the scope of application was included in the first part of the treaty. The Protocol's scope of application is formulated with reference to the Convention's articles dealing with scope of application. These articles remained where they were placed by the drafters of the Convention.

Paragraph 1

The first phrase of the paragraph was added by the Drafting Committee at the proposal of the Working Group.[92] The paragraph not only specifies that the Protocol applies in the event of armed conflict but also includes several provisions which must be applied in time of peace. In this respect, the Protocol refers in particular to the articles concerning the safeguarding of cultural property (art. 5), the Committee (art. 24), the Secretariat (art. 28), the Fund (art. 29), the dissemination of information (art. 30), Assistance of UNESCO (art. 33), translation and reports (art. 37), and in all other situations when the Articles of the Protocol are applied in time of peace. By using the words 'in addition', the legislators wanted to convey that the Protocol was to be implemented mainly during peacetime and that its application during conflicts (in accordance with the corresponding articles) was an exceptional circumstance.

Therefore, the term 'in addition' refers only to Article 18, paragraphs 1 and 2 of the Convention and to Article 22 of the Second Protocol concerning non-international armed conflicts. In this respect, there is no difference in the scope of application between the Convention and the Protocol. The Second Protocol uses the same method of reference to the main Convention as Article 1, paragraph 2 of the 1977 Additional Protocol I.

The inclusion of the scope of application and the reference to Articles 18 and 22 was proposed by the delegates of Ireland and the UK at the Plenary Sessions of the Conference.[93]

---

91 See the report of the First Hague Meeting of Experts of 1993, para. 6.1 and 6.2.
92 Working Group on Chapters 1 and 5. Chair's Note of Meeting of 25 March 1999, p. 2.
93 1999 Hague Conference, Plenary Session, 19 March 1999, pp. 237 and 239.

The comments on Article 18 of the 1954 Convention[94] were included in the 1996 Commentary. They indicated that the Article was almost entirely taken from the text of Article 2 common to the four 1949 Geneva Conventions. Paragraph 1 of Article 18 was more modest in its modification of Article 2 of the Geneva Conventions, substituting the phrase 'taking effect' for 'implementation'.

Earlier conventions on international humanitarian law did not define the situations to which they applied: the mere reference to war or armed conflict seemed sufficient. This was the case with the Geneva Conventions of 1864, 1906 and 1929. The Hague Conventions of 1899 and 1907 also adhered to this principle. Furthermore, the conventions concerning cultural property – the Fourth and Ninth Hague Conventions of 1907 and the Washington Pact of 1935 – followed the same format.

With regard to the Geneva Conventions, it was self-evident that they applied in time of war. The outbreak of hostilities should be preceded by a declaration, but when this was not the case, or when, for one reason or another (such as non-recognition by one of the Parties of the government of the other), the state of war was not recognized by one of the two sides, the applicability of the Convention might be contested. It was for this reason that the ICRC and the Conference of Government Experts recommended that the Conventions should apply to any armed conflict, whether or not the latter is recognized as a state of war by the Parties concerned. Such conflict included the occupation of territory even in the absence of any state of war.

Article 18, paragraph 1 taken from the Geneva Conventions deprives belligerents of the pretexts they might invoke for evasion of their obligations. War that is declared, or otherwise recognized, means that the Convention and the Protocol are applied (even in the absence of hostilities). The declaration of war required by the 1907 Hague Convention Relative to the Opening of Hostilities (Convention III) has been disregarded for many decades. There

---

94   Article 18 reads as follows:
Article 18 Application of the Convention
1. Apart from the provisions which shall take effect in time of peace, the present Convention shall apply in the event of declared war or of any other armed conflict which may arise between two or more of the High Contracting Parties, even if the state of war is not recognized by, one or more of them.
2. The Convention shall also apply to all cases of partial or total occupation of the territory of a High Contracting Party, even if the said occupation meets with no armed resistance.
3. If one of the Powers in conflict is not a Party to the present Convention, the Powers which are Parties thereto shall nevertheless remain bound by it in their mutual relations. They shall furthermore be bound by the Convention, in relation to the said Power, if the latter has declared that it accepts the provisions thereof and so long as it applies them.

is no longer any need for a formal declaration of war, or for recognition of the state of war, as preliminaries to the application of the Convention. The Convention becomes applicable from the actual opening of hostilities. The existence of armed conflict between two or more Contracting Parties or any dispute between States when armed forces are used automatically brings the Convention into operation.[95]

Armed conflict consisting of any difference arising between two States and leading to the intervention of armed forces or similar forces constitutes a situation in which the Convention and the Protocol are applied. Thus, the length of the conflict, the loss of life entailed, a simple police operation, acts of legitimate self-defence, undeclared hostilities and so on, all indicate the presence of armed conflict.

In comparison with Article 2 common to the Geneva Conventions, which states that the Conventions shall apply 'even if the state of war is not recognized by one of them', the 1954 Hague Convention refers to 'one or more of them'. This drafting change in no way alters the meaning of this provision as compared with Article 2 common to the 1949 Geneva Conventions. On the contrary, it expresses even more clearly the fact that the Convention shall be applied even if all parties to the conflict deny the existence of the state of war. According to Jean Pictet, 'even in that event it would not appear that they could, by tacit agreement, prevent the Conventions from applying. It must not be forgotten that the Conventions have been drawn up first and foremost to protect individuals and not to serve State interests'.[96]

According to paragraph 2, the Convention and the Protocol also apply to all cases of partial or total occupation of the territory of a High Contracting Party, even if such occupation meets with no armed resistance. This provision was introduced into the text of Geneva Conventions in response to the experiences of the Second World War. It does not refer to occupation during hostilities, for in such a case the Conventions would be applicable immediately upon the outbreak of hostilities or the declaration of war (as stated in paragraph 1). Paragraph 2 refers solely to situations in which occupation takes place without war being declared and in the absence of hostilities or military operations.[97]

To maintain an overview of the scope of application, paragraph 1 also includes a reference to Article 22, paragraph 1 of the Second Protocol, which

---

95 Pictet (1952–60), Vol. I, p. 32.
96 Ibid., Vol. IV, p. 21. See also Commentary on the Additional Protocols of 8 June 1977, para. 63, p. 40.
97 Ibid., para. 65, p. 40.

deals with 'the event of an armed conflict not of an international character, occurring within the territory of one of the Parties'. We shall examine this provision in detail under the heading of Article 22.[98]

Paragraph 2

The draft of this paragraph was included in the Preliminary Draft of October 1998, in Article 2, paragraph 2. Paragraph 1 of this Article became Article 2 of the Second Protocol.

The formulation of paragraph 3 of Article 18 of the Convention made simple reference to this paragraph impossible.[99] As suggested by Germany and Norway in the comments on the Preliminary Draft, the Article follows the language of Article 96(2) of the 1977 Additional Protocol I.[100] At the Plenary Session of the Conference, the use of the formula of Article 18, paragraph 3 of the Convention was also proposed by the delegate of Lebanon.[101] The paragraph was exclusively formulated to be used when 'one of the Powers in conflict is not a Party to the present Convention'. It was therefore deemed indispensable to rewrite the provision so as to make it applicable only to the situation 'when one of the Parties to an armed conflict is not bound by this Protocol'. Otherwise, the content and sense of the Article remains identical to Article 18, paragraph 3 of the Convention. Because we have been dealing with these issues in the Commentary on the Convention, we shall return shortly to the two phrases included in paragraph 2.

First sentence of Article 3, paragraph 2

The first sentence deals with the old *clausula si omnes*, which was included in the 1899 and 1907 Hague Conventions and the 1906 Geneva Convention. This *clausula* meant that the Convention was applicable only if all parties in

---

98 From the purely redactional point of view, it would have been better if the end of this paragraph had been formulated as follows: 'referred to in Article 18 paragraphs 1 and 2 and in Article 22 paragraph 1 of this Protocol'.

99 Article 18(3) reads as follows: '3. If one of the Powers in conflict is not a Party to the present Convention, the Powers which are Parties thereto shall nevertheless remain bound by it in their mutual relations. They shall furthermore be bound by the Convention, in relation to the said Power, if the latter has declared that it accepts the provisions thereof and so long as it applies them.'

100 Article 92(2) reads as follows: '2. When one of the Parties to the conflict is not bound by this Protocol, the Parties to the Protocol shall remain bound by it in their mutual relations. They shall furthermore be bound by this Protocol in relation to each of the Parties which are not bound by it, if the latter accepts and applies the provisions thereof.'

101 Plenary Session of the Conference, 19 March 1999, p. 237.

the conflict were Parties to it and were bound by it.[102] Thus, if at least one belligerent was not Party to the Convention, the Convention would not be applicable to any of the belligerent parties to the conflict, regardless of whether those parties were also Parties to the Convention. The 1929 and 1949 Conventions therefore included the provision that 'although one of the Powers in conflict may not be a party to the [present] Convention, the Powers who are Parties thereto shall remain bound by it in their mutual relations'.[103] The first sentence of Article 18, paragraph 3, and Article 3, paragraph 2, reproduce the provision from Article 2, paragraph 3 of the 1949 Geneva Convention.

Second sentence of paragraph 2 of Article 3

Likewise, the second sentence of Article 3, paragraph 2 is similar to the wording of the second sentence of Article 18, paragraph 3 of the Convention. The wording of this sentence of the Protocol is adapted to the needs of the Protocol, referring to the States Parties to it.

The formulation used in the Second Protocol is even closer to the original meaning and wording of the second sentence of Article 2, paragraph 3 common to the Geneva Conventions. In the light of the 1996 Commentary on the 1954 Convention, we have extensively detailed the discussions that took place at the Geneva Diplomatic Conference of 1949. The legislator was willing to ensure that the Convention's application was in accordance with the Convention's spirit. He also had the ability to recognize that the Convention should be applied to the non-Contracting adverse State insofar as the latter accepted and applied the provision. The Commentary on the 1949 Geneva Convention states the following:

> The spirit and character of the Conventions conclusively indicate that the Contracting Party must apply their provisions from the moment

---

102 During the First World War, Montenegro was not a party to the 1907 Hague Conventions and was only signatory to the 1906 Geneva Convention. No one invoked this strict application of the law, and Paul de Goutte (1930, p. 188), in his Commentary on the 1929 Geneva Convention noted only that 'le fait, appuyé sur l'honneur de la signature comme aussi sur l'intérêt humanitaire de tous, l'a donc emporté sur le droit'.

103 Article 2(2) of the common Article 2 of the 1949 Geneva Conventions. See also Article 25 of the 1929 Geneva Convention for the Amelioration of the Condition of the Wounded and Sick in Armies in the Field, and Article 82 of the 1929 Geneva Convention relative to the Treatment of prisoners of war. For more information on the discussion at the Geneva Diplomatic Conference of 1949, see Toman (1996), pp. 197–98.

hostilities break out until such time as the adverse Party has had the time and an opportunity to state his intentions. That is not perhaps a strictly legal solution based on a literal exegesis of the text; but it is to our thinking the only honorable and reasonable solution. It follows from the spirit of the Conventions, and is in accordance with their character, as we have already stated. It is in accordance with the moral interest of the Contracting Party insofar as it invites the latter to honor the signature he has given before the world. It is in accordance even with his practical interest, because the fact of his making a beginning himself with the application of the Convention will encourage the non-Contracting Party to declare his acceptance, whereas any postponement of the application of the Convention by the Contracting Party is likely to give non-Contracting Party a pretext for reserving his decision.[104]

The second sentence of the aforementioned paragraph includes two conditions laid out for the non-Contracting Power: it should *accept* and *apply* the provisions of the Convention:

> In the absence of any further indication, there is no reason to assume that 'acceptance' necessarily implies an explicit declaration. It can equally well be tacit. It may be implicit in *de facto* application. These considerations do not in any way minimize the importance of an explicit declaration by the non-Contracting Power. The latter should always make such a declaration, and with the least possible delay. . . . In practice any Contracting Power in conflict with a non-Contracting Power will begin by complying with the provisions of the Convention pending the adverse Party's declaration. It will be guided first and foremost by the latter's actions. [105]

These comments concerning the Geneva Conventions are enlightening when viewed in the context of the 1954 Hague Convention. We can see that the wording of the second sentence of Article 18, paragraph 3 has been slightly modified as compared with the 1949 Conventions. Instead of *accepts* and *applies*, the provisions thereof Article 18, paragraph 3 of the 1954 Hague Convention states: 'if the latter has declared that it accepts the provisions

---

104 Pictet (1952–60), Vol. I, p. 35.
105 Ibid., p. 37.

thereof and so long as it applies them'. As compared with Article 2 of the Geneva Conventions, acceptance has to be in the form of a declaration accompanied by effective application. The phrase 'accepts and applies' is far less formalistic, and 'accepts' may be interpreted in conjunction with 'applies' as a single unit. By applying it, the Power concerned accepts it without any formal declaration. As we have indicated in our 1996 Commentary, the version adopted in the 1954 Convention was a step backward in comparison with the provision of the Geneva Conventions and was inspired by the Belgian proposal submitted to the 1949 Geneva Conference, according to which the signatories were bound by the Convention only from the moment that the non-signatory Party gave its formal acceptance.[106]

The wording of the Second Protocol returned to the original formulation under the Geneva Conventions. In addition, the earlier quotation from Pictet's comments fully applies to this provision.

---

106 Toman (1996), p. 200. See also Pictet (1952–60), Vol. I, p. 36.

Article 4

RELATIONSHIP BETWEEN CHAPTER 3 AND OTHER PROVISIONS OF THE CONVENTION AND THIS PROTOCOL

The application of the provisions of Chapter 3 of this Protocol is without prejudice to:

a. *the application of the provisions of Chapter I of the Convention and of Chapter 2 of this Protocol;*

b. *the application of the provisions of Chapter II of the Convention save that, as between Parties to this Protocol or as between a Party and a State, which accepts and applies this Protocol in accordance with Article 3 paragraph 2, where cultural property has been granted both special protection and enhanced protection, only the provisions of enhanced protection shall apply.*

Preparatory works

UNESCO, Third Meeting of the High Contracting Parties to the Convention for the Protection of Cultural Property in the Event of Armed Conflict (The Hague, 1954). UNESCO House, Paris, 13 November 1997. *Final Report*, CLT-97/CONF.208/3, Paris, November 1997, para. 5(vii), p. 4.

1999 Hague Conference, Plenary Session, 19 March 1999.

Working Group on Chapter 1 and 5. Chair's Note of Meeting of 25 March 1999, p. 2.

Bibliography

Chamberlain, K. 2004. *War and Cultural Heritage*. Leicester: Institute of Art and Law, p. 177.

O'Keefe, R. 2006. *The Protection of Cultural Property in Armed Conflict*. Cambridge: Cambridge University Press.

PREPARATORY WORK AND ANALYSIS OF THE TEXT

The representatives of the High Contracting Parties to the 1954 Convention discussed at the Third Meeting in 1997 the possibility of adopting a new legal instrument independent of but having a close relationship with the Convention. They also expressed the need to further examine the relationship that would exist between the new instrument and the Convention:

> It was proposed to draft a new instrument independent of the 1954 Hague Convention (but having a close relationship with it). States wishing to obtain an enhanced level of protection would become party to it. It was agreed that States Parties to the 1954 Hague Convention wishing to keep the present level of protection would be still bound by the provisions of that Convention. States which are not yet party to this instrument and wishing to have the basic level of protection would be still able to join. Most of the delegates expressed the need to carefully consider the question of the relations between the two instruments when drafting the new text.[107]

The wish of the High Contracting Parties is expressed in the present Article, which was drafted by the Working Group:

> The United Kingdom introduced the third Article on the relationship between Chapter 3 and other provisions of the Convention and of the Protocol, and said that this matter had been referred to the Working Group by the Working Group on Chapter 3. The purpose of the Article was twofold. It was intended to make it clear, first, that the loss of enhanced protection under the Protocol did not affect the regime of general protection from which cultural property benefited under the Convention and the Protocol; and secondly that, in relations between Parties to the Protocol, the provisions of the Protocol on enhanced protection would apply where cultural property had been granted both special protection under the Convention and enhanced protection under the Protocol, but that otherwise the provisions on enhanced protection would not affect the regime of special protection under the Convention.[108]

The Article concerns the application of the provisions of the Protocol's Chapter 3, that is, the chapter concerning enhanced protection. It is quite obvious

---

107 UNESCO, Third Meeting of the High Contracting Parties to the Convention for the Protection of Cultural Property in the Event of Armed Conflict (The Hague, 1954), UNESCO House, Paris, 13 November 1997. *Final Report.* CLT-97/CONF.208/3, Paris, November 1997, p. 4.

108 Working Group on Chapter 1 and 5. Chair's Note of Meeting of 25 March 1999, p. 2.

that the introduction of this new form of protection and its co-existence with another form of protection – special protection – can create problems of understanding and application. For this reason, all necessary precautions had to be taken to avoid confusion.

The drafters preferred to include this provision in the introductory Chapter 1 instead of placing it in Chapter 3 itself. This was a good solution since this provision is closely related to the scope of application and, moreover, greater attention will be paid to it if it is placed at the front of the Convention.

The application of enhanced protection is therefore without prejudice to the application of sub-paragraphs (a) and (b).

We shall discuss in detail the application of the provisions concerning enhanced protection later when we comment on Articles 10–14.

The words 'without prejudice' mean that the application of Chapter 3 will in no way affect or modify in a positive or negative manner the provisions included in two sub-paragraphs (a) and (b). In addition, it leaves all other provisions completely intact and unchanged. The use of the phrase is not limited to the English version;[109] its definition also applies to the Arabic, Chinese, French,[110] Spanish and Russian versions of Article 4.

---

109 The usual meaning of *prejudice* is 'damage or detriment to one's legal rights or claims' (*Black's Law Dictionary*, 8th edn. [St. Paul, Minn.: Thomson-West, 1999], p. 1218). In its ordinary meaning, it is 'a judicial act without effect as a final determination or res judicata . . . The term imports that no right or remedy of the parties is affected' (*Ballentine's Law Dictionary*, 3rd edn. [San Francisco: Bancroft-Witney, 1969], p. 1374). Mellinkoff defines it as 'a legal expression that should never be used in the presence of non lawyers. . . . Without prejudice is something special. For non-lawyers, confusing nonsense. For the profession, an important device – a reservation, a precaution, a warning . . . Lawyers and judges use "without prejudice" to describe action that does not decide a case nor result in a loss of rights.' (*Mellinkoff's Dictionary of American Legal Usage* [St.Paul, Minn.: West Pub. Co.,1992], p. 689.) In the US, the Uniform Commercial Code, Section 1-207, states: 'Performance or Acceptance Under Reservation of Rights: A party who with explicit reservation of rights performs or promises performance or assents to performance in a manner demanded or offered by the other party does not thereby prejudice the rights reserved. Such words as "without prejudice", "under protest" or the like are sufficient.'

110 'ne porte pas atteinte'; Synonyme des mots également utilisé en français: 'sans préjudice' définit dans le dictionnaire juridique de la manière suivante: 'Expression couramment employée dans les textes de loi pour indiquer que la règle posée laisse intégralement subsister telle autre disposition'. (Gérard Cornu, *Vocabulaire juridique*, 2nd edn. [Paris: Presse Universitaire de France, 1987], p. 617.) This definition expresses best the sense of the word in the present article.

Sub-paragraph (a) concerning the general provisions regarding protection

The application of the provisions of Chapter 3 (enhanced protection) is without prejudice to the provisions of:
- Chapter I of the Convention, entitled 'General provisions regarding protection', and;
- Chapter 2 of the Second Protocol, with the same title.

Introduction of enhanced protection will therefore *not affect* in any way the articles in these two chapters.

Chapter I of the Convention, entitled 'General provisions regarding protection', contains the following provisions:
- Definition of cultural property (art. 1 of the Convention);
- Protection of cultural property (art. 2);
- Safeguarding of cultural property (art. 3);
- Respect of cultural property (art. 4);
- Occupation (art. 5);
- Distinctive marking of cultural property (art. 6);
- Military measures (art. 7).

Chapter 2 of the Protocol also entitled 'General provisions regarding protection':
- Safeguarding of cultural property (art. 5 of the Protocol);
- Respect for cultural property (art. 6);
- Precautions in attack (art. 7);
- Precautions against the effects of hostilities (art. 8);
- Protection of cultural property in occupied territory (art. 9).

As Roger O'Keefe has observed with regard to Article 4(a),

> In practical terms, this means that cultural property under enhanced protection is protected not just by Article 12 of the Protocol, as refined by Article 13, but also by articles 3, 4(3), 4(4), 4(5) and 5 of the Convention and by articles 5, 7, 8 and 9 of the Protocol. It also means that it is protected by Article 4(1) of the Convention to the extent that the expression 'act of hostility' used in this provision is more compendious than the term 'attack' used in articles 12 and 13 of the Protocol.[111]

---

111 O'Keefe (2006), p. 244

These two chapters and the provisions they include are independent of the provisions on enhanced protection for the States Parties also to the Second Protocol. Chapter I of the Convention is obviously not affected by the Second Protocol with regard to the States non-Parties to the Second Protocol.

Sub-paragraph (b) is relating exclusively to the second sentence of the Article 3, paragraph 2 of the Protocol

This paragraph concerns only the specific situation mentioned in our comments on Article 3, paragraph 2, second sentence of the Protocol. In this situation, one State Party to the Protocol enters into a conflict with another State not bound by the Protocol. If the latter State (not bound by the Protocol) accepts the provisions of the Protocol and applies the Protocol, the State then becomes bound by the Protocol for as long as that State continues to apply it. If in this case special protection according to the Convention was granted at the same time as enhanced protection under the Protocol, only the provisions of enhanced protection shall apply.

Another complex situation arises when there are two States (A and B) involved in the same conflict that are not parties to the same instruments. For instance, suppose State A is Party to both the Convention and the Protocol. State A could choose to benefit from special protection according to the Convention, enhanced protection as determined in the Protocol, or both provisions. Conversely, assume State B is Party only to the Convention. State B could choose to benefit only from special protection according to the Convention, for the Protocol's provisions do not apply to a non-party. However, State B could also choose to accept and apply the Protocol. If this is allowed, both States will benefit from special protection in its unaltered form despite the existence of enhanced protection. However, if only State A benefits from both special and enhanced protection, only enhanced protection will be applied.

Finally a situation may arise in which one party to the conflict is also a Party to the Convention and to the Protocol, but for whatever reason did not request enhanced protection before the conflict started. Under Article 12, paragraph 9, this Party may request, on an emergency basis, enhanced protection of cultural property under its jurisdiction or control. If provisional enhanced protection is granted to such a Party, it will replace the special protection, if such protection existed before.

The preparatory works and the 1999 Hague Conference did not examine the use of the distinctive emblem created by the 1954 Hague

Convention (art. 10, 16 and 17).[112] Kevin Chamberlain examined this issue in his commentary and raised the question:

> does this mean that property subject to enhanced protection need not bear the distinctive emblem? It would certainly be logical for such property to bear the distinctive emblem, and for it to be compulsory to do so. Paragraph (b) of Article 4 states that the application of Chapter 3 is 'without prejudice' to the application of Chapter II of the Convention (which includes Article 10). If the effect of this is that the distinctive emblem may, by analogy, be applied to property under enhanced protection, a further question then arises as to whether the emblem should in accordance with Article 17 of the Convention be repeated three times as for property under special protection, or be used alone. Unfortunately, the Protocol does not provide a clear answer to these questions. Article 27, paragraph 1 (a) of the Protocol provides for the Committee for the Protection of Cultural Property in the Event of Armed Conflict, established by Article 24, to develop guidelines for the implementation of the Protocol. Guidelines for the use of the distinctive emblem for property under enhanced protection might be a suitable topic for the Committee to consider at an early meeting.[113]

The Committee for the Protection of Cultural Property in the Event of Armed Conflict effectively dealt with this important issue. During discussion of the Draft Guidelines for the Implementation of the Second Protocol, the relevant provision stated that Parties are entitled to mark cultural property under enhanced protection with the distinctive emblem of the Convention because such property is, by definition, cultural property.

---

112 Toman (1996), pp. 141–42.
113 Chamberlain (2004), p. 177.

GENERAL PROVISIONS REGARDING PROTECTION

INTRODUCTION

The Second Protocol followed very closely the structure of the Hague Convention. Chapter 2 of the 1999 Protocol keeps the same title as Chapter I of the Convention: 'General provisions regarding protection'.

a) It retains the main issues included in the Convention but modifies and augments them based on experience gained from the application of the Convention and where improvement is needed. This is particularly the case for provisions on the safeguarding of cultural property, respect for cultural property, and occupation. The additions and modifications are applicable only to Parties to the Protocol and remain unmodified for High Contracting Parties to the Convention.

b) The Protocol introduces some new provisions that the drafters considered important as they relate to the codification of international humanitarian law and represent progress in the codification of humanitarian issues. This is the case for the provisions on precautions in attack, and precautions against the effects of hostilities.

c) The Protocol keeps unchanged other provisions that were considered satisfactory. This is particularly the case for the definition of cultural property, its distinctive marking, and military measures.

Issues of general protection were not the main focus of the experts meetings, as can be seen by a comparison of the proposals. At the Second Expert meeting held in Lauswolt in 1994, the draft concentrated mostly on Special Protection (later changed to Enhanced Protection), jurisdiction and responsibility, non-international armed conflict, institutional issues, and dissemination and assistance. General protection was covered in two articles, one of which, concerning precautionary measures, was based on the Slovenia's proposal and became Article 7 of the Protocol.

Article 5
SAFEGUARDING OF CULTURAL PROPERTY

Preparatory measures taken in time of peace for the safeguarding of cultural property against the foreseeable effects of an armed conflict pursuant to Article 3 of the Convention shall include, as appropriate, the preparation of inventories, the planning of emergency measures for protection against fire or structural collapse, the preparation for the removal of movable cultural property or the provision for adequate in situ protection of such property, and the designation of competent authorities responsible for the safeguarding of cultural property.

Preparatory works

UNESCO document: A working document prepared by the Secretariat, CLT/94/608/1 of 28 November 1994, pp. 2–3.

UNESCO document: A working document prepared by the Secretariat, CLT/94/608/1 of 28 November 1994, p. 3. The document referred to the original UNESCO draft of 1954 mentioned in the Commentary of 1996, pp. 60–61.

UNESCO. Meeting of Governmental Experts. Summary of comments received from States Parties to the Hague Convention and from International Council on Archives. UNESCO document CLT-96/CONF.603/INF.4, Paris, December 1996, p. 2.

Preliminary Draft Second Protocol to the 1954 Hague Convention. UNESCO document HC/1999/1, October 1998 (English, French and Russian), art. 4.

Draft Second Protocol to the 1954 Hague Convention for the Protection of Cultural Property in the Event of Armed Conflict, UNESCO document HC/1999/1/rev.1, February 1999, art. 3.

1999 Hague Conference, Plenary Session, 16 March 1999.

Working Group on Chapter 2. Chairman's Draft Working Paper, 22 March 1999, 09.00, Article 3 Safeguarding of cultural property.

Bibliography

Boylan, P. J. 1993. *Review of the Convention for the Protection of Cultural Property in the Event of Armed Conflict (The Hague Convention of 1954).* Paris: UNESCO, pp. 61–73.

Büchel, R. 2004. Swiss measures to protect cultural property. *IRRC*, No. 854, June, pp. 325–36.

Chamberlain, K. 2004. *War and Cultural Heritage*. Leicester: Institute of Art and Law, pp. 173–74.

Desch, T. 1999. The Second Protocol to the 1954 Hague Convention for the Protection of Cultural Property in the Event of Armed Conflict. *Yearbook of International Humanitarian Law*, Vol. 2, pp. 71–72.

Henckaerts, J.-M. 1999. New rules for the protection of cultural property in armed conflict: the significance of the Second Protocol to the 1954 Hague Convention for the Protection of Cultural Property in the Event of Armed Conflict. *IRRC*, No. 835, p. 597.

Office fédéral de la protection civile. 1984–1985. *La protection des biens culturels*. Berne: Office fédéral de la protection civile. See also several issues of the review of *Kulturgüterschutz Forum*, No. 1/2001, 2/2002, 3/2003, 4/2004, 5/2004.

Toman, J. 1984. *La protection des biens culturels en cas de conflit armé: projet d'un programme d'action. Etude et commentaire*. Paris: UNESCO, p. 86 et seq.

Toman, J. 1996. *The Protection of Cultural Property in the Event of Armed Conflict: Commentary on the Hague Convention of 14 May 1954*. Aldershot: Dartmouth/Paris: UNESCO, pp. 59–66.

UK Ministry of Defence. 2004. *The Manual of the Law of Armed Conflict*. Oxford: Oxford University Press, para. 5.26.7, p. 73.

PREPARATORY WORK AND ANALYSIS OF THE TEXT

Conventions dealing with situations of armed conflict and conventions of international humanitarian law also refer to measures undertaken in time of peace. This is the case of the common Article 2 of the 1949 Geneva Conventions, which starts with the words: 'In addition to the provisions which shall be implemented in peacetime'. Several such measures are included in the text of the Conventions.[114]

As indicated in our previous Commentary, the idea for preparatory measures in peacetime comes from the draft of the Netherlands Archaeological Society of 15 May 1919 sent to foreign cultural organizations with a proposal to convene an international conference on the protection of historic and artistic monuments and objects against the dangers of war. This draft drew

---

114 See, in particular, the provisions concerning the dissemination of the text, establishment of hospitals, safety and demilitarized zones, etc. See Solf and Roach (1987), p. 186.

attention to this omission in the 1899 and 1907 Hague Conventions, which did not recommend any preparation for protection in peacetime. Similarly, the 1938 Preliminary Draft of the International Convention referred to peacetime preparation in its Preamble and in Article 1, stating that 'the High Contracting Parties deem it to be incumbent upon every government to organize the defence of historic buildings and works of art against the foreseeable effects of war, and undertake, each for its own part, to prepare that defence in time of peace.'[115]

The 1954 Hague Convention has a specific provision concerning safeguarding measures to be undertaken in time of peace. Article 3, entitled 'Safeguarding of cultural property', states: 'The High Contracting Parties undertake to prepare in time of peace for the safeguarding of cultural property situated within their own territory against the foreseeable effects of an armed conflict, by taking such measures as they consider appropriate.'

The draft of the Convention communicated by the Director-General to all States, by letter CL/717 of 5 February 1953, referred to safeguarding as a series of positive measures for ensuring the best possible material arrangements for the protection of cultural property. It included some examples of safeguarding.[116] The final version of the provisions concerning safeguarding was whittled down.[117] The Article left to each Party to the Convention the freedom to take and choose the measure it holds to be appropriate.[118]

The 1996 Commentary deals extensively with the preparation of Article 3 and its interpretation.[119]

State reports concerning the implementation of the Conventions of 1962, 1967, 1970, 1979, 1984, 1989 and 1995 provide valuable information

---

115 Toman (1996), p. 59.

116 The UNESCO draft set out some examples of safeguarding:

(a) Special measures of an architectonic nature designed to ensure the protection, particularly against the dangers of fire and collapse, of a certain number of buildings of great value and of *buildings containing collections of cultural property* (museums, archives, libraries, etc.).

(b) Special measures designed to ensure the protection of *movable property* of cultural value in the building where it is generally to be found or in the immediate neighbourhood of the latter (organization, stocking of packing material, etc.).

(c) The establishment of *refuges* for the shelter, in case of armed conflict, of the most important and most seriously endangered movable cultural property, and organization of the necessary transport to these refuges.

(d) The institution of a *civilian service* which in case of war or threat of war would put into execution the measures taken or prepared under paragraphs (a), (b) and (c) above. (*Records*, p. 308).

117 Amendments tabled by the US, the UK and the draft proposed by Belgium, France, the Netherlands and Switzerland. Toman (1996), p. 60.

118 Doc. CBC/DR/33, *Records*, p. 374; the UK delegate stressed that 'measures taken in peace-time would that be decided entirely by the country concerned' (*Records*, para. 881, p. 201).

119 Toman (1996), pp. 59–66.

and a number of ideas. It was further suggested that the handbook containing the safeguarding provisions undertaken in peacetime would prove useful.[120]

UNESCO, NGOs and certain States paid attention to protection and preparatory measures in peacetime. It is important to mention, in particular, the experiences of Austria,[121] Germany and Switzerland.[122] Also noteworthy are the substantial paper by A. Noblecourt on the protection of museum objects during armed conflict, the Belgian national manual, and the Lavachery and Noblecourt practical manual published by UNESCO in its Museums and Monuments series. The text was updated in 1956 by A. Noblecourt and the final English edition was published in 1958.[123]

Improvement of safeguarding measures in the 1999 Second Protocol

The limited nature of Article 3 of the Hague Convention, which provides little or no guidance on the adoption and development of safeguarding measures, was criticized during the preparatory works of the 1999 Second Protocol.

Patrick Boylan made several recommendations for the improvement of safeguarding, and provided descriptions of the practice of some States – in particular, France and the Netherlands – in the field of safeguarding measures and national actions for the protection of cultural property.

The First Hague Meeting of Experts in 1993 and the Lauswolt meeting in 1994 made no proposals on safeguarding. The first mention of this issue was made in the working document prepared by the UNESCO Secretariat for the Second Expert Meeting in 1994, suggesting that some thought should be given to strengthening the provision on safeguards

> which is consistent with action being taken during the decade for reduction of the effects of natural disasters, for general contingency planning. It is also consistent with the establishment of management plans for World Heritage sites, as part of the nomination process for inscription on the World Heritage List.[124]

---

120 Boylan (1993), para. 5.14, p. 64.
121 See, e.g., Micewski and Sladek (2002).
122 See, e.g., Büchel (2004), pp. 325–36. See also Office fédéral de la protection (1984–1985), as well as the review *Kulturgüterschutz Forum*, No. 1/2001, 2/2002, 3/2003, 4/2004 and 5/2004.
123 Noblecourt (1958). See Boylan (1993), para. 5.6–5.12, p. 62. Boylan stresses that this publication offers much practical information of great value and recommends that UNESCO publish an up-to-date manual on the practical measures.
124 Expert meeting on the Review of the 1954 Hague Convention for the Protection of Cultural Property in the Event of Armed Conflict. Paris, 28 November–2 December 1994. A working document prepared by the Secretariat. CLT/94/608/1, 28 November 1994, p. 3.

The Secretariat proposed a working draft of the article:

> Preparatory action will be taken to safeguard cultural property by
> the preparation of inventories, the planning of emergency measures
> for protection against fire or structural collapse, removal of movable
> cultural property from areas likely to be damaged in military action
> and appointment of wardens who have specially prescribed duties in
> time of grave threat to the safety of cultural property.[125]

In 1997 the comments of the States Parties were submitted in view of the
Third Meeting of Government Experts in Paris. Two proposals were made
under Article 3 of the Convention. The first proposal, made by Guinea,
related to Articles 25 and 7 of the Convention (dissemination and military
measures, respectively).[126] The second proposal, submitted by Slovenia,
concerned precautionary measures; it was inspired by Article 57 of the 1977
Additional Protocol I and aimed at reinforcing provisions of Article 4, para.
1 of the Hague Convention. This proposal, as we shall see, was the origin of
Article 7 of the Second Protocol.[127]

Fundamental progress on the preparation of the present Article was
made at the Meeting of Government Experts in 1997. Draft articles of the
'revised Lauswolt document' included the new provision, which complemented
Article 3 of the Convention and was based on the UNESCO proposal in
1954.[128] These were reintroduced at the Lauswolt meeting of experts.

---

125 UNESCO document: A working document prepared by the Secretariat, CLT/94/608/1 of 28
November 1994, p. 3. The document referred to the original UNESCO draft of 1954 mentioned in
the Toman (1996), pp. 60–61.

126 'II. 1 *Guinea* proposes that Article 3 of the Convention concerning measures in time of peace be
complemented by a number of measures listed below: 1. introduction of the notion 'heritage' into
school and university curricula; 2. dissemination of the Convention to military and paramilitary
units; 3. publication of maps containing cultural property situated in the territories of the High
Contracting Parties and dissemination of such maps to military and paramilitary units; 4. transfer of
military targets (camps and powder factories) and all other strategic installations such as power
stations, factories, telecommunication and broadcasting stations out of towns; 5. fortifications of
public buildings, in particular those that contain art, ethnographic and scientific objects; and 6.
meticulous conservation of plans, models and photographs of important art, historic and scientific
objects.' (UNESCO, Meeting of Governmental Experts. Summary of comments received from
States Parties to the Hague Convention and from the International Council on Archives. UNESCO
document CLT-96/CONF.603/INF.4, Paris, December 1996, p. 2).

127 Ibid., p. 2. Slovenia proposal referred to the precautionary measures to be taken in the conduct of
military operations.

128 UNESCO Secretariat working document CLT/94/608/1, p. 3. See Toman (1996), p. 60.

The Preliminary Draft of October 1998 includes the provision (art. 4), which has nearly the same wording as the text proposed by the Secretariat.[129] Comments by governments submitted before the Conference concern the reduction of the paragraphs with few additional proposals. These were taken into consideration in the preparation of the new draft submitted to the Conference. During the general debate on Chapter 2, eight delegations intervened regarding the Article's wording, and the Working Group submitted the new draft to the Plenary Session:

> Preparatory action taken in time of peace for the safeguarding of cultural property against the foreseeable effects of an armed conflict pursuant to Article 3 of the Convention shall include, as appropriate, the preparation of inventories, the planning of emergency measures for protection against fire or structural collapse, the preparation for the removal of movable cultural property or the provision for adequate *in situ* protection of such property, and the designation of competent authorities responsible for the safeguarding of cultural property.[130]

During the discussion at the Plenary Session of the Conference, most of the delegates expressed their support, considering these new elements to be sufficient to justify the autonomous nature of the regulation of general protection.[131] There was little discussion in the Working Group,[132] and no changes were made in the Drafting Committee and at the Plenary Session of the Conference.

Interpretation of the text

The Second Protocol refers to Article 3 of the Convention and does not change the content of this article. It leaves the adoption of preparatory measures to the discretion of the Parties.

---

129 'Preparatory action shall be taken to safeguard cultural property by undertaking such measures as the preparation of inventories, the planning of emergency measures for protection against fire or structural collapse, removal of movable cultural property from areas likely to be damaged in military action and the appointment of wardens who have specially prescribed duties in time of grave threat to the safety of cultural property.' (Article 4 of Preliminary Draft Second Protocol, October 1998, HC/1999/1, October 1998).

130 Working Group on Chapter 2 Chairman's Draft Working Paper, 22 March 1999, 09.00, Article 3 Safeguarding of cultural property.

131 1999 Hague Conference, Plenary Session, 16 March 1999: Italy, p. 60; Switzerland, p. 61; Lebanon, p. 86.

132 Result of discussion in Working Group 2, Plenary Session, 24 March 1999, p. 252.

The purpose of this Article is to help the Parties to the Protocol identify preparatory measures by providing them with examples of such measures. These measures should be chosen in view of the 'foreseeable effects of an armed conflict'. The foreseeable effects can be ascertained based on previous experience – not only of the Party's own country but also that of other countries, including their practical knowledge and understanding.

The taking of safeguarding measures is left to the exclusive decision of the Parties, including the possible danger that no measure will be taken at all. But the wording is positive. The Article speaks about preparatory measures taken in time of peace, without leaving any doubt that such measures will be taken. These words are completed by another very affirmative proclamation that these measures 'shall include' and not 'should include'. As we know, 'shall' in use with a third-person subject occurs in legal and quasi-legal discourse in stipulating regulations or legal requirement.[133]

Non-exhaustive examples of safeguarding measures

The authors of this Article based the choice of measures on their experience and also on examples that can be taken from the reports that States presented on the implementation of the Convention. In our 1996 Commentary on the Convention, we included a list based on a study of country reports.[134]

---

133 'Here shall is close in meaning to must'. R. Quirk, S. Greenbaum, G. Leech and J. Svartvik, *A Comprehensive Grammar of the English Language* (London: Longman, 1985), para. 4.58, p. 230.

134 Toman (1996), p. 64. For more information, see Toman (1984), p. 86 et seq. On the basis of the State reports, our 1996 Commentary indicated several examples of safeguarding and protection policy, including action programmes, legislative measures, creation of an infrastructure of protection, and adoption of appropriate financial and budgetary measures, including the opportunity of creating an international fund. The following examples can be culled from the State reports: 1) archaeological excavations, sheltering the objects; 2) restoration work; 3) inventories: survey, identification, classification and registration of movable and immovable property, drawing up of lists, publication of maps, preparation of indexes; 4) documentation: scientific and technical studies designed to identify and describe the property and preserve a record of it in the event of damage or destruction (microfilming, microfiche records, photography, photogrammetry, cartography; constitution of scientific files, and so on), with a view to ensuring the preservation of the information and documentation compiled in this way, some measures might be taken at the international or regional level; 5) storage of movable property: some reports contain information on schemes for the location of refuges (decentralization, intermediate stores) and for the security of these refuges; 6) special measures: these relate to the arrangements made to ensure protection against theft, pillage (alarm device), fire, natural disasters, and special measures to be applied in the event of armed conflict (packaging, evacuation and transport of the prop6 special shelters); 7) studies, drawing up of standards and technical directives which may also be of use to other countries. A documentation centre should be set up in which all the technical and legal documentation would be available. That centre might also answer inquiry and serve as an advisory centre with experts available to it.

Among them is the reference to some examples included in the State reports to UNESCO.

The Second Protocol only suggests measures that could be taken. The list is not exhaustive:

a) preparation of inventories, which could mean, according to our 1996 Commentary, 'survey, identification, classification and registration of moveable and immovable property, drawing up of lists, publication of maps, preparation of indexes';[135]

b) planning of emergency measures for protection against fire or structural collapse;

c) preparation for the removal of movable cultural property; and

d) provision for adequate *in situ* protection of such property.

Before mentioning the different examples, the authors of this provision included the words 'as appropriate', based on the wording used in Article 3 of the Convention. In this context, this confirms the same approach taken by the 1954 Hague Conference, that is, it leaves the choice of measure to the High Contracting Parties, which must take measures they consider appropriate according to context, conditions and circumstances. It also reduces the feeling of obligation to take such measures.

To these examples of safeguarding measures, the Article adds an important provision concerning the authority responsible for such measures: '*and the designation of competent authorities responsible for the safeguarding of cultural property.*'

In our 1996 Commentary we indicated the gap in Article 3 of the Convention, which refers to the High Contracting Parties without indicating which national authority will assume responsibility for safeguarding measures.[136] It was recalled that such a role could be played by the national advisory committee, recommended by Resolution II of the 1954 Hague Conference, or by private national associations created alongside the government committee, similar to that proposed in Article 17 of the 1972 Convention.

---

135 Ibid., p. 64.
136 Boylan described in detail the management structure in the Netherlands Ministry of Defence where the Director of the Cultural Heritage Policy is developing an integrated policy for protection using the network of volunteers throughout the country. Boylan (1993), para. 5.26–5.35, pp. 67–69. See also the 1991 Handbook published by the Government of the Netherlands, 1991.

The damage and destructive effects of war are not very different from the consequences of natural disasters. UNESCO,[137] the Office of the United Nations Coordinator for Disaster Relief[138] and the UN Office of Humanitarian Assistance should undertake joint efforts for the protection of cultural property.

Patrick Boylan recommended that all those responsible at any level for cultural property 'should adopt an integrated approach to peacetime planning for the possible consequences of all disasters and serious emergencies, including natural disasters, civil disasters and armed conflicts (including terrorist attacks)', and that such protection should be included in the disaster preparedness and disaster relief plans.[139] A very important role can be played by NGOs and in particular by the International Committee of the Blue Shield and its national committees. They can provide know-how and voluntary assistance.

The ICRC's legal advisor rightly made the following observations:

> These measures are of great practical importance for the protection of cultural property in the event of armed conflict. Cleary, they also require financial resources and know-how. With these requirements in mind, the Second Protocol provides for the setting up of a Fund for the Protection of Cultural Property in the Event of Armed Conflict (Article 29 of the Protocol). The Fund was specifically established to provide financial or other assistance in support of preparatory or other measures to be taken in peacetime. It will be managed by the Committee for the Protection of Cultural Property in the Event of Armed Conflict, which was set up pursuant to the Second Protocol (Article 24 of the Protocol). The resources of the Fund shall consist *inter alia* of voluntary contributions made by States party to the Second Protocol (Article 29 (4)). Some States sought the inclusion of compulsory contributions, but in the end that proposal was rejected.[140]

States can also address their requests to UNESCO in accordance with Article 23 of the Hague Convention and Article 33 of the Second Protocol.

---

137 See, e.g., the Preliminary Study, submitted by the Director-General to the Executive Board in April 1983, on the technical and legal aspects of preservation of cultural heritage against disasters and other major calamities (UNESCO, Executive Board, 116th Session, Report of the Programme and External Relations Commission, 116 EX/50, Paris, 25 July 1983, Item 5.4.4, pp. 27–29). See also Toman (1996), p. 65, n. 4.
138 Boylan (1993), para. 5.37, p. 70.
139 Ibid., para. 5.42–5.43, p. 71.
140 Henckaerts (1999), p. 597.

Article 6
RESPECT FOR CULTURAL PROPERTY

With the goal of ensuring respect for cultural property in accordance with Article 4 of the Convention:

a. *a waiver on the basis of imperative military necessity pursuant to Article 4 paragraph 2 of the Convention may only be invoked to direct an act of hostility against cultural property when and for as long as:*

    i. *that cultural property has, by its function, been made into a military objective; and*

    ii. *there is no feasible alternative available to obtain a similar military advantage to that offered by directing an act of hostility against that objective;*

b. *a waiver on the basis of imperative military necessity pursuant to Article 4 paragraph 2 of the Convention may only be invoked to use cultural property for purposes which are likely to expose it to destruction or damage when and for as long as no choice is possible between such use of the cultural property and another feasible method for obtaining a similar military advantage;*

c. *the decision to invoke imperative military necessity shall only be taken by an officer commanding a force the equivalent of a battalion in size or larger, or a force smaller in size where circumstances do not permit otherwise;*

d. *in case of an attack based on a decision taken in accordance with sub-paragraph (a), an effective advance warning shall be given whenever circumstances permit.*

Preparatory works

For the preparatory work of the 1954 Hague Convention, see:

Toman, J. 1996. The Protection of Cultural Property in the Event of Armed Conflict: Commentary on the Hague Convention of 14 May 1954. Aldershot: Dartmouth/Paris: UNESCO, p. 67.

Review of the application of the Convention for the Protection of Cultural Property in the Event of Armed Conflict (The Hague, 14 May 1954), 140 EX/26, p. 6.

Expert Meeting on the Review of the 1954 Hague Convention for the Protection of Cultural Property in the Event of Armed Conflict. Paris, 28 November–2 December 1994, A working document prepared by the Secretariat, HC/608/1, 28 November 1994.

UNESCO, Meeting of Governmental Experts. Summary of comments received from States Parties to the Hague Convention and from the

International Council on Archives. UNESCO document CLT-96/CONF.603/INF.4, Paris, December 1996, p. 2

UNESCO, Meeting of Governmental Experts on the Review of the 1954 Hague Convention for the Protection of Cultural Property in the Event of Armed Conflict 1954, UNESCO Headquarters, Paris, 24–27 March 1997, *Final Report*, UNESCO document CLT-96/CONF.603/INF.4, p. 4.

Draft provisions for the revision of the 1954 Hague Convention and commentary from the UNESCO Secretariat. CLT-97/CONF.208/2, Paris, October 1997, p. 3.

UNESCO, Meeting of Governmental Experts on the Review of the 1954 Hague Convention for the Protection of Cultural Property in the Event of Armed Conflict 1954, UNESCO Headquarters, Paris, 24–27 March 1997. *Final Report*. UNESCO document CLT-96/CONF.603/5, Paris, 30 April 1997, p. 2.

Preliminary Draft Second Protocol to the 1954 Hague Convention, HC/1999/1, October 1998, distributed by the Netherlands in preparation for the Diplomatic Conference to be held in the Netherlands in March 1999.

Draft Second Protocol to the 1954 Hague Convention for the Protection of Cultural Property in the Event of Armed Conflict, UNESCO document HC/1999/1/rev. 1.

1999 Hague Conference, Plenary Session, 16 March 1999.

Bibliography

Boylan, P. J. 1993. *Review of the Convention for the Protection of Cultural Property in the Event of Armed Conflict (The Hague Convention of 1954)*. Paris: UNESCO, pp. 53–61.

Breucker, J. de. 1975. La réserve des nécessités militaires dans la Convention de La Haye du 14 mai 1954 sur la protection des biens culturels. *Revue de droit pénal militaire et de droit de la guerre*, Vol. 14, No. 3–4, pp. 225–69.

Chamberlain, K. 2004. *War and Cultural Heritage*. Leicester: Institute of Art and Law, pp. 178–79.

Desch, T. 1999. The Second Protocol to the 1954 Hague Convention for the Protection of Cultural Property in the Event of Armed Conflict. *Yearbook of International Humanitarian Law*, Vol. 2, pp. 71–75.

Dinstein, Y. 1982. Military necessity. R. Bernhardt (ed.), *Encyclopedia of Public International Law*, Vol. 3. Amsterdam: North-Holland Publishing, pp. 274–76.

Dunbar, N. C. H. 1952. Military necessity in war crimes trials. *British Yearbook of International Law*, Vol. 29, pp. 442–52.

Eustathiades, C. 1960. La réserve des nécessités militaires et la Convention de La Haye pour la protection des biens culturels en cas de conflit armé. *Hommage d'une génération de juristes au Président Basdevant*. Paris: Pédone, pp. 183–209.

Henckaerts, J.-M. 1999. New rules for the protection of cultural property in armed conflict: the significance of the Second Protocol to the 1954 Hague Convention for the Protection of Cultural Property in the Event of Armed Conflict. *IRRC*, No. 835, pp. 593–620, here 598–606.

Hladík, J. 1999. The 1954 Hague Convention for the Protection of Cultural Property in the Event of Armed Conflict and the notion of military necessity. *IRRC*, No. 835, pp. 621–35.

Article 6 of the Second Protocol is the *complement* to Article 4 of the Hague Convention and cannot be read or understood without appropriate knowledge of that article. For this reason, we have divided the commentary on Article 6 into the following sections:

1. Military necessity in international law and humanitarian law
2. Military necessity at the 1954 Hague Conference (Article 4 of the Hague Convention)
3. The review of the 1954 Convention 1991–1999.
4. The 1999 Hague Diplomatic Conference
5. Analysis of Article 6 of the Second Protocol.

1. MILITARY NECESSITY IN INTERNATIONAL HUMANITARIAN LAW

As we indicated in the Commentary of 1996,[141] international humanitarian law embodies no general reservation of military necessity which might justify failure to observe a rule of international law. The extreme theory advanced by the old military manual of the German Supreme Headquarters *(Kriegsbrauch im Landkriege, 1902)* at the beginning of twentieth century of the primacy of *Kriegsraison* over *Kriegsmanier* has been rejected and is regarded as destructive to the entire body of the law of war. Moreover, such concepts are incompatible with the principle of the law of war embodied in Article 22 of the Hague Regulations, according to which belligerents do not have an unlimited choice

---

141 Toman (1996), p. 73 et seq.

as to the means they may deploy in order to harm the enemy. Case law on war crimes and legal theory both confirm this point of view.[142] It is therefore widely conceded that no general clause of necessity exists either in the treaties or in customary law. It follows that military necessity may only be invoked when an express provision so permits.

> The laws of war are based on the subtle balance between two opposing considerations: military necessity, on the one hand, and humanitarian sentiments, on the other. If military necessity were to prevail completely, no limitation of any kind would be imposed on the freedom of action of belligerents. Conversely, if humanitarianism were the only guide to conduct in warfare, war would entail no human suffering, but then it would not be war. In reality, the laws of war take a middle road, giving belligerents much leeway, although only within certain accepted parameters.[143]

In the treaties, military necessity may only appear in two specific cases. Firstly, when the considerations of military necessity are part of the drafting process as, for example, in the 1868 Declaration of Saint Petersburg, where reference is made to the reconciliation of the necessities of war with the principles of humanity. Secondly, it may be invoked when the reservation of military necessity is included *expressis verbis* in the text of the legal rule either by making reference directly to military necessity or by using an equivalent term.[144]

---

142 See the trials after the Second World War: trial of Krupp (in two separate publications) and others, Lauterpacht (1953), pp. 620 et seq., *War Crimes Reports*, Vol. 10, 1949, pp. 69 et seq.; Friedman (1972), Vol. II, pp. 1344–72; trial of W. List and others (Hostages Trial), Lauterpacht (1953), pp. 632 et seq.; *War Crimes Reports*, Vol. 8, 1949, p. 34 et seq., Friedman (1972), Vol. II, pp. 1303–43 (and on p. 1325: 'the rules of international law must be followed even if it results in the loss of a battle or even a war. Expediency or necessity cannot warrant their violation'); trial of Wilhelm von Leeb and others, *War Crimes Reports*, Vol. 12, 1949, pp. 1–95, Friedman (1972), Vol. II, pp. 1421–70. For the doctrine, see Weidenbaum (1939).

143 Dinstein (1982), p. 395.

144 For example, the following expressions are used: 'as far as possible' (art. 27, 43, 48 and 51 of the Hague Regulations); 'the officer in command . . . must . . . do all in his power' (ibid., art. 26); 'absolute necessity' (art. 4(6), art. 13 and 17 of Convention X of The Hague; art. 11 of Convention XI of The Hague; art. 19(2) of Geneva Convention 1 of 1949); 'except where and to the extent that it is absolutely necessary' (art. 19 of Convention V of The Hague, 1907); 'if important circumstances require it' (art. 4(5) of Convention X of The Hague, 1907); 'as far as possible' or 'so far as military interests permit' (art. 7(1) and 16, respectively, of Convention X of The Hague, 1907); 'as far as circumstances permit' (Art. 17 of Geneva Convention I of 1949); 'to the fullest extent practicable' (art. 71(3) of Protocol 1, 1977).

The reservation of military necessity is not admitted in any other case. Conventions must be respected in all circumstances, as is also pointed out in Article 1 common to the Geneva Conventions of 1949. The clause of military necessity is never implicit and must always be expressly stipulated. The application of military necessity is admissible only in the limits well expressed in the *Hostages case* by the US Military Tribunal in Nuremberg that 'military necessity permits a belligerent, subject to the laws of war, to apply any amount and kind of force to compel the complete submission of the enemy with the least possible expenditure of time, life and money.'[145] The use of force is strictly limited to the behaviour authorized and permissible by the laws of war. The connection between the forcible action and the necessity of war is required.

When applied, the exception of military necessity intervenes not only *on the level of the Parties to the conflict* but also *on the level of individual members of the armed forces*, when the law expressly grants them a degree of latitude in their conduct.

'As history shows, however, the concept of military necessity *has not limited warfare in any significant way*. The Second World War, for example, was fought under the restriction that no property could be destroyed unless there was an imperative military necessity to do so. Yet entire cities were destroyed.'[146]

Another example from the Second World War is relevant here. In the 1943 Italian mainland campaign, the Allied Supreme Commander in Europe, General Dwight D. Eisenhower, issued clear directions requiring his forces to respect and preserve cultural property. However, following widespread criticism of the destruction of the Monastery of Monte Cassino in February 1944, Eisenhower promulgated even more explicit rules of engagement on 26 May 1944 in advance of the Normandy landings:

1. Shortly we will be fighting out way across the Continent of Europe in battles designed to preserve our civilization. Inevitably, in the path of our advance will be found historical monuments and cultural centres which symbolize to the world all that we are fighting to preserve.

2. It is the responsibility of every commander to protect and respect these symbols whenever possible.

---

145 Trial of W. List and others (Hostages Trial), see Lauterpacht (1953), p. 646.
146 Henckaerts (1999), p. 599.

3. In some circumstances the success of the military operation may be prejudiced in our reluctance to destroy these revered objects. Then, as at Cassino,[147] where the enemy relied on our emotional attachments to shield his defence, the lives of our men are paramount. So, where military necessity dictates, commanders may order the required action even though it involves destruction of some honoured site.

4. But there are many circumstances in which damage and destruction are not necessary and cannot be justified. In such cases, through the exercise of restraint and discipline, commanders will preserve centres and objects of historical and cultural significance. Civil Affairs Staffs and higher echelons will advise commanders of the locations of historical monuments of this type, both in advance of the front lines and in occupied areas. This information, together with the necessary instruction, will be passed down through command channels to all echelons.[148]

And more important and in more direct language, General Eisenhower set out his view of military necessity in his Staff Orders of 29 December 1943 relating to the Italian mainland campaign:

> Today we are fighting in a country which has contributed a great deal to our cultural inheritance, a country rich in monuments which by their creation helped and now in their old age illustrate the growth of the civilization which is ours. If we have to choose between destroying a famous building and sacrificing our own men, then our men's lives count infinitely more and the buildings must go. But the choice is not always so clear-cut as that. In many cases the monuments can be spared without any detriment to operational needs. Nothing can stand against the argument of military necessity. That is an accepted principle. But the phrase 'military necessity' is sometimes used where it would be more truthful to speak of military convenience or even of personal convenience. I do not want it to cloak slackness or indifference.[149]

---

147 Referring to enemy's use of Cassino to 'shield his defense'.

148 Eisenhower had copies of this memorandum sent to the War Office, Air Ministry, Admiralty and the Forward Echelon, Communications Zone, at ETOUSA. See Chandler (1970), Vol. III, pp. 1890–91.

149 Quoted by Boylan (1993), p. 55.

2. MILITARY NECESSITY AT THE 1954 HAGUE CONFERENCE

The provisions of the 1954 Conference were drafted in the atmosphere that followed the experience of the Second World War, where the destruction of whole cities – full of cultural monuments – was still considered an acceptable way to conduct hostilities. The 1954 Conference sought to eliminate, or at least limit, these destructive practices, but the delegates could not completely abandon the basic notions of the law of war.

Military necessity was discussed on several occasions at the Hague Conference: in the Preamble and Articles 4, 8 and 11.[150] As the discussion first arose in connection with Article 4, our 1996 Commentary dealt with it under this provision.[151] Here, we will refer only to the major point of the discussion at the 1954 Diplomatic Conference.

Two tendencies were manifested at the Conference: the opposition between the 'realists', who favoured the clause of military necessity, and the 'idealists', who wanted, if not to eliminate, at least to curtail its use.

- The 'realistic' delegations insisted on the retention of a waiver of military necessity that would make the Convention militarily applicable. The delegates of Belgium, Israel and the Netherlands spoke out against a utopian approach and in favour of a text that would be acceptable to the military authorities of every country.
- Other reputedly 'idealistic' countries (USSR, Greece) asked for the words 'military necessity' to be deleted or at least restricted. The introduction of a waiver was regarded as a retrograde step in relation to previous international law, in particular to Article 56 of the Hague Regulations.

Compromise was necessary and it came from the delegates of Spain and France. The Spanish delegate felt that if the Convention was to be widely applied and to receive the real and effective support of the largest possible number of countries, including the great powers, it was preferable to work out a compromise formula that would avoid radical positions and recognize, but only by way of exception, military necessity in the text of Article 4. Most of the delegations accepted, then, the French delegate's opinion that only cultural property of high value should be protected and that everything should be done to ensure its safeguarding. Many delegations at the Conference favoured maintenance of the reservation – first and foremost, to make adoption of the

---

150 It was referred to somewhat less during the examination of art. 5, 13 and 15.
151 Toman (1996), pp. 74–82.

Convention more probable and also for humanitarian reasons, taking into account situations where 'the lives of thousands of soldiers might depend on it, and in such an event no military leader would hesitate'.[152]

The waiver had to be applied solely to the obligations expressed in the first paragraph and under no circumstances to the prohibitions set out in paragraphs 3 and 4 of the Article (theft, pillage, misappropriation, reprisals). In these instances, the ban remained absolute and unconditional. This waiver included in paragraph 2 also stipulated that military necessity must be 'imperative'. But from what point does a military necessity become imperative in qualitative terms? And who is to decide and assess this necessity? The answer must be sought in the concept of military necessity embodied in international law.[153]

These were also the issues to which the 1999 Hague Conference had to respond. Several other points discussed at the 1954 Diplomatic Conference of interest to the drafting of Article 6 of the Second Protocol were mentioned in the discussion.

Attention was also drawn to the fact that the *concept of military necessity was not clear.* The Swiss representative at the 1954 Diplomatic Conference felt that this was of no great importance, 'as the Convention was above all an affair of good faith. Honesty alone compelled reservations to be made but provisions could be made for brochures which, distributed by UNESCO, would be designed to explain the meaning of the Convention to soldiers'.[154]

Some delegates also felt that the judgement on existence and extent of military necessity is necessarily *subjective* and opens the door to arbitrary

---

152 *Records,* para. 277, p. 145 (Roeling), CBC/SR/10, p. 8. The proposal to delete any reference to military necessity was rejected by 22 votes to eight with eight abstentions, eight delegates being absent.

153 We also find the expression 'imperative military necessity' once again in Articles 54(5) and 62(1) of Additional Protocol 1 of 1977. In relation to Article 54(5), the Commentary on this Protocol concluded that 'the "scorched earth" policies exercised by an Occupying Power withdrawing from occupied territory were judged legitimate if required by imperative military necessity' (*Commentary on the Additional Protocols of 8 June 1977,* p. 659). The commentary points out that Article 54 did not change this situation, except with regard to objects indispensable to the survival of the civilian population, as this reservation did not apply to the Occupying Power who may not destroy property situated in occupied territories. The 'scorched earth' policy pursued by an Occupying Power, even when withdrawing from the occupied territory, should not affect such property. On the other hand, a belligerent power may, if imperative military necessities so require, destroy – in extreme cases – objects that are indispensable to the survival of the population in the part of its national territory it controls. However, it may not effect such destruction in the part of its territory under enemy control. Article 62(1) states that civil defence organizations shall be entitled to perform their tasks 'except in case of imperative military necessity' and such situations can be justified by security reasons and in the light of imperative operational choices.

154 *Records,* para. 281, pp. 146–47.

action and to a situation in which the military, which has no qualifications in this matter, might set itself up as judge of cultural values.[155] The representative of Byelorussian SSR raised the following problem: 'Who will decide on this imperative military necessity: a colonel, a captain or a mere lieutenant?'[156] Spain's representative felt that this decision must rest with General Staff[157] and the Israeli delegate proposed that 'decisions in case of really imperative military necessity would have to be taken by high military authorities'.[158] Contrary to Article 8 of the Convention on special protection, the assessment of military necessity is left to the military with no stipulation of special conditions. That opens the door to arbitrary action. Stanislaw E. Nahlik pointed out in 1986 that the decision could be taken by 'any officer of the adverse party, acting merely upon his subjective judgement, perhaps on the spur of the moment, who is competent enough, to decide that such or such other property is to be pulled down.'[159]

Pursuant to Article 4, as adopted by the Conference, the reservation of imperative military necessity no longer referred to all obligations concerning respect for cultural property. This reservation was not adopted with respect to the prohibition of acts of theft, pillage, misappropriation, vandalism and requisition. In those cases, the ban remains absolute.

One important aspect arising from the discussion at the 1954 Conference should be mentioned. On the initiative of Mr Saba, UNESCO's Legal Adviser, the Legal Committee examined the possibility of adding to paragraph 2 of Article 4 a provision which would introduce into it a clause similar to that appearing in Article 11: 'However, if one of the Parties to the conflict violates the obligation laid down in the preceding paragraph and as long as this violation persists, the opposing Party shall be released from the obligation to respect the cultural property against which the violation has been committed.' However, a majority of members of the Legal Committee opposed this proposal since they held that Article 4, paragraph 2 already referred to the possibility of the Parties being freed from their obligation to respect cultural property in the event of imperative military necessity and that it was therefore preferable to make no further provision freeing the Parties from their obligation of respect. That rule would remain applicable except in the case of military necessity, even if the opposing Party did not adhere

---

155 CBC/SR/10, p. 12.
156 CBC/SR/10, p. 4.
157 *Records*, para. 293, p. 148.
158 *Records*, para. 300, pp. 150–51.
159 S. E. Nahlik, Convention, p. 90.

to its undertaking.[160] At the request of Mr Saba, the minutes included an observation that Article 4 was to be interpreted as follows: 'The obligation to respect an item of cultural property remains even if that item is used by the opposing Party for military purposes. The obligation of respect is therefore only withdrawn in the event of imperative military necessity.'[161]

The imperative military necessity to use cultural property was conceived in the 1954 Convention as a *measure of exception*. Cultural property could be used for military purposes if such use is required by imperative military necessity, which is precisely what Mr Saba wanted to avoid by the interpretation he included in the minutes. The content of the exception remained obscure during the entire existence of the Convention and proved very difficult to explain.

Military necessity was criticized after the adoption of the 1954 Convention.

> If imperative requirements of military necessity can trump the protection of cultural property, no real progress has been achieved since the days of the 'as far as possible' exhortation, since the attacking force is prone to regard almost any military necessity as 'imperative'. No doubt, there are occasions when a belligerent Party may decide to forgo an attack after weighing potential damage to cultural property as against minor military necessity. Thus, in the 1991 hostilities the US chose not to attack Iraqi fighter aircraft positioned adjacent to the ancient temple of Ur; but in that case the aircraft (left without servicing equipment or a runway nearby) were deemed out of action and therefore not worth the risk of damaging the temple[162] (the Ur temple seems to have sustained some damage anyhow).[163] The restraint shown might have been overridden by imperative requirements of military necessity had there been an operational runway nearby. The outcome might well have been that irreparable damage to irreplaceable monuments would have occurred by dint of transient perceptions of military necessity.[164]

---

160 *Records*, para. 1167, p. 221.
161 Ibid.
162 See Birov (1998), pp. 201 and 234.
163 Meyer (1993), pp. 349, 376–77.
164 Dinstein (2004a), p. 158.

At the start of the review, Patrick Boylan also mentioned the lack of clear definition as a serious weakness and recommended waiving the provision on military necessity.[165]

Jan Hladík, in his study on military necessity summarizes the two understandings of this notion as they appear at the 1954 Convention:

> The reference to 'imperative military necessity' in Article 4, para. 2 of the Convention enables the States party to use cultural property and its immediate surroundings or appliances for military purposes and to conduct hostilities against such property 'where military necessity imperatively requires such a waiver'. In view of these not very strict conditions, the scope for invoking the waiver is quite large. UNESCO has no information, however, about the practice of States.
>
> The notion of 'unavoidable military necessity' in Article 11, para. 2 has stricter conditions for its application to cultural property placed under special protection. In particular, immunity may be withdrawn 'only in exceptional cases of unavoidable military necessity' and 'only for such time as that necessity continues'; it is further provided that such necessity can only be established at a higher command level. At the moment, six cultural sites are granted special protection under the 1954 Convention. They are all registered in the International Register of Cultural Property under Special Protection (Article 8, para. 6 of the Convention).
>
> The definition of 'imperative military necessity' (applicable to cultural property under general protection) differs from that of 'unavoidable military necessity' (in cases of special protection) in two respects: the rank of the military officer who may invoke the exception (battalion commander or division commander, respectively) and the obligation to give a warning prior to a military operation (recommended or obligatory, respectively).'[166]

The lack of definition of 'military necessity' had the consequence that it was up to each State party to interpret the concept in a concrete case. Hladík provides an example:

---

165 Boylan, (1993), para. 4.16, p. 57.
166 Hladík (1999b), pp. 621–35.

Croatia stated in its latest report on the implementation of the Convention that 'as for Article 4, paragraph 2, of the Convention, cases should be mentioned where relentless enemy attacks necessitated some deviations from the Convention. An example of it is the defense of Vukovar, which, besieged for many months, had to organize defense against incessant air and artillery attacks intended to take the town. It is obvious that in the event of armed hostilities the interpretation of such a provision may vary and may even lead to abuse. For this reason, the question came up again in the course of the review of the Convention, which began in the early 1990s, mainly as a reaction to the destruction of cultural heritage during the conflict in the former Yugoslavia.' [167]

3. THE REVIEW OF THE 1954 CONVENTION 1991–1999

The aforementioned description of the content and elaboration of Article 4 of the Convention is indispensable to a proper understanding of the meaning of Article 6 of the Second Protocol. Article 4 continues to govern general protection of cultural property and new Article 6 of the Second Protocol is only the explanatory complement to it.

Several drafts of Article 6 presented to committees of experts included reference and repetition of provisions of Article 4. But these repetitions were ultimately abandoned, as Article 4 of the Convention remains binding on all States, including those who are parties to the Second Protocol. Such repetitions were unnecessary and even confusing.

Article 6 is therefore exclusively limited to the new understanding of paragraph 2 of Article 4. The whole of Article 6 is nothing but a new version and new interpretation of paragraph 2, which will be binding only on States that became party to the Second Protocol.

Legally speaking, we are therefore now faced with two situations:

1. The application of Article 4, paragraph 2 of the Convention, as explained above and applied to the States Parties to the Convention only.

---

167 Ibid. Hladík is quoting the UNESCO document Information on the implementation of the Convention for the Protection of Cultural Property in the Event of Armed Conflict (The Hague, 1954), 1995 Reports, UNESCO document CLT-95/WS/13, Paris, December 1995, p. 23.

2. A new concept and new interpretation introduced by the Second Protocol which will be used only among States Parties to both the Convention and Second Protocol.

Practically speaking, Article 6 will undoubtedly exert an influence on the interpretation of Article 4 of the Convention.

Preparatory work

General protection and its improvement was one of the major issues of the process of review of the Convention. Let us look at the different phases of this review process.

In the explanatory note submitted to the *140th Session of UNESCO's Executive Board*, the Netherlands questioned, *inter alia*, the adequacy of the exceptions regarding 'military necessity' in the sense of Article 4, paragraph 2, and their conformity with the present state of international humanitarian law.[168] The *Hague Experts Meeting in 1993* and the *Lauswolt document of 1994* did not mention this issue. This led to the conclusion that:

> the fact that the experts at Lauswolt repeated in Article 1 of their draft text most of the legal rules contained in Article 4 of the Hague Convention, without mentioning the waiver in cases of military necessity and adding Article 2 on precautionary measures directly inspired by Protocol I of the Geneva Conventions, leaves no doubt as to their desire to omit any mention of military necessity.[169]

The expert meetings did not bring forth new ideas for the improvement of general protection, but instead concentrated on more attractive issues, such as enhanced protection, jurisdiction and responsibility, and the establishment of new institutions. The Expert meeting in Lauswolt in 1994 adopted only one article on the general protection of cultural property, which was very much a repetition of the provisions of Article 4 of the Convention with only few new ideas. First, two paragraphs announced that:

- the property should not be used for purposes likely to expose it to destruction or damage (art. 4, para. 1 of the Convention);

---

168 Review of the application of the Convention for the Protection of Cultural Property in the Event of Armed Conflict (The Hague, 14 May 1954), 140 EX/26, p. 6.
169 Expert Meeting on the Review of the 1954 Hague Convention for the Protection of Cultural Property in the Event of Armed Conflict. Paris, 28 November–2 December 1994, a working document prepared by the Secretariat, HC/608/1, 28 November 1994.

- prohibiting acts of hostility against it (art. 4, para. 1), and prohibiting its use in support of military effort (inspired by art. 53 and 16 of the Additional Protocols and strengthening the text of the Hague Convention), and prohibiting reprisals (art. 4, para. 4 requiring to refrain from reprisals).

Two other paragraphs prohibited:
- theft pillage and misappropriation (already present in art. 4, para. 3); the only addition was 'prohibition of any other breach of integrity';
- export from an occupied territory (First Protocol) or from a part of the territory of a State Party (new provision).

The UNESCO Commentary specified in relation to this paragraph:

> The fact that it has been included in Article 1 side by side with respect for cultural property is an indication of the importance that the experts at Lauswolt attached to this prohibition to export in view of the multitude of cases of exportation of cultural property that have occurred during recent conflicts (e.g. Iraq-Kuwait, and former Yugoslavia). This paragraph also extends prohibition to movements of cultural property inside the borders of a territory.[170]

The only new provision was the Article concerning precautionary measures included in the Lauswolt document (which became Article 7 of the Protocol) and was supported by Slovenia.

In the comments received from the States Parties to the Hague Convention in 1996,[171] Croatia and Slovenia were in favour of deleting the sub-paragraph of Article 4, paragraph 2 of the Convention. Slovenia further supported its position by stating that military necessity violates the principle of proportionality. The Czech Republic requested either deletion or insertion of the following provision: 'The obligation mentioned in paragraph 1 of the present Article cannot be waived in case of cultural property under special protection as defined in Article 8 of the Convention.' Belgium proposed to insert the word 'unavoidable' in sub-paragraph 2. Kuwait proposed to reconsider the concept of military necessity so as to protect cultural heritage under any circumstances. The International Council on Archives expressed concern that this notion may be misused or interpreted abusively. The conclusion reached by the UNESCO Secretariat from the Expert Meeting

---

170 Ibid., p. 4.
171 CLT-96/CONF.603/INF.4, p. 4.

in Paris in November and December 1994 was that 'some experts wished to exclude it to reinforce the protection of cultural property in the event of armed conflict, others felt that its deletion might interfere with the conduct of military operations.'[172]

The *1997 Meeting of Governmental Experts* on the review of the Hague Convention for the Protection of Cultural Property in the Event of Armed Conflict 1954 (UNESCO Headquarters, Paris, 24–27 March 1997) and its drafting group elaborated the revised version of the Lauswolt document – important for future codification work – and the Secretariat was charged with preparing a working document.[173] The document dealt with the protection of cultural property, the issue of military necessity and illicit export of cultural property from occupied territories.[174] It was pointed out that:

> certain military legal advisers favoured including such a phrase in the new instrument because, according to their views, such a concept has been a part of international customary and treaty law of armed conflicts and the exclusion of this concept would not be accepted by their military. Those observers pointed out that there were close links between 'military necessity' and the corresponding obligation not to use cultural property for military purposes.[175]

The Israeli observer suggested that the following provision be inserted into the new draft: 'The provisions of this instrument shall not prejudice or derogate from accepted customary principles of the Laws of War, including, *inter alia*, the principles of proportionality, distinction and military necessity.'[176]

---

172 UNESCO, Meeting of Governmental Experts on the Review of the 1954 Hague Convention for the Protection of Cultural Property in the Event of Armed Conflict 1954, UNESCO Headquarters, Paris, 24–27 March 1997. *Final Report.* UNESCO document CLT-96/CONF.603/INF.4, p. 4.

173 *Draft provisions for the revision of the 1954 Hague Convention and commentary from the UNESCO Secretariat.* CLT-97/CONF.208/2, Paris, October 1997. The document included the text of the 'revised Lauswolt document'. Draft articles are followed by a Secretariat's comments comparing the original provisions of the Lauswolt document with the revised provisions resulting from the deliberation of participants. Such comments are entitled 'Reasons for change'. The Secretariat has also summarized the main points raised in the discussions in the sections entitled 'Main points of discussion'. Some parts of the revised Lauswolt document were put into square brackets because the discussion did not achieve unanimity on these issues. These had to be subjects of further negotiation.

174 The new draft included another paragraph 5: 'The occupying power shall not encourage, tolerate or facilitate, either directly or indirectly, illicit export of cultural property from the occupied territory.'

175 Draft provisions for the revision of the 1954 Hague Convention and commentary from the UNESCO Secretariat. CLT-97/CONF.208/2, Paris, October 1997, p. 3.

176 Ibid.

The *Revised Lauswolt document* made only a few additions to Article 1, paragraph 3, inserting the words 'any illicit purchase', and adding 'illicit removal' to paragraph 4 concerning occupied territories.

During the discussions at the *1997 Meeting of Government Experts*, Austria, Israel and the UK were in favour of taking military necessity under consideration, but their view was not shared by other experts. The Italian observer considered that general protection could only be waived for self-defence and protection of human lives. The Israeli observer suggested a new article: 'The provisions of this instrument shall not prejudice or derogate from accepted customary principles of the laws of war, including, *inter alia*, the principles of proportionality, distinction and military necessity.' The Iraqi delegate proposed a new paragraph to Article 1: 'Assistance intended to help cultural property in danger shall not be prevented under any circumstances or on any pretext.'[177]

The concept evolved very slowly: the report of the 1997 Meeting of Experts included a wide variety of opinions. Some participants wished to exclude this notion on the ground that it might be misinterpreted and serve as a pretext for non-compliance with the provisions of the Convention. It was also claimed that recent developments in the law of armed conflicts have tended to grant stronger protection to cultural property during hostilities. However, certain military legal advisers favoured including such a phrase in the new instrument because, they contended, such a notion has been part of international customary and treaty law of armed conflicts and the exclusion of this notion would not be accepted by the military. These observers pointed out that there were close links between 'military necessity' and the corresponding obligation not to use cultural property for military purposes.[178]

The *1997 Third Meeting of High Contracting Parties* did not go much further. It was recalled that military necessity must not be confused with military convenience, while the tendency was to accept military necessity but define it precisely and narrowly in order to prevent its abuse and retain its applicability in only a limited number of cases, such as the protection of human lives or self-defence.[179]

---

177 Ibid.

178 UNESCO, Meeting of Governmental Experts on the Review of the 1954 Hague Convention for the Protection of Cultural Property in the Event of Armed Conflict 1954, UNESCO Headquarters, Paris, 24–27 March 1997. *Final Report*. UNESCO document CLT-96/CONF.603/5, Paris, 30 April 1997, p. 2.

179 CLT-97/CONF.208/3, p. 3.

The *1998 Vienna Experts Meeting* followed the same pattern but made reference to the 1977 Additional Protocol. Special attention was also given to the written proposals submitted by several delegations as to the meaning of the concept. The Preliminary Draft of October 1998 reflects the progress made during these discussions.[180] Article 3 of the Preliminary Draft states:

Article 3 Respect for cultural property
1. In order to ensure respect for cultural property it is prohibited:
   a. to use cultural property, its immediate surroundings or its appliances in use for its protection, for purposes which are likely to expose it to destruction or damage in the event of armed conflict.
   b. to commit any acts of hostility directed against cultural property.
   c. to use cultural property in support of the military effort.
2. Cultural property shall never be made the object of reprisals.
3. Any form of theft, pillage or misappropriation of, any archaeological excavation, any act of vandalism directed against, any illicit purchase, or any other breach of integrity [variant: any breach of authenticity] or any transformation of cultural property is prohibited.
4. Without limiting the provisions of the 1954 Protocol, it is prohibited to export or otherwise illicitly remove cultural property from occupied territory or from a part of the territory of a State Party.
[5. The occupying power shall not encourage, tolerate or facilitate, either directly or indirectly, illicit exports of cultural property from the occupied territory.]
6. The obligations in paragraph 1 and 2 may only be waived in the case of imperative military necessity under the following conditions:
   a. only that degree of force may be applied that is not otherwise prohibited by the law of armed conflict and that is required for partial or complete submission of the enemy with a minimum expenditure of time, life and physical resources;
   b. warning is given to the opposing forces;

---

180 Preliminary Draft Second Protocol to the 1954 Hague Convention, HC/1999/1, October 1998, distributed by the Netherlands in preparation for the Diplomatic Conference to be held in the Netherlands in March 1999.

c. a minimum time to redress the situation is given to the opposing forces;
d. the decision to attack is taken on battalion level;
e. no alternative means are reasonably available;
f. means and methods are limited to those which are strictly necessary to counter the threat posed.

This new draft included several elements that can be found in the final text. The governments presented numerous suggestions and substantial comments requesting clarification of the relationship between this article and Article 4 of the Convention (Norway and the UK). The ICRC proposed a new article on the 'loss of general protection'. Several remarks were focused on the problem of occupied territories. The ICRC proposed the inclusion of paragraphs 3, 4 and 5 in a separate article entitled 'Additional protection of cultural property in occupied territories', which later became Article 9 of the Protocol. These comments were taken into consideration when the Secretariat prepared the Final Draft Second Protocol to the Convention for the Diplomatic Conference.

The Final Draft submitted to the 1999 Conference included more precise definitions and included the clause of proportionality.[181] It comprised three articles:

Article 4 Standard of general protection of cultural property
1. Objects constituting cultural property are civilian objects and it is prohibited to commit any act of hostility against such objects provided they are not military objectives.
2. Cultural property may never be made the objects of reprisals.

[Article 5 Loss of general protection
Objects (or sites) constituting cultural property lose their general protection from the moment they become military objectives, that is, when they are used to make an effective contribution to military action and when their total or partial destruction offers a definite military advantage in the circumstances ruling at the time.]

---

181 Draft Second Protocol to the 1954 Hague Convention on the Protection of Cultural Property in the Event of Armed Conflict. UNESCO document HC/1999/1/rev.1.

[Article 6 Conditions for military operations
An attack against cultural property which has lost its general protection according to Article 5 may only be undertaken on the following conditions:

   a. the attack is ordered by an officer commanding a force equivalent to a battalion;

   b. where circumstances permit, a minimum time is given to the opposing forces to redress the situation;

   c. where circumstances permit an effective prior warning shall be communicated to the opposing forces;

   d. no other feasible alternative is available;

   e. the means and methods chosen are limited to those which are strictly necessary to counter the threat posed; and

   f. the damage caused is not excessive in relation to the concrete and direct military advantage anticipate from the attack.]

This article formed the basis of the discussion at the Diplomatic Conference. It was one of the most debated issues and, as usual in the case of this controversial subject, two tendencies dominated the discussion: the advocates of military necessity and those with a humanitarian orientation willing to protect as efficiently as possible the cultural property and eliminate or at least reduce the exception of military necessity.

4. THE 1999 HAGUE DIPLOMATIC CONFERENCE

Nearly two days of the Conference were reserved for discussion of Chapter 2 of the Second Protocol and most of the interventions concerned the question of military necessity.

Even if some delegations were still in favour of deleting the clause of imperative military necessity, most wanted to keep it but wished to clarify the conditions under which imperative military necessity may be invoked[182] and prevent it from being abused.[183] Many delegates recommended following the recent evolution in international humanitarian law – in particular, Article 52, para. 2, second phrase of the 1977 Additional Protocol I and the concept of the 'military objective', which determines clearly the behaviour leading to loss

---

182 1999 Hague Conference, Plenary Session, 16 March 1999: e.g. the delegates of Germany, p. 59; Italy, p. 60; Switzerland, p. 62.
183 Ibid., Indonesia, p. 63.

of protection. The adoption of this new approach, which is clearer and more coherent, does not mean the abandonment of military necessity but rather makes this vague notion understandable and applicable.[184] The ICRC delegate stressed that this article is considered as customary law. According to the US delegate, Chapter 2 should 'reflect accurately and completely the language of current instruments of the law of armed conflict and in particular, those of Additional Protocol I . . . and incorporate the full terms of the condition contained in Article 52 of Protocol I.'[185]

The UK delegate summarized the position of certain delegations:

> Perceptions of the concept of military necessity . . . vary from delegation to delegation. For example, to Austria it was a higher standard than the rules in Article 52 of Protocol I, whereas to others it was seen simply as a let-out clause which allowed commanders to justify almost any attack. The starting point for his delegation was that there had to be some military flexibility of a limited kind both for the attackers and defenders. Any State represented in the room could be either an attacker or a defender. These terms would be neutral and no moral value would be attached to them. It might be helpful to insert in the text the definition of 'attacks' contained in Article 49(1) of Protocol I 1977 so that 'attacks mean acts of violence against the adversary whether in offence or in defence'. Given the differences in approach to the concept of military necessity, he asked how the situation could be clarified and made clear that the standard of protection would be a high one. One option was the suggestion of the delegate of the ICRC, and which was partly adopted in the UNESCO draft to replace the term 'imperative military necessity' with the language of Article 52 of Additional Protocol I of 1977 concerning military objectives. That would however, only work for offensive attacks and not for the use of cultural property by a defender. Another option was to preserve the 1954 text but clarify it by saying what 'imperative military necessity' means, such as that there would be no feasible alternative for achieving the military goal in question. One could also add more qualifications such as conditions and precautions along the lines set out in Articles 6, 7 and 8 of the UNESCO draft. The two options could also be combined, as suggested by Switzerland, and include the

---

184 Ibid., Switzerland, p. 62.
185 Ibid., US delegate, p. 65.

concept of military necessity and Article 52 of Protocol I. He preferred the second option which was outlined by Austria. Like Austria and Argentina, he believed that the present text was over complex and could be simplified.[186]

After the long discussion in the Plenary Session, a Working Group – presided over by Thomas Desch from Austria – was constituted to deal with Chapter 2 of the Protocol. The group dealt with Articles 5–9 and 10. The discussion of the present Article 6 of the Protocol was mostly based on the proposals of Austria and the ICRC.

The Austrian proposal read: 'Imperative military necessity under Article 4, paragraph 2 of the Convention may only be invoked when there is no other feasible alternative for fulfilling the mission and for as long as the reasons for its invocation prevail'.

The ICRC proposal read: 'Objects constituting cultural property lose their general protection from the moment they become military objectives, i.e. when they are used to make an effective contribution to military action and when their total or partial destruction, capture or neutralization offers a definite military advantage in the circumstances ruling at the time'.

The group decided not to repeat the provisions of Article 4 of the Convention and focused on clarifying imperative military necessity. The task was to combine the Austrian and ICRC proposals since the delegates felt that both had merit and were in fact complementary.

The Austrian proposal sought to define the 'imperative' character of military necessity whereas the ICRC proposal sought to use the concept of military objective to give content to the principle of military necessity. A criticism of the ICRC proposal was that it singled out the use of cultural property that could make an effective contribution to military action, whereas Article 52(2) of Additional Protocol I specifies that the nature, location, purpose or use of objects can make an effective contribution to military action. Many delegates, mostly from NATO countries, observed that any definition of military objective had to correspond exactly to the definition given in Article 52(2) of Protocol I.

As a result, the Working Group decided to provide a definition of military objective at the beginning of the Protocol, while Article 4

---

186 Ibid., UK delegate, pp. 94–95.

would limit acts of hostility against cultural property to property 'which, by its use, has become a military objective'. But even in the Working Group, several delegations expressed concern about the restriction 'by its use', whereby cultural property could become a military objective by its use only and not by its location, for example. When the draft prepared by the Working Group on Chapter 2 came back to the plenary, the issue of use and location was clearly too controversial and the text was not acceptable to a significant number of delegations.[187]

The German delegate stated that:

> Article 6 a(i) only retained the word 'use' and omitted the words 'nature, location and purpose' thus leaving the realm of accepted language. Article 52(2) of Additional Protocol I contained language which was the result of a long and difficult debate, as any reader of ICRC authoritative commentary on Additional Protocol I might see.[188]

He added:

> For example, an historic bridge might by its mere location make an effective contribution to military action and its total or partial destruction, capture or neutralization offer a definite military advantage. The same could be said for an historic park which qualified as cultural property under the Convention and its Protocol ,or an historic castle or airport building that is of cultural value may by its mere nature also offer a definite military advantage.[189]

The Egyptian[190] and Greek[191] delegations, supported by some other delegations,[192] were the most active in supporting the restriction whereby cultural property could become a military objective by its use only:

---

187 Henckaerts (1999), p. 602.
188 Plenary Session of the Conference, 24 March 1999: German delegate, p. 258. Supported by the delegates of France, p. 260, Turkey, p. 266, the UK, p. 268, Sweden, p. 270, Denmark and the US, p. 271. The ICRC delegate also supported this view, pp. 273–74.
189 Ibid., German delegate, p. 258.
190 Ibid., Egyptian delegate, p. 261: 'Only by its use could cultural property be considered military objective.'
191 Ibid., Greek delegate, p. 270.
192 Ibid., delegates of Cameroon, Romania, Thailand, Libyan Arab Jamahiriya, Syria, pp. 259, 267, 273.

The argument was that cultural property, which was not used in any way for military action, should never be the object of attack. If mere location could turn a cultural property into a military objective, the protection of cultural property would be greatly diminished. Some positive action should be required from the holder of the property before it could become a military objective. The ICRC supported this approach. Since it was agreed that the nature and purpose of cultural property could never turn it into a military objective, the entire debate centered on the issue of location. The ICRC Commentary to 1977 Protocol I notes that the Working Group of Committee III introduced the location criterion without giving reasons.[193] The same thing could be said of the Second Protocol. No real reasons were given why location had to be included. One example commonly cited at the Diplomatic Conference was that of historic bridges. This example is misleading, however, because it is really the use of such bridges that can make an effective contribution to military action.

The Canadian delegation offered another specific example: the retreat of troops could be blocked by a historic wall and there might be no way around the wall if it was located in a valley or a mountain pass. To go around the wall would take too much time, and the commander would therefore either have to take casualties or break through the wall. In such case, the historic wall would not be used for military action and would become a military objective merely because of its location. This example does not seem realistic as such walls are not usually built in valleys or mountain passes. The need for the criterion of location was not well explained, yet several delegations, mostly from NATO countries, strongly insisted on it.

The ICRC Commentary on Additional Protocol I gives the following examples of objects which by virtue of their location make an effective contribution to military action: a bridge or other construction or a site which is of special importance for military operations in view of its location, either because it is a site that must be seized or because it is important to prevent the enemy from seizing it, or otherwise because it is a matter of forcing the enemy to retreat from it.[194]

As mentioned above with respect to historic bridges, it is really the use of a construction or site that turns it into a military objective.

---

193 Commentary on the Additional Protocols of 8 June 1977, para. 2021, p. 636.
194 Ibid., para. 2021, p. 636.

With regard to sites that must be seized because of their location, the question arose at the CDDH what the situation would be if a belligerent in a combat area wished to prevent the enemy army from establishing itself in a particular area or from passing through that area, for example, by means of barrage fire.[195] There can be little doubt, according to the Commentary, that in such a case the area must be considered as a military objective and treated as such. Of course, such a situation could only concern limited areas and not vast stretches of territory. It applies primarily to narrow passages, bridgeheads or strategic points such as hills or mountain passes.[196]

None of these examples constitute convincing evidence of the need to target cultural property because of its location. There is convincing legal evidence, on the other hand, to say that what turns cultural property into a military objective is ultimately its use. In 1907, Article 27 of the Regulations Respecting the Laws and Customs of War on Land already stipulated that 'in sieges and bombardments all necessary steps must be taken to spare, as far as possible, buildings dedicated to religion, art, science, or charitable purposes, historic monuments, hospitals, and places where the sick and wounded are collected, provided they are not being used at the time for military purposes.' This text confirms that it is their use which makes these objects lose their protection.

The ICRC Commentary on Article 53 of Additional Protocol I confirms this view. Article 53 prohibits the use of cultural property in support of the military effort.[197] The Commentary notes that 'if protected objects were used in support of the military effort, this would obviously constitute a violation of Article 53 of the Protocol, though it would not necessarily justify attacking them. To the extent that it is admitted that the right to do so does exist with regard to objects of exceptional value, such a right would depend on their being a military objective, or not, as defined in Article 52, paragraph 2.'[198] For example, 'it is not permitted to destroy a cultural object whose use does not make any contribution to military action, nor a cultural object which

---

195 Ibid., para. 1955, p. 621.
196 Ibid.
197 Although Article 53 deals with the use of very special cultural property only – e.g. cultural property on the International Register of Cultural Property under Special Protection or the new List of Cultural Property under Enhanced Protection – the author will argue below that there is no need to differentiate between the ways in which special or enhanced protection on the one hand and general protection on the other is lost.
198 Commentary on the Additional Protocols of 8 June 1977, para. 2079, p. 648.

has temporarily served as a refuge for combatants, but is no longer *used as such*'.[199] [200]

Another meeting of the Working Group found the compromise: the phrase 'which, by their use, have become military objects' was changed and replaced by the sentence 'which, by their function, have been made into military objects' in the Second Protocol.[201]

> This represents a twofold change. First, the word 'use' was replaced by 'function', which does not appear in the definition of a military objective. Secondly, 'become' was replaced by the words 'been made into'.
>
> With regard to the new text, there was a clear understanding that the word 'function' referred at the same time to something that was in fact functioning. For example, an old fortification which was not functioning as a fortification could not be considered a military objective. In addition, the new text sought to convey the requirement of an active role on the part of the holder of the cultural property in that the holder made the property into a military objective. This could only happen through use.
>
> It is only by a stretch of imagination that function could cover location: the example of the historic wall blocking retreating soldiers could fall under the new text in that the circumstances make the wall, which functions to block a retreat, into a military objective. But in real life this is not the problem faced by cultural property on the battlefield. In real life the problem is that cultural property is attacked even when it is not used for any military action or is attacked indiscriminately. In real life the rule should be simple: cultural property, which is not used to make an effective contribution to military action and whose destruction, seizure or neutralization does not offer a definite military advantage, cannot be attacked. It is difficult to imagine how military commanders could teach their soldiers anything else.
>
> It is remarkable that military lawyers who call for texts that are simple to teach and apply argue at such length about a minor difference that will be difficult to apply and teach. The reason why some delegates

---

199 Ibid. See Bothe, Partsch and Solf (1982), p. 334, para. 2.6.
200 Henckaerts (1999), p. 604-605.
201 Mr Desch, Austria, Chairman of the Working Group, Plenary Session of the Conference, 24 March 1999, p. 19.

strongly argued for use only was clear. The mere location of pyramids in Egypt or temples on Greek islands should never serve as a pretext to attack those objects. The insistence on changing use to function is difficult to understand if the only example that could be given was that of an ancient wall blocking a pass. This example could easily have been dealt with under the exception of the prohibition on use of cultural property, thus leaving the overall system consistent, clear and simple. It is to be hoped that it will be taught and applied in that way.'[202]

5. ANALYSIS OF ARTICLE 6 OF THE SECOND PROTOCOL

The 1999 Diplomatic Conference maintained the wording of Article 4 of the 1954 Convention. Instead of choosing to revise the wording, as some delegates requested, the majority chose to supplement it. For this reason, 'imperative military necessity' did not disappear from the law concerning the protection of cultural property and continues to be binding for all States Parties to the 1954 Hague Convention and the 1999 Second Protocol. This is expressed in the first phrase of Article 6: '*With the goal of ensuring respect for cultural property in accordance with Article 4 of the Convention.*'

The Conference participants missed the opportunity to adapt the law protecting cultural property to the evolution undertaken in the process of reaffirmation and development of international humanitarian law. Instead of adopting the new way forward based exclusively on the definition of the military objective, military necessity was maintained. The 1999 Diplomatic Conference did not follow the path taken by the CDDH in 1974–77, when the notion of imperative military necessity was considered too vague to constitute an effective limitation on warfare:

> Even military lawyers at the Diplomatic Conference [1974–1977] admitted that it was difficult to teach their troops how to interpret and work with the concept. In general, matters left to discretionary clauses based on military necessity are those which could not be regulated; and matters which are not regulated provide a field for the law to develop. In order to do so, the military philosophy behind the maxim 'Have confidence in the wisdom of the generals' had to be replaced with objective criteria that were binding on the military. The goal of

---

202 Henckaerts (1999), p. 605-606.

the Diplomatic Conference was to give a content to the notion of imperative military necessity with a view to enhancing its meaning and effect.[203]

The new path taken during the 1974–77 Diplomatic Conference abandoned the classic approach to military necessity and chose the approach of defining the military objective. Instead of allowing subjectivity and uncertainty to characterize the clause of military necessity, the Conference choose the definite, material and identifiable approach to the military objective. The ICRC delegate described this new approach as follows:

> In 1977, the Protocol additional to the Geneva Conventions of 12 August 1949, and relating to the Protection of Victims of International Armed Conflicts (Protocol I) did away with this approach. Henceforth, only military objectives – more clearly defined and more carefully selected – were to be made the object of attack. Civilians and civilian objects were not to be made the object of a direct attack. This approach is a clear example of how international humanitarian law balances military necessity and humanitarian needs: it allows attacks that are necessary but establishes strict humanitarian limits.
>
> It was therefore obvious that any improvement of the 1954 Convention should reflect this modern approach: cultural property is generally civilian property and as such should not be attacked; it may be attacked only if and when it becomes a military objective. This approach also has the advantage of providing a clearer answer to the question of when cultural property may be attacked.
>
> The definition of military objective in Article 52(2) of Additional Protocol I was one of the major achievements of the Diplomatic Conference on the Reaffirmation and Development of International Humanitarian Law Applicable in Armed Conflicts (CDDH), which was convened by the Swiss Government in 1974 and adopted Additional Protocol I on 8 June 1977. States not party to Additional Protocol I, such as the United States, Turkey and India, confirmed the customary law nature of this provision during the 1999 Diplomatic Conference that adopted the Second Protocol. This illustrates how the Diplomatic Conference also sought to reaffirm certain rules of humanitarian law while developing others.

---

203 Ibid.

The definition of military objective contains two criteria which have to be fulfilled cumulatively before objects can be destroyed, captured or neutralized. They deal with the nature, location, purpose or use of objects and with the military advantage to be gained by destroying, capturing or neutralizing them. The nature, location, purpose or use of the object has to be such that it makes an 'effective contribution to military action'. The military advantage has to be 'definite, in the circumstances ruling at the time'. These criteria were as clear as it was possible to negotiate during the CDDH and they are fairly strict.

As such, the notion of military objective incorporates the idea of military necessity. Once an object has become a military objective it can be destroyed, captured or neutralized, subject to certain exceptions. This simple rule recognizes the military necessity of attacking certain objects during war. By limiting those objects to those which are military objectives it incorporates the notion that war has a limit. As a result, the concept of military objective embodies the balance that humanitarian law establishes between military interests and humanitarian concerns.[204]

The new definition of imperative military necessity by reference to the military objective

Paragraph (a)

The new definition of imperative military necessity formulated in Article 6 will apply to States who become party to the Second Protocol.

> (a) a waiver on the basis of imperative military necessity pursuant to Article 4 paragraph 2 of the Convention may only be invoked to direct an act of hostility against cultural property when and for as long as:
>
> i. that cultural property has, by its function, been made into a military objective; and
> ii. there is no feasible alternative available to obtain a similar military advantage to that offered by directing an act of hostility against that objective.

---

204 Ibid.

This first paragraph concerns *the attacker*, who must fulfil two conjunctive conditions:

a) Cultural property is military objective by its function; and

b) No other feasible alternative is available.

Paragraph 2 of Article 4 referred to the waiver 'only in the cases where military necessity imperatively requires such a waiver'. No definition of the notion of 'imperative military necessity' was given, nor were any other conditions, precisions or clarifications. We have seen that the delegates at the 1954 Conference were concerned about this lack of precision, but, as this provision was a result of compromise, it was probably impossible to go further. The lack of precision of this term also preoccupied delegates at the 1999 Conference. For this reason, they included conditions for the application of military necessity and specified 'when and for as long as' an 'act of hostility against cultural property' can take place.

By using the words 'when and for as long as', the Article specifies not only the times when these conditions must be complied with but also the duration of these conditions. If the circumstances in question exist only for a very short time, the existence of these conditions will not be satisfied. It is necessary that these conditions continue to exist for the duration of the act of hostility. If these conditions disappear or cease to exist, it will no longer be possible to accomplish the act of hostility under the clause of imperative military necessity. The party to the conflict responsible for the use of the cultural property as military objective may realize that it is creating the situation in which the application of military necessity could take place and find another alternative. It can also benefit from the warning given to it according to sub-paragraph (d). It can therefore change the situation and avoid the acts of hostilities directed against the cultural property.

What is the meaning of 'act of hostility'? The expression is usually used in the plural form of 'hostilities'. The *Dictionary of the International Law of Armed Conflict* defines hostilities as 'acts of violence by a belligerent against an enemy in order to put an end to his resistance and impose obedience'.[205] It adds that 'Positive international law does not define hostilities but often uses the word in, for example, the phrases: Opening of hostilities, conduct of hostilities, acts of hostility, persons taking or not taking part in hostilities, effects of hostilities, suspension of hostilities, end of hostilities.'[206]

---

205 Pietro Verri, *Dictionary of the International Law of Armed Conflict*, Geneva, ICRC, 1992, p. 57.

206 Id., p. 57. The dictionary mentions the treaties in which the word 'hostilities' is used: 1907 Hague Convention III; Hague Regulations, art. 220–41; Hague Convention VI; Geneva Conventions,

'Act of hostility', as used in Article 6, should not be understood as only a single act but as several acts that could be, in this case, directed against cultural property during the existence of the conditions mentioned in the two cumulative sub-paragraphs (i) and (ii). Both conditions specified in these two paragraphs must be present in order to apply the waiver based on imperative military necessity.

Sub-paragraph (a) (i)

(i) that cultural property has, by its function, been made into a military objective; and

Imperative military necessity comes under consideration only when the cultural property becomes, is used as or is transformed into a military objective – in other words, is used for military purposes.

Military objective

The distinction should be made between 'military objectives' and 'military objects'. A military object is military by definition, and attack or military action can be directed against it. A civilian object is protected by its very nature, but it can become a military objective if it is used in a way that deprives it of its civilian character and transforms it into a military objective. Article 6, Paragraph (a) i) rightly respects this distinction.

It was generally recognized that only military objectives can be attacked, but there was no agreed definition of such objectives. In such situations, even during the Second World War and the conflicts that followed, it was up to the belligerents themselves to determine and define the military objectives.

The definition of military objectives has formed part of codification efforts since the very beginning. Before the attempt made in the 1954 Hague Convention, an attempt at a simple definition was included in the non-binding 1922 Hague Rules, making air bombardment legitimate 'only when directed against a military objective, i.e. an objective whereof the total or partial destruction would constitute an obvious military advantage for the belligerent.'[207] No such attempts were made in the 1929 and the 1949 Geneva Conventions,

---

common art. 3; Convention I, art. 17; Convention III, art. 67, 118, 119; Convention IV, art. 44, 49, 130 and 133–35; Additional Protocol I, art. 33, 34, 45, 47, 59 and 60.

207 Hague Rules, art. 24.

which nevertheless referred to military objectives, without defining them. The 1956 ICRC Draft Rules for the Limitation of Dangers incurred by the Civilian Population in Time of War took a new approach in its Article 7:

> Art. 7. In order to limit the dangers incurred by the civilian population, attacks may only be directed against military objectives.
>
> Only objectives belonging to the categories of objective which, in view of their essential characteristics, are generally acknowledged to be of military importance, may be considered as military objectives. Those categories are listed in an annex to the present rules.[208] However, even

---

208 The ICRC, with the help of military experts, drew up and presented as a model, subject to modification, the 'List of Categories of Military Objectives according to Article 7, paragraph 2'. It reads as follows:
I. The objectives belonging to the following categories are those considered to be of generally recognized military importance:
(1) Armed forces, including auxiliary or complementary organizations, and persons who, though not belonging to the above-mentioned formations, nevertheless take part in the fighting.
(2) Positions, installations or constructions occupied by the forces indicated in sub-paragraph 1 above, as well as combat objectives (that is to say, those objectives which are directly contested in battle between land or sea forces including airborne forces).
(3) Installations, constructions and other works of a military nature, such as barracks, fortifications, War Ministries (e.g. Ministries of Army, Navy, Air Force, National Defense, Supply) and other organs for the direction and administration of military operations.
(4) Stores of arms or military supplies, such as munition dumps, stores of equipment or fuel, vehicles parks.
(5) Airfields, rocket launching ramps and naval base installations.
(6) Those of the lines and means of communication (railway lines, roads, bridges, tunnels and canals) which are of fundamental military importance.
(7) The installations of broadcasting and television stations; telephone and telegraph exchanges of fundamental military importance.
(8) Industries of fundamental importance for the conduct of the war:
(a) industries for the manufacture of armaments such as weapons, munitions, rockets, armored vehicles, military aircraft, fighting ships, including the manufacture of accessories and all other war material.
(b) industries for the manufacture of supplies and material of a military character, such as transport and communications material, equipment for the armed forces;
(c) factories or plants constituting other production and manufacturing centers of fundamental importance for the conduct of war, such as the metallurgical, engineering and chemical industries, whose nature or purpose is essentially military;
(d) storage and transport installations whose basic function it is to serve the industries referred to in (a)–(c);
(e) installations providing energy mainly for national defense, e.g. coal, other fuels, or atomic energy, and plants producing gas or electricity mainly for military consumption.
(9) Installations constituting experimental, research centers for experiments on and the development of weapons and war material.
II. The following however, are excepted from the foregoing list:
(1) Persons, constructions, installations or transports which are protected under the Geneva Conventions I, II, III, of August 12, 1949;
(2) Non-combatants in the armed forces who obviously take no active or direct part in hostilities.

if they belong to one of those categories, they cannot be considered as a military objective where their total or partial destruction, in the circumstances ruling at the time, offers no military advantage.'

The fundamental step forward was the adoption of Article 52 of the 1977 Additional Protocol I.

'Military objectives' – as defined, for example, in the ICRC commentary on the Additional Protocol I – are considered to:

> include the armed forces and their installation and transports. As far as objects are concerned, military objectives are limited, according to Article 52 (*General protection of civilian objects*), paragraph 2: to those objects which by their nature, location, purpose or use make an effective contribution to military action and whose total or partial destruction, capture or neutralization, in the circumstances ruling at the time, offers a definite military advantage.[209]

In its reservation of 20 November 1990, expressed on ratification, Canada stated its understanding in relation to Article 52 as follows:

> a. a specific area of land may be a military objective if, because of its location or other reasons specified in the Article as to what constitutes a military objective, its total or partial destruction, capture or neutralization in the circumstances governing at the time offers a definite military advantage; and
>
> b. the first sentence of paragraph 2 of the Article is not intended to, nor does it, deal with the question of incidental or collateral damage resulting from an attack directed against a military objective.

W. Hays Parks, Special Assistant for Law of War Matters to the US Army Judge Advocate General, has criticized the Protocol I definition of 'military objective' as being focused too narrowly on definite military advantage and

---

III. The above list will be reviewed at intervals of not more than ten years by a group of Experts composed of persons with a sound grasp of military strategy and of others concerned with the protection of the civilian population.

209 *Commentary on the Additional Protocols of 8 June 1977*, para. 1874, p. 600. Article 48 of the 1977 Additional Protocol I imposes at all times the distinction between the civilian objects and military objectives and this in order to ensure respect for a protection of the civilian population and civilian objects.

paying too little heed to war-sustaining capability, including economic targets, such as export industries.[210]

Some critics of Coalition conduct in the Gulf War have suggested that the Coalition air campaign, directed admittedly against legitimate military objectives within the scope of the Protocol I definition, caused excessive long-term damage to the Iraqi economic infrastructure with consequential adverse effects on the civilian population.[211]

'Although the Protocol I definition of military objective is not beyond criticism, it provides the contemporary standard which must be used when attempting to determine the lawfulness of particular attacks. That being said, it must be noted once again neither the USA nor France is party to Additional Protocol I. The definition is, however, generally accepted as part of customary law.'[212]

Sub-paragraph (a) (ii)

> ii. there is no feasible alternative available to obtain a similar military advantage to that offered by directing an act of hostility against that objective;

The decision-maker has to make every efforts to avoid an attack on cultural property whenever it is possible to find an alternative. As the ICRC commentary describes it: it is necessary to find 'the lesser of two evils'. This rule already existed in Article 8(a), paragraph 2 of the ICRC Draft Rules for the Limitation of the Dangers incurred by the Civilian Population in Time of War of 1956: 'When the military advantage to be gained leaves the choice open between several objectives, he[213] is required to select the one, an attack on which involves least danger for the civilian population.'

In the Additional Protocol I, a similar provision was included in Article 57, paragraph 3: 'When a choice is possible between several military objectives for obtaining a similar military advantage, the objective to be selected shall be that the attack on which may be expected to cause the least danger to civilian lives and to civilian objects.'

---

210 Parks (1990), pp. 135–45.
211 See Middle East Watch (1991); Gardam (1993).
212 Final Report to the Prosecutor by the Committee Established to Review the NATO Bombing Campaign Against the Federal Republic of Yugoslavia, p. 12, para. 42 (www.un.org/icty/pressreal/ nato0613 00.htm).
213 The person responsible for ordering or launching an attack.

The CDDH accepted this provision without much discussion, and the same occurred at the 1999 Hague Conference.

Paragraph (b)

> (b) a waiver on the basis of imperative military necessity pursuant to Article 4 paragraph 2 of the Convention may only be invoked to use cultural property for purposes which are likely to expose it to destruction or damage when and for as long as no choice is possible between such use of the cultural property and another feasible method for obtaining a similar military advantage;

This second condition concerns the *defending party*, the party that has control of such property and decides to expose it to destruction and damage when the defender has no choice in order to obtain similar military advantage:

> The requirement of the 1954 Convention that the military necessity has to be 'imperative' is made sufficiently clear in Article 4 of the Second Protocol by the second condition, namely that no other alternative is available. Military necessity could therefore virtually never be invoked to justify an attack on cultural property standing in the way of an advancing army, as there are almost always alternatives to circumvent the property. This means that when there is a choice between several military objectives and one of them is a cultural property, the latter shall not be attacked. In fact, this provision adds cultural property to the military objectives which, under Article 57(3) of Protocol I, should not be attacked. The protection of cultural property is enhanced in that the concept of military objective – so widely recognized and used that it has become part of customary international law – is used to define the exception of military necessity. The rule that only military objectives can be targeted is now part and parcel of military manuals and military training worldwide. As many delegates stated at the Diplomatic Conference, it is important to have a simple text which is easy to use and to teach. The concept of military objective fulfils these requirements far better than the vague notion of military necessity.[214]

---

214 Henckaerts (1999), p. 601.

Paragraph (c)

> (c) the decision to invoke imperative military necessity shall only be taken by an officer commanding a force the equivalent of a battalion in size or larger, or a force smaller in size where circumstances do not permit otherwise;

As we have seen, the 1954 Conference was not able to reach a decision on level of command concerning the waiver on military necessity. It was only in relation to special protection that such a decision was given to 'the officer commanding a force equivalent of a division in size or larger'. Concerning general protection, the first Preliminary Draft[215] based on the meetings of government experts and the final Preliminary Draft submitted to the Conference stated that 'the attack is ordered by an office commanding a force equivalent to a battalion'.[216] The first Preliminary Draft stated in Article 3, paragraph 6 (d) that 'the decision to attack is taken on battalion level'. In the comments of the Governments, Austria and Slovenia proposed to insert the words 'at least' after the word 'taken'; China and Israel proposed to add the words 'or higher' at the end; Finland would delete the words 'to attack' and replace them with the words 'to take military action' if needed; Norway questioned the battalion level and the reasoning behind this choice. These comments convey the atmosphere and attitude in the prelude to the Conference.

The Working Group maintained the battalion level. However, the group also took into account that situations might emerge whereby no battalion commanded the theatre of operations; therefore some flexibility in decision-making was felt to be necessary.[217]

At the Plenary Session several delegates proposed the deletion of the last part of the sentence: 'force smaller in size where circumstances do not permit otherwise'.[218]

---

215 HC/1999/1.

216 HC/1999/1/rev.1, art. 6.

217 Desch, Austria, Chairman of the Working Group, Plenary Session of the Conference, 24 March 1999, p. 252.

218 1999 Hague Conference, Plenary Session, 24 March 1999: Poland, Hungary, China, Romania, p. 267.

Paragraph (d)

> (d) in case of an attack based on a decision taken in accordance with sub-paragraph (a), an effective advance warning shall be given whenever circumstances permit.

The first Preliminary Draft based on the meetings of government experts[219] and the final Preliminary Draft submitted to the Conference included the paragraph on conditions of military operations, stating that 'where circumstances permit as effective prior warning shall be communicated to the opposing forces'.[220] In their comments on the first draft, Israel and Norway questioned the obligatory warning to opposing forces, and Israel even doubted its feasibility. The Working Group on Chapter 2 deemed this provision to be necessary in order to provide flexibility in an armed conflict.[221] The delegates of China, Libya and Hungary proposed the deletion of the words 'whenever circumstances permit'.[222]

---

219 HC/1999/1.

220 HC/1999/1/rev.1, art. 6.

221 Desch, Austria, Chairman of the Working Group, Plenary Session of the Conference, 24 March 1999, p. 253.

222 1999 Hague Conference, Plenary Session, 24 March 1999, p. 273.

Article 7
PRECAUTIONS IN ATTACK

Without prejudice to other precautions required by international humanitarian law in the conduct of military operations, each Party to the conflict shall:

a. do everything feasible to verify that the objectives to be attacked are not cultural property protected under Article 4 of the Convention;

b. take all feasible precautions in the choice of means and methods of attack with a view to avoiding, and in any event to minimizing, incidental damage to cultural property protected under Article 4 of the Convention;

c. refrain from deciding to launch any attack which may be expected to cause incidental damage to cultural property protected under Article 4 of the Convention which would be excessive in relation to the concrete and direct military advantage anticipated; and

d. cancel or suspend an attack if it becomes apparent:

   i. that the objective is cultural property protected under Article 4 of the Convention;

   ii. that the attack may be expected to cause incidental damage to cultural property protected under Article 4 of the Convention which would be excessive in relation to the concrete and direct military advantage anticipated.

Preparatory works

The Second Expert meeting on the 1954 Hague Convention for the Protection of Cultural Property in the Event of Armed Conflict. Lauswolt, The Netherlands, 9–11 February 1994.

UNESCO, Meeting of Governmental Experts on the Review of the 1954 Hague Convention for the Protection of Cultural Property in the Event of Armed Conflict 1954, UNESCO Headquarters, Paris, 24–27 March 1997. *Final Report*, UNESCO document CLT-96/CONF.603/5, Paris, 30 April 1997, p. 2.

Draft provisions for the revision of the 1954 Hague Convention and commentary from the UNESCO Secretariat. CLT-97/CONF.208/2, Paris, October 1997.

1998 Vienna Governmental Experts Meeting on the revision of the Hague Convention for the Protection of Cultural Property in the Event of Armed Conflict of 1954. Vienna, 11–13 May 1998. UNESCO document Paris, March 1998, *Final Report*, p. 2

Preliminary Draft Second Protocol to the 1954 Hague Convention. UNESCO document HC/1999/1, October 1998, distributed by the Netherlands in preparation for the Diplomatic Conference to be held in the Netherlands in March 1999.

Draft Second Protocol to the 1954 Hague Convention on the Protection of Cultural Property in the Event of Armed Conflict. UNESCO document HC/1999/1/rev.1.

1999 Hague Conference, Plenary Session, 16 March 1999.

Bibliography

Bothe, M., Partsch, K. J. and Solf, W. A. 1982. *New Rules for Victims of Armed Conflicts: Commentary on the Two 1977 Protocols Additional to the Geneva Conventions of 1949*. The Hague: Martinus Nijhoff, pp. 357–75.

Chamberlain, K. 2004. *War and Cultural Heritage*. Leicester: Institute of Art and Law, pp. 186–88.

Sandoz, Y., Swiniarski, C. and Zimmermann, B. (eds.). 1987. *Commentary on the Additional Protocols of 8 June 1977 to the Geneva Conventions of 12 August 1949*. Geneva: ICRC, Martinus Nijhoff, pp. 677–95.

Desch, T. 1999. The Second Protocol to the 1954 Hague Convention for the Protection of Cultural Property in the Event of Armed Conflict. *Yearbook of International Humanitarian Law*, Vol. 2, p. 75.

Henckaerts, J.-M. 1999. New rules for the protection of cultural property in armed conflict: the significance of the Second Protocol to the 1954 Hague Convention for the Protection of Cultural Property in the Event of Armed Conflict. *IRRC*, No. 835, pp. 593–620, here 613.

ANALYSIS OF THE TEXT

Article 7 must be viewed in connection with Articles 4 and 13 of the Hague Convention. Article 4 is a general provision requiring that the High Contracting Parties refrain 'from any act of hostility directed against such property'. 'Refraining' also means taking all appropriate precautions. Article 13 of the Convention is even more explicit, but only in relation to transportation. According to this article, 'the High Contracting Parties shall take, so far as possible, the necessary precautions to avoid acts of hostility directed against the transport described in paragraph 1 of the present Article and displaying the distinctive emblem'.

As the ICRC legal advisor pointed out, by introducing the notion of military objective, other rules concerning the conduct of hostilities contained in the 1977 Additional Protocol could also be introduced.[223] Article 7 on precautions in attack codifies and elaborates further the principle of distinction between military objectives and cultural property, and is based on Article 57 of the 1977 Additional Protocol I. This last Article codified and developed conventional and customary law in order to exclude collateral casualties and damages. Earlier attempts at codifying these exclusions are found in Article 25 of the 1922 Hague Rules of Air Warfare and Articles 8–10 of the ICRC draft rules of 1956. These formed a good basis for discussion at the 1971 and 1972 Governmental Experts Conferences.

We can trace the origin of this provision in the comments of States Parties to the Hague Convention, in particular Slovenia's proposal that the following paragraph from the Lauswolt document be incorporated into the new draft:

> In order to ensure the protection of cultural property, precautionary measures shall be taken in the conduct of military operations, such as verifying that the objects likely to be used for military purposes or likely to be attacked are not cultural property, taking all feasible precautions in the choice of means and methods with a view to protect cultural property and all other reasonable precautions to avoid losses of or damage to cultural property.

This paragraph was included in the draft adopted at the Second Expert meeting in Lauswolt in 1994 as Article 2.[224] At the 1997 Paris Meeting of Governmental Experts, most of 'the participants stressed the need, when planning military operations, for a scrupulous verification of the character of possible targets to avoid the destruction of cultural property.'[225]

The revised Lauswolt document[226] included a modified version of the provision:

---

223 Henckaerts (1999), p. 613.
224 The Second Expert meeting on the 1954 Hague Convention for the Protection of Cultural Property in the Event of Armed Conflict. Lauswolt, The Netherlands, 9–11 February 1994, art. 2.
225 UNESCO, Meeting of Governmental Experts on the Review of the 1954 Hague Convention for the Protection of Cultural Property in the Event of Armed Conflict 1954, UNESCO Headquarters, Paris, 24–27 March 1997. *Final Report*. UNESCO document CLT-96/CONF.603/5, Paris, 30 April 1997, p. 2.
226 Draft provisions for the revision of the 1954 Hague Convention and commentary from the UNESCO Secretariat. CLT-97/CONF.208/2, Paris, October 1997.

Article 2 Precautionary measures

In order to ensure the protection of cultural property, *the following* precautionary measures shall be taken in *the preparation and* conduct of military operations:

    (i) *all feasible measures* to verify that the object likely to be used for military purposes or likely to be attacked are not cultural property;

    (ii) all feasible precautions in the choice of *targets*, means and methods of attack with a view to protect cultural property; and,

    (iii) all *feasible* precautions to avoid losses of or damage to cultural property.

The Secretariat indicated that the separation was made to clarify the text and included the modification proposed by the experts or participants. At the Vienna Experts Meeting, the participants requested that this provision be strengthened and also asked for clarification of the terms.[227] The Comments of Governments at the end of 1998 expressed their support for the provision, and the ICRC proposed to split the article into two provisions: 'precaution in attack' and 'precaution against the effect of attack'. Israel proposed to add the words 'and location' after 'objects', and Switzerland recommended following more closely the terminology of Article 57(2) of Protocol I.

The following draft was included in the Final Document presented to the Conference:

Article 7 Precautions against attack

In order to ensure the protection of cultural property:

    a. the cultural property shall not be used in direct support of military action;

    b. the cultural property, its immediate surroundings or its appliances in use for its protection, shall not be used for purposes which are likely to expose it to destruction or damage in the event of armed conflict.

---

227 1998 Vienna Governmental Experts Meeting on the revision of the Hague Convention for the Protection of Cultural Property in the Event of Armed Conflict of 1954. Vienna, 11–13 May 1998. UNESCO document Paris, March 1998, *Final Report*, p. 2.

Article 8 Precautions against the effects of hostilities
The parties to the conflict shall, to the maximum extent possible:

a. remove movable cultural property from the vicinity of military objectives or provide for adequate *in situ* protection of cultural property;

b. avoid locating military objectives near cultural property.

Article 9 Precautions in military operations
Without prejudice to other precautions required by international law, the following precautionary measures shall be taken during the preparation and conduct of military operations:

a. all feasible measures to verify that the objectives likely to be attacked are not cultural property;

b. all feasible precautions in the choice of means and methods of attack with a view to avoid, and in any event to minimise, incidental damage to cultural property;

c. cancellation or suspension of an attack if it becomes apparent that the objective constitutes cultural property and not a military objective; and,

d. all other [feasible] [reasonable] precautions to avoid [losses of, or] damage to cultural property.

At the Diplomatic Conference, most of the delegates expressed their support for the proposed provisions as enhancing the protection of cultural property[228] and considered them a logical follow-up to the concept of protection.[229]

Comparison with Article 57 of the 1977 Additional Protocol I

The wording of Article 7 is almost identical to Article 57 of the 1977 Additional Protocol I; it adapts the protection of civilian populations and objects more specifically to the protection of cultural property. Article 7 of the Second Protocol is the specific provision for cultural property.

Article 57 of the 1977 Additional Protocol I protects civilian populations but also civilian objects, and as such it also covers cultural property, which is by its nature also a civilian object. It is important to mention this twofold coverage, for Article 57 will be applied to all States Parties of the 1977

---

228 1999 Hague Conference, Plenary Session, 16 March 1999: Germany, p. 59.
229 Ibid., Switzerland, p. 62.

Additional Protocol, regardless of whether they are party to the 1999 Second Protocol.

The purpose of this commentary is not to comment on Articles 57 or 58 of Additional Protocol I, since excellent commentaries on these provisions are available elsewhere.[230] But we are obliged to use and extensively refer to the codification and development at the CDDH and to the commentaries on these articles, since they very much explain the substance of these provisions, which constitutes the basis of all paragraphs of Article 7.

When dealing with Article 57, the ICRC Commentary on the Additional Protocols noted that 'to some extent Article 57 reaffirms rules which are already contained explicitly or implicitly in other articles',[231] referring in particular to Articles 48, 51, 52 and 54 of Protocol I. The same statement is valid for Article 7, which is based on Article 6 of the Second Protocol.

Article 57 was the result of lengthy discussions and difficult negotiations at the CDDH and the text finally agreed upon was the result of laborious compromise. As Article 7 of the Second Protocol specifically reproduces several paragraphs of Article 57, we have to see each of these provisions in the light of the discussions that took place in Geneva during the CDDH in 1974–77.

The authors of this provision at the 1999 Hague Conference nevertheless considered it important to reaffirm the provision regarding precautions in attack specifically for cultural property. This useful provision will undoubtedly attract the attention of military commanders and act as an *aide memoire* for their duties.

This is mentioned at the outset of Article 7: 'without prejudice to other precautions required by international humanitarian law in the conduct of military operations'. These words refer not only to Articles 57 and 58 (dealing with precautions) but to all provisions included in international humanitarian law as a whole; in other words, the 1907 Hague Regulations and other 1907 Hague Conventions, the 1949 Geneva Conventions and the 1977 Additional Protocols to them (in particular, art. 48–58 of Protocol I), as well as other conventions and treaties, particularly the Convention on Prohibition or Restriction on the Use of Certain Conventional Weapons

---

230 Commentary on the Additional Protocols of 8 June 1977, pp. 677–95; Bothe, Partsch and Solf (1982), pp. 357–75.
231 Commentary on the Additional Protocols of 8 June 1977, para. 2189, p. 679.

which May be Deemed to be Excessively Injurious or to Have Indiscriminate Effects of 1980 and its Protocols.

The first phrase of Article 7 uses the term 'military operations', which are usually defined to mean 'any movements, manoeuvres and other activities whatsoever carried out by the armed forces with a view of combat'.[232]

Article 7 imposes additional limits on attacks directed against legitimate military objectives. It prohibits indiscriminate attacks, as mentioned in other provisions of international humanitarian law: art. 51(4c) and (5b) concerning the civilian population, art. 52 on civilian objects, but also art. 35(1) and (2) and 49(3) and (4) of Protocol I, and art. 3, para 8 of Protocol II to the 1980 Convention.[233]

Article 7 (as well as art. 57 of Protocol I) constitutes an extension of the principle of proportionality already included in Article 6 (art. 52 of Protocol I). During the CDDH, the ICRC persisted, in the face of opposition, in proposing and extending the principle of proportionality.

Article 7 specifies in four paragraphs the choice of precautionary measures, taken nearly *expressis verbis* from Article 57

One provision, paragraph 1 of Article 57, is missing from Article 7. This paragraph indicates that constant care shall be taken in military operations 'to spare the civilian population, civilians and civilian objects'. This paragraph will nevertheless be applied to cultural property on the basis of application of Additional Protocol I, though it is missing from Article 7. It is difficult to explain why such a general provision, often referred to as the 'golden rule', was not included, particularly as it is useful for interpreting all the other paragraphs.

---

232 Ibid., para. 2191, p. 680.

233 Protocol II, as amended in 1996 to the Convention of 1980, defines indiscriminate attacks in case of use of mines, booby-traps or other devices:

Indiscriminate use is any placement of such weapons:

(a) which is not on, or directed against, a military objective. In case of doubt as to whether an object which is normally dedicated to civilian purposes, such as a place of worship, a house or other dwelling or a school, is being used to make an effective contribution to military action, it shall be presumed not to be so used;

(b) which employs a method or means of delivery which cannot be directed at a specific military objective; or

(c) which may be expected to cause incidental loss of civilian life, injury to civilians, damage to civilian objects, or a combination thereof, which would be excessive in relation to the concrete and direct military advantage anticipated.

Article 7 also modified the structure of the provisions of Article 57, placing paragraph 2 and its sub-paragraphs (a) and (b) on the same hierarchical level. The three further sub-paragraphs of sub-paragraph (a), marked by the roman numerals (i), (ii) and (iii), became paragraphs (a), (b) and (c) in Article 7. These sub-paragraphs deal, as we shall see later, with verification of objectives (i), choice of means and methods of combat (ii), and refrain from attack (iii). These three sub-paragraphs are introduced in paragraph (a) of Article 57 with the words: 'Those who plan or decide upon an attack shall:'

In Article 57 this means that, for these three sub-paragraphs, the burden of responsibility is placed at the higher level of military commanders.[234] Such a burden is not left to subordinates, and decisions on these issues should be taken by higher-ranking officers.[235] This responsibility must be viewed also in relation to Article 85 on repression of breaches. It is only the cancellation and suspension of attacks that is left to all levels of command, including the lower levels.

This significant phrase disappeared in the drafting of Article 7,[236] which talks only about 'each Party to the conflict' and not about those who takes the decisions and plans the operations. The authors of Article 7 wanted to enlarge the circle of those who take such important decisions and included not only those responsible for planning and deciding at a high level of command but also those who execute the orders at lower levels. This change also enlarges the circle of those who will assume criminal responsibility according to Article 15, para. 1(c) and (d) concerning serious violations of the Convention and the Protocol. The violation of these provisions will be committed not by the abstract unit 'Party to the conflict' but by those who are acting on its behalf – commanders and other military personnel in charge of military operations.

---

234 The issue of the level on which obligations have to be addressed was an important point of discussion at the CDDH.

235 The ICRC Commentary indicates that 'a very large majority of delegations at the Diplomatic Conference wished to cover all situations with a single provision, including those which may arise during close combat where commanding officers, even those of subordinate rank, may have to take very serious decisions regarding the fate of the civilian population and civilian objects. It clearly follows that the high command of an army has the duty to instruct personnel adequately so that the latter, even if of low rank, can act correctly in the situation envisaged'. (*Commentary on the Additional Protocols of 8 June 1977*, para. 2197, p. 681.)

236 In fact, the text included in the Preliminary Draft Second Protocol was formulated such that no reference was made to the party to the conflict, stating that 'the following precautionary measures shall be taken in the preparation and conduct of military operation'. It was closer to the formulation of Article 57.

Paragraph (a)

This paragraph is adapted according to sub-paragraph 2(a)(i) of Article 57, which states:

> (i) do everything feasible to verify that the objectives to be attacked are neither civilians nor civilian objects and are not subject to special protection but are military objectives within the meaning of paragraph 2 of Article 52 and that it is not prohibited by the provisions of this Protocol to attack them.'

Paragraph (a) of Article 7 applies the same wording on cultural property:

> (a) do everything feasible to verify that the objectives to be attacked are not cultural property protected under Article 4 of the Convention.

This provision imposes on the attacker the duty to verify and identify the objective towards which the attack is directed. Here we are dealing with a civilian object that may eventually be under special protection and should be protected. To avoid the errors of past wars, particularly the Second World War, decisions must be based on accurate information. If doubt subsists, the decision-maker must request additional information, which should be provided by subordinates or those responsible for such information and are answerable to them, such as aerial reconnaissance and intelligence units.[237]

> The evaluation of the information obtained must include a serious check of its accuracy, particularly as there is nothing to prevent the enemy from setting up fake military objectives or camouflaging the true ones. In fact it is clear that no responsible military commander would wish to attack objectives which were of no military interest. In this respect, humanitarian [and cultural] interests and military interests coincide.[238]

---

237 The discussion at the CDDH also noted that identification depends on the technical means available, which may be disproportionate between the parties to the conflict.

238 Commentary on the Additional Protocols of 8 June 1977, para. 2195, p. 681.

In close combat on land, the information provided will be more direct, supplied by a commander's own troops. The presence of enemy troops in a building structure or installation will make an attack legitimate, taking into account all the other precautions included in paragraphs (b) to (d). If a belligerent places troops in sites that are cultural property, these places are exposed to the danger of destruction, and the belligerent assumes full responsibility for these acts.

The words 'everything feasible' were discussed at length at the CCDH.[239] The final choice of words was a response to the divide between those who desired absolute requirement and those who wanted practical measures. When the Article was adopted,

> some delegations stated that they understood these words to mean everything that was practicable or practically possible, taking into account all the circumstances at the time of the attack, including those relevant to the success of military operations.[240] The last-mentioned criterion seems to be too broad, having regard to the requirements of this Article. There might be reason to fear that by invoking the success of military operations in general, one might end up by neglecting the humanitarian obligations prescribed here. Once again the interpretation will be a matter of common sense and good faith. What is required of the person launching an offensive is to take the necessary identification measures in good time in order to spare the population as far as possible. It is not clear how the success of military operations could be jeopardized by this.[241]

---

239 In the draft, the ICRC had used the expression 'take all reasonable steps'. This wording was not retained by the Diplomatic Conference, which opted for the words 'everything feasible'. The translation of 'feasible' into French by *possible* did not seem satisfactory, even though this is one meaning of the English term. According to the *Oxford English Dictionary*, 'feasible' means 'capable of being done, accomplished or carried out, possible, practicable'. Finally agreement was reached on the present French text *tout ce qui est pratiquement possible*, which seems to translate the intent of the drafters of the English version (*Commentary on the Additional Protocols of 8 June 1977*, para. 2198, p. 681 n. 6).

240 India expressed the understanding that Article 57 as a whole will apply in accordance with the limit of capability, practical possibility and feasibility of each Party to the conflict . . . These capabilities will vary, and 'this Article does not require a Party to undertake to do something which is not within its means or its methods or its capability. In its practical application, a Party would be required to do whatever is practical or possible'. Italy also expressed the view that the term is basic to the whole structure of Article 57, and that the obligations are conditional on the actual circumstances really allowing the proposed precautions to be taken, on the basis of available information and the imperative needs of national defence. CDDH/SR.42, annex.

241 Commentary on the Additional Protocols of 8 June 1977, para. 2198, pp. 681–82.

Verification requires the collection and evaluation of timely target intelligence, which the adverse party may frustrate and confuse.

It is also important to mention that the Article refers to cultural property protected under Article 4 of the Convention, that is, to the provisions concerning general protection which the High Contracting Parties have to respect within their own territory, as well as within the territory of other High Contracting Parties. This concerns the property defined in Article 1 of the Convention. The drafters referred to Article 4 in order to make a distinction from the provisions concerning special protection, which have a distinct definition of cultural property.

Paragraph (b)

This paragraph is adapted according to sub-paragraph 2(a)(ii) of Article 57, which states:

> (ii) take all feasible precautions in the choice of means and methods of attack with a view to avoiding, and in any event to minimizing, incidental loss[242] of civilian life, injury to civilians and damage to civilian objects.

Paragraph (b) of Article 7 applies the same wording on the cultural property:

> (b) take all feasible precautions in the choice of means and methods of attack with a view to avoiding, and in any event to minimizing, incidental damage to cultural property protected under Article 4 of the Convention.

In this paragraph we are dealing with the choice of means and methods of attack. In the choice of weapons, it is necessary to take into account the force of such weapons, their precision and range.

At the CDDH, the ICRC warned that there is always a risk that any attack, even when directed against a clearly determined military objective, might affect civilian population and objects, as well as cultural objects. Several factors may influence the accuracy of bombardment: the configuration of

---

242 The ICRC Commentary suggested that it would be better to say 'with a view to reducing incidental loss to a minimum'. (*Commentary on the Additional Protocols of 8 June 1977*, para. 2203, p. 683.)

the terrain (danger of landslides or ricocheting), the relative accuracy of the weapons used (relative dispersion according to the trajectory, ammunition used, condition of equipment, meteorological conditions, effect of wind on atmospheric pressure, clouds), the specific nature of the military objective (ammunition stores, fuel tanks), and the standard of technical training of the combatants and their technical ability in handling weapons.[243] These different factors must be taken into consideration by those who are planning, deciding and executing the attacks. The ICRC's efforts to introduce a reference to the 'immediate vicinity of military objectives' were rejected at the CDDH, and it was necessary to be satisfied with the affirmative duty of doing what is feasible. These rules should be included in military and technical manuals and instructions.

The ICRC commentary considers that:

> such precautions coincide with the concerns of military commanders wishing to economize on ammunition and to avoid hitting points of no military interest. When a well-placed 500 kg projectile is sufficient to render a military objective useless, there is no reason to use a 10-ton bomb or a series of projectiles aimed without sufficient precision. However, it is clear that the circumstances of combat and the control of airspace may render it more difficult to observe this rule. Finally, mention may be made of the precautionary measures taken by the Allied Forces during bombardments carried out during the Second World War against factories located in territories occupied by German forces; in order to avoid hitting the people working in these factories, the attacks took place on days or at times when the factories were empty; the desired effect was to destroy the factories without killing the workers.[244]

This rule does not imply any prohibition of specific weapons. It imposes on commanders a duty to make a choice when they have before them different possible alternatives. The most important option is the general rule: avoid any incidental damage to cultural property. As a complement to the rule of imperative military necessity, they have in any event (i.e. in all possible circumstances) to minimize incidental damage. Here again, Article 15 on individual criminal responsibility is the obligatory reminder.

---

243 CDDH/III/SR. 21, para. 3.
244 Commentary on the Additional Protocols of 8 June 1977, para. 2200, p. 682.

To this end it is necessary to interpret the words 'all feasible precautions'. Protocol II on Prohibitions or Restrictions on the Use of Mines, Booby-traps and Other Devices, as amended on 3 May 1996 at the Convention of 10 October 1980 on Prohibition or Restrictions on the Use of Certain Convention Weapons, gives a new definition of these words in Article 3, paragraph 10:

> All feasible precautions shall be taken to protect civilians from the effects of weapons to which this Article applies. Feasible precautions are those precautions which are practicable or practically possible taking into account all circumstances ruling at the time, including humanitarian and military considerations. These circumstances include, but are not limited to:
> (a) the short- and long-term effect of mines upon the local civilian population for the duration of the minefield;
> (b) possible measures to protect civilians (for example, fencing, signs, warning and monitoring);
> (c) the availability and feasibility of using alternatives; and
> (d) the short- and long-term military requirements for minefield.[245]

Paragraph (c)

The paragraph is adapted according to sub-paragraph 2(a)(iii) of Article 57, which states:

> (iii) refrain from deciding to launch any attack which may be expected to cause incidental loss of civilian life, injury to civilians, damage to civilian objects, or a combination thereof, which would be excessive in relation to the concrete and direct military advantage anticipated.

Paragraph (c) of Article 7 applies the same wording on cultural property:

> c) refrain from deciding to launch any attack which may be expected to cause incidental damage to cultural property

---

245 See also Protocol III on Prohibitions and Restrictions on the use of incendiary weapons (Protocol III), art. 1.

protected under Article 4 of the Convention which would be excessive in relation to the concrete and direct military advantage anticipated.

As in paragraph (d) which follows, the present sub-paragraph includes the rule of proportionality[246] and fixes limits for military action in order to maintain the balance between military necessity and humanitarian, civilian and cultural requirements.

As the ICRC states: 'Even if this system is based to some extent on a subjective evaluation, the interpretation must above all be a question of common sense and good faith for military commanders. In every attack they must carefully weigh up the humanitarian and military interests at stake.'[247]

The ICRC commentary also explains the use of words in this paragraph. Instead of 'which may be expected to cause', some delegates expressed a preference for the expression 'which risks causing', but this was not adopted by Committee III of the CDDH.[248]

The expression 'concrete and direct' was 'intended to show that the advantage concerned should be substantial and relatively close, and that advantages which are hardly perceptible and those which would only appear in the long term should be disregarded';[249] '"concrete" means specific, not general; perceptible to the senses. Its meaning is therefore roughly equivalent to the adjective "definite" used in the two-pronged test prescribed by Article 52(2). "Direct", on the other hand, means "without intervening condition of agency". Taken together the two words of limitation raise the standard set by Art. 52 in those situations where civilians may be affected by the attack';[250] they impose stricter conditions on the attacker than those implied by the criteria defining military objectives in Article 52, and 'there can be no question of creating conditions conducive to surrender by means of attacks which incidentally harm the civilian population.'[251]

Military advantage 'can only consist in ground gained and in annihilating or weakening the enemy armed forces';[252] it refers to the advantage anticipated

---

246 The formulation the ICRC proposed in the 1973 draft read as follows: 'not disproportionate to the direct and substantial military advantage anticipated'. We find similar provisions also in Article 51, para. 5(b) and in Protocol II as amended in 1996, Article 3, para. 8(c) to the 1980 Convention.

247 Commentary on the Additional Protocols of 8 June 1977, para. 2208, p. 684.

248 See Levie (1980), pp. 324–26.

249 Commentary on the Additional Protocols of 8 June 1977, para. 2209, p. 684.

250 Bothe, Partsch and Solf (1982), para. 2.7.2, p. 365.

251 Commentary on the Additional Protocols of 8 June 1977, para. 2218, p. 685.

252 Ibid.

from a specific military operation of which the attack is taken as a whole and not from isolated or particular parts of that operation.[253]

Several delegations at the CDDH regretted that this provision allows a fairly broad margin of judgement and interpretation, while others considered that it provides a useful guideline for military commanders.[254] Similar reservations were expressed in relation to the words 'which would be excessive in relation to the concrete and direct military advantage anticipated', but the provision was maintained by Committee III.[255] This phrase was the object of several interpretative statements at the CDDH; for example, the Italian delegation stated: 'As to the evaluation of the military advantage expected from an attack, referred to in sub-paragraph 2(a)(iii), the Italian delegation wishes to point out that expected advantage should be seen in relation to the attack as a whole, and not in relation to each action regarded separately.'[256] For the ICRC commentary,

> this does not mean that during such an attack actions may be undertaken which would lead to severe losses among the civilian population or to extensive destruction of civilian objects. Not does it mean that several clearly distinct military objectives within an urban area may be considered as a single objective.[257]

Such actions will be considered as indiscriminate attacks[258] and 'not strictly limited to military objectives' as required by Article 52, paragraph 2 and by the principles of distinction (civilian objects).

An interesting consideration of the principle of proportionality was included in the Final Report to the Prosecutor by the Committee Established to Review the NATO Bombing Campaign Against the Federal Republic of Yugoslavia. It describes the principle of proportionality in the following way:

> 48. The main problem with the principle of proportionality is not whether or not it exists but what it means and how it is to be applied.

---

253 CDDH/SR.41, para. 141 (Netherlands); annex: Canada, Germany; SR.42, annex: Germany, Italy and the US.
254 OR Vol. VI, pp. 211 ff. CDDH/SR.42.
255 OR XIV, p. 303, CDDH/III/SR.31, para. 31. Romanian delegates objected to this wording.
256 OR, VI, p. 231, CDDH/SR.42, Annex (ad art. 50). See also the declaration of the Netherlands on Article 3(8) of Protocol II of the 1980 Convention.
257 Commentary on the Additional Protocols of 8 June 1977, para. 2218, p. 685.
258 See n. 233 above.

It is relatively simple to state that there must be an acceptable relation between the legitimate destructive effect and undesirable collateral effects. For example, bombing a refugee camp is obviously prohibited if its only military significance is that people in the camp are knitting socks for soldiers. Conversely, an air strike on an ammunition dump should not be prohibited merely because a farmer is plowing a field in the area. Unfortunately, most applications of the principle of proportionality are not quite so clear cut. It is much easier to formulate the principle of proportionality in general terms than it is to apply it to a particular set of circumstances because the comparison is often between unlike quantities and values. One cannot easily assess the value of innocent human lives as opposed to capturing a particular military objective.

49. The questions which remain unresolved once one decides to apply the principle of proportionality include the following:
    (a) What are the relative values to be assigned to the military advantage gained and the injury to non-combatants and or the damage to civilian objects?
    (b) What do you include or exclude in totaling your sums?
    (c) What is the standard of measurement in time or space? and,
    (d) To what extent is a military commander obligated to expose his own forces to danger in order to limit civilian casualties or damage to civilian objects?

50. The answers to these questions are not simple. It may be necessary to resolve them on a case by case basis, and the answers may differ depending on the background and values of the decision maker. It is unlikely that a human rights lawyer and an experienced combat commander would assign the same relative values to military advantage and to injury to noncombatants. Further, it is unlikely that military commanders with different doctrinal backgrounds and differing degrees of combat experience or national military histories would always agree in close cases. It is suggested that the determination of relative values must be that of the 'reasonable military commander'. Although there will be room for argument in close cases, there will be many cases where reasonable military commanders will agree that the

injury to noncombatants or the damage to civilian objects was clearly disproportionate to the military advantage gained.[259]

'Incidental damage', used in paragraph (c) of Article 7, is equivalent to 'incidental loss' in Article 57. The danger to the cultural property may also depend on several factors: location (within or in the vicinity of a military objective), the terrain (landslides, floods, etc.), accuracy of the weapons used, weather conditions (visibility), the specific nature of the military objective concerned (ammunition depot, fuel reservoir, main road of military importance), and the technical skill of the combatants. These different factors must be taken into consideration in the evaluation of incidental damage.

As in the case of Protocol I,[260] violations of paragraph (c) will constitute serious violations under Article 15, paragraphs (c) and (d) of the Second Protocol when committed intentionally and in violation of the Convention and the Second Protocol.

Paragraph (d)

The paragraph is adapted according to sub-paragraph 2(b) of Article 57, which states:

> (b) an attack shall be cancelled or suspended if it becomes apparent that the objective is not a military one or is subject to special protection or that the attack may be expected to cause incidental loss of civilian life, injury to civilians, damage to civilian objects, or a combination thereof, which would be excessive in relation to the concrete and direct military advantage anticipated.

Paragraph (d) of Article 7 applies the same wording on cultural property:

> (d) cancel or suspend an attack if it becomes apparent:
>
> (i) that the objective is cultural property protected under Article 4 of the Convention;

---

259 Final Report to the Prosecutor by the Committee Established to Review the NATO Bombing Campaign Against the Federal Republic of Yugoslavia (http://www.un.org/icty/pressreal/nato061300.htm).

260 And according to Article 85 of Protocol I.

(ii) that the attack may be expected to cause incidental damage to cultural property protected under Article 4 of the Convention which would be excessive in relation to the concrete and direct military advantage anticipated.

Article 57, paragraph 2(i), (ii) and (iii) applies, according to the text, to those who are planning or deciding upon attacks. Paragraph 2 applies to all who are undertaking the attacks – in other words, to those who are planning and deciding, but also and primarily to those who are executing the attacks. As we have seen, such a distinction was not adopted by the authors of Article 7. The obligation is addressed to the attacker at all echelons, including higher ones (who usually have better intelligence at their disposal). The lower echelons are particularly concerned with the duty to cancel or suspend the attack.

This provision is a complement, but also an appropriate warning, to all attackers who can otherwise be held responsible for serious violations according to Article 15 of the Second Protocol.

We have dealt with this wording in the commentary on the previous paragraphs, so it is not necessary to return to these explanations here. Article 57 of Protocol I and Article 7 of the Second Protocol concern the fire aspect of military operations. Fire must cease if the object of attack has been mistakenly identified as a military objective.

The proportionality rule is concerned with the identification and evaluation of concrete and direct military advantage:

> In a coordinated military operation, the relative importance of the military objective under attack in relation to the concrete and direct military advantage anticipated is not a matter which can be determined by individual tank leader, the commanders of lower echelon units or individual attacking bomber aircraft. If assigned a fire or bombing mission they must assume that an appropriate assessment had been made by those who assigned the mission. Thus, in this situation, the decision to cancel will have to be made at the level where the decision to initiate the attack was made.[261]

On the other hand, the ICRC commentary provides a practical example in relation to this provision:

---

261 Bothe, Partsch and Solf (1982), para. 2.8.1.3, pp. 366–67.

It is principally by visual means – in particular, by means of aerial observation – that an attacker will find out that an intended objective is not a military objective, or that it is an object entitled to special protection. Thus, to take a simple example, an airman who has received the order to machine-gun troops traveling along a road, and who finds only children going to school, must abstain from attack. However, with the increased range of weapons, particularly in military operations on land, it may happen that the attacker has no direct view of the objective, either because it is very far away, or because the attack takes place at night. In this case, even greater caution is required.[262]

For obvious reasons, the authors of the provision were not inclined to introduce into Article 7 the other paragraphs of Article 57: paragraphs 2(c), 3, 4 and 5. All these provisions apply to cultural property regarded as civilian objects. There was probably even less reason to include them among the specific provisions of the Second Protocol.

Paragraph 2(c) concerns effective advanced warnings and is addressed mainly to the possible evacuation of civilian populations. Its application is less realistic and practical for the transport of movable cultural property, mainly because of time limits.

Paragraph 3 deals with the choice between different military objectives. It requires the attacker, when in a position to obtain similar military advantage, to select objectives 'which may be expected to cause least danger to civilian lives and to civilian objects'. Such a choice is largely academic in relation to cultural property as it is unlikely that the attacker will be confronted with a choice between two or even several objects of cultural value. If the choice is between cultural property and a civilian population, the choice will be made in favour of civilians. Concerning a choice between civilian objects, where one object constitutes cultural property, the choice depends on the specific circumstances, and we must express the hope that the soldier making the decision has received sufficient instruction to be able to make the most appropriate choice.

Paragraph 4 concerns military operations at sea and in the air and was introduced into Protocol I by the CDDH Working Group of Committee III. It was not considered necessary to include this provision in the Second Protocol, since the provision is applicable to cultural property, which is in principle a civilian object. On the other hand, Article 7 of the Second

---

262 Commentary on the Additional Protocols of 8 June 1977, para. 2221, p. 686.

Protocol is obviously applicable to such military operations. It is interesting that the codification of the law of sea warfare already includes provisions concerning cultural property,[263] as do the Rules of Air Warfare, drafted by the Commission of Jurists in 1922 and 1923, and these correspond largely to the customary rules and general principles underlying conventions on the law of war on land and at sea.[264]

Paragraph 5 only confirms the evidence that nothing in the provisions could be misused for the justification of attacks.

Reservations concerning Article 57, paragraph 2

Because Article 7 of the Second Protocol was fundamentally influenced by Article 57 of the 1977 Additional Protocol I, it may be important to indicate that several High Contracting Parties noted reservations about this Article during the process of signature, ratification or accession to Additional Protocol I. Even if such reservations were not reiterated in relation to the 1999 Second Protocol, their expression in relation to a document of fundamental importance to humanitarian law may help us better understand the attitudes of certain States towards expressions used in the Additional Protocol, which may influence the understanding of legal and military terms used in Article 7.

Military advantage

For Australia, references to 'military advantage' are intended to mean advantage anticipated from a military attack considered as a whole,[265] not from isolated or particular parts of that attack,[266] and that the term 'military advantage' involves a variety of considerations, including the security of attacking forces. Furthermore, it is Australia's understanding that the term 'concrete and direct military advantage anticipated', used in Articles 51 and 57, means a *bona fide* expectation that the attack will make a relevant and proportional contribution to the objective of the military attack involved. New Zealand expressed a similar reservation.

---

263 1907 Convention (IX) concerning Bombardment by Naval Forces in Time of War, art. 5. See Schindler and Toman (2004), p. 1081. See also Doswald-Beck (1995), art. 47.

264 See, in particular, Articles 24, 25 and 26 of the Hague Rules of Air Warfare. See Schindler and Toman (2004), pp. 319–20.

265 Or in 'its totality', as mentioned in Belgium's reservation at ratification, and 'not from the isolated or particular parts of the attack' (France, Italy).

266 Germany, Spain and the UK.

Decision of the military commander

Austria expressed a reservation about Article 57, paragraph 2, stating 'the understanding that, with respect to any decision taken by a military commander, the information actually available at the time of the decision is determinative'. Furthermore, 'it is the understanding of Australia that military commanders and others responsible for planning, deciding upon, or executing attacks, necessarily have to reach their decisions on the basis of their assessment of the information from all sources, which is available to them at the relevant time.' Similarly for Canada, Ireland, Italy, the Netherlands, New Zealand, Spain and the UK.

Feasible precautions

Belgium: 'those that can be taken in the circumstances prevailing [practicable or practically possible] at the moment, which include military considerations as much as humanitarian ones'. Similarly for Canada, Germany, Ireland, Italy, the Netherlands, Spain and the UK (including the words in brackets).

Due precautions

France indicates that it 'will take all due precautions referred to in the provisions of Article 56, of Article 57, paragraph 2(a)(iii) and of paragraph 3(c) of Article 85 in order to avoid severe collateral losses among the civilian populations, including possible direct attacks.'

Cancellation or suspension of the attack

France considers that 'the duty to cancel or suspend an attack according to the provisions of paragraph 2(b) of Article 57 requires only the application of normal proceedings for cancellation or suspension of this attack on the basis of information available to those deciding on an attack.' Similarly for the UK.

Article 8
PRECAUTIONS AGAINST THE EFFECTS OF HOSTILITIES

The Parties to the conflict shall, to the maximum extent feasible:

a. *remove movable cultural property from the vicinity of military objectives or provide for adequate in situ protection;*

b. *avoid locating military objectives near cultural property.*

Preparatory works

UNESCO, Meeting of Governmental Experts on the Review of the 1954 Hague Convention for the Protection of Cultural Property in the Event of Armed Conflict 1954, UNESCO Headquarters, Paris, 24–27 March 1997. *Final Report,* UNESCO document CLT-96/CONF.603/5, Paris, 30 April 1997, p. 2.

1998 Vienna Governmental Experts Meeting on the revision of the Hague Convention for the Protection of Cultural Property in the Event of Armed Conflict of 1954. Vienna, 11–13 May 1998. UNESCO document Paris, March 1998, *Final Report,* p. 2.

Preliminary Draft Second Protocol to the 1954 Hague Convention, HC/1999/1, October 1998, distributed by the Netherlands in preparation for the Diplomatic Conference to be held in the Netherlands in March 1999.

Draft Second Protocol to the 1954 Hague Convention on the Protection of Cultural Property in the Event of Armed Conflict. UNESCO document HC/1999/1/rev.1.

1999 Hague Conference, Plenary Session, 16 March 1999.

Bibliography

Bothe, M., Partsch, K. J. and Solf, W. A. 1982. *New Rules for Victims of Armed Conflicts: Commentary on the Two 1977 Protocols Additional to the Geneva Conventions of 1949.* The Hague: Martinus Nijhoff, pp. 357–75.

Chamberlain, K. 2004. *War and Cultural Heritage.* Leicester: Institute of Art and Law, pp. 188–89.

Sandoz, Y., Swiniarski, C. and Zimmermann, B. (eds.). 1987. *Commentary on the Additional Protocols of 8 June 1977 to the Geneva Conventions of 12 August 1949.* Geneva: ICRC and Martinus Nijhoff, pp. 691–96.

Desch, T. 1999. The Second Protocol to the 1954 Hague Convention for the Protection of Cultural Property in the Event of Armed Conflict. *Yearbook of International Humanitarian Law*, Vol. 2, p. 75.

Henckaerts, J.-M. 1999. New rules for the protection of cultural property in armed conflict: the significance of the Second Protocol to the 1954 Hague Convention for the Protection of Cultural Property in the Event of Armed Conflict. *IRRC*, No. 835, pp. 593–620, here 613.

ANALYSIS OF THE TEXT

The provisions of Article 8 were closely related to those of Article 7 during the preparatory work. This is largely due to the ICRC proposal for the original article, 'Precautionary measures', to be divided into two separate articles, following the example of Additional Protocol I. This evolution is described in the introductory section on Article 7.

Article 8 of the Second Protocol is the specific provision for cultural property. As was the case for Article 7, it is inspired by its respective article in the 1977 Additional Protocol I, Article 58, its wording adapted to suit the needs of cultural property. As such, the wording of Article 8 is almost identical to that of Article 58.

Article 58 of the 1977 Additional Protocol I provides precautions and protects civilian populations and civilian objects; as such, it also covers cultural property, which is by nature a civilian object. This twofold coverage is significant since Article 58 applies to all States Parties to the 1977 Additional Protocol I, as well as to those States that are not and will not be party to the 1999 Second Protocol.

The purpose of the present commentary is not to comment on Article 58 of Additional Protocol, for excellent commentaries on these provisions are available elsewhere. [267] But we are obliged to use and extensively refer to the codification and development at the CDDH and the commentaries on these articles, as they very much explain the substance of these provisions, which constitutes the basis of all the paragraphs in Article 8.

The title of Article 8 was modified. It refers not to the effects of attacks but to the effects of hostilities, which are substantially larger.

The Article is a complementary measure to the more active precautions taken by parties to the conflict according to Article 7. It ensures respect for the

---

267 *Commentary on the Additional Protocols of 8 June 1977*, pp. 677–95; Bothe, Partsch and Solf (1982), pp. 357–75.

principle of distinction but is independent of Article 7 since it concerns only the party that has control over the territory in which the cultural property is located. Article 7 is mostly addressed to the party actively involved in military operations, even if the attacks can be both offensive and defensive. Article 8 is concerned not with attacks and active participation in hostilities but with precautionary measures against hostilities of a passive character.

Parties to the conflict may expect that their adversaries will behave in accordance with their obligations (including respect for Article 7). But they must also cooperate regarding these aims by taking all possible precautions for the benefit of cultural property located within their territory.

For Article 58 of Protocol I there was a precedent provision in the 1956 Draft Rules, namely Article 11, that included such precautionary measures, though only for civilian populations, not for civilian objects. Only a few measures can be cited concerning civilian objects and their safeguarding,[268] but these are of a different nature. Essentially two measures establish such precautionary measures: Articles 12 and 13 of the 1954 Convention concerning the transport of cultural property. Both were deemed insufficient. Lastly, Article 8 is closely linked to Article 5 of the 1999 Second Protocol.

Provisions concerning the removal of cultural property were included in the Lieber Code in 1863. According to its Article 36, 'the ruler of the conquering State or nation may order them to be seized or removed for the benefit of the said nation'. The Preliminary Draft Convention of 1938 included a provision on immunity for means of transportation taking place under international supervision. The 1954 Hague Convention included two provisions: Article 12 on transport under special protection, which builds on Article 17 and 18 of the Regulations for Execution of the Convention, and Article 13 on transport in urgent cases.[269]

As noted in our 1996 Commentary:

> There are many reasons for expressing doubts about the feasibility of the kind of transport operations described in Article 12. It seems to us that such protection will not be easy to carry out. We can see that in practice, the organization of the system of supervision and the designation of the Protecting Powers and Commissioners-General are not easy to put into effect.[270]

---

268 1907 Hague Regulations, art. 27; 1907 Hague Convention No. IX, art. 5; Fourth 1949 Geneva Convention, art. 18 and 28; 1954 Hague Convention, art. 4 and 8.
269 Toman (1996), pp. 151–67.
270 Ibid., p. 165

It was therefore helpful that a more flexible, practical and realistic formula was included within Article 13 of the Convention, 'though naturally without foreseeing the obstacles that arose subsequently when the Convention came to be applied'.[271] But even if a simple form of transport is used, Article 13 of the Convention may still encounter other obstacles, such as the issue of the distinctive emblem, and notification of the opposing side, as indicated in the comments on this Article. For these reasons, the general and simple provision on removal of the property included in Article 8, first part of the paragraph 1, is very useful. Furthermore, in cases where removal is impossible, particularly with regard to immovable property, adequate forms of *in situ* protection should be envisaged and are encouraged. However, it must be kept in mind that all these forms of precaution are limited by the clause 'maximum extent feasible'; but, as we shall see, the insertion of this limitation was the condition *sine qua non* for acceptance of this provision.

Concerning the 'mother provision' of Article 58, the Governmental Expert Meetings in 1971 and 1972 manifested little enthusiasm for these complementary measures. The imposition of mandatory obligations to take precautions with respect to nationals and property in national territory was considered an infringement on sovereignty. Several delegations at the CDDH defended their freedom to organize their national defence in the most effective way, according to their own judgment.[272] This was particularly the case for the placement of military objectives outside densely populated areas. For this reason, they insisted on the phrase 'to the maximum extent feasible', where 'feasible' means 'practicable or practically possible, taking into account all circumstances at the time, including those relevant to the success of military operations'.[273]

The introductory phrase encourages parties to the conflict to do their utmost in taking precautions: 'to the maximum extent feasible' to minimize

---

271 Ibid.
272 Delegate of the Republic of Korea: 'it is the understanding of my delegation that this provision does not constitute a restriction on a State's military installations on its own territory. We consider that military facilities necessary for a country's national defense should be decided on the basis of the actual needs and other considerations of that particular country'. Official Records, Vol. VI, pp. 234–35, CDDH/SR.42, annex: Republic of Korea. In their reservations, Austria and Switzerland indicated that paragraph (a) and (b) will be applied subject to requirements for their defense of the national territory.
273 See, e.g., the report of the Committee CDDH/215/rev.1, para 102. See also CDDH/SR.42, para. 41, 59, 61 (Turkey, the UK, Netherlands), annex: Canada, Germany, Italy, Republic of Korea, Cameroon and the US.

the collateral effects of hostilities. As the ICRC Commentary put it, 'no one can be required to do the impossible'.[274]

Articles 8 and 58 apply to all territories under the effective *de facto* control of a party, including national territory 'which is under its control and any foreign territory under its control'.[275]

Paragraph (a)

This paragraph includes two different measures that are dependent on the practical and concrete circumstances of each case:

remove movable cultural property from the vicinity of military objectives,

or

provide for adequate in situ protection.

'Removal' refers to transport out of the area close to the military objective, the alternative being provision of protection at the place where the cultural property is located. The best choice depends on the specific circumstances of each individual case. Removal and transportation should be carried out under the most appropriate conditions possible for movable cultural property. It is probable that removal will not require long-distance transportation; otherwise the Convention provisions concerning transportation could apply (art. 13). Immovable property cannot be removed and is in danger when situated close to a military objective. The only solution is to undertake protective measures where such cultural property is located.

But, as we have seen, Article 13 includes certain conditions that constitute an obstacle to effective removal. This is why the present provision – simple, general and without specific conditions – is most welcome in the interests of cultural property.

It may be useful to recall our previous comments on Article 13 of the Convention: In the event of the inapplicability of Article 12 of the Convention, mentioned above, Article 13 is better suited for the transfer of cultural property. This Article is designed at the outset:

a) to provide for evacuation to safe refuge at the opening of hostilities;

---

274 Commentary on the Additional Protocols of 8 June 1977, para. 2245, p. 692.
275 The report of the Committee CDDH/215/rev.1, para. 103.

b) to be applied in the case of transport not planned in peacetime but necessitated, in the course of a conflict, by unforeseen circumstances requiring immediate action.

In the first case (a) – transfers of property at the beginning of a conflict – the point was made that, in theory, it would be desirable for evacuation transport to take place before the outbreak of a conflict. However, there will often be many justifiable reasons, especially psychological, militating against such transport being effected before general mobilization of armed forces, which explains why measures of this type might not be taken. Moreover, in most cases hostilities break out suddenly or unforeseeably, so that such transfers cannot take place at the most suitable moment. It is precisely for these reasons that this kind of situation needs to be anticipated in peacetime and the evacuation and movement of cultural property planned in detail.[276]

These measures and plans of action could also be relevant in the second case (b) – transport and evacuation during a conflict – when unforeseen circumstances make it necessary. This would include, for example, transport to the improvised refuges referred to in the Regulations for the Execution of the Convention.[277] In all cases where, for various reasons, a transfer cannot be notified in advance or placed under international control – and therefore cannot be effected according to the requirements set out in Article 12 and the Regulations for the Execution of the Convention – Article 13 provides for a minimum of protection: the High Contracting Parties shall take 'so far as possible the necessary precautions to avoid acts of hostility directed against the transport described in paragraph 1 of the present Article and displaying the distinctive emblem'. In such cases, the Convention requires that transport

---

276 This is the duty of all persons with responsibility for this property in peacetime. The measures to be taken need to be thought out well in advance in the same way as precautions against fire, flood and so on. The civil authorities responsible for cultural property accordingly need to have close peacetime liaison with the military authorities, so that if such a situation does arise, the experts and technical staff, packing materials, trucks, trains and/or aircraft may be made available to the authorities responsible for civil protection and those responsible for cultural property. Evacuation plans and programmes need to be drawn up, those places where the property can be appropriately protected (in the country or abroad) identified, and the most suitable routes selected away from main roads, since these will be congested with military traffic or exposed to enemy attack. Provision will also need to be made for military escorts, and so on.

277 It has to be realized that the movement of cultural property always involves exposure to serious risk. One has only to think of the risks involved when there is no urgency at all in the transport arrangements, as with exhibits being conveyed for display at exhibitions. Such transfers therefore should not be contemplated unless they are imperative for the safety of the property to be protected and in cases of extreme urgency. The experts all consider that these risks are to be treated as greater than those arising from enemy occupation. It will be a matter for the civil authorities, in cooperation with the military authorities, to weigh these risks and assume their responsibilities, bearing in mind all the circumstances and not simply the importance of the physical protection of the property.

display the emblem. In fact, even admitting that military necessities prevent the conferring of immunity on the transports as provided for in Article 12 of the Convention, it is desirable, because of the very great value of most property transferred to a refuge, that the transports enjoy the right to bear the emblem in order that the armed forces of the parties to the conflict may realize that property is being transferred whose safeguarding is of concern to the international community as a whole.

We should also mention paragraph 5 of the Protocol for the Protection of Cultural Property in the Event of Armed Conflict, signed at The Hague on 14 May 1954. It reads:

> 5. Cultural property coming from the territory of a High Contracting Party and deposited by it in the territory of another High Contracting Party for the purpose of protecting such property against the dangers of an armed conflict, shall be returned by the latter, at the end of hostilities, to the competent authorities of the territory from which it came.

This paragraph, proposed by Poland, applies when cultural property has been transported abroad without benefiting from the provisions of Articles 12 and 13 of the Convention. The paragraph deals with precautionary measures in relation to property, before an armed conflict breaks out.

Paragraph (b)

> *avoid locating military objectives near cultural property.*

The ICRC commentary states: 'It is to be expected that in future armed conflict, as in the past, military objectives will continue to be attacked wherever they are located'.[278] This last requirement will not be easily implemented. As we have seen, the provisions of Article 8 of the Convention faced various difficulties, and 'adequate distance' was one of the major obstacles to the implementation of special protection.

If paragraph (a) is applied mostly in pre-conflict or conflict situations, paragraph (b) also requires measures to be taken in peacetime. It is in the State's own interest to take such measures.

---

278 Bothe, Partsch and Solf (1982), para. 2.9, p. 375.

Article 9
PROTECTION OF CULTURAL PROPERTY IN OCCUPIED TERRITORY

1. *Without prejudice to the provisions of Articles 4 and 5 of the Convention, a Party in occupation of the whole or part of the territory of another Party shall prohibit and prevent in relation to the occupied territory:*
   a. *any illicit export, other removal or transfer of ownership of cultural property;*
   b. *any archaeological excavation, save where this is strictly required to safeguard, record or preserve cultural property;*
   c. *any alteration to, or change of use of, cultural property which is intended to conceal or destroy cultural, historical or scientific evidence.*
2. *Any archaeological excavation of, alteration to, or change of use of, cultural property in occupied territory shall, unless circumstances do not permit, be carried out in close co-operation with the competent national authorities of the occupied territory.*

Preparatory works

Draft Second Protocol to the 1954 Hague Convention on the Protection of Cultural Property in the Event of Armed Conflict. UNESCO document HC/1999/1/rev.1.
1999 Hague Conference, Plenary Session, 16, 24 and 26 March 1999.

Bibliography

Chamberlain, K. 2004. *War and Cultural Heritage.* Leicester: Institute of Art and Law, pp. 189–91.
Desch, T. 1999. The Second Protocol to the 1954 Hague Convention for the Protection of Cultural Property in the Event of Armed Conflict. *Yearbook of International Humanitarian Law,* Vol. 2, p. 75.
Toman, J. 1996. *The Protection of Cultural Property in the Event of Armed Conflict: Commentary on the Hague Convention of 14 May 1954.* Aldershot: Dartmouth/Paris: UNESCO, pp. 359–60.

ANALYSIS OF THE TEXT

The 1954 Hague Convention includes specific provision for the protection of cultural property in occupied territory. Article 5 is simply entitled 'Occupation'. The 1996 Commentary provided details on useful characteristics of this provision.[279]

Article 9 of the 1999 Second Protocol is composed of two paragraphs. Paragraph 1 completes Article 5 of the Convention by imposing on the Occupying Power several prohibitions and preventive measures relating to the occupied territory. Paragraph 2 underlines the exclusive competence of the national authorities of the occupied territory in the event that any archaeological excavation of, alteration to, or change of use of cultural property is undertaken, 'unless circumstances do not permit'. The title of the Article and the introductory phrase of the paragraph 1 indicate that two elements must be kept in mind:

- protection of cultural property, regulated in particular by Article 4 of the Convention, and
- occupied territory, regulated in principle by Article 5 of the Convention.

These two elements are not modified by the Second Protocol and continue to be applied. Article 9 indicates that the prohibitions and preventive measures included within it are 'without prejudice' to the two articles of the Convention.

Occupation

Before dealing with the provisions of this Article, it may be useful to remember the meaning of the words 'occupation' and 'occupied territory'.

The basic provisions defining 'occupation' are the articles of the 1907 Hague Regulations, which are part of customary international law and therefore are binding on all States. Article 42 of the Regulations gave the following definition of 'occupation': 'Territory is considered occupied when it is actually placed under the authority of the hostile army. The occupation extends only to the territory where such authority has been established and

---

279 Toman (1996), pp. 83–89.

can be exercised.' Article 56 is of particular concern to cultural property, since it prohibits seizure, destruction or wilful damage.[280]

> The property of municipalities, that of institutions dedicated to religion,[281] charity and education, the arts and sciences, even when State property, shall be treated as private property.[282] All seizure of, destruction or willful damage done to institutions of this character, historic monuments, works of art and science,[283] is forbidden, and should be made the subject of legal proceedings.[284]

According to Article 2 common to the 1949 Geneva Conventions, its humanitarian provisions 'also apply to all cases of partial or total occupation of the territory of a High Contracting Party even if the said occupation meets with no armed resistance.'

The establishment of mandatory direct administration is only a *de facto* administration and does not release the Occupying Power from its duties under the law of occupation. Article 47 of the Fourth Geneva Convention specifies:

> Protected persons who are in occupied territory shall not be deprived, in any case or in any manner whatsoever, of the benefits of the present Convention by any change introduced, as the result of the occupation of a territory, into the institutions or government of the said territory, nor by any agreement concluded between the authorities of the occupied territories and the Occupying Power, nor by any annexation by the latter of the whole or part of the occupied territory.

---

280 This provision has its origin in the Russian draft submitted to the 1874 Brussels Conference and included within the draft declaration, which also refered to 'scientific museums'.

281 This formulation (in French, 'établissements consacrés aux cultes') replaces the reference to 'churches' on the proposal of Caratheodory-Effendi, first delegate of Turkey (*Actes de la Conference de Bruxelles* [Brussels: F. Hayez, 1874], Protocol XVIII, pp. 207–8). The report of Mr. Rolin at the second commission of the Conference stated that Article 56 will be applied to institutions of this nature, churches, temples, mosques, synagogues, etc.

282 As such, it is subject to requisitions.

283 The question of archives was also discussed in Brussels in 1874, but was finally not included because of the danger of incomplete enumeration and the possibility that the occupant may always take military plans serving the purposes of war (General Voigt-Rhentz, German delegate) (*Actes de la Conference de Bruxelles* [Brussels: F. Hayez, 1874], Protocol IV, pp. 243–44).

284 Colonel Count Lanza (Italy) required criminal sanctions to be included, and said clause removes any doubt about the intentions of the Conference. (*Actes de la Conference de Bruxelles* [Brussels: F. Hayez, 1874], Protocole XVIII, p. 215).

Article 9 of the Protocol must be seen in this context: the protection of cultural property should not be changed as a result of occupation and the aim of Article 9 is to eliminate by prohibition and preventive measures significant interference in the cultural environment of the occupied territory. This Article, based on the existing international law of occupation, protects cultural property against arbitrary decisions based on military strength and force, and requires that the decisions of national authorities of an occupied territory or State be respected. The Hague Regulations not only respected the population of a territory, but also its institutions and laws.[285] The Occupying Power is only a trustee, not a sovereign power.[286]

Paragraph 1

Articles 4 and 5 of the Convention are not modified by the adoption of Article 9 and remain binding on States Parties to the Convention and the Second Protocol.

The Article addresses the Occupying Power, in other words, 'a Party in occupation of the whole or part of the territory of another Party.'

An Occupying Power has a responsibility to 'prohibit and prevent' the series of acts mentioned in sub-paragraphs (a), (b) and (c), but only in relation to the occupied territory. The sub-paragraphs do not concern the territory of the Occupying Power itself, nor the territory of another party which is not occupied. Prohibition and prevention are the full responsibility of the Occupying Power and do not impose any duties on the national authorities. But as they result from other provisions concerning occupation, we can suppose that implementation of prohibition and preventive measures will take place in conjunction with the national authorities, when by the character of the provision such cooperation is really necessary. However, it is not a duty of the Occupying Power to do so provided that it respects the prohibitions and preventions.

We can also say that the involvement of national authorities is fully respected in Article 5 of the Convention. The authors of the Convention were very much preoccupied with the respect for and role of the national authorities of the occupied territory. In paragraph 1 of Article 5 the safeguarding and preservation of cultural property in occupied territory is undertaken by the 'competent national authorities'. The Occupying Power has to provide support

---

285 Pictet (1952–60), Vol. IV, p. 274.
286 Wilson (1933), p. 38.

to the national authorities – though this duty is limited by the clause 'as far as possible'. Exclusive responsibility is fully left to the national authorities. But assistance by the Occupying Power is restricted and limited, and left very much to their own discretion. It was therefore necessary to reinforce the responsibility of the Occupying Power and limit the possible benefits from the occupation.

Paragraph 2 of Article 5 of the Convention creates the secondary responsibility of the Occupying Power to preserve cultural property, leaving primary responsibility for preservation to the competent national authorities. The Occupying Power is involved only when 'proved necessary' and when national authorities are unable to take such measures. Here again the Occupying Power is involved only 'as far as possible' and in close cooperation with the national authorities.

The paragraph uses the word 'prohibit' (*interdit*), clearly defining the proscribed acts as illegal and outlawed. It uses also the word 'prevent' (*empêche*), meaning to take all appropriate measures to avoid the realization of the acts mentioned in the sub-paragraphs. It also means putting stop to an action, impede, obstruct, preclude, pre-empt and disallow. But which acts are prohibited and must be prevented? The answer lies in the three sub-paragraphs.

Sub-paragraph 9(a)

As we have indicated in our 1996 Commentary, the seizure of works of art was a customary practice in past conflicts and was regarded as an addition to the glory of the victor and the humiliation of the vanquished. But there are also example of condemnation of such practices and requirements for restitution. Furthermore, a distinction must be made between prohibitions on illicit exportation, other forms of removal, and transfers of ownership.

Prevention according to the First Hague Protocol

This paragraph must be viewed in connection with the *First Protocol* for the Protection of Cultural Property in the Event of Armed Conflict, signed at The Hague on 14 May 1954. Most of its provisions deal with return and restitution and eventually with indemnification. Only paragraph 1 of section I deals with the prevention of exportation:

1. Each High Contracting Party undertakes to *prevent* [emphasis added] the exportation, from a territory occupied by it during an armed conflict, of cultural property as defined in Article 1 of the Convention for the Protection of Cultural Property in the Event of Armed Conflict, signed at The Hague on 14 May, 1954

It is important to stress that the Protocol deals only with prevention of exportation and does not include prohibition of exportation and removal or transfer of ownership, as in the case of Article 9 of the Second Protocol.

As we have indicated, the adoption of the Protocol was a response to the events of the Second World War, which saw not only the destruction of cultural property but also systematic pillage of occupied territories: 'The occupying powers practised a new technique to cloak the dispossession of the rightful owners of works of art with a semblance of legality. By demanding huge daily indemnities from the occupied countries, they made deliberately forced transactions appear free commercial dealings.'[287]

The 1907 Hague Regulations prohibited pillage and 'all seizure'. During the Second World War, Eighteen Powers in the Joint Declaration of 5 January 1943 warned

all concerned, and in particular to persons in neutral countries, that they intend to do their utmost to defeat the methods of dispossession practiced by the government with which they are at war against the countries and peoples who have been so wantonly assaulted and despoiled,

and they reserved

all their rights to declare invalid any transfers of, or dealings with, property rights and interests of any description whatsoever, which are, or have been, situated in the territories which have come under the occupation or control, direct or indirect, of the governments with which they are at war, or which belong, or have belonged, to persons (including juridical persons) resident in such territories. This warning applies whether such transfers or dealings have taken the form of open looting or plunder or of transactions apparently legal in form, even when they purport to be voluntarily effected.

---

287 CBC/3, *Records*, p. 319.

The UNESCO draft was based on the Joint Declaration of 1943. But aside from the first introductory paragraph, the Protocol deals with questions of return, restitution and indemnification which are not the direct object of Article 9. We have dealt with these issues in our 1996 Commentary on the Convention.[288] As we have seen, questions of return and restitution were not included within the text of the Convention. Although several countries requested their inclusion, it was feared that some States would decline to sign the Convention if these provisions are included in the text of the Convention. As a result, these provisions were included in the separate Protocol.[289] This concession was made by the Main Commission.[290]

According to paragraph 1 of the First Protocol, each High Contracting Party undertakes to prevent the exportation of cultural property (as defined in Article 1 of the Hague Convention) from a territory occupied by it during an armed conflict. The paragraph thus covers all cultural property, movable and immovable, irrespective of its origin or ownership.

This paragraph deals with the exportation of cultural property from an occupied territory by a High Contracting Party, irrespective of whether that territory belongs to a Contracting Party. The paragraph does not say how the Contracting Party is to prevent exportation, the measures to be taken being left to its own judgement and discretion. On this point, the 1970 Convention on the means of prohibiting and preventing the illicit import, export and transfer of ownership of cultural property is much more precise: see Articles 6 and 7 of the 1970 Convention.

Prohibition and prevention by 1970 Convention on the Means of Prohibiting and Preventing the Illicit Import, Export and Transfer of Ownership of Cultural Property

Article 9, paragraph 1(a) took its wording from the 1970 Convention: export and transfer of ownership.

As the title of the Convention indicates, it deals both with prevention and prohibitions. Its aim is to protect movable cultural property, without distinction between peacetime and time of war. The 1970 Convention leaves implementation of protection of cultural property to States Parties.

---

288 Toman (1996), pp. 336–51.
289 For example, the difference in attitude between the Netherlands on the one side and Belgium on the other, which favoured the adoption of the separate protocol. (*Records*, p. 350).
290 *Records*, pp. 260–61. This concession was made in particular to the UK, which nevertheless declined to ratify the Convention, and did so only recently.

Article 3 of the 1970 Convention considers illicit the import, export or transfer of ownership that is made contrary to provisions adopted by the States Parties to the Convention. National legislation is decisive in this matter.

A special provision concerning occupation was included within the Convention. Even though the Convention is not restricted to occupation in time of war, Article 11 is particularly relevant for periods of armed conflict. According to Article 11, 'the export and transfer of ownership of cultural property under compulsion arising directly or indirectly from the occupation of a country by a foreign power shall be regarded as illicit'.

Whereas Article 3 defines the illicit character in relation to national legislation, by indicating that the acts in question are contrary to provisions adopted under the Convention by the States Parties thereto, Article 11 defines the illicit character arising from occupation without linking it with or referring to national law.

Article 11 of the 1970 Convention supplements Articles 1–4 of the 1954 Hague Protocol. It reinforces the undertaking of the High Contracting Parties to 'prevent the exportation [of cultural property] from an occupied territory' as far as the movable property defined in Article 1 of the 1970 Convention is concerned. The prohibition on export concerns not only the territories occupied by the Occupying Power, but is addressed to all States Parties to the 1970 Convention: Article 1 of the 1954 Protocol is intended to prevent 'the exportation [of cultural property] from a territory occupied by it'. Article 11 treats as illicit 'the export and transfer of ownership of cultural property under compulsion arising directly or indirectly from the occupation of a country by a foreign power'. Export and transfer are thus regarded as illicit not only with respect to the Occupying Power but also with respect to all other Parties to the Convention.

Contrary to Article 1 of the 1954 Protocol, Article 11 of the present Convention concerns not only the export but any transfer of ownership of cultural property under compulsion.

In Article 1 of the 1954 Protocol, prohibition is restricted to periods of armed conflict. The occupation referred to in Article 11 may take place even outside the context of an armed conflict. The term 'occupied country' must be understood to mean the permanent control of a given territory by armed forces.

Export and transfer of ownership are deemed to be under compulsion when effected against the will of the lawful owner. In recognizing the illicit situation of these operations, the 1970 Convention thereby declares any such transfers null and void and thus makes possible the recovery of property when the occupation is over.[291]

The inclusion of the prohibition of 'any illicit export, other removal or transfer of ownership' in the Second Protocol is not fortuitous. It was suggested by the Polish delegate at the first meeting of the High Contracting Parties in 1962 in the form of a chapter on restitution or reparations.[292] The continuing violations of the First Hague Protocol, most particularly in recent conflicts, are another reason why this paragraph is so important.

In this context it is also important to mention Article 24, paragraph 2 of the 1954 Convention prohibiting special agreements that 'diminish the protection afforded by the . . . Convention to cultural property and to the personnel engaged in its protection'. The Occupying Power may be tempted to use its advantage and its position to conclude agreements with the authorities of the occupied party in order to allow, for example, export of cultural property from the occupied territory or to proceed with archaeological excavations.

Sub-paragraph 9(b)

Sub-paragraph 9(b) imposes on the Occupying Power the duty to prohibit and prevent 'any archeological excavation, save where this is strictly required to safeguard, record or preserve cultural property'.

Archaeological sites at the 1954 Conference

Issues of an archaeological nature were discussed several times during the 1954 Hague Conference.

The protection of 'archaeological sites'[293] and 'manuscripts, books and other objects of artistic, historical or archaeological interest' is mentioned in

---

291 Toman (1996), p. 361.
292 Nahlik (1967), p. 142.
293 The inclusion of archeological sites was requested by Israel (CBC/DR/1), and was included in the drafts of Switzerland (DR/2, Spain (DR/4), USA (DR/22), the UK (DR/31), Italy (DR/42) and Greece (DR/100). The Israeli delegate said that 'it was absurd to protect museums and allow their sources, which were the sources of history itself, to be exposed to the ravages of war' (*Records*, para. 135, p. 117). The inclusion of archeological sites was adopted by 30 votes to one, with five abstentions.

Article 1 of the 1954 Hague Convention, definition of cultural property.[294] It is also mentioned in Article 1 of the 1970 Convention.[295]

During the Plenary Session of the 1954 Conference, the representative of Greece proposed the following provision:

> The Occupying Power shall refrain from excavations or other action for the discovery of unknown cultural property save with the consent and participation of the competent national authorities of the occupied country.[296] Partly because of the fact that it was formulated orally in the closing phase of the Conference, this amendment (supported by the Federal Republic of Germany, France, Iraq and Yugoslavia) was finally rejected by a narrow majority of nine votes to eight, with 22 abstentions.

The country report on the implementation of the 1954 Convention, submitted by Jordan, refers to the problems posed by archaeological excavations conducted by Israel in the occupied territories. With regard to the character of the conflict, Jordan felt that the purpose of these excavations was to conceal and misrepresent the facts for political ends. A problem of interpretation therefore arose as to the entitlement of the Occupying Power to make reference – in its report pursuant to Article 26(2) – to measures taken in the occupied territory.[297]

1956 Recommendation

Two years later, at its 9th Session, the UNESCO General Conference adopted, on 5 December 1956, a Recommendation on International Principles Applicable to Archaeological Excavations. The Recommendation stresses the interests of individual States, but also of the international community in the protection of cultural property.

---

294 See also the European Convention for the Protection of Archeological Heritage of 6 May 1969 (*UNTS*, Vol. 788, p. 227); and the Convention on the Protection of Archeological, Historical and Artistic Heritage of the American Nations, signed in San Salvador on 16 June 1976 (*International Legal Materials*, Vol. XV, No. 6, p. 1350).

295 Toman (1996), pp. 359–60.

296 *Records*, para. 1641, p. 257.

297 Information on the implementation of the Convention for the Protection of Cultural Property in the Event of Armed Conflict, The Hague 1954, 1979 REPORTS, pp. 20–24, 1989 REPORTS, p. 21.

It is important to mention a few provisions of this recommendation with regard to the clarification of Article 9, as it provides a definition of archaeological excavation and property protected in Chapter 1, entitled 'Definitions':

Archaeological excavations

1. For the purpose of the present Recommendation, by archaeological excavations is meant any research aimed at the discovery of objects of archaeological character, whether such research involves digging of the ground or systematic exploration of its surface or is carried out on the bed or in the sub-soil of inland or territorial waters of a Member State.

Property protected

2. The provisions of the present Recommendation apply to any remains, whose preservation is in the public interest from the point of view of history or art and architecture, each Member State being free to adopt the most appropriate criterion for assessing the public interest of objects found on its territory. In particular, the provisions of the present Recommendation should apply to any monuments and movable or immovable objects of archaeological interest considered in the widest sense.

3. The criterion adopted for assessing the public interest of archaeological remains might vary according to whether it is a question of the preservation of such property, or of the excavator's or finder's obligation to declare his discoveries.

   (a) In the former case, the criterion based on preserving all objects originating before a certain date should be abandoned, and replaced by one whereby protection is extended to all objects belonging to a given period or of a minimum age fixed by law.

   (b) In the latter case, each Member State should adopt far wider criteria, compelling the excavator or finder to declare any object, of archaeological character, whether movable or immovable, which he may discover.

Chapter II, dealing with general principles, includes a set of principles entitled 'Protection of the archaeological heritage', which read:

Protection of the archaeological heritage

4. Each Member State should ensure the protection of its archaeological heritage, taking fully into account problems arising in connection with excavations, and in conformity with the provisions of the present Recommendation.

5. Each Member State should in particular:

    (a) Make archaeological explorations and excavations subject to prior authorization by the competent authority;

    (b) Oblige any person finding archaeological remains to declare them at the earliest possible date to the competent authority;

    (c) Impose penalties for the infringement of these regulations;

    (d) Make undeclared objects subject to confiscation;

    (e) Define the legal status of the archaeological sub-soil and, where State ownership of the said sub-soil is recognized, specifically mention the fact in its legislation;

    (f) Consider classifying as historical monuments the essential elements of its archaeological heritage.

Other principles provide descriptions of the protecting body, careful supervision, education of the public, regulations governing excavations and international cooperation, and so on.

The most important chapter for our consideration is Chapter VI, entitled 'Excavations in occupied territory'. Article 32 of this chapter states:

> In the event of an armed conflict, any Member State occupying the territory of another State should refrain from carrying out archaeological excavations in the occupied territory. In the event of chance finds being made, particularly during military works, the Occupying Power should take all possible measures to protect these finds, which should be handed over, on the termination of hostilities, to the competent authorities of the territory previously occupied, together with all documentation relating thereto.

These principles were drafted by the Committee of Governmental Experts which met in Palermo, 4–19 May 1956. It was the experts' unanimous wish that the principle concerning archaeological excavations in occupied territory 'and the necessary implementing regulations, be embodied in an addendum to the International Convention for the Protection of Cultural Property in the Event of Armed Conflict which should be revised accordingly'. The

Committee's report noted that 'it was clear from the discussion that this question raised complex problems which should be given the most careful study and which could be finally settled only by the adoption of provisions having the force of a convention.'[298]

Chapter V includes provisions on the repression of clandestine excavations and the illicit export of archaeological finds:

> Protection of archaeological sites against clandestine excavations and damage
> 29. Each Member State should take all necessary measures to prevent clandestine excavations and damage to monuments defined in paragraphs 2 and 3 above, and also to prevent the export of objects thus obtained.
>
> International co-operation in repressive measures
> 30. All necessary measures should be taken in order that museums to which archaeological objects are offered ascertain that there is no reason to believe that these objects have been procured by clandestine excavation, theft or any other method regarded as illicit by the competent authorities of the country of origin. Any suspicious offer and all details appertaining thereto should be brought to the attention of the services concerned. When archaeological objects have been acquired by museums, adequate details allowing them to be identified and indicating the manner of their acquisition should be published as soon as possible.
>
> Return of objects to their country of origin
> 31. Excavation services and museums should lend one another assistance in order to ensure or facilitate the recovery of objects derived from clandestine excavations or theft, and of all objects exported in infringement of the legislation of the country of origin. It is desirable that each Member State should take the necessary measures to ensure this recovery. These principles should be applied in the event of temporary exports as mentioned in paragraph 23(c), (d) and (e) above, if the objects are not returned within the stipulated period.

---

298 Report by the Committee of Governmental Experts, doc. 9C/PRG/7, particularly para. 62–63, p. 16, Annex II.

Neither the UNESCO Recommendation of 1956 nor national legislation contains any provisions on the philosophy to be adopted in the area of archaeological research. The few provisions existing on this subject include the Bulgarian directives of 19 July 1956 specifying the purpose of excavations.[299]

In our 1996 Commentary on the Convention, we mentioned some examples: the UNESCO mission sent to Lebanon to visit the archaeological site of the city of Tyre, and the recommendations of this mission.[300]

1999 Second Protocol

Archaeological excavations were discussed during the preparatory works of the Hague Conference and at the Conference itself.

At the 1997 Meeting of Experts, participants to the discussion frequently raised the question of illicit export of cultural property from occupied territories. Several participants expressed their concern about this issue and pointed out that the Protocol to the Convention, which prevents such export, is not legally binding for all States Parties to the Convention. A provision to this end was therefore incorporated in the draft Article 1 of the revised Lauswolt document:

> Article 1 paragraph 5: 'The occupying power shall not encourage, tolerate or facilitate, either directly or indirectly, illicit exports of cultural property from the occupied territory.'

The issue of occupied territories continued to be discussed within the framework of the Article concerning general protection.

---

299 Directions on archaeological probes and excavations, 19 July 1956, cited by Prott and O'Keefe (1984), p. 232. According to these directives, 'the aim of excavations is to find and study the archaeological monuments underground so as to explain the basic questions of historical development, the history of the development of the production forces of a given society, the characteristics of the state and development of its economic basis, social relations, specific traits in the development of the culture of a given society, its interrelations with neighbouring peoples and many other questions related to the life and culture of the tribes and peoples who have created the material monuments excavated. In view of (1) the great scientific importance of the archaeological monuments unearthed as prime historical sources of given epochs, (2) the fact that the excavations of such monuments are frequently connected by necessity with their demolition, and (3) the fact that any mishandling of finds is irreparable, archaeological excavations should be carried out according to present-day methods of archaeological studies by trained persons only, employing all necessary scientific methods and observations which guarantee the further scientific utilization of the results of the excavations as fully valuable historical sources.'

300 Toman (1996), p. 265, UNESCO Rapport de la mission à Tyr.

The ideas expressed at the 1998 Vienna Experts Meeting were later included within the Preliminary Draft of October 1998, which reflects the progress accomplished during these discussions. Article 3 of the Preliminary Draft concerning the respect for cultural property included several paragraphs on occupied territories:

> Article 3 Respect for cultural property
> 3. Any form of theft, pillage or misappropriation of, any archaeological excavation, any act of vandalism directed against any illicit purchase, or any other breach of integrity [variant: any breach of authenticity] or any transformation of cultural property is prohibited.
> 4. Without limiting the provisions of the 1954 Protocol, it is prohibited to export or otherwise illicitly remove cultural property from occupied territory or from a pan of the territory of a State Party.
> [5. The occupying power shall not encourage, tolerate or facilitate, either directly or indirectly, illicit exports of cultural property from the occupied territory.]

This new draft elaborated on the basis of the 1998 Vienna Expert Meeting, and the remarks of governments submitted at the end of 1998 included several elements that we find in the final text. Several proposals were made by the governments relating to occupied territories. The ICRC proposed the inclusion of paragraphs 3–5 in the separate Article entitled 'Additional protection of cultural property in occupied territories', which later became Article 9.

The Final Draft Second Protocol (HC/1999/1/rev.1) followed the ICRC recommendation and included the new Article 10:

> Article 10 Protection of cultural property in occupied territory
> 1. Any form of theft, pillage or misappropriation of, any archaeological excavation in occupied territory, any act of vandalism directed against, any illicit purchase, any transformation of cultural property or any [other breach of integrity] [breach of authenticity] is prohibited.
> 2. Without limiting the provisions of the First Protocol, it is prohibited to [illicitly] export or otherwise illicitly remove cultural property from occupied territory or from a part of the territory of a Party.

[3. The occupying power shall not encourage, tolerate or facilitate, either directly or indirectly, illicit exports of cultural property from the occupied territory.]

This text was discussed extensively at the 1999 Hague Diplomatic Conference.

Discussion at the Conference

The Second Protocol reinforces the protection of archaeological excavations. As we have seen, the 1956 Recommendation encourages a Member State occupying the territory of another State to refrain from carrying out excavation on the occupied territory. Article 9, paragraph 1 goes further by prohibiting and preventing such excavations.

There is only one exception, and this exception exists only in the interest of the cultural property itself: such excavation can be undertaken when it is strictly required for the following purposes:
- safeguarding,
- recording, or
- preservation of cultural property.

The US delegate considered the reference to 'any archaeological excavation in Article 10 as too broad in its formulation and should be limited to excavation of cultural property and permit those which are necessary to preserve and protect cultural property'. He also considered such terms as 'transformation', 'breach of integrity' and 'breach of authenticity' too ambiguous and proposed that these terms should be deleted.[301] The Israeli delegate also felt that the prohibition went far beyond the provisions of the Convention.[302] The Lebanese delegate proposed to separate theft and pillage from archaeological excavations and considered that excavation should be completely prohibited in the occupied territory.[303] The UK delegate did not understand

> Article 5 of the Convention as forbidding all archaeological activity in occupied territory. It was permitted where it was necessary to safeguard or preserve cultural property. His delegation preferred clarifying the prohibition so that it had a limited exception where necessary to

---

301 1999 Hague Conference, Plenary Session, 16 March 1999: US delegate, p. 66.
302 Ibid., Israeli delegate, p. 70.
303 Ibid., Lebanese delegate, p. 87.

safeguard and to preserve. He agreed with Professor Boylan that there would be situations where this may occur. For example, in an occupied territory an occupier might quite legitimately propose to build a road and while building the road the occupier discovers remnants of an earlier civilisation. The question would then be what is he has to do. Is the occupier supposed to put the concrete over the remnants or, as he would suggest, properly investigate and preserve them so that they can be carefully catalogued for posterity. An exception should be admitted in this regard rather than having a total prohibition. Further, some of the terms in Article 10 were unfamiliar to those whose discipline was humanitarian law rather than cultural law, for example the term of 'illicit transfer'. This could be clarified by borrowing from the wording of Article 11 of the 1970 UNESCO Convention.[304]

With regard to Article 9, on the protection of cultural property in occupied territory, the Working Group on Chapter 2[305] decided to split the ideas expressed in the draft Article and make a distinction between protection in occupied territory and the idea of having a provision on non-international armed conflict. A decision was finally taken to deal only with occupied territory in international armed conflict. The main ideas contained in the Article were: the question of export, removal or transfer of ownership of cultural property; the issue of archaeological excavations in occupied territory; and the concept of 'breach of integrity' or 'breach of authenticity' of cultural property in occupied territory. The use of the term 'breach of integrity' was avoided because the precise legal meaning was not clear. It was replaced by 'alteration to' or 'change of views of cultural property with the intent to conceal or destroy cultural, historical or scientific evidence'.

With regard to paragraph (a), the Group used the term 'illicit' in order to make it clear that not all export, removal or transfer of ownership should be prohibited, but only that which is illicit. As a result, the Working Group felt it was necessary to define 'illicit' in that context and to include the definition in Article 1 of the Protocol. It was considered necessary to cover both the domestic law of the occupied territory and international law.

With paragraph (b) on archaeological excavation, the Working Group discussed not only the need to include such a provision in the Protocol but

---

304 Ibid., UK delegate, p. 95.
305 Desch, Austria, Chairman of the Working Group on Chapter 2, 1999 Hague Conference, Plenary Session, 24 March 1999, pp. 253–54.

also the question of whether archaeological excavation should be prohibited absolutely or whether there should be exceptions for necessary excavations. The Working Group finally decided to allow some flexibility and to permit excavations where strictly required to safeguard, record or preserve cultural property. The introductory phrase 'without prejudice to Articles 4 and 5 of the Convention' avoids repetition of these provisions, since it 'seemed unrealistic to completely prohibit excavations, particularly since Article 5 of the Convention allows for excavations under certain circumstances, such as where cultural property has been damaged by military operations and it is necessary to safeguard the property'.[306]

Not all delegates accepted this conclusion. It was contested at the Plenary Session by the delegate of Palestine and a few other States.[307] The delegate of Palestine expressed his opposition to the Article as suggested by the Working Group and suggested making a distinction between territory under national control and control by an occupying power. In the spirit of compromise, the Palestinian delegate withdrew his opposition.[308]

Paragraph 2

At the 1999 Conference, Article 9, paragraph 2 was discussed by the Working Group. The group decided that any such activity by an Occupying Power should be carried out in close cooperation with the competent national authorities.[309] To reflect the Occupying Power's obligation, the word 'shall' was employed, and to ensure flexibility, the phrase 'shall as far as possible be carried out' was included.

Archaeological excavations are also mentioned in paragraph 2 of Article 9: excavations that take place in the event of the aforementioned case (i.e. when it is strictly required) should be carried out in close cooperation with the competent national authorities of the occupied territory. This is a confirmation of one of the principles of the 1956 Recommendation, expressed in the Preamble, that individual States are more directly concerned with archaeological discoveries made in their territory. But this requirement is not absolute and is accompanied by the reservation 'unless circumstances do not

---

306 Ibid., p. 262.
307 1999 Hague Conference, Plenary Session, 24 March 1999: Palestinian delegate, p. 256; but also the delegates of Yemen, p. 259, Egypt, p. 261, and Syria, p. 266.
308 1999 Hague Conference, Plenary Session, 26 March 1999, pp. 72–73.
309 Supported by the Egyptian and Libyan delegates in the 1999 Hague Conference, Plenary Session, 24 March 1999, pp. 261, 273.

permit'. The 1956 Recommendation is not absolute. As the Chairman of the Working Group also indicated, neither is it binding.[310]

The two paragraphs of the Preamble, while underlining the role of national authorities, also speaks in favour of the interests of the international community:

> *Considering* that, while individual States are more directly concerned with the archaeological discoveries made on their territory, the international community as a whole is nevertheless the richer for such discoveries

> *Being of the opinion* that, though the regulation of excavations is first and foremost for the domestic jurisdiction of each State, this principle should be brought into harmony with that of a liberally understood and freely accepted international co-operation,

This paragraph also includes a more general reference to alteration or change of use of cultural property in occupied territory, which must be done 'in close co-operation with the competent national authorities of the occupied territory'. This paragraph confirms the role of national authorities in all questions relating to cultural property. It also confirms the rules that govern occupation since the adoption of the 1907 Hague Regulations. At the very last moment of the Plenary Session, the provision concerning national authorities was reinforced through the replacement of the words 'as far as possible' with the words 'unless circumstances do not permit'.[311]

---

310 Desch, Austria, Chairman of the Working Group on Chapter 2, Plenary Session of the Conference, 24 March 1999, p. 263. See also the Greek delegate, p. 271.
311 Desch, ibid., p. 19.

Chapter 3

ENHANCED PROTECTION

INTRODUCTION

The 1907 Hague Conventions and the Hague Regulations deal with general protection and make no distinction between different categories of cultural monuments, such as 'buildings dedicated to religion, art, science or charitable purposes' and 'historic monuments'. All are protected on two conditions: that they are not used for military purposes, and that their status is clearly indicated by a distinctive and visible sign. These requirements are present in the Hague Regulations (art. 27 and 56) and in Article 5 of the 1907 Convention IX concerning Bombardment by Naval Forces in Time of War.

In the Roerich Pact of 1935, under Article IV, 'the signatory Governments . . . shall send to the Pan American Union . . . a list of the monuments and institutions for which they desire the protection agreed to in this treaty'. The protection was absolute and concerned all the cultural monuments indicated in the list. No specific categories were stated among the monuments and institutions.

The Hague Rules 1922–1923[312]

The first appearance of a distinction between the general protection of monuments and the protection of a monument of great historic value appeared in the Hague Rules concerning the Control of Wireless Telegraphy in Time of War and Air Warfare, drafted by a Commission of Jurists at The Hague (11 December 1922–17 February 1923). Never adopted in legally binding form, they are nevertheless regarded 'as an authoritative attempt to clarify and formulate rules of law governing the use of aircraft in war'.[313] If Article 25 referred to 'buildings dedicated to public worship, art, science, and charitable purposes, historic monuments', Article 26 speaks of 'the efficient protection of monuments of great historic value situated on their territory provided they are disposed to abstain from using for military purposes not only such

---

312 Schindler and Toman (2004), pp. 315–25.
313 Oppenheim (1952), p. 519.

monuments and also the area surrounding them, and to accept a special system for control to this end'.[314]

The Preliminary Draft of 1938

Most probably based on this precedent, the distinction of monuments and the introduction of special protection was made in the Preliminary Draft of the International Convention for the Protection of Historic Buildings and Works of Art in Time of War, proposed by the International Museums Office in October 1938.[315] But special protection was not granted on the basis of evaluation of monuments from an historic or artistic standpoint. This task was left to the Contracting Parties, and specific conditions were set for monuments based on their situation (position), use, previous notification and openness to inspection.

Article 4 describes the establishment of refuges and the conditions for their immunity as follows:

1. The High Contracting Parties undertake to refrain from any act of hostility directed against any refuge that a High Contracting Party may have designated in his territory to shelter in time of war works of art or of historic interest that may be threatened by military operations.
2. The number of such refuges shall be limited; they may take the form either of buildings erected for the purpose or of existing historic buildings or groups of buildings.
3. To secure immunity, refuges must:
    (a) be situated at a distance of not less than 20 kilometres from the most likely theatres of military operations, from any military objective, from any main line of communication, and from any large industrial centre (this distance may be reduced in certain cases in countries with a very dense population and small area);
    (b) have already been notified in time of peace;
    (c) not be used directly or indirectly for purposes of national defence;

---

314 Schindler and Toman (2004), pp. 319–20; O'Keefe (2006), pp. 44–51.
315 This draft was prepared by a group of eminent lawyers convened by the International Museums Office during the years 1936–1938.

(d) be open to international inspection during hostilities.

4. The military authorities shall have access to the refuges at any time for the purpose of satisfying themselves that they are not being used in any way contrary to the present Convention.

Article 5 of the draft included specific conditions for the protection of monuments, which read:

1. The High Contracting Parties, acknowledging it to be their joint and several duty to respect and protect all monuments of artistic or historic interest in time of war, agree to take all possible precautions to spare such monuments during operations and to ensure that their use or situation shall not expose them to attack.

2. Special protection shall be given to monuments or groups of monuments which:
   (a) are isolated from any military objective within a radius of 500 metres;
   (b) are not directly or indirectly used for purposes of national defence;
   (c) have already been notified in time of peace;
   (d) are open to international inspection during hostilities.

As we have seen, the drafting of the Hague Convention was also largely influenced by this Draft and the idea of special protection, but in a different sense. The idea of special protection was taken up by the Italian delegation at the UNESCO General Conference in Florence in 1950, where they presented the draft of an international convention based on the 1938 International Museums Office project.

The Hague Convention of 1954

As we have seen, general protection according to Article 1 of the Convention refers to movable and immovable property that is of great importance to the cultural heritage of peoples. The decision concerning protection depends entirely on the authorities of the country in whose territory the property is located. The UNESCO draft spoke of cultural value, but the Conference maintained the reference to 'importance', which enabled national authorities to draw up a list of property to be protected. The term is also very subjective.[316]

Article 8, paragraph 1 of the Convention limited further the categories of property to be protected, citing only cultural properties of 'very great importance':

> 1. There may be placed under special protection a limited number of refuges intended to shelter movable cultural property in the event of armed conflict, of centres containing monuments and other immovable cultural property of very great importance, provided that they:
> (a) are situated at an adequate distance from any large industrial centre or from any important military objective constituting a vulnerable point, such as, for example, an aerodrome, broadcasting station, establishment engaged upon work of national defence, a port or railway station of relative importance or a main line of communication;
> (b) are not used for military purposes.

'Special protection', as defined in the Hague Convention, was among the foremost issues in need of attention when the process of revision started. The process began shortly after signature of the Convention. The first Meeting of the High Contracting Parties in 1962 asked for clarification of the term 'adequate distance'. The delegates adopted a resolution on this point, expressing the hope

> that in evaluating the "adequate distance" for purposes of special protection, the High Contracting Parties will bear in mind first and foremost the very purpose of the Convention, which is to provide the widest possible protection for cultural property throughout the world.[317]

The matter was referred to the consultative committee, which was never formed.[318] The impossibility of determining such distance and the fact that

---

316 Toman (1996), pp. 49–50.

317 First meeting of the High Contracting Parties to the Convention for the Protection of Cultural Property in the Event of Armed Conflict, UNESCO document UNESCO/CUA/120, Paris, 3 September 1962, p. 4.

318 Ibid., p. 101.

many valuable cultural properties are situated in the large, industrial cities was one of the reasons for the limited number of requests for registration of cultural property under special protection. But there was another important reason: political motivations, when the authority requesting the registration was not considered by some States as the legitimate representative of the country (e.g. the case of Cambodia).

Inspiration from the 1972 World Heritage Convention

Comparison between the success of the 1972 Convention and World Heritage List and the very limited progress, if not failure, of the 1954 Convention acted as an incentive for those who wished to improve protection for cultural property in the event of armed conflict. Protection under the World Heritage Convention was used in the case of Dubrovnik and had positive results. The only way to ensure improvement was to eliminate the shortcomings of the 1954 regime and to improve the system of sanctions for those who act against the protection regime.

Review of the Hague Convention in the 1990s

Efforts for the better implementation of existing instruments and the reinforcement of UNESCO's actions[319] began at the 139th Session of the UNESCO Executive Board (May 1992), with the endorsement of a draft resolution, submitted by Italy, calling for the creation of a consultative group of experts. In its report to the 140th Executive Board session (1992), the Director-General indicated that the 1954 Hague Convention no longer met current requirements and, in particular, that the special protection regime had not been properly implemented and applied, with only a small number of entries in the International Register and a cumbersome registration procedure.[320]

Patrick Boylan was asked by the UNESCO Secretariat to prepare an in-depth analysis of the issues and to present a set of recommendations to the members of the Executive Board.[321] He considered the narrow definition of protected property to be the reason why, after many years of existence, only one cultural centre – Vatican City – had been included on the Register. He

---

319 Resolution 26C/Res. 3.9, adopted on 6 November 1991.
320 Report by the Director-General on the reinforcement of UNESCO's action for the Protection of the World Cultural and Natural Heritage, 140 EX/13 Corr.
321 Boylan (1993).

recommended that 'the most important museums, galleries, special libraries and archives repositories' be included in future updating.[322] He also explained that one of the reasons for lack of interest in registration according to Article 8 of the Convention may well be that some States Parties chose to switch their priority to proposals for the World Heritage List, following the adoption of the UNESCO World Heritage Convention in 1972. He accordingly recommended that States review their policies and priorities.[323]

The Executive Board, at its 141st Session (1992), adopted Decision 5.5.1, which acknowledges, *inter alia*, the opinion expressed by the Director-General that the 1954 Convention no longer meets current requirements and invited States Parties to the 1954 and 1972 Conventions to examine the possibility of nominating sites on the World Heritage List for the International Register of Cultural Property under Special Protection.[324]

At the first Meeting of Experts on the application and effectiveness of the Convention for the Protection of Cultural Property in the Event of Armed Conflict (The Hague, 14 May 1954),[325] which took place in The Hague on 5–7 July 1993, some doubts were expressed about the usefulness of the special protection regime and the overly complicated procedure for entering names on the International Register. If the regime was to be maintained, it should be simplified, namely by revising its conditions and making them more objective. Also, certain institutional arrangements, similar to those of the 1972 Convention, should be made: an organ modelled along the lines of the World Heritage Committee could contribute to the more effective application of the Convention, having a role in evaluating requests for (new) entries on the International Register.

The 27th Session of the General Conference, which met in Paris in October and November 1993, invited the High Contracting Parties to the 1954 Hague Convention to consider:

---

322 Ibid., para. 6.6, p. 76.

323 Ibid., para. 6.24, p. 81.

324 UNESCO contacted the States Parties to the 1954 and 1972 Conventions and asked them to consider the possibility of nominating their cultural sites on the World Heritage List for the International Register of Cultural Property under Special Protection. By June 1995, 'seven States have replied positively but have not yet provided the Secretariat with sufficient details to proceed with the inscription'. Information note to the second meeting of the States Parties to the 1954 Hague Convention, CLT-95/CONF.009/INF.1, p. 1

325 UNESCO document 142 EX/15, Annex. http://unesdoc.unesco.org/images/0009/000958/095820Eo.pdf

(a) entering into further consultations on the validity of the distinction between the general and special protection regimes in the Convention and, in this regard, on the procedure for entering cultural property in the International Register of Cultural Property under Special Protection;

(b) the need for an institutional mechanism under the 1954 Hague Convention that could perform both advisory and operational functions, taking into account the functions performed by the existing organs established under other UNESCO instruments for the protection of cultural property.[326]

The General Conference also addressed the States not party to the Hague Convention but Parties to the 1972 World Cultural and Natural Heritage Convention, and reminded them that the Hague Convention 'offers protection of cultural property that is of national and local importance as well as to sites of outstanding universal importance'. The Director-General also invited States Parties to both of these Conventions 'to nominate these sites [of 1972 Convention] for the International Register of the Hague Convention'.[327] At the 1999 Hague Diplomatic Conference, Lyndel Prott, representative of the UNESCO Secretariat, explained the reaction of States to this letter:

> There were 47 States in this situation who were Parties to both Conventions and which had cultural sites on the World Heritage List. Eleven replies were received. Many of the original signatories and early participants in the Convention had never approached the Secretariat with an application to put the site on the Register, and many of them had never reported, thus making it difficult to know why they never approached the Secretariat to put a site on the Register. Of the eleven replies, all lacked the information which was required by the provisions relating to special protection. As a result, UNESCO had not been able to add one site to the Special Protection Register.[328]

---

326 Records of the General Conference. 27th session, Paris, 25.10–16.11.1993, Vol. 1. Resolutions. Resolution 3.5. Convention for the Protection of Cultural Property in the Event of Armed Conflict (The Hague, 1954). Resolution adopted on the report of Commission IV at the 28th plenary meeting, on 13 November 1993.

327 UNESCO Executive Board, 145th Session. Report by the Director-General on the Review of the Convention for the Protection of Cultural Property in the Event of Armed Conflict, 145 EX/21, 20 July 1994, para. 3, p. 2.

328 1999 Hague Conference, Plenary Session, 17 March 1999, p. 131.

The second meeting of experts, held at Lauswolt (9–11 February 1994), included three articles that indicate the orientation of future codification:

Article 3 Special Protection
1. Cultural property, as defined in Article 1 of the Convention, may be placed under special protection in accordance with the provisions of this instrument, provided that it is of great importance to humankind.
2. Special protection is granted to cultural property by its entry in the International Register of Cultural Property under Special Protection. This entry shall only be made, in accordance with the provisions of this instrument on the basis of the criteria defined by the Committee under Article [...]
3. Such cultural property is included in the International Register for Cultural Property under Special Protection at the request of the State Party in whose territory the cultural property is located.
4. States Parties may object [to] [sic] the inclusion into the International Register for Cultural Property under Special Protection under this instrument. Objections must be submitted to the Committee and can be made only on the basis of the criteria mentioned in paragraph 2. They shall be specific and related to facts.
5. If in case of emergency a State Party requests the special protection of cultural property, it shall communicate this request to the Committee. Provisional special protection can be granted by the Committee pending the outcome of the regular procedure for the granting of special protection.

Article 4 Immunity of cultural property under special protection
1. The States Parties shall ensure at all times the immunity of cultural property specially protected under this instrument by refraining, from the time of entry into the International Register for Cultural Property under Special Protection, from any act of hostility directed against such property and from using such property in support of the military efforts.
2. Article 11, paragraph 1 of the Convention, is applicable *mutatis mutandis* for the withdrawal of immunity of cultural property specially protected under this instrument.

3. The Committee and the Director-General of UNESCO shall be informed by the State concerned of such withdrawal, stating the reasons.

Article 5 Cancellation of special protection
1. In cases of serious and continuous violations of the obligations under this instrument with respect to special protection, or in case of loss of intrinsic cultural value of the cultural property, the Committee may decide to cancel such protection.
2. The Committee may invite the Director-General of UNESCO to apply Article 16, paragraph 2, of the Regulations for the execution of the Convention *mutatis mutandis*.

At the Meeting of Governmental Experts on the Review of the Hague Convention for the Protection of Cultural Property in the Event of Armed Conflict 1954 (UNESCO Headquarters, Paris, 24–27 March 1997),[329] the Secretariat submitted the summary of comments received from States Parties. A number of States expressed the desire to widen the scope of cultural property to be placed under special protection.

Croatia noted that the conditions for obtaining special protection should be more liberal and a registration procedure more simple. The *Czech Republic* and *Poland* stated that the notion 'adequate distance' was too vague and therefore should be precisely defined, possibly in an Annex to a new instrument. The Secretariat considered that with the development of more sophisticated weapons it may be difficult to define such distance. One attempt has been made in the past to clarify this issue: it was discussed at the first meeting of State Parties to the Hague Convention in Paris in July 1962.

Guinea and *Poland* wished to widen the scope and include the cultural sites entered in the World Heritage List on the Register. *Guinea* proposed that the scope of Article 8, paragraph 1 be enlarged as follows:

There may be placed under special protection all cultural property inscribed in the World Heritage List regardless of its location, refuges containing ethnographic, art and scientific collections (e.g. museums,

---

329 UNESCO, Meeting of Governmental Experts on the Review of the 1954 Hague Convention for the Protection of Cultural Property in the Event of Armed Conflict 1954, UNESCO Headquarters, Paris, 24–27 March 1997. *Final Report.* UNESCO document CLT-96/CONF.603/5, Paris, 30 April 1997.

archives and libraries), parks and all other cultural property being of artistic, scientific or historic importance.

The Secretariat indicated that it was contacting States Parties to both instruments.

At this expert meeting, the participants mentioned the difficulties of the present system. One of the participants indicated that according to the present conditions of entry, no city in his country might be entered on the Register. Two new elements were introduced: first, it was decided that special protection should be extended to cultural property of great importance to humankind; second, it was proposed that the nomination of cultural sites for entry on the Register be submitted to the Committee, a body in charge of the administration of the new instrument, which would also be responsible for the Register and eventually consider whether objections to entry of cultural sites in the Register are admissible. The expert meeting prepared the revised Lauswolt document, which was submitted again to the States Parties for comments and constituted the basis of discussion at the 1998 Vienna Meeting of Governmental Experts.

The comments of governments were summarized by the Secretariat. The following were the comments concerning special protection.

Austria stated that draft Articles 3, 4 and 5 of the revised Lauswolt document contain no improvement in comparison with Article 8 of the Convention. *Croatia* proposed that cultural property entered in the World Heritage List under the 1972 World Heritage Convention should also be specially protected. *France* was in favour of maintaining the system of special protection for cultural property of great importance for humankind and wished to keep the provisions of Article 11, paragraph 2 of the Convention concerning the withdrawal of immunity for cultural property under special protection as part of the new instrument. The French comment also links the granting of special protection to a supervisory body responsible for implementation of the Convention and/or the new instrument. *Germany* wished to simplify the conditions of entry of cultural property on the International Register and stated that the choice of registering or not registering cultural property for special protection must be left to the discretion of States Parties. *Israel* favoured reproduction of the wording of Article 11, paragraphs 1 and 2 of the Convention for the new Article 4, paragraph 2 of the revised Lauswolt document, because the relationship between the Convention and the new instrument is subject to discussion. The ICA expressed its readiness to contribute, in the way specified by the Director-General of UNESCO, to identifying archival institutions or holdings that might be included on the International Register.

At the next Meeting of Governmental Experts on the revision of the Hague Convention for the Protection of Cultural Property in the Event of Armed Conflict of 1954 in Vienna, 11–13 May 1998,[330] two documents formed the basis of discussion: draft provisions from the Secretariat[331] and the aforementioned 1998 *Summary of comments* received from States and organizations.[332]

Most delegates were in favour of the creation of an intergovernmental committee closely related to special protection. Several delegates pointed out that an efficient special protection regime demands a solid institutional basis. At the Vienna meeting, a proposal was made to establish an enhanced regime of special protection providing more flexibility regarding the eligibility of cultural property for special protection:

> A majority of delegations expressed the view that any special regime on an intergovernmental level has to be complemented by appropriate national legislation. It was even proposed that national legislation on this matter be a further prerequisite for entering a site in the list of specially protected property under the new regime. In this context it was pointed out that the new instrument should include the obligation to provide assistance for States that do not yet have national legislation in place. One delegation pointed out that a special protection regime should not lead to a downgrading of the 'normal' protection regime. Therefore there should be a thorough consideration of the impact of the special protection regime on cultural property not falling under this special regime.[333]

The meeting asked the UNESCO Secretariat to prepare a comprehensive working document to be distributed in good time before the Diplomatic Conference, to be held in The Hague from 14 to 26 March 1999 at the invitation of the Netherlands.

---

330 UNESCO document Paris, March 1998, *Final Report*.
331 Draft provisions for the revision of the 1954 Hague Convention and commentary from the UNESCO Secretariat. CLT-97/CONF.208/2, Paris, October 1997.
332 UNESCO, Meeting of Governmental Experts. Summary of comments received from States Parties to the Hague Convention, the International Committee of the Red Cross and the International Council on Archives. UNESCO document Paris, March 1998.
333 UNESCO document Paris, March 1998, *Final Report*, para. 12, pp. 2–3.

The UNESCO Secretariat prepared the document based on the meetings of government experts and particularly on the discussions that took place at the May 1998 Vienna Meeting.[334] It was sent to Member States of UNESCO and the UN, and to selected international organizations with a request for comments to be taken into account in the preparation of a final draft for the Diplomatic Conference to be held at The Hague.

The Secretariat received 15 replies from High Contracting Parties to the Convention, several of which expressed their views on enhanced protection in their comments. We shall return to the comments of governments under the different provisions of the articles, as they often relate to the formulation and wording. We shall also return to the oral presentations of delegates at the 1999 Diplomatic Conference. On the basis of the comments of governments, the UNESCO Secretariat elaborated a new draft Second Protocol, to which delegates of the 1999 Hague Conference referred[335] in their interventions.

Discussion of 'enhanced special protection', as enhanced protection was called in the Draft Second Protocol, started on 17 March 1999, the third day of the Conference. During the general discussion, many States underlined the importance of this new chapter of the Protocol, which demonstrates, together with Chapter 4 (Jurisdiction and responsibility), fundamentally new elements and the supplementary nature of the Protocol in relation to the Convention. It constituted a new level of protection.

The Israeli delegate summarized the view of the delegations by saying that some questioned the necessity of Chapter 3 entirely, others believed that Chapter 3 should be linked to the Convention's existing special protection regime, and the remainder understood that Chapter 3 contained a new regime:

> Under Article 8 of the Convention, special protection may be given either a refuge for immovable property or a centre for immovable property or immovable monuments. The new Chapter 3 did not contain such criteria and was almost the same as the criteria for normal cultural property. Assuming the draft was supplementary, then countries who signed the document and acknowledged its contents could designate a site as an enhanced special protection site, whilst the same site for a non-signatory country could be viewed as normal cultural property,

---

334 *Preliminary Draft Second Protocol to the 1954 Hague Convention.* UNESCO document HC/1999/1, October 1998 (English, French and Russian).

335 Draft Second Protocol to the 1954 Hague Convention for the Protection of Cultural Property in the Event of Armed Conflict, HC/1999/1/rev.1, Original: English, February 1999, 52 articles.

resulting in two combatants under two different regimes in relation to the same site. This would be a very unfortunate situation in wartime which would be almost unprecedented in the law of war. Therefore, it would be a problem calling the draft a supplement because a new regime would be added which most countries would apply in wartime, but may still not apply to all combatants, thus potentially creating a misunderstanding. He shared the concerns of other delegations about the implementability of this regime.[336]

He considered it necessary to clarify the level of the protection:

> His delegation had thought that the enhanced special protection would either be equal to or stronger than, the existing special protection of the Convention. However, he noted that the delegate of Germany had explained that the actual enhanced special protection would be a lower level of protection than the one of 1954.[337]

Other delegates, such as the delegate of Finland, considered enhanced protection to be higher than general protection.[338] This was also the opinion of the British delegate: 'For him it was a new level of special protection which was higher than that in the Convention where the scope was restricted to a category of highly important world-class objects'.[339]

Some States felt, however, that the protection provided should extend to the surroundings of cultural property under enhanced protection.

Two tendencies were expressed in this general debate. One group of States considered the introduction of a new level of protection unnecessary, but others, responding to the criticisms of special protection, considered Chapter 3 to be necessary and essential to ensure better protection of important cultural properties.

Several delegates referred to the weaknesses and insufficiencies of special protection, as stated in Article 8 of the Convention (Austria, Germany and Ireland), and welcomed the creation of a new level of protection by the Protocol (Argentina, Austria, Canada, China, Finland, Germany, Hungary, Italy, Ireland, Sweden and Switzerland). These delegates considered protection

---

336 1999 Hague Conference, Plenary Session, 17 March 1999: Israeli delegate, p. 126.
337 Ibid.
338 Ibid., Finnish delegate, p. 127.
339 Ibid., UK delegate, p. 128.

for cultural property of great importance to be essential,[340] but noted that special protection should not divert attention from the need for effective general protection as provided for in the Convention, in addition to any supplementary provisions regarding general protection which may emerge from the Conference.[341]

But some delegates were not in favour of the new regime,[342] which had 'the same faults and was just as bureaucratic as the old one'.[343] The Spanish delegate was against the multiplication of protective regimes and considered that practical measures should be adopted for the implementation of Article 8 of the Convention and its conditions of application.[344] The French delegate favoured the improvement of the existing system by amending the Convention.[345] Many States felt that Articles 10 and 11 should reflect the provisions of Chapter II of the Convention and better distinguish the higher level of protection. They considered that Article 10 should reflect Article 8 of the Convention, which requires that property under special protection must not be situated near a military objective nor used for military purposes.

The Hungarian delegate considered enhanced special protection to be a subcategory of special protection and proposed the following article:

> Cultural property may be placed under the enhanced special protection provided that it meets the following conditions, and is in full conformity with the provision of Article 8 of the 1954 Hague Convention.
>
> (a) is immovable and movable heritage of very great importance and of outstanding universal value.

The UK delegate suggested that an additional text be included to make clear the relationship and differences between enhanced special protection and special protection under the Convention. In particular, where cultural property has been granted both special protection and enhanced special protection, it should in all cases enjoy the higher level of protection. As we have seen this situation was settled by Article 4, paragraph (b) of the Protocol.

---

340 Ibid., Irish delegate, p. 104.
341 Ibid., French delegate, p. 129.
342 Ibid., delegates of Denmark, p. 116, Turkey, p. 115.
343 Ibid., Danish delegate, p. 116.
344 Ibid., Spanish delegate, p. 121.
345 Ibid., French delegate, p. 129.

The Belgian delegate noted an important gap: no distinctive sign was mentioned in relation to enhanced protection.[346] During discussion on the report of the Working Group, the Austrian delegate reiterated this point and considered that in cases of new enhanced protection 'the use of the emblem repeated three times should also be mentioned to avoid ambiguity'.[347]

One delegate felt that the right of the country to protect its cultural property should be a human right and that the sub-paragraphs should be amended accordingly.

As we have said, the preparation of the draft of the Protocol was influenced by the World Heritage Convention, and some delegates continued to request an alignment with that Convention[348] with respect to the definition of cultural property or creation of the List. The ICRC delegate said:

> It was important to realize that the sites which are put on the World Heritage List have been put there for another purpose. They may meet some conditions for inclusion but being on the World Heritage List would not of itself be the only criterion for inclusion. In addition, there must be an undertaking not to use them for military purposes. The list would be limited only to sites for which governments would be ready to say that they must never be used for military action. The list would be reduced to extremely important sites.[349]

Some delegates felt that Article 11 should better clarify the relationship between special protection under the Convention and 'enhanced special protection' under the Draft Second Protocol, perhaps by using the term 'enhanced protection' (*protection renforcée*). This term was first proposed by the German delegate and was endorsed by the Working Group and retained.[350]

After a long day's discussion, the Chairman summarized the results. He pointed out that the discussion had demonstrated the need for a higher

---

346 Ibid., Belgian delegate, p. 134.
347 1999 Hague Conference, Plenary Session, 25 March 1999: Austrian delegate, p. 27.
348 Argentina, Hungary. It is interesting to note that draft Article 17 of the Preliminary Draft of October 1998 even included among the reasons for cancellation 'loss of intrinsic value', which the delegate of Lebanon found unnecessary saying that it would be useful only if the cultural property was totally destroyed, but otherwise would be impossible to consider during military operations (1999 Hague Conference, Plenary Session, 17 March 1999: Lebanese delegate, p. 110). This reference was not included in the final text.
349 1999 Hague Conference, Plenary Session, 17 March 1999: ICRC delegate, pp. 137–38.
350 Ibid., German delegate, p. 119.

level of protection, although the provisions of Chapter 3 might be revised to better reflect the higher level of 'enhanced special protection', and define its relationship with the Hague Convention protection regime.

The ICRC expressed its full support for efforts to improve special protection:

> the 1954 regime reflects the atmosphere which prevailed after the Second World War. In particular, there were too many instances of area bombardments resulting in either entire cities or significant parts of them being eliminated. The Geneva Conventions of 1949 and the Convention tended to deal with that problem by suggesting that specially protected objects should be placed far away from cities. This way of thinking changed with the Additional Protocol 1. Rather than having the approach that virtually anything of some kind of industrial utility could be bombed, there was the opposite approach that only military objectives could be attacked and everything else must be spared. Keeping this in mind it was therefore inappropriate to retain the conditions in Article 8(1)(a) of the Convention. In particular, certain sites of outstanding global value would be frequently either in the very centre of a large city or very much on the outskirts. In light of modern humanitarian law and warfare, this should not be a reason for saying that they cannot have special protection. Rather, areas or objects which should never be attacked must never be used for military action. It should be clear in all armed conflicts that unless there was a very clear undertaking and a trust that this undertaking was meaningful, that a certain area or object would not be used for military action, otherwise any protection might be illusory. In her view it was this undertaking, proven to be genuine where there was legislation or clear abstention, which would give the protection which was required.[351]

The Chairman announced that Mrs. Louise Terrillon-Mackay (Canada) had agreed to chair an informal Working Group on the provisions of Chapter 3. This was a very large group and it was therefore necessary to create a smaller drafting group of approximately 12 persons who addressed the various Articles of Chapter 3 and submitted two working papers to the larger group for further discussion. We shall see that the draft of Chapter 3 prepared by the Working Group was accepted by the Plenary Meeting of the Conference with very

---

351 Ibid., ICRC delegate, p. 137.

few editorial changes.[352] The term 'enhanced special protection' used in the drafts was definitively replaced by 'enhanced protection'.

In the discussion on the Working Group draft, the Argentine delegate was not satisfied with the three-tiered system of protection, 'which in his view, would bring confusion and be detrimental to the system of special protection'.[353]

Enhanced protection was discussed at the Plenary Sessions of the Conference on 17, 25 and 26 March. On the last day of the Conference, the articles concerning enhanced protection were adopted.[354]

The Second Protocol is only additional and supplementary to the provisions of the Convention. This supplementary character is distinguished from any form of amendment to the Convention. This supplementary character was stressed by many delegates at the 1999 Conference.[355] It is important to state that special protection, as created by the Convention, continues to exist without any modification. The Convention will retain its High Contracting Parties, and it is hoped that a very large number of these Parties will progressively join the Second Protocol, and that enhanced protection will be used with success.

The exact relationship between special protection and enhanced protection lies in the hands of the Parties to the Second Protocol. Will they be willing to adopt the new regime and consider submitting cultural property for enhanced protection instead of special protection? The authors of this provision hope that this will be the case. Will they establish the liaison between the 1972 World Heritage Convention and register property currently on the World Heritage List on the newly created List under enhanced protection? This is the response which all participants of the Hague Conference expect.

---

352 HC/1999/5/Add.7.
353 1999 Hague Conference, Plenary Session, 25 March 1999: Argentine delegate, p. 25.
354 Ibid., 26 March 1999, p. 81.
355 In particular, Argentina, Azerbaijan, Germany and Ireland.

Article 10
ENHANCED PROTECTION

Cultural property may be placed under enhanced protection provided that it meets the following three conditions:

a. it is cultural heritage of the greatest importance for humanity;

b. it is protected by adequate domestic legal and administrative measures recognizing its exceptional cultural and historic value and ensuring the highest level of protection;

c. it is not used for military purposes or to shield military sites and a declaration has been made by the Party which has control over the cultural property, confirming that it will not be so used.

Preparatory work

1999 Hague Conference, Plenary Session, 17 March 1999.

Bibliography

Boylan, P. *Draft procedures*. (This study is on file at the UNESCO Secretariat.)

Henckaerts, J.-M. 1999. New rules for the protection of cultural property in armed conflict: the significance of the Second Protocol to the 1954 Hague Convention for the Protection of Cultural Property in the Event of Armed Conflict. *IRRC*, No. 835, pp. 593-620.

Hladík, J. 1999. The 1954 Hague Convention for the Protection of Cultural Property in the Event of Armed Conflict and the notion of military necessity. *IRRC*, No. 835, pp. 621–35.

ANALYSIS OF THE TEXT

Before starting to study the content of Article 10, we should underline the importance of Articles 1 and 8 of the Convention, which are binding on all States Parties to the Convention and obviously on those that are Parties to the Second Protocol. These two articles form the point of departure for our analysis. Article 1 constitutes the definition of cultural property under general protection. Article 8 concerns property under special protection:

> 1. There may be placed under special protection a limited number of refuges intended to shelter movable cultural property in the event

of armed conflict, of centres containing monuments and other immovable cultural property of very great importance, provided that they:

(a) are situated at an adequate distance from any large industrial centre or from any important military objective constituting a vulnerable point, such as, for example, an aerodrome, broadcasting station, establishment engaged upon work of national defence, a port or railway station of relative importance or a main line of communication;

(b) are not used for military purposes.

2. A refuge for movable cultural property may also be placed under special protection, whatever its location, if it is so constructed that, in all probability, it will not be damaged by bombs.

3. A centre containing monuments shall be deemed to be used for military purposes whenever it is used for the movement of military personnel or material, even in transit. The same shall apply whenever activities directly connected with military operations, the stationing of military personnel, or the production of war material are carried on within the centre.

The objective of Article 10 and the following articles of the Second Protocol is to remove the obstacles created by the restrictive definition and unrealistic conditions preventing larger registration of property under special protection.

Article 10 refers to cultural property defined under Article 1 of the Convention:

For the purposes of the present Convention, the term 'cultural property' shall cover, irrespective of origin or ownership:

(a) movable or immovable property of great importance to the cultural heritage of every people, such as monuments of architecture, art or history, whether religious or secular; archaeological sites; groups of buildings which, as a whole, are of historical or artistic interest; works of art; manuscripts, books and other objects of artistic, historical or archaeological interest; as well as scientific collections and important collections of books or archives or of reproductions of the property defined above;

(b) buildings whose main and effective purpose is to preserve or exhibit the movable cultural property defined in sub-paragraph (a) such as

> museums, large libraries and depositories of archives, and refuges
> intended to shelter, in the event of armed conflict, the movable
> cultural property defined in sub-paragraph (a);
>
> (c) centres containing a large amount of cultural property as defined
> in sub-paragraphs (a) and (b), to be known as 'centres containing
> monuments'.

This definition remained unchanged in the new Protocol. Article 10 provides no further details about such property, aside from that given in paragraphs (a), (b) and (c). Only these three criteria will be applied for registration on the new List of Cultural Property under Enhanced Protection (the List). Objections against the decision to grant or deny enhanced protection shall be made with respect to specific and related facts.[356]

Before the 1999 Hague Conference, several proposals (amendments) were submitted by States to the UNESCO Draft of October 1998. Australia signalled a lack of reference to proximity of military targets and the ICRC proposed the redrafting of the Article.

The drafting of articles on enhanced protection, as we have seen, was inspired by the 1972 World Heritage Convention; this is also the case for Article 10. The experience associated with its almost 30 years of existence at the moment of the 1999 Hague Conference, undoubtedly made the World Heritage Convention a valuable guide for the drafting of the new Protocol. Before and during the Conference the possibility of automatically transferring enhanced protection to World Heritage cultural sites (586 at the moment of the Conference) was discussed, but this idea was finally abandoned for several reasons, including practical objections. But the existence of cultural sites (689 cultural sites were listed on the World Heritage List at the time of this writing) will function as a practical guide in defining the 'greatest importance for humanity', a criterion included in Article 10(a), and will also act as a good example for the new Committee established by the Second Protocol.

If a good parallel exists for cultural property protected by the 1972 Convention and the 1954 Convention, there are fewer examples for museums, archives and libraries. For this reason, Patrick Boylan suggested that benefit could be drawn from the 'Memory of the World' programme created by UNESCO's Communication and Information Sector.[357] While some of the

---

356 Article 11(5) and 11(7) of the Second Protocol.
357 UNESCO has launched the Memory of the World programme to guard against collective amnesia, calling upon the preservation of valuable archive holdings and library collections all over the world, ensuring their wide dissemination. The programme was launched in 1997. The Memory of the

museums or libraries in this programme are included on the World Heritage List, others will certainly seek the possibility of adding their names to the enhanced protection list.[358]

Boylan noted a significant difference between cultural property inscribed on the World Heritage List and that which in the future may be granted enhanced protection. Without in any way minimizing or denigrating the status of World Heritage sites, the effects of inscription on the World Heritage List are essentially moral ones; breaches of the principles of the World Heritage Convention carry no explicit sanctions other than the possibility (still under debate) that a World Heritage Site might be removed from the List in the event of serious degradation or neglect of proper protection and management.[359] As we shall see later, the Second Protocol introduces serious sanctions for violation of provisions of the Protocol.

The role of the Secretariat will be fundamental in providing the necessary background and information to the Committee. Patrick Boylan made an estimation of the workload of the Secretariat and the Committee, coming to the conclusion that an urgent study was needed across the Cultural Heritage Division of UNESCO to ascertain whether the technical expertise and related resources of the World Heritage Centre could be used on behalf of the International Standard Section[360] (and perhaps the Information Society Division of the Communication and Information Sector in relation to 'Memory of the World' inscription), to make available online the necessary detailed information concerning the List of Cultural Property under Enhanced Protection.'[361]

Mr. Walden from Canada, replacing the Chair of the Working Group, stated that paragraphs (a) and (b) 'concerned time of peace and possibly time

---

World Register lists documentary heritage, which has been identified by the International Advisory Committee in its meetings in Tashkent (September 1997), in Vienna (June 1999) and in Cheongju City (June 2001), and has been endorsed by the Director-General of UNESCO as corresponding to the selection criteria for world significance. At present, the Register lists 68 collections of world significance from 33 countries. (Boylan, *Draft procedures*, para. 4.11, p. 20).

358 Boylan suggested that provision should be made in the work programme of the Secretariat and the International Committee for the processing and consideration of perhaps 150 nominations for enhanced protection in respect of archives, libraries and museums from the 15 States that already ratified the Second Protocol, and a further 415 from the other 31 'signatory' States in due course, as they in turn ratify the Protocol.' (Ibid., para. 4.28, p. 28).

359 Ibid., para. 4.3, p. 17.

360 The International Standards Section has been dissolved and, in consequence, responsibility for the administration of the 1954 Hague Convention and its two Protocols now lies with the Section of Museums and Cultural Objects of the Division of Cultural Objects and Intangible Cultural Heritage.

361 Boylan, *Draft procedures*, para. 4.35, p. 32.

of war, while paragraph (c) implicitly related almost exclusively to enhanced protection during time of war. He considered Article 10(c) to be crucial to Chapter 3 as it contained the requirement that cultural property under enhanced protection should not be used for military purposes'.[362]

Paragraph (a)

This paragraph refers to 'cultural heritage' without defining it. The definition of cultural property is provided in Article 1 of the Protocol and refers us to Article 1 of the Convention.

But to understand the notion of 'cultural heritage of the greatest importance for humanity', we should first turn to the 1972 World Heritage Convention, which was for the legislators the example and inspiration behind improvement of the 1954 Convention.

The World Heritage Convention provides the following definition of cultural heritage in Article 1:

> For the purposes of this Convention, the following shall be considered as 'cultural heritage':
> - monuments: architectural works, works of monumental sculpture and painting, elements or structures of an archaeological nature, inscriptions, cave dwellings and combinations of features, which are of outstanding universal value from the point of view of history, art or science;
> - groups of buildings: groups of separate or connected buildings which, because of their architecture, their homogeneity or their place in the landscape, are of outstanding universal value from the point of view of history, art or science;
> - sites: works of man or the combined works of nature and of man, and areas including archaeological sites which are of outstanding universal value from the historical, aesthetic, ethnological or anthropological points of view.

In case of enhanced protection created under the Second Protocol, the situation is more complicated. This covers not only immovable cultural monuments, groups of buildings, sites and zones, but also important archives, libraries, museums and also movable property. Certain comments provided

---

362 1999 Hague Conference, Plenary Session, 25 March 1999, p. 21.

in the draft Guidelines for the Implementation of the Second Protocol expressly requested the inclusion in the draft Guidelines of a specific section pointing out that movable cultural property may be eligible for the granting of enhanced protection.

Application for the granting of enhanced protection may be made by the State Party that has jurisdiction or control over the territory in which the cultural property concerned is located (see later, Article 11, para 1). It may then be granted only in relation to the fixed, clearly identifiable, geographical location.

In the comments submitted before the Conference, Norway and Sweden questioned the reasoning behind the expression 'great importance for humankind' and proposed that the same language be used as that of the Convention. Australia even considered that the phrase might give less protection than the Convention.

This paragraph and the definition of cultural property drew the attention of delegates at the Conference. Nearly all expressed their views on the issue and most[363] preferred the reference to humanity or humankind instead of the reference to 'all peoples' proposed as an alternative in the UNESCO draft submitted to the Conference.[364] Some delegates wished to align the definition with that of the World Heritage Convention and the term 'outstanding universal value'[365] and introduce a reference to the World Heritage List.[366] The Hungarian delegate presented the following draft:

Article 11. Enhanced special protection
Cultural property may be placed under enhanced special protection provided that it meets the following conditions and is in full conformity with the provisions of Article 8 of the 1954 Hague Convention.

a. It is *immovable or movable heritage of very great importance and of outstanding universal value;* [367]

---

363 In particular, Azerbaijan, Belarus, Belgium, China, Egypt, India, Portugal, Romania, Syria, Switzerland and the UK.
364 The second alternative was supported by Turkey (1999 Hague Conference, Plenary Session, 17 March 1999, p. 115).
365 Argentina, Belarus, Hungary and Syria. Lyndel Prott from the UNESCO Secretariat considered this term inappropriate because some sites on the World Heritage List were probably not sites which should be protected under this kind of Convention.
366 Argentina.
367 Italics indicate the inserted text.

According to the Hungarian delegate, enhanced special protection

> is a subcategory of special protection. The reference to Article 8 of
> the 1954 Hague Convention provides the conditions, under which
> special protection can be granted. When enhanced special protection
> is to be granted, conditions of the above Article must be met at least.
> The next prerequisite for eligibility of enhanced special protection is
> the outstanding universal value of the cultural property. While only
> a limited number of World Heritage sites will be eligible or even
> nominated for enhanced special protection by the State Parties to this
> Protocol, the use of the language of the World Heritage Convention
> is advantageous. It suggests that already a great deal of legal, technical
> and professional work have been accumulated and scrutinized to
> avoid the unacceptably high degree of subjectivity in defining the
> judgement 'of very great importance'. Nevertheless to emphasize the
> difference between the criteria of selection in the two Conventions, we
> re-introduced the well-defined concepts of immovable and movable
> cultural heritage.[368]

The Indian delegate pointed out 'that it was extremely difficult in cases of
ancient civilizations like India, which have more than five thousand years of
recorded history, to establish a ranking of higher or lower important cultural
property'.[369]

The US delegate considered that the paragraph 'should be designed
to cover a special category of a limited number of cultural items of unusually
great importance and therefore the standard should be revised to reflect a
high level of importance'.[370]

The Syrian delegate considered the threshold too high, and preferred
as an expression: 'cultural property shall be considered for inclusion in the
list at the request of the Party in whose territory the cultural property is
located'.[371] The Lebanese delegate made a comparison of expressions used by
the Convention and the draft Protocol and raised an important question. Who
will determine the importance for humanity: the Committee or other bodies

---

368 HC/1999/CRP.3.
369 1999 Hague Conference, Plenary Session, 17 March 1999: Indian delegate, p. 136.
370 Ibid., US delegate, p. 113.
371 Ibid., 25 March 1999: Syrian delegate, p. 35.

or simply the State requiring the registration?[372] In this respect the answer seems clear: it will be the Committee on the basis of the State request.

The paragraph maintains the reference to 'greatest importance' to which we expressed some objections as being too subjective. As we have seen, Article 1 of the Convention used the words 'great importance', Article 8 characterized the property as of 'very great importance', and paragraph (a) of Article 10 of the Protocol speaks about 'greatest importance'. This means that the words used in the Protocol indicate a slightly higher level of significance than the 'very great importance' associated with special protection. The use of the absolute adjective 'greatest' was raised again at the end of the Conference.[373]

As we have said in the 1996 Commentary on the provisions of the Convention, the decision was placed in the hands of national authorities, who would judge more on the basis of criteria of importance than of value: 'Certain objects, although of limited value, may be important for the national culture while others, even though of great value, can be replaced and are therefore less important.'[374] This was the case of the Convention. The formulation of the Protocol gives less liberty to national authorities, as it requires that the cultural property be of the 'greatest importance for humanity'. Judgments can no longer be passed with reference only to limited national criteria. It is necessary to take into consideration the 'higher standard' of humanity and the international community.

A similar situation now exists with respect to 'cultural heritage'. The selection will be made only by the States requesting enhanced protection and the Committee which will take the final decision concerning the granting or denial of enhanced protection, according to Article 11, paragraph 7 of the Second Protocol. The text of the paragraph is clear: the Committee may decide *only* on the basis of criteria mentioned in Article 10.

To clarify the first criterion, it may be important for the Committee to adopt a practice of 'general comments' in order to provide clarification of certain notions or situations. But States, as usual, will apply their own criteria and views. The consideration of 'greatest value' will in most cases be determined by national views. This will constitute the first stage of the nomination process, decided at the level of the requesting State.

To limit the subjectivity and exclusivity of decisions, Article 11(3) gives the right of initiative to other States Parties to the Protocol, to the

---

372 Ibid., 17 March 1999: Lebanese delegate, p. 109.
373 1999 Hague Conference, Plenary Session, 25 March 1999. See the delegate of the UK, p. 28.
374 Toman (1996), p. 50.

International Committee of the Blue Shield (ICBS), and to NGOs with relevant expertise, 'to recommend specific cultural property to the Committee'. But in this case, the decision remains in the hands of the Committee, which 'may decide to invite a Party to request inclusion of that cultural property in the List'. Yet the final decision concerning the request remains in the hands of the State which has the jurisdiction or control over the cultural property. As we shall see, several delegates at the 1999 Conference insisted upon this point.

Paragraph (b)

But the 'greatest importance for humanity' is not the only element taken into consideration. It is accompanied by the national criterion, that is, recognition of the importance of the cultural property concerned at the national level. This national level is expressed in terms of the fact that such cultural property will also be protected by 'adequate domestic legal and administrative measures' and adequate information on existing arrangements for the protection of the site, building or zone under local, national, regional and international legal and administrative measures. These measures are taken because the national authorities have committed to 'recognizing its exceptional cultural and historic value and ensuring the highest level of protection'. It is interesting to note that this paragraph does not use the subjective term 'importance', but the more objective word 'value'.

A study on national legislation relating to cultural property would be very helpful, in addition to the creation of a special database, similar to that which exists for international humanitarian law created by the ICRC. The World Heritage Centre has a specific database related to World Heritage sites which could be used by the Committee for the purposes of the Second Protocol.[375] The former UNESCO International Standards Section commissioned a study of national legislation for the purposes of Chapter 4 of the Second Protocol.[376] The UNESCO draft contained two separate paragraphs on this issue:

---

375 UNESCO Cultural Heritage Laws Database: http://portal.unesco.org/culture/en/ev.php-URL_
    ID=33928&URL_DO=DO_TOPIC&URL_SECTION=201.html
376 O'Keefe (2002).

(b) adequate legislation at the national level exists, recognizing its exceptional cultural-historical value and ensuring its legal and sustainable protection at the highest national level; and

(c) such legislation is effectively implemented, and includes preventive and organisational measures for emergency situations.[377]

Norway, in its comments before the Conference, asked for clarification of the term 'adequate legislation', and Sweden[378] modified it by proposing 'adequate legislative and administrative measures', which was adopted in the final text.[379]

During discussion at the Conference, it was noted that dependence on legislative and administrative actions taken at the national level, removed the superior level as accorded by paragraph (a) to a level not higher than the protection stated in Article 8 of the Convention. We should not go so far. The provision of Article 1, paragraph (b) simply means that if a State wishes to benefit from the highest protective level, it must also demonstrate a national effort to ensure protection at the domestic level by providing for that purpose legislative and administrative infrastructures and recognition of exceptional cultural and historic value. The requesting State must ensure the highest level of protection at home before proceeding to the international level.

Some States considered that paragraph (b) did not take into consideration the difficulties that could arise in a federal state,[380] or difficulties that developing countries can encounter in implementation of these provisions, especially without international and technical assistance.[381]

Paragraph (c)

This paragraph was not included in the Preliminary Draft of October 1998 (HC/1999/1). In its comments on the draft, Israel proposed a new

---

377 Preliminary Draft Second Protocol to the 1954 Hague Convention, HC/1999/1, October 1998, p. 3.
378 Letter of Ministry of Foreign Affairs of Sweden of 15 December 1998.
379 The Draft of the Protocol of 1998 also included paragraph (c) referring to legislation and stating: 'such legislation is effectively implemented, and includes preventive and organizational measures for emergency situations'. It was not included in the final text.
380 1999 Hague Conference, Plenary Session, 17 March 1999: India and Canada, p. 116. The Canadian delegate suggested that such legal protection may exist and be effective below the national level, or at multiple levels such as provincial and municipal.
381 Ibid., Indonesia, p. 120; Ethiopia, p. 123.

paragraph (d): 'is not used for military purposes'. Austria also wanted to include a prohibition 'to use cultural property in support of military effort'. Australia signalled the lack of a reference to the proximity of military targets and the ICRC simply proposed that the article be redrafted.

In the final text, more practical elements relating to military activity are included in this third paragraph. The paragraph requires two additional tests:

a) the property is not being used for military purposes, or to shield military sites; and,

b) declaration has been made by the Party that has control over the cultural property, confirming that it will not be so used.

The first test: the property is not being used for military purposes, or to shield military sites

The first test concerns the elimination of any doubt that the cultural property in question is not used as a military objective.[382] We should recall the definition of military objectives provided by Article 52(2) of the 1977 Additional Protocol I:

> Insofar as objects are concerned, military objectives are limited to those objects which by their nature, location, purpose or use make an effective contribution to military action and whose total or partial destruction, capture or neutralization, in the circumstances ruling at the time, offers a definite military advantage.

It was not necessary to include in paragraph (c) of Article 10 a reference to *nature*, for by its very nature cultural property – by definition – will not be a military objective.

As we have seen in the case of special protection according to Article 8 of the Convention, the location[383] of cultural property and requirement of 'adequate distance' were the major obstacles to the registration of cultural property. But it proved impossible to find an acceptable definition for

---

382 The definition of the military objective is contained in Article 1(f) of the Second Protocol.

383 Location was introduced into Article 52(2) of the Additional Protocol I, as it may constitute an effective contribution to military action, such as a bridge, but the Working Group which introduced it gave no particular reasons. *Commentary on the Additional Protocols of 8 June 1977*, para. 2021, p. 636.

'adequate distance'.[384] This was replaced by the second test: a declaration made by the Party that has control over the cultural property, confirming that it will not be so used for military purposes.

The first test includes in the definition two remaining elements: *purpose and use*.

At the 1999 Conference the delegations felt that the declaration of non-use of cultural property for military purposes should be a criterion for the granting of enhanced protection to any cultural property. The US delegate

> remarked that Article 11 [of the draft] did not include the two conditions contained in Article 8 of the Convention, which he considered essential namely that the property in question must not be located in the immediate proximity of the military objectives and that the property is in use for military purposes. The language of Article 12(4) [of the draft] should follow the Convention and use the phrase 'use for military purposes' which was carefully defined in Article 8 (3) of the Convention.[385]

When the paragraph uses the words 'military purpose', it is close to the original definition that the ICRC proposed to the 1974–1977 Diplomatic Conference: the objects should be recognized to be of military interest.[386] The ICRC Commentary explains these two words:

> The criterion of 'purpose' is concerned with the intended future use of an object, while that of 'use' is concerned with its present function. Most civilian objects can become useful objects to the armed forces. Thus, for example, a school or a hotel is a civilian object, but if they are used to accommodate troops or headquarters staff, they become military objectives. It is clear from paragraph 3 that in case of doubt, such places must be presumed to serve civilian purposes.[387]

---

384 The meeting of the High Contracting Parties in 1962 asked for this notion to be clarified, but the matter was referred to a consultative committee, which was never formed. See Toman (1996), p. 101.
385 1999 Hague Conference, Plenary Session, 17 March 1999: US delegate, p. 114.
386 Commentary on the Additional Protocols of 8 June 1977, para. 2019, p. 635.
387 Ibid., para. 2022, p. 636.

For Yoram Dinsten,

> the purpose of an object – as a separate ground for classifying it as a
> military target – is determined after the crystallization of its original
> nature, albeit prior to actual use. In other words, the military purpose
> is assumed not to be stamped on the objective from the outset
> (otherwise, the target would be military by nature). Military purpose
> is deduced from an established intention of a belligerent as regards
> future use.[388]

Paragraph (c) of Article 10 is quite affirmative: cultural property 'is not to be
used for military purposes'. If it is used for such purposes, enhanced protection
cannot be granted.

The second part of condition (1) is that the cultural property *does not*
'shield military sites'. If it does, the granting of enhanced protection is also
excluded.

The word 'shield' must be explained in more detail. The words 'military
sites' could be assimilated to the notion of military objectives as explained
in relation to Article 6, paragraph 1, sub-paragraph (i). The phrase 'shield
military sites' refers to the location of military installations very close or inside
cultural property.[389] This provision therefore relates in a more general way to
the condition and requirement of Article 8, paragraph 1 of the Convention,
where 'adequate distance' was required:

> adequate distance from any large industrial centre or from any important
> military objective constituting a vulnerable point, such as, for example,
> an aerodrome, broadcasting station, establishment engaged upon work
> of national defence, a port or railway station of relative importance or
> a main line of communication.

It may be recalled that this provision created serious problems of interpretation
and was, for this reason, a major obstacle to the use of special protection under the
Convention. The legislators therefore simplified the wording rather than refining
the details. The Swedish delegate at the Conference mentioned that the

---

388 Dinstein (2004a), p. 89.
389 Patrick Boylan characterizes this expression by saying that 'shield genuine military objective during
   a conflict will by no means be confined to deliberate action taken by a defending States e.g. by
   locating military installations very close to important cultural property'. (Boylan, *Draft procedures*,
   para. 4.14, p. 22.)

lack of adequate distance from industrial centres and military objectives should not be as obstacle to placing an object on the list. The adoption of this concept represented an important step forward in the protection of cultural property because objects on this list would be known and there would or should be individual criminal responsibility attached to breaches of this protection. The prohibition of the use of such property should also be extended to the surroundings of the property, otherwise it may be endangered by hostilities.[390]

The general provision, on the other hand, imposes greater responsibility on the Committee to take into consideration possible situations with respect to cultural property in relation to military objectives. [391] A serious preliminary study will be necessary in determining such situations and the responsibility for this important task will again fall on the Secretariat in consultation with international and NGOs. It will require adequate documentation, maps, military or geographic grid coordinates or GIS data. The experience of the World Heritage Committee and Centre will be of fundamental importance for the Secretariat of this new committee.[392]

---

390 1999 Hague Conference, Plenary Session, 17 March 1999: Swedish delegate, p. 104.

391 Patrick Boylan, mentioning the arrangement agreed by Italy in relation to the Vatican City, said that 'the International Committee would ultimately have to take a view as to whether such measures would be sufficient or whether certain buildings and sites, regardless of their outstanding importance, could not be granted enhanced protection because of their very close proximity to a potential legitimate military objective'. (Boylan, *Draft procedures*, para. 4.15, p. 22.)

392 4.18 […] An examination of the documentation of a sample of current World Heritage List sites has demonstrated three very important facts. First, the maps and other location documentation and descriptions submitted for World Heritage Convention purposes are often nowhere near sufficient or detailed enough for military planning purposes, so even in very well established World Heritage List cases additional work will be needed to improve this documentation.

4.19. Second, very many World Heritage sites, especially 'serial' or 'multiple' listings, are much too large and complex for Enhanced Protection purposes, and the larger or dispersed sites may well have potential military objectives within them. A good example from one of the States that has already ratified the Second Protocol is the World Heritage listing as a single World Heritage site of the isolated painted churches in the Troodos Mountains of Cyprus. These are spread over a distance of some tens of kilometres, and there is a major international military communications installation more or less in the centre of the group on the Troodos summit. In cases such as this the applicant State is likely to need guidance from the Secretariat in breaking down one overall World Heritage (or other) designated zone into several or perhaps very many separate Enhanced Protection proposals.

4.20. Conversely, in other cases where there is a clear and contiguous boundary around a World Heritage List designation which can in principle form the boundary of an Enhanced Protection designation as well, there may be buildings or installations within this which could form a legitimate military objective in the event of war. Though in the limited time available it has not been possible to do detailed research on the point, it seems very likely that within large historic city World Heritage designations, such as Vienna, Austria – a State that has already ratified the Second Protocol – or the city centres of e.g. Florence and Rome, Italy (a signatory State), there are likely to be

To illustrate the important role that the experience of the World Heritage Convention and List can play, we include here Patrick Boylan's analysis of the possible use of existing lists, the Main List and the Tentative List for the future work of the Committee:

4.22.   [...] I have therefore analysed in some detail both the definitive cultural World Heritage listings and the Tentative Lists deposited with the World Heritage Centre for the 15 States that have already ratified the Second Protocol, on the assumption that these are likely to be among the earliest submissions to the Second Protocol International Committee, starting soon after the Second Protocol comes into force (i.e. three months after the deposit of the 20th Instrument of Ratification or Accession). I have also analysed the same listings for the 31 other States that have signed the Second Protocol but not yet completed the process of formal ratification under their respective national procedures. It seems reasonable to suppose that so far as cultural monuments are concerned these two groups will form the bulk of the likely submissions for the granting of enhanced protection over the first three or four years after the Second Protocol comes into force.

4.23.   I have at the same time examined the details of World Heritage 'serial' or 'multiple' inscriptions and made estimates of the number of individual Enhanced Protection submissions that each of these might generate. Spain, which has already ratified the Second Protocol, has several good examples of such World Heritage List inscriptions.

4.24.   For example, the ancient pilgrimage Route of Santiago de Compostella is on the World Heritage List as a single inscription. However, this is essentially an historic route which crosses the whole of northern Spain west to east, and along much of the Route the World Heritage designation is of just that route – a strip just 70 metres wide at its narrowest.

---

potential legitimate military, politico-military or communications targets. If this proves to be the case such buildings or other facilities, (probably with appropriate buffer zones around each of these), would have to be excluded from the enhanced protection provision. Similar considerations would probably apply in relation to e.g. naval and airport facilities among the more than 100 islands and approx. 100 km of coastline of the Venice Lagoon World Heritage site, and the very large Bay of Naples and Isle of Capri World Heritage nomination on Italy's current Tentative List under the World Heritage Convention. (Boylan, *Draft procedures*, para. 4.18–4.20, pp. 23–24.)

However, there would clearly be the strongest possible military objections to an Enhanced Protection designation of the whole of the World Heritage List route, since this would – in effect – create a legally protected barrier cutting off the whole of mainland Spain from its Atlantic coast in terms of ground-level military communication and movements in the event of a conflict. On the other hand it would be totally impracticable to designate separately for Enhanced Protection every one of the more than 1,800 individual buildings and monuments protected under Spanish law as part of the Santiago route. Instead, after detailed examination of the World Heritage designation files, I estimate that in practical terms Enhanced Protection is likely to be sought in respect of a total of just under one hundred sites: towns, villages and other clusters of buildings, within the single World Heritage designation.

4.25. Another Spanish example is the World Heritage inscription as a single World Heritage 'site' of a total of 723 caves containing important Palaeolithic art, stretching across all four of Spain's Mediterranean provinces. Also, Spain's Tentative List of future World Heritage site nominations includes a proposal to extend the single site of the Altamira Cave, Cantabria, northern Spain to cover all 48 caves with important Palaeolithic art within the region. Caves have very considerable military potential in infantry and guerrilla operations – for shelter, stores of military materiel, as well as in direct fighting – and it seems very likely that Spain would in due course want to see all the World Heritage List and Tentative List cave art sites under Enhanced Protection. Thus, just two World Heritage inscriptions could generate no less that 771 Enhanced Protection proposals, which would have to be processed by the Secretariat, and then ruled on by the International Committee for the Protection of Cultural Property in the Event of Armed Conflict.

4.26. Taking these factors into account, I estimate that the 16 Second Protocol 'ratification' States and the 31 other signatory States are likely to generate, simply from their existing World Heritage Listing and Tentative Lists, the following:[393]

---

393 Boylan, *Draft procedures*, pp. 25–27.

	World Heritage List Cultural Inscriptions	World Heritage List: Individual Properties	Tentative List: Individual Properties	Total
15 'Ratification' States	64	938	126	1064
31 'Signatory' States	178	315	273	598
TOTAL	242	1253	399	1662

The second test: declaration has been made by the Party that has control over the cultural property, confirming that it will not be so used.

It is therefore not merely sufficient that cultural property 'is not being used for military purposes, or to shield military sites'; it is also necessary that the Party which has control over the cultural property confirms that the property will not be used for military purposes or to shield military sites.

This condition constitutes a fundamental difference from paragraph 5 of Article 8 of the Convention:

> If any cultural property mentioned in paragraph 1 of the present Article is situated near an important military objective as defined in the said paragraph, it may nevertheless be placed under special protection if the High Contracting Party asking for that protection undertakes, in the event of armed conflict, to make no use of the objective and particularly, in the case of a port, railway station or aerodrome, to divert all traffic there from. In that event, such diversion shall be prepared in time of peace.

Article 10, paragraph (c) is based on a different premise. This Article imposes on the Party willing to register the cultural property under enhanced protection the duty not to use it for military purposes or to shield military sites. Article 8(5) of the Convention starts with the affirmation that such property is situated near an important military objective:

Even if this may also be the case in the situation of Article 10(c), the first step would be for the State to make an effort to remove the military objective far from the cultural property. It should make this attempt before presenting the request for enhanced protection. Should this prove impossible for material reasons, such as the existence of a port, railway station or aerodrome, the State must make a declaration confirming that the cultural property will not be used for military purposes or to shield military sites. Only if these conditions are fulfilled could enhanced protection eventually be granted. Article 10(c) is thus more explicit than Article 8(5).

During the Hague Conference, one State expressed a preference for deletion of this last part of the sub-paragraph (referring to the confirmation of a State, by declaration, that cultural property will not be used for military purposes or to shield military sites). Other States, however, stressed the necessity for its inclusion – that the latter part of the sub-paragraph explains its importance: the declarations refer not only to present non-use but also to future non-use. Some other States questioned whether 11(c) (now 10(c)) refers only to 'control' and not to 'jurisdiction'. One participant in the Working Group explained that this use was correct in this instance because only the State that has control of a territory can make the required declaration.[394] The Syrian delegate also preferred the use of 'control or jurisdiction' in this paragraph.[395]

---

394 1999 Hague Conference, Plenary Session, 25 March 1999: Lyndel Prott, p. 29. Ms Prott pointed out that the question of 'jurisdiction or control' also came up in Articles 11(c), 12(2) and 12 (9) of the draft. Article 10(c) of the final text, as was pointed out by the delegate of the UK, referred only to 'control' because only the person in control would be able to declare that the property was not being used and would not be used in the future. Only they would able to give that guarantee. This provision was important to reassure other Parties to the Convention that there was to be no misuse of cultural property. She emphasized that Articles 11(2) and 11(9) of the final text were both concerned with the possibility of requesting inscription on the list. The idea presented by the Working Group for both those procedures was that these were objects of very great importance to all humanity and therefore both States should be allowed the possibility of making a request. A request by the Party in control for nomination should be considered by the Committee as well as a request by the Party which has jurisdiction. The Committee would then try and reach agreement between these Parties that this cultural property should be spared the effects of conflict by being entered in the list. She stressed that before the text was sent to the Drafting Committee, the Conference had to make sure whether the terms 'control' in Article 10(c), and 'Jurisdiction and control' in Article 11(2) should be retained, and whether that same condition in Article 11(2) applied equally to a request for the list under Article 11(9).

395 Ibid., pp. 36 and 29.

Article 11

THE GRANTING OF ENHANCED PROTECTION

1. *Each Party should submit to the Committee a list of cultural property for which it intends to request the granting of enhanced protection.*

2. *The Party which has jurisdiction or control over the cultural property may request that it be included in the List to be established in accordance with Article 27 sub-paragraph 1(b). This request shall include all necessary information related to the criteria mentioned in Article 10. The Committee may invite a Party to request that cultural property be included in the List.*

3. *Other Parties, the International Committee of the Blue Shield and other non-governmental organizations with relevant expertise may recommend specific cultural property to the Committee. In such cases, the Committee may decide to invite a Party to request inclusion of that cultural property in the List.*

4. *Neither the request for inclusion of cultural property situated in a territory, sovereignty or jurisdiction over which is claimed by more than one State, nor its inclusion, shall in any way prejudice the rights of the parties to the dispute.*

5. *Upon receipt of a request for inclusion in the List, the Committee shall inform all Parties of the request. Parties may submit representations regarding such a request to the Committee within sixty days. These representations shall be made only on the basis of the criteria mentioned in Article 10. They shall be specific and related to facts. The Committee shall consider the representations, providing the Party requesting inclusion gives a reasonable opportunity to respond before taking the decision. When such representations are before the Committee, decisions for inclusion in the List shall be taken, notwithstanding Article 26, by a majority of four-fifths of its members present and voting.*

6. *In deciding upon a request, the Committee should ask the advice of governmental and non-governmental organizations, as well as of individual experts.*

7. *A decision to grant or deny enhanced protection may only be made on the basis of the criteria mentioned in Article 10.*

8. *In exceptional cases, when the Committee has concluded that the Party requesting inclusion of cultural property in the List cannot fulfill the criteria of Article 10 sub-paragraph (b), the Committee may decide to grant enhanced protection, provided that the requesting Party submits a request for international assistance under Article 32.*

9. *Upon the outbreak of hostilities, a Party to the conflict may request, on an emergency basis, enhanced protection of cultural property under its jurisdiction*

or control by communicating this request to the Committee. The Committee shall transmit this request immediately to all Parties to the conflict. In such cases the Committee will consider representations from the Parties concerned on an expedited basis. The decision to grant provisional enhanced protection shall be taken as soon as possible and, notwithstanding Article 26, by a majority of four-fifths of its members present and voting. Provisional enhanced protection may be granted by the Committee pending the outcome of the regular procedure for the granting of enhanced protection, provided that the provisions of Article 10 sub-paragraphs (a) and (c) are met.

10.*Enhanced protection shall be granted to cultural property by the Committee from the moment of its entry in the List.*

11.*The Director-General shall, without delay, send to the Secretary-General of the United Nations and to all Parties notification of any decision of the Committee to include cultural property on the List.*

Preparatory work

1999 Hague Conference, Plenary Session, 17 March 1999, pp. 103–39.

Bibliography

Henckaerts, J.-M. 1999. New rules for the protection of cultural property in armed conflict: the significance of the Second Protocol to the 1954 Hague Convention for the Protection of Cultural Property in the Event of Armed Conflict. *IRRC*, No. 835, pp. 593-620

ANALYSIS OF THE TEXT

Article 11 of the Protocol elaborates in detail the procedure for granting enhanced protection.

During the 1999 Hague Conference, a view was expressed by certain delegates that some provisions of Article 11 should be moved to Chapter 6 dealing with institutional issues, since they concerned procedural matters under the responsibility of the Committee.[396] The drafting of operational guidelines was also considered in order to supersede those of the Regulations to

---

396 1999 Hague Conference, Plenary Session, 17 March 1999: Argentina, p. 134, Austria, p. 118, Belgium, p. 134, Canada, p. 116.

the Hague Convention.[397] However, operational guidelines cannot supersede the Regulations for the Execution of the Convention. The regulations are an integral part of the Convention and can be modified only by the procedure explained in Article 39 of the Convention – in other words, by the unanimity of the States Parties to the Convention.

The Working Group included these procedural issues in Article 11 and determined who could request inclusion on the List. Only a party that has control over a cultural property could make the declaration required by Article 11(c) (renumbered 10(c) in the final text). However, a Party with either 'jurisdiction or control' could request the inscription of cultural property on the List. This was in keeping with the importance of these properties for all humankind. The representative of the Chairperson of the informal Working Group on Chapter 3 did, however, draw the attention of the Plenary to the fact that in certain instances when only 'control' was used, a minority of delegations would still have preferred the use of 'jurisdiction or control'.

Paragraphs 1–4: request for the granting of enhanced protection

The granting of enhanced protection is made on the basis of an application, which each party should submit to the Committee for the Protection of Cultural Property in the Event of Armed Conflict (the Committee), created by Article 24 of the Second Protocol.

The UNESCO draft presented to the 1999 Conference kept two options: the Committee or the restraint Bureau. At the Conference, most States favoured the creation of the Intergovernmental Committee, including those who favoured amending the Convention rather than adoption of the additional Protocol.[398]

An application submitted to the Committee should identify precisely the property; any uncertainty would be totally unacceptable as serious penal consequences are related to the violation of such property under enhanced protection.

---

397 Argentina. This suggestion requires serious consideration. The Regulations for the Execution of the Convention are part of the Hague Convention and cannot be superseded by a lower instrument, such as operational guidelines.

398 Italy. The delegate of France who was not in favour of the new protection regime welcomed the creation of the Committee and its responsibilities for the implementation of the special protection of the Convention. 1999 Hague Conference, Plenary Session, 17 March 1999, p. 130.

Such an application, according to paragraph 1, should be submitted by each party exclusively to the Second Protocol. The application is addressed to the Committee, but will be received by the UNESCO Secretariat. The Secretariat will inform the members of the Committee and submit the dossier to the next session of the Committee. The request will be submitted to the Committee with all information required by the criteria of Article 10.

Paragraph 2 indicates the ways by which requests for the granting of the enhanced protection come to the Committee. There are three possible ways.

First method for submitting requests

A request may be submitted by the party to the Second Protocol that has jurisdiction or control over the cultural property. The Party is not obliged to do so, although it is its right. Possessing jurisdiction or control over the cultural property is a prerequisite for submitting a request. By using the reference 'jurisdiction and control', the authors of the provision opted for a concept which is usually used in relation to the exercise of territorial power.[399] Independently of the concept of bases of jurisdiction, 'a State must be able to identify a sufficient nexus between itself and the object of its assertion of jurisdiction'[400] – the territorial jurisdiction with which we are concerned in this Article and which is also most often invoked by States. We must take into consideration the scope of this jurisdiction, which will cover the entire territory of the State as defined by international law. The reference to control indicates that the request for enhanced protection may concern cultural property which is not in the territory where the requesting State is exercising its exclusive jurisdiction, but also the territory analogous to the territorial jurisdiction: areas leased by a State in accordance with the lease, areas under military occupation, and so on.

We should also add that the formulation used in this paragraph does not refer only to territory, although this will primarily be the case. As the paragraph states, a Party that has jurisdiction or control in the form of ownership of a cultural object (movable property), located in the territory of

---

399 For example, the International Court of Justice states: 'The existence of the general obligation of States to ensure that activities within their jurisdiction and control respect the environment of other States or of areas beyond national control is now part of the corpus of international law relating to the environment.' (*Legality of the threat or use of nuclear weapons, Advisory opinion of 8 July 1996, I.C.J.Reports 1996*, para. 29, p. 242).

400 Oxman (1987), p. 55.

another State, may be able to request protection. Several delegates were in favour of maintaining the words 'jurisdiction or control'.[401]

In relation to the List of Cultural Property under Enhanced Protection, the paragraph refers to Article 27, sub-paragraph 1(b).

Submission by invitation

The Committee may invite a Party to request that a cultural property be included on the List. This is an innovative form of submission, by which the Committee has the power to initiate a submission in the interests of a cultural property of the greatest importance for humanity.

Such an initiative may draw the interest of the State and its authorities to the cultural property in its territory or a territory under its control, and which for whatever reason registration was not submitted. It is easy to imagine that a property, situated in a territory where an ethnic minority is living, may not be presented for political reasons relating to the majority population. In such cases, the initiative of the Committee may be valuable. But simple bureaucratic reasons may also lie behind the lack of registration.

The advantage of such an initiative is that it places State authorities in a position whereby refusing is difficult.

Submission via recommendation

The third method for submission – included separately in paragraph 3 – is via a recommendation, addressed to the Committee on behalf of:
- *States parties to the Second Protocol.* At the 1999 Conference, one State proposed that Article 11(2) should allow Parties from one State to request inscription of cultural property located in a second State on the International List of Cultural Property under the enhanced special protection in order to protect the cultural property of minorities. The provision of paragraph 3 was probably considered as sufficient.
- *International Committee of the Blue Shield (ICBS).*
- *Other NGOs with relevant expertise.* In this last case, a limit is imposed on organizations that have no particular competence in the field of cultural values. The Austrian delegation particularly welcomed this provision.

---

401 1999 Hague Conference, Plenary Session, 25 March 1999: Armenia, India, p. 26.

In this case, it will be up to the Committee to decide whether to follow such a recommendation and invite a Party that has jurisdiction or control over a cultural property to present a request for inclusion of a cultural property on the List. Three delegates suggested amending Article 11(3) to make it clear that the recommendation of an NGO had no effect without a request by a State (Article 11(2)) and a decision by the Committee.[402] This was also confirmed by the Chairman of the Conference. The granting of enhanced protection will always be an 'intergovernmental exercise', affirmed by the delegate of Argentina.[403] It is important to stress that exclusive powers are left to the Party that has jurisdiction or control over the cultural property in question.

In the last Plenary Session on 25 March, one State was concerned by the power that Article 11(2) seemed to give the Committee to 'invite' Parties to request the inclusion of a cultural property on the List. Another State was concerned that 11(2) did not seem to consider the situation of a State that, though it has jurisdiction over a certain territory (and by extension the cultural property contained therein), does not have control over that territory. The situation was clarified when another State indicated that when 11(2) is taken with 11(3), it becomes clear that no State could abuse the provisions of sub-paragraph 11(2).

Paragraph 4: existence of dispute when cultural property lies in the territory of more than one State

Based on past experiences relating to special protection, the present paragraph was included in order to allow Parties to resolve territorial disputes without taking into consideration actions which were undertaken under the present Article. As we have seen, situations may arise when one or more States will claim sovereignty or jurisdiction over a territory or a cultural property. In such cases, neither the fact that the request for inclusion was deposited nor the inclusion itself of the property on the List 'shall in any way prejudice the rights of the parties to the dispute', in other words, will have no influence on the settlement of such dispute.

---

402 1999 Hague Conference, Plenary Session, 17 March 1999: Azerbaijan, China and Turkey, p. 115.
403 Ibid., Argentina, p. 112. This was also a preoccupation of some delegates who proposed new wording giving all power to the Committee. Ibid., Syria, p. 113, Austria, p. 118, Egypt.

Paragraphs 5–8: deliberation and decision by the Committee

Paragraph 5 follows the World Heritage Convention Model. When the Committee receives a request for inclusion on the List it has a responsibility to consider proposals from the States Parties. The following steps have to be accomplished:

1. The first step, before taking any decision, is to inform all Parties to the Protocol of the request received.

2. States Parties may submit representations, but they are not obliged to do so. They must respect the time limit fixed for such representation which is 60 days. Contrary to the objections under special protection, representations shall be made only on the basis of the criteria mentioned in Article 10. There is one more requirement: representations shall be specific and related to facts. A proposal to limit objections to 'relevant specific facts' was made by Israel in its comments on the UNESCO Draft from October 1998. China, in these comments, also required that objections 'be made only on the basis that the property is not cultural property'.[404] In this way, authors of this provision aimed to eliminate objections of a political character that had nothing to do with the cultural property itself and were opposed rather to the protection of cultural property.

3. The committee itself will discuss and consider representations.

4. While the Committee is considering representations, the Party directly concerned, namely the Party requesting inclusion, has a reasonable opportunity to respond before the Committee takes its decision on the inclusion of the property on the List.

5. The Committee decides by a majority of two-thirds of its members present and voting on whether a property shall be granted or denied enhanced protection, or whether the request should be referred or deferred. In two exceptional cases, a majority of four-fifths of the members of the Committee present and voting is needed:

    (i) when Parties make a representation to the Committee on the basis of another Party's request for inclusion in the List; and

    (ii) when a Party requests enhanced protection on an emergency basis.[405]

---

404 China, Comments, December 1998.
405 Cf. Articles 11(5) and 11(7) of the Second Protocol.

The procedure will also require adequate preparation of each file, in other words, the collection of all documentation and information concerning in particular with respect to conditions prescribed by Article 10. This will require not only documentation that will be provided by the Party directly concerned but also additional research and evaluation of the available facts. During this procedure, the burden of documentation submitted to the Committee, original applications with any responses, counter-arguments and expert advice, and so on, will rest on the Secretariat and crucial professional and administrative activity will be required.[406]

. According to the 2008 Draft Guidelines, Parties are entitled and encouraged to submit to the Committee requests for granting enhanced protection to cultural property under their jurisdiction or control. The Committee, which establishes and maintains the List, decides in each particular case whether the criteria set out above are met. The requests will be sent to the Committee through the Secretariat, which will also acknowledge the receipt, check for completeness, register the request, and will eventually ask for additional information. The Secretariat will forward complete requests to the Bureau of the Committee. The Bureau may consult organizations with relevant expertise to evaluate the requests.

Once the Committee has received a request it informs all Parties of the request for inclusion in the List. Parties may submit a representation concerning the request to the Committee within sixty days. These representations may only concern the criteria mentioned in Article 10, and will be specific and related to facts. The Committee considers the representations, providing the requesting Party with a reasonable opportunity to respond before taking a decision. The Committee may decide to invite a Party to request inclusion of cultural property on the List. Other Parties as well as ICBS and other NGOs with relevant expertise may recommend cultural property to the Committee for inclusion on the List. In such cases, the Committee may decide to invite the Party concerned to request inclusion of that property on the List.[407]

In its comments on the 1998 Draft, Italy noted the need for a more cooperative attitude on the part of States Parties when raising objections to inclusion in the Register.

---

406 Boylan, *Draft procedures*, para. 4.2, p. 16

407 See 2008 Draft Guidelines for Implementation of the 1999 Second Protocol to the Hague Convention of 1954 for the Protection of Cultural Property in the Event of Armed Conflict, developed by the Committee for the Protection of Cultural Property in the Event of Armed Conflict, chap. 3, 3.1.2, para. 44–51, pp. 17–18.

In the Draft Protocol submitted to the Conference, the question of objections (later called representations) was placed in square brackets. The position of the States differed. Some wished to eliminate the brackets and keep the possibility of objections with some limitations as indicated in the UNESCO draft,[408] [409] while others were even against the maintenance of objections.[410] Some States felt that it was necessary for a belligerent State to abstain during a vote on inclusion of cultural property on the List, while others felt that the provision should be clarified to show that the Committee could overrule objections. The US delegate 'considered that it was important to retain the provision in Article 14 of the Regulations, which required a vote of two-thirds of the High Contracting Parties to overrule an objection made by one of the Parties'.[411]

Paragraph 6 contains a rather strong recommendation to the Committee ('should')[412] to ask the advice of governmental and non-governmental organizations, as well as of individual experts. Some States felt that the use of 'should' in relation to Article 11(6) was to encourage consultation of specialized NGOs by the Committee rather than leaving the decision to consult on a completely discretionary basis. The delegate of China proposed the replacement of 'should' by 'may'.[413] 'The delegate of the United Kingdom explained that the word "should" in this Article did not convey an obligation; rather it was an encouragement or a moral persuasion. Only the word "shall" would convey such an obligation'.[414]

The present paragraph is an appeal to the high professionalism of the Committee requesting that it not hesitate to seek the advice of other bodies, including individuals. As we shall see later, the Committee, as with every institution of this type, is an abstract entity composed not of individual

---

408 Article 12, para. 5 of the draft said: '[5. Parties may object to an inclusion on the List. Objections must be submitted to the Committee [Bureau] and can be made only on the basis of criteria mentioned in Article 11. They shall be specific and related to facts.]'

409 Switzerland. The Italian delegate considered that a final decision must be left to the Committee. The States directly interested in the decision should abstain during the vote in order to insure objectivity. (1999 Hague Conference, Plenary Session, 17 March 1999: Italy, p. 108; see also the delegate of Syria, p. 113).

410 Ibid., Indonesia, p. 120, Armenia, p. 125.

411 Ibid., US delegate, p. 115.

412 'In this use, *should* + infinitive is often equivalent to the mandative subjunctive. In using *should*, the speaker entertains, as it were, some 'putative' world, recognizing that it may well exist or come into existence'. See R. Quirk et al. (eds.), *A Comprehensive Grammar of the English Language* (London: Longman, 1985), para. 4.64, p. 234.

413 1999 Hague Conference, Plenary Session, 25 March 1999, p. 25. See also the delegate of India, p. 26.

414 Ibid., UK delegate, p. 28.

experts chosen because of their expertise[415] but from State representatives, who should be knowledgeable in the field of cultural values, although this would not necessarily be the case for all. Professional knowledge will be indispensable in these cases, which is why the legislators strongly suggested that the Committee not to hesitate to seek advice.

Paragraph 7 concerns the criterion for the decision, which may be positive, but could also be negative. The only criterion for the decision and appreciation of the request will be Article 10 of the Protocol. This is the most important paragraph of the Article as it limits the scope of representation. It is also an insurance against cases, such as those of Cambodia and Libya, from reoccurring.[416]

Paragraph 8 includes the exception and facility for countries with limited resources that will not be in a position to give satisfaction to sub-paragraph (b) of Article 11. As we recall, this sub-paragraph states:

(b) it is protected by adequate domestic legal and administrative measures recognizing its exceptional cultural and historic value and ensuring the highest level of protection.

---

415 At the 1954 Hague Conference, it was mainly Italy and Belgium who suggested the creation of the permanent or consultative committee responsible for the monitoring the execution of the Convention. Italy proposed the intergovernmental committee. Italy also wanted coordination in the execution of the Convention: 'Most multilateral conventions, e.g. the Red Cross Convention, the Universal Convention for the Protection of Copyright, referred to the establishment of a permanent committee to ensure the application of the convention. No qualified body for such a task existed within UNESCO and it was from that fact that the idea arose of establishing, within the UNESCO framework, a body ensuring the application of the Convention which would make it possible for recourse to a complicated arbitration procedure to be avoided. The choice of property to be placed under general protection had been left to each country. How could their number be reduced if the list submitted by every country was too long? While in cases of disagreement, recourse might be had to the objection procedure, the latter was unpleasant and to avoid it required preliminary control by a body comprising the main Contracting Parties to the Convention. That body would have other duties, such as the choice of the Commissioners-General and other permanent tasks. The meetings referred to in Article 26 of the Draft would thus be more frequent. The name, whether council, coordinating committee or permanent bureau was of little importance. What was important was that such a body should be representative of the governments and should enjoy some discretion in the compilation of the lists of property falling under general protection. While an exchange of such lists was essential – it was also provided for in the Washington Pact – a general examination with the object of making recommendations to those governments that had submitted lists which were too long was also necessary.' (*Records*, para. 1201, p. 244).
Belgium, on the contrary, had in mind a committee composed of individual delegates, appointed *ad personam*. The Secretary-General of the Belgian National Commission for UNESCO suggested later the establishment of a Consultative Committee responsible for monitoring the execution of the Convention and for interpreting it. Such a committee might be composed of two delegates from the International Committee for Monuments and the International Council of Museums, together with two jurists (in line with the example of the Universal Copyright Convention).
416 See Toman (1996), pp. 108–11.

This paragraph recognizes that this provision refers only to exceptional situations. The Committee may decide to grant enhanced protection even when the State concerned is not in a position to fulfill this requirement, but on one condition: the requesting Party must at the same time submit a request for international assistance under Article 32. As we have seen at the Diplomatic Conference, several States considered that this paragraph (b) did not take into consideration the difficulties that could arise in a federal state,[417] or the difficulties that developing countries can encounter in implementation of these provisions, especially without international and technical assistance.[418]

Paragraph 9: request upon the outbreak of hostilities

In relation to States Parties to the Second Protocol, the present paragraph supplements the provision of Article 11 of Regulations of Execution of the Convention. After discussion on the even more complicated procedures at the 1954 Conference,[419] it was finally agreed to adopt Article 11.

The procedure according to Article 11 of the Regulations remain very complicated:

1. During armed conflict, the High Contracting Party, induced by unforeseen circumstances, sets up an improvised refuge and desires to place it under special protection.
2. The High Contracting Party communicates this desire to the Commissioner-General. The designation of the Commissioner-General was practically inexistent and the provisions of the Regulation fail on this point.
3. If the Commissioner-General considers the request justified, he/she may authorize the Party to display the distinctive emblem of the Convention.
4. The Commissioner-General communicates the decision to the delegates of the Protecting Powers, also inexistent in the absolute majority of conflicts.
5. The delegates may within 30 days order the withdrawal of the emblem, and if they do so, the granting of special protection is impossible.

---

417 1999 Hague Conference, Plenary Session, 17 March 1999: India, Canada, p. 116. The Canadian delegate suggested that such legal protection may exist and be effective below the national level, or at multiple levels such as provincial and municipal.
418 1999 Hague Conference, Plenary Session, 17 March 1999: Indonesia, p. 120, Ethiopia, p. 123.
419 *Records*, p. 316; Toman (1996), pp. 113–14.

6. If, on the contrary, they agree or do not respond within the time limit, the Commissioner General must ascertain whether the improvised refuge fulfils the conditions of Article 8 of the Convention.
7. If the decision is positive, the Commissioner-General will ask the Director-General of UNESCO to enter the refuge in the Register of Cultural property under special protection.[420]

Due to the impossibility of fulfilling these conditions, the provision was never applied. For this reason, paragraph 9 of the Second Protocol adopted a new and substantially simplified and more realistic system:

1. Usage of the broader term 'upon the outbreak of hostilities', rather than only during armed conflict, which is more restrictive.
2. A Party to the conflict may request, on an emergency basis, placement of the cultural property (under its jurisdiction or control).[421] The request will be communicated directly to the Committee.

    Sweden in its comments to the 1998 draft considered that such 'application should be severely circumvented to situations in which there is great need and in which the responsible government had valid reasons for its failure to include the object on the list prior to the outbreak of the conflict'.[422] In the views of certain delegates at the 1999 Conference, the UNESCO draft needed to be simplified,[423] others considered that it should remain unchanged. Others considered it 'too bureaucratic' and insufficient and in need of redrafting.[424]

    a) The Committee shall transmit the request to all Parties to the conflict and will consider representations on an expedited basis. The Rules of Procedure should specify the form of such consideration (teleconference, rapid communication by e-mail, etc.).

    b) The decision to grant provisional enhanced protection shall be taken as soon as possible and, notwithstanding Article 26, by a majority of four-fifths of its members present and voting.

---

420 For more information, see Toman (1996), pp. 113–16.
421 As a member of the Working Group, the delegate of Israel described the discussion as follows: Originally, it was requested to delete the word 'jurisdiction' in paragraph 9 due to the fact that there was a possibility that the property would be put on the list immediately without discussion. However, later it was understood that the process would be similar to that in paragraph 3, but would be quicker. And therefore the problem would not arise and symmetry between paragraphs 3 and 9 seems logical. (1999 Hague Conference, Plenary Session, 25 March 1999: Israeli delegate, p. 31.)
422 Letter of the Ministry of Foreign Affairs of Sweden, 15 December 1998.
423 1999 Hague Conference, Plenary Session, 17 March 1999: Switzerland.
424 Ibid., Argentina, Belgium.

With respect to sub-paragraph 11(9), the Swedish delegate questioned the four-fifths majority required to grant provisional enhanced protection to a cultural property as opposed to a two-thirds majority. Such a majority is too high and illogical given that the Committee would consist of twelve States.[425] The explanation for this was that since this constituted a higher level of protection, a higher level of agreement was required, even in emergency situations.[426]

A rapid emergency meeting of the members of the Committee will be required under these circumstances (Rules of Procedure of the Committee, Rule 2: Ordinary and Extraordinary Sessions). The Canadian delegate at the Conference considered implementation of this difficult and suggested 'that perhaps the Bureau of the Committee would be a better vehicle for meeting in an emergency'.[427]

c) Provisional enhanced protection may be granted by the Committee pending the outcome of the regular procedure for the granting of enhanced protection, provided that the provisions of Article 10, sub-paragraphs (a) and (c) are met.

Paragraphs 10–11: entry on the List and notification

Paragraph 10 fixes the moment of the beginning of enhanced protection: from the moment of entry on the List.[428] This provision ensures the rapid commencement of protection, within hours after the decision taken by the Committee. This differs from provisions concerning special protection of the Convention. Entries for special protection became effective thirty days after certified copies have been dispatched by the Director-General to the Secretary-General of the UN, to the High Contracting Parties and, at the request of the Party applying for registration, to all other States referred to in Article 30 and 32 of the Convention[429] (Article 15 of the Regulations for the Execution of the Convention). This highly administrative and bureaucratic provision of the Convention was abandoned in the Second Protocol.

---

425 Ibid., 25 March 1999, Swedish delegate, p. 35
426 Ibid., US delegate, p. 36.
427 Ibid., 17 March 1999, Canada, p. 117.
428 The Chinese delegate also wished to include a reference to provisional enhanced protection. Ibid., Chinese delegate, p. 122.
429 The States referred to in Articles 30 and 32 are as follows: 1) all the States invited to the Conference which met at The Hague from 21 April to 14 May 1954; 2) any other State invited to accede to the Convention by the Executive Board of UNESCO.

The Protocol nevertheless maintained notification of copies as indispensable. According to paragraph 11, the Director-General shall, without delay, send notification of any decision of the Committee to include cultural property on the List to the Secretary-General of the UN and to all Parties (meaning the Parties to the Second Protocol).

Article 12
IMMUNITY OF CULTURAL PROPERTY UNDER ENHANCED PROTECTION

The Parties to a conflict shall ensure the immunity of cultural property under enhanced protection by refraining from making such property the object of attack or from any use of the property or its immediate surroundings in support of military action.

Preparatory work

1999 Hague Conference, Plenary Session, 17 March 1999.

Bibliography

Chamberlain, K. 2004. *War and Cultural Heritage.* Leicester: Institute of Art and Law, p. 201.

Henckaerts, J.-M. 1999. New rules for the protection of cultural property in armed conflict: the significance of the Second Protocol to the 1954 Hague Convention for the Protection of Cultural Property in the Event of Armed Conflict. *IRRC,* No. 835, pp. 606–13.

Hladík, J. 1999. The 1954 Hague Convention for the Protection of Cultural Property in the Event of Armed Conflict and the notion of military necessity. *IRRC,* No. 835, pp. 621–35.

ANALYSIS OF THE TEXT

What are the reasons for creating a specific form of protection for cultural property? This is what Article 12 explains.

We have seen in the past considerations of forms of protection granted to cultural property in general.[430] The reason for the creation of special protection in the 1954 Hague Convention was to provide immunity to cultural property. Article 9 of the Convention defines this immunity:

> Article 9. Immunity of cultural property under special protection
> The High Contracting Parties undertake to ensure the immunity
> of cultural property under special protection by refraining, from the

---

430 See page 75 ff.

time of entry in the International Register, from any act of hostility directed against such property and, except for the cases provided for in paragraph 5 of Article 8, from any use of such property or its surroundings for military purposes.

The immunity, according to the Convention consists of two acts:

(1) refraining, from the time of entry in the International Register, from any act of hostility directed against such property and,

(2) except for the cases provided for in paragraph 5 of Article 8, refrain from any use of such property or its surroundings for military purposes.

The drafters of Article 12 of the Second Protocol modified the wording to state that the Parties to a conflict shall ensure the immunity of cultural property under enhanced protection:

a) by refraining from making such property the object of attack, or
b) refraining from any use of the property or its immediate surroundings in support of military action.

The Preliminary draft of October 1998 (HC/1999/1), included the following draft:

Article 8 Immunity of cultural property under special protection
1. The States Parties shall ensure the immunity of cultural property specially protected under this Protocol by refraining, from the time of entry into the International Register for Cultural Property under Special Protection, from any act of hostility directed against the property and from using the property in support of the military effort, except for the cases provided for in para. 2.
2. Cultural property under special protection must be protected in all circumstance unless the opposing party has emplaced, within the property or its immediate surroundings, command, control, communications, computers and intelligence systems (C-4-I systems) or operational weapon systems or essential parts thereof, which from the location in question can bring substantial force to bear on opposing forces.
3. In using force against cultural property under special protection in one of the exceptional cases mentioned in para. 2 the attacking forces

shall only attack the property concerned if no alternative means are reasonably available and under the following conditions:

a. warning is given to the opposing forces;
b. a minimum time to redress the situation is given to the opposing forces;
c. the decision to attack is taken on national command level;
d. means and methods are limited to those which are strictly necessary to counter the threat posed.

When the States responded to the Preliminary Draft of October 1998 (HC/1999/1), the ICRC proposed to divide the draft of Article 8 into three separate articles. This was undertaken in the final version of the text. At the 1999 Conference, the view was expressed that Article 13 of the draft (which later became Article 12) should be restructured to clarify when immunity could be lost. The delegates recommended inspiration be drawn from Articles 9 and 11 of the Convention.[431] Others thought that Article 13 should clearly indicate 'Party' in the singular in order to remove any interpretation of action being collective.

Article 12 is the key article for understanding the fundamental concept of enhanced protection. It states the obligations of both the attacker and the defender in respect of the property under enhanced protection. This Article relates directly to Article 10(c).[432]

Let us examine this new wording in Article 12 in comparison with Article 9 of the Convention.

Refraining from making such property the object of attack

The Preliminary Draft of October 1998 (HC/1999/1) used the term 'refraining . . . from any act of hostility', which was also used in Article 9 of the Convention. In the comments to Article 8 of the Preliminary Draft, Israel proposed the formulation 'totally refraining from using the property in support of the military effort and from any act of hostility directed against the property'.

In the 1996 Commentary on the Convention, we defined acts of hostility as follows:

---

431 1999 Hague Conference, Plenary Session, 17 March 1999: US delegate, p. 114.
432 Working Group, p. 22.

Acts of hostility constitute the whole range of actions and operations of war in the broad sense, regardless of whether they are committed by the opposing Party or by the Party to the conflict which has cultural property in its possession. The authors of Protocol I to the Geneva Conventions of 1977 preferred the term 'attack', which is defined in the military instructions of many countries as an offensive act whose purpose is to destroy enemy forces and gain ground. The definition adopted by the Protocol is wider since it also covers defensive acts (particularly, 'counter-attacks') and offensive acts since both of them may affect the protected objectives, in this case cultural property. The Commentary of the ICRC seems to identify both terms when it defines attacks as 'the use of armed force to carry out a military operation at the beginning or during the course of armed conflict.'

The fact that the Convention uses the term 'acts of hostility' signifies that the prohibition also extends to the cultural property in its own possession or on its own territory. The Convention therefore protects cultural property against destruction committed by all the Parties to the conflict, regardless of whether such destruction is the result of an attack or of the deterioration of objects under the control of a Party.[433]

The drafters of the Second Protocol opted for the terminology used in the 1977 Additional Protocol I.

Refraining from any use of the property or its immediate surroundings in support of military action

The only change, along the line of the discussion on improvement, was to add the word 'immediate' to surroundings. This was the proposal of Sweden, made in the comments to the Preliminary Draft.[434] This narrowed the notion of surroundings, close to the cultural property itself. The restrictive approach is also found in the replacement of the word 'purpose',[435] which is present in the Article 9 of the Convention. The Preliminary Draft of the Secretariat of October 1998 (HC/1999/1) referred to the use of property 'in support of the military effort'. In its comments, Austria proposed to replace this by the

---

433 Toman (1996), p. 139.
434 Comments of the Ministry of Foreign Affairs of Sweden, 15 December 1998, p. 4.
435 The 'purpose' in the sense of motives means motivate, grounds, basis or justification; it can also mean objective, role or motivation.

wording 'in direct support of military action'.[436] The reference to 'action'[437] is substantially narrower than purpose and effort. The Syrian Arab Republic proposed the insertion of the words 'aimed directly or indirectly' after the word 'hostility'. The Austrian formulation was included in the final text, but without the word 'direct'.

The Preliminary Draft of October 1998 (HC/1999/1) included in Article 8 of the draft another paragraph, paragraph 2, which was finally not included in the text of the Protocol:

> 2. Cultural property under special protection must be protected in all circumstance unless the opposing party has emplaced, within the property or its immediate surroundings, command, control, communications, computers and intelligence systems (C-4-I systems) or operational weapon systems or essential parts thereof, which from the location in question can bring substantial force to bear on opposing forces.

In the comments to the draft some States suggested additional circumstances be added to the text. Israel proposed 'use as staging ground for attack, or as troop quarters', while Sweden drew the attention to the fact that 'the enumeration in paragraph 2 doesn't cover "troops" and that the reasons for that lacuna will have to be explained'.[438] Germany considered the conditions of paragraphs 2 and 3 militarily less realistic than paragraphs 1 and 2 of Article 11 of the Convention. Qatar proposed deleting the rest of the paragraph after the word 'circumstances'.

At the 1999 Conference the Lebanese delegate noticed that the condition of distance had disappeared and was not mentioned in the draft. He very much supported the idea of a declaration attached to the request for enhanced protection, that cultural property will not be used for the support of military action (art. 10, para. (c)).

The Working Group adopted the text of the Article, as did the Plenary Session of the Conference.

---

436 Comments of the Ministry of Foreign Affairs of Austria, CFSP/BON/0834/98 of 30 December 1998, para. 6, p. 2.
437 The 'action' means act, move, maneuver, activity, movement. In the military sense it can be replaced by synonyms: battle, conflict, combat, engagement. See C. A. Lindberg (ed.), *Oxford American Writer's Thesaurus* (Oxford: Oxford University Press, 2004), p. 14.
438 Letter of Ministry of Foreign Affairs of Sweden, Stockholm, 15 December 1998.

Article 13
LOSS OF ENHANCED PROTECTION

1. *Cultural property under enhanced protection shall only lose such protection:*
    a. *if such protection is suspended or cancelled in accordance with Article 14; or*
    b. *if, and for as long as, the property has, by its use, become a military objective.*
2. *In the circumstances of sub-paragraph 1(b), such property may only be the object of attack if:*
    a. *the attack is the only feasible means of terminating the use of the property referred to in sub-paragraph 1(b);*
    b. *all feasible precautions are taken in the choice of means and methods of attack, with a view to terminating such use and avoiding, or in any event minimizing, damage to the cultural property;*
    c. *unless circumstances do not permit, due to requirements of immediate self-defense:*
        (i). the attack is ordered at the highest operational level of command;
        (ii). effective advance warning is issued to the opposing forces requiring the termination of the use referred to in sub-paragraph 1(b); and
        (iii). reasonable time is given to the opposing forces to redress the situation.

Preparatory work

1999 Hague Conference, Plenary Session, 17 March 1999.

Bibliography

Henckaerts, J.-M. 1999. New rules for the protection of cultural property in armed conflict: the significance of the Second Protocol to the 1954 Hague Convention for the Protection of Cultural Property in the Event of Armed Conflict. *IRRC*, No. 835, pp. 593-620.

Hladík, J. 1999. The 1954 Hague Convention for the Protection of Cultural Property in the Event of Armed Conflict and the notion of military necessity. *IRRC*, No. 835, pp. 621–35.

PREPARATORY WORK AND ANALYSIS OF THE TEXT

Article 13 of the Second Protocol does not follow the same structure as Article 11 of the Convention. Already the title of the provision, which removes the special form of protection, is different. The term used in the Convention is 'withdrawal'. But the authors of the provision in the Second Protocol turned to a more neutral and also more appropriate title for the paragraph, calling it 'Loss of Enhanced Protection', and establishing two exclusive situations under which protection can be lost:

a) if such protection is suspended or cancelled in accordance with Article 14; or

b) if, and for as long as, the property has, by its use, become a military objective.

Before analyzing the present article, it may be useful to briefly summarize Article 11 of the Convention.

Article 11 of the Convention: Withdrawal of Immunity

Article 11 of the Convention uses the term 'withdrawal', but because withdrawal requires an action to be taken, we can ask, 'withdrawal by whom?' The most logical answer would be that such action should be taken by the authority which granted such immunity. But this was not the case.[439]

In the case of special protection, such decision is taken by the opposing party itself which, in cases of violation and its persistence, are released from the obligation to ensure the immunity of the property concerned. As such action is taken exclusively between two opposing parties without any neutral and impartial verification, the doors are open to subjective judgement by the opposing party. This paragraph introduces reciprocity into evaluation of the use of special protection.[440]

As in paragraph 1 of Article 11, we are at the level of High Contracting Parties in conflict; the decision should be taken by high national authorities only.

If paragraph 1 is a kind of political affirmation, paragraph 2 of the same Article has more of an executive nature, prescribing the conditions of such withdrawal in the battlefield. According to paragraph 2, the withdrawal

---

439 In fact, the Commissioner-General (who plays a fundamental role in the determination of special protection, even if entry on the Register is formally made by the Director-General) is only informed of withdrawal, according to paragraph 3 of Article 11.

440 Toman (1996), p. 144.

of immunity will be done 'only in exceptional cases of unavoidable military necessity and only for such time as that necessity continues'. It is the practical expression that – in paragraph 1 – is formulated 'so long as this violation persists'.

One important question raised during the 1954 Conference was: Who – among the national authorities – will have power to take such a decision? And after long discussion, such power was attributed – in the case of special protection – to 'the officer commanding a force the equivalent of a division in size or larger'.[441] Notification was required 'whenever circumstances permit'.

The ICRC delegate at the 1999 Hague Conference raised the question:

> Under the 1954 Convention special protection consists of the fact that the immunity of such property can only be withdrawn 'in exceptional cases of unavoidable military necessity'. The wording implied a stricter standard than for cultural property under general protection, where a waiver on the basis of 'imperative military necessity' was in place. In practice, however, it was not clear what 'exceptional cases of unavoidable military necessity' were.[442]

Many States thought that there was a need to clarify the conditions under which 'enhanced special protection' would be lost (art. 13). Some expressed the view that any possible loophole to justify the loss of 'enhanced special protection' should be removed from the provisions of Article 13 by making the conditions for loss 'direct and indirect support of military operations'. Others felt that the wording of Article 13 gave an unacceptable advantage to the owner of cultural property.

The UNESCO draft of the Second Protocol, included two provisions which were more or less merged into the final text of Article 13.[443] Article 14

---

441 Ibid., pp. 145–47.
442 Henckaerts (1999), p. 609; Toman (1996), pp. 145–46.
443 See Articles 14 and 15 of the UNESCO draft:
   Article 14 Loss of enhanced special protection
   Cultural property under enhanced special protection loses this enhanced special protection only if it is used for other than its normal function and in regular, significant and direct support of military operations and if military action is the only feasible way to terminate such support.
   Article 15 Conditions for military operations
   An attack against cultural property which has lost its enhanced special protection according to Article 14 may only be undertaken on the following conditions:
      a. the attack is ordered by the highest level of government;

of the draft was formulated along the basis of Article 56 of the 1977 Additional Protocol I concerning the protection of works and installations containing dangerous forces. Paragraph 2, sub-paragraph (a) of Article 56 states that special protection against attacks ceases for a dam or a dyke 'only if it is used for other than its normal function and in regular, significant and direct support of military operations and if such attack is the only feasible way to terminate such support'. This wording provoked numerous interventions of delegates mainly concerning the words 'normal function'.

It was suggested that phrases such as 'other than normal function' and 'significant and direct support' be reconsidered. Some delegations considered the UNESCO draft not totally clear, in particular, with respect to the phrase 'being used for other than normal functions', which could be eliminated.[444]

This is a good example of the point that formulations, however attractive, cannot be simply transplanted from one legal text to another, and require more attentive formulation according to the subject-matter.

Paragraph 1

As we have indicated, the first paragraph of Article 13 is composed of two elements and indicates two situations under which the property protected by enhanced protection may lose this protection:[445]

a) if such protection is suspended or cancelled in accordance with Article 14.

It is most appropriate to deal with this first sub-paragraph under Article 14.

b) A situation whereby the cultural property becomes by its use a military objective and as long as it is used as such.

---

b. a minimum time is given to the opposing forces to redress the situation;

c. an effective prior warning is communicated to the opposing forces;

d. no other feasible alternative is available;

e. the means and methods chosen are limited to those which are strictly necessary to counter the threat posed; and

f. the damage caused is not excessive in relation to the concrete and direct military advantage anticipated.

444 Austria, Lebanon, Switzerland and the US. The Austrian delegate gave an example: 'a particular cultural site could be used as a hospital although it was not the normal function'. For loss of protection he proposed the wording 'if it is used for significant and direct support of military operations'. See 1999 Hague Conference, Plenary Session, 17 March 1999, p. 118.

445 These two elements were included on the suggestion of the delegate of the UK (1999 Hague Conference, Plenary Session, 17 March 1999, p. 128).

In paragraph (c) of Article 10 we have seen the broad prohibition against the use of cultural property for military purposes or to shield military sites as a condition for granting enhanced protection.

Article 13, paragraph 1(b) states that if the situation of a cultural property under enhanced protection changes and the property is used as a military objective, and as long as it is used as such, the enhanced protection is lost. What does this mean? Can cultural property be then attacked and destroyed without any limitation?

The authors of these exceptional provisions were aware that their first duty was to spare cultural property and that any action contrary to the provisions will be severely punished. The loss of protection does not necessarily mean that any action and attack against the property is permitted. Here we must turn to the second paragraph of Article 13, which limits the possibility of attack on the cultural property, which was placed under enhanced protection on the grounds of being of the 'greatest importance for humanity'.

With regard to the new Article 13(1)(b), the delegate of Egypt preferred to see the word 'function' replaced by 'use', when defining the conditions under which immunity under enhanced protection can be lost. He felt that this would make for a more coherent text and bring Chapter 3 in line with the provisions of Chapter 2, by treating cultural property in both chapters on the same footing. The majority of States said that the discussions on Chapter 3 had only ever centred around 'function'. They said that if 'function' was used in Chapter 2 and 'use' in Chapter 3, this was specifically to mark the distinction between the different levels of protection that each Chapter provides for – general protection in Chapter 2, and enhanced protection of cultural property of greatest importance to humanity in Chapter 3 – and to form a symmetry between this chapter and the provisions of Article 10(c) regarding the declaration of non-use of cultural property for military purposes. The Chairman confirmed that he had understood that the difference in language between Chapters 2 and 3 had been deliberate. He appealed to the opposing delegate to yield to the observations made in this respect. The delegate was however not in agreement that the application of the word 'use' granted a higher level of protection than 'function' and he felt that this was not in line with the compromise that had been made in the informal Working Groups on Chapter 2 and 3. He felt that the distinction between the two levels of protection should not be made in this manner but rather, by inserting other conditions for protection within the provisions of Chapter 3. Although some States expressed an understanding for these observations concerning the chapter, the decision was nevertheless taken to adopt the chapter in view of its consensual nature and the fact that this correctly reflected the discussions which took place during the informal Working Group. In a spirit of compromise, the State concerned agreed to withdraw its objections.

The Second Protocol established more clearly when cultural property can lose enhanced protection; when the cultural property becomes used as a military objective and, as paragraph 2 indicates, 'an attack is the only feasible means of terminating the use of the property', which has made it a military objective.

The 2008 Draft Guidelines for the Implementation of 1999 Second Protocol provide important details about suspension and cancellation. According to paragraph 82 suspension is defined as 'a provisional measure which does not result in a permanent loss of the enhanced protection but in an interruption of the protection when the conditions for granting it are no longer met. When the conditions are met again, the Committee will decide on the resumption of enhanced protection.'[446] On the contrary, cancellation 'is a definitive measure. It leads to the permanent loss of the enhanced protection.'[447]

The procedure on suspension and cancellation is elaborated in the 2008 draft Guidelines, Chapter 3, point 3.4.[448]

Paragraph 2

This paragraph includes numerous conditions for an attack. Only if these conditions are satisfied will the highest operational authority be authorized to take such an important and irreversible decision. We have to keep in mind that Article 28 of the Convention already required States Parties to the Convention to introduce into their legislation provisions punishing breaches to the Convention, and that the Second Protocol includes very severe punishments for serious violations of the Convention and the Protocol. Those who are then authorizing the attack must be aware of their individual criminal responsibility.

We should start by examining the notion of attack. When introducing this notion, the drafters were undoubtedly inspired by Additional Protocol I. The term 'attack' is used in Part IV and several other provisions of the Protocol. Concerning the notion of 'attack', the ICRC Commentary said

---

446 *2008 Draft Guidelines*, chap. 3, 3.3, para. 80.
447 Ibid., para. 86.
448 Ibid., chap. 3.4, para. 89–93.

that the meaning given to it in Article 49 is not exactly the same as the usual meaning of the word.[449]

> The definition given by the Protocol has a wider scope since it – justifiably – covers defensive acts (particularly 'counter-attacks') as well as offensive acts, as both can affect the civilian population. It is for this reason that the final choice was a broad definition. In other words, the term 'attack' means 'combat action'. This should be taken into account in the instruction for armed forces who should clearly understand that the restrictions imposed by humanitarian law on the use of force should be observed both by troops defending themselves and by those who are engaged in an assault or taking the offensive.[450]

As we have seen, Articles 14 and 15 of the UNESCO draft, which later more or less merged in Article 13 of the Protocol, were based on Article 56, para. 2, letter (a) of the Additional Protocol I. At the Diplomatic Conference of 1999, the ICRC delegate stated:

> that it was important that there were some conditions before an attack occurs, over and above the fact that it is used for military action by the other side. For example, one could have a group of soldiers which used a centre for military action in a way which higher levels were unaware of, or for which there was no clearance. Because of the political implications it would be inappropriate in these circumstances for it to be attacked. If the loss of the protection is a result of behaviour of [draft] Article 13 (b) [using the property in support of military action] then care should be taken that in [draft] Article 15 there is a warning and a time given to redress the situation. [Draft] Article 15

---

449 In the larger dictionaries the idea of instigating combat and striking the first blow is predominant. The second definition given in the *Shorter Oxford Dictionary* (1978, p. 127) is closest to the meaning of the term as used in the Protocol, 'to set upon with hostile action'. In this respect it is interesting to refer to an investigation conducted amongst its members by the International Society of Military Law and the Law of War. (Questionnaire on the subject of armed forces and the development of the laws of war, presented during the 9th International Conference of the International Society of Military Law and the Law of War, held at Lausanne from 2–6 September 1982. Text in 'Forces armées et développement du droit de la guerre', *op. cit.*, pp. 51–55; see also p. 303). The questions that were raised included one relating to this question of terminology. In general, the replies indicated that the meaning given by the Protocol to the word 'attacks' did not give rise to any major problems, even though military instruction manuals in many countries define an attack as an offensive act aimed at destroying enemy forces and gaining ground. See *Commentary on the Additional Protocol* I, para. 1879, p. 603.

450 Ibid., para. 1880, p. 603

should not indicate 'where conditions permit', rather they are absolute conditions.[451]

In the comments to the Preliminary Draft from October 1998 (HC/1999/1), Germany and Australia expressed concern as to the conditions included. Qatar and Syria favoured deletion of the paragraph. Israel questioned why the limitations set forth in paragraphs 3(6)a–3(6)e of the draft (later Article 6, para. 2) are not repeated here and whether those conditions weakened the protection in some way.

Finland considered that 'the list should also include, in addition to what is mentioned now, also the principle of proportionality of use of force'.[452] Switzerland proposed a new sub-paragraph 'including the principles of proportionality between damage and concrete military advantage'. Italy proposed a new paragraph that would refer to the necessity of self-defense and the protection of human life.

At the 1999 Conference, the Representative of the ICRC pointed out that in the Additional Protocol I to the Geneva Conventions, protection is no longer limited to only a few unique objects with all others being legitimate military objectives. Rather, attack is now only allowed on military objectives, with all other objects being protected. Therefore, the protection accorded these significant items needed to be substantially higher than general protection. Some delegates recommended following Articles 9 and 11 of the Convention. The US delegate

> believed that there must be some provision for the possibility of extraordinary circumstances in which there may be an urgent need for commanders to take action. He therefore proposed the inclusion of the provision that would permit action in exceptional cases of unavoidable military necessity for as long as the necessity continues as provided for in Article 11 of the Convention.[453]

The delegate of Finland considered that the criteria of paragraph 2 were sufficient.[454]

As pointed out by the Working Group, the Article on the loss of enhanced protection reflects the language of Additional Protocol I.

451 1999 Hague Conference, Plenary Session, 17 March 1999: ICRC delegate, p. 138.
452 Helsinki, 15 December 1998.
453 1999 Hague Conference, Plenary Session, 17 March 1999: US delegate, p. 114.
454 Ibid., Finnish delegate, p. 127.

Loss of enhanced protection can occur only *in wartime* for breach of the conditions.

Paragraph 2 imposes three restrictive conditions if cultural property is to become the object of attack.

Sub-paragraph (a)

> (a) the attack is the only feasible means of terminating the use of the property referred to in sub-paragraph 1(b).

This provision supposes that the decision-maker made a preliminary effort to avoid the attack, and must have reasons to come to the conclusion that an attack is the only way to stop the use of cultural property as a military objective, and that such use will be particularly harmful to his/her own forces. The recourse to an attack must be, in short, inevitable.

Loss of enhanced protection is conditional on the fact that it is used as a military objective.

It is the *bona fide* duty of the attacker to verify by all available means the situation of the enhanced cultural property in question before launching an attack.

This paragraph maintains the word 'use' instead of the word 'function' employed in the case of general protection.

With regard to Article 13(i)(b) of the final text, some States felt that this sub-paragraph should be aligned to Article 6(a)(i) with the word 'use' being replaced by the word 'function'.[455] Some Working Group members were able to explain that 'use' was the appropriate term to use in this case, since it was entirely possible that a State might request enhanced protection for a military museum, for example, whose function would then be military, but whose use is clearly not. The Chairman of the Conference also explained that the difference between Articles 6 and 13 was deliberate as Chapter 3 of the Protocol is dealing with cultural property at the level of very great importance for humanity.[456]

The ICRC delegate at the Conference explained the issue in the following terms:

---

455 Ibid., 26 March 1999, Egyptian delegate, p. 74.
456 Ibid., Chairman, p. 74, German delegate, p. 74.

the *quid pro quo* of enhanced protection was non-use in exchange for enhanced protection. . . . one of the conditions for registration of cultural property for enhanced protection is abstention from its use for military purposes and a declaration confirming that it will not be so used. The argument was that since there is a promise not to use, enhanced protection can only be lost through use. It was further argued that limiting loss of protection for cultural property under enhanced protection to instances of use only was an essential part of the 'enhanced' level of protection offered by an enhanced protection system. This argument is, however, mistaken.

A common misunderstanding is that there is a difference in the levels of protection afforded cultural property under general and enhanced protection – and the names indeed do suggest that such a difference exists. But there is, in fact, no lower or higher level of protection. The basic protection is the same: the object cannot be destroyed, captured or neutralized. Once protection is lost, it is lost for good: 'you use, you lose'. There are minor differences in the level of command at which an attack has to be ordered, the warning to be given and the requirement that a reasonable time be given to the opposing forces to redress the situation (see below), but these differences do not change the basic loss of protection.

There is no difference in the level of protection and there is no need to differentiate between two different ways in which cultural property can become a military objective. What is the difference then between enhanced protection and general protection? The main difference lies not in the obligations of the attacker but in the obligations of the holder of the cultural property. In the case of general protection, the holder of the property has the right, if need be, to convert the property into a military objective, by using it for military action. In the case of enhanced protection, the holder of the property has absolutely no right ever to convert the property into a military objective by using it for military action. Registration on the List therefore requires the State party to seriously study whether it would ever be in need of that property for military purposes and to answer in the negative.

Using property on the List for military purposes would amount to a serious violation of the Second Protocol, and the offender would be liable to criminal sanction as a war criminal. The term 'enhanced protection' is therefore misleading. The essence of the system is that it concerns some form of 'registered' or 'certified protection'. The holder of the property registers or certifies his promise that the property will never be used for military purposes. As a result, the property can never become the object of an attack. The advantage of putting property on the List is that an adversary will be particularly aware of it and any attack on the property will have serious consequences for the perpetrator (see below).

The registration of an object on the List of Cultural Property under Enhanced Protection can be compared to an internationally recognized declaration establishing a non-defended locality. It is best to make such declaration in peacetime as it guarantees that everything is in place if and when an armed conflict breaks out.[457]

Sub-paragraph (b)

(b) all feasible precautions are taken in the choice of means and methods of attack, with a view to terminating such use and avoiding, or in any event minimizing, damage to the cultural property.

This sub-paragraph details the instructions concerning the precautions that have to be taken regarding the choice of means (e.g. weapons) and the methods for putting an end to the use of cultural property as a military objective: two steps should be taken into consideration:
- terminating such use and avoiding damage to the cultural property;
- terminating such use and, at least, minimizing the damage.

With regard to practical decisions concerning an attack, the attacker should employ the first step and, only if unavoidable, proceed to the second step, that is, only minimizing the damage instead of avoiding it totally.

The Preliminary Draft of October 1998 spoke about the condition 'means and methods are limited to those which are strictly necessary to counter the threat posed'. In its comments, Switzerland proposed to delete the words 'to counter the threat posed'.

Sub-paragraph (c)

(c) unless circumstances do not permit, due to requirements of immediate self-defense.

---

457 Henckaerts (2001), p. 43.

Three supplementary conditions are required (see below). However, the US delegate proposed a caveat at the 1999 Conference, that these conditions 'should not apply in circumstances where this is not possible'.[458] In such cases, their use may eventually be abandoned. There is only one situation in which circumstances are recognized as creating a prejudice for use of these conditions; that an attack must be undertaken as a measure of self-defence. The three conditional requirements for the attack are as follows:

i) the attack is ordered at the highest operational level of command;

As we have seen, the 1954 Conference discussed extensively the definition of the decision-maker in relation to waiver of protection in cases of military necessity.

Such discussion took place in relation to general protection (Article 4) and in relation to withdrawal of special protection under Article 11 of the Convention.

During the discussion relating to Article 4, proposals were made varying from the General Staff to high military authorities, before the matter was finally left open without any decision being taken.[459]

Article 11 was more precise stating that unavoidable military necessity 'can be established only by the officer commanding a force the equivalent of a division in size or larger'.[460] The following phrase specified that 'whenever

---

458 1999 Hague Conference, Plenary Session, 17 March 1999: US delegate, p. 114.

459 Some also felt that the 'judgement on the existence and extent of military necessity must necessarily be subjective and open the door to arbitrary action and to a situation in which the military, who have no qualifications in this matter, might set themselves up as judges of cultural values' (CBC/SR.10, p. 12). The representative of Belarus raised the following problem: 'Who will decide on this imperative military necessity: a colonel, a captain or a mere lieutenant?' (CBC/SR.10, p. 4). The representative of Spain felt that this decision must rest with General Staff (*Records*, para. 293, p. 148) and the delegate of Israel proposed that decisions in case of really imperative military necessity would have to be taken by high military authorities (*Records*, para. 300, pp. 150–51). Contrary to Article 8 of the Convention on special protection, the assessment of military necessity is left to the military with no stipulation of special conditions. That opens the door to arbitrary action. S. Nahlik pointed out in 1986 that the decision could be taken by 'any officer of the adverse party, acting merely upon his subjective judgement, perhaps on the spur of the moment, who is competent enough to decide that such or such other property is to be pulled down' (S.E. Nahlik (1986a), p. 90). See Toman (1996), p. 79.

460 The discussion which took place at the 1954 Conference is very instructive for the present formulation. It started with a reference to the 'staff of the large formation in charge of the operation involved' (UNESCO Draft). The UK proposed 'the officer commanding a force the equivalent of a division in size or larger', which was finally included in the text. The intention was to prevent a situation in which any officer was able to judge the existence of an unavoidable military necessity. There is no great difference between the two formulas except for the fact that the reference to 'staff' would have meant that an individual decision would have been replaced by a collective decision.

circumstances permit, the opposing Party shall be notified, a reasonable time in advance, of the decision to withdraw immunity'.

Sub-paragraph (c)(i) also effectively refers to circumstances, but imposes limits through the clause of self-defense. The reference to 'highest operational level of command' is close to the proposal made by Israel at the 1954 Conference.

The Preliminary Draft of October 1998 (HC/1999/1) referred in Article 8, paragraph 3(c) to 'the decision to attack is taken on national command level'. In the comments on the draft, Israel preferred 'some identifiable military level such as division level'. Turkey petitioned for the words 'highest possible' to be inserted before the words 'national command level' and the words 'in theatre' to be added at the end.

The UNESCO draft submitted to the Conference (HC/1999/1/Rev.1) referred to orders 'by the highest level of government'. The US delegate considered that this reference 'may not be practical in some circumstances'.[461] Several other delegates expressed their view on this issue and requested clarification.[462] The Swiss delegate proposed the replacement of this wording with 'the highest level of the army'.[463] The Italian delegate also considered that responsibility lies in the hands of military officers who must assume such responsibility without transmitting the decision to a political level. He proposed that the decision be placed at the highest level of an operation

---

In addition, the UK proposed additional wording: that 'or in exceptional circumstances confirmed' should be added after 'such necessity can be established'. This addition was not accepted. (This new clause would have placed the decision on military necessity in the hands of an officer of a force equivalent of a division in size or larger, but *post factum* (that is, once it had been taken by a military commander of a rank lower than that of a divisional commander). Approval of this proposal would have rendered the reservation completely ineffectual since it would have allowed the decision to lift immunity to be taken by any local commanding officer. For the same reason, the representatives at the Conference did not accept the UK proposal to the effect that unavoidable military necessity could be established by a commanding officer 'whenever military circumstances permit'. Had this clause been adopted, the establishment of a case of unavoidable military necessity by the officer commanding a force at least equivalent to a division would no longer have been a condition for governing the legality of the waiver. The lifting of immunity as it is defined in this paragraph leads us to take up the fundamental question which was raised by the delegate of Ecuador: 'does the military commander, even at divisional level, have the necessary competence to assess the significance of what will be sacrificed by his decisions?' Despite this dilemma, the clause exists in the Convention. When we were writing the Commentary we also stated that there is little likelihood of it being deleted even on the occasion of a reaffirmation and possible development of the rules relating to the protection of cultural property. (Text based on Toman [1996], pp. 146–47.)

461 1999 Hague Conference, Plenary Session, 17 March 1999: US delegate, p. 114. See also the Turkish delegate, p. 115.

462 Ibid., Syrian delegate, p. 113.

463 Ibid., Swiss delegate, p. 106.

zone, brigade or division.[464] Others preferred the reference to operational command.[465] The Argentinean delegate, on the contrary, noted 'that the conditions for enhanced protection were almost the same as those for general protection and that the only distinction was on relation to the level of government'.[466] Some delegates also wished to add the provision 'where the circumstances permit' to this paragraph. The ICRC representative stated that 'enhanced special protection' would apply only to supremely important cultural property (other cultural property being covered by the 'general protection provisions') and thus, any attack on such objects would have very significant political implications and should therefore only be authorized at the highest possible level. Because of the political implications, care should be taken before such a condition was swept aside.[467]

The ICRC delegate later commented:

> The Second Protocol seeks to tighten these conditions, but an effort to change the relative duty of notice into an absolute duty and a concomitant effort, supported by the ICRC, to have the decision to attack taken at the highest level of government failed. It would indeed make sense to have the decision taken at the highest level of government because of the political implications thereof. Several delegates, however, argued against this proposal. While they recognized that in some countries such a decision would probably be taken at the highest level of government, for example if the Head of State is the Commander-in-Chief of the armed forces, they felt that the political structures of countries around the world were too diverse to impose such an obligation. Hence, the Second Protocol requires that an attack be ordered at the highest operational level of command.[468]

ii) effective advance warning is issued to the opposing forces requiring the termination of the use referred to in sub-paragraph 1(b); and

This condition concerning advance warning is also inspired by the Convention. Article 11, paragraph 2 includes the following phrase: 'Whenever circumstances

---

464 Ibid., Italian delegate, p. 107.
465 Ibid., Austria, Belgium, Canada, the UK.
466 Ibid., Argentinean delegate, p. 112.
467 Ibid., ICRC delegate, p. 138.
468 Henckaerts (2001), p. 48.

permit, the opposing Party shall be notified, a reasonable time in advance, of the decision to withdraw immunity'.

Paragraph (c)(ii) of the Protocol is an equivalent provision using the more modern terminology of 'warning'.

In its Comments to the Preliminary Draft of October 1998 (HC/1999/1), Israel repeated its comments to Article 6:[469]

> The requirement is to give advance warning in any and all cases. Not only is such a total requirement not feasible in the field (no advance warning is usually given when returning fire at an enemy position) but it would seem to be an attempt to grant cultural property more protection than that granted to *civilians* under the law of war (Article 57 (2)(c)) of the 1977 Geneva Protocol I which refers to 'effective advance warning... *unless circumstances do not permit.*' As the idea of granting cultural property more protection than that granted to civilian men, women and children seems to us unjustified, we suggest using similar language to that used in the Geneva Protocol I.[470]

The ICRC delegate wrote in his Article on the Conference:

> In addition, a proposal to make it an absolute obligation to order the attack at such level, to give effective advance warning and to give reasonable time to the opposing forces to redress the situation, was rejected. Several delegates argued that if their troops came under fire from cultural property under enhanced protection they would deem it excessive to have to comply with those conditions without being able to return fire immediately. Hence, the three obligations are waived if circumstances do not permit 'due to requirements of immediate self-defense'. This still represents progress over the 1954 Convention, as the level at which the attack has to be ordered is much higher and as the vague 'whenever circumstances permit' has been narrowed considerably. In addition, the requirement that a reasonable time be given to the opposing forces to redress the situation is new and adds an extra layer of protection.[471]

---

469 Article 3(6)(b) of the Preliminary Draft.
470 Israel comments of 15 December 1998.
471 Henckaerts (2001), p. 48.

iii) Reasonable time is given to the opposing forces to redress the situation.

The time-limit for redress of the situation is also inspired by the Hague Convention. It was formulated in the second phrase of Article 11, paragraph 1: 'Nevertheless, whenever possible, the latter Party shall first request the cessation of such violation within a reasonable time'.

Here the formulation is a little different: the time limit will be fixed by the adverse Party. Such time limit will not be requested, but will be given, fixed in advance. The reference to 'whenever possible' was inserted in front of the three conditions, but was formulated, as we have seen, in a much more restrictive way: 'unless circumstances do not permit, due to requirements of immediate self-defense'.

In its comments to the Preliminary Draft of October 1998 (HC/1999/1), Israel repeated its comments to Article 6.[472] Israel considered that 'it is impossible to expect military commanders in all cases to refrain from returning fire (or taking similar military action) until the enemy has been given an opportunity to vacate the premises.'[473]

The ICRC delegate later noted the following:

> An earlier ICRC proposal to approximate the protection of cultural property under enhanced protection to that given to medical units was not considered. Under Article 21 of the 1949 Geneva Convention for the Amelioration of the Condition of the Wounded and Sick in Armed Forces in the Field, the protection to which medical units are entitled shall not cease 'unless they are used to commit, outside their humanitarian duties, acts harmful to the enemy. Protection may, however, cease only after a due warning has been given, naming, in all appropriate cases, a reasonable time limit and after such warning has remained unheeded'. It was felt that hospitals deserved an exceptional level of protection, beyond that enjoyed by other civilian objects.[474]

---

472 Article 3(6)(c) of the Preliminary Draft.
473 Israel comments of 15 December 1998.
474 Henckaerts (2001), p. 49.

Article 14
SUSPENSION AND CANCELLATION OF ENHANCED PROTECTION

1. *Where cultural property no longer meets any one of the criteria in Article 10 of this Protocol, the Committee may suspend its enhanced protection status or cancel that status by removing that cultural property from the List.*
2. *In the case of a serious violation of Article 12 in relation to cultural property under enhanced protection arising from its use in support of military action, the Committee may suspend its enhanced protection status. Where such violations are continuous, the Committee may exceptionally cancel the enhanced protection status by removing the cultural property from the List.*
3. *The Director-General shall, without delay, send to the Secretary-General of the United Nations and to all Parties to this Protocol notification of any decision of the Committee to suspend or cancel the enhanced protection of cultural property.*
4. *Before taking such a decision, the Committee shall afford an opportunity to the Parties to make their views known.*

Preparatory work

1999 Hague Conference, Plenary Session, 17 March 1999.

Bibliography

Henckaerts, J.-M. 1999. New rules for the protection of cultural property in armed conflict: the significance of the Second Protocol to the 1954 Hague Convention for the Protection of Cultural Property in the Event of Armed Conflict. *IRRC*, No. 835, pp. 593–620.

ANALYSIS OF THE TEXT

The UNESCO draft submitted to the Conference (HC/1999/1/Rev.1) dealt with suspension and cancellation in two separate articles (art. 16 and 17). Several delegates were unable to perceive a difference with Article 13 (loss of the protection) and suggested the alignment of these two notions.[475] The view was expressed that Articles 14–16 should be placed in a normative package

---

475 1999 Hague Conference, Plenary Session, 17 March 1999: Austria, Switzerland, p. 106.

since they deal with conditions where 'enhanced special protection' could be waived.[476] The Secretariat explained that Articles 16 and 17 could be applied by the Committee in peacetime and even when conflict was not threatening, while Articles 14 and 15 regulated conflict situations only.

Article 13 of the Second Protocol specified two conditions for the loss of enhanced protection:

(a) if such protection is suspended or cancelled in accordance with Article 14; or

(b) if, and for as long as, the property has, by its use, become a military objective.

Article 14 is a development of sub-paragraph (a) of Article 13(1) and it deals with two situations, other than sub-paragraph (b), under which enhanced protection can be lost: suspension or cancellation. Suspension and cancellation are dealt with together in this Article.[477] Suspension is a temporary measure giving the hope that the situation may be reversed and enhanced protection will again become fully operative. Suspension 'is basically meant to provide in a great number of cases an acceptable alternative to termination while avoiding its radical effects'.[478]

Sub-paragraph (b) of Article 13(1) describes loss of protection when a cultural property becomes a military objective. But loss of enhanced protection, as we have indicated, does not mean that the cultural property in question shall automatically become an object of attack. Other limitations are imposed on attacks by paragraph 2 of the same article.

The Committee, created according to Article 24, is the only competent organ to proceed with suspension or cancellation. Whether the Committee will proceed with suspension or cancellation as described in paragraphs 1 and 2 of Article 14 depends upon the degree of alteration taking place. Two situations exist:

1.   Cultural property no longer meets any one criteria in Article 10;
2.   Serious violations of Article 12.

---

476 Ibid., Argentina.
477 Similarly, in the case of termination and suspension of treaties, in Articles 54, 57, 58 and 59 of the 1969 Vienna Convention on the Law of Treaties, Paul Reuter noted that dealing in parallel with termination and suspension was done 'probably in order to increase the number of situations where the principle of the treaty is safeguarded, although this endeavor has hardly been so far sanctioned by practice'. See Reuter (1995), para 213, p. 138.
478 Ibid., para. 238, p. 166.

Several comments were expressed regarding the provision on suspension in the Preliminary Draft. Australia asked whether a State could seek cancellation of special protection against its own designated cultural property, how a matter should be brought before the Committee, how the Committee should decide on the cancellation of special protection, and whether a State adversely affected by violation could bring the matter before the Committee. Israel would differentiate between suspension of immunity on the ground (favouring a provision similar to Article 11 of the Convention) and suspension (or even cancellation) of inclusion of a specific property in the Register:

> We believe that this Article should deal only with the latter. As for the former – in our opinion, a provision similar to Article 11 of the 1954 Convention should be included, clarifying that immunity of specially protected cultural property is automatically suspended on the ground in the cases of abuse specified in para. 2 of Article 8 [of the draft].[479]

Norway considered that the suspension of immunity of cultural property under special protection may contradict the provisions of Article 3(2) regarding the prohibition of reprisals. Sweden recommended adding at the end of paragraph 1 the following phrase: 'on condition that such suspension does not unjustifiably benefit a Party which has violated the immunity of that property.'

In the UNESCO draft submitted to the Conference (HC/1999/1/ rev.1), these two criteria were included in the two separate Articles 16 and 17, and representatives of the Secretariat explained that these criteria could also be effective in peacetime. Articles 14 and 15 of the draft dealing with loss of protection (which were merged in Article 14 of the Second Protocol) 'would operate in a theatre of conflict which explained the layout and philosophy behind these Articles'.[480] Loss of enhanced protection can only occur in wartime as a result of breach of the conditions. On the other hand, the Committee has the power to suspend or cancel enhanced protection in peacetime in cases where any of the conditions of the Article 10 are not being met.

---

479 Israel comments of 15 December 1998, p. 9.
480 1999 Hague Conference, Plenary Session, 17 March 1999: Lyndel Prott, p. 119.

Paragraph 1: cultural property no longer meets any one of the criteria in Article 10

Article 10 prescribed the following criteria for the granting of enhanced protection:

(a) it is cultural heritage of the greatest importance for humanity;

(b) it is protected by adequate domestic legal and administrative measures recognizing its exceptional cultural and historic value and ensuring the highest level of protection;

(c) it is not used for military purposes or to shield military sites and a declaration has been made by the Party which has control over the cultural property, confirming that it will not be so used.

If one or several of these conditions no longer exist, the Committee will evaluate the situation and take a decision according to the importance of the change in the situation. It is this importance of the change that will guide the Committee in deciding the importance of the measures to be taken:

a) The Committee will suspend enhanced protection. The suspension will be a temporary measure. When the situation is redressed and respect of the conditions completed, the suspension will be cancelled and enhanced protection will be renewed.

b) If the Committee comes, on the basis of facts, to the conclusion that the situation cannot be redressed and that the mission criteria cannot anymore be realized, it will proceed to the much more drastic and definitive measure of cancellation of enhanced protection. In this situation only, will the Committee proceed with the decision to remove the cultural property from the List of cultural property under enhanced protection. One proposal concerned reformulating Article 16 to include informing a State that its cultural property has had its 'enhanced special protection' removed.

Paragraph 2: serious violation of Article 12

Suspension or cancellation can occur also in cases of serious violations of Article 12 of the Second Protocol. According to this Article, the Parties to a conflict ensure the immunity of cultural property under enhanced protection by refraining from making such property the object of attack or from any use of the property or its immediate surroundings in support of military action.

Nevertheless, paragraph 2 includes greater precision by referring to serious violations committed in relation to cultural property under enhanced protection.

The Lebanese delegate raised the following question at the Conference: who is the author of the serious violations? Will it be determined by the Committee? Who may request that the Committee suspend the protection? Or is it suspended automatically?[481]

This paragraph also limits the violation only to situations when such violations are 'arising from its use in support of military action'.

Suspension or cancellation is not enforced when the property is made the object of an attack. In such cases, the cultural property is probably being used as a military objective and could become the object of an attack if the provisions of paragraph 2 of Article 13 are applied. It will therefore lose its enhanced protection and there will no longer be any reason to apply the provisions on suspension or cancellation.

But in the event that the cultural property is used in support of military action, suspension or cancellation can constitute a sanction for such behaviour, and in such a way discourage the Party from such further use. The Party must in such a case consider seriously abandoning such misuse under the threat of sanctions undertaken according to Chapter 4 of the Second Protocol (Article 15, paragraph 1 (a)).

Only in the case of continuing violations may the Committee be obliged to take the exceptional measure of cancelling the enhanced protection status and removing the cultural property from the List. The Chairman of the Working Group also indicated that cancellation would occur only in exceptional circumstances.[482] The Party committing such a violation would be subjected to sanctions according to Article 15, paragraph 1(b).

The Canadian delegate replacing the Chairman of the Working Group stated:

> that it must be understood that suspension or cancellation under Article 14 was seen as taking place most often during peacetime and not in an emergency or an armed conflict. For this reason, the Group was of the view that cancellation or suspension should be left to the discretion of the Committee.[483]

---

481 Ibid., Lebanese delegate, p. 110.
482 Ibid., 25 March 1999, p. 22.
483 Ibid., oral report of the Working Group, p. 22.

Lyndel Prott from the UNESCO Secretariat added that in the Working Group, the view was not to apply Article 15(2) during wartime. Article 15 'was a general clause and was not talking about specific military conflict. Rather, it envisaged action in peacetime such as use of this property for military stores'.[484]

Paragraph 3: notification of suspension and cancellation

We have seen that according to Article 11, paragraph 11, the Director-General sends, without delay, to the Secretary-General of the UN and to all Parties (meaning the Parties to the Second Protocol) notification of any decision by the Committee to include cultural property on the List. Paragraph 3 of this Article exists as a parallel to this obligation. The suspension and cancellation of enhanced protection by the decision of the Committee must also be notified, without delay, to the same addresses; in other words, to the Secretary-General of the UN and to all Parties to the Second Protocol.[485]

Paragraph 4: rights of the Parties to express their views

The final paragraph of this Article is rather procedural in nature. When the Committee is called upon to make an important decision concerning suspension or cancellation of enhanced protection for a 'cultural heritage of the greatest importance for humanity', it should take all possible precautions, one of which is to give to the Parties the possibility to express their views. This provision is just a procedural remainder to the Committee to give the Parties the right to explain the situation and eventually defend their approach. It is essentially an expression of the basic right to be heard in any forum for decision-making.

---

484 Ibid., Lyndel Prott, p. 23.
485 It is interesting to note that in the Article 11, paragraph 11 a reference is made to the notifications to all Parties, and it was our logical interpretation that only the Parties to the Second Protocol are concerned. In this paragraph the reference is more precise.

Chapter 4
CRIMINAL RESPONSIBILITY AND JURISDICTION

INTRODUCTION

Historical background

In the past, the protection of cultural property in the event of armed conflict was included in legal instruments concerning the laws and customs of war. A very limited number of these provisions included prosecution of violations of these laws and customs of war.

The development of codified laws of war was influenced in the early stages by national provisions, in particular those adopted in the US during the Civil War. The *Lieber Instructions*, initiated by President Abraham Lincoln, represent the first attempt to codify laws of war. They were prepared by Francis Lieber, then a professor at Columbia College in New York, and influenced the codification of laws of war at the international level and the adoption of similar instructions by other States.[486] According to Articles 34–36, museums of fine arts, classical works of art, libraries and scientific collections 'must be secured against all avoidable injury' and are 'not to be considered public property'. Article 44 fixes the penalty:

> All wanton violence committed against persons in the invaded country, all destruction of property not commanded by the authorized officer, all robbery, all pillage or sacking, even after taking a place by main force, all rape, wounding, maiming, or killing of such inhabitants, are prohibited under the penalty of death, or such other severe punishment as may seem adequate for the gravity of the offense. A soldier, officer or private, in the act of committing such violence, and disobeying a superior ordering him to abstain from it, may be lawfully killed on the spot by such superior.[487]

---

486 Hertigan (1983).
487 Ibid., p. 54; Schindler and Toman (2004), p. 9.

Lieber's Swiss correspondent, J.-G. Bluntschli, considered the 'degradation of monuments and works of art' barbarous acts to be severely punished.[488] The first step towards the codification of laws and customs of war, the Project of an International Declaration Concerning the Laws and Customs of War of 1874 (492A),[489] includes the protection of works of art in Articles 8 and 17, without providing specific sanctions. A private codification, the *Oxford Manual* on the laws of war on land, adopted by the Institute of International Law in 1880,[490] which ensures protection against bombardment (art. 34) and during occupation (art. 53), is more specific about penal sanctions in Part III 'Penal Sanctions':

> If any of the foregoing rules be violated, the offending parties should be punished, after a judicial hearing, by the belligerent in whose hands they are. Therefore

Art. 84. Offenders against the laws of war are liable to the punishments specified in the penal law.

> This mode of repression, however, is only applicable when the person of the offender can be secured. In the contrary case, the criminal law is powerless, and, if the injured party deem the misdeed so serious in character as to make it necessary to recall the enemy to a respect for law, no other recourse than a resort to reprisals remains.
>
> Reprisals are an exception to the general rule of equity that an innocent person ought not to suffer for the guilty. They are also at variance with the rule that each belligerent should conform to the rules of war, without reciprocity on the part of the enemy. This necessary rigor, however, is modified to some extent by the following restrictions:

It then refers to provisions concerning reprisals (Art. 85 and 86).

The *Second Hague Convention* (1899) and the *Fourth Hague Convention* (1907) deal only with the responsibility of the belligerent Party (art. 3) but leave States entirely free to punish or not to punish the actions of their

---

488 Bluntschli (1874), art. 649, 656 and 657.
489 Schindler and Toman (2004), pp. 23–28.
490 *The Laws of War on Land*, Oxford, September 9, 1880 [= *Oxford Manual*]. In Schindler and Toman (1988), pp. 36–48. http://www.icrc.org/ihl.nsf/385ec082b509e76c41256739003e636d/6a5d425d2 9d9d6dbc125641e0032ec97?OpenDocument

own troops or enemy soldiers. Individual responsibility is included only in national legislation:

> Art. 3. A belligerent Party which violates the provisions of the said Regulations shall, if the case demands, be liable to pay compensation. It shall be responsible for all acts committed by persons forming part of its armed forces.

The solution proposed was inadequate when major armed conflicts started. In keeping with the spirit of the Fourth Hague Convention, the *Peace Treaty with Germany, signed at Versailles on, 28 June 1919,* ordered the return of property, rights, and interests to the rightful owners. The joint Arbitration Tribunal had to determine the amount of reparations. According to Article 228:

> The German Government recognizes the right of the Allied and Associated Powers to bring before military tribunals persons accused of having committed acts in violation of the laws and customs of war. Such persons shall, if found guilty, be sentenced to punishments laid down by law. This provision will apply notwithstanding any proceedings or prosecution before a tribunal in Germany or in the territory of her allies. The German Government shall hand over to the Allied and Associated Powers, or to such one of them as shall so request, all persons accused of having committed an act in violation of the laws and customs of war, who are specified either by name or by the rank, office or employment which they held under the German authorities.

The Treaty did not go beyond this general reference. It did not provide a definition of violations and referred to the general provisions of the laws and customs of war, in other words, to the primary norms of the international law of armed conflicts.

No individual was punished for any of the great acts of destruction that took place during the First World War, such as the burning of the library of Louvain, the bombardment of Rheims Cathedral, or the destruction of the Town Hall of Arras. The Commission on Responsibility for War and Guarantees was set up on 25 January 1919, and all available information was assembled on illegal attacks on objects of cultural property, but the lack of sanctions prevented action.[491] Persons accused of crimes were not handed

---

491 Williams (1978), p. 21.

over. Germany itself tried some of the accused in its own courts. Of the 896 claimed war criminals, only 45 were tried and 9 were condemned by the Supreme Court of Leipzig, created under German law. The sentences were light and the convicted were pardoned a few years later.

Not much attention was paid to aspects of individual responsibility for the destruction of cultural values. But nevertheless, on 15 May 1919 the Netherlands Society of Archaeology (Nederlandsche Oudheidkundige Bond) made a set of proposals[492] in which it raised the following question in point 11: 'Is it desirable to impose the special penal sanction for the violation of the rules to be formulated and should the judgment in this matter be pronounced by the international judge or national judge?'[493] This was probably the first time this important issue was raised at the international level.

The 1923 Hague Rules concerning the Control of Wireless Telegraphy in Time of War and Air Warfare made progress in the establishment of control, but not in prosecution.[494] The Roerich Pact of 1935 also left it to governments to adopt the internal legislative measures necessary to ensure that cultural property was respected and protected (art. 2).[495]

The *Preliminary Draft International Convention* for the Protection of Historic Buildings and Works of Art in Time of War (1938) stated that '[t]he High Contracting Parties undertake to take steps to punish in time of war any person looting or damaging monuments and works of art' (art. 3, para. 3). But the Preliminary Draft also contains another interesting provision: Article 11 stipulates that:

1. International Commissions of Inspection shall satisfy themselves while military operations are proceeding that no breach of the provisions of this Convention is committed.
2. Offences committed in breach of the provisions of this Convention shall be established by the International Commission of Inspection operating in the territory in which they were committed.

The draft went no further than the previous provisions. This demonstrates how difficult it was to overcome the sovereign domination of States with

---

492 Pays-Bas (1919), pp. 329–36.
493 '11. Est-il désirable de frapper d'une sanction pénale spéciale la violation des règles à établir et le jugement, en cette matière, devra-t-il être prononcé par un juge international ou par un juge national?'
494 Schindler and Toman (2004), p. 320.
495 Ibid., p. 992.

regard to international sanctions. International criminal law still had a long way to go.

During the Second World War,[496] the Allied Powers sent a warning to the Germans concerning prosecution for atrocities committed during war. This was then developed into the Charter of International Military Tribunal.[497] The Charter established individual responsibility for crimes against peace, war crimes and crimes against humanity (Article 6 of the Charter). Paragraph (b) of Article 6 deals with Crimes, 'namely violations of the laws and customs of war'. According to this paragraph,

> such violations shall include, but not be limited to, murder, ill-treatment or deportation to slave labor or for any other purposes of civilian population of or in occupied territory, murder or ill-treatment of prisoners of war or persons on the seas, killing of hostages, plunder of public and private property, wanton destruction of cities, towns or villages, or devastation not justified by military necessity.[498]

From the point of view of cultural property, the references to 'plunder of public and private property, wanton destruction of cities, towns or villages, or devastation not justified by military necessity', are important. The Charter of the Tokyo Tribunal was less explicit. It referred in Article 5 to 'Conventional war crimes: Namely violations of the laws or customs of war'.[499] Subsequent war crimes trials clarified certain issues relating to cultural property. The post-war courts followed the provisions of the Hague regulations concerning the protection of private property. Restitution was considered to be more important than traditional concepts concerning the *bona fide* purchasers.[500]

---

496 Moscow Declaration of 30 October 1943 in particular.

497 Agreement for the Prosecution and Punishment of the Major War Criminals of the European Axis, signed in London on 8 August 1945; Schindler and Toman (2004), pp. 1253–61.

498 Ibid., p. 1256.

499 The International Military Tribunal for the Far East was established in Tokyo by the Supreme Commander for the Allied Powers in the Pacific, General D. MacArthur, by the Proclamation of 19 January 1946. The Charter under the same date is parallel to the Charter of London. See Lauterpacht (1953), pp. 357–58; Friedman (1972), Vol. I, p. 894. *A Decade of American Foreign Policy: Basic Documents*, 1941–49. Prepared at the request of the Senate Committee on Foreign Relations. By the Staff of the Committee and the Department of State. Washington, DC: Government Printing Office, 1950. http://www.yale.edu/lawweb/avalon/imtfech.htm.

500 *Menzel v. List* (1966), 49 Misc. 2d 300, 267 N.Y.S. 2d 804 (Sup.Ct), aff'd *per curiam* (1967), 28 A.D. 516, 279 N.Y.S. 2d 608. Quoted in Williams (1978, p. 19). She also quotes Law 59 of the US Military Government for Germany of 10 November 1947: 'Provisions of law for the protection of purchasers in good faith which would defeat restitution of property confiscated by the Nazi regime shall be disregarded'.

The Nuremberg Judgment of major war criminals before the International Military Tribunal (1945–46) declared in particular that the general laws and customs of war laid down in the Hague Convention, were in 1939 'regarded as being declaratory of the laws and customs of war which are referred to in Article 6(b) of the Charter.'[501] French and Soviet prosecutions at the main Nuremberg Trial presented an extensive documentary testimony on Einsatzstab Rosenberg, an organization set up in 1940 under the auspices of the Nazi Party to seize art objects and other valuable properties abandoned by or taken from Jews and other disfavoured owners.[502] The judgement recognized Rosenberg, Reich Minister for the Occupied Eastern Territories, as 'responsible for a system of organized plunder of both public and private property throughout the invaded countries of Europe.' He directed the 'Einsatzstab Rosenberg', which plundered museums and libraries, confiscated art treasures and collections, and pillaged private houses. His own reports show the extent of the confiscations. In 'Aktion-M' (Möbel), instituted in December 1941 at Rosenberg's suggestion, 69,619 Jewish homes were plundered in the West, 38,000 of them in Paris alone, and it took 26,984 railroad cars to transport the confiscated furnishings to Germany. As of 14 July 1944, more than 21,903 art objects, including famous paintings and museum pieces, had been seized by the Einsatzstab in the West. The Tribunal found Rosenberg guilty.

The principles of international law recognized by the Charter of the Nuremberg Tribunal and the judgement of the Tribunal were affirmed by unanimous UN General Assembly resolution 95(I) of 11 December 1946.[503] The resolution directed the International Law Commission to deal with the International Criminal Code, and the Commission considered that as the principles were affirmed by the General Assembly, its task was to formulate them. It did so in a document adopted in July 1950 under the title 'Principles of International Law recognized in the Charter of the Nuremberg Tribunal and in the Judgment of the Tribunal', which included the same text concerning the protection of public or private property as the Charter itself.[504]

With this limited experience it was unsurprising that the 1954 Hague Conference did not go further in the preparation of sanctions for violations committed against cultural property. Only one article, Article 28, concerns sanctions. The fact that such limited attention was paid to sanctions was the

---

501 Friedman (1972), Vol. 2, p. 961.
502 Taylor (1992), p. 365.
503 Schindler and Toman (2004), p. 1263.
504 Ibid., pp. 1265–66.

source of criticism, which started immediately after its adoption at the First Meeting of the High Contracting Parties in 1962.

Sufficient protection for cultural property was lacking in both world wars. There was a need for special rules for protection and penal provisions for the enforcement of such rules. In general international humanitarian law, such attempts were made by the 1949 Geneva Conventions.

Grave breaches and other violations of the 1949 Geneva Conventions

The need for penal provisions was felt at the 1949 Geneva Conference. Grave breaches provisions were included in Articles 49 and 50 of Geneva Convention I;[505] Articles 50 and 51 of Geneva Convention II;[506] Articles 129 and 130 of Geneva Convention III;[507] and Articles 146 and 147 of Geneva Convention IV.[508] Two major categories of provisions were instituted for violations committed against provisions of the Conventions.

1.   **Grave breaches**, defined in articles 50/51/130/147:
     a) enact and adopt *national legislation* necessary to provide effective penal sanctions for persons committing, or ordering to be committed, any of the grave breaches of the [present] Convention, which are included in 50/51/130/147;
     b) take the following measures:
        (i)   obligation to *search* such persons alleged to have committed, or to have ordered to be committed such grave breaches;
        (ii) bring such persons, regardless of their nationality, *before its own courts*; or
        (iii) if it prefers, *hand such persons over* for trial to another High Contracting Party concerned provided such High Contacting Party has made out a 'prima facie' case.
2.   **Other violations** than grave breaches which do not reach the gravity of grave breaches. Very little is said about these other violations: the Contracting Parties are under obligation to suppress these other acts

---

505 Convention (I) for the Amelioration of the Condition of the Wounded and Sick in Armed Forces in the Field, Geneva, 12 August 1949, 75 UNTS 31.
506 Convention (II) for the Amelioration of the Condition of Wounded, Sick and Shipwrecked Members of Armed Forces at Sea, Geneva, 12 August 1949, 75 UNTS 85.
507 Convention (III) relative to the Treatment of Prisoners of War, Geneva, 12 August 1949, 75 UNTS 135.
508 Convention (IV) relative to the Protection of Civilian Persons in Time of War Geneva, 12 August 1949, 75 UNTS 287.

which are contrary to the Conventions. The nature of this suppression is a matter for the national legislation of each State, and can comprise administrative, disciplinary and even penal measures.

In all circumstances, the accused persons shall benefit from *safeguards*: fair trial and defence (not less favourable than those provided by Article 105 of Geneva Convention III).

Definition of grave breaches

A definition of grave breaches is provided in Articles 50/51/130/147. No specific reference to cultural property is given in these articles and only the following text, included in Articles 50, 51 and 147, may affect cultural property: 'and extensive destruction and appropriation of property, not justified by military necessity and carried out unlawfully and wantonly'.[509]

The 1954 Hague Conference and sanctions for violation of the Convention

The next step in the protection of cultural property, as we have seen, was the adoption of the 1954 Hague Convention. The UNESCO Draft prepared in the light of the 1954 Hague Conference stressed the necessity for an effective system of sanctions. It contained the only modest proposal to be included in the Convention. The Secretariat has not yet been in a position to confront the hesitation of States to move forward towards a more improved

---

509 *No possibility of absolution from liability incurred*: According to Article 148, '[n]o High Contracting Party shall be allowed to absolve itself or any other High Contracting Party of any liability incurred by itself or by another High Contracting Party in respect of breaches referred to in the preceding Article'. The Article concerns only grave breaches and not other violations. As the Commentary to the 1949 Geneva Convention indicates, the obligation to prosecute and punish those committing breaches of the Convention is absolute. If, however, any doubt existed on that point, this Article would clear it up entirely. For a better understanding of the sense of this provision, the Commentary compares this provision with Article 3 of the Fourth Hague Convention of 1907, which reads: 'A belligerent Party which violates the provisions of the said Regulations shall, if the case demands, be liable to pay compensation. It shall be responsible for all acts committed by persons forming part of its armed forces.' According to the Commentary, 'Article 148 is intended to prevent the vanquished from being compelled in an armistice agreement or a peace treaty to renounce all compensation due for breaches committed by persons in the service of the victor. As regards material compensation for breaches of the Convention, it is inconceivable, at least as the law stands today, that claimants should be able to bring a direct action for damages against the State in whose service the person committing the breach was working. Only a State can make such claims on another State, and they form part, in general, of what is called "war reparations". It would seem unjust for individuals to be punished while the State in whose name or on whose instructions they acted was released from all liability.' (Pictet [1952–1960], Vol. IV, p. 603.)

system of sanctions. The UNESCO Secretariat itself described this as an extremely simple approach, accounted for largely by the fact that criminal international law is still in its infancy. Thus, according to the UNESCO Draft, the aim of the Conference should be to induce the Contracting Parties to take 'all necessary measures to prosecute and impose penal or disciplinary sanctions upon those persons . . . who committed or order to be committed a breach of the present Convention'. A detailed list of breaches that might be committed was considered dispensable. To meet the objections of certain States whose penal systems depend on the principles of public law, which it was not intended to change, it was decided that States would undertake repressive measures only within the framework of their criminal jurisdiction.[510] In this respect the Hague Conference did not even follow the progressive developments accomplished by the 1949 Geneva Conference and included in the Geneva Conventions.

During the Hague Conference, several delegates took a stand on the issue of sanctions. The UK delegate pointed out that 'because of the vague and all-embracing definition of cultural property in Article 1, there is a danger that people might break the Convention quite unwittingly. It is wrong that sanctions should apply to breaches committed through ignorance'. Referring to the draft articles, he proposed that the word 'knowingly' should, therefore, be inserted between 'who' and 'commit'.[511] For his part, the delegate of Italy considered that the word 'prosecute' was superfluous.[512] The Conference did not take up these two requests.

On the other hand, the delegate of the USSR proposed a more detailed article[513] based on Article 146 of the Fourth Geneva Convention. It is useful to remember in this context the attitude of the Soviet delegation at the 1949 Geneva Conference. The experience of the Second World War and the post-war attitude led the Soviet delegate to insist on the improvement and development of sanctions in the law of war. The question of criminal responsibility constituted one of the main contributions of the USSR to the development of the rule of international humanitarian law at this time. In the opinion of the Soviet delegate at the 1954 Hague Conference, the Article should comprise, in particular, effective sanctions and the possibility of the accused persons being handed over for trial to another Party concerned, if that Party were to possess evidence constituting counts of indictment against

---

510 *Records*, p. 314.
511 Ibid., p. 344.
512 Ibid., p. 347.
513 Ibid., CBC/DR/71, p. 390.

such persons. His draft included a definition of acts contrary to Article 11 of the Convention and sanctions to be imposed in the event of misuse of the distinctive emblem. Finally, the delegate of the USSR asked that the necessary measures be taken to put an end to any other acts contrary to the provisions of the Convention. The Conference decided to base the text on the UNESCO Draft and did not take these progressive proposals into account.

The discussion that took place at the Conference bears witness to the restrictive attitude on the part of governments: for example, when reference was made to cases of *force majeure*, or when a proposition was made to have no provision concerning sanctions. The experts who prepared the UNESCO text added a list of possible breaches. They understood that they had no chance of having this text accepted by all the States, particularly those with a federal constitution.

As a result, the 1954 Hague Conference adopted only a very modest provision on sanctions, Article 28. It reads as follows:

> The High Contracting Parties undertake to take, within the framework of their ordinary criminal jurisdiction, all necessary steps to prosecute and impose penal or disciplinary sanctions upon those persons, of whatever nationality, who commit or order to be committed a breach of the present Convention.

The 1954 Convention therefore did not go much beyond previous provisions concerning the protection of cultural property, whether the Fourth Hague Convention of 1907 or the Roerich Pact of 1935. According to Article 28, sanctions are left to national, domestic legal systems.

The wording of the text is modelled on paragraph 1 of Article 49/50/129/146 common to the Geneva Conventions. The States undertake to enact the necessary legislation. This legislation must already be implemented in time of peace. In our opinion, such legislation should lay down a sanction for each breach.

Practical application of Article 28 of the Convention

The reports submitted according to Article 26 by the High Contracting Parties throw little light on this subject. Some States merely note in their reports that the provisions of the penal code or the military penal code are consistent with the spirit of the Convention (Austria, Hungary, Switzerland). Others cite laws or articles of the pertinent laws (Byelorussian SSR, Iran,

Italy, the Netherlands, Yugoslavia). The Federal Republic of Germany indicated, for example, that criminal law provides for sanctions against the commanding officers and members of the armed forces. Special penal provisions are envisaged to supplement the general body of laws in force (penal code, military penal law and regulations governing members of the armed forces). The following acts are considered to be offences: damaging or looting property; misusing or damaging the distinctive emblem; interfering with, assaulting, insulting or threatening persons charged with the protection of property and control tasks. Article 261 (offences against international law) of Chile's Criminal Code defines offences as acts against places of worship, libraries, museums, archives and works of art.[514]

The representative of one government raised the question as to whether a Party to the Convention was obliged to prosecute and impose penal sanctions upon those who have committed breaches outside the territory subject to the criminal jurisdiction of the State in question. The answer is yes, because that is the aim of this provision. It may reasonably be assumed that the country has at its disposal general legislation concerning the protection of its own cultural property, and that the criminal act directed against that property would, in any event, be covered by those provisions. What remains to be done – according to Article 28 of the Convention – is *to prosecute those who have committed criminal acts outside the territorial jurisdiction of the State*. Because the provision is so succinct and leaves all regulating to national legislation, it is impossible to give it a uniform interpretation. There is one positive side to the Article: it is made quite clear that the Convention may not be infringed with impunity.

The limited nature of sanctions provided for by the Convention has been criticized as a step backwards relative to the previous provisions. However, it was pointed out that, even though the Convention fails to deal with the civil consequences, that is, with the State responsibility for a wrongful act and the corresponding obligation either to provide restitution or to pay compensation, Article 3 of the Fourth 1907 Hague Convention is still applicable. According to this provision, 'A belligerent Party which violates the provisions of the said Regulations shall, if the case demands, be liable to pay compensation. It shall be responsible for all acts committed by persons forming part of its armed forces.' Stanislaw E. Nahlik has rightly remarked that the restitution of the

---

514 The recent study prepared by Roger O'Keefe (2002) does not provide in its second part (12 case studies) any specific examples of the existing penal provisions for the protection of cultural property.

object removed or, if it can no longer be returned, the restitution of another object of the same kind and the same cultural (and not economic) value is likely to satisfy the owner.[515] In fact, this is the solution that for centuries has generally been recognized under customary law. The reluctance on the part of the Conference to venture further along the path of sanctions has been attributed to the fact that the ILC was in the process of drawing up an International Code, though it contained only a very general clause: in its Article 2, paragraph 12, it mentions 'acts committed in violation of the laws and customs of war'.

Post-Convention efforts for the improvement of sanctions

We should not forget the important place of the doctrine of international law.[516] Some authors hold that the history of case-law and international relations reveals a trend that should logically lead to the singling out, among international crimes, of those that more particularly threaten humanity's cultural heritage. These criminal acts are called 'crimes against cultural heritage'.

It was mostly in connection with the *First Meeting of the High Contracting Parties in 1962* that the lack of appropriate sanctions for violations of the rules for protection of cultural property was revealed. This criticism came mostly from countries that had already wanted to develop the rules of sanctions during the 1954 Hague Conference but that were not able to do so because of the opposition of other States.

Among the States in favour of sanctions were the countries of the Socialist block. As often happened in the sphere of international relations, the socialist countries undertook the repartition of tasks among their members and it seems that the role relating to protection of cultural property was assigned to Poland. In preparation for the First Meeting of the High Contracting Parties, the outstanding expert in this field was Stanislaw E. Nahlik, Professor of International Law at Krakow University. He elaborated a list of crimes against cultural property based on the 1954 Hague Convention, but also on the rules of the 1907 Hague Conventions. This list was published in 1959

---

515 Nahlik (1967), p. 148.
516 Bassiouni (1983) and (1986), Vol. 2, pp. 195–227; Boylan (1993), para. 9.1–9.25, pp. 91–98; Breucker (1975b); Nahlik (1959).

and distributed at the 1962 Meeting of the Parties to the 1954 Convention. We include his draft in the footnote.[517]

---

517 Nahlik (1959):

I. General Injunctions

1. General principle of respect for private property; institutions dedicated to religion, charity and education, the arts and sciences, even when State property, shall be treated as private property (Articles 46, para. 1 and 56, para. 1 of the 1907 Regulations).

2. Prohibition of any act of hostility directed against cultural property (Articles 4, para. 1, and 9 of the 1954 Convention).

3. Prohibition of any act directed by way of reprisals against cultural property (Article 4, para. 4 of the 1954 Convention).

4. Prohibition of any act of hostility directed against transport under special protection (Article 12, para. 3 of the 1954 Convention).

5. Principle of respect for and facilities to be accorded to personnel engaged in the protection of cultural property (Article 15 of the 1954 Convention).

II. Prohibition of Destruction

6. General prohibition of the destruction of enemy property, unless such destruction is imperatively demanded by the necessities of war (Article 23, letter (g) of the 1907 Regulations).

7. Prohibition of any wilful destruction of institutions dedicated to religion, charity and education, the arts and sciences, and of historic monuments and works of art and science (Article 56 of the 1907 Regulations).

8. Prohibition of attack or bombardment, by whatever means, of towns, villages, dwellings or buildings which are undefended (Article 25 of the Regulations and Article 1, para. 1 of the Ninth Convention of 1907).

9. Injunction, before commencing a bombardment, except in the case of assault, to do everything within the power of the officer in command of an attacking force to warn the authorities (of the place to be bombarded) (Article 26 of the Regulations and Article 6 of the Ninth Convention of 1907).

10. Injunction, during sieges and bombardments, to take all necessary steps to spare, as far as possible, buildings dedicated to religion, art, science, or charitable purposes, historic monuments [...] provided that they are not being used at the time for military purposes (Article 27, para. 1 of the Regulations and Article 5, para. 1 of the Ninth Convention of 1907).

11. Injunction, in the event of occupation of the territory of the other belligerent, to ensure that its cultural property is safeguarded and preserved (Article 5, paras 1 and 2 of the 1954 Convention).

III. Prohibition of Pillage

12. Prohibition of the pillage of a town or place, even if taken by assault (Article 28 of the Regulations and Article 7 of the Ninth Convention of 1907).

13. Prohibition of pillage during the exercise of military authority over the territory of a hostile State (Article 47 of the Regulations of 1907).

14. General prohibition of the seizure of the property of institutions dedicated to religion, charity and education, the arts and sciences (Article 46, para. 2, Article 56, para. 1, and Article 53, *a contrario*, of the Regulations of 1907).

15. Prohibition of the capture of vessels charged with religious, scientific or philanthropic missions (Article 4 of the Eleventh Convention of 1907).

16. Prohibition of the requisitioning of movable cultural property situated in the territory of a Contracting Party (Article 4, para. 3, second sentence of the 1954 Convention; cf. Article 52 of the Regulations of 1907).

17. General prohibition of the seizure of enemy property, unless such seizure is imperatively demanded by the necessities of war, and a special prohibition of any seizure of institutions dedicated to religion, charity and education, the arts and the sciences and of historic monuments

and works of art and science (Article 23, letter (g) and Article 56, para. 1 and 2 of the Regulations of 1907).

18. Prohibition of the seizure, capture or placing in prize of cultural property being transported and means of transport exclusively engaged in the transfer of such cultural property (Article 14 of the 1954 Convention).

19. Injunction addressed to States in occupation of enemy territory to regard themselves only as the administrator or ususfructuary of public buildings and immovable property belonging to the hostile State (Article 55 of the Regulations of 1907).

20. Injunction addressed to States in occupation of enemy territory to prohibit, prevent and, if necessary, put a stop to any form of theft, pillage or misappropriation of, and any acts of vandalism directed against, cultural property (Article 4, para. 3, first sentence of the 1954 Convention).

21. Injunction addressed to all the Parties to prevent the exportation of cultural property from an occupied territory, to take into custody cultural property imported either directly or indirectly from any occupied territory and, at the close of hostilities, to return such property to the competent authorities of the territory previously occupied (para. 1, 2, 3 and 5 of the 1954 Protocol).

IV. Prohibition of Wilful Damage

22. Prohibition of any wilful damage done to institutions dedicated to religion, charity and education, the arts and sciences, and to historic monuments and works of art and science (Article 56, para. 1 and 2 of the Regulations of 1907).

V. Injunctions Concerning Property Belonging to the Enjoined State Itself

23. Injunction addressed to all the Contracting Parties to prepare in time of peace for the safeguarding of cultural property situated within their own territory against the foreseeable effects of an armed conflict (Article 3 of the 1954 Convention).

24. Prohibition (by hypothesis) of the use for military purposes of buildings dedicated to religion, art, science or charitable purposes and historic monuments, and of the use of cultural property and its surroundings either for military purposes or for purposes likely to expose it to destruction or damage in the event of armed conflict (Article 27, para. 1 of the Regulations and Article 5, para. 1 of the Ninth Convention of 1907, Articles 4, para. 1 and 9 of the 1954 Convention).

25. Injunction to mark with distinctive emblems at least the cultural property under special protection (Article 10 of the 1954 Convention; cf. Articles 27, para. 2 of the Regulations and 5, para. 2 of the Ninth Convention of 1907).

26. Injunction addressed to any Contracting Party whose government is considered their legitimate government by members of a resistance movement to draw, if possible, their attention to the obligation to respect cultural property (Article 5, para. 3 of the 1954 Convention).

VI. Abuse of Privileges Granted by the Convention

27. Prohibition of the use of the distinctive emblem in cases other than those specified by the Convention (Article 17, para. 3 of the 1954 Convention).

28. Prohibition (by hypothesis) of the lifting of the immunity to which the cultural property of the opposing Party is entitled in circumstances other than those specified by the Convention and of taking advantage of the military necessity clause in circumstances other than those specified by the Convention (Article 4, para. 2 of the 1954 Convention).

VII. Injunction to Take the Necessary Measures to Ensure the Application of the Convention

29. Injunction to take all necessary measures to ensure the effective application of the Convention within a period of six months after its entry into force, and in particular to disseminate the text, to include the study of the text in training programmes, to introduce the principles into military regulations, and so on (Articles 34, para. 1, 25 and 7 of the Convention and para. 11 of the Protocol of 1954).

VIII. Injunction Addressed to the International Control Personnel

30. Injunction addressed to the Commissioners-General for Cultural Property, delegates of the Protecting Powers, inspectors and experts in no case to exceed their mandates, to take account of the security needs of the Contracting Party to which they are accredited and so on (Article 8 of the 1954 Regulations).

1977 Protocols Additional to the Geneva Conventions

The 1977 Protocols Additional to the Geneva Conventions adopted two important articles on the protection of cultural property: Article 53 of Protocol I and Article 16 of Protocol II. These articles define more precisely the nature of these crimes and represent a step forward.

Even though it deals extensively with sanctions for violations of the rules of international humanitarian law, Additional Protocol I did not establish a special category of crimes against cultural property. Such sanctions were formulated on the basis of the 1907 Hague Regulations, even if not enforced by penalties at that time.

This paragraph is constructed in relation to Article 53 of Protocol I, which states:

> Without prejudice to the provisions of the Hague Convention for the Protection of Cultural Property in the Event of Armed Conflict of 14 May 1954, and of other relevant international instruments, it is prohibited:
> a. to commit any acts of hostility directed against the historic monuments, works of art or places of worship which constitute the cultural or spiritual heritage of peoples;
> b. to use such objects in support of the military effort;
> c. to make such objects the object of reprisals.

Article 85, paragraph 4 of Protocol I refers to such acts of hostility as follows:

> d. making the clearly recognized historic monuments, works of art or places of worship which constitute the cultural or spiritual heritage of peoples and to which special protection has been given by special arrangement, for example, within the framework of a competent international organization, the object of attack, causing as a result extensive destruction thereof, where there is no evidence of the violation by the adverse Party of Article 53, sub-paragraph (b), and when such historic monuments, works of art and places of worship are not located in the immediate proximity of military objectives.

These acts are regarded as a serious breach of the Protocol when committed deliberately and in violation of the Geneva Conventions and Protocol I.

According to paragraph 5 of the same Article: 'Without prejudice to the application of the Conventions and of this Protocol, grave breaches of these instruments shall be regarded as war crimes.'

International Law Commission Drafts (1954, 1996)

In the atmosphere of the post-Nuremberg trials, the General Assembly of the UN gave to the newly created ILC the task 'to study the desirability and possibility of establishing an international judicial organ for the trial of persons charged with genocide or other crimes over which jurisdiction will be conferred upon that organ by international conventions'.[518] At its first session, in 1949, the Commission drew up a provisional list of topics selected for codification. Among these was 'jurisdiction with regard to crimes committed outside national territory'. The Commission started to draft the Code of Crimes against the Peace and Security of Mankind. In 1950, the General Assembly set up a Committee on International Criminal Jurisdiction, which was charged with preparing concrete proposals on the establishment of an international criminal court that could administer the Code to be elaborated by the ILC.[519]

At its 1954 session, the General Assembly considered the draft Code[520] and decided to postpone further consideration until the new special committee on the definition of aggression had submitted its report. The 1954 Draft enumerates in Article 2 the acts considered to be offences against the peace and security of mankind and includes among them under paragraph 12 'Acts in violation of the laws and customs of war'.[521]

However, this main obstacle (non-definition of aggression) disappeared with the adoption of Resolution 3314 (XXIX) on 14 December 1974. The path was open to restart work on the Code. However, it was only in 1981 that the General Assembly invited the ILC to resume its work on the draft

---

518 UN General Assembly Resolution 260 B (III) of 9 December 1948.

519 For more on the elaboration of the draft, see UN (1996), pp. 38–41.

520 The text was adopted by the ILC at its 6th Session, in 1954, and submitted to the General Assembly as part of the Commission's report covering the work of that session. The report, which also contains commentaries on the draft articles, appears in *Yearbook of the International Law Commission*, Vol. II (1954). http://untreaty.un.org/ilc/publications/yearbooks/Ybkvolumes(e)/ILC_1954_v2_e.pdf

521 In Article 2, paragraph 13, the Drafts specify that it considers among the acts the following:
(i) Conspiracy to commit any of the offences defined in the preceding paragraphs of this article; or (ii) Direct incitement to commit any of the offences defined in the preceding paragraphs of this article; or (iii) Complicity in the commission of any of the offences defined in the preceding paragraphs of this article; or (iv) Attempts to commit any of the offences defined in the preceding paragraphs of this article.

Code of Offences against the Peace and Security of Mankind. It took several years before the Commission accomplished its work.[522] When it submitted its draft, it was understood that work on the draft Code and the draft statute of an international criminal court should be coordinated by the Special Rapporteur on the draft Code and by the Chairman and members of the Drafting Committee and of the Working Group on a Draft Statute for an International Criminal Court. The Commission adopted the text of the draft Code at its 48th Session in 1996, and submitted it to the General Assembly as part of its report.[523]

The draft Code provided an extensive definition for individual responsibility. According to Article 2, paragraph 3:

> An individual shall be responsible for a crime set out in Article 17, 18, 19 or 20 if that individual:
> (a) intentionally commits such a crime;
> (b) orders the commission of such a crime which in fact occurs or is attempted;
> (c) fails to prevent or repress the commission of such a crime in the circumstances set out in Article 6;
> (d) knowingly aids, abets or otherwise assists, directly and substantially, in the commission of such a crime, including providing the means for its commission;
> (e) directly participates in planning or conspiring to commit such a crime which in fact occurs;
> (f) directly and publicly incites another individual to commit such a crime which in fact occurs;
> (g) attempts to commit such a crime by taking action commencing the execution of a crime which does not in fact occur because of circumstances independent of his intentions.

Article 20 is entitled 'War crimes' and includes the following paragraph concerning the protection of property and civilian objects, including the classic 1907 Hague provision on 'institutions dedicated to religion, charity and education, the arts and sciences, historic monuments and works of art and science':

---

522 For more on the elaboration of the draft, see UN (1996), pp. 142–49.
523 UN Doc. A/48/10. The report contains the commentaries which were published in the *Yearbook of the International Law Commission*, 1996, Vol. II, Part 2.

Any of the following war crimes constitutes a crime against the peace and security of mankind when committed in a systematic manner or on a large scale:

(a) any of the following acts committed in violation of international humanitarian law: [...]

    (iv) extensive destruction and appropriation of property, not justified by military necessity and carried out unlawfully and wantonly;

(b) any of the following acts committed wilfully in violation of international humanitarian law and causing death or serious injury to body or health: [...]

    (ii) launching an indiscriminate attack affecting the civilian population or civilian objects in the knowledge that such attack will cause excessive loss of life, injury to civilians or damage to civilian objects;

    (iii) launching an attack against works or installations containing dangerous forces in the knowledge that such attack will cause excessive loss of life, injury to civilians or damage to civilian objects; [...]

(e) any of the following acts committed in violation of the laws or customs of war: [...]

    (ii) wanton destruction of cities, towns or villages, or devastation not justified by military necessity;

    (iii) attack, or bombardment, by whatever means, of undefended towns, villages, dwellings or buildings or of demilitarized zones;

    (iv) seizure of, destruction of or wilful damage done to institutions dedicated to religion, charity and education, the arts and sciences, historic monuments and works of art and science;

    (v) plunder of public or private property;

(f) any of the following acts committed in violation of international humanitarian law applicable in armed conflict not of an international character: [...]

    (vi) pillage.

The Commentary indicates that Article 20:

reproduces, *inter alia*, the categories of war crimes provided for by the 1907 and 1929 Conventions as well as the 1949 Geneva Conventions and Protocols Additional thereto. However, the Commission considered that the above-mentioned acts must also meet the general criteria indicated in the chapeau of Article 20 or, in other words, that they must have been committed in a systematic manner or on a large scale in order to constitute crimes under the present Code, i.e. crimes against the peace and security of mankind.[524]

The Commission insisted on the seriousness of the crime in order to qualify as a crime against the peace and security of mankind: 'A crime is committed on a *large scale* when it is directed against a multiplicity of victims, either as a result of a series of attacks or of a single massive attack against a large number of victims.'

Paragraph (e) sub-paragraph (iv) is of particular concern to us. The Commentary of the Draft Code indicates that the Commission noted:

> that subparagraph (e)(iv) would cover, *inter alia*, the cultural property protected by the 1954 Hague Convention for the Protection of Cultural Property, as well as the literary and artistic works protected by the Berne Convention for the Protection of Literary and Artistic Work. This provision is based on the Nürnberg Charter (Article 6 (c)) and the Statute of the International Criminal Tribunal for the former Yugoslavia (Article 3). In contrast to those instruments, the present provision provides an exhaustive list of violations of the laws or customs of war to provide a greater degree of certainty in terms of the conduct covered by the present Code.

States were invited to comment on the Draft Code of Crimes against the Peace and Security of Mankind. Among them, Turkey referred to the issue of cultural values:

> Under the heading 'exceptionally serious war crimes', paragraph 2 (f) of Article 22 foresees that acts of aggression against religious, historical and cultural values shall be considered as war crimes. It will be appropriate to expand this paragraph to include the theft, smuggling and destruction of those items of religious, historical, cultural and

---

524 Commentary to the Draft Code of 1996, http://www.un.org/law/ilc/texts/dccomfra.htm.

scientific or technological value as well, carried out in the chaotic atmosphere of times of war.[525]

International tribunals

Thanks to fundamental changes in the international community following the end of the cold war, a new area of development in international criminal law began. The first step was the creation of the International Criminal Tribunal for the former Yugoslavia. This was a test of the new political atmosphere and proved positive. The second step was the creation of the International Criminal Tribunal for Rwanda. The success of these tests constituted sufficient encouragement to proceed with the project of the International Criminal Court. After several years of preparatory work, the Rome Statute was adopted on 17 July 1998.

Provisions concerning violations committed against cultural property were included in the statute of the International Criminal Tribunal for the former Yugoslavia.[526]

Before examining the different provisions, we should indicate that all these rules concerning the punishment of crimes against cultural property and against war crimes in general are secondary in relation to the primary rules that continue the rules of international humanitarian law prohibiting certain behaviour in situations of armed conflicts. However, these primary rules are on occasion quite general and vague. In order to respect the basic rule of criminal law *nulla poena sine lege*, it is necessary to reach a precise definition of the crimes penalized under the secondary rules.

These secondary rules, once established and tested in practice, exercise an influence on the future formulation of primary rules.[527] The States participating in the drafting of the Statutes turned first to the primary rules generally recognized by the international community. The US, the only superpower left after the dissolution of the Soviet Union, played the major role in the preparation of the Statute of the International Tribunal for the former Yugoslavia, and also (at least in the very beginning) of the Rome Statute. The result – in other words, the formulation of concrete rules – was largely influenced by lawyers from the US, or at least of Anglo-Saxon origin.

---

525 Bassiouni and Manikas (1996), p. 519.
526 No such provision exists in the Statute of the International Criminal Tribunal for Rwanda.
527 Cassese (1996), p. 227 et seq.

This was the case for the protection of cultural property, the formulation of which was based upon the 1907 Hague Regulations and not on the 1954 Hague Convention, to which neither the US nor the UK are Parties.

The International Criminal Tribunal for the former Yugoslavia

Following the serious violations of international humanitarian law committed on the territory of the former Yugoslavia as from 1991, the UN Security Council in Resolution 746 (1992) of 3 July 1992 reaffirmed that all parties to the conflict in the territory of the former Yugoslavia were bound to comply with the obligations under international humanitarian law and that persons who commit or order the commission of grave breaches are individually responsible for such breaches. By Resolution 780 (1992) of 6 October 1992, the Security Council asked the Secretary-General to establish an impartial commission of experts to report on the evidence of grave breaches and other violations committed in the territory of the former Yugoslavia. The Commission of Experts submitted its Final Report on 24 May 1994.[528]

It is striking that the *Final Report of the Commission of Experts* referred to Article 19 of the 1954 Hague Convention on cultural property in relation to internal conflicts, but did not mention Article 18 in relation to international armed conflicts (it refers only to the 'Hague Convention IV of 1907, the Geneva Conventions of 1949 and, to some extent, the provisions of Additional Protocol I'), and concludes: 'It must be observed that the violations of the laws or customs of war referred to in Article 3 of the statute of the International Tribunal are offences when committed in international, but not internal armed conflict'.[529] The experts did not pay much attention to the 1954 Hague Convention, which includes Article 18 concerning international conflicts. M. Cherif Bassiouni, who was Chairman of the Commission, stated:

---

528 *Final Report of the Commission of Experts Established pursuant to Security Council Resolution 780 (1992)*, UN SCOR, Annex, UN Doc. S/1994/674 (27 May 1994). The UN published the annexes to this report for public dissemination in August 1995 as UN Doc. S/1994/674/Add. 2 (Vol. I) (31 May 1995) (Vol. II–V) (28 December 1994). Annex XI, 'Destruction of cultural property', was prepared by Commissioner M'Baye. The summary of this annex and Annex XI-A, 'The Battle of Dubrovnik and the law of armed conflict', is published in Bassiouni and Manikas (1996), pp. 177–78. The Commission of Experts, created by Resolution 780 (1992), specifically lists the 1954 Hague Convention as part of applicable 'customary international law' (Interim Report of Commission of Experts, p. 13, para. 39–40, annexed to the Report of the Secretary-General to the Security Council dated 9 February 1993, UN Doc. No. S/2574; quoted in Boyland (1993), para. 9.3, p. 91).

529 *Final Report of the Commission of Experts Established pursuant to Security Council Resolution 780 (1992)*, UN SCOR, Annex, UN Doc. S/1994/674 (27 May 1994); quoted in Bassiouni and Manikas (1996), pp. 508–9.

Article 3(d) of the Statute, which relates to religious and cultural, objects, should be interpreted in light of the 1954 Cultural Property Convention, although Article 3(d) and Report of the Secretary-General failed to explicitly include this convention. The Cultural Property Convention substantially expands Article 27 of the Hague Convention. It requires member states to take international and national measures in times of peace to organize the protection of cultural property. The SFRY[530] became a party to the Cultural Property Convention in 1954.[531]

He then summarizes Articles 3, 4 and 19 of the 1954 Hague Convention and points out the relevance of these provisions in the case of the former Yugoslavia.[532]

After considering the report of the Commission of Experts, the UN Security Council authorized, by Resolution 808 of 22 February 1993, the establishment of the Tribunal 'for the sole purpose of prosecuting persons responsible for serious violations of international humanitarian law' and asked the Secretary-General to produce a report on the Statute within 60 days. The report was submitted on 3 May 1993, and the resolution establishing

---

530 Socialist Federative Republic of Yugoslavia.

531 Bassiouni and Manikas (1996), p. 512. Article 27 of the Hague Convention of 1907.

532 Bassiouni and Manikas (1996), pp. 513–14 (footnotes ommitted): 'The protection of cultural and religious property is especially relevant to the conflict in the former Yugoslavia because many Catholic and Orthodox churches, mosques, and historic monuments of all sides have been the objects of deliberate attack.' According to one report, 800 mosques in Bosnia and Hercegovina (BiH) have been completely or partially destroyed. One of BiH's oldest mosques, the Ferhadija Dzamija mosque in Banja Luka, built in 1583, reportedly was destroyed deliberately in 1993. Even older mosques, such as the Euin Turhan Bey Mosque in Ustikolina, which was built in the fifteenth century, also have been demolished. Other important buildings in Sarajevo have been damaged during the siege of the city. The Institute of Oriental Studies was badly damaged by missiles on 17 May 1992, and the Sarajevo City Hall was severely damaged from consistent bombardments. Other cities have also lost significant cultural property. The old town in Dubrovnik was severely damaged during the battle of Dubrovnik. Finally, the ancient Mostar Bridge over the Neretva River was destroyed. The Commission of Experts determined that neither of these last two examples had legitimate aims. While violations of the laws of war do not require showing that war crimes were committed pursuant to state policy, a link between the offender and one warring faction must be proven. Proving this link may be problematic where victims and offenders are of the same nationality or from countries which are on the same side in the conflict. Part of the problem is that the definition of nationality is unsettled. It is unclear whether Bosnian Serbs, Bosnian Muslims and Bosnian Croats are the same or different nationalities. Thus, it is unclear whether crimes committed by Bosnian Serbs against Bosnian Muslims would be war crimes (most likely they would). Furthermore, because of the strong correlation between membership in an ethnic group and loyalty to a particular side in the conflict, it is also likely that there will be a presumption that crimes committed by members of that ethnic group against other members of that same ethnic group will not be war crimes. This presumption could be rebutted by evidence of any other factor which would make an ordinary crime or a crime against humanity into a war crime.

the Tribunal was adopted on 25 May 1993, approving the Statute of the Tribunal (Resolution 827, 1993). The transition from the Commission to the Prosecutor of the Tribunal was completed in 1995.

The Statute defines the competence of the Tribunal by referring to violations of international humanitarian law, both conventional and customary. It refers *expressis verbis* to the 1949 Geneva Conventions. No reference was made to the 1954 Hague Convention, but the violation of cultural property is included in Article 3 of the Statute, 'Violations of the laws and customs of war'. The Article says, *inter alia*:

> The International Tribunal shall have the power to prosecute persons violating the laws and customs of war. Such violations shall include, but not be limited to: . . .
>
> (b) wanton destruction of cities, towns or villages, or devastation not justified by military necessity;
>
> (c) attack, or bombardment, by whatever means, of undefended towns, villages, dwellings, or buildings;
>
> (d) seizure of, destruction or wilful damage done to institutions dedicated to religion, charity and education, the arts and sciences, historic monuments and works of art and science;
>
> (e) plunder of public or private property.

In this Article the authors of the Statute expressed the customary rules of international law, as interpreted and applied by the Nuremberg Tribunal in the wording used by the 1907 Hague Regulations. No reference is made to the 1954 Hague Convention.

The International Criminal Tribunal for the former Yugoslavia (ICTY) has referred, in several judgments, to the protection of cultural property according to the Statute. The jurisprudence of the ICTY will be analyzed in detail in a separate chapter at the end of this Commentary.[533]

The International Criminal Court

The most recent development is the Statute of the International Criminal Court (ICC). After several decades of efforts[534] to develop international

---

533 See p. 736–765.
534 See Schindler and Toman (2004), pp. 1309–10. See also the extensive literature concerning the International Criminal Court. We mention in particular the following: Cassese (2003); Cassese et

criminal jurisdiction, the Statute of the Court was adopted in Rome on 17 July 1998.[535] The Rome Statute includes two major provisions concerning the protection of cultural property and the formulation of both of them is influenced by the wording used in the Statute of the ICTY. Article 8 of the Statute is entitled 'War crimes'.

Paragraph 2 of this Article is divided into three major sections, which provide the definition of 'war crimes'; two of them include thr provisions relating to cultural property:

(b)   Other serious violations of the laws and customs applicable in *international armed conflict, within the established framework of international law,* [emphasis added] namely, any of the following acts:

[Among these other violations are mentioned, points (ii), (iv), (ix) and (xvi) the following acts:]

(ii)   *Intentionally directing attacks against civilian objects, that is, objects which are not military objectives;* . . .

(iv)   Intentionally launching an attack in the knowledge that such attack will cause incidental loss of life or injury to civilians or damage to civilian objects or widespread, long term and severe damage to the natural environment which would be clearly excessive in relation to the concrete and direct overall military advantage anticipated; . . .

(ix)   Intentionally directing attacks against buildings dedicated to religion, education, art, science or charitable purposes, historic monuments, hospitals and places where the sick and wounded are collected, provided they are not military objectives; . . .

(xvi)   Pillaging a town or place, even when taken by assault;
. . .

e. Other serious violations of the laws and customs applicable in *armed conflicts not of an international character, within the established framework of international law,* [emphasis added] namely, any of the following acts:

---

al. (2002); Crawford (2003); Lee (2001); Dörmann et al. (2002), p. 524; Knoops (2003); Schabas (2004).

535 UN Doc. A/CONF.183/9; http://www.un.org/law/icc/statute/romefra.htm. See Cassese et al. (2002) for the text of the Rome Statute of the International Criminal Court, Rules of Procedure and Evidence, Elements of Crimes.

[Among these other violations are mentioned, in points (iv) and (v), the following acts:]

> (iv)   Intentionally directing attacks against buildings dedicated to religion, education, art, science or charitable purposes, historic monuments, hospitals and places where the sick and wounded are collected, provided they are not military objectives;
>
> (v)   Pillaging a town or place, even when taken by assault.

This is an important step, one that placed the prosecution of the crimes against cultural property in the general context of international criminal law.

In Additional Protocol I, violations directed against cultural property appear among additional grave breaches, according to paragraph 4 of Article 85, and in the reference made to 'the cultural or spiritual heritage of peoples and that enjoy a special protection under international agreement'. It does not appear as such in the Statute:

> During the Diplomatic Conference, a reasonable proposal to include attacks against cultural property in the list of war crimes was made by Spain (A/CONF.183/C.1/L.4 of 17 June 1998). Most regretfully, this item was not a priority for the 'like-minded' countries and could neither be approved, nor extensively discussed.[536]

In this document, Spain proposed a new formulation that not only would include protection based on the Hague Convention formula but also would refer to the Hague Convention of 1954. Spain wanted to include the following text: '(g) [...] attacks against internationally protected cultural property [...]', leaving the remaining text unchanged.[537]

---

536 Venturini (2001), p. 99.
537 DOCUMENT A/CONF.183/C.1/L.4 Spain: proposal regarding Article 5 – [Original: Spanish] [17 June 1998]:
War crimes
Section B, sub-paragraph (g)
Amend to read:
'(g)[...] attacks against internationally protected cultural property... [remainder of the text unchanged];'
Section B, sub-paragraph (r)
Add the following:
', as well as against personnel of the Protecting Power or its substitute and impartial humanitarian organizations carrying out activities to protect and assist the victims of an armed conflict in accordance with the Geneva Conventions;'
Section D, sub-paragraph (b)

The protection of cultural property is a specific case in relation to the general principle concerning the protection of civilian objects that are not military objectives (art. 8(2)(b)(ii)). The wording is based on the articles of the Hague Regulations of 1907, which continue to mix unnecessarily the protection of cultural property with the protection of the sick and wounded and hospitals. These issues are different and should be treated under separate provisions. The situation was different in 1899 and in 1907 as protection of the sick and wounded already had a separate legal basis under the 1864 Geneva Convention. There was no connection between the subject of this Convention and the newly introduced protection of historical monuments. The authors of this provision were inspired by the 1864 precedent and used it as a basis for the benefit of 'buildings dedicated to religion, education, art, science or charitable purposes, historic monuments'. The same comment can be applied in relation to the wording of the Statute of the ICTY.

As mentioned above, the definitions adopted in the Statute may influence the future application and interpretation of the primary rules:

> In some respects, the definitions perpetuate the *lacunae* or deficiencies of the primary rules, but in other respects, they also remedy some of those deficiencies. Thus, Articles reflect the link between primary and secondary rules in a very specific, albeit some times confusing way which cannot be explained without reference to the historic development of these rules. This will serve as a basis for analyzing this relationship further below with regard to specific war crimes.[538]

After long discussion at the Conference, Article 9 of the Rome Statute introduced *elements of crimes* that 'shall assist the Court in the interpretation and application of the Articles 6, 7 and 8 dealing with crimes'.[539] It was agreed that the Elements of Crimes would guide but not bind the Court.[540] The draft

---

Add the following:
'as well as against personnel of impartial humanitarian organizations carrying out activities to protect and assist the victims of the conflict.'

538 Bothe (2002), p. 381.

539 Elements have to be adopted by a two-thirds majority of members of the Assembly of States Parties to the Statute (Article 9, paragraph 1 of the Rome Statute).

540 Lee (2001), p. xlviii. In this context, it is interesting to note the declaration made by the ICRC: If such a document is drafted, it is imperative that it be done with extreme care. A great deal of existing law is to be found in detailed treaty provisions and in both international and national case law that interprets international humanitarian law provisions. Any inaccuracy could give rise to the danger that such a document would amount to unintended international legislation rather than being a reflection of existing law. The experience of the ICRC in its advisory service work (which

Elements of Crimes were adopted by the Preparatory Commission for the International Criminal Court on 30 June 2000 (PCNICC/2000/1/Add.2). The following text was included in these Elements for Article 8(2)(b)(ix):

> War crime of attacking protected objects[541]
> Elements
> 1. The perpetrator directed an attack.
> 2. The object of the attack was one or more buildings dedicated to religion, education, art, science or charitable purposes, historic monuments, hospitals or places where the sick and wounded are collected, which were not military objectives.
> 3. The perpetrator intended such building or buildings dedicated to religion, education, art, science or charitable purposes, historic monuments, hospitals or places where the sick and wounded are collected, which were not military objectives, to be the object of the attack.
> 4. The conduct took place in the context of and was associated with an international armed conflict.
> 5. The perpetrator was aware of factual circumstances that established the existence of an armed conflict.

The elements of crimes as defined here are identical with the elements concerning Article 8(2)(e)(iv) (non-international armed conflicts).

During the discussion at the Preparatory Commission, the US, which drew up the main draft on the elements of crimes, proposed 'largely identical elements for both these crimes'.[542] This is not surprising, as this formulation is used in US military manuals, for example, *US Army Field Manual FM 27-10*.[543]

---

helps governments to incorporate humanitarian law in their domestic legislation) is that national legal systems, concepts and vocabulary vary widely. Care should therefore be taken in this international document intended for the Court to avoid approaching such elements from a primarily domestic law perspective and instead to concentrate on international law and practice (A/CONF.183/C.1/L.53).

541 The following note was added to the title under No. 45 in the original text: The presence in the locality of persons specially protected under the Geneva Conventions of 1949 or of police forces retained for the sole purpose of maintaining law and order does not by itself render the locality a military objective.

542 Pfirter (2001), p. 163.

543 Para. 45, p. 21, using the same wording as the 1907 Hague Regulations. At the time, the US was not yet party to the 1954 Hague Convention, and for this simple reason it could hardly propose any other formulation. This task had to be accomplished by other States bound by the 1954 Hague

Comments on the elements of crimes rightly pointed out that material elements were not contentious and that any specific damage to protected buildings was not required, but was not excluded. 'In doing so, it followed the US and Swiss proposals. The Japanese proposal had required extensive destruction whereas the Spanish proposal had required on the contrary that the attack not cause any harm or damage. Both proposals were rejected by clear majorities'.[544]

The element depends on the intention of the perpetrator, and it is this intention that establishes the seriousness of the crime. The *mens rea* element is of fundamental importance:

> This specific intent does not however require any legal appreciation of the protected status of the attacked objects. The perpetrator only needs to know the factual circumstances, which give the attacked building special protection. It can be argued that this element is unnecessary in light of the application of Article 30. It was however maintained, in order to provide clarity and to reflect the explicit mention of intent in the definition of the crime, as is the case for mental elements in some other crimes, such as in the war crime of attacking civilians (art. 8(2)(b)(i)), and the war crime of attacking civilian objects (Art. 8(2)(b)(ii)).[545]

On the road to the 1999 Second Protocol

In an effort to improve implementation of the Convention, UNESCO decided to consult with legal experts, who met in Vienna in October 1983. They considered that a meeting of the High Contracting Parties would be useful – if one were convened – in order to examine important developments in the practical application of the Convention, new developments in the nature of conflicts, the results of the reaffirmation and development of humanitarian international law in the years 1974–1977, and, above all, the adoption of two articles concerning the protection of cultural property in the

---

Convention and Parties to the 1954 Hague Convention, participating in the drafting of the 1998 Rome Statute and in the preparation of the elements of crimes.

544 Pfirter (2001), p. 163. In the footnote, the references to the proposals are given: PCNICC/1999/DP.4/Add.2, PCNICC/1999/WGEC/DP.8, PCNICC/1999/WGEC/DP.12, PCNICC/1999/WGEC/DP.9.

545 Pfirter (2001), p. 163.

context of the 1977 Additional Protocols to the Geneva Conventions. The issue of sanctions was certainly among the subjects to be discussed. In the examination of proposals and suggestions based on the consultant's report, the experts underlined the importance of Article 28 of the Convention but 'noted that no information was available on the extent to which States had complied with the obligations' and encouraged UNESCO to 'endeavour to obtain information on this question and publish it'.[546]

In the process of the review of the Convention, Patrick Boylan was asked by the UNESCO Secretariat and the Government of the Netherlands to prepare an in-depth analysis of the issues and to present a set of recommendations to the members of the Executive Board.[547] Regarding sanctions, he referred in particular to the recent experience with the punishment of violations in Yugoslavia. He suggested close cooperation between the UN and UNESCO in the investigation and preparation of cases for proposed war crimes trials, recommending to the UN the acceptance of the offer of the Director-General to assist in this investigation. He further pointed to the lack of provisions for resolving serious differences between States Parties in relation to the application of either the Convention or the Protocol: 'The issues of appropriate balance of law and jurisdictional systems need to be studied closely by experts in both international and criminal law before proposals could be made for a text to give competence to a court to prosecute offenders specifically under the provisions of the 1954 Convention.'[548] He recommended that a high priority be given to that verification that national military and criminal law measures have been adopted, and that criminal law measures be adopted to prevent trafficking in cultural property from war zones.

The question of sanctions was raised at the first meeting of experts on the application and effectiveness of the Convention for the Protection of Cultural Property in the Event of Armed Conflict[549] (The Hague, July 1993). The need to strengthen sanctions was affirmed, with suggestions that two aspects of the question of sanctions be taken into account: on the one hand,

---

546 UNESCO, Meeting of legal experts on the Convention for the Protection of Cultural Property in the Eevent of Armed Conflict (The Hague, 1954), Vienna, 17–19 October 1983, CLT-83/CONF.641/1, para. 33, p. 11.

547 Boylan (1993).

548 Ibid., para. 9.25, p. 98.

549 Report by the Director-General on the Reinforcement of UNESCO's action for the Protection of the World Cultural and Natural Heritage. UNESCO document 142 EX/15, Annex: Hague Meeting of Experts on the application and effectiveness of the Convention for the Protection of Cultural Property in the Event of Armed Conflict (The Hague, 14 May 1954), *Final Report*. http://unesdoc.unesco.org/images/0009/000958/095820Eo.pdf

the responsibility of the State for a violation of the Hague Convention and, on the other, individual responsibility, in which case those involved should be prosecuted either by an international tribunal or by national tribunals.[550] The role of the International Fact-Finding Commission (Article 90 of the 1977 Additional Protocol I) was also invoked in relation to the inquiry concerning violation of the rules concerning the protection of cultural property.

But it was at the 1994 Lauswolt Meeting of Experts, in particular, that the first legal instruments constituting the beginning of the process of codification were drafted and became known as the 'Lauswolt document'. Chapter 2 of this document was entitled 'Jurisdiction and Responsibility' and included the following articles:

Chapter 2. Jurisdiction and responsibility
- Article 6. Jurisdiction[551]
- Article 7. Responsibility of States[552]
- Article 8. Individual criminal responsibility[553]

---

550 Ibid., para. 6.3, p. 3.

551 Article 6. Jurisdiction
  1. States Parties undertake to prosecute, bring to trial and punish, persons present in their territory responsible for, or accused of, [the acts] defined in Article[s] [....] of this instrument.
  2. To that end States Parties shall adopt, whenever necessary, appropriate legislative and administrative measures.
  3. Persons charged with [the acts] enumerated in Article[s] [...] of this instrument may be tried by a competent court of any State Party which may acquire jurisdiction over the person of the accused or by an international tribunal as may have jurisdiction.
  4. A State Party in whose territory a person alleged to have committed grave breach under Article[s] [...] of this instrument is present shall either try or extradite that person.
  5. The provisions of paragraph 3 do not prejudice the establishment and the jurisdiction of an international tribunal.

552 Article 7. Responsibility of States
  1. States Parties are responsible for serious violations of the provisions of this instrument, which are attributable to a State under international law.
  2. Prosecution of an individual for [a grave breach] [an act] under Article[s] [...] of this instrument does not relieve a State Party of any responsibility under international law for an act or omission attributable to it.

553 Article 8. Individual criminal responsibility
  1. Without prejudice to the Convention and its Protocol the commission of any [acts] in violation of the provisions of this instrument entails individual criminal responsibility.
  2. In relation to grave breaches under this instrument the planning preparation, initiation, ordering, commission, or otherwise aiding and abetting in the planning, preparation or execution of such breaches entails individual criminal responsibility.
  3. The official position of any accused person, whether as Head of State or Government or as a responsible Government official, shall not relieve such person of criminal responsibility nor mitigate punishment, for grave breaches under this instrument.
  4. Any [acts) prohibited under this instrument committed by a subordinate does not relieve a superior of criminal responsibility if he knew or had reason to know that the subordinate was about to commit such acts or had done so and the superior failed to take the necessary and reasonable measures to prevent such acts or to punish the perpetrators thereof.

- Article 9. Grave breaches[554]
- Article 10. Other violations[555]
- Article 11. Mutual assistance in criminal matters.[556]

As this table of content shows, the draft elaborated in Lauswolt included the first series of provisions to become a basis for the formulation of articles concerning criminal responsibility and jurisdiction. It constituted the first substantial draft of these provisions. We shall return to them when we discuss the individual articles. The document was inspired by the 1977 Additional Protocol to the Geneva Conventions. The most developed parts of the Lauswolt proposal concerned the responsibility of States and individual responsibility, reflecting new developments relating to the creation of the ICTY and the preparatory work for the ICC.

The Director-General informed the 145th Session of the Executive Board (1994) about the proposals of the Lauswolt meeting and contended that these proposals needed 'to be further discussed by technical, military and legal experts before any written proposal could be presented to the States Parties to the Convention for their consideration'. He decided to organize at least one meeting of experts before the next session of the General Conference.

---

5. The fact that an accused person acted pursuant to an order of a Government or of a superior shall not relieve that person of criminal responsibility, but may be considered in mitigation of punishment.

554 Article 9. Grave breaches
The extensive destruction, misappropriation or damage carried out wilfully or wantonly to cultural property specially protected by this instrument, contrary to the laws and customs of war, shall be regarded as a grave breach.

555 Article 10. Other violations
The following shall be regarded as violations of this instrument:
(a) the theft, pillage or misappropriation or any other breach of integrity of cultural property protected by this instrument;
(b) acts of vandalism directed against property protected by this instrument;
(c) the export of cultural property from occupied territory or from a part of the territory of a State Party, without prejudice to the provisions of the 1954 Protocol;
(d) the extensive destruction or damage carried out wilfully or wantonly to cultural property, as defined in Article 1 of Convention, contrary to the laws and customs of war.

556 Article 11. Mutual assistance in criminal matters
1. The States Parties shall assist one another in detecting, arresting and bringing to trial persons suspected of having committed grave breaches under this instrument.
2. States Parties shall cooperate in the matter of extradition and they shall give due consideration in particular to the request of the State in whose territory the grave breaches under this instrument have occurred.
3. The States Parties shall cooperate in all other cases of violations of this instrument under the same conditions.
4. The law of the States Parties requested shall apply in all cases. The provisions of the preceding paragraphs shall not, however, affect the obligations arising from the provisions of any other treaty of a bilateral or multilateral nature which governs or will govern the whole or part of the subject of mutual assistance in criminal matters.

The 1994 Expert Meeting was held in Paris at UNESCO Headquarters from 28 November to 2 December 1994.[557] The UNESCO Secretariat prepared an excellent working document for this expert session. This document made use of our 1996 Commentary on the Convention, Patrick Boylan's Report, and the reports of the Hague and the Lauswolt expert meetings, and provided the UNESCO Secretariat's comments on each issue.[558] The discussion concentrated on a few major issues, including the responsibility of States, individual criminal responsibility, extradition and the role of international tribunals. It also drew a distinction between grave breaches and other violations of the Convention:

> On the question of responsibility, the participants generally agreed that much broader provisions should be formulated requiring the States Parties to implement their obligations, to establish jurisdiction and to prosecute. In particular, the experts agreed that it was extremely important that the States Parties should undertake to adopt adequate penal sanctions, seek to detain persons accused of violating the provisions of the Convention and to actively bring them to trial.
>
> It was generally agreed that, in cases where a State does not in fact prosecute, it should be bound to co-operate in the extradition of accused persons so that they may be handed over to a State that is willing to put them on trial. The objection that a special agreement would be required in order to authorize extradition was met by the proposal that a provision could be inserted in the Convention that would have the effect of such an agreement.
>
> It was hoped too that tribunals could be set up along the lines of the one that had been instituted for the purpose of trying war crimes committed on the territory of the former Yugoslavia. In this connection reference was made to the draft statute for an international criminal court which was considered by the International Law Commission at its forty-sixth session. One view was that there should be an exhaustive enumeration of crimes being of international concern in an international treaty. Another view expressed was that there should be universal jurisdiction to serious crimes committed against cultural property. The

---

557 Expert meeting on the review of the 1954 Hague Convention for the Protection of cultural property in the Event of Armed Conflict. Paris, UNESCO Headquarters, 28 November–2 December 1994. UNESCO document CLT/CH/94/608/2, *Final Report*.

558 UNESCO document a working document prepared by the Secretariat, CLT/94/608/1 of 28 November 1994.

experts expressed their satisfaction that Article 3 of the Statute of the International Tribunal for the Prosecution of Persons Responsible for Serious Violations of International Humanitarian Law Committed in the Territory of the Former Yugoslavia reiterates *expressis verbis* in its paragraph d that 'seizure of, destruction or wilful damage done to institutions dedicated to religion, charity and education, the arts and sciences, historic monuments and works of art and science' constitutes a violation of the laws or customs of war.

It was acknowledged that, in accordance with international law, the responsibility of States could be considered from the legal and financial points of view (restitution and compensation), but not from the political standpoint. It was important that the State itself take responsibility for compliance with the Convention; it was not sufficient if it punished individuals after a violation occurred. One participant raised the question of the responsibility of a State for failure to mark cultural property, to report to UNESCO or to disseminate information concerning the application of the Hague Convention. The distinction between 'violations' and 'serious violations' ought to be looked at. Some experts felt that 'serious violations' should follow the definition of 'grave breaches' in Protocol I to the Geneva Conventions.

The debate then moved on to examine the matter of individual responsibility. Some of the participants stated that, in this matter, no mention should be made of the responsibility of Heads of State or Government: they felt it preferable to adopt a more general definition. There was overall consensus on the principle of individual responsibility. The importance of inclusion of guarantees for accused persons should be included into a new text.

The experts then proceeded to examine the matter of grave breaches and other violations of the Convention. Some of the participants thought it necessary to further clarify the notion of gravity of violations. Others pointed out the need to highlight the psychological aspect, in other words, the wilful nature of violations of the Convention in order that any such violations could be attributed to the person responsible.[559]

---

559 Expert meeting on the review of the 1954 Hague Convention for the Protection of Cultural Property in the Event of Armed Conflict. Paris, UNESCO Headquarters, 28 November–2 December 1994. UNESCO document CLT/CH/94/608/2, *Final Report*, pp. 4–5.

The resolution adopted by the Second Meeting of the High Contracting Parties held in November 1995, *inter alia*, invited the Parties to submit to the Secretariat written comments on the substantive proposals of improvement of the Convention by 1 September 1996. The meeting also emphasized the importance of organizing a meeting of a limited number of governmental experts to further discuss the improvement of the Convention and to submit proposals to that effect to the Director-General for transmission to the High Contracting Parties.

The Secretariat received comments from nine States and from the ICA. The 1996 *Summary of the comments*, prepared by the Secretariat in December, was submitted to the meeting of governmental experts in March 1997.[560] In these comments, Guinea proposed a new formulation of Article 28 of the Convention concerning the costs of restoration or reconstruction of damaged or destroyed cultural property. Belgium considered that the review of the Convention should include sanctions against deliberate destruction of immovable and movable cultural property carried out to eliminate peoples' cultural heritage. Poland recommended an amendment to Article 28 so that deliberate damage to or destruction of cultural property in the event of an armed conflict would be considered a war crime and fall under the jurisdiction of international or national tribunals. The ICA wished to reinforce punishment for crimes against cultural property. Croatia stressed that grave breaches of the Convention should be subject to universal jurisdiction, including international tribunals, ad hoc or permanent. Kuwait wished to amend the Convention so that any crime against historical or other valuable cultural property would be considered a war crime. Slovenia insisted on the insertion of Article 8(2–5) of the Lauswolt document.

The 1997 Governmental Experts Meeting on the review of the Hague Convention for the Protection of Cultural Property in the Event of Armed Conflict 1954 was held at UNESCO Headquarters, Paris, 24–27 March 1997.[561]

---

560 UNESCO, Meeting of Governmental Experts. Summary of comments received from States Parties to the Hague Convention and from the International Council on Archives. UNESCO document CLT-96/CONF.603/INF.4, Paris, December 1996.
   As of 28 November 1996, the Secretariat has received replies from nine States from the total number of 88 States Parties to the Convention.
561 UNESCO, Meeting of Governmental Experts on the Review of the 1954 Hague Convention for the Protection of Cultural Property in the Event of Armed Conflict 1954, UNESCO Headquarters, Paris, 24–27 March 1997. *Final Report*. UNESCO document CLT-96/CONF.603/5, Paris, 30 April 1997.

Besides the *Summary of comments* from governments, the experts also received an Information Note suggesting the points on which they might focus their work,[562] the provisional agenda,[563] and provisional rules of procedure.[564] The discussion was based on the Lauswolt document and attention was paid to comments presented by States. The Secretariat was charged with preparing a working document,[565] known as the 'revised Lauswolt document'. The meeting dealt extensively with issues concerning responsibility and jurisdiction:

- *Grave breaches and other violations* (draft Articles 6 and 7). The participants mentioned the destruction of property in recent conflicts and stressed the need to strengthen prosecution and punishment of violations in the new instrument. This would reflect more recent developments such as Article 85 of Additional Protocol I and the relevant provision of the Statute of the ICTY. Concern over archaeological excavations undertaken by an Occupying Power in occupied territory was also mentioned.
- *The responsibility of States* (draft Article 8) for violations of norms of international humanitarian law, with a focus on the importance of the work of the ILC in this respect.
- *Individual criminal responsibility* (draft Article 9), with the need for a provision to exceed the scope of Article 28 of the Convention.
- *Jurisdiction* (draft Article 10), suggesting that jurisdiction over crimes against cultural property be given to the ICC.
- *Mutual assistance in criminal matters* (draft Article 11), based on Article 88 of Additional Protocol I, aiming towards closer cooperation among States Parties to ensure that perpetrators of crimes against cultural property would be either tried or extradited.

---

562 Information Note, UNESCO document CLT-96/CONF.603/INF.3, Paris, November 1996. Several points were suggested for discussion, among them the reinforcement of sanctions for violation of the Convention, and individual and state criminal responsibility.

563 UNESCO document CLT-96/CONF.603/1.

564 UNESCO document CLT/96/CONF.603/3.

565 *Draft provisions for the revision of the 1954 Hague Convention and commentary from the UNESCO Secretariat.* CLT-97/CONF.208/2, Paris, October 1997. This document included the text of the 'revised Lauwolt document'. Draft articles are followed by a Secretariat's comments comparing the original provisions of the Lauswolt document with the revised provisions resulting from the deliberation of participants. Such comments are entitled 'Reasons for change'. The Secretariat also summarized the main points made and issues raised in the discussions in sections entitled 'Main points of discussion'. Some parts of the revised Lauswolt document were put into square brackets because the discussion did not result in unanimity on these issues. They would be subject to further negotiation.

The Third Meeting of the High Contracting Parties in November 1997[566] was informed of the results of the four previous expert meetings (Hague 1993, Lauswolt 1994, Paris 1994 and Paris 1997). During the general debate, some participants were in favour of elaboration of the provision on individual criminal responsibility in order to prosecute and punish persons who committed crimes against cultural property, thus implementing Article 28 of the Convention which had proved insufficient. Others preferred to link this issue to the work of the International Law Commission or the United Nations Preparatory Committee on the Establishement of an International Criminal Court with the aim of avoiding duplication.

The discussion at the next *1998 Vienna Governmental Experts Meeting*[567] was based on two documents: 'Draft provisions for the revision of the 1954 Hague Convention and commentary from the UNESCO Secretariat'[568] and the 'Summary of comments received from the States Parties to the Hague Convention, the International Committee of the Red Cross and the International Council on Archives'.[569] We shall deal here with the draft provisions and comments received from States and international organizations during the commentary to each article of the Second Protocol.

The experts were less than unanimous on the issues of jurisdiction and responsibility, particularly those concerning the responsibility of States. The UNESCO Secretariat prepared the document based on the outcomes of several meetings of governmental experts, and particularly on the discussions that took place at the May 1998 Vienna Meeting: *Preliminary Draft Second Protocol*,[570] which was sent to the Member States and international organizations concerned for comments.

Based on their responses the UNESCO Secretariat and the Government of the Netherlands drew up the final draft of the Second Protocol: *Draft Second Protocol to the 1954 Hague Convention for the Protection of Cultural Property*

---

566 UNESCO, Third Meeting of the High Contracting Parties to the Convention for the Protection of Cultural Property in the Event of Armed Conflict (The Hague, 1954), UNESCO House, Paris, 13 November 1997. *Final Report.* CLT-97/CONF.208/3, Paris, November 1997. See also Hladik (1998b).

567 UNESCO, Meeting of Governmental Experts on the Revision of the Hague Convention for the Protection of Cultural Property in the Event of Armed Conflict of 1954. Vienna, 11–13 May 1998. UNESCO document Paris, May 1998, *Final Report.*

568 Draft provisions for the revision of the 1954 Hague Convention and commentary from the UNESCO Secretariat. CLT-97/CONF.208/2, Paris, October 1997.

569 UNESCO, Meeting of Governmental Experts. Summary of comments received from States Parties to the Hague Convention, the International Committee of the Red Cross and the International Council on Archives. UNESCO document Paris, March 1998.

570 *Preliminary Draft Second Protocol to the 1954 Hague Convention.* UNESCO document HC/1999/1, October 1998 (English, French and Russian).

in the Event of Armed Conflict (UNESCO doc. HC/1999/1/rev.1, February 1999). We shall return to this and other documents when commenting on the different provisions of Chapter 4.

The 1999 Hague Diplomatic Conference

The Diplomatic Conference on the Second Protocol to the Hague Convention of 1954 for the Protection of Cultural Property in the Event of Armed Conflict took place in The Hague from 15 to 26 March 1999.

Chapter 4 of the Protocol was discussed at the Plenary Session of the Conference on 18 March 1999. This session examined the draft provisions in document HC/1999/1/rev1. After the exchange of views on the draft Articles 18–23, an informal Working Group was created to work on reformulating the provisions of Chapter 4 in light of all the observations made. The Working Group was chaired by Professor Horst Fischer (Germany).[571]

The draft submitted to the Conference was substantially rewritten by the Working Group. In his presentation of the results of the Working Group, Fischer declared that national jurisdiction is dependent upon three elements:

* normative rules
* criminalizing violations, and
* concrete obligations of States to establish jurisdiction, particularly to try or to extradite.

On Wednesday, 24 March, two days before the end of the Conference, Fischer, as Chairman of the Working Group, informed the Plenary Session that, for the first time, 'cultural property has only now received its criminal law protection in particular with regard to cultural objects of universal value'. A balance had been painfully struck between the rights of the attacker and those of the defender (art. 18(1)(a) and (b)),[572] and the Hague Convention had been given the enforcement machinery that it had lacked. Certain offences had been criminalized, and the responsibility of States to try or to extradite had been emphasized. The Chairman of the informal Working Group on Chapter 4 made the following interpretative declaration: 'Nothing in this

---

571 The following documents were distributed to the Working Group on Chapter 4: the Chairman's Working Paper, 22 March 1999, 19.00 hours; Draft Articles prepared by the Working Group, HC/1999/5/Add.8, March 1999; Consensus text, Working Group on Chapter 4, 23 March 1999, 18.00 Hours; *Presentation of the results of the Working Group on Chapter 4*. H. Fischer, coordinator of the Working Group, 25 March 1999. HC/1999/INF.5, 3 p. Précis of the Conference, Wednesday, 24 March 1999.
572 This is Article 15(1)(a) and (b) of the Protocol.

Protocol, including Article 19, in any way limits the State's ability to legislate, criminalize or otherwise deal with any substantive offences including conduct addressed in this Protocol. Nothing in Article 19(2) should be interpreted as in any way affecting the application of Article 19(1)(a).'[573]

Consensus was reached, and the revised document was transmitted to the Drafting Committee and adopted on the last day by the Plenary Session.

Chapter 4 of the 1999 Protocol imposes on States Parties two distinct obligations:

- the first is to adopt legislative measures of a specifically penal nature, and
- the second is to adopt legislative and other measures that may include measures of a penal nature.

The first range of obligations are those attaching to the five 'serious violations' of the Protocol defined in Article 15(1). These obligations are to be found in Articles 15(2) to 19. The second set of obligations are those attaching to the two 'other violations' referred to in Article 21; they are to be found in Article 21 itself.[574]

Structure of Chapter 4

It is useful to say a few words about the structure of Chapter 4. Article 15 is the basic provision that defines serious violations directed against cultural property. It was followed immediately in the preparatory work by the provision concerning other violations. In the final stage, the Article concerning violations other than serious ones was placed at the end of Chapter 4 as Article 21. The reason for this was that several provisions concerning jurisdiction (art. 16), prosecution (art. 17), extradition (art. 18), mutual legal assistance (art. 19), and grounds for refusal (art. 20) were mostly directly related to serious violations, and it was logical to place these immediately after Article 15.

Certain doubts can be expressed, however, regarding the placement of Articles 18 and 19. It would probably be more logical to place the provision on mutual legal assistance (art. 19) before that of extradition (art. 18), because extradition is one of the forms of mutual legal assistance. In this case, Article 20 (concerning grounds of refusal) would have followed the provision of extradition, to which it is more closely connected. The authors had different views on this question, which we must certainly respect.

---

573 *Presentation of the results of the Working Group on Chapter 4.* H. Fischer, coordinator of the Working Group, 25 March 1999. HC/1999/INF.5, p. 3. Précis of the Conference, Wednesday, 24 March 1999, pp. 4–5.

574 O'Keefe (2002), pp. 4–5.

Article 15
SERIOUS VIOLATIONS OF THIS PROTOCOL

1. *Any person commits an offence within the meaning of this Protocol if that person intentionally and in violation of the Convention or this Protocol commits any of the following acts:*
    a. *making cultural property under enhanced protection the object of attack;*
    b. *using cultural property under enhanced protection or its immediate surroundings in support of military action;*
    c. *extensive destruction or appropriation of cultural property protected under the Convention and this Protocol;*
    d. *making cultural property protected under the Convention and this Protocol the object of attack;*
    e. *theft, pillage or misappropriation of, or acts of vandalism directed against cultural property protected under the Convention.*
2. *Each Party shall adopt such measures as may be necessary to establish as criminal offences under its domestic law the offences set forth in this Article and to make such offences punishable by appropriate penalties. When doing so, Parties shall comply with general principles of law and international law, including the rules extending individual criminal responsibility to persons other than those who directly commit the act.*

Preparatory works

Report by the Director-General on the Reinforcement of UNESCO's Action for the Protection of the World Cultural and Natural Heritage. UNESCO document 142 EX/15. Annex. The Hague Meeting of Experts on the application and effectiveness of the Convention for the Protection of Cultural Property in the Event of Armed Conflict (The Hague, 14 May 1954), *Final Report*, para. 6.3, p. 3. http://unesdoc.unesco.org/images/0009/000958/095820Eo.pdf

A working document prepared by the Secretariat, CLT/94/608/1 of 28 November 1994, p. 3.

UNESCO, Meeting of Governmental Experts. Summary of comments received from States Parties to the Hague Convention and from the International Council on Archives. UNESCO document CLT-96/CONF.603/INF.4, Paris, December 1996, p. 2.

Expert meeting on the review of the 1954 Hague Convention for the Protection of Cultural Property in the Event of Armed Conflict. Paris,

UNESCO Headquarters, 28 November–2 December 1994. UNESCO document CLT/CH/94/608/2, *Final Report*, pp. 4–5.

UNESCO, Meeting of Governmental Experts. Summary of comments received from States Parties to the Hague Convention and from the International Council on Archives. UNESCO document CLT-96/CONF.603/INF.4, Paris, December 1996.

Draft provisions for the revision of the 1954 Hague Convention and commentary from the UNESCO Secretariat. CLT-97/CONF.208/2, Paris, October 1997.

UNESCO, Meeting of Governmental Experts. Summary of comments received from States Parties to the Hague Convention, the International Committee of the Red Cross and the International Council on Archives. UNESCO document Paris, March 1998.

Preliminary Draft Second Protocol to the 1954 Hague Convention. UNESCO document HC/1999/1, October 1998 (English, French and Russian).

Draft Second Protocol to the 1954 Hague Convention for the Protection of Cultural Property in the Event of Armed Conflict. UNESCO document HC/1999/1/rev.1, February 1999 (original: English).

Presentation of the results of the Working Group on Chapter 4. H. Fischer, coordinator of the Working Group, 25 March 1999. Conference document HC/1999/INF.5.

Bibliography

Boylan, P. J. 1993. *Review of the Convention for the Protection of Cultural Property in the Event of Armed Conflict (The Hague Convention of 1954).* Paris: UNESCO, para. 9.1–9.25, pp. 91–98.

Cassese, A. 2003. *International Criminal Law.* Oxford: Oxford University Press.

Chamberlain, K. 2004. *War and Cultural Heritage.* Leicester: Institute of Art and Law, 2004, pp. 205–10.

Desch, T. 1999. The Second Protocol to the 1954 Convention for the Protection of Cultural Property in the Event of Armed Conflict. *Yearbook of International Humanitarian Law,* Vol. 2, pp. 79–82.

Henckaerts, J.-M. 1999. New rules for the protection of cultural property in armed conflict: the significance of the Second Protocol to the 1954 Hague Convention for the Protection of Cultural Property in the Event of Armed Conflict. *IRRC,* No. 835, pp. 593–620, here 613–15.

O'Keefe, R. 2002. *National Implementation of the Penal Provisions of Chapter 4 of the Second Protocol of 26 March 1999 to the Hague Convention of 1954 for the Protection of Cultural Property in the Event of Armed Conflict.* 29 March (UNESCO document CLT/CIH/MCO/2002/PI/H/1). (A French version is also available: *Mise en oeuvre nationale des dispositions pénales du chapitre 4 du deuxième Protocole relatif à la Convention de La Haye de 1954 pour la protection des biens culturels en cas de conflit armé.* Report edited by R. O'Keefe, Cambridge University, 29 March 2002.)

Schabas, W. A. 1997. Sentencing by international tribunals: a human rights approach. *Duke Journal of Comparative and International Law*, Vol. 7, p. 461.

Toman, J. 1996. *The Protection of Cultural Property in the Event of Armed Conflict: Commentary on the Hague Convention of 14 May 1954.* Aldershot: Dartmouth/Paris: UNESCO, pp. 59–66.

Statutes of the international criminal tribunals

Statute of the International Criminal Tribunal for the former Yugoslavia, adopted on 25 May 1993 by Resolution 827, as amended by Resolution 1166 (13 May 1998), Resolution 1329 (30 November 2000), Resolution 1411 (17 May 2002), Resolution 1431 (13 August 2002) and Resolution 1481 (19 May 2003); UN Doc. S/25704 as amended. http://www.un.org/icty/legaldoc-e/index.htm

Statute of the International Criminal Tribunal for Rwanda, adopted on 8 November 1994 by resolution of the UN Security Council S/RES/955 (1994), with numerous amendments. http://www.ictr.org/default.htm

Rome Statute of the International Criminal Court. (UN Doc. A/CONF.183/9*).[575]

---

575 Several corrections were made to the Statute. United Nations, *Treaty Series*, Vol. 2187, p. 3; depositary notifications C.N.577.1998. TREATIES-8 of 10 November 1998 and CN.604.1999. TREATIES-18 of 12 July 1999 [*procès-verbaux* of rectification of the original of the Statute (Arabic, Chinese, English, French, Russian and Spanish authentic texts)]; C.N.1075.1999.TREATIES-28 of 30 November 1999 [*procès-verbal* of rectification of the original text of the *Statute* (French and Spanish authentic texts)]; *C.N.266.2000. TREATIES-8 of 8 May 2000* [*procès-verbal* of rectification of the original text of the Statute (French and Spanish authentic texts)]; C.N.17.2001.TREATIES-1 of 17 January 2001 [*procès-verbal* of rectification of the Statute (authentic French, Russian and Spanish texts)]; C.N.765.2001.TREATIES-18 of 20 September 2001 (Proposals for corrections to the original text of the Statute (Spanish authentic text)] and C.N.1439.2001.TREATIES-28 of 16 January 2002 (*Procès-verbal*). http://www.un.org/law/icc/statute/romefra.htm

PREPARATORY WORK BEFORE THE 1999 HAGUE CONFERENCE

The UNESCO Draft presented to the 1954 Hague Conference considered that the Contracting Parties should take 'all necessary measures to prosecute and impose penal or disciplinary sanctions upon those persons . . . who committed or order to be committed a breach of the present Convention'. In order to meet the objections of certain States whose penal systems depend on the principles of public law – which the Draft was not intended to change – it was decided that States would undertake repressive measures only within the framework of their criminal jurisdiction.[576] The Hague Conference did not follow the progressive developments accomplished in the 1949 Geneva Conventions[577] by making these violations an international crime.

As a result, the 1954 Hague Conference adopted only a very modest provision on sanctions: Article 28,[578] which states:

> *The High Contracting Parties undertake to take, within the framework of their ordinary criminal jurisdiction, all necessary steps to prosecute and impose penal or disciplinary sanctions upon those persons, of whatever nationality, who commit or order to be committed a breach of the present Convention.*

As Jean-Marie Henckaerts put it, this Article remained 'a dead letter, mainly because it does not list the violations which require a criminal sanction. The experience of the ICRC Advisory Service on International Humanitarian Law proves that such a list is essential if a coherent and complete system of criminal repression of war crimes is to be instituted worldwide.'[579]

The first meeting of experts on the application and effectiveness of the Convention for the Protection of Cultural Property in the Event of Armed Conflict at The Hague in July 1993[580] required the strengthening of sanctions and suggested that:

---

576 *Records*, p. 314.
577 See the general introduction to this Chapter, p. 257 ff.
578 For more details, see the Introduction to the Chapter 4, pp. 265-267 above.
579 Henckaerts (1999), p. 613.
580 Report by the Director-General on the Reinforcement of UNESCO's Action for the Protection of the World Cultural and Natural Heritage. UNESCO document 142 EX/15, Annex: Hague Meeting of experts on the application and effectiveness of the Convention for the Protection of Cultural Property in the Event of Armed Conflict (The Hague, 14 May 1954), *Final Report*. http://unesdoc.unesco.org/images/0009/000958/095820Eo.pdf

attacks on cultural property were already defined as war crimes in the 1977 Protocol I to the Geneva Conventions of 1949, and that under the 1954 Convention State Parties were under an obligation to impose sanctions at national level on those who breach the Convention. It was suggested that such attacks should also be described as war crimes in The Hague Convention itself, for instance by formulating an additional instrument, such as a Protocol to the Convention. It was acknowledged that two aspects of the question of sanctions had to be taken into account: on the one hand the responsibility of the State for a violation of The Hague Convention, and on the other individual responsibility, in which case those involved should be prosecuted either by an international tribunal or by national tribunals.[581]

This was the basic mission which, according to the experts, should be followed in the process of review of the Convention.

The first draft of the legal provision, having as its purpose the initiation of this mission, was formulated at the Lauswolt Meeting of Experts, held in the small Dutch town of Lauswolt in February 1994.[582] Article 9, entitled 'Grave breaches', stated:

> Article 9 Grave breaches
> The extensive destruction, misappropriation or damage carried out wilfully or wantonly to cultural property specially protected by this instrument, contrary to the laws and customs of war, shall be regarded as a grave breach.

It also included an Article on other violations:

> Article 10 Other violations
> The following shall be regarded as violations of this instrument:
> (a) the theft, pillage or misappropriation or any other breach of integrity of cultural property protected by this instrument;
> (b) acts of vandalism directed against property protected by this instrument;

---

581 Ibid., para. 6.3, p. 3.
582 The Second Expert meeting on the 1954 Hague Convention for the Protection of Cultural Property in the Event of Armed Conflict. Lauswolt, The Netherlands, 9–11 February 1994.

(c) the export of cultural property from occupied territory or from a part of the territory of a State Party, without prejudice to the provisions of the 1954 Protocol;

(d) the extensive destruction or damage carried out wilfully or wantonly to cultural property, as defined in Article 1 of the Convention, contrary to the laws and customs of war.

This was a very different approach in comparison with Article 28 of the Convention. The violations committed against cultural property had to be identified in the international treaty and the perpetrators of such violations had to be prosecuted and punished. Two categories of violations had been established: grave breaches and other violations. This separation of the two categories was even better expressed in the drafts which follow.

In his report to the 145th Session of the Executive Board (1994) about the proposals of the Lauswolt meeting, the Director-General considered that these proposals 'need to be further discussed by technical, military and legal experts before any written proposal could be presented to the States Parties to the Convention for their consideration'. This was done at the 1994 Expert Meeting held in Paris, where:

'the participants generally agreed that much broader provisions should be formulated requiring the States Parties to implement their obligations, to establish jurisdiction and to prosecute. In particular, the experts agreed that it was extremely important that the States Parties should undertake to adopt adequate penal sanctions, seek to detain persons accused of violating the provisions of the Convention and to actively bring them to trial'. Some experts considered 'that there should be universal jurisdiction to serious crimes committed against cultural property'. The experts expressed their satisfaction that Article III of the Statute of the International Tribunal for the Prosecution of Persons Responsible for Serious Violations of International Humanitarian Law Committed in the Territory of the Former Yugoslavia reiterates *expressis verbis* in its paragraph (d) that 'seizure of, destruction or wilful damage done to institutions dedicated to religion, charity and education, the arts and sciences, historic monuments and works of art and science' constitute a violation of the laws or customs of war.' The experts thought it necessary to further clarify the notion of gravity of violations.[583]

Following the discussion at the 1997 Governmental Experts Meeting,[584] the Secretariat prepared two documents: 'Draft provisions for the revision of the 1954 Hague Convention and commentary from the UNESCO Secretariat'[585] and the 1996 *Summary of comments* received from the States and organizations. In this summary,[586] several comments insisted upon the need to include sanctions against deliberate destruction of immovable and movable cultural property, which should be considered as war crimes and fall under the jurisdiction of international or national tribunals. Grave breaches of the Convention should be subject to universal jurisdiction.

Following the discussion at the 1998 Vienna Governmental Experts Meeting,[587] the UNESCO Secretariat prepared a document based on

---

583 Expert meeting on the review of the 1954 Hague Convention for the Protection of Cultural Property in the Event of Armed Conflict. Paris, UNESCO Headquarters, 28 November–2 December 1994. UNESCO document CLT/CH/94/608/2 Final Report, pp. 4–5.

584 UNESCO, Meeting of Governmental Experts on the Review of the 1954 Hague Convention for the Protection of Cultural Property in the Event of Armed Conflict 1954, UNESCO Headquarters, Paris, 24–27 March 1997. *Final Report*. UNESCO document CLT-96/CONF.603/5, Paris, 30 April 1997.

585 Draft provisions for the revision of the 1954 Hague Convention and commentary from the UNESCO Secretariat. CLT-97/CONF.208/2, Paris, October 1997. In relation to Article 15, but also to Article 21, based on the previous Lauswolt proposal, the following Articles were adopted:
Article 6 (formerly Article 9): Grave breaches
1. The [extensive] destruction, misappropriation or *damage* carried out wilfully [or wantonly] to cultural property specially protected by this instrument, contrary to the laws and customs of war, shall be *regarded* as a grave breach.
Article 7 (formerly Article 10): Other violations
Violations of this instrument shall include but not be limited to:
   (a) Any form of theft, pillage or misappropriation of, any acts of vandalism directed against any illicit *purchase*, or any other breach of integrity of cultural property with *reference to both its form and its function*;
   (b) the illicit export or other illicit removal of cultural property from occupied territory or from a part of the territory of a State Party, but the dispositions of the 1954 Protocol, if in force, shall continue to apply;
   (c) the destruction or damage carried out wilfully or wantonly to cultural property, as defined in Article 1 of the Convention, contrary to the laws and customs of war.
In the discussion two other proposals were made: one concerning the archaeological excavations (as para. (d)), and breaches of the respect of persons engaged in the protection of cultural property (para. (e)).

586 UNESCO, Meeting of Governmental Experts. Summary of comments received from States Parties to the Hague Convention and from the International Council on Archives. UNESCO document CLT-96/CONF.603/INF.4, Paris, December 1996. As of 28 November 1996, the Secretariat has received replies from nine States of the total number of 88 States party to the Convention.

587 UNESCO, Meeting of Governmental Experts on the Revision of the Hague Convention for the Protection of Cultural Property in the Event of Armed Conflict of 1954. Vienna, 11–13 May 1998.

several meetings of government experts, and particularly on the discussions that took place at the May 1998 Vienna Meeting: the *Preliminary Draft Second Protocol*,[588] which was sent to the Member States and international organizations concerned for new comments.[589]

The following major comments were made before the beginning of the Conference. Austria required the definition of grave breaches, criminal liability for grave breaches, establishment of jurisdiction and a statement of the principle *aut dedere aut judicare*, a clear definition of other offences, and consequences for the commission of other offences mentioned. Australia preferred to remove the notion of grave breaches from the Draft Protocol and, for non-international armed conflict, would introduce an appropriate alternative called 'serious violations'. Germany thought that Articles 10–15 should be in line with existing instruments of international humanitarian law, including the Rome Statute of the International Criminal Court. The Syrian Arab Republic would combine Articles 10 and 11. Switzerland wished to delete the word 'wantonly' and to include intent in paragraph 2. The UK would reconsider the extensive treatment of criminal liability in Articles 10–13, having regard, *inter alia*, to the existing grave breach provision in Article 85(4)(d) of Protocol I.

UNESCO document Paris, May 1998, *Final Report*.

588 *Preliminary Draft Second Protocol to the 1954 Hague Convention*. UNESCO document HC/1999/1, October 1998 (English, French and Russian). The new draft, concerning Articles 15 and 21 of the Second Protocol, was formulated in the following way:
Article 10 Grave breaches
1. The wilful violation of the provisions of Article 8 [immunity under special protection] shall be regarded as a grave breach.
2. The extensive destruction, misappropriation or extensive damage carried out unlawfully and wantonly to cultural property shall be regarded as a grave breach.
Article 11 Other violations
Violations of this Protocol shall include but not be limited to:
a. Any form of theft, pillage or misappropriation of, any archaeological excavation, any acts of vandalism directed against, any illicit purchase, or any other breach of integrity of cultural property with reference to both its form and its function;
b. the illicit export or other illicit removal of cultural property from occupied territory or from a part of the territory of a State Party, but the dispositions of the 1954 Protocol, if in force, shall continue to apply;
c. the intentional destruction or damage of cultural property.
d. the commission of any acts of hostility directed against cultural property not justified by Article 3 [respect of cultural property];
e. the use of cultural property in support of military effort or as object of reprisals.

589 UNESCO, Summary of comments on Preliminary Draft Second Protocol to the 1954 Hague Convention received from High Contracting Parties to the Hague Convention for the Protection of Cultural Property in the Event of Armed Conflict 1954, other UNESCO Member States and international organizations, Paris, 15 January 1999.

On the basis of the responses from States, the UNESCO Secretariat and the Government of the Netherlands drew up the final draft of the Second Protocol: *Draft Second Protocol to the 1954 Hague Convention for the Protection of Cultural Property in the Event of Armed Conflict* (UNESCO doc. HC/1999/1/rev.1, February 1999), which constituted the basis of discussion at the 1999 Hague Diplomatic Conference.

Chapter 4 was still entitled 'Jurisdiction and responsibility [enforcement]', though this was later changed to 'Criminal responsibility and jurisdiction'.

Articles 18 and 19 were the basis for the final formulation of Articles 15 and 21 of the Second Protocol:

Article 18 Grave breaches

A person who
   a. wilfully, and in violation of this Protocol, commits a breach of the immunity of cultural property under enhanced special protection, or
   b. abuses the enhanced special protection of cultural property by using it for military purposes, or
   c. systematically destroys, misappropriates or damages cultural property, or
   d. unlawfully and wantonly destroys, misappropriates or damages cultural property causing extensive destruction, loss or damage to the cultural heritage of humanity,

or
   e. makes cultural property the object of reprisals has committed a grave breach of this Protocol.

Article 19 Other violations
1. Other violations of this Protocol include all those acts and omissions for which Parties or individuals are responsible and those which engage the liability of the parties to the conflict.
2. The Parties shall adopt all necessary legislative and administrative measures to give effect to this Protocol, in particular the penal legislation necessary to give effect to Article 18 [and Article 19] of this protocol.
[3. Parties shall adopt, whenever necessary, appropriate legislative and administrative measures.]

Discussion and drafting of Article 15 at the 1999 Hague Conference

The delegates that took the floor at the Plenary Session of the Conference agreed with the two-tier approach,[590] as expressed in the draft and which followed the method adopted by other instruments of humanitarian law and international criminal law. Several delegates considered this Article as important[591] and a 'difficult technical area'.[592] One group of States (France, Switzerland, the UK and the US) favoured provisions similar to those used in Protocol I (Art. 85), whereas other delegations wanted the Second Protocol linked to recent developments in international law, in particular international criminal law.[593]

The draft of Articles 15–21 based on the text submitted to the Conference was substantially rewritten by the Working Group under the chair of Professor Horst Fischer. The group also followed the recommendations of the Plenary Session of the Conference (which discussed this chapter on 18 March 1999).

Instead of the term 'grave breaches' used in the Geneva Conventions and Additional Protocols, the Working Group proposed the term 'serious violations of this Protocol', which was accepted by the Conference. The group's report was discussed on 24 March at the afternoon session. Introducing the report, the Chairman indicated that consensus was reached in the consideration of different aspects of international law, including cultural property, humanitarian and criminal law.

'The list of the serious violations was based on the proposals submitted by Austria and the ICRC to the Working Group on Chapter 4. This explains why it contains two types of violations'.[594]

ANALYSIS OF THE TEXT

Paragraph 1

The identification of crimes was included in paragraph 1 of Article 15 of the Protocol. The acts included in this paragraph were criminalized. According to

---

590 Germany, Greece, Italy, Sweden, Switzerland, Syria and the ICRC, in particular.
591 Austria calling it the most avant-garde chapter, Belgium, 1999 Hague Conference, Plenary Session, 24 March 1999, pp. 15–16.
592 Ibid., UK delegate, p. 15.
593 Desch (1999), p. 79.
594 Henckaerts (1999), p. 615.

the presentation of the Chairman of the Working Group, this point should be highlighted, 'as contrary to other recent events, we were not only able to reaffirm existing rules on international crimes but also to make certain objects of cultural property better protected, including those under enhanced protection, a term which has not yet been used in state practice.'[595]

According to the draft submitted to the Conference, serious violations of the Protocol can be committed by anybody, that is, any person. The following phrase specifies that this concerns only the field of the Second Protocol: 'an offence within the meaning of this Protocol'. Only those States that are Parties to the Protocol are specifically concerned and bound by this provision. The States Parties to the Convention that are not party to the Second Protocol are bound only by the modest provision of Article 28 of the Convention.

What kind of offences do we have in mind? Only offences which are committed:

- intentionally, and
- in violation of the Convention or this Protocol.

Intentionally, as used in this paragraph, refers to intentional and knowing behaviour, often described by the Latin expression *mens rea* (*actus non facit reum nisi mens sit rea*). The criminal act must be intentional, but there are different degrees and levels of intention in different national legal systems – in interpretation, practice, use and theory. The definition of crime and punishable violation involves two different aspects: objective and subjective.[596] Article 30 of the ICC Statute states in paragraph 1: 'Unless otherwise provided, a person shall be criminally responsible and liable for punishment for a crime within the jurisdiction of the Court only if the material elements are committed with intent and knowledge.' Paragraph 2 defines *intent* in the following way: 'For the purposes of this article, a person has intent where: (a) In relation to conduct, that person means to engage in the conduct; (b) In relation to a consequence, that person means to cause that consequence or is aware that it will occur in the ordinary course of events.' Intention 'should be distinguished from negligence where the result is foreseeable but the accused acts carelessly without having his mind on the act or its consequences. Such a case would not entail criminal responsibility but would be more appropriately dealt with by disciplinary sanctions'.[597]

---

595 *Presentation of the results of the Working Group on Chapter 4*. H. Fischer, coordinator of the Working Group, 25 March 1999. Conference document HC/1999/INF.5, p. 2.
596 Lee (2001), pp. 24–28.
597 Chamberlain (2004), p. 206.

Violations concern not only offences committed against the Protocol but also violations against the provisions of the Convention. Parties to the Protocol are also bound by the Convention.

The sub-paragraphs (a) to (e) indicate when such violations are committed against the Convention, and when they are committed against the Protocol:

- Sub-paragraphs (a) and (b) deal with violations against enhanced protection. Only the Second Protocol includes provisions on enhanced protection and these violations obviously concern the provisions of the Protocol alone.
- Sub-paragraph (c) and (d) are concerned with 'extensive destruction or appropriation' committed against protected cultural property and making such property an 'object of attack', and refer both to the Convention and the Second Protocol.
- The acts mentioned in sub-paragraph (e) are prohibited by the Convention and these prohibitions are not repeated in the Protocol. It refers only to the Convention where the violation was already expressed.

As Kevin Chamberlain rightly points out:

> Accordingly, where cultural property under enhanced protection has been made the object of an attack, an offence would not be committed if the attack fell within the conditions of paragraph 2 of Article 13, since such attack would not be in violation of the Convention or Protocol. Similarly, an attack on cultural property subject to general protection would not constitute an offence where 'imperative military necessity' can be invoked. Conversely, an attack on cultural property that did not fall within any of the exceptions of the Convention or Protocol, for example because the use of force was judged to be excessive, would be a violation of the Convention or Protocol but would not necessarily entail criminal responsibility unless done 'intentionally'. The question whether the attack was done 'intentionally' in any given case would depend on the evidence.[598]

As we have mentioned, the list of serious violations was established on the basis of the proposals of Austria and the ICRC, submitted to the Working Group. As one of the participants at the Working Group described it:

---

598 Ibid.

The first three violations correspond to what are called 'grave breaches' under the Geneva Conventions and Additional Protocol I, and are based on a proposal by Austria. States have a duty to try or extradite anyone charged with having committed any of these violations on the basis of universal jurisdiction. Specific and detailed provisions regulate the prosecution and extradition of offenders. According to the Chairman of the Working Group, from the point of view of international criminal law, these provisions are a major achievement as all elements to form a coherent system of prosecution and extradition are included.

With respect to the specific violations included in this category, it is interesting to note that the first two violations concern cultural property under enhanced protection, and that both an attack on and the use of such property or its immediate surroundings in support of military action are established as serious violations. Under Protocol I of 1977, only an attack on such property is defined as a grave breach and only insofar as it causes extensive destruction. The Second Protocol establishes a balance in criminalizing acts of both the attacker and the defender.

A proposal by the delegate from China to prohibit collateral damage to cultural property under enhanced protection was not acted upon. This would have been a significant improvement of the existing system. Since the Second Protocol requires parties to a conflict to refrain from any use of such property or its immediate surroundings in support of military action, such a rule could have fitted into the Second Protocol.[599]

The third serious violation concerns the destruction or appropriation of all cultural property, but the extensive nature of such acts make them serious violations on a par with grave breaches.[600]

The last two serious violations were added to the list at the suggestion of the ICRC. The reason for this was that these acts had been recognized as war crimes subject to criminal sanction in the Rome Statute of the International Criminal Court. As such, they could not be included in a general provision on 'other violations' which would only require States to suppress such acts without specifying the means of doing so. As indicated above, the experience of the ICRC has shown that the

599 Henckaerts (1999), p. 615.
600 Ibid., pp. 615–16 (footnotes omitted).

vagueness of the category of 'other violations' makes it very difficult to convince States that certain of those other violations are indeed war crimes which have to be penalized with a criminal sanction under domestic law.

These two serious violations amount to war crimes, but States only have the obligation to repress them by criminal sanctions using the most common grounds for jurisdiction, namely when the offence is committed in the territory of the State or when the alleged offender is a national of the State. There is no obligation to establish jurisdiction over cases where the alleged offence was committed abroad by a non-national, although States may exercise such jurisdiction.[601]

Distinction according to the character of the protected property

A distinction is made according to the character or sort of the cultural property: enhanced protection on the one hand, and general protection of cultural property on the other.

Violations directed against enhanced protection as provided in Chapter 3 of the Protocol

The first two sub-paragraphs refer exclusively to the new category of protection: *enhanced protection*. This is the case of sub-paragraph (a), which concerns the attacker:

> making cultural property under enhanced protection the object of attack,

and sub-paragraph (b), which concerns the *defender*:[602]

> using cultural property under enhanced protection or its immediate surroundings in support of military action.

The Working Group in its presentation of the draft stated that it created in these two paragraphs 'a balance in criminalizing acts of the attacker and

---

601 Ibid., p. 617 (footnotes omitted).
602 See also the explanation of Lyndel Prott (UNESCO Secretariat), 1999 Hague Conference, Plenary Session, 18 March 1999, p. 162.

the defender, a new development in humanitarian law, which only recently began and which takes into account the experience of actual conflicts in which objects were endangered by being used to protect military objectives.'[603]

Violations directed against general cultural property ('extensive destruction clause')

    c. extensive destruction or appropriation of cultural property protected under the Convention and this Protocol;

    d. making cultural property protected under the Convention and this Protocol the object of attack;

    e. theft, pillage or misappropriation of, or acts of vandalism directed against cultural property protected under the Convention.

Sub-paragraphs (c), (d) and (e) of paragraph 1 concern cultural property under general protection, as indicated, and formulate violations on the basis of existing law and give to them criminal law form. These paragraphs 'reaffirmed customary law'.[604]

Paragraph (c) and (d) cover the protection of cultural property in the Convention and the Protocol and formulate crimes committed against them. Paragraph (e) criminalizes acts committed in violation of the Convention, as such acts are prohibited by the Convention and are not repeated in the Second Protocol. It is naturally fully sufficient as all States Parties to the Protocol are also Parties to the Convention.

Another categorization may be made in relation to extradition or rather *'extradibility'* of persons alleged to commit crimes, as it is specified in Article 18 concerning extradition. Only criminals committing serious violations of sub-paragraphs (a), (b) and (c) are subject to extradition as mentioned in Article 18.

Even if the ICC Statute does not create a hierarchy of crimes *per se*, crimes against civilians are inherently more serious than offences against combatants, and some distinctions, like that concerning international and non-international armed conflicts will be confronted with 'a reluctance of States to permit international humanitarian law to encroach upon their sovereign domain, rather than any objective gradation in the seriousness of the crime'.[605] Nevertheless, a simple look at the offences enumerated in

---

603 *Presentation of the results of the Working Group on Chapter 4.* H. Fischer, coordinator of the Working Group, 25 March 1999. Conference document HC/1999/INF.5, p. 2.

604 H. Fischer, coordinator of the Working Group, Plenary Session, 24 March 1999, p. 11.

605 Schabas (2002b), p. 1507.

Article 15, paragraph 1 will permit such a distinction, already mentioned in the foregoing categorization of crimes, particularly the distinction between property protected by enhanced protection and generally protected cultural property.

A comparison can be made between Article 85, sub-paragraph (4)(d) of Protocol I, which defines grave breaches against cultural property,[606] and Article 8, sub-paragraph 2(b)(ix) of the ICC Statute:

> Although Article 85, subparagraph (4)(d) of Additional Protocol I and Article 8, sub-paragraph 2(b)(ix) of the ICC Statute go some way towards the criminalisation of serious violations of the laws and customs of war as they apply to the protection of cultural property, the offences in Article 15 are in a number of respects wider than these offences. In the first place, as regards Article 85(4)(d) offence, that offence only covers cases of armed conflict to which Additional Protocol I is applicable, namely international armed conflicts. Additional Protocol II (which applies to internal conflicts) contains a provision (Article 16) prohibiting acts of hostility directed against cultural objects and places of worship or using them in support of the military effort but unlike Additional Protocol I there is no provision making such acts 'grave breaches'.[607]

The Second Protocol and the ICC Statute apply to both categories of armed conflicts:

> A further difference is that the offences covered by Article 15 are more precisely defined, and acts that would constitute offences under Article 15 would not necessarily constitute offences under either Additional Protocol I or the ICC Statute. For example, it would not be an offence under Article 85(4)(d) for cultural property to be the object of an attack if the adverse Party is using the property in support of the military effort, or if the property is located in the immediate proximity of a military objective, nor if the attack caused damage that was not 'extensive'. Article 8 of the ICC Statute also would permit such an attack if the cultural property was a 'military objective'. As seen from the preceding chapters, the mere fact that cultural property

---

606 See pp. 307-308 above.
607 Chamberlain (2004), pp. 207–8.

is a military objective or its location is near a military objective, or it is used by the adverse Party in support of the military effort would not justify an attack. All the other conditions required by the Protocol must be present before an attack can be launched, namely that no feasible alternatives exist to secure a similar military objective, the attack must be proportionate etc. An intentional failure to comply with these more stringent conditions could give rise to an offence under Article 15 but not necessarily an offence under Additional Protocol I or the ICC Statute. Finally, there are a number offences covered by Article 15 that do not find any place either in Article 85 of Additional Protocol I or in the ICC Statute. It is not an offence under these provisions to use cultural property under enhanced protection or its immediate surroundings in support of military action, whereas the offence under Article 15 is regarded, along with the offences in sub-paragraphs (a) and (c) as of the utmost gravity, justifying under Article 16 the exercise of so-called universal jurisdiction. Nor is the offence covered in sub-paragraph (e) included in the offences covered by Additional Protocol I or the ICC Statute.[608]

Paragraph 2

If the first paragraph provided the identification of crimes, the second paragraph provides the *rationale* for this identification. Why have we identified these violations? What are the obligations of States when they become Party to the Protocol?

First phrase of paragraph 2

Each Party to the Protocol has the duty to 'adopt such measures as may be necessary':
1) to establish as criminal offences under its domestic law the offences set forth in this Article (Criminalization), and
2) to make such offences punishable by appropriate penalties.

---

608 Ibid.

Criminalization of serious violations

By stating that Parties to the Protocol may 'adopt such measure as may be necessary' leaves to the Party to the Protocol the freedom to adopt measures according to its own legislation or legal system. This is in some ways a response to a question the Thai delegate raised at the Plenary Session of the Conference:

> (...) the basic question was whether the sanctions provided for in the Second Protocol should be in more general terms, along the lines of Article 28 of the Convention. Difficulties may arise with a number of State Parties if the Second Protocol required them to adopt new legislative measures in order to implement its provisions. For example, in Thailand any international agreement which involves changes to territorial limits or requires legislations to be passed, must be submitted to parliament. For a number of countries this would be quite difficult and the result would be unpredictable.[609]

These measures are taken with the purpose of establishing that these violations and offences, mentioned in paragraph 1, become 'criminal offences under the domestic law'. It applies to all the offences defined in sub-paragraphs (a) to (e) of that Article. Only the degree of responsibility and culpability will differ according to the level of importance of the social damage.

Some authors complained about the lack of precision regarding the definition of offences in paragraph 1, which leaves to State Parties the task 'to make them sufficiently strict when establishing these offences as criminal offences under their domestic law in order to comply with the general principles of criminal law, in particular the principle *nullum crimen sine lege*'.[610]

Penalties

The following interesting guideline was given by Robert H. Jackson during the first international criminal prosecution after the Second World War:

> Punishment of war criminals should be motivated primarily by its deterrent effect, by the impetus which it gives to improved standards of international conduct and, if the theory of punishment is broad enough, by the implicit condemnation of ruthlessness and unlawful

---

609 1999 Hague Conference, Plenary Session, 18 March 1999, p. 161 (M. Wichiencharoen).
610 Desch (1999), pp. 80–81.

force as instruments of attaining national ends. The satisfaction of instincts of revenge and retribution for the sake of retribution are obviously the least sound basis of punishment. If punishment is to lead to progress, it must be carried out in a manner which world opinion will regard as progressive and as consistent with the fundamental morality of the Allied case.[611]

The first sentence of Article 15, paragraph 2 of the Second Protocol states: 'and to make such offences punishable by appropriate penalties'. Each State Party is obliged to adopt such appropriate penalties. The acts mentioned in paragraph 1 will not only be identified as serious violations and criminalized, but will be followed by an appropriate penalty.

To be deemed 'appropriate' compared with the serious character of the violations, 'the expectation is that the penalty to be prescribed should be on a par with the penalties for offences of a similar gravity under the criminal law of the Contracting party concerned.'[612]

Chamberlain adds that 'it should be noted there is nothing in the Protocol itself that would prevent a Contracting Party from prescribing the death penalty for the most serious violations of the Protocol', but he tempers this statement in a footnote: 'However, a State that imposed the death penalty would have some difficulty in securing the extradition of the offender from States that did not have the death penalty, unless the requesting State were able to give assurances that in the event of the offender being found guilty the death penalty would not be carried out'.[613]

We have serious doubts that even those who are not necessarily against capital punishment would include the death penalty among the penalties for material damage of even the most prestigious cultural values without the loss of life. As we know, the aim of the 1949 Geneva Conventions was not to regulate but rather to eliminate the death penalty, as was the case of the Universal Declaration of Human Rights and the International Covenant of Civil and Political Rights, especially its Second Protocol. The Statutes of the international criminal tribunals (ICTY, ICTR and ICC) exclude the death penalty, as does Protocol No. 13 of the European Convention of Human

---

611 Memorandum of Proposals for the Prosecution and Punishment of Certain War Crimes and Other Offenders, 1946; quoted in Bassiouni (1992), p. 14.
612 Chamberlain (2004), p. 208.
613 Ibid., p. 208 and n. 3.

Rights and Fundamental Freedoms of 3 May 2002, which abolishes it 'in all circumstances'.[614]

The determination of the penalty will be a matter decided by national legislators, judged in comparison with usual practice for the determination of penalties in other domestically punishable crimes. However, we can be confident that capital punishment will not be among them. In this respect, the spirit of the Second Protocol follows the practice established by recent international criminal courts (ICTY, ICTR, ICC), choosing not to establish the precise range of sanctions for specific offences and crimes, which is, on the contrary, the usual practice of national criminal codes. This has led some authors to the conclusion the requirements of the principle of legality may be doubted:

> The principle of legality not only stipulates that crimes have to be
> defined before the conduct in question was committed to be punishable
> – *nullum crimen sine praevia lege poenali*, which is often seen as the main
> element of the principle of legality – but also that punishment is clear
> beforehand: *nulla poena sine praevia lege poenali*. Not only no crimes,
> but also no punishments without previous law.[615]

As the author of this opinion states, the reverse argument of some authors is that 'this question was supposedly well settled at Nuremberg'.[616] The practice of determination of penalties will probably not change in the foreseeable future.

The recent development of international criminal law in the Statutes of the international criminal tribunals will be a good guide for national legislators. International practice cannot go far beyond respect of national sovereignty. International tribunals must be aware of national sensibility and Article 24 of the Statute of the ICTY is a good example.[617] When referring

---

614 See esp. Schabas (2002a).

615 Haveman, Kavran and Nicholls (2003), p. 64.

616 Schabas (1997), p. 469.

617 The penalties are included in the Statutes of the international criminal tribunals. Statute of the International Criminal Tribunal for the former Yugoslavia, art. 24 Penalties:

  1. The penalty imposed by the Trial Chamber shall be limited to imprisonment. In determining the terms of imprisonment, the Trial Chambers shall have recourse to the general practice regarding prison sentences in the courts of the former Yugoslavia.

  2. In imposing the sentences, the Trial Chambers should take into account such factors as the gravity of the offence and the individual circumstances of the convicted person.

  3. In addition to imprisonment, the Trial Chambers may order the return of any property and proceeds acquired by criminal conduct, including by means of duress, to their rightful owners.

to the determination of the sentence, it refers not only to 'the general practice regarding prison sentences in the courts of the former Yugoslavia'[618] to which the tribunal has to have recourse, but also to the return of the property and proceeds acquired by criminal conduct. '[Such] factors as the gravity of the offence and the individual circumstances of the convicted person' are taken into account. As crimes against cultural property were included in the Statute, the rules of the ICTY are a useful guide.[619]

The ICC Statute reserves Part 7 for Penalties. The most important are Articles 77 and 78. Article 77 states:

1. Subject to Article 110, the Court may impose one of the following penalties on a person convicted of a crime referred to in Article 5 of this Statute:
   (a) Imprisonment for a specified number of years, which may not exceed a maximum of 30 years; or
   (b) A term of life imprisonment when justified by the extreme gravity of the crime and the individual circumstances of the convicted person.
2. In addition to imprisonment, the Court may order:
   (a) A fine under the criteria provided for in the Rules of Procedure and Evidence;
   (b) A forfeiture of proceeds, property and assets derived directly or indirectly from that crime, without prejudice to the rights of bona fide third parties.

Rules of Procedure and Evidence states in the Rules 101 A and B: Penalties (Adopted on 11 February 1994, amended on 10 July 1998, amended on 1 December 2000 and on 13 December 2000) states:

(A) A convicted person may be sentenced to imprisonment for a term up to and including the remainder of the convicted person's life. (Revised on 12 November 1997).

(B) In determining the sentence, the Trial Chamber shall take into account the factors mentioned in Article 24, paragraph 2, of the Statute, as well as such factors as: (i) any aggravating circumstances; (ii) any mitigating circumstances including the substantial cooperation with the Prosecutor by the convicted person before or after conviction; (iii) the general practice regarding prison sentences in the courts of the former Yugoslavia; (iv) the extent to which any penalty imposed by a court of any State on the convicted person for the same act has already been served, as referred to in Article 10, paragraph 3, of the Statute. (Revised on 30 January 1995, amended on 10 July 1998).

618 It is interesting to note that the ICTY confirmed sentences as high as 40 years, but the prior legislation of Yugoslavia excluded life imprisonment and allowed only incarceration of 15–20 years. Schabas (2002b), p. 1508.

619 Statute of the International Criminal Tribunal for Rwanda (ICTR), art. 23, uses the similar formulation as the Statute of the ICTY. The Statute of the ICTR has no provision on the protection of cultural property.

As with the ICTY Statute, the ICC Statute refers for determination of the sentence to 'factors [such] as the gravity of the offence and the individual circumstances of the convicted person'. In cases where the person who committed the serious violations according to Article 15 of the Second Protocol is prosecuted and punished in the ICC, the aforementioned articles will apply to their punishment.

Views will certainly differ in different legal systems, as is already the case in academic writings. Roger O'Keefe considers it 'clear at least . . . that imprisonment is the only appropriate penalty for war crimes.[620] Fines and forfeiture alone are inappropriate, although they may be imposed in addition to a custodial sentence.'[621] [622] We do not think that it is necessary to adopt such a restrictive attitude. Both fines and forfeitures can be used in the domestic system, as they are used already at the international level.

We have to remain cognizant of the fact that during the drafting of rules in national legal systems, the legislators will be under the overwhelming influence of their own legal theory and practice; of its concept, history, legal culture and past experience. This was also the experience of the drafting of the Statutes and Rules of Procedure or Evidence of the international criminal courts, where the delegates of countries praised and underlined the merits of their own system in relation to and in comparison with other legal systems. This is probably also the reason why the provisions of the statutes remain very general and leave great discretion to the judges of the international courts.

Imprisonment will be the normal form of sanctions according to Article 15. The capital penalty is excluded. Additional forms of penalties, fines and forfeitures, even if accompanying the imprisonment, as required by the ICC Statute, may play a role as a response to certain specific crimes mentioned in Article 15. This is particularly the case for sub-paragraph (c) and (e) of Article 15 concerning the appropriation of cultural property or theft, pillage and misappropriation. This punishment is not new. The International Military Tribunal in Nuremberg could also 'deprive the convicted person of any stolen property and order its delivery to the Control Council for

---

620 See Rome Statute of the International Criminal Court (UN Doc. A/CONF.183/9, English text as corrected), art. 77(1); Statute of the International Criminal Tribunal for the former Yugoslavia (UN Doc. S/25704, Annex, as amended), art. 24(1); Statute of the International Criminal Tribunal for Rwanda (UN Doc. S/RES/955 (1994), Annex), art. 23(1). Note that these provisions all pertain to trial by international criminal tribunals (and, for that matter, by the specific tribunals in question). All the same, they are indicative of the principles one might expect to be embodied in analogous national legislation.
621 See ICC Statute, art. 77(2); ICTY Statute, art. 24(3); ICTR Statute, art. 23(3).
622 O'Keefe (2002), p. 6.

Germany'.[623] A fine was also authorized as Article 27 indicates that 'such other punishment as shall be determined by it to be just'.[624]

Fines and forfeiture are included in the ICC Statute, Article 77, paragraph 2 as an addition to imprisonment. Rule 147 of the Rules of Procedure and Evidence of the ICC states that 'a Chamber shall hear evidence as to identification and location of specific proceeds, property or assets which have been derived directly or indirectly from the crime.'[625]

The national lawmakers will decide themselves whether they will include these forms of punishment into the national legislation.

The determination of the sentence will be the decision of the court exercising the jurisdiction. The purpose of the sanction will 'include such aims as just punishment, deterrence, incapacitation of the dangerous and rehabilitation'.[626] The mitigating and aggravating circumstances will be an important balance in all cases. It is interesting to quote the proposal made by the Committee of French Jurists during the drafting of the ICTY Statute, which urged respect for:

> The fundamental principles of proportionality and individualization and suggested the Tribunal could consider the gravity of the offence (intention, premeditation, motives and goals of the perpetrator, state of mind, etc.), the values safeguarded by treating the act as serious crime (human dignity, right to life, right to physical and/or moral integrity, right to own property), the extent of harm caused (either actual or threatened, number of persons involved, value of property affected), as well as the personality of the offender, his or her background and personal situation, and his or her conduct following the offence.[627]

---

623 Agreement for the Prosecution and Punishment of Major War Criminals of the European Axis, and Establishing the Charter of the International Military Tribunal (IMT). *UNTS*, Vol. 82, p. 279, art. 28.

624 Ibid., art. 27.

625 Lee (2001), p. 569.

626 *Prosecutor v. Tadic.* IT-94-1-T, Sentencing Judgment, 14 July 1997.

627 Letter dated 10 February 1993 from the Permanent Representative of France to the United Nations Addressed to the Secretary-General, UN Doc. S/25266 (1993), para. 129–31; quoted in Schabas (2002b), pp. 1523–24.

Second sentence of sub-paragraph 2: General principles of law and
international law

As expressed by the words 'when doing so', the details concerning criminalization, that is, establishment of the criminal offence, and the punishment by appropriate penalties were left to the 'general principles of law and international law'. This is a form of instruction (not only advice) given by the Protocol (international treaty) to the Party to the Protocol ('shall comply' with the 'general principles of law and international law').

The delegates at the Hague Conference were not willing to include in the Protocol the rules that had been already extensively discussed in relation to the International Criminal Tribunals for the former Yugoslavia and Rwanda, and especially in the drafting of the ICC Statute. The presentation of the Working Group interprets this second sentence, stating that paragraph 2:

> makes reference to the well established principles of international criminal law such as command responsibility, without listing all the elements explicitly. This would have meant not only making this Chapter longer but also discussing in depth rules which have already been discussed in other forums recently and for which there exists almost universal consensus among states.[628]

Many delegates felt that there was no need to repeat the rules in a 'mini criminal code'.[629]

The first phrase of paragraph 2 uses the very general wording 'general principles of law and international law'. This is not referring to the principles of criminal law or international criminal law.

The draft submitted by the Chairman of the Working Group on 22 March 1999 used a different formulation: it referred to 'general principles of law, *including* international law with respect to the imputation of individual criminal responsibility under international humanitarian law *to persons other than those who directly commit the relevant act.*'[630] The Chairman's proposal was more explicit. It referred to the general principles of law – in other words,

---

628 *Presentation of the results of the Working Group on Chapter 4.* H. Fischer, coordinator of the Working Group, 25 March 1999. Conference document HC/1999/INF. 5, p. 2.

629 1999 Hague Conference, Plenary Session, 18 March 1999: W. H. Parks, US, p. 169. See Henckaerts (1999), p. 615.

630 Chairman's Working Paper, 22 March 1999, 19.00 Hours (document distributed to the members of the Working Group), p. 1 (In bold in the original text of the Chairman's Working Paper.)

to the principles of national legal systems concerning this issue. It refers to international law (and not to the principles of international law), though only to the part of international law that deals with criminal responsibility: 'with respect to the imputation of individual criminal responsibility under international humanitarian law' and therefore more particularly to the 1977 Additional Protocol I, which deals with the issues of secondary forms of responsibility ('to persons other than those who directly commit the relevant act').

According to the Chairman of the Working Group, some delegates nevertheless found this general reference to 'established principles of international criminal law'[631] to be broad and ambiguous. The delegate of Thailand even asked 'whether the phrase could be stopped after the words 'international law', which would naturally create even more ambiguity.[632] According to Horst Fischer:

> the majority of delegations found it useful to add the second part in order to make it clear what paragraph (2) was about. He said that the second part indicated to the reader that this paragraph dealt with the major developments in international criminal law in respect of command responsibility and others. He was of the view that even though it was broad it would not be harmful as it indicated the specific topic of Article.[633]

This reference helps us to understand the real sense and content of this provision. Nevertheless, if we limit interpretation of the text together with the reference to *travaux preparatoires*,[634] we can arrive at the conclusion that the general formulation was used probably because the drafters did not want to limit the reference to criminal law but also wanted it to include other rules of international law, particularly international humanitarian law and the international law of human rights. The reference to the general principles of international law may lead us to the conclusion that the authors also had in mind a reference to Part 3 of the Rome Statute on 'General principles

---

631 1999 Hague Conference, Plenary Session, 24 March 1999: H. Fischer (Working Group on Chapter 4), p. 11.

632 Ibid., p. 14.

633 Ibid., p. 17: the Finnish delegate stated that the last sentence 'included very specific language which was important to many delegations'.

634 The formulation of the phrase is sufficiently 'ambiguous or obscure' to allow us to have recourse 'to supplementary means of interpretation, including the preparatory works' (1969 Vienna Convention on the Law of Treaties, art. 32).

of criminal law'. These principles are based on the traditions of continental Europe and many other countries. We shall refer to these principles in the following considerations. These principles were also a result of previous experience with the Nuremberg principles and rules included in the ILC Draft Code of Crimes against Peace and Security of Mankind.

Individual criminal responsibility in the preparatory work for the review of the Convention and at the 1999 Hague Conference

The spirit of economy that directed the drafters in the final stage of the Conference to avoid formulation of a new 'mini-criminal code', as W. Hays Parks put it, does not prevent us from briefly mentioning this prior process of evolution. Rules on individual criminal responsibility were present in the drafts of the new instrument from the very beginning of the review process.

The first draft formulated at the Lauswolt Meeting of Experts included Article 8, on individual criminal responsibility.[635] Following the discussion at the 1997 Governmental Expert Meeting, the Secretariat prepared the 'Draft provisions for the revision of the 1954 Hague Convention and commentary from the UNESCO Secretariat',[636] which slightly improved on the Lauswolt

---

635 Article 8. Individual criminal responsibility
   1. Without prejudice to the Convention and its Protocol the commission of any [acts] in violation of the provisions of this instrument entails individual criminal responsibility.
   2. In relation to grave breaches under this instrument the planning preparation, initiation, ordering, commission, or otherwise aiding and abetting in the planning, preparation or execution of such breaches entails individual criminal responsibility.
   3. The official position of any accused person, whether as Head of State or Government or as a responsible Government official, shall not relieve such person of criminal responsibility nor mitigate punishment, for grave breaches under this instrument.
   4. Any [acts] prohibited under this instrument committed by a subordinate does not relieve a superior of criminal responsibility if he knew or had reason to know that the subordinate was about to commit such acts or had done so and the superior failed to take the necessary and reasonable measures to prevent such acts or to punish the perpetrators thereof.
   5. The fact that an accused person acted pursuant to an order of a Government or of a superior shall not relieve that person of criminal responsibility, but may be considered in mitigation of punishment.
   (The Second Expert Meeting on the 1954 Hague Convention for the Protection of Cultural Property in the Event of Armed Conflict. Lauswolt, The Netherlands, 9–11 February 1994.)
636 Draft provisions for the revision of the 1954 Hague Convention and commentary from the UNESCO Secretariat. CLT-97/CONF.208/2, Paris, October 1997. In relation to Article 15, but also to Article 21, based on the previous Lauswolt proposal, were adopted:
   Article 6. (formerly Article 9) Grave breaches
   1. The [extensive] destruction, misappropriation or *damage* carried out wilfully [or wantonly] to cultural property specially protected by this instrument, contrary to the laws and customs of war, shall be *regarded* as a grave breach.

document and included the new wording of paragraph 2 based on Article 7(1) of the ICTY Statute. This new wording introduced a new notion – an attempt to commit a violation, and by that, reinforced responsibility for violation (paragraph 3) and moved paragraph 7(2) of the Lauswolt draft to this Article as paragraph 7.[637]

Several comments were transmitted to the UNESCO Secretariat before the 1998 Vienna Meeting of Governmental Experts,[638] requesting more details and links to the Geneva Convention, the work of the International Law Commission and the preparation of the ICC Statute. The ICRC presented a new draft of the provision. More comments[639] were presented

---

Article 7 (formerly Article 10): Other Violations

Violations of this instrument shall include but not be limited to:

(a) Any form of theft, pillage or misappropriation of, any acts of vandalism directed against any illicit *purchase,* or any other breach of integrity of cultural property with *reference to both its form and its function*;

(b) the illicit export or other illicit removal of cultural property from occupied territory or from a part of the territory of a State Party, but the dispositions of the 1954 Protocol, if in force, shall continue to apply;

(c) the destruction or damage carried out wilfully or wantonly to cultural property, as defined in Article 1 of the Convention, contrary to the laws and customs of war.

In the discussion two other proposals were made: one concerning the archaeological excavations (as para. (d), and the breaches of the respect of persons engaged in the protection of cultural property (para. (e)).

637 Article 9. (formerly Article 8) Individual criminal responsibility

1. The commission of any violation of a provision of this instrument entails individual criminal responsibility.

2. A person who planned, instigated, ordered, committed or otherwise aided and abetted in the planning, preparation or execution of a grave breach [any violation of] this instrument, shall be individually responsible.

3. Any attempt in respect of acts referred to in para. (1) and (2) of this Article entails individual criminal responsibility.

4. The official position of any accused person, whether as Head of State or Government or as a responsible Government official, shall not relieve that person of criminal responsibility nor mitigate punishment for any grave breach under this instrument.

5. *The commission of any act* prohibited under this instrument by a subordinate *shall* not relieve a superior of criminal responsibility if the superior knew or had reason to know that the subordinate was about to commit the act or had done so and the superior failed to take the necessary and reasonable measures to prevent the act or to punish the perpetrators.

6. The fact that an accused person acted pursuant to an order of a Government or of a superior shall not relieve that person of criminal responsibility but may be considered in mitigation of punishment.

7. (formerly Article 7(2)) Prosecution of an individual for [a grave breach] [an act] under Article[s] . . . of this instrument shall not relieve a State Party of any responsibility under international law for an act or omission attributable to it.

638 UNESCO, Meeting of Governmental Experts on the Revision of the Hague Convention for the Protection of Cultural Property in the Event of Armed Conflict of 1954. Summary of comments received from States Parties to the Hague Convention, the ICRC, and from the ICA. Paris, March 1998. The comments were presented by Argentina, Croatia, Germany, Hungary and the ICRC.

639 UNESCO, Summary of comments on Preliminary Draft Second Protocol to the 1954 Hague Convention received from High Contracting Parties to the Hague Convention for the Protection of

on the Preliminary Draft Second Protocol.[640] On that basis the UNESCO Secretariat and the Government of the Netherlands drew up the final draft of the Second Protocol: *Draft Second Protocol to the 1954 Hague Convention for the Protection of Cultural Property in the Event of Armed Conflict* (UNESCO doc. HC/1999/1/rev.1, February 1999), which constituted the basis of discussion at the 1999 Hague Diplomatic Conference and included the text discussed at the Conference.[641]

The delegates at the Conference suggested following closely the ICC Statute on this issue, others considered the elaboration of a 'mini-criminal code' unnecessary as these are matters normally undertaken when setting up an international criminal court.[642] As we have seen, the Working Group abandoned this provision by making only a general reference to the 'general principles of law and international law'.

Rules extending individual criminal responsibility to persons other than those who directly commit the act

The 'general principles of law and international law' not only had to direct Parties in respect of criminalization and penalties, but also in terms of

---

Cultural Property in the Event of Armed Conflict 1954, other UNESCO Member States and international organizations, Paris, 15 January 1999.

640 *Preliminary Draft Second Protocol to the 1954 Hague Convention.* UNESCO document HC/1999/1, October 1998 (English, French and Russian).

641 Article 20 Individual criminal responsibility
   1. A person who violates [a provision of this Protocol] [Article 18] shall be individually responsible.
   2. A person who plans, instigates, orders, commits or otherwise aids and abets the planning, preparation or execution of any violation of this Protocol, shall be individually responsible.
   3. Any attempt in respect of acts referred to in para. (1) and (2) of this Article entails individual criminal responsibility.
   4. The official position of any accused person, whether as Head of State or Government or as a responsible Government official, shall not relieve that person of criminal responsibility nor mitigate punishment for any violation under this Protocol.
   5. The commission of any act prohibited under this Protocol by a subordinate shall not relieve a superior of criminal responsibility if the superior knew or, owing to the circumstances at the time, should have known that the subordinate was committing or about to commit the act or had done so and the superior failed to take the necessary and reasonable measures to prevent or repress the act or to punish the perpetrators.
   6. The fact that an accused person acted pursuant to an order of a Government or of a superior shall not relieve that person of criminal responsibility but may be considered in mitigation of punishment.
   7. No provision in this Protocol relating to individual criminal responsibility shall affect the responsibility of States under international law.

642 1999 Hague Conference, Plenary Session, 18 March 1999: W. H. Parks, US, pp. 169–70. Similarly, the UK delegate found it 'not necessary to invent a new criminal code'. Ibid., p. 182.

establishing rules concerning degree of responsibility and involvement in acts of violence – as well as various forms of conduct, by stating that the reference also includes 'the rules extending individual criminal responsibility to persons other than those who directly commit the act'. The drafters wanted to cover not only those who commit the offence, but also all other forms of criminal responsibility.

These secondary forms of criminal responsibility can be derived from different national legal systems, the experience and traditions of international criminal tribunals following the Second World War, recent experience with the ICTY and ICTR and, in particular, the ICC.[643] Some authors felt that the lack of specific definition for categories of persons left an element of uncertainty.[644]

Primary responsibility: direct commission of the offence

The primary form of criminal responsibility in national systems of criminal law and international criminal law is commission of the offence, 'those who directly commit the act' (as also mentioned in art. 15, para. 2, second phrase).

This form of responsibility is included in Article 25(3)(a)[645] of the Rome Statute:

> In accordance with this Statute, a person shall be criminally responsible and liable for punishment for a crime within the jurisdiction of the Court if that person:
> (a) Commits such a crime, whether as an individual, jointly with another or through another person, regardless of whether that other person is criminally responsible.

Perpetration of the offence is committed either by individuals, jointly with other persons (more than one person working together), or through indirect perpetratorship.

---

643 1999 Hague Conference, Plenary Session, 24 March 1999: Italian delegate referring to Articles 25 and 28 of the ICC Statute, p. 18.

644 Chamberlain (2004), pp. 209–10: 'However, in view of the fact that the Conference did not consider it necessary to elaborate further on Article 23(3) of the ICC Statute, it would be reasonable to argue that in implementing paragraph 2 of Article 15, Contracting Parties should cast the net as widely as possible and include, as a minimum, all the participants in the offence listed in Article 25 (3).'

645 See also the Statutes of ICTY (Article 7(1)) and ICTR (Article 6(1)).

Secondary, auxiliary criminal responsibility of persons other than those who directly commit the act

Instigation (*complicité par instigation*) (Article 25(3)(b) of the Rome Statute)[646]

> (b) Orders, solicits or induces the commission of such a crime which in fact occurs or is attempted.

Instigation must remain connected to the main crime. It is a form of inducement, encouragement or persuasion. No special intent is required and general provision of Article 30 of the ICC Statute must be observed. The intent of the instigator must be concretely directed at a certain crime and perpetrator.

Aiding, Abetting or Otherwise Assisting (*complicité par aide et assistance*) (Article 25(3)(c) of the Rome Statute)[647]

> (c) For the purpose of facilitating the commission of such a crime, aids, abets or otherwise assists in its commission or its attempted commission, including providing the means for its commission.

Classical complicity by assistance does not reach the level of instigation. It is also accessorial to the main crimes. Preparatory contribution remains unpunishable if the intended principal crime is not carried out.

Complicity in group (Article 25 (3) (d) of the Rome Statute)[648]

> (d) In any other way contributes to the commission or attempted commission of such a crime by a group of persons acting with a common purpose. Such contribution shall be intentional and shall either: (i) Be made with the aim of furthering the criminal activity or criminal purpose of the group, where such activity or purpose involves the commission of a crime within

---

646 Eser (2002), pp. 795–98.
647 Ibid., pp. 798–801.
648 Ibid., pp. 802–7.

the jurisdiction of the Court; or (ii) Be made in the knowledge of the intention of the group to commit the crime.

This form of participation, close to the concept of conspiracy of the Nuremberg Trials,[649] finds its expression in the International Convention of the Suppression of Terrorist Bombings.[650]

Most legal systems will consider that all participants in a common criminal action are equally responsible if these two conditions are realized.[651]

Attempt and abandonment (Article 25 (3) (f) of the Rome Statute)[652]

> (f) Attempts to commit such a crime by taking action that commences its execution by means of a substantial step, but the crime does not occur because of circumstances independent of the person's intentions. However, a person who abandons the effort to commit the crime or otherwise prevents the completion of the crime shall not be liable for punishment under this Statute for the attempt to commit that crime if that person completely and voluntarily gave up the criminal purpose.

Omission

Legal provisions after the Second World War did not refer to omission, but some criminals were convicted for omissions on the basis of Article 1 of the 1907 Hague Regulations, which provides that members of the armed forces must 'be commanded by a person responsible for his subordinates'.

Article 86(1) of the 1977 Additional Protocol I, entitled 'Failure to act', states:

---

649 Articles 9 and 10 of the Charter of the International Military Tribunal. See Schindler and Toman (2004), p. 1257.
650 UN Doc. A/RES/52/164 (1998), annex. Article 2(3(c)): 'In any other way contributes to the commission of one or more offences as set forth in paragraph 1 or 2 of the present Article by a group of persons acting with a common purpose; such contribution shall be intentional and either be made with the aim of furthering the general criminal activity or purpose of the group or be made in the knowledge of the intention of the group to commit the offence or offences concerned'.
651 Cassese (2003), pp. 181–88.
652 Eser (2002), pp. 807–18.

1. The High Contracting Parties and the Parties to the conflict shall repress grave breaches, and take measures necessary to suppress all other breaches, of the Conventions or of this Protocol which result from a failure to act when under a duty to do so.

As the ICRC commentary indicates, there are several provisions of the Convention and in particular of Protocol I that state that many breaches may be committed simply by a failure to act.[653] Article 86 was adopted by the Committee and the Plenary Session of the Geneva Conference by consensus. But as the ICRC commentary indicates, 'determining the limits of responsibility for acts of omission gives rise to a number of problems of criminal law which have not been yet resolved.'[654]

The situation at the drafting of the statutes of the international criminal tribunals was no better. Regulations of omission were included neither in the ICTY nor in the ICTR Statutes. No provision is made in the Rome Statute. But the Draft Statute and Draft Final Act, proposed by the Preparatory Committee, contained the general regulation of omission and the Model Draft Statute recommended the following definition: 'Conduct . . . can constitute either an act or an omission, or a combination thereof', criminal responsibility for the result of an omission to act is given only 'if person was under a legal obligation to avoid that result'.[655] But this definition was not included in the final text of the Statute. We find reference to the omission in some decisions of the Tribunals, such as in the judgments of the ICTY.[656]

International criminal liability may arise not only as a result of a positive act or conduct (killing of an enemy civilian, unlawfully destroying works of art, etc.) but also from an omission that is failure to take action. Omission is only criminalized when the law imposed a clear

---

653 Commentary on the Additional Protocols, para. 3534–36, pp. 1008–9.

654 Ibid., para. 3527, p. 1007. This Commentary indicates in a note: On this subject, see 'Le projet de code pénal international, commentaires', *Revue internationale de droit pénal*, 1981, pp. 553–56. A distinction is made in particular between 'infractions d'omission proprement dites', 'les infractions de commission par omission' and 'la conduite omissive et participation'.

655 Eser (2002), p. 819.

656 In the case of Kunarac, Kovac and Vukovic, the Tribunal stated: '390. An individual can be said to have "committed" a crime when he or she physically perpetrates the relevant criminal act or engenders a culpable omission in violation of a rule of criminal law. There can be several perpetrators in relation to the same crime where the conduct of each one of them fulfills the requisite elements of the definition of the substantive offence.' (Kunarac et al. (IT-96-23&23/1) 'Foca', Trial Chamber, Judgment, 22 February 2001, para. 390). See also *Tadic*, IT-94-1, Appeals Chamber, Judgment, 15 July 1999, para 188. See also the judgments of the ICTR: Rutaganda, ICTR-96-3, Trial Chamber, Judgment, 6 December 1999, para. 41.

obligation to act and the person wilfully or recklessly failed to do what was legally required.[657]

Superior responsibility

Several decisions after the Second World War were based on the doctrine of superior responsibility.[658] National military laws also include the principle of superior responsibility.[659] But most the important provisions are Articles 86 and 87 of Additional Protocol I and Article 28 of the Rome Statute:

> Responsibility of commanders and other superiors:
> In addition to other grounds of criminal responsibility under this Statute for crimes within the jurisdiction of the Court:
> 1. A military commander or person effectively acting as a military commander shall be criminally responsible for crimes within the jurisdiction of the Court committed by forces under his or her effective command and control, or effective authority and control as the case may be, as a result of his or her failure to exercise control properly over such forces, where:
>   (a) That the military commander or person either knew or, owing to the circumstances at the time, should have known that the forces were committing or about to commit such crimes; and
>   (b) That military commander or person failed to take all necessary and reasonable measures within his or her power to prevent or repress their commission or to submit the matter to the competent authorities for investigation and prosecution.
> 2. With respect to superior and subordinate relationships not described in paragraph 1, a superior shall be criminally responsible for crimes within the jurisdiction of the Court committed by subordinates under his or her effective authority and control, as a result of his or her failure to exercise control properly over such subordinates, where:

657 Cassese (2003), p. 200.
658 Ambos (2002), pp. 823–32.
659 Ibid., pp. 841–43.

(a) The superior either knew, or consciously disregarded information which clearly indicated that the subordinates were committing or about to commit such crimes;

(b) The crimes concerned activities that were within the effective responsibility and control of the superior; and

(c) The superior failed to take all necessary and reasonable measures within his or her power to prevent or repress their commission or to submit the matter to the competent authorities for investigation and prosecution.

We should also remember that Article 28 of the 1954 Hague Convention already includes prosecution and punishment for breaches of the Convention, not only for those who commit the breach but also for those who give the order to commit such breaches.

Non-prescriptibility[660]

The fear that German war criminals of the Second World War might escape prosecution because of the expiration of the period of limitation applicable to their crimes resulted in the adoption of two conventions: the Convention on the Non-applicability of Statutory Limitations to War Crimes and Crimes Against Humanity, adopted by Resolution 2391 (XXIII) of the UN General Assembly on 26 November 1968, and the European Convention on the Non-applicability of Statutory Limitations to Crimes against Humanity and War Crimes, opened for signature at Strasbourg on 25 January 1974. The number of ratifications remained modest.[661]

> It is difficult to suggest that customary international law prohibits statutory limitations in respect of all international crimes in the light of the silence of multilateral treaties creating international crimes on this subject. The position is different in the case of 'core' crimes of genocide, war crimes, crimes against humanity, and aggression. There is support for the view that the prohibitions on these crimes constitute norms of *ius cogens*, and that a necessary consequence of such a characterization is the inapplicability of statutory limitations.[662]

---

660 Van den Wyngaert and Dugard (2002), pp. 873–88.
661 On 1 October 2009, 53 States parties to the United Nations Convention, and five States Parties to the European Convention.
662 Van den Wyngaert and Dugard (2002), p. 887.

The authors consider arguable the assertion that Article 29 of the Rome Statute reflects customary international law.

Article 29 of the Rome Statute includes the provision on non-applicability of the statute of limitations: *The crimes within the jurisdiction of the Court shall not be subject to any statute of limitations.*

Article 16
JURISDICTION

1. *Without prejudice to paragraph 2, each Party shall take the necessary legislative measures to establish its jurisdiction over offences set forth in Article 15 in the following cases:*
   a. *when such an offence is committed in the territory of that State;*
   b. *when the alleged offender is a national of that State;*
   c. *in the case of offences set forth in Article 15 sub-paragraphs (a) to (c), when the alleged offender is present in its territory.*
2. *With respect to the exercise of jurisdiction and without prejudice to Article 28 of the Convention:*
   a. *this Protocol does not preclude the incurring of individual criminal responsibility or the exercise of jurisdiction under national and international law that may be applicable, or affect the exercise of jurisdiction under customary international law;*
   b. *except in so far as a State which is not Party to this Protocol may accept and apply its provisions in accordance with Article 3 paragraph 2, members of the armed forces and nationals of a State which is not Party to this Protocol, except for those nationals serving in the armed forces of a State which is a Party to this Protocol, do not incur individual criminal responsibility by virtue of this Protocol, nor does this Protocol impose an obligation to establish jurisdiction over such persons or to extradite them.*

Preparatory works

Report by the Director-General on the Reinforcement of UNESCO's Action for the Protection of the World Cultural and Natural Heritage. UNESCO document 142 EX/15, Annex: Hague Meeting of experts on the application and effectiveness of the Convention for the Protection of Cultural Property in the Event of Armed Conflict (The Hague, 14 May 1954), *Final Report*, para. 6.3, p. 3. http://unesdoc.unesco.org/images/0009/000958/095820Eo.pdf

A working document prepared by the Secretariat, CLT/94/608/1 of 28 November 1994, p. 3.

UNESCO, Meeting of Governmental Experts. Summary of comments received from States Parties to the Hague Convention and from the International Council on Archives. UNESCO document CLT-96/CONF.603/INF.4, Paris, December 1996, p. 2

Expert Meeting on the review of the 1954 Hague Convention for the Protection of Cultural Property in the Event of Armed Conflict. Paris, UNESCO Headquarters, 28 November–2 December 1994. UNESCO document CLT/CH/94/608/2, *Final Report*, pp. 4–5.

UNESCO, Meeting of Governmental Experts. Summary of comments received from States Parties to the Hague Convention and from the International Council on Archives. UNESCO document CLT-96/CONF.603/INF.4, Paris, December 1996.

Draft provisions for the revision of the 1954 Hague Convention and commentary from the UNESCO Secretariat. UNESCO document CLT-97/CONF.208/2, Paris, October 1997.

UNESCO, Meeting of Governmental Experts. Summary of comments received from States Parties to the Hague Convention, the International Committee of the Red Cross and the International Council on Archives. UNESCO document Paris, March 1998.

Preliminary Draft Second Protocol to the 1954 Hague Convention. UNESCO document HC/1999/1, October 1998 (English, French and Russian).

Draft Second Protocol to the 1954 Hague Convention for the protection of cultural property in the event of armed conflict. UNESCO document HC/1999/1/rev.1, February 1999 (original: English).

Presentation of the results of the Working Group on Chapter 4. H. Fischer, coordinator of the Working Group, 25 March 1999. Conference document HC/1999/INF.5.

1999 Hague Conference. Plenary Sessions. 18 March 1999 and 24 March 1999. Electronic version. Full text proceedings, part 2.

Bibliography

Boylan, P. J. 1993. *Review of the Convention for the Protection of Cultural Property in the Event of Armed Conflict (The Hague Convention of 1954).* Paris: UNESCO, para. 9.1–9.25, pp. 91–98.

Chamberlain, K. 2004. *War and Cultural Heritage.* Leicester: Institute of Art and Law, pp. 210–11.

Desch, T. 1999. The Second Protocol to the 1954 Convention for the Protection of Cultural Property in the Event of Armed Conflict. *Yearbook of International Humanitarian Law*, Vol. 2, p. 81.

Henckaerts, J.-M. 1999. New rules for the protection of cultural property in armed conflict: the significance of the Second Protocol to the 1954 Hague

Convention for the Protection of Cultural Property in the Event of Armed Conflict. *IRRC*, No. 835, pp. 593–620, here 613–15.

O'Keefe, R. 2002. *National Implementation of the Penal Provisions of Chapter 4 of the Second Protocol of 26 March 1999 to the Hague Convention of 1954 for the Protection of Cultural Property in the Event of Armed Conflict.* 29 March (UNESCO document CLT/CIH/MCO/2002/PI/H/1).

Statutes of the international criminal tribunals

See the documentation under the commentary to Article 15.

PREPARATORY WORK BEFORE THE 1999 HAGUE CONFERENCE

Article 28 of the 1954 Hague Conference stated that 'the High Contracting Parties undertake to take, within the framework of their ordinary criminal jurisdiction, all necessary steps to prosecute and impose penal or disciplinary sanctions upon those persons, of whatever nationality, who commit or order to be committed a breach of the present Convention.'

As previously mentioned, this provision had very limited application and remained within the framework of ordinary criminal jurisdiction, not extending prosecution for crimes committed outside national territory by a non-national.

The need to improve this situation as part of the review process was affirmed from the beginning, at the first meeting of experts on the application and effectiveness of the Convention for the Protection of Cultural Property in the Event of Armed Conflict at The Hague in July 1993. The experts requested the establishment of 'individual responsibility, in which case those involved should be prosecuted either by an international tribunal or by national tribunals.'[663]

The first draft of the legal provision had for its purpose to implement this task. The document drafted at the Lauswolt Meeting of Experts in February 1994 included Article 6, entitled 'Jurisdiction', which stated:

---

663 Report by the Director-General on the Reinforcement of UNESCO's action for the Protection of the World Cultural and Natural Heritage. UNESCO document 142 EX/15, Paris, 18 August 1993; Annex: Meeting of experts on the application and effectiveness of the Convention for the Protection of Cultural Property in the Event of Armed Conflict (The Hague, 14 May 1954), *Final Report*, para. 6.3, p. 3. http://unesdoc.unesco.org/images/0009/000958/095820Eo.pdf

1. States Parties undertake to prosecute, bring to trial and punish, persons present in their territory responsible for, or accused of, [the acts] defined in Article[s] . . . of this instrument.
2. To that end States Parties shall adopt, whenever necessary, appropriate legislative and administrative measures.
3. Persons charged with [the acts] enumerated in Article [s] . . . of this instrument may be tried by a competent court of any State Party which may acquire jurisdiction over the person of the accused or by an international tribunal as may have jurisdiction.[664]
4. State Party in whose territory a person alleged to have committed a grave breach under Article[s] . . . of this instrument is present shall either try or extradite that person.
5. The provisions of paragraph 3 do not prejudice the establishment and the jurisdiction of an international tribunal.[665]

This was a substantial development in comparison with Article 28, corresponding to the new era in international criminal law that began in the early 1990s.

Further deliberation by experts was required by the 145th Session of the Executive Board (1994) and a further Expert Meeting was held in Paris in 1994. The UNESCO Secretariat prepared a working document based on the previous reports and meetings, which showed the growing tendency and support for universal jurisdiction in relation to war crimes.[666] The draft Article from Lauswolt 'is still less onerous than the current obligation to repress piracy, according to which States have jurisdiction not only over accused within their territory, but over such persons wherever taken. However, it is notable that the jurisdiction proposed is not restricted to persons of the nationality of one of the Contracting States.'[667] At the 1994 Paris Expert Meeting, 'the participants generally agreed that much broader provisions should be formulated requiring the States Parties to implement their obligations, to establish jurisdiction and to prosecute.' Some experts considered 'that there

---

664 An attempt to make a general universal jurisdiction.
665 The ILC prepared the draft Code of Crimes against Peace and Security of Mankind and the draft Statute for an international criminal court. See UN (1996), p. 149.
666 Bassiouni (1983), p. 308; Prott (1983).
667 UNESCO document a working document prepared by the Secretariat, CLT/94/608/1 of 28 November 1994, p. 11.

should be universal jurisdiction for serious crimes committed against cultural property.'[668]

At the 1997 Governmental Experts Meeting[669] a number of participants were in favour of giving jurisdiction over such crimes to the ICC, which was in the process of being created by the UN, and emphasized that the punishment of offenders committing crimes against cultural property during armed conflicts should be in the interest of the whole international community.[670] The revised Lauswolt document distributed at the closure of the Expert Meeting[671] only incorporated paragraph 5 of the Lauswolt document into paragraph 3.[672]

After the 1998 Vienna Governmental Expert Meeting,[673] the UNESCO Secretariat prepared a draft based on several meetings of government experts, and particularly on the discussions that took place at the May 1998 Vienna

---

668 Expert meeting on the Review of the 1954 Hague Convention for the Protection of Cultural Property in the Event of Armed Conflict. Paris, UNESCO Headquarters, 28 November–2 December 1994. UNESCO document CLT/CH/94/608/2. *Final Report*, pp. 4–5.

669 UNESCO, Meeting of Governmental Experts on the Review of the 1954 Hague Convention for the Protection of Cultural Property in the Event of Armed Conflict 1954, UNESCO Headquarters, Paris, 24–27 March 1997. *Final Report*. UNESCO document CLT-96/CONF.603/5, Paris, 30 April 1997.

670 Ibid., para. 18, p. 3.

671 Draft provisions for the revision of the 1954 Hague Convention and commentary from the UNESCO Secretariat. CLT-97/CONF.208/2, Paris, October 1997.

672 '3. Persons charged with [the acts] enumerated in Article[s] . . . of this instrument may be tried by a competent court of any State Party which may acquire jurisdiction over the accused or by any international tribunal which *may* have jurisdiction. *This does not preclude the jurisdiction of any international tribunal which may be established.*'

673 UNESCO, Meeting of Governmental Experts on the Revision of the Hague Convention for the Protection of Cultural Property in the Event of Armed Conflict of 1954. Vienna, 11–13 May 1998. UNESCO document Paris, May 1998, *Final Report*. The summary of comments received from States Parties, ICRC and the International Council on Archives submitted to the 1998 Vienna Expert meeting included mainly the following: *Austria* underlined the overlap of paragraphs 1 and 4. *France* considered the Article incompatible with French national legislation. *Germany* reiterated the need to improve the possibilities of prosecution in the new instrument and recommended a linkage with the Geneva Conventions. *Israel* questioned the whole concept of universal jurisdiction and particularly the extension of jurisdiction to a State Party to the new instrument or an international tribunal which may have jurisdiction. It would prefer to omit the possibility of extradition. *Mexico* underlined the importance of Article 28 of the Convention on sanctions and would like to have included a provision on the way in which a good faith purchaser would receive compensation for an object surrendered under Article 1(4) of the existing Protocol. (UNESCO, Meeting of Governmental Experts on the Revision of the Hague Convention for the Protection of Cultural Property in the Event of Armed Conflict of 1954. Vienna, 11–13 May 1998. UNESCO document, *Summary of comments received from States Parties to The Hague Convention, the International Committee of the Red Cross and the International Council on Archives*. Paris, March 1998, p. 6.)

Meeting: *Preliminary Draft Second Protocol*.[674] The draft was sent to Member States and international organizations for a new round of comments.[675]

On the basis of these responses, the UNESCO Secretariat and the Government of the Netherlands drew up the final draft of the Second Protocol: *Draft Second Protocol to the 1954 Hague Convention for the Protection of Cultural Property in the Event of Armed Conflict* (UNESCO doc. HC/1999/1/rev.1, February 1999), which was presented to the 1999 Hague Diplomatic Conference.

Chapter 4 was still entitled 'Jurisdiction and responsibility [enforcement]', though it was later changed to 'Criminal responsibility and jurisdiction'.

Article 16 [21 in the draft] was presented to the Conference with the following wording:

Article 16 [21] Jurisdiction
1. A Party on whose territory a person alleged to have committed a grave breach under Article 18 of this Protocol is present shall search for that person and either bring to trial or extradite that person.
2. Parties undertake to [prosecute, bring to trial and punish persons responsible for, or accused of, the acts defined in Article 19] [repress other violations] of this Protocol.

---

674 *Preliminary Draft Second Protocol to the 1954 Hague Convention*. UNESCO document HC/1999/1, October 1998 (English, French and Russian).

675 UNESCO, Synoptic report of comments on the Preliminary Draft Second Protocol to the 1954 Hague Convention received from High Contracting Parties to the Hague Convention for the Protection of Cultural Property in the Event of Armed Conflict 1954, other UNESCO Member States and international organizations, Paris, 15 January 1999.
The following are the most important comments presented by governments on the Preliminary Draft Second Protocol to the 1954 Hague Convention: *Germany* suggested this Article not broaden the scope of the jurisdiction of the ICC. *Sweden* proposed to harmonize this Article with the relevant provisions of the Geneva Conventions and Protocol I. Regarding paragraph 1, *Australia* would clarify the relation between paragraphs 1 and 4 by combining them in a single provision imposing an obligation to 'prosecute or extradite' on a State Party where an alleged offender is found on its territory. It would make use of precedents of the terrorism conventions such as Article 8(1) of the Convention for the Suppression of Terrorist Bombings and would substitute 'alleged to have committed' for 'accused of'. The *Syrian Arab Republic* would delete the reference to Article 11. In relation to *Paragraph: Austria, Australia, China, Israel and Sweden* preferred not to make reference to the International Criminal Court. Israel wished to clarify the criteria of jurisdiction. *Norway* called for clarification of the reference to international courts/tribunals and *Sweden* questioned universal jurisdiction. The *Syrian Arab Republic* proposed to delete the words 'or by any international tribunal which may have jurisdiction' in the first phrase and to add the word 'other' after the word 'any' in the second phrase of this paragraph. In relation to *Paragraph 4, Israel* wished to exclude the possibility of extradition. The *Syrian Arab Republic* proposed to add the phrase 'in accordance with the relative provisions of the Rome Statute of the International Criminal Court' at the end of this paragraph.

3. Persons charged with the acts enumerated in Article 18 of this Protocol may be tried by a competent court of any Party which may acquire jurisdiction over the accused, or by the International Criminal Court or any other international tribunal which may have jurisdiction. This does not preclude the jurisdiction of any international tribunal which may be established in the future.

Discussion and drafting of Article 16 at the 1999 Hague Conference

Only a few delegates referred to Article [21] on jurisdiction, comparing it with Article 28 of the Convention and taking note of the innovative paragraph 3.[676] The Chinese delegate proposed to delete the words after 'accused', considering it 'more appropriate to retain the national court mechanism in the Convention, the Geneva Conventions 1949 and their Additional Protocol I 1977'. In his view, such a provision would 'make it difficult for non-States Parties to the Statute of the International Criminal Court to become Party to the present Protocol.'[677] Some delegates were opposed to the introduction of the ICC;[678] others, on the contrary, accepted the complementary role of the ICC.[679] The Swedish delegate considered that the obligation 'to search for and bring to trial or extradite the person' was going too far and that States should submit said person to the competent authorities for prosecution.[680] Israel was opposed to universal jurisdiction.[681] The ICRC representative noted that the notion of international jurisdiction is one that is already embedded in existing instruments of international law, namely Article 8(a) of the ICC Statute.

The draft Articles 15–21 of the actual Protocol, based on the text submitted to the Conference, were substantially rewritten by the Working Group under the chairmanship of Professor Fischer. The group followed the recommendations of the Plenary Session of the Conference (which discussed this chapter on 18 March 1999). The Article on jurisdiction was considered at the Working Group under the number [19] and became Article 16 of the Second Protocol.[682] The basis for discussion of the Working Group was

---

676 Switzerland.
677 1999 Hague Conference, Plenary Session, 18 March 1999: China, p. 165.
678 Ibid., US, Peru, pp. 169–70, 190.
679 Ibid., Argentina, Cambodia, France, Morocco, pp. 168, 177, 186.
680 Ibid., Sweden, France, Romania, pp. 172, 174, 177.
681 Ibid., Israel, p. 180.
682 Article 18 of the draft was replaced by Article 15 in the final text.

the draft prepared by the Chairman,[683] but only a few modifications were introduced.

In the written report to the Plenary Session of the Conference, Professor Fischer underlined the particular importance of this Article and made an important declaration which explained its content and significance. In his opinion, the Article dealing with jurisdictional questions was carefully balanced in its paragraphs 1 and 2, highlighting basic universally accepted jurisdiction (art. [19](1) and (2)(a)), and adding an exception clause for non-State Parties to the Protocol (art. [19](2)(b)). Article [19] paragraph 1 sets out the obligations of States Parties to establish jurisdiction in three specific cases, which from the point of view of international criminal law is a major achievement. All elements of a coherent system of prosecution and extradition are present. The specific combination of Articles [18], [19] and the prosecution and extradition clauses, present in Articles [21–23], has not been achieved so far at a treaty level for important crimes of a *new* nature committed in war. It also reaffirms the prosecution and extradition regime with regard to customary law. Article [19](2)(b) includes an exception. This exception clause is only of relevance when Article [19](2)(a) is not applicable. With the following statement, the Chairman expressed the basis of the compromise reached by the Working Group:

> Nothing in the Protocol, including Article [19], would in any way limit the States ability to legislate, criminalize or otherwise deal with any substantive offences even if they were addressed by the Protocol. Nothing in Article [19](2)(b) should be interpreted as affecting the application of Article [19] (1)(a).[684]

With this document began a process, which may sooner or later lead to an acceptance of all crimes listed in Article [18] (which became Article 15 of the final text) as crimes under customary law. Taking into account the specific circumstances of the negotiations, what occurred can not really be interpreted as setting a precedent for the future. Following the Chairman's appeal, the

---

683 Chairman's Working Paper – 22 March 1999 – 19.00 Hours (Document distributed to the members of the Working Group).

684 At the Plenary Session, the delegate of the UK insisted on this point declaring that 'Article 19(2)(b) should not be interpreted as in any way affecting the application of Article 19(1)(a). That was also how he interpreted this provision and how his delegation would apply it.' The UK, supported by the delegate of Finland, 1999 Hague Conference, Plenary Session, 24 March 1999, pp. 15, 17.

delegations realized the advantages of the text as described some minutes before and therefore accepted it in its present form.[685]

In the Plenary Session on 24 March, Horst Fischer again insisted on the fact that the application of paragraph (2)(a) renders paragraph (2)(b) irrelevant. [686]The draft Article elaborated by the Working Group was adopted by the Plenary Session on 24 March 1999, transmitted to the Drafting Committee, and included in the final text of the Protocol.

ANALYSIS OF THE TEXT

Paragraph 1

The whole text of this paragraph must be viewed in connection with paragraph 2, sub-paragraph (a), which refers to the 'exercise of jurisdiction under the national and international law that may be applied or affect the exercise of jurisdiction under customary international law'. It also includes an important exception concerning members of the armed forces and nationals of a State, which is not party to the Protocol. This is the meaning of the words 'without prejudice to paragraph 2'. This is a reference to the global concept of jurisdiction in national and international law to which paragraph 1 is a specific provision.

General jurisdiction

According to this paragraph, jurisdiction is not automatically conferred by the Protocol, but imposes only on States Parties the duty ('shall') to take 'the necessary legislative measures to establish its jurisdiction'.

A few remarks may be made regarding this introductory part of the paragraph:

- the paragraph is referring to *necessary legislative measures*, i.e. to legislative measures, which are necessary for the establishment of jurisdiction according to the constitutional system of each of the States Parties to the Protocol. Such measures will be taken by the legislative body in charge of the adoption of laws on criminal matters. As we are dealing in this paragraph only with serious violations of cultural property, this will be the legislative body, according to the constitution,

---

685 Abridged text of H. Fischer. See *Presentation of the results of the Working Group on Chapter 4*. H. Fischer, coordinator of the Working Group, 25 March 1999. Conference document HC/1999/ INF.5, p. 2.

686 1999 Hague Conference, Plenary Session, 24 March 1999, p. 12.

responsible for the adoption of criminal laws and not for administrative and disciplinary sanctions. In some countries such measures can be taken either at the federal or at the state level.

- Such measures must be taken in relation to *all offences* set forth in Article 15 of the Protocol:
  a) making cultural property under enhanced protection the object of attack;
  b) using cultural property under enhanced protection or its immediate surroundings in support of military action;
  c) extensive destruction or appropriation of cultural property protected under the Convention and this Protocol;
  d) making cultural property protected under the Convention and this Protocol the object of attack;
  e) theft, pillage or misappropriation of, or acts of vandalism directed against cultural property protected under the Convention.
- The competent forum for the exercise of jurisdiction will be the national court or the ICC. Among the national courts it will most probably be the court in charge of criminal matters or a military tribunal, depending on the structure of the judicial system in each country.

The general jurisdiction established for all these offences is specified in paragraph 1, sub-paragraph (a) and (b) of Article 16 of the Second Protocol. There is jurisdiction:

a) *when such an offence is committed in the territory of that State:*
Each State Party to the Protocol must provide jurisdiction of its courts over all offences set forth in Article 15(1) on the basis of territoriality, i.e. according to the territorial principle. This universally recognized principle, based on the notion of sovereignty, means that the State may assert jurisdiction over any conduct or offence committed within its territory. States may prescribe and enforce its rules within their territory.[687]

b) *when the alleged offender is a national of that State:*
Each State Party to the Protocol must provide jurisdiction of its courts over all offences set forth in Article 15(1) on the basis of the nationality of offender, i.e. according to the principle of active nationality.[688] An offender 'who commits a crime anywhere in the world, irrespective of whether the conduct constitutes a crime in the legal system of the

---

687 See esp. Bassiouni (1983).
688 See Cassese (2003), p. 281.

country of origin, is subject to the penal jurisdiction of his country of citizenship. Consequently, where conduct constitutes a crime in the territory in which it occurred, any violation would subject an actor to the jurisdiction of his national state, in addition to the jurisdiction of the state in which the conduct took place'.[689]

According to these two paragraphs, the State exercises ordinary criminal jurisdiction, which is also mentioned in Article 28 of the Convention. The notion of 'ordinary criminal jurisdiction' in the Second Protocol seems to be more restrictive as penalties for serious violations will be of the nature of criminal law and not disciplinary. Administrative and disciplinary sanctions will be applied in relation to other violations according to Article 21 of the Protocol.

In cases of paragraphs (d) and (e) – namely, the last two serious violations according to Article 15, paragraph 1 – these violations were not transferred to the category of 'other violations', which would only require States to suppress them without specifying the means by which they will do it. These two violations are recognized as war crimes and are also subject to sanctions according to the ICC Statute. But States have an obligation only to suppress them through criminal sanctions on the basis of general jurisdiction, according to the aforementioned paragraphs (a) and (b); in other words, when such offences are committed in the territory of the State or when the offender is a national of the State. As one of the participants of the Working Group said:

> There is no obligation to establish jurisdiction over cases where the alleged offence was committed abroad by a non-national, although States may exercise such jurisdiction. This reflects the principle of permissive universal jurisdiction for war crimes, according to which all States have jurisdiction to try non-nationals for war crimes committed abroad but are under no obligation to do so if the crimes do not amount to grave breaches. This also follows clearly from the acknowledgement that States may establish jurisdiction over such persons under applicable national or international law, including customary international law, and from the statement by the Chairman of the Working Group[690] on Chapter 4, referred to above, that nothing in the Protocol limits in

---

689 Bassiouni (1983), p. 308.
690 *Presentation of the results of the Working Group on Chapter 4.* H. Fischer, coordinator of the Working Group, 25 March 1999. Conference document HC/1999/INF.5, p. 3.

any way the ability of the State to legislate, criminalize or otherwise deal with any of the serious violations of the Protocol.[691]

Universal jurisdiction as established by paragraph (c) of Article 16(1) in relation to sub-paragraphs (a) to (c) of paragraph 1 of Article 15

> (c) in the case of offences set forth in Article 15 sub-paragraphs
> (a) to (c), when the alleged offender is present in its territory:

The Hague Conference established universal jurisdiction over this category of violations, that is, serious violations according to Article 15, paragraph 1, sub-paragraphs (a) to (c). This universal principle recognizes that certain offenses are so heinous and so widely condemned that 'any state if it captures the offender may prosecute and punish that person on behalf of the world community regardless of the nationality of the offender or victim or where the crime is committed'.[692]

This is the jurisdictional competence termed 'universal by treaty', which is established by States Parties to a multilateral treaty in regard to 'offences of an international character of serious concern to the international community as a whole, which it is accepted may be punished by whichever state has custody of the offender'.[693]

> Universal jurisdiction over the specified offenses is a result of universal condemnation of those activities and general interest in cooperating to suppress them, as reflected in widely-accepted international agreements and resolutions of international organizations. These offences are subject to universal jurisdiction as a matter of customary law. Universal jurisdiction for additional offenses is provided by international agreements, but it remains to be determined whether universal jurisdiction over a particular offence has become customary law for states not party to such an agreement.[694]

---

691 Henckaerts (1999), p. 617 (footnotes omitted).
692 Bassiouni (1986), Vol. II, p. 298.
693 Jennings and Watts (1996), p. 469.
694 *Restatement of the Law, Third: The Foreign Relations Law of the United States* (Philadelphia, Pa.: American Law Institute, 1987), Vol. 1, para. 404, Comment, pp. 254–55.

Sub-paragraph (c) means that the delegates at the 1999 Hague Conference established:

> jurisdiction not only when the offence is committed in the territory of the State or when the alleged offender is a national of the State, but also when the offence is committed abroad by a non-national. This reflects the principle of mandatory universal jurisdiction for grave breaches, which implies that all States have to establish jurisdiction to try or extradite non-nationals for war crimes committed abroad who are present in their territory.[695]
> [This is] prescriptive jurisdiction over impugned conduct taking place outside the territory of the prosecuting state by a person not a national of that state, where the conduct does not constitute an attack on the fundamental interests of that state.[696] In this respect, what is mandated by Article 16(1)(c) is what might be called universal custodial jurisdiction – that is, the exercise of universal jurisdiction over offences in the event that the offender is subsequently present in the territory of the prosecuting state. There is no obligation on States Parties to make legislative provision, where domestically permissible, for trial *in absentia* pursuant to universal jurisdiction.[697]

The Austrian delegate at the Conference also affirmed that 'it was the clear understanding of the Diplomatic Conference that jurisdiction has only been established when the State concerned does not extradite the alleged offender to another State having established jurisdiction according to Article 16(1) (a) and (b).'[698]

Paragraph 2: Exercise of jurisdiction

Paragraph 2 concerns the exercise of jurisdiction as established in paragraph 1. It excludes any modification or change of Article 28 of the Convention by the words 'without prejudice to Article 28 of the Convention'. The establishment of jurisdiction according to Article 28 is independent of jurisdiction in Article 16 of the Protocol. As the 1999 Hague Conference did

---

695 Henckaerts (1999), p. 616 (footnotes omitted).
696 See the definition of universal jurisdiction given in Pradelle (2000), chap. 74, § 1. The last would justify extraterritorial jurisdiction over non-nationals on the basis of the 'protective principle'.
697 O'Keefe (2002), pp. 9–10.
698 Desch (1999), p. 81.

not draft details of individual criminal responsibility and referred to general principles, it is important to underline that Article 28 required prosecution and punishment not only of offenders who commit violations, but also of those who give the order to commit breaches of the Convention.

Sub-paragraph (a)

This sub-paragraph goes even further than affirmation of the prosecution according to Article 28. It simply reaffirms the freedom of States to exercise ordinary jurisdiction in their national law, or according to international law, whether conventional or customary. This sub-paragraph reaffirms that States Parties are not precluded from establishing individual criminal responsibility or exercising their jurisdiction according to national and international law. This does not affect the exercise of jurisdiction according to customary international law.[699] The Protocol, in particular Article 16, does not prevent a Contracting Party from exercising jurisdiction on any other basis, either under national or international law. According to the Chairman of the Working Group on Chapter 4, nothing in the Second Protocol in any way limits the ability of States to legislate, criminalize or otherwise deal with any offence under the Protocol, and by the fact that the entire jurisdictional regime is without prejudice to Article 28 of the 1954 Convention.

Sub-paragraph (b)

Sub-paragraph (b) was included on the request of the US. The US delegate at the 1999 Hague Conference, W. H. Parks, said that:

> Members of armed forces of States which did not adhere to the Protocol should not be subjected to criminal sanctions for which they would not otherwise be liable under current agreements or customary law. To do so would violate not only the normal rules of treaty law but would constitute an amendment to the Convention which was not the purpose of the present exercise. Further, it should not be attempted

---

699 For example, the International Military Tribunal at Nuremberg determined that violations of the Hague Regulations amounted to war crimes because the treaty rules had crystallized into customary law by the time of the Second World War. See other examples in Henckaerts and Doswald-Beck (2005), p. 572.

to prescribe the jurisdiction, of international tribunals such as the International Criminal Court.[700]

The sub-paragraph

excludes nationals of States not party to the Second Protocol from the regime of mandatory universal jurisdiction. This would mean that States have no obligation to try or extradite such persons. The extent of this exception is greatly diminished, however, by the acknowledgement that States may establish jurisdiction over such persons under applicable national or international law, including customary international law, by the statement of the Chairman of the Working Group on Chapter 4 that nothing in the Second Protocol in any way limits the ability of States to legislate, criminalize or otherwise deal with any offence under the Protocol, and by the fact that the entire jurisdictional regime is without prejudice to Article 28 of the 1954 Convention.[701]

---

700 1999 Hague Conference, Plenary Session, 18 March 1999, p. 169. The position of the US on the issue of international criminal jurisdiction and the ICC is well known. It was stated succinctly by Ambassador D. J. Scheffer (1998): 'So why did the United States vote against the agreement reached last month in Rome to establish a permanent court? Because the agreement that was reached puts at risk the vital efforts of the United States and others to promote international peace and security, while the worst perpetrators of atrocities may go unpunished. Such an outcome hardly promotes the interests of justice. . . . Thus, the US delegation, which I headed, went to the Rome conference with twin goals: continue the progress towards international justice, while protecting the critical roles of the United States and other responsible members of the international community in maintaining peace and security through humanitarian action, peacekeeping, and, when necessary, collective military action. We sought a court that would be empowered by the UN Security Council to pursue those responsible for heinous crimes, whoever and wherever they are, but also a court whose ability to act without a Security Council mandate would be shaped in such a way as to protect against a misguided exercise of authority that might harm legitimate national and international interests. . . . This was a reasonable approach that had been initially proposed by a UN team of international law experts. In Rome, we indicated our willingness to be flexible as to how cases would be referred to the court, but we felt it was essential to recognize a government's right to assess the court's fairness and impartiality before allowing its people to come under the court's jurisdiction in the absence of a referral from the Security Council. This approach guaranteed the ability of responsible governments to undertake life-saving missions without fear that their troops would be dragged before a tribunal that had yet to stand the test of time. Unfortunately, a small group of countries, meeting behind closed doors in the final days of the Rome conference, produced a seriously flawed take-it-or-leave-it text, one that provides a recipe for politicization of the court and risks deterring responsible international action to promote peace and security. Most problematic is the extraordinary way the court's jurisdiction was framed at the last moment. A country whose forces commit war crimes could join the treaty but escape prosecution of its nationals by "opting out" of the court's jurisdiction over war crimes for seven years. By contrast, a country that does not join the treaty but deploys its soldiers abroad to restore international peace and security could be vulnerable to assertions that the court has jurisdiction over acts of those soldiers.'

701 Henckaerts (1999), p. 616 (footnotes omitted).

It is also reduced by sub-paragraph (a) itself as, according to which, States may exercise jurisdiction under national and international law that may be applicable, or affect the exercise of 'jurisdiction under customary international law', among others on the basis of Additional Protocol I or the ICTY and ICC Statutes.

Article 28 of the 1954 Convention was in fact already intended to provide for mandatory universal jurisdiction. As we have affirmed in the Commentary:

> The representative of one government raised the question of whether a Party to the Convention was obliged to prosecute and impose penal sanctions upon persons having committed breaches outside the territory subject to the criminal jurisdiction of the State in question. The answer is yes, because that is the aim of this provision. It may reasonably be assumed that the country has at its disposal general legislation concerning the protection of its own cultural property and that the criminal act directed against that property would, in any event, be covered by those provisions. What remains to be done – according to Article 28 of the Convention – *is to prosecute those who have committed criminal acts outside the territorial jurisdiction of the State.* [702]

---

702 Toman (1996), p. 294 (emphasis in original).

Article 17
PROSECUTION

1. *The Party in whose territory the alleged offender of an offence set forth in Article 15 sub-paragraphs 1 (a) to (c) is found to be present shall, if it does not extradite that person, submit, without exception whatsoever and without undue delay, the case to its competent authorities, for the purpose of prosecution, through proceedings in accordance with its domestic law or with, if applicable, the relevant rules of international law.*

2. *Without prejudice to, if applicable, the relevant rules of international law, any person regarding whom proceedings are being carried out in connection with the Convention or this Protocol shall be guaranteed fair treatment and a fair trial in accordance with domestic law and international law at all stages of the proceedings, and in no cases shall be provided guarantees less favourable to such person than those provided by international law.*

Preparatory works

Preliminary Draft Second Protocol to the 1954 Hague Convention. UNESCO document HC/1999/1, October 1998 (English, French and Russian).

UNESCO, Summary of comments on Preliminary Draft Second Protocol to the 1954 Hague Convention received from High Contracting Parties to the Hague Convention for the Protection of Cultural Property in the Event of Armed Conflict 1954, other UNESCO Member States and international organizations, Paris, 15 January 1999.

Draft Second Protocol to the 1954 Hague Convention for the Protection of Cultural Property in the Event of Armed Conflict. UNESCO document HC/1999/1/rev.1, February 1999 (original: English).

Presentation of the results of the Working Group on Chapter 4. H. Fischer, coordinator of the Working Group, 25 March 1999. Conference document HC/1999/INF.5.

Bibliography

Chamberlain, K. 2004. *War and Cultural Heritage*. Leicester: Institute of Art and Law, 2004, pp. 205–10.

Desch, T. 1999. The Second Protocol to the 1954 Convention for the Protection of Cultural Property in the Event of Armed Conflict. *Yearbook of International Humanitarian Law*, Vol. 2, p. 79.

Human Rights Committee General Comment 13, Article 14 (Twenty-first session, 1984, para. 10, Compilation of General Comments and General Recommendations adopted by Human Rights Treaty Bodies, UN Doc. HRI/GEN/1/rev.1 at 14 (1994))

O'Keefe, R. 2002. *National Implementation of the Penal Provisions of Chapter 4 of the Second Protocol of 26 March 1999 to the Hague Convention of 1954 for the Protection of Cultural Property in the Event of Armed Conflict.* 29 March (UNESCO document CLT/CIH/MCO/2002/PI/H/1).

Statutes of the international criminal tribunals

See the documentation under the commentary to Article 15.

PREPARATORY WORK BEFORE THE 1999 HAGUE CONFERENCE

Article 17 does not find its origin in any of the pre-conference drafts. The only place from which the idea could have come is the proposal of Australia concerning paragraph 1 of Article 16 on jurisdiction to 'clarify the relationship between the paragraphs 1 and 4 by combining them in a single provision imposing an obligation to "prosecute or extradite" on a State Party where an alleged offender is found on its territory'. It would make use of the precedent of the terrorism conventions such as Article 8(1) of the Convention for the Suppression of Terrorist Bombings[703] and would substitute 'alleged to have committed' for 'accused of'.[704]

During the Conference, the delegate of Sweden 'stressed that there should also be a provision for a fair trial such as that contained in Article 146(4) of Geneva Convention IV or subsequent developments in international law'.[705]

---

703 'The State Party in the territory of which the alleged offender is present shall, in cases to which Article 6 applies, if it does not extradite that person, be obliged, without exception whatsoever and whether or not the offence was committed in its territory, to submit the case without undue delay to its competent authorities for the purpose of prosecution, through proceedings in accordance with the laws of that State. Those authorities shall take their decision in the same manner as in the case of any other offence of a grave nature under the law of that State'. (International Convention for the Suppression of Terrorist Bombings, G.A. Res. 164, UN GAOR, 52nd Sess., Supp. No. 49, at 389, UN Doc. A/52/49 (1998). Entered into force on 23 May 2001.)

704 UNESCO, Summary of comments on Preliminary Draft Second Protocol to the 1954 Hague Convention received from High Contracting Parties to the Hague Convention for the Protection of Cultural Property in the Event of Armed Conflict 1954, other UNESCO Member States and international organizations, Paris, 15 January 1999.

705 1999 Hague Conference, Plenary Session, 18 March 1999, pp. 172–73. Article 146, paragraph 4 of the Geneva Convention IV states: 'In all circumstances, the accused persons shall benefit by

The Article was first formulated in the Chairman's Working Paper on 22 March 1999 and was included in the draft articles prepared by the Working Group.[706]

ANALYSIS OF THE TEXT

The Article constitutes a unit comprising two parts, as envisaged by the Australian delegation: one covers prosecution and the refers to extradition, which although mentioned in this article, is developed further in the following Article 18, entitled 'Extradition'. Here, only a reference is made to extradition according to the principles *aut dedere aut judicare*. This Article deals only with the second part, *judicare*.

The two different parts of the Article are logically connected: the first part concerns prosecution; the second part deals with 'fair treatment' and 'fair trial' which could also be called 'fundamental guarantees of the due process'. Prosecution in this sense includes not only prosecution in the narrow sense, but also trial and punishment. The Parties to the Protocol which 'adopt such measures as may be necessary to establish criminal offence' for all offences mentioned in Article 15, paragraph 1, have also the duty to provide fair treatment and fair trial. This concerns not only the offences in sub-paragraphs (a) to (c), but all offences, that is, offences (a) to (e).

Paragraph 1

As regards the serious violations of the Protocol embodied in Article 15(1) sub-paragraphs (a) to (c), Article 17(1) imposes on Parties to the Protocol the obligation to try or extradite any alleged offender found in their respective territories, according to the well-known principle *aut dedere au judicare*. Each Party to the Protocol must, 'if it does not extradite the alleged offender, submit, without exception whatsoever and without undue delay, the case to its competent authorities for the purpose of prosecution, through proceedings in accordance with its domestic law or with, if applicable, the relevant rules of international law'.

---

safeguards of proper trial and defense, which shall not be less favourable than those provided by Article 105 and those following of the Geneva Convention relative to the Treatment of Prisoners of War of August 12, 1949'.

706 1999 Hague Conference. Conference document HC/1999/5/Add.8. Only one modification was made in the first phrase of the draft Article: instead of 'serious offence' the final text of the Working Group referred to 'offence'. The world 'serious' was probably considered as redundant as the Article is referring to Article 1(a) and (c) and this Article is already entitled 'serious violations'.

The Party can avoid having recourse to prosecution, if the conditions for extradition are available, and if it considers such extradition preferable. This is a matter of consideration to be evaluated by the State authorities.

The basic inspiration for this provision is Article 146, paragraph 2 of the Fourth Geneva Convention:

> Each High Contracting Party shall be under the obligation to search for persons alleged to have committed, or to have ordered to be committed, such grave breaches, and shall bring such persons, regardless of their nationality, before its own courts. It may also, if it prefers, and in accordance with the provisions of its own legislation, hand such persons over for trial to another High Contracting Party concerned, provided such High Contracting Party has made out a 'prima facie' case.

This paragraph goes further than Article 28 of the Hague Convention and is completed by the requirement of extradition in the present paragraph.

In cases where the Party does not proceed with extradition because it is not willing to do so and the conditions for extradition are not met, it has a duty to submit the case to 'its competent authorities', in other words, to the determined authorities according to its domestic law.

Prosecutions 'without exception'

Submission for the purpose of prosecution must be done 'without exception whatsoever and without undue delay'. The legislators considered it important to mention that such submission must be done 'without exception'. These words were included in the International Convention for the Suppression of Terrorist Bombings of 1998 and other similar treaties. The legislators of this provision simply wanted to be certain that nobody would escape sanctions for serious violations committed against cultural property. Criminal law knows of several exceptions and limits to criminal proceedings which the authors of this provision wished to avoid. Among these limitations several can be mentioned.

Amnesty laws

Laws granting amnesty for broad categories of crimes are one such limitation. Amnesty laws preclude investigation or cancel sentences already passed.

Non-prescriptibility[707]

The legislation of many States provides that after a certain number of years no prosecution may be initiated even with regard to certain very serious crimes. A sentence which has not been served is no longer applicable.[708]

> It is difficult to suggest that customary international law prohibits statutory limitations in respect of all international crimes in the light of the silence of multilateral treaties concerning international crimes on this subject. The position is different in the case of 'core' crimes of genocide, war crimes, crimes against humanity, and aggression. There is support for the view that the prohibitions on these crimes constitute norms of *ius cogens*, and that a necessary consequence of such a characterization is the inapplicability of statutory limitations. [709]

Immunities

Courts may be barred from the exercise of their jurisdiction if national or foreign agents benefit from the immunity.

> National courts are obliged by international rules to set aside any functional immunity the accused may invoke, any time he is charged with an international crime. In contrast, if he pleads personal immunities (for instance diplomatic immunities), courts are bound to respect them, hence to refrain from initiating prosecution, whether or not the accused is on an official mission on the territory of the courts or in transit.[710]

---

707 Van den Wyngaert and Dugard (2002), p. 873–88; Frulli (2002), pp. 251–53.

708 The fear that the German war criminals of the Second World War might escape prosecution because of the expiration of the period of limitation applicable to their crimes had as a result the adoption of two conventions: the Convention on the Non-applicability of Statutory Limitations to War Crimes and Crimes Against Humanity, adopted by Resolution 2391 (XXIII) of the United Nations General Assembly on 26 November 1968 (G.A. res. 2391 (XXIII), annex, 23 UN GAOR Supp. (No. 18) at 40, UN Doc. A/7218 (1968), entered into force on 11 November 1970), and the European Convention on the Non-Applicability of Statutory Limitations to Crimes against Humanity and War Crimes, opened for signature at Strasbourg on 25 January 1974 (ETS, No. 082; entered into force on 27 June 2003). The number of ratifications remained modest. As of 1 April 2009, 52 States parties to the United Nations Convention and three States Parties to the European Convention.

709 Cassese (2003), p. 316. Van den Wyngaert and Dugard (2002), p. 887. Both authors consider arguable the view that Article 29 of the Rome Statute reflects customary international law. Article 29 of the Rome Statute includes the provision on: *Non-applicability of statute of limitations: The crimes within the jurisdiction of the Court shall not be subject to any statute of limitations.*

710 Cassese (2003), p. 322.

In a recent case, the ICJ examining the immunities of the Heads of States, Head of Government and the Minister for Foreign Affairs according to the customary international law concluded

> that the functions of a Minister for Foreign Affairs are such that, throughout the duration of his or her office, he or she when abroad enjoys full immunity from criminal jurisdiction and inviolability. The immunity and that inviolability protect the individual concerned against any act of authority of another State which would hinder him or her in the performance of his or her duties.[711]

A contrario, the Rome Statute of the International Criminal Court of 1998 states in Article 27 Irrelevance of official capacity:

1. This Statute shall apply equally to all persons without any distinction based on official capacity. In particular, official capacity as a Head of State or Government, a member of a Government or parliament, an elected representative or a government official shall in no case exempt a person from criminal responsibility under this Statute, nor shall it, in and of itself, constitute a ground for reduction of sentence.
2. Immunities or special procedural rules which may attach to the official capacity of a person, whether under national or international law, shall not bar the Court from exercising its jurisdiction over such a person.

'Undue delay' is a widely accepted clause in State practice,[712] in the international law of human rights,[713] international humanitarian

---

711 Arrest Warrant of 11 April 2000 (Democratic Republic of the Congo v. Belgium), Judgment, *ICJ Reports 2002*, p. 22, para. 54.

712 According to the Canadian Federal Court 'The classic test to be applied in these matters is threefold: first, whether there has been inordinate delay; secondly, is the delay inexcusable; and thirdly, whether the defendants are likely to be seriously prejudiced by the delay'. Mr. Justice Dube in Nichols v. Canada (1990) 36 F.T.R. 77.

713 International Covenant on Civil and Political Rights (1966), art. 9, para. 2–4, art. 14, para. 3(a) and (c). According to the Human Rights Committee General Comment 13, 'the guarantee of the "undue delay" relates not only to the time by which a trial should commence, but also the time by which it should end and judgment be rendered; all stages must take place "without undue delay". To make this right effective, a procedure must be available in order to ensure that the trial will proceed "without undue delay", both in the first instance and on appeal'. (Human Rights Committee General Comment 13, Article 14 (Twenty-first session, 1984, para. 10, Compilation of General Comments and General Recommendations Adopted by Human Rights Treaty Bodies, UN Doc. HRI/GEN/1/

law[714] and international criminal law.[715] The purpose is to insure that the pre-trial process and trial proceedings will take place as quickly as possible according to the circumstances of the case. In the Statutes of the International Criminal Tribunals, as in this paragraph, the evocation of 'undue delay' appears as a right of the accused:

> in practice, however, the judges' expeditiousness is not just a right of the accused but also the guarantee for the victims and a necessity in order for the institution to be able to carry out its role in relation to everyone, both persons coming under its jurisdiction, victims of crimes committed and their principals, and more generally world public opinion. Reasonable times are thus both a right of the accused, of the parties to the trial and of the victims, and for the judges an obligation '*erga omnes*', as well as a principle of sound administration of justice.[716]

The practice of international criminal tribunals demonstrates, however, that rapidity is not always easy to attain.

> It is notable that very often in international criminal trials both questions of fact and those relating to law prove extremely complex, thereby requiring much time for their proper consideration. In particular, it may prove necessary to call a great number of witnesses, coming from different countries. Furthermore, normally international courts must rely on State co-operation for investigations, the gathering of evidence, the apprehension of accused, and so on. All this necessarily complicates and slows down the whole process. In addition, language barriers prolong the proceedings, as normally the language of the witnesses and the accused is different from that of the court, and, on top of that, the court is bound to employ more than one official language. Often the defendant contributes to the length of proceedings by filing many

---

Rev.1 at 14 (1994)). European Convention on Human Rights speaks in Article 6(1) of 'hearing in reasonable time' which depends on the particular circumstances of the case (*König v. FRG* A 27 para 99 (1978)) and factors that are always taken into account are the complexity of the case, the conduct of the applicant and the conduct of the competent administrative and judicial authorities (*Ruotolo v. Italy* A 230-D (1992)).

714 Article 75, para. 3 and 4 of the 1977 Additional Protocol I.

715 Art. 67, para. 1 of the ICC Statute, art. 21, para. 4 of the ICTY Statute, art. 20, para. 4 of the ICTR Statute.

716 Terrier (2002), pp. 1264–65.

procedural motions, as he is entitled to do, but which inevitably delay the outcome of the trial.[717]

The case is transmitted to the competent authorities for prosecution. The Protocol, as an international treaty, established the duty for the Parties to the Protocol to exercise criminal jurisdiction. The Parties accomplish this duty by submitting such cases to their national authorities. This is a very important provision as prosecution can be exercised only on the basis of an international treaty. There is 'no customary rule with a general content, no general international principle can be found that might be relied upon to indicate that an obligation to prosecute international crimes has crystallized in the international community'.[718]

Prosecution is exercised on the basis of national statutes and laws, which provide the definitions of crimes and establish the rules of jurisdiction and the proceedings. National courts usually require the implementation of legislation drawn from treaties that have been ratified. This is the meaning of the reference that prosecution will be carried on 'through proceedings in accordance with its domestic law'. The courts of some States adopt an *expansive approach* that has resulted in a broadening of their jurisdiction over international crimes'.[719]

The present paragraph goes a step further. It refers not only to 'proceedings in accordance with its domestic law', but 'with, if applicable, the relevant rules of international law'. In this respect, Antonio Cassese points out that

> there exist many international customary and treaty rules, which impose upon States the obligation to respect a core of procedural standards, when national courts prosecute and try persons accused of international

---

717 Cassese (2003), pp. 399–400. From the experience of the ICTY, Antonio Cassese mentions 'several mechanisms and procedures to reduce the length of proceedings. Among other things, (1) a pre-trial judge as well as pre-trial conferences have been provided for, (ii) time limits for the filing of procedural or preliminary motions have been set, and (iii) provision has been made for admission of written evidence and in particular for the filing of affidavits. Furthermore, (iv) the number of judges has been increased, in particular through the election of *ad litem* judges (that is, non-permanent judges, or not-full-time judges, who only sit in one or two cases), which required an amendment to the ICTY Statute by the Security Council Resolution No. 1329 (2000) of 30 November 2000 (a similar amendment has recently been adopted for the ICTR)'.
718 Cassese (2003), p. 302.
719 Ibid., p. 307.

crimes, regardless of the specific legal ground of jurisdiction on which the courts assert their jurisdiction.[720]

He is referring to two sets of rules: rules on human rights based essentially on human rights treaty provisions,[721] and the customary and treaty rules of international humanitarian law.[722]

Paragraph 2

The present paragraph is inspired by Article 146, paragraph 4 of the Fourth Geneva Convention. According to this paragraph, invoked during the discussion at the 1999 Hague Conference by the Swedish delegate: 'In all circumstances, the accused persons shall benefit by safeguards of proper trial and defense, which shall not be less favourable than those provided by Article 105 and those following of the Geneva Convention relative to the Treatment of Prisoners of War of August 12, 1949'.

Paragraph 2 embodies certain fundamental procedural safeguards and guarantees for any person against whom proceedings are being carried out in connection with the Convention or this Protocol, in other words, the alleged offenders. Such persons, like any persons, shall be guaranteed fair treatment and a fair trial in accordance with domestic law and international law at all stages of the proceedings.

These guarantees are provided not only according to the safeguards provided by the domestic legal system, but also by international law. A combination of both systems is required. And to be sure that guarantees are provided at the level of both of these systems, the paragraph adds that in no cases will such guarantees not be less favourable to such persons than the guarantees provided by international law. The guarantees according to international law constitute the minimum guarantees to which additional guarantees may be provided by domestic law. These guarantees apply to proceedings in respect of all serious violations of the Protocol set forth in Article 15(1), that is, to violations of sub-paragraphs (a) and (e). They also

---

720 Ibid., p. 309.

721 Rules of the International Covenant on Civil and Political Rights (art. 15 and 16 in particular) and regional conventions: European Convention (art. 6 and 7), American Convention (art. 8 and 9), African Charter (art. 7).

722 See also Fischer, Kress and Lüder (2001). Horst Fischer was the author of paragraph 1 of Article 17 and introduced the reference to the rules of international law, which were not mentioned in the model provision of the International Convention for the Suppression of Terrorist Bombings (New York, 12 January 1998).

apply to proceedings pursuant to legislative measures of a penal nature taken by States Parties in accordance with Article 21. The guarantees in question are not restricted to prosecution but apply equally to extradition proceedings.

This constitutes the basic meaning of this paragraph. But in the introduction, the paragraph is saying more: 'Without prejudice to, if applicable, the relevant rules of international law...' Is this just a repetition of the phrase 'in no cases shall be provided guarantees less favourable to such person than those provided by international law'? Or does it mean more? We think it unlikely that the authors wanted to repeat the reference to international law twice. Once, at the end of the phrase is sufficient and perfectly clear. By adding the reference to the relevant rules of international law, they probably had in mind the reference to the international criminal court, which if used for prosecution of serious violation will obviously apply the relevant rules of international law. This will happen in cases where International Criminal Court is charged with the prosecution of violations.

Fair treatment and fair trial

It is probably not necessary to comment on the meaning of these two terms, which have a definite meaning in international criminal law.

There is a great variety of meaning regarding these terms in the domestic law of States, and their content depends on the constitutional law and criminal law of each country. The Human Rights Committee in its General Comment 13 encouraged States to provide relevant information on their legal systems, as the laws and practices dealing with these matters vary widely from State to State. This is a requirement of natural justice and international criminal justice, to minimize the risk of innocent individuals being convicted. 'In order to protect innocent individuals one needs to incorporate safeguards, to ensure that nobody is convicted, unless there is proof beyond reasonable doubt that the person in question is guilty of the crimes with which he or she is charged'.[723] According to Professor Bassiouni, the provisions which explicitly guarantee the right to a fair trial or hearing in criminal cases, exist in no less than forty-one national constitutions.[724]

Guarantees, according to this paragraph, are provided to 'any person'. As we are concerned with situations of armed conflict, international or non-international, this refers to civilians as well as to combatants. The rules

---

723 Buisman (2003), p. 167.
724 Bassiouni (2003), p. 605.

determining fair treatment and fair trial, in this context, will not only be the rules of international humanitarian law, but also the international law of human rights.

The 1949 Geneva Conventions and the 1977 Additional Protocols provide rules for fair treatment and fair trial, according to the category of persons involved or not involved in the armed conflict. The Third Geneva Convention provides such rules for combatants, the Fourth Geneva Convention for civilians. Article 75 of Additional Protocol I is supplementary, not only for civilians but also for combatants who are denied prisoner-of-war status in case of capture. The first paragraph of this Article states clearly that:

> Insofar as they are affected by a situation referred to in Article 1 of this Protocol, persons who are in the power of a Party to the conflict and who do not benefit from more favourable treatment under the Conventions or under this Protocol shall be treated humanely in all circumstances and shall enjoy, as a minimum, the protection provided by this Article without any adverse distinction based upon race, colour, sex, language, religion or belief, political or other opinion, national or social origin, wealth, birth or other status, or on any other similar criteria. Each Party shall respect the person, honour, convictions and religious practices of all such persons.

In comparison with human rights treaties, which are subject to derogations in time of war or emergencies, Article 75 is not subject to any possibility of derogation or suspension, and consequently it is these provisions which will play a decisive role in cases of armed conflict.[725] It is important to stress paragraph 7 of Article 75, which states:

> in order to avoid any doubt concerning the prosecution and trial of persons accused of war crimes or crimes against humanity, the following principles shall apply:
> (a) persons who are accused of such crimes should be submitted for the purpose of prosecution and trial in accordance with the applicable rules of international law;[726] and

---

725 Commentary on the Additional Protocols of 8 June 1977, pp. 878–80.

726 These words 'undoubtedly meant that the national law applicable in such cases must be strictly in conformity with the respective rules of international law' as the delegate of Germany pointed out (Official Records, Vol. XV, p. 205 – CDDH/III/SR.58, para 11).

(b) any such persons who do not benefit from more favourable treatment under the Conventions or this Protocol shall be accorded the treatment provided by this Article, whether or not the crimes of which they are accused constitute grave breaches of the Conventions or of this Protocol.

The international law of human rights includes provisions concerning fair treatment and fair trial. These rights are deeply rooted in the history of human rights and are included in the Universal Declaration, which states in Article 10: 'Everyone is entitled in full equality to a fair and public hearing by an independent and impartial tribunal, in the determination of his rights and obligations and of any criminal charge against him.' These rights are included in the International Covenant on Civil and Political Rights (art. 14), the European Convention (art. 5–6), the American Convention (art. 8) and the African Charter of Human and Peoples' Rights (art. 7). 'All of these provisions are aimed at ensuring the proper administration of justice, and to this end uphold a series of individual rights such as equality before the courts and tribunals and the right to a fair and public hearing by a competent, independent and impartial tribunal established by law.'[727] Fair treatment and fair trial include also the customary law principles *non bis in idem* and no punishment without law.

> In addition to the usual guarantees of an independent and impartial tribunal, public hearing, the presumption of innocence and the rights of the defense, it also provides for protection against self-incrimination, the right of appeal, and compensation for miscarriage of justice, and lays down the principles that no one may be tried twice for the same offence.[728]

---

727 Human Rights Committee General Comment 13, Article 14 (Twenty-first session, 1984, para. 10, Compilation of General Comments and General Recommendations Adopted by Human Rights Treaty Bodies, UN Doc. HRI/GEN/1/Rev.1 at 14 (1994), para. 1).
728 Robertson and Merrills (1996), p. 38.

Article 18
EXTRADITION

1. *The offences set forth in Article 15 sub-paragraphs 1 (a) to (c) shall be deemed to be included as extraditable offences in any extradition treaty existing between any of the Parties before the entry into force of this Protocol. Parties undertake to include such offences in every extradition treaty to be subsequently concluded between them.*

2. *When a Party which makes extradition conditional on the existence of a treaty receives a request for extradition from another Party with which it has no extradition treaty, the requested Party may, at its option, consider the present Protocol as the legal basis for extradition in respect of offences as set forth in Article 15 sub-paragraphs 1 (a) to (c).*

3. *Parties which do not make extradition conditional on the existence of a treaty shall recognize the offences set forth in Article 15 sub-paragraphs 1 (a) to (c) as extraditable offences between them, subject to the conditions provided by the law of the requested Party.*

4. *If necessary, offences set forth in Article 15 sub-paragraphs 1 (a) to (c) shall be treated, for the purposes of extradition between Parties, as if they had been committed not only in the place in which they occurred but also in the territory of the Parties that have established jurisdiction in accordance with Article 16 paragraph 1.*

Preparatory works

Report by the Director-General on the Reinforcement of UNESCO's action for the Protection of the World Cultural and Natural Heritage. UNESCO document 142 EX/15, Annex: Hague Meeting of Experts on the application and effectiveness of the Convention for the Protection of Cultural Property in the Event of Armed Conflict (The Hague, 14 May 1954), *Final Report*, para. 6.3, p. 3. http://unesdoc.unesco.org/images/0009/000958/095820Eo.pdf

The Second Expert Meeting on the 1954 Hague Convention for the Protection of Cultural Property in the Event of Armed Conflict. Lauswolt, The Netherlands, 9–11 February 1994.

A working document prepared by the Secretariat, CLT/94/608/1 of 28 November 1994, p. 3.

UNESCO, Meeting of Governmental Experts. Summary of comments received from States Parties to the Hague Convention and from the

International Council on Archives. UNESCO document CLT-96/ CONF.603/INF.4, Paris, December 1996, p. 2.

Expert Meeting on the review of the 1954 Hague Convention for the Protection of Cultural Property in the Event of Armed Conflict. Paris, UNESCO Headquarters, 28 November–2 December 1994. UNESCO document CLT/CH/94/608/2, *Final Report*, pp. 4–5.

UNESCO, Meeting of Governmental Experts. Summary of comments received from States Parties to the Hague Convention and from the International Council on Archives. UNESCO document CLT-96/ CONF.603/INF.4, Paris, December 1996.

Draft provisions for the revision of the 1954 Hague Convention and commentary from the UNESCO Secretariat. UNESCO document CLT-97/CONF.208/2, Paris, October 1997.

UNESCO, Meeting of Governmental Experts. Summary of comments received from States Parties to the Hague Convention, the International Committee of the Red Cross and the International Council on Archives. UNESCO document Paris, March 1998.

Preliminary Draft Second Protocol to the 1954 Hague Convention. UNESCO document HC/1999/1, October 1998 (English, French and Russian).

Draft Second Protocol to the 1954 Hague Convention for the protection of cultural property in the event of armed conflict. UNESCO document HC/1999/1/rev.1, February 1999 (original: English).

Presentation of the results of the Working Group on Chapter 4. H. Fischer, coordinator of the Working Group, 25 March 1999. Conference document HC/1999/INF.5.

Bibliography

Boylan, P. J. 1993. *Review of the Convention for the Protection of Cultural Property in the Event of Armed Conflict (The Hague Convention of 1954).* Paris: UNESCO, para. 9.1–9.25, pp. 91–98.

Chamberlain, K. 2004. *War and Cultural Heritage.* Leicester: Institute of Art and Law, pp. 205–10.

Desch, T. 1999. The Second Protocol to the 1954 Convention for the Protection of Cultural Property in the Event of Armed Conflict. *Yearbook of International Humanitarian Law,* Vol. 2, pp. 79–82.

Henckaerts, J.-M. 1999. New rules for the protection of cultural property in armed conflict: the significance of the Second Protocol to the 1954

Hague Convention for the Protection of Cultural Property in the Event of Armed Conflict. *IRRC*, No. 835, pp. 613–15.

O'Keefe, R. 2002. *National Implementation of the Penal Provisions of Chapter 4 of the Second Protocol of 26 March 1999 to the Hague Convention of 1954 for the Protection of Cultural Property in the Event of Armed Conflict.* 29 March (UNESCO document CLT/CIH/MCO/2002/PI/H/1).

Schabas, W. A. 1997. Sentencing by international tribunals: a human rights approach. *Duke Journal of Comparative and International Law*, Vol. 7, p. 461.

Toman, J. 1996. *The Protection of Cultural Property in the Event of Armed Conflict: Commentary on the Hague Convention of 14 May 1954.* Aldershot: Dartmouth/Paris: UNESCO, pp. 59–66.

Statutes of the international criminal tribunals

See the documentation under the commentary to Article 15.

PREPARATORY WORK BEFORE THE 1999 HAGUE CONFERENCE

Although the discussion on prosecution of violations commenced at the very beginning of the review process, extradition was only mentioned for the first time in the draft elaborated at the Lauswolt Expert Meeting in February 1994.[729] Extradition is one of the main forms of legal assistance that States provide to one other, and as such it was included in Article 11, which concerns mutual assistance in criminal matters. However, only paragraph 2 is reserved for extradition:

> 2. States Parties shall cooperate in the matter of extradition and shall give due consideration in particular to the request of the State whose territory the grave breaches under this instrument have occurred.

Following the discussion at the 1997 Governmental Experts Meeting, the Secretariat prepared 'Draft provisions for the revision of the 1954 Hague Convention and commentary from the UNESCO Secretariat'.[730] To ensure

---

729 The Second Expert Meeting on the 1954 Hague Convention for the Protection of Cultural Property in the Event of Armed Conflict. Lauswolt, The Netherlands, 9–11 February 1994.

730 Draft provisions for the revision of the 1954 Hague Convention and commentary from the UNESCO Secretariat. CLT-97/CONF.208/2, Paris, October 1997.

clarity, the last part of the phrase, following 'State', was replaced with 'in whose territory any grave breach under this instrument has occurred.'

After the discussion at the 1998 Vienna Governmental Expert Meeting, the UNESCO Secretariat prepared a document based on several meetings of government experts, and particularly on the discussions that took place at the May 1998 Vienna Meeting: the *Preliminary Draft Second Protocol*.[731] This was then sent to Member States and international organizations for a new round of comments.[732]

Extradition remained in Article [15] on mutual assistance on criminal matters in the same form as the text included in the 1997 Draft Provisions:

2. States Parties shall cooperate in the matter of extradition and shall give due consideration in particular to the request of the State in whose territory any grave breach under this instrument has occurred.

The final draft of the Second Protocol – *Draft Second Protocol to the 1954 Hague Convention for the Protection of Cultural Property in the Event of Armed Conflict* (UNESCO doc. HC/1999/1/rev.1, February 1999), which constituted the basis of discussion at the 1999 Hague Diplomatic Conference – included only one modification: 'instrument' was replaced by 'Protocol'.

THE DRAFTING OF ARTICLE 18 AT THE 1999 HAGUE CONFERENCE

The delegates that took the floor at the Plenary Session of the Conference concentrated on the main articles concerning serious violations. A few of them expressed views on mutual legal assistance, but not specifically on extradition. Chaired by Horst Fischer, the Working Group was tasked with establishing the final text. Several delegates recommended avoiding the drafting of texts relating to criminal procedures, which are already well covered by other international treaties. As a result, the chairman's draft separated the paragraph on extradition from the article on mutual assistance, and presented to the

---

731 *Preliminary Draft Second Protocol to the 1954 Hague Convention.* UNESCO document HC/1999/1, October 1998 (English, French and Russian).
732 UNESCO, Summary of comments on Preliminary Draft Second Protocol to the 1954 Hague Convention received from High Contracting Parties to the Hague Convention for the Protection of Cultural Property in the Event of Armed Conflict 1954, other UNESCO Member States and international organizations, Paris, 15 January 1999.

Working Group a new article on extradition based on the wording of other international treaties dealing with criminal matters, in particular in relation to terrorism.[733] The draft Fischer proposed was adopted by the Working Group and also by the Plenary Session of the Conference. With minor modifications, it was included in the Second Protocol as Article 18.

ANALYSIS OF THE TEXT

Article 18 contains a range of provisions relevant to extradition. These provisions apply only to those serious violations of the Protocol set forth in Article 15, paragraph 1, sub-paragraphs (a) to (c).

As mentioned above, the formulation of Article 18 is practically identical to Article 9 of the International Convention for the Suppression of Terrorist Bombing of 1998.[734] This Convention was the last to be adopted before the 1999 Hague Conference, and it is for this reason that the wording of the Convention inspired the authors of the provision adopted and included in the Second Protocol.

It is not our purpose here to analyze the international conventions on criminal matters, but it is nevertheless useful to trace the history of this wording. The first formulation used for future drafting was found in Article 8 of the Convention for the Prevention and Punishment of Terrorism, signed in Geneva, 16 November 1937.[735] This formulation is then found in other

---

733 This Article is almost identical to Article 8 of the International Convention for the Suppression of Terrorist Bombing, General Assembly Resolution 164, UN GAOR, 52nd Session, Supp. No. 49, at 389, UN Doc. A/52/49 (1998).

734 Ibid. Article 9 states: '1. The offences set forth in Article 2 shall be deemed to be included as extraditable offences in any extradition treaty existing between any of the States Parties before the entry into force of this Convention. States Parties undertake to include such offences as extraditable offences in every extradition treaty to be subsequently concluded between them. 2. When a State Party which makes extradition conditional on the existence of a treaty receives a request for extradition from another State Party with which it has no extradition treaty, the requested State Party may, at its option, consider this Convention as a legal basis for extradition in respect of the offences set forth in Article 2. Extradition shall be subject to the other conditions provided by the law of the requested State. 3. States Parties which do not make extradition conditional on the existence of a treaty shall recognize the offences set forth in Article 2 as extraditable offences between themselves, subject to the conditions provided by the law of the requested State. 4. If necessary, the offences set forth in Article 2 shall be treated, for the purposes of extradition between States Parties, as if they had been committed not only in the place in which they occurred but also in the territory of the States that have established jurisdiction in accordance with Article 6, paragraphs 1 and 2. 5. The provisions of all extradition treaties and arrangements between States Parties with regard to offences set forth in Article 2 shall be deemed to be modified as between State Parties to the extent that they are incompatible with this Convention.'

735 *League of Nations Official Journal*, Vol. 19 (1938), p. 23, League of Nations Doc. C.546(I).1937.V (1938). This convention never entered into force.

conventions that prohibit terrorist activities[736] with a similar provision also found in Article 10 of the Draft Code of Crimes against the Peace and Security of Mankind, adopted by the ILC at its 48th session in 1996.

In the international context, extradition is defined as a legal process, based on treaty and/or national law, by which one State delivers to another State an accused offender or a convicted individual, charged or convicted of a criminal offence against the laws of the requesting State, or in violation of international criminal law, in order to be tried or punished in the requesting State with respect to the crime stated in the request:

> While usually the wanted person will have been physically present on the territory of the requesting state, when the crime was committed, this is not necessarily the case, for example in relation to offences committed on board ships or aircraft, or in a place under the control of, but not under the *de jure* sovereignty of, the requesting state, or offences constructively committed in that state by someone outside it, as where the effects of an offence occur within its territory or a constituent element of the offence takes place there.[737]

Extradition has a long history, dating back to pre-Christian times, but its basic rules were developed at the end of the 19th century and form part of contemporary international law, while never becoming part of customary international law. There is no duty imposed on States to extradite common criminals or to prosecute or punish fugitive offenders when extradition does not take place.

The provisions of Article 18 enable the State where the offender is present – the custodial State – to select and implement a legal basis for extradition. This Article ensures that the custodial State will have such a legal basis to grant a request for extradition and fulfill its obligation under Article 17.

Extradition is based on bilateral agreements or multilateral treaties. Article 18 is one such international provision.

---

736 Article 8 of the Convention for the Suppression of Unlawful Seizure of Aircraft (The Hague, 16 December 1970); Article 8 of the Convention for the Suppression of Unlawful Acts Against the Safety of Civil Aviation (Montreal, 23 September 1971), Article 8 of the Convention on the Prevention and Punishment of Crimes Against Internationally Protected Persons, Including Diplomatic Agents (New York, 14 December 1973); Article 15 of the Convention on the Safety of United Nations and Associated Personnel (New York, 9 December 1994); Article 10 of the International Convention Against the Taking of Hostages (New York, 17 December 1979).

737 Jennings and Watts (1996), p. 949.

Paragraph 1

The first paragraph of this Article addresses situations in which an extradition treaty exists between the States concerned but that does not cover the crime for which extradition is requested.

First phrase of paragraph 1

According to this paragraph, the serious violations against cultural property included in paragraphs (a), (b) and (c) of Article 15, paragraph 1 shall be considered to be included as extraditable offences in any extradition treaty that the Parties have concluded and that entered into force before the entry into force of this Protocol.

International law allows States to grant extradition for any crime they consider appropriate. This happens only for the most serious crimes, as is shown in the present paragraph. National laws and international treaties have sometimes included an agreed list of offences, called 'extraditable offences'. This was mainly the practice of older treaties, but the different definitions of crimes and variety of terminologies in national penal codes proved an impediment. For this reason, more recent treaties have referred to a certain category of punishment (deprivation of liberty) as the criterion for extradition. Recent bilateral treaties have mostly abandoned the practice of a list of extraditable offences in favour of a reference to punishability, that is, the requirement of deprivation of liberty for at least one year,[738] without taking into consideration the existence of extenuating or aggravating circumstances.

Many States adopted special laws that enumerate the crimes for which extradition can be granted. These laws constituted a useful basis for the conclusion of extradition treaties, formulated in ways consistent with the

---

738 This is also the practice used in the European Convention on Extradition of 13 December 1957 (ETS 024), art. 2, para. 1: 'Extradition shall be granted in respect of offences punishable under the laws of the requesting Party and of the requested Party by deprivation of liberty or under a detention order for a maximum period of at least one year or by a more severe penalty. Where a conviction and prison sentence have occurred or a detention order has been made in the territory of the requesting Party, the punishment awarded must have been for a period of at least four months.' The Convention entered into force on 18 April 1960. As of 1st October 2009, 49 States are Parties to this Convention.

laws.[739] These laws also decided whether extradition treaties take precedence over national extradition acts.[740]

In the past, extradition was included in certain peace treaties, but it was only in the second part of the 18th century that such treaties were concluded to any great extent. In the 19th century, numerous bilateral treaties were concluded and constituted the first form of cooperation between States with respect to the surrender of fugitive criminals to States which had the jurisdiction to try and punish them. The number of these treaties has increased and is currently estimated at around 1,500.[741]

With the growing tendency towards codification of international law, multilateral extradition treaties began to develop in different regions of the world. As usual, the process started among the American States, which concluded such treaties in 1889, 1902,[742] 1911[743] and 1933,[744] the most important being the Inter-American Convention on Extradition of 1981.[745] The European Convention on Extradition was adopted on 13 December 1957[746] and was followed by two additional protocols (1975, 1978). Extradition conventions were also concluded by the Arab States (1952)[747] and the African States (Tananarive, 1961).[748]

In cases where the offender is in the territory of the States Party to these conventions, the States are encouraged, though not necessarily obliged,

---

739 Belgium was the first state to adopt such a law in 1833.

740 European laws usually state that the extradition treaty takes precedence: Austrian Extradition Act (*Bundesgesetzblatt*, 1979, No. 529), Germany (*Bundesgesetzblatt*, 1982, I, 2071), Switzerland ILM, Vol. 20, 1981, p. 1339). In the UK, the Extradition Act prevails.

741 According to the index of treaties published in 1983, approximately 484 extradition treaties were concluded after 1945. See Rohn (1997). During the period of the League of Nations, 112 bilateral treaties were registered and published by the League of Nations Treaty Series (LNTS).

742 Treaty for the Extradition of Criminals and for the Protection against Anarchism, 28 January 1902; Consolidated Treaty Series (CTS), Vol. 190, p. 411.

743 Caracas Agreement on Extradition, 18 July 1911, CTS, Vol. 214, p. 129.

744 Montevideo Convention on Extradition, 26 December 1933, LNTS, Vol. 165, p. 45.

745 International Legal Materials, Vol. 20, 1981, p. 723.

746 CETS 024, UNTS, Vol. 359, p. 273. Entered into force on 18 April 1960. Convention was ratified by 49 States (two non-Member States of Council of Europe, Israel and South Africa). The European Convention supersedes existing bilateral treaties, but permits future bilateral treaties supplementing the provisions of the Convention (art. 28).

747 An agreement between the Arab League States Concerning the Extradition of Fugitive Offenders. This agreement was approved by the Council of the League of Arab States on 14 September 1952, opened for signature on 3 November 1952, and signed by Egypt, Iraq, Jordan, Lebanon, Saudi Arabia and Syria. BFSP, Vol. 159 (1952), p. 606. Only Egypt, Jordan and Saudi Arabia ratified the agreement.

748 General Convention on the Cooperation in judicial matters of OCAM (Organisation Communale Africaine et Malgache) concluded by 14 former French colonies, signed at Tananarive on 12 September 1961. See Sohn (1971–1974), Vol. 2, p. 616.

to proceed with extradition. The legal basis of the extradition is either the Convention itself, or references to extradition in other existing treaties or future conventions on extradition. This is the case for this provision.

Numerous multilateral treaties on specific offences (drugs, hijacking, terrorism) contain provisions on extradition or consider that such specific crimes are deemed to be included in existing extradition treaties. This is also stated in Article 18, paragraph 1: such offences 'are deemed to be included as extraditable offences in any extradition treaty existing between any of the Parties before the entry into force of the Protocol'.

What is the legal significance of this provision in relation to bilateral and multilateral treaties on extradition? The phrase 'shall be deemed to be included' is a unilateral interpretative clause, which binds only the State taking such engagement when becoming party to the Protocol. It is neither an amendment to the previous extradition treaty nor a modification of its text. According to the 1969 Vienna Convention, amendment and modification require accomplishment of the procedures stated in Article 40. With the development of this practice following adoption of the 1969 Vienna Convention, we can qualify this engagement as supplementary: 'The right to become a party to a supplementary treaty is not necessarily extended and limited to parties to the earlier treaty. This will be so if the supplementary treaty, although linked to the earlier treaty, stands alone and to be effective does not need the parties to it to be parties to the earlier treaty'.[749] This problem did not escape the attention of the legislators at the Vienna Conference in 1968–1969. The ILC submitted a draft of Article 38, which provided that '[a] treaty may be modified by subsequent practice in the application of the treaty establishing the agreement of the parties to modify its provisions'. According to the Commission's final report,[750] the case contemplated amounted to a tacit agreement rather than a custom. The 1968–1969 Vienna Conference rejected the draft Article by 53 votes to 15, with 26 abstentions,[751] for several reasons: first, to avoid officially recognizing a situation which must remain exceptional; second, to reinforce the requirements of constitutional law against the encroachments of international law; and finally, to resist unwritten international agreements in general (all the more fiercely as the requirements of practice prevail over any such resistance).[752]

---

749 Aust (2000), p. 221.
750 Yearbook of the International Law Commission, 1966, Vol. II, p. 238.
751 United Nations Conference on the Law of Treaties, *Official Records, Reports of the Committee of the Whole*, p. 158
752 Reuter (1995), para. 212, p. 138.

Second phrase of paragraph 1

The second phrase of paragraph 1 declares the engagement of Parties to the Protocol engage to include the offences set forth in Article 15, paragraph 1, sub-paragraphs (a), (b) and (c) in every future extradition treaty 'to be subsequently concluded between them'. It is therefore the obligation of the Parties to the Protocol to include offences (a), (b) and (c) in every future extradition treaty, whether bilateral or multilateral. Paragraphs (2) to (4) refine this obligation.

Paragraph 2

This paragraph does not need much comment. It deals with situations in which, under the law of the requested State, extradition is conditional on the existence of an extradition treaty, and there is no such extradition treaty between the States concerned when extradition is requested.

It refers to situations when States that are Parties to the Second Protocol make possible extradition only when an extradition treaty exists. As I. A. Shearer says:

> For those States whose laws or established practices prevent them from extraditing in the absence of a formal international agreement, extradition treaties are the sole means by which they co-operate with other States in surrendering fugitive criminals to jurisdictions competent to try and punish them. The number and effectiveness of such treaties is therefore of vital importance.[753]

Extradition takes place only if there is a request for it. The formalities to be accomplished may be stipulated in treaties or in the domestic extradition laws of the requesting State. The 1957 European Convention on Extradition requires the following formalities:

> Article 12 The request and supporting documents
> 1. The request shall be in writing and shall be communicated through the diplomatic channel. Other means of communication may be arranged by direct agreement between two or more Parties.
> 2. The request shall be supported by:

---

753 Shearer (1971), pp. 34–35.

(a) the original or an authenticated copy of the conviction and
sentence or detention order immediately enforceable or of the
warrant of arrest or other order having the same effect and
issued in accordance with the procedure laid down in the law
of the requesting Party;

(b   a statement of the offences for which extradition is requested.
The time and place of their commission, their legal descriptions
and a reference to the relevant legal provisions shall be set out
as accurately as possible; and

(c) a copy of the relevant enactments or, where this is not possible,
a statement of the relevant law and as accurate a description
as possible of the person claimed, together with any other
information which will help to establish his identity and
nationality.

Article 13 Supplementary information
If the information communicated by the requesting Party is found
to be insufficient to allow the requested Party to make a decision
in pursuance of this Convention, the latter Party shall request the
necessary supplementary information and may fix a time-limit for the
receipt thereof.

The laws of some States require that the lawfulness of the extradition be
determined by the courts when domestic law so requires. This is not a
requirement of customary international law.[754]

When a Party to the Protocol receives a formal request for extradition
and no extradition treaty exists between the requested and requesting State,
this paragraph of the Protocol establishes a legal basis for extradition, but
only if the requested Party wishes so. The paragraph simply confirms that
in situations where the Contracting Parties to the Protocol have no bilateral
extradition treaty between themselves or are not Contracting Parties to a
multilateral treaty on extradition, they have the possibility, if they so wish and
depending on their exclusive sovereign decision, to regard the Second Protocol
as a legal basis for extradition. This provision can help them to overcome and
respond to the requirements of their domestic laws on extradition and creates
an appropriate legal basis. This legal basis is limited to the offences set forth
in Article 15, paragraph 1, sub-paragraphs (a), (b) and (c).

---

754 Jennings and Watts (1996), p. 960.

The paragraph is based on the usual practice that the subject-matter of the extradition is left entirely to the requested State.

Paragraph 3

Paragraph 3 of the Article on Extradition deals with the situation of States, mostly countries of civil law, that have no treaties for extradition. Under the law of the States concerned, extradition is not conditional on the existence of a treaty.

Based on the practice of civil law countries, the Institute of International Law, in the Resolution adopted on 9 September 1880 at the session in Oxford, favoured the adoption of treaties, but did not consider these indispensable. It considered that extradition can operate in the absence of contractual relations: '*Il est à desirer que, dans chaque pays, une loi règle la procédure de la matière, ainsi que les conditions auxquelles les individus réclamés comme malfaiteurs seront livrés aux gouvernements avec lesquels il n'existe pas de traité.*'[755] This view corresponded to the continental view, particularly to French legal doctrine and practice. The laws of several other countries also required a guarantee of reciprocity as a condition precedent to the operation in the absence of a formal treaty. According to present practice and doctrine in most of the States,

> the national law represents an auxiliary and subsidiary factor in relations to treaties. The pre-eminence of international law, be it conventional or customary, is thus recognized by practically all the states of Western Europe. As an example, the French law on extradition of 1927 must abide by contrary clauses of a treaty. The French law is applicable only when there exists no convention, or in order to make up for *lacunae*. Article 1 of the Swiss law on International Cooperation in Criminal Matters, which entered into force on 1 January 1983, expressly reserves the international conventions that bind Switzerland.[756]

Even if serious violations of sub-paragraphs (a), (b) and (c) are not included in national laws of extradition and, in the absence of an extradition treaty, the Parties to the Protocol recognize these offences as extraditable ones, the

---

755 Extradition. Résolutions d'Oxford, 9 septembre 1880, Session d'Oxford. Résolutions de l'Institut de droit international. Tableau général des résolutions (1873–1956) publié par Hans Wehberg. Bâle, Editions juridiques et sociologiques, 1957, p. 380.
756 Poncet and Gully-Hart (1986), p. 466.

conditions of extradition and the extradition procedure will be governed by the law of the requested State.

Paragraph 4

This provision is a safety valve bridging any potential gap. The words 'if necessary' mean that in situations where the basis of extradition expressed in the previous three paragraphs is confronted by obstacles, the present paragraph provides an additional guarantee ensuring that extradition takes place. Paragraph 4 extends the principle of universal jurisdiction to such situations by enlarging the application of the territorial principle included in Article 16, paragraph 1, sub-paragraph (a), to Parties that have established jurisdiction in accordance with that paragraph.

A paragraph of a similar nature[757] was included in the Draft Code of Crimes Against the Peace and Security of Mankind adopted by the ILC in 1996.[758] Paragraph 4 of Article 10 of the Draft states:

> Each of those crimes shall be treated, for the purpose of extradition between States Parties, as if it had been committed not only in the place in which it occurred but also in the territory of any other State Party.[759]

In the Commentary of the International Law Commission, it was stated:

> Under some treaties and national laws, the custodial State may only grant requests for extradition coming from the State in which the crime occurred. However, several anti-terrorism conventions contain provisions which are designed to secure the possibility for the custodial State, notwithstanding any such restriction, to grant requests for

---

757 The question was raised during the discussion by one of the members of the Commission, Mr. Rosenstock: '[giving] the priority to request of the State in whose territory the crime had been committed was not always justified …. Recourse to national courts would be preferable' (2347th meeting of the ILC, 3 June 1994, *Yearbook of the International Law Commission*, 1994, Vol. I, para. 34, p. 130).

758 *Yearbook of the International Law Commission*, 1996, Vol. II, Part 2. http://www.un.org/law/ilc/texts/dcodefra.htm

759 It is interesting to note that the draft of Article included the same formulation as the present paragraph, i.e. 'territories of the States Parties which have established their jurisdiction in accordance with Article 5 bis', but was replaced by the words 'any other State Party' by the Drafting Committee. Mr. Calero Rodriguez, Chairman of the Drafting Committee. *Yearbook of the International Law Commission*, 1996, Vol. I, para. 70, p. 53.

extradition received from certain States which have an obligation to establish their primary jurisdiction over the relevant offences.[760] The more recent Convention on the Safety of United Nations and Associated Personnel also secures the possibility for the custodial State to grant such a request received from a State that intends to exercise jurisdiction on a permissive basis, for example, the passive personality principle. Paragraph 4 secures the possibility for the custodial State to grant a request for extradition received from any State Party to the Code with respect to the crimes covered in Part II. This broader approach is consistent with the general obligation of every State Party to establish its jurisdiction over the crimes set out in articles 17 to 20 in accordance with Article 8 and finds further justification in the fact that the present Code does not confer primary jurisdiction on any particular States nor establish an order of priority among extradition requests.[761]

---

760 The question of whether these provisions also extend to States seeking to exercise jurisdiction on a permissive basis has been raised in relation to paragraph 4 of Article 10 of the Hostages Convention in the following terms: 'This provision was added to the Hague Convention and each of the subsequent anti-terrorism conventions to cover the case of any requirement which may exist in treaties or domestic laws wherein extradition may only be had when the offence was committed in the territory of the requesting State. It may be noted that this fiction relates only to those States which are required to establish primary jurisdiction pursuant to Article 5(1). It would not appear to relate to those States which have established their jurisdiction pursuant to that provision on a permissive basis, i.e., the passive personality principle, and over stateless persons resident in their territory.' Lambert (1990), p. 243.

761 *Yearbook of the International Law Commission*, 1996, Vol. II, Part 2, pp. 32–33. http://www.un.org/law/ilc/texts/dcodefra.htm

Article 19
MUTUAL LEGAL ASSISTANCE

1. *Parties shall afford one another the greatest measure of assistance in connection with investigations or criminal or extradition proceedings brought in respect of the offences set forth in Article 15, including assistance in obtaining evidence at their disposal necessary for the proceedings.*
2. *Parties shall carry out their obligations under paragraph 1 in conformity with any treaties or other arrangements on mutual legal assistance that may exist between them. In the absence of such treaties or arrangements, Parties shall afford one another assistance in accordance with their domestic law.*

Preparatory works

Report by the Director-General on the Reinforcement of UNESCO's action for the Protection of the World Cultural and Natural Heritage. UNESCO document 142 EX/15, Annex: Hague Meeting of Experts on the application and effectiveness of the Convention for the Protection of Cultural Property in the Event of Armed Conflict (The Hague, 14 May 1954), *Final Report*, para. 6.3, p. 3. http://unesdoc.unesco.org/images/0009/000958/095820Eo.pdf

A working document prepared by the Secretariat, CLT/94/608/1 of 28 November 1994, p. 3.

UNESCO, Meeting of Governmental Experts. Summary of comments received from States Parties to the Hague Convention and from the International Council on Archives. UNESCO document CLT-96/CONF.603/INF.4, Paris, December 1996, p. 2

Expert meeting on the review of the 1954 Hague Convention for the Protection of Cultural Property in the Event of Armed Conflict. Paris, UNESCO Headquarters, 28 November–2 December 1994. UNESCO document CLT/CH/94/608/2, *Final Report*, pp. 4–5.

UNESCO, Meeting of Governmental Experts. Summary of comments received from States Parties to the Hague Convention and from the International Council on Archives. UNESCO document CLT-96/CONF.603/INF.4, Paris, December 1996.

Draft provisions for the revision of the 1954 Hague Convention and commentary from the UNESCO Secretariat. CLT-97/CONF.208/2, Paris, October 1997.

UNESCO, Meeting of Governmental Experts. Summary of comments received from States Parties to the Hague Convention, the International Committee of the Red Cross and the International Council on Archives. UNESCO document Paris, March 1998.

Preliminary Draft Second Protocol to the 1954 Hague Convention. UNESCO document HC/1999/1, October 1998 (English, French and Russian).

Draft Second Protocol to the 1954 Hague Convention for the Protection of Cultural Property in the Event of Armed Conflict. UNESCO document HC/1999/1/rev.1, February 1999.

Presentation of the results of the Working Group on Chapter 4. H. Fischer, coordinator of the Working Group, 25 March 1999. Conference document HC/1999/INF.5.

Bibliography

Boylan, P. J. 1993. *Review of the Convention for the Protection of Cultural Property in the Event of Armed Conflict (The Hague Convention of 1954).* Paris: UNESCO, para. 9.1–9.25, pp. 91–98.

Chamberlain, K. 2004. *War and Cultural Heritage.* Leicester: Institute of Art and Law, pp. 205–10.

Desch, T. 1999. The Second Protocol to the 1954 Convention for the Protection of Cultural Property in the Event of Armed Conflict. *Yearbook of International Humanitarian Law,* Vol. 2, pp. 79–82.

Henckaerts, J.-M. 1999. New rules for the protection of cultural property in armed conflict: the significance of the Second Protocol to the 1954 Hague Convention for the Protection of Cultural Property in the Event of Armed Conflict. *IRRC,* No. 835, pp. 593–620, here 613–15.

O'Keefe, R. 2002. *National Implementation of the Penal Provisions of Chapter 4 of the Second Protocol of 26 March 1999 to the Hague Convention of 1954 for the Protection of Cultural Property in the Event of Armed Conflict.* 29 March (UNESCO document CLT/CIH/MCO/2002/PI/H/1).

Schabas, W. A. 1997. Sentencing by international tribunals: a human rights approach. *Duke Journal of Comparative and International Law,* Vol. 7, p. 461.

Toman, J. 1996. *The Protection of Cultural Property in the Event of Armed Conflict: Commentary on the Hague Convention of 14 May 1954.* Aldershot: Dartmouth/Paris: UNESCO, pp. 59–66.

Statutes of the international criminal tribunals

See the documentation under the commentary to Article 15.

PREPARATORY WORK BEFORE THE 1999 HAGUE CONFERENCE

The Article on mutual assistance in criminal matters was included by the experts who met in Lauswolt for the Second Expert Meeting in February 1994. It formed part of the first provision on sanctions. Article 11 was drafted as follows:

> Article 11. Mutual assistance in criminal matters
> 1. The States Parties shall assist one another in detecting, arresting and bringing to trial persons suspected of having committed grave breaches under this instrument.
> 2. States Parties shall cooperate in the matter of extradition and shall give due consideration in particular to the request of the State whose territory the grave breaches under this instrument have occurred.
> 3. The States Parties shall cooperate in all other cases of violations of this instrument under the same conditions.
> 4. The law of the States Parties requested shall apply in all cases. The provisions of the preceding paragraphs shall not, however, affect the obligations arising from the provisions of any other treaty of a bilateral or multilateral nature which governs or will govern the whole or part of the subject of mutual assistance in criminal matters.

Only a few, rather stylistic changes were made in the draft elaborated by the Secretariat on the basis of the discussion at the 1997 Governmental Experts Meeting: 'Draft provisions for the revision of the 1954 Hague Convention and commentary from the UNESCO Secretariat'.[762] These provisions were also included along with these changes, in the *Preliminary Draft Second Protocol*,[763] which the UNESCO Secretariat prepared after the 1998 Vienna

---

762 Draft provisions for the revision of the 1954 Hague Convention and commentary from the UNESCO Secretariat. CLT-97/CONF.208/2, Paris, October 1997. The word 'suspected' was replaced by 'accused'.
763 *Preliminary Draft Second Protocol to the 1954 Hague Convention*. UNESCO document HC/1999/1, October 1998 (English, French and Russian), art. [15]:

Governmental Experts Meeting. The *Preliminary Draft Second Protocol*, which also includes a few editorial modifications, was sent to the UNESCO Member States and international organizations for comments.[764]

In their comments the States proposed an Article to include mutual assistance and extradition. The States proposed to examine it with reference to relevant provisions of the terrorist conventions (Australia), Part 9 of the ICC Statute (Norway), and Article 88 of Protocol I (Sweden). Several drafting modifications were also proposed. On the basis of the States' responses, the UNESCO Secretariat and the Government of the Netherlands drew up the final draft of the Second Protocol: *Draft Second Protocol to the 1954 Hague Convention for the Protection of Cultural Property in the Event of Armed Conflict* (UNESCO doc. HC/1999/1/Rev.1, February 1999), which provided the basis of discussion at the 1999 Hague Diplomatic Conference. Only paragraph 3 was substantially modified in comparison with the previous text:

Article [23]. Mutual assistance in criminal matters
1. The States Parties shall assist one another to detect, arrest and bring to trial any person accused of having committed any grave breach under this Protocol.
2. States Parties shall cooperate in the matter of extradition and shall give due consideration in particular to the request of the State in whose territory any grave breach under this Protocol has occurred.
3. The States Parties shall provide all possible means of mutual assistance in connection with investigations or proceedings taken in respect of all violations of this Protocol including the obtaining of evidence for use in such proceedings.

Article [15]. Mutual assistance in criminal matters
1. The States Parties shall assist one another to detect, arrest and bring to trial any person accused of having committed any grave breach under this Protocol.
2. States Parties shall cooperate in the matter of extradition and shall give due consideration in particular to the request of the State in whose territory any grave breach under this Protocol has occurred.
3. The States Parties shall provide mutual assistance in all other cases of violation of this Protocol.
4. The law of the State Party which requested to provide assistance shall apply.
5. The provisions of the preceding paragraphs shall not affect the obligations arising from the provisions of any other treaty with regard to cooperation and mutual assistance in criminal matters.
764 UNESCO, Summary of comments on Preliminary Draft Second Protocol to the 1954 Hague Convention received from High Contracting Parties to the Hague Convention for the Protection of Cultural Property in the Event of Armed Conflict 1954, other UNESCO Member States and international organizations, Paris, 15 January 1999.

4. The law of the State Party which requested to provide assistance shall apply.

5. The provisions of the preceding paragraphs shall not affect the obligations arising from the provisions of any other treaty with regard to cooperation and mutual assistance in criminal matters.

Discussion and drafting of Article 19 at the 1999 Hague Conference

The delegates that took the floor at the Plenary Session of the Conference concentrated on the main articles on serious violations but welcomed the provision on mutual assistance (France, Italy and Switzerland). Argentina proposed to merge this Article with Article [21], which concerned jurisdiction.[765] The US delegate, supported by Israel, Spain and Sweden, suggested drawing on those provisions that were already accepted in other instruments 'rather than attempting to innovate and to go into matters of criminal procedure which was not the business of the present exercise'.[766]

The real drafting work lay in the hands of the Working Group, chaired by Professor Horst Fischer. Taking into account the recommendation to adapt the provisions of this Protocol to the basic codification work done by others, Fischer included a new draft in his Working Paper of 22 March 1999. This was based on the previous draft but its wording was adapted to take into account provisions used in other international treaties dealing with criminal matters, in particular, those concerning terrorism.[767] The draft Fischer proposed was adopted by the Working Group and afterwards by the Plenary Session of the Conference. Apart from minor editorial changes, this text figures in the Protocol as Article 19.

ANALYSIS OF THE TEXT

Similar provisions are included in other international treaties dealing with international crimes, that are relevant to paragraph 1.[768] Article 10 of

---

765 Hague Conference, Plenary Session, 18 March 1999, p. 168.

766 Ibid., p. 170.

767 The article is essentially identical to Article 10 of the International Convention for the Suppression of Terrorist Bombing, General Assembly resolution 164, UN GAOR, 52nd Session, Supp. No. 49, at 389, UN Doc. A/52/49 (1998).

768 Relevant to paragraph 1 of this Article are the following: Article 10, paragraph 1 of the Convention for the Suppression of Unlawful Seizure of Aircraft (The Hague, 16 December 1970); Article 11,

the International Convention for the Suppression of Terrorist Bombing of 1998[769] states that:

1. States Parties shall afford one another the greatest measure of assistance in connection with investigations or criminal or extradition proceedings brought in respect of the offences set forth in Article 2, including assistance in obtaining evidence at their disposal necessary for the proceedings.
2. States Parties shall carry out their obligations under paragraph 1 of the present Article in conformity with any treaties or other arrangements on mutual legal assistance that may exist between them. In the absence of such treaties or arrangements, States Parties shall afford one another assistance in accordance with their domestic law.

Paragraph 1

Paragraph 1 obliges States Parties to the Protocol to afford one another the greatest measure of assistance in connection with the following proceedings:
*   investigations,
*   criminal proceedings, or
*   extradition proceedings brought in respect of the offences.
This is set forth in Article 15, paragraph 1, sub-paragraphs (a), (b) and (c), that is, in relation to serious violations subject to universal jurisdiction.

This duty of assistance includes assistance in obtaining evidence at the disposal of the States that is necessary for the proceedings.

It is important to stress that paragraph 1 is not limited to most serious violations of sub-paragraphs (a), (b) and (c), but bears on all serious violations as included in Article 15, paragraph 1.

---

paragraph 1 of the Convention for the Suppression of Unlawful Acts Against the Safety of Civil Aviation (Montreal, 23 September 1971), Article 10, paragraph 1 of the Convention on the Prevention and Punishment of Crimes Against Internationally Protected Persons, Including Diplomatic Agents (New York, 14 December 1973); Article 11, paragraph 1 of the European Convention on the Suppression of Terrorism (Strasbourg, 27 January 1977); Article 11, paragraph 1 of the International Convention Against the Taking of Hostages (New York, 17 December 1979).
769 General Assembly Resolution 164, UN GAOR, 52nd Session, Supp. No. 49, at 389, UN Doc. A/52/49 (1998).

The need for legal assistance became apparent with the growth in movement of persons. Even if cooperation established by police-to-police channels helped to provide basic information for dealing with criminal matters, such assistance at the police and informal level proved insufficient, for insurmountable obstacles arose when legal process and judicial intervention were required. Such judicial activities in the territory of foreign States were impossible; and those engaged in such activities were confronted by the need to respect the territorial sovereignty of States. The legal assistance of State prosecutors and courts was necessary to permit the organs and courts of foreign States to accomplish investigating and prosecuting activities in the territory of that State.

This paragraph constitutes a legal basis for legal assistance between Parties to the Protocol, even in circumstances when no specific bilateral or multilateral treaty exists for mutual legal assistance. Legal cooperation requires a broad range of assistance, including: taking evidence or statements from persons involved; search and seizure of property; transmittal of information, documents or evidentiary items; and temporary transfer of persons to assist in investigations or to appear as witnesses.

The assistance provided consists in different acts, usually described in detail in treaties and conventions. The information, documents and materials transmitted through diplomatic channels and ministries of foreign affairs or justice, or other central organs and conditions of legal assistance, are regulated by the legal provisions of each State.

The legal assistance is executed in the manner provided by the law of the requested State. National law might prescribe various conditions, such as the obligation of reciprocity, admissibility of the request and double criminality, and the principle of specialty, meaning that the legal assistance may not be used in the prosecution of crimes omitted from the request or excluded by the treaty. Sometimes, the requested State allows a judge or prosecutor from the requesting State to conduct the investigation in its territory, but under the supervision of the judicial authorities of the requested State.

The requesting State, for its part, will prepare the request in a way that will facilitate its implementation. The request requires the details of the authority making the request, the object and the reason for the request, and, when possible, the identity and nationality of the person concerned and the name and address of the person to be served. The request and documentation must be translated into the language of the requested State.

Paragraph 2

Paragraph 2 provides more details on the practical realization of mutual legal assistance. It is useful to say that, according to international law, there is no general legal obligation to provide legal assistance. Legal doctrine agrees that States have only an obligation to take into consideration requests for such assistance.[770]

Mutual legal assistance can be realized in two basic forms:
- In conformity with treaties, or other arrangements, and
- In accordance with domestic laws, in case of absence of such treaties or arrangements.

Treaties and other arrangements[771]

Bilateral treaties

After national laws, the main source for the regulation of the legal assistance is bilateral treaties: treaties on mutual legal assistance[772] or extradition treaties. The US has 19 mutual legal assistance treaties and 15 more have been signed but are not yet in force. The 1973 Treaty between Switzerland and the US on Mutual Assistance in Criminal Matters[773] is often mentioned as an influential instrument for the elaboration of other bilateral treaties.

The UN General Assembly also adopted the Model Treaty on Mutual Assistance[774] as a guide for States who wish to develop treaties.

Multilateral treaties

a) International multilateral treaties concerning legal assistance

There are practically no general universal treaties concerning legal assistance in criminal law matters. Such treaties exist in the field of civil and commercial law.[775]

---

770 Geiger (1997), p. 202.

771 The extradition legislation of Great Britain applies only 'where an arrangement has been made with any foreign State' (33 and 34 Vict.c. 52, s.2 (1870)). The world 'arrangement' is arguably of wide meaning and might extend to an exchange of diplomatic correspondence concerning a particular individual, but this view has never been tested. It would seem most unlikely that such was the meaning of the Act, especially since in any event an order-in-council must follow the 'arrangement' in bringing the Act into force in respect of that foreign State for the duration of the agreement'. See Shearer (1971), p. 28.

772 Rohn (1997) lists approximately 93 such bilateral treaties.

773 Entered into force on 23 January 1977. UST 2019, TIAS 8302. See Frei and Freschal (1990).

774 UN General Assembly Resolution 45/117 of 14 December 1990.

775 Hague Conventions on Private International Law: Convention of 15 November 1965 on the Service Abroad of Judicial and Extrajudicial Documents in Civil or Commercial Matters, Convention of 18 March 1970 on the Taking of Evidence Abroad in Civil or Commercial Matters.

The only treaties elaborating mutual legal assistance in detail are the UN Convention Against Illicit Traffic in Narcotic Drugs and Psychotropic Substances of 20 December 1988[776] and the UN Convention against the Transnational Organized Crime of 2001,[777] but this refers more to category (c) concerning specific crimes (see below).

b) Regional multilateral treaties

Cooperation on a regional basis was much more successful. The first such treaty was concluded in 1959 with the Council of Europe: the European Convention on Mutual Assistance in Criminal Matters of 20 April 1959.[778] Two Protocols completed the Convention. The Convention also served as basis for the adoption of more specific bilateral agreements between Member States. Noteworthy is also the European Convention on Offences relating to Cultural Property of 23 June 1985, which includes provisions on legal assistance in Articles 8–11.[779]

States, members of the Organization Commune Africaine et Malgache (OCAM)[780] signed the Convention on Cooperation in Judicial Matters in 1961, the content of which was inspired by the European Convention.

The Inter-American Convention on the Taking of Evidence Abroad (1975)[781] and the additional Protocol (1985)[782] were adopted by States from the American continents.

The Model Bilateral Arrangement by Mutual Assistance on Letters Rogatory in Criminal Matters was elaborated by the group of experts of the Asian-African Legal Consultative Committee in 1983.

c) Treaties concerning specific crimes of international concern including provisions of legal assistance

See, for example, the following treaties:

---

776 Entry into force: 11 November 1990, No 27627. At 1st October 2009, 187 States were Parties to the Convention.

777 Adopted by the United Nations General Assembly Resolution 55/25 on 8 January 2001. The Convention included several articles concerning legal assistance, esp. art. 18–31. *UNTS.* Vol. 2225, p. 209. At 1st October 2009, 150 States were Parties to this Convention

778 ETS No. 030. Entry into force: 12.06.1962. 48 States, Members of the Council of Europe are parties to this treaty which was also ratified by Israel, as at 1st October 2009. Additional Protocol of 17 March 1978 and Second Additional Protocol of 8 November 2001.

779 Article 8 stated: 'Each party shall execute in the manner provided for by its law any letters rogatory relating to proceedings addressed to it by the competent authorities of a Party that is competent in accordance with Article 13 for the purpose of procuring evidence or transmitting articles to be produced in evidence, records or documents'. ETS No. 119. The Convention was signed by six States, but not ratified by any State and is not yet in force (as of 1st October 2009).

780 Organization of the French-speaking States of Africa and Mauritius.

781 International Legal Materials, Vol. 14, 1975, p. 328.

782 Ibid., Vol. 24, 1985, p. 472.

- Article 10 of the Convention for the Suppression of Unlawful Seizure of Aircraft (The Hague, 16 December 1970);
- Article 11 of the Convention for the Suppression of Unlawful Acts Against the Safety of Civil Aviation (Montreal, 23 September 1971);
- Article 8 of the European Convention on the Suppression of Terrorism (Strasbourg, 27 January 1977);
- Article 10 of the Convention on the Prevention and Punishment of Crimes against Internationally Protected Persons, including Diplomatic Agents (New York, 14 December 1973);
- Article 11 of the International Convention Against the Taking of Hostages (New York, 17 December 1979);
- Article 13 of the Convention on the Physical Protection of Nuclear Material (Vienna, 26 October 1979);
- Article 10 of the International Convention for the Suppression of Terrorist Bombing (New York, 15 December 1997);

Laws concerning legal assistance

In the absence of treaties or other arrangements, the conditions of judicial assistance are determined exclusively by the internal law of each State. Even if mutual legal assistance is relatively new (having started in the late 1950s), the practice already existed more than a century ago in the form of 'Letters Rogatory'[783] (or commission rogatory, *commission rogatoire*), which continue to exist and are based on the principle of comity. The provisions of this form of cooperation are included in special statutes,[784] or the criminal code or codes of criminal procedure.

---

783 See Bassiouni (2003), p. 352: 'the courts of one State address a request to those of another State for judicial assistance in the form of taking the testimony of a witness or securing tangible evidence. The courts than transmit the oral or tangible evidence to the requesting court, certifying that the evidence has been secured in accordance with the legal requirements of the requested State.'

784 See, e.g., the recent Law of Luxembourg on International Judicial Assistance in Criminal Matters, adopted on 13 July 2000 and entered into force on 8 August 2000 (La loi du 8 juillet 2000 sur l'entraide judiciaire internationale en matière pénale), and the Swiss Federal Act on International Mutual Assistance in Criminal Matters, 20 March 1981.

Article 20
GROUNDS FOR REFUSAL

1. *For the purpose of extradition, offences set forth in Article 15 sub-paragraphs 1 (a) to (c), and for the purpose of mutual legal assistance, offences set forth in Article 15 shall not be regarded as political offences nor as offences connected with political offences nor as offences inspired by political motives. Accordingly, a request for extradition or for mutual legal assistance based on such offences may not be refused on the sole ground that it concerns a political offence or an offence connected with a political offence or an offence inspired by political motives.*

2. *Nothing in this Protocol shall be interpreted as imposing an obligation to extradite or to afford mutual legal assistance if the requested Party has substantial grounds for believing that the request for extradition for offences set forth in Article 15 sub-paragraphs 1 (a) to (c) or for mutual legal assistance with respect to offences set forth in Article 15 has been made for the purpose of prosecuting or punishing a person on account of that person's race, religion, nationality, ethnic origin or political opinion or that compliance with the request would cause prejudice to that person's position for any of these reasons.*

Preparatory works

Report by the Director-General on the Reinforcement of UNESCO's action for the Protection of the World Cultural and Natural Heritage. UNESCO document 142 EX/15, Annex: Hague Meeting of Experts on the application and effectiveness of the Convention for the Protection of Cultural Property in the Event of Armed Conflict (The Hague, 14 May 1954), *Final Report*, para. 6.3, p. 3. http://unesdoc.unesco.org/images/0009/000958/095820Eo.pdf

A working document prepared by the Secretariat, CLT/94/608/1 of 28 November 1994, p. 3.

UNESCO, Meeting of Governmental Experts. Summary of comments received from States Parties to the Hague Convention and from the International Council on Archives. UNESCO document CLT-96/CONF.603/INF.4, Paris, December 1996, p. 2.

Expert meeting on the review of the 1954 Hague Convention for the Protection of Cultural Property in the Event of Armed Conflict. Paris, UNESCO Headquarters, 28 November–2 December 1994. UNESCO document CLT/CH/94/608/2, *Final Report*, pp. 4–5.

UNESCO, Meeting of Governmental Experts. Summary of comments received from States Parties to the Hague Convention and from the International Council on Archives. UNESCO document CLT-96/CONF.603/INF.4, Paris, December 1996.

Draft provisions for the revision of the 1954 Hague Convention and commentary from the UNESCO Secretariat. UNESCO document CLT-97/CONF.208/2, Paris, October 1997.

UNESCO, Meeting of Governmental Experts. Summary of comments received from States Parties to the Hague Convention, the International Committee of the Red Cross and the International Council on Archives. UNESCO document Paris, March 1998.

Preliminary Draft Second Protocol to the 1954 Hague Convention. UNESCO document HC/1999/1, October 1998 (English, French and Russian).

Draft Second Protocol to the 1954 Hague Convention for the Protection of Cultural Property in the Event of Armed Conflict. UNESCO document HC/1999/1/rev.1, February 1999.

Presentation of the results of the Working Group on Chapter 4. H. Fischer, coordinator of the Working Group, 25 March 1999. Conference document HC/1999/INF.5.

Bibliography

Boylan, P. J. 1993. *Review of the Convention for the Protection of Cultural Property in the Event of Armed Conflict (The Hague Convention of 1954).* Paris: UNESCO, para. 9.1–9.25, pp. 91–98.

Chamberlain, K. 2004. *War and Cultural Heritage.* Leicester: Institute of Art and Law, pp. 205–10.

Desch, T. 1999. The Second Protocol to the 1954 Convention for the Protection of Cultural Property in the Event of Armed Conflict. *Yearbook of International Humanitarian Law,* Vol. 2, pp. 79–82.

Henckaerts, J.-M. 1999. New rules for the protection of cultural property in armed conflict: the significance of the Second Protocol to the 1954 Hague Convention for the Protection of Cultural Property in the Event of Armed Conflict. *IRRC,* No. 835, pp. 593–620, here 613–15.

O'Keefe, R. 2002. *National Implementation of the Penal Provisions of Chapter 4 of the Second Protocol of 26 March 1999 to the Hague Convention of 1954 for the Protection of Cultural Property in the Event of Armed Conflict.* 29 March (UNESCO document CLT/CIH/MCO/2002/PI/H/1).

Schabas, W. A. 1997. Sentencing by international tribunals: a human rights approach. *Duke Journal of Comparative and International Law*, Vol. 7, p. 461.

Toman, J. 1996. *The Protection of Cultural Property in the Event of Armed Conflict: Commentary on the Hague Convention of 14 May 1954*. Aldershot: Dartmouth/Paris: UNESCO, pp. 59–66.

Statutes of the International Criminal Tribunals

See the documentation under the commentary to Article 15.

PREPARATORY WORK DURING THE 1999 HAGUE CONFERENCE

There was no mention of the content of the present Article in the drafts and discussion that preceded the Hague Conference. This issue was not mentioned at the discussion at the Plenary Session of the Conference. It was during discussion of extradition and mutual legal assistance at the Working Group that this provision was added to the Articles concerning extradition and legal assistance. As we have seen, both of these Articles were taken from the conventions and treaties concerning criminal matters, since certain delegates at the Conference suggested their relation to other articles concerning criminal responsibility and jurisdiction.

The Article entitled 'Grounds for Refusal' appeared for the first time in the Chairperson's working paper on Chapter 4, submitted to the Working Group on 22 March 1999. Both paragraphs proposed by the Chairperson, Horst Fischer, were adapted from Articles 11 and 12 of the 1997 International Convention for the Suppression of Terrorist Bombing and were inspired by other similar international treaties from which Articles 11 and 12 had already been taken. As mentioned previously, among the conventions against terrorism, the Convention against Terrorist Bombing was the closest in time to the sessions of the 1999 Hague Conference.

Working Group 4 of the Conference was occupied mostly with the first Articles of Chapter 4. Because the provisions on extradition and mutual legal assistance remained unmodified, grounds for refusal followed the same pattern and was submitted as such to the Plenary Session of the Conference. These provisions had already been discussed extensively during the process of adoption of the Conventions that inspired the present provision, and there was sufficient agreement on these provisions within the international community. This also simplified the process of adoption of this Article at the final Plenary Session of the Conference.

ANALYSIS OF THE TEXT

Article 20 clarifies the permissible grounds on which a State Party to the Protocol may refuse a request for extradition with regard to the offences set forth in Article 15(1), sub-paragraphs (a) to (c), or for mutual legal assistance regarding any serious violation set forth in Article 15(1).

As extradition is possible in relation to the offences set forth in Article 15, paragraph 1 and sub-paragraphs (a), (b) and (c), refusal of extradition for the reasons mentioned in paragraph 1 and 2 of the present Article is possible only in relation to the serious violations according to these sub-paragraphs.

Because mutual legal assistance is connected to all serious violations set forth in Article 15, it may be refused with respect to all these violations.

Paragraph 1

Article 20(1) concerns the so-called 'political offence exception' commonly invoked in relation to obligations of extradition and mutual legal assistance. It is broadly formulated by stating that the offences in question 'shall not be regarded as political offences or as offences connected with political offences or as offences inspired by political motives'. Article 20(1) makes it clear that 'a request for extradition or for mutual legal assistance based on such offences may not be refused on the sole ground that it concerns a political offence or an offence connected with a political offence or an offence inspired by political motives'.

The purpose of paragraph 1 of this Article is to eliminate the political offence clause from the consideration of extradition and mutual legal assistance of serious violations against the cultural property.

In past centuries, the surrender of political enemies was considered more important than the handing over of common criminals. Later, the interdependence of nations, international cooperation and humanistic ideas precluded the surrender of political offenders. The political offence exception accompanied the extradition notes and treaties of France with other countries and was included in the Belgium extradition law of 1833. It continues to be included in extradition treaties[785] and statutes to this day, though without having the character of customary law.

The problem was the definition of what constitutes 'political offences or offences connected with political offences or offences inspired by political motives'. Many writers consider a crime to be 'political'

> if committed from a political motive, others call 'political' any crime committed for a political purpose; again, others recognize such a crime only as 'political' as was committed both from political motive and at the same time for a political purpose; and thirdly, some writers confine the term 'political crime' to certain offences against the State only, such as high treason, *lèse-majesté*, and the like. Up to the present day, all attempts to formulate a satisfactory conception of the term have failed, and the reason of the thing will probably forever exclude the possibility of finding a satisfactory definition.[786]

It is less problematic to define 'absolute' or 'purely' political offences, which are directed exclusively against a political order, against a State, its organs and political organization. But it is much more difficult to define 'relative' and 'related' acts designated sometimes as *délit complexe*, which are characterized in this paragraph as 'offences connected with political offences or as offences inspired by political motives'. The same act is directed against the political order, but also against private rights. These uncertain,

> [relative] political offences are *in se* common crimes assimilated to political offences because the perpetrator pursued a political purpose or was politically motivated (the subjective definition) or because the common crime fell into a political context in that it was committed incidentally to or in the course of and in furtherance of civil war, insurrection or political commotion. A more rigid definition confines relative political offences to those common crimes having a

---

785 For example, the European Convention on Extradition (1957), art. 3, para. 1: 'Extradition shall not be granted if the offence in respect of which it is requested is regarded by the requested Party as a political offence or as an offence connected with a political offence.' This provision was not accepted by all delegations because of its mandatory character. The International Law Institute stated in its resolution on new problems of extradition that 'where the extradition treaty does not expressly contain the right to refuse extradition for political offences, a State may nevertheless invoke this defense in support of its refusal.' (Resolution adopted on 1 September 1983). Annuaire de l'Institut de droit international. *Résolutions 1957–1991*. Paris: Pédone, 1992, p. 161.

786 Oppenheim (1955), pp. 707–8.

'predominantly' political character[787] or being directly connected to a purely political offence by preparing, facilitating or ensuring the impunity of the latter. The 'predominance' or 'proportionality' test, requiring consideration of such factors as the seriousness of the offence or its consequences, the indiscriminate use of violence against innocent victims and the futility of the attempt to further the political object claimed for the offence, appears to be the most reasonable approach, but none of the others is excluded by law, and even the strict subjective definition, though mostly rejected in theory, has been frequently applied in practice. A requested State's decision affirming the political character of an offence may be challenged, if at all, only in clear cases of abuse.[788]

The determination of whether a crime is political has been left to the internal law of each country, and the final determination is still a matter for the requested State.[789]

With the development of international criminal law after the Second World War and the human rights movement, a new tendency emerged in relation to the most heinous crimes, the non-recognition of the political offence exception. This is the case of the 1948 Genocide Convention and the conventions against international crimes concerning terrorist activities.[790] The Second Protocol, which prohibits serious violations directed against cultural property, falls within this tendency.

Torsten Stein drew the following conclusion on these matters:

> In sum, neither the kind nor the number of particular restrictions to the political offence exception reflect a general consensus as to what is worthy of the protection offered by the exception, and what cannot be tolerated by the community of nations and therefore ought not be

---

787 'A request shall not be granted if the subject of the proceeding is an act which, according to the Swiss concept, has a predominantly political character, constitutes a violation of the obligation to perform military or similar service or appears to be directed against the national defense or military strength of the requesting State.' Swiss Federal Act on International Mutual Assistance in Criminal Matters, 20 March 1981, art. 3.

788 Stein (1997), p. 332.

789 As in the case of Article 3, paragraph 1 of the European Convention on Extradition. See note (1).

790 See, e.g., Article 2, paragraph 1 of the European Convention on the Suppression of Terrorism (Strasbourg, 27 January 1977); Articles 11 and 12 of the International Convention for the Suppression of Terrorist Bombing (1997). See also Article IV of the Draft Articles on Extradition in Relation to Terrorist Offences, adopted by the Committee of International Law Association. Report of the 63rd Conference held at Warsaw, 1988, p. 1038.

privileged in extradition law. There are increasing doubts as to whether the political offence exception in its traditional wording is still a timely concept, if indeed it ever was.[791]

Paragraph 2

As we indicated in the comments to the previous paragraph, lack of definition of the political offence led to attempts in national laws and international treaties to replace it with a provision corresponding to the requirements of the international law of human rights.[792] This is expressed in paragraph 2 by the statement that nothing in this Protocol

> shall be interpreted as imposing an obligation to extradite or to afford mutual legal assistance if the requested Party has substantial grounds for believing that the request for extradition . . . or for mutual legal assistance . . . has been made for the purpose of prosecuting or punishing a person on account of that person's race, religion, nationality, ethnic origin or political opinion or that compliance with the request would cause prejudice to that person's position for any of these reasons.

This change from the indefinable political offence clause to a reference to the human rights approach and a non-discrimination clause is defined in the Swiss Extradition Act, which excludes an act from the political offence exception if it

> (a) was aimed at the extermination or oppression of a segment of the population on account of nationality, race, religion, or ethnic, social or political affiliation; or
> (b) appears particularly reprehensible because the offender, for the purpose of extortion or duress, placed or threatened to place under jeopardy the freedom, life or limb of persons, especially

---

791 Stein (1997), p. 332.

792 The authors of an Article on the Soering case concluded that as this case shows 'in extradition proceedings, . . . state-oriented interests are not of exclusive relevance. Moreover, it is a convincing illustration that the fundamental and human rights of the person extradited must also be considered. The Strasbourg organs considerably strengthened the legal philosophy aiming at the defense, protection, and safeguard of human rights in the field of extradition by granting the fugitive a legal right of his own' (Breitenmoser and Wilms (1990), p. 881).

by hijacking planes, taking hostages or using means of mass extermination.[793]

It is defined in the same way in the 1989 Extradition Act of the United Kingdom. The European Convention of Extradition (1957),[794] which accepted the political offence exception, also stated:

> The same rule [that the extradition shall not be granted] shall apply if the requested Party has substantial grounds for believing that a request for extradition for an ordinary criminal offence has been made for the purpose of prosecuting or punishing a person on account of his race, religion, nationality or political opinion, or that that person's position may be prejudiced for any of these reasons.

The Institute of International Law stated in its resolution in 1983 that '[in] cases where there is a well-founded fear of the violation of the fundamental human rights of an accused in the territory of the requesting State, extradition may be refused, whoever the individual whose extradition is requested and whatever the nature of the offence of which he is accused.'[795]

---

793 Swiss Federal Act on International Mutual Assistance in Criminal Matters, 20 March 1981, art. 3.
794 A similar provision is also found in Article 9, paragraph 1(a) of the International Convention against the Taking of Hostages (1979).
795 Annuaire de l'Institut de droit international. *Résolution 1957–1991*. Paris: Pédone, 1992, p. 163.

Article 21
MEASURES REGARDING OTHER VIOLATIONS

Without prejudice to Article 28 of the Convention, each Party shall adopt such legislative, administrative or disciplinary measures as may be necessary to suppress the following acts when committed intentionally:

a. *any use of cultural property in violation of the Convention or this Protocol;*

b *any illicit export, other removal or transfer of ownership of cultural property from occupied territory in violation of the Convention or this Protocol.*

Preparatory works

Expert meeting on the review of the 1954 Hague Convention for the Protection of Cultural Property in the Event of Armed Conflict. Paris, UNESCO Headquarters, 28 November–2 December 1994. UNESCO document CLT/CH/94/608/2, *Final Report*, pp. 4–5.

UNESCO, Meeting of Governmental Experts. Summary of comments received from States Parties to the Hague Convention and from the International Council on Archives. UNESCO document CLT-96/CONF.603/INF.4, Paris, December 1996.

UNESCO, Meeting of Governmental Experts on the Review of the 1954 Hague Convention for the Protection of Cultural Property in the Event of Armed Conflict 1954, UNESCO Headquarters, Paris, 24–27 March 1997, *Final Report*, UNESCO document CLT-96/CONF.603/5, Paris, 30 April 1997.

Draft provisions for the revision of the 1954 Hague Convention and commentary from the UNESCO Secretariat. UNESCO document CLT-97/CONF.208/2, Paris, October 1997.

UNESCO, Meeting of Governmental Experts on the Revision of the Hague Convention for the Protection of Cultural Property in the Event of Armed Conflict of 1954. Vienna, 11–13 May 1998. UNESCO document Paris, May 1998, *Final Report.*

UNESCO, Meeting of Governmental Experts. Summary of comments received from States Parties to the Hague Convention, the International Committee of the Red Cross and the International Council on Archives. UNESCO document Paris, March 1998.

Preliminary Draft Second Protocol to the 1954 Hague Convention. UNESCO document HC/1999/1, October 1998 (English, French and Russian).

UNESCO, Summary of comments on Preliminary Draft Second Protocol to the 1954 Hague Convention received from High Contracting Parties to the Hague Convention for the Protection of Cultural Property in the Event of Armed Conflict 1954, other UNESCO Member States and international organizations, Paris, 15 January 1999.

Draft Second Protocol to the 1954 Hague Convention for the Protection of Cultural Property in the Event of Armed Conflict. UNESCO document HC/1999/1/rev.1, February 1999.

Presentation of the results of the Working Group on Chapter 4. H. Fischer, coordinator of the Working Group, 25 March 1999. Conference document HC/1999/INF.5.

Bibliography

Chamberlain, K. 2004. *War and Cultural Heritage.* Leicester: Institute of Art and Law, pp. 205–10.

Desch, T. 1999. The Second Protocol to the 1954 Convention for the Protection of Cultural Property in the Event of Armed Conflict. *Yearbook of International Humanitarian Law,* Vol. 2, pp. 79–82.

O'Keefe, R. 2002. *National Implementation of the Penal Provisions of Chapter 4 of the Second Protocol of 26 March 1999 to the Hague Convention of 1954 for the Protection of Cultural Property in the Event of Armed Conflict.* 29 March (UNESCO document CLT/CIH/MCO/2002/PI/H/1).

Statutes of the International Criminal Tribunals

See the documentation under the commentary to Article 15.

PREPARATORY WORK BEFORE THE 1999 HAGUE CONFERENCE

Most of the preparatory work relating to the drafting of this Article was covered in the description of and comments on Article 15, to which this provision is closely related.

Originally these Articles were systematically close and followed one other. This was one conceivable structure. Instead, these provisions were divided and the two Articles were separated. The reason for doing so was probably that Articles 16–20 are related to Article 15 on serious violations, and it is therefore more appropriate to link them with Article 15 and place Article 21, which concerns other violations, at the very end of Chapter 4. This separation of Articles 15 and 21 was made at the very final stage of discussion at the Working Group meetings.[796]

However, during preparatory work, these Articles were dealt with together. This corresponded better, at that stage, to the ongoing discussion regarding definition of serious and other violations, during which several points changed places between these two Articles.

The first draft of legal provisions was formulated at the Lauswolt Meeting of Experts in February 1994. This draft included Article 9, entitled 'Grave breaches', which included the following text: 'The extensive destruction, misappropriation or damage carried out wilfully or wantonly to cultural property specially protected by this instrument, contrary to the laws and customs of war, shall be regarded as a grave breach'. The most important forms of violations were included in this article. The next article, Article 10, included other violations, but, as we have seen, some of these were moved and were included among serious violations. This was the case for paragraphs (a) and (b), which merged into paragraph (e) of Article 15, and for paragraph (c), which became, in modified form, sub-paragraph (c) of Article 15.

Article 10 of the Lauswolt draft was formulated as follows:

Article 10 Other violations
The following shall be regarded as violations of this instrument:
(a) the theft, pillage or misappropriation or any other breach of integrity of cultural property protected by this instrument;
(b) acts of vandalism directed against property protected by this instrument;
(c) the export of cultural property from occupied territory or from a part of the territory of a State Party, without prejudice to the provisions of the 1954 Protocol;
(d) the extensive destruction or damage carried out wilfully or wantonly to cultural property, as defined in Article 1 of the Convention, contrary to the laws and customs of war.

Following the discussion at the 1997 Governmental Experts Meeting,[797] the Secretariat prepared 'Draft provisions for the revision of the 1954 Hague

---

796 Consensus text. Working Group on Chapter 4, 23 March 1999.
797 UNESCO, Meeting of Governmental Experts on the Review of the 1954 Hague Convention for the Protection of Cultural Property in the Event of Armed Conflict 1954, UNESCO Headquarters, Paris, 24–27 March 1997. *Final Report.* UNESCO document CLT-96/CONF.603/5, Paris, 30 April 1997.

Convention and commentary from the UNESCO Secretariat'.[798] The draft kept the same form as the previous Article 10. Only the wording of the paragraph concerning the export of property from occupied territories was improved, to include the reference 'the illicit export or other illicit removal', which is also now found, along with other improvements, in Article 21 of the Protocol.

Comments received from States and the ICA[799] insisted on the need to include sanctions against the deliberate destruction of immovable and movable cultural property, and that such actions should be considered as war crimes falling under the jurisdiction of international or national tribunals. In other words, grave breaches of the Convention should be subject to universal jurisdiction.

After the discussion at the 1998 Vienna Governmental Experts Meeting,[800] the UNESCO Secretariat prepared a document based on several meetings of government experts, and particularly on the discussions that took place at the May 1998 Vienna Meeting: the *Preliminary Draft Second*

---

798 Draft provisions for the revision of the 1954 Hague Convention and commentary from the UNESCO Secretariat. CLT-97/CONF.208/2, Paris, October 1997.
In relation to Article 15, but also to Article 21, based on the previous Lauswolt proposal, was adopted:
Article 6. (formerly Article 9) Grave breaches
1. The [extensive] destruction, misappropriation or *damage* carried out wilfully [or wantonly] to cultural property specially protected by this instrument, contrary to the laws and customs of war, shall be *regarded* as a grave breach.
Article 7 (formerly Article 10): Other Violations
Violations of this instrument shall include but not be limited to:
(a) Any form of theft, pillage or misappropriation of, any acts of vandalism directed against any illicit *purchase*, or any other breach of integrity of cultural property with *reference to both its form and its function*;
(b) the illicit export or other illicit removal of cultural property from occupied territory or from a part of the territory of a State Party, but the dispositions of the 1954 Protocol, if in force, shall continue to apply;
(c) the destruction or damage carried out wilfully or wantonly to cultural property, as defined in Article 1 of the Convention, contrary to the laws and customs of war.
During the discussion two other proposals were made: one concerning archaeological excavations (as para. (d), and breaches of the respect of persons engaged in the protection of cultural property (para. (e)).
799 UNESCO, Meeting of Governmental Experts. Summary of comments received from States Parties to the Hague Convention and from the International Council on Archives. UNESCO document CLT-96/CONF.603/INF.4, Paris, December 1996.
As at 28 November 1996, the Secretariat has received replies from nine States of the total number of 88 States party to the Convention.
800 UNESCO, Meeting of Governmental Experts on the Revision of the Hague Convention for the Protection of Cultural Property in the Event of Armed Conflict of 1954. Vienna, 11–13 May 1998. UNESCO document Paris, May 1998, *Final Report*.

Protocol.[801] This was sent to Member States and international organizations for a new round of comments.[802] We find in the provision again few additional improvements, and the two Articles are still together, one following the other.

In its comments, Austria requested a clear definition of other offences. Australia preferred to remove the notion of grave breaches from the Draft Protocol and introduce an appropriate alternative entitled 'serious violations'.

On the basis of the responses from States, the UNESCO Secretariat and the Government of the Netherlands drew up the final draft of the Second Protocol: *Draft Second Protocol to the 1954 Hague Convention for the Protection of Cultural Property in the Event of Armed Conflict* (UNESCO doc. HC/1999/1/rev.1, February 1999), which formed the basis of the discussion at the 1999 Hague Diplomatic Conference. It is in this final pre-Conference draft that the provisions were moved from the Article on 'other violations' to the Article on 'grave beaches', which later became the Article on serious violations. Articles 18 and 19 were the basis for the final formulation of Article 15 and 21 of the Second Protocol:[803]

---

801 *Preliminary Draft Second Protocol to the 1954 Hague Convention*. UNESCO document HC/1999/1, October 1998 (English, French and Russian). The new draft, concerning Articles 15 and 21 of the Second Protocol was formulated in the following way:
Article 10 Grave breaches
1. The wilful violation of the provisions of Article 8 [immunity under special protection] shall be regarded as a grave breach.
2. The extensive destruction, misappropriation or extensive damage carried out unlawfully and wantonly to cultural property shall be regarded as a grave breach.
Article 11 Other Violations
Violations of this Protocol shall include but not be limited to:
a. Any form of theft, pillage or misappropriation of, any archaeological excavation, any acts of vandalism directed against, any illicit purchase, or any other breach of integrity of cultural property with reference to both its form and its function;
b. the illicit export or other illicit removal of cultural property from occupied territory or from a part of the territory of a State Party, but the dispositions of the 1954 Protocol, if in force, shall continue to apply;
c. the intentional destruction or damage of cultural property;
d. the commission of any acts of hostility directed against cultural property not justified by Article 3 [respect of cultural property];
e. the use of cultural property in support of military effort or as object of reprisals.
802 UNESCO, Summary of comments on Preliminary Draft Second Protocol to the 1954 Hague Convention received from High Contracting Parties to the Hague Convention for the Protection of Cultural Property in the Event of Armed Conflict 1954, other UNESCO Member States and international organizations, Paris, 15 January 1999.
803 Draft Second Protocol to the 1954 Hague Convention for the Protection of Cultural Property in the Event of Armed Conflict. UNESCO document HC/1999/1/rev.1, February 1999 (original: English).

Article 18 Grave breaches

A person who

    a. wilfully, and in violation of this Protocol, commits a breach of the immunity of cultural property under enhanced special protection, or

    b. abuses the enhanced special protection of cultural property by using it for military purposes, or

    c. systematically destroys, misappropriates or damages cultural property, or

    d. unlawfully and wantonly destroys, misappropriates or damages cultural property causing extensive destruction, loss or damage to the cultural heritage of humanity, or

    e. makes cultural property the object of reprisals has committed a grave breach of this Protocol.

Article 19 Other violations

1. Other violations of this Protocol include all those acts and omissions for which Parties or individuals are responsible and those which engage the liability of the parties to the conflict.

2. The Parties shall adopt all necessary legislative and administrative measures to give effect to this Protocol, in particular the penal legislation necessary to give effect to Article 18 [and Article 19] of this protocol.

[3. Parties shall adopt, whenever necessary, appropriate legislative and administrative measures.]

DISCUSSION AND DRAFTING OF ARTICLES 15 AND 21 AT THE 1999 HAGUE CONFERENCE

As we have seen, the delegates at the Plenary Session of the Conference agreed with the two-tier approach,[804] as expressed in the draft, which followed the method adopted by other instruments of humanitarian law and international criminal law. One group of States (France, Switzerland, the UK and the US) preferred provisions similar to those used in Additional Protocol I (art. 85), whereas other delegations wanted to link the Second Protocol to

---

804 Germany, Greece, Italy, Sweden, Switzerland, Syria and the ICRC in particular.

recent developments in international law, particularly international criminal law.[805]

The draft of Article 21, based on the text submitted to the Conference, was partially rewritten by the Working Group chaired by Horst Fischer. The Group also followed the recommendations of the Plenary Session of the Conference (which discussed this article on 18 March 1999). Article 15 was given the title 'Serious violations of this Protocol'. In the case of Article 21 [24 in the draft], 'dealing with so called other violations [gave] an additional level of protection if States wish to use the additional measures'.[806]

The report of the Working Group was discussed on 24 March at the afternoon session. Introducing the report, Fischer indicated that consensus had been reached in the consideration of different aspects of international law, including cultural property, humanitarian and criminal law.

ANALYSIS OF THE TEXT

Paragraph 1

Other violations

The term 'other violations' in Article 21 is used in contradistinction to the expression 'serious violations' of the Protocol, set forth in Article 15(1).

Without prejudice to Article 28 of the Convention

Article 21 does not modify in any way the provision of Article 28 of the Convention. As previously noted, Article 28 requested that: 'The High Contracting Parties undertake to take, within the framework of their ordinary criminal jurisdiction, all necessary steps to prosecute and impose penal or disciplinary sanctions upon those persons, of whatever nationality, who commit or order to be committed a breach of the present Convention.' Comparing this text with Article 21, the following differences emerge:

- Article 28 refers to ordinary criminal jurisdiction, which can adopt penal or disciplinary sanctions. This is not the case for Article 21 of the Protocol, which is broader and refers not only to legislative and disciplinary measures but also to administrative measures. It refers to

---

805 Desch (1999), p.79.
806 *Presentation of the results of the Working Group on Chapter 4*. H. Fischer, coordinator of the Working Group, 25 March 1999. Conference document HC/1999/INF.5, p. 3.

measures and not to sanctions, which are naturally much stronger. Criminal jurisdiction and legislative measures are the basic measures taken under Article 15 of the Protocol.

- Application of these measures is limited to Parties to the Protocol, and Article 28 covers all the High Contracting Parties that are Party to the Protocol.
- The purpose of the measures under Article 21 is 'to suppress' violations; they do not possess a punitive or socially reform-oriented character, as is the case for Article 15.
- Articles 21 and 28 are addressed to persons of 'whatever nationality' (this is not mentioned in Article 21).
- Article 28 concerns breaches of the Convention. Article 21 has a less limited material scope: it addresses only the use of cultural property in violation of the Convention and the Protocol. Other forms of violations, such as extensive destruction, or appropriation, making cultural property an object of attack, theft, pillage, misappropriation or vandalism, are covered by Article 15.
- Article 21 includes a specific form of violation under paragraph (b).

This short comparison and summary of differences between these two Articles demonstrates that, in many respects, Article 28 of the Convention is broader than Article 21 of the Second Protocol, and the latter Article should not constitute an obstacle to application of Article 28. Therefore, Article 21 is 'without prejudice to Article 28 of the Convention'.

Possible adoption of legislative, administrative and disciplinary measures

Parties to the Protocol shall adopt such measures 'as may be necessary'. Thus, this leaves them a certain discretion. States are not obliged to take such measures; they may consider that such measures are not necessary, and that they can be satisfied with the existing measures they undertake and are obliged to undertake according to Article 15 or according to the aforementioned Article 28 of the Convention.

As we have seen, the draft of this Article includes only legislative and administrative measures, in other words, measures that are established by the relevant State organs. This means either parliament, when legislative measures are being adopted, or executive organs (government or ministries/departments), which adopt measures of an administrative nature.

Among the measure the Parties can undertake are those of a penal nature. Roger O'Keefe considers that the imposition of penal sanctions in respect of the violations set forth in Article 21 would be an appropriate means of giving effect to the obligation laid down in that article, given the gravity of the violations in question.

First, it would be appropriate for each State Party, in pursuance of the obligation of suppression laid down in Article 21, to adopt such measures as may be necessary to establish as criminal offences under its domestic law the violations referred to in that article. The gravity of such offences would properly be reflected in their designation by each State Party as non-prescriptible.

Second, it would be appropriate for each State Party to establish its jurisdiction over the violations set forth in Article 21 when such violations are committed in the territory of that State and, in the event of extraterritorial commission, when the alleged offender is a national of that State.

Finally, it would be appropriate for States Parties to deem the violations set forth in Article 21 as extraditable offences in any extradition treaty existing between any of them, to include such offences in every extradition treaty subsequently concluded between them and to afford one another the greatest measure of assistance in connection with investigations or criminal or extradition proceedings brought in respect of them, including assistance in obtaining evidence at their disposal necessary for the proceedings. In this regard, such offences should not be regarded as political offences nor as offences connected with political offences nor as offences inspired by political motives[807]

Disciplinary measures were added only at the very final stage of the Working Group discussion.[808] The ICRC commentary on the Fourth Geneva Convention's Article 119, entitled 'Disciplinary punishments', states that '[disciplinary] penalties are aimed at repressing minor breaches such as offences against discipline or internment regulations. Since they are not designed to punish ordinary offences against the law, they must not be as serious as judicial punishments.'[809] Based on this definition, we can say that the reference to administrative and disciplinary measures will be designed for minor violations that bear on cultural property or to disciplinary offenses that

---

807 O'Keefe (2002), p. 11.
808 1999 Hague Conference. Document HC/1999/5/Add.8. The reference to disciplinary measures was not included in the Chairman's Working Paper of 22 March 1999.
809 Pictet (1952–1960), Vol. IV, p. 482.

endanger properties or cause minor damage. It will be the role of national courts or administrative authorities to take a decision on the basis of the specific circumstances.

As in the case of Article 28, disciplinary sanctions can be envisaged for acts of less gravity. However, Article 28 uses the qualification 'within the framework of their ordinary criminal jurisdiction', which is not an obstacle to the use of disciplinary sanctions, 'since many states routinely use military law and tribunals for the prosecution and punishment of certain crimes committed by certain categories of persons, especially in relation to crimes committed during armed conflict.'[810]

Measures to suppress other violations

The only reason for a decision to take such legislative, administrative and disciplinary measures is 'to suppress the following act'. The acts to be suppressed must be 'committed intentionally'.[811] But what are the acts that are committed intentionally and have to be suppressed?

> a. any use of cultural property in violation of the Convention or [the] Protocol.

The Article refers to 'any use' of cultural property in violation of the Convention or the Protocol. This paragraph is a 'catch-all provision' suppressing all other violations.[812] 'Any use' does not include other forms of condemnable behaviour, which are covered by the provisions of Article 15: other forms of violations, such as destruction, appropriation, making the property the object of the attack, theft, pillage, misappropriation or vandalism.

> b. any illicit export, other removal or transfer of ownership of cultural property from occupied territory in violation of the Convention or [the] Protocol.

Kevin Chamberlain rightly points out that this paragraph (b) should be read in conjunction with Article 9, sub-paragraph 1(a) of the Protocol, which requires Parties to 'prohibit and prevent' any illicit export, other removal or transfer

---

810 Ibid., p. 12.
811 We have defined these words 'intentionally' under Article 15 on p. 310.
812 This expression is used by Chamberlain (2004), p. 215.

of ownership of cultural property. The acts in sub-paragraph 1(b) and 1(c) of Article 9 (archaeological excavation and change of use) would constitute use of cultural property in violation of the Protocol, and would therefore fall within the scope of paragraph (a) of Article 21 of the Protocol.

Chapter 5

THE PROTECTION OF CULTURAL PROPERTY IN ARMED CONFLICT NOT OF AN INTERNATIONAL CHARACTER

INTRODUCTION

The emergence of rules of international law on the protection of cultural property in situations of non-international armed conflicts took a long time. It is well known that the only way that provisions concerning international armed conflict could be applied in the field of civil war or non-international armed conflict was through the recognition of belligerency. This recognition is granted under several conditions: the existence of a civil war accompanied by general hostilities, occupation accompanied by a measure of orderly administration of a substantial part of the national territory by insurgents, observance of the rules of warfare on the part of the insurgent forces acting under a responsible authority, and the practical necessity for third States to define their attitude towards the civil war.[813] But as international law had so few provisions concerning cultural property, even recognition of belligerency did little to change the situation concerning its protection.[814]

During the Spanish Civil War (1936–1939), recognition of belligerency was correctly refused for the reason that the accepted rules concerning recognition of belligerency did not apply to a situation in which – as a result of the illegal intervention of foreign States – hostilities had lost the character of a civil war, in the accepted meaning of the term.[815] This was the attitude of powers such as the UK.

The Director's Committee of the International Museums Office (OIM), part of the International Institute of Intellectual Co-operation of the League of Nations, considered that

> [in] the absence of generally accepted regulations, the Director's Committee took the view that it did not possess the requisite powers

---

813 Oppenheim (1952), p. 249.
814 For recognition of belligerency see ibid., pp. 249–54; Riedel (1982), pp. 47–50.
815 Oppenheim (1952), p. 251.

and means to take any systematic action [for the protection of artistic and cultural treasures]; it expresses the wish that the Spanish authorities will continue to take all appropriate measures for the preservation of the testimonies of the cultural grandeur of the country and that they will exert every effort, more particularly, to conform to the rules which the Office had laid down through its international conferences of experts.[816]

Thus it was thanks to this unsuccessful initiative during the Spanish Civil War that the process of codification of specific rules for the protection of cultural property began. It was a new start for a process of codification that had previously been all but abandoned.[817]

In view of this new situation, the Director's Committee recalled the recommendations that the Assembly of the League of Nations addressed on October 10, 1932 to the States Members and non-Members of the League of Nations, following the 1931 Athens Conference, and considered that 'public opinion is, in fact, one of the most powerful instruments that can be used . . . and . . . it has been seriously alarmed at the menaces with which monuments and works of art have been faced as a result of acts of violence due either to civil disorder or international wars.'[818] It considered it 'necessary to complete the technical and juridical study of the protection of monuments and works of art in time of war or civil disorder, with a view to arriving at an international agreement and, if necessary, at the setting up of a body that would be responsible for its application'.[819] It recommended taking into consideration the conclusions of the Committee of Jurists, set up in 1922 by the Washington Conference. The Director's Committee convened the Committee of Experts, presided over by Professor Charles de Visscher, and produced the Preliminary Draft of the International Convention for the Protection of Historic Buildings and Works of Art in Time of War. Its

---

816 League of Nations, International Institute of Intellectual Co-operation, Report of the Director's Committee of the International Museum Office. *Protection on Monuments and Works of art in Time of War and Civil Disorder.* 21 August 1936, p. 2. Geneva: Archives of the League of Nations.

817 At the meeting of 6 and 7 December 1933, the same Director's Committee, relying on the opinion expressed by the League of Nations, asserted that 'it could in no circumstances give its support to an action of this kind [education of the public to respect cultural property in time of war], which it deemed both impossible to apply and undispensible in principle'. It referred to the Athens Conference of 1931. *Commentary*, p. 18.

818 League of Nations. Ibid., p. 3.

819 Ibid., p. 4.

authors made a first attempt to create a provision for situations of internal conflict in Article 10 of the Draft:

> The High Contracting Parties, recognizing the necessity of extending the protection contemplated by this Convention to historic buildings and works of art threatened by disturbance or armed conflicts within a country, agree as follows:
>
> 1. They may lend their friendly assistance to the contending parties for the purpose of safeguarding the threatened and artistic treasures.
> 2. They may receive and shelter, in their respective territories, works of art coming from a country in which civil strife is prevalent and endangered by acts arising out of such strife.
> 3. Museums and collections of a public character may store works of art abroad during a period of civil strife.
>   So long as such works remain abroad, the museums which deposited them shall be deemed their owners.
>   Such deposits shall not be restored until the civil strife is at an end. During transport and for the period of their deposit, such work of art shall be exempt from confiscation, and may not be disposed of either by the depositor or by the depositary.
> 4. Works of art in private ownership may receive protection in foreign territory, provided that they are there deposited on the responsibility of and through the agency of a national museum or collection of public character. The same rule concerning deposit and restoration shall apply and restoration may be affected only through the agency of the depositing institution.[820]

Article 11 of the Regulations for the Execution of this Draft Convention, which was annexed to the Preliminary Draft, stated that 'for the purposes of the application of Article 10 of the Convention, the Standing Committee of the Conference shall lend its good offices to the contending parties with a view to taking all necessary steps for the protection of cultural monuments and works of art threatened by the operations.'[821]

---

820 *Avant-projet de la Convention internationale pour la protection des monuments et oeuvres d'art au cours des conflits armés.* Preliminary draft International Convention for the protection of historic buildings and works of art in time of war. League of Nations, 13 January 1939. Geneva: Archives of the League of Nations. R 40 44, 5 B 36624/30433, documents 193901940, p. 3.
821 Ibid., p. 7.

In the field of international humanitarian law, the first provision dealing directly with non-international armed conflict was Article 3 of the 1949 Geneva Conventions. This Article does not include any reference to property or cultural property.[822]

Article 10 of the Preliminary Draft of 1938 and Article 3 common to the four 1949 Geneva Conventions were both used by the authors of the 1954 Convention as inspiration for the new provision. These two precedents constituted a good example for the authors of the 1954 Convention, who did not want to incorporate situations of internal conflict, where cultural values suffer as much as in international wars. These two provisions help us to better understand Article 19 of the 1954 Hague Convention.

The 1949 Geneva Diplomatic Conference on the Protection of Victims of War

Before studying in detail the provisions concerning protection of cultural property in the event of armed conflict, it may be useful to examine how the provisions for the protection of victims of internal armed conflicts became part of international humanitarian law.

All international Conventions are primarily the affair of governments. Governments discuss them and sign them, and it is on governments that the

---

822 In the case of armed conflict not of an international character occurring in the territory of one of the High Contracting Parties, each Party to the conflict shall be bound to apply, as a minimum, the following provisions:
(1) Persons taking no active part in the hostilities, including members of armed forces who have laid down their arms and those placed 'hors de combat' by sickness, wounds, detention, or any other cause, shall in all circumstances be treated humanely, without any adverse distinction founded on race, colour, religion or faith, sex, birth or wealth, or any other similar criteria.
To this end, the following acts are and shall remain prohibited at any time and in any place whatsoever with respect to the above-mentioned persons:
(a) violence to life and person, in particular murder of all kinds, mutilation, cruel treatment and torture;
(b) taking of hostages;
(c) outrages upon personal dignity, in particular humiliating and degrading treatment;
(d) the passing of sentences and the carrying out of executions without previous judgment pronounced by a regularly constituted court, affording all the judicial guarantees which are recognized as indispensable by civilized peoples.
(2) The wounded and sick shall be collected and cared for.
An impartial humanitarian body, such as the International Committee of the Red Cross, may offer its services to the Parties to the conflict.
The Parties to the conflict should further endeavour to bring into force, by means of special agreements, all or part of the other provisions of the present Convention.
The application of the preceding provisions shall not affect the legal status of the Parties to the conflict.

duty of applying them devolves. But it was a non-governmental body, the Red Cross, that played an important role in the initiation of the process of codification. According to the ICRC Commentary:

> There is nothing astonishing, therefore, in the fact that the Red Cross has long been trying to aid the victims of internal conflicts, the horrors of which sometimes surpass the horrors of international wars by reason of the fratricidal hatred which they engender. But the difficulties which the Red Cross encountered in its efforts in this connection – as always when endeavoring to go a step beyond the text of the Conventions – were enhanced in this case by special obstacles arising out of the internal politics of the States in which the conflict raged. In a civil war the lawful Government, or that which so styles itself, tends to regard its adversaries as common criminals. This attitude has sometimes led governmental authorities to look upon relief given by the Red Cross to war victims of the other Party to the conflict as indirect aid to those who are guilty. Applications by a foreign Red Cross or by the International Committee of the Red Cross have more than once been treated as unfriendly attempts to interfere in the internal affairs of the country concerned.[823]

The Red Cross was not discouraged, and despite frequent lack of understanding on the part of governments, it carried out its humanitarian mission in civil conflicts. Several resolutions were adopted by the International Red Cross Conferences in 1921 and 1938. The last conference requested the International Committee, making use of its practical experience, to continue its general study of the problems raised by civil war as regards the Red Cross.

At the Preliminary Conference of National Red Cross Societies in 1946, the International Committee proposed that, in the event of civil war in a country, the parties should be invited to state that they were prepared to apply the principles of the Convention on the basis of reciprocity. In the Draft Conventions for the Protection of War Victims, which the ICRC submitted to the XVIIth International Red Cross Conference in Stockholm, a fourth and last paragraph read as follows:

> In all cases of armed conflict which are not of an international character, especially cases of civil war, colonial conflicts, or wars of religion, which

---

823 Pictet (1952–1960), Vol. IV, p. 27.

may occur in the territory of one or more of the High Contracting Parties, the implementing of the principles of the present Convention shall be obligatory on each of the adversaries. The application of the Convention in these circumstances shall in no ways depend on the legal status of the Parties to the conflict and shall have no effect on that status.[824]

At the Diplomatic Conference of 1949, divergences of views became apparent,[825] and a considerable number of delegations were opposed to such a provision. Those who were opposed raised the following arguments:

It was said that it would cover in advance all forms of insurrection, rebellion, anarchy, and the break-up of States, and even plain brigandage. Attempts to protect individuals might well prove to be at the expense of the equally legitimate protection of the State. To compel the Government of a State in the throes of internal convulsions to apply to these internal disturbances the whole body of provisions of a Convention expressly concluded to cover the case of war would mean giving its enemies, who might be no more that a handful of rebels or common brigands, the status of belligerents, and possibly even a certain degree of legal recognition. There was also a risk of common or ordinary criminals being encouraged to give themselves a semblance of organization as a pretext for claiming the benefit of the Conventions, representing their crimes as 'acts of war' in order to escape punishment for them. A party of rebels, however small, would be entitled under the Conventions to ask for the assistance and intervention of a Protecting Power. Moreover, it was asked, would not the *de jure* Government be compelled to release the captured rebels as soon as the troubles were over, since the application of the Convention would place them on the same footing as prisoners of war? Any such proposals giving insurgents a legal status, and consequently increased authority, would hamper and handicap the Government in its perfectly legitimate measures of repression.[826]

---

824 Ibid., p. 30.
825 Final Record of the Diplomatic Conference of Geneva, 1949, Vol. II-B, on Article 2, pp. 9–15.
826 Pictet (1952–1960), Vol. IV, p. 31.

By contrast, those in favour of the Stockholm draft regarded the proposals in that instrument as courageous and a step forward in the development of humanitarian law:

> Insurgents, said some, are not all brigands. It sometimes happens in a civil war that those who are regarded as rebels are in actual fact patriots struggling for the independence and the dignity of their country. Others argued that the behaviour of the insurgents in the field would show whether they were in fact mere brigands, or, on the contrary, genuine soldiers deserving of the benefit of the Conventions. Again, it was pointed out that the inclusion of the reciprocity clause in all four Conventions, and not merely (as had been proposed at Stockholm) in the Third and Fourth Conventions, would be sufficient to allay the apprehensions of the opponents of the Stockholm proposals. It was not possible to talk of 'terrorism', 'anarchy' or 'disorders' in the case of rebels who complied with humanitarian principles. Finally, the adoption of the Stockholm proposals would not in any way prevent a *de jure* Government from taking measures under its own laws for the repression of acts judged by it to be dangerous to the order and security of the State.[827]

After long discussions in the Working Groups on the French, Italian and Soviet proposals, the Joint Committee and the Conference adopted the final text:

> To borrow the phrase of one of the delegates, Article 3 is like a 'Convention in miniature'. It applies to non-international conflicts only, and is only applicable to them until such time as a special agreement between the Parties has brought into force between them all or part of the other provisions of the Convention. It is very different from the original draft produced by the International Committee of the Red Cross and adopted at Stockholm, the latter providing for the application of the Conventions in their entirety. But, as the representative of the International Committee at the Diplomatic Conference remarked, since the text originally adopted at Stockholm had no chance of being accepted by the Governments and it was necessary to fall back on an intermediate solution, the text finally

---

827 Ibid., p. 31.

adopted was the one which was to be preferred amongst the various drafts prepared during the Conference. It has the merit of being simple and clear. It at least ensures the application of the rules of humanity which are recognized as essential by civilized nations and provides a legal basis for charitable interventions by the International Committee of the Red Cross or any other impartial humanitarian organization – interventions which in the past were all too often refused on the ground that they represented unfriendly interference in the internal affairs of a State. The text in question has the additional advantage of being applicable automatically, without any condition of reciprocity. Its observance does not depend upon preliminary discussions as to the nature of the conflict or the particular clauses to be respected, as would have been the case with the other drafts discussed. It is true that it merely provides for the application of the principles of the Convention and not for the application of specific provisions, but it defines those principles and in addition lays down certain imperative rules. Finally, it has the advantage of expressing, in each of the four Conventions, the common principle which governs them.[828]

The 1954 Hague Conference

UNESCO Draft CBC/3, submitted to the 1954 Hague Conference, borrowed its basic structure from the common Article 3 of the 1949 Geneva Conventions. According to the UNESCO Commentary, the Article concerned provided

> that at least the principles of the Convention relating to respect for cultural property should be applied in the event of a conflict not of an international character, i.e. generally, in fact, in the event of civil war. These provisions are based on those found in the Geneva Conventions of 1949. They may be thought to be imperfect; but the Red Cross faced with the same textual difficulties, decided that they should not, for that reason, be omitted. The basis of the obligation prescribed by Article 19 for each adversary is that each of the latter is bound by contractual engagements undertaken by a community of which he is a part.[829]

---

828 Pictet (1952–1960), Vol. IV, pp. 33–34.
829 *Records*, p. 313.

At the 1954 Hague Conference, the only opposing voice came from the UK. Its delegate was alone in proposing the deletion of Article 19 (judging it to be unworkable) or at least its weakening, inviting parties to the conflict to 'endeavour' – rather than 'to be bound' – to apply the provisions of the Convention, and removing UNESCO's right take the initiative. The Legal Committee of the Conference did not agree with the UK's reasoning.[830]

The USSR delegate, whose delegation had played an important role in the adoption of Article 3 at the 1949 Geneva Diplomatic Conference, replied to the UK to the effect that

> the Article was perfectly clear. Paragraph 1 referred to the necessity of respecting and safeguarding cultural property and paragraph 4 implied that the application of its provisions would not affect the legal status of the Conflicting Parties. The subject had already been examined in sufficient detail at the 1949 Geneva Conference where a Special Committee and two Working Parties had worked on it for 20 days. A very detailed report had been submitted. Delegates from all countries had spoken and an Article 3 had finally been adopted, which appeared in all Geneva Conventions and listed the provisions to be respected. While the question under discussion then had been the sick and wounded, and was now that of cultural property, the principle was the same and it should be remembered that the decisions then taken were adopted by 61 countries. It was a sufficiently weighty precedent and should be taken into consideration.[831]

Article 19 of the Hague Convention and its short analysis

This Article was adopted in its original form, with two changes for stylistic reasons:

> Conflicts Not of an International Character
> Article 19.
> 1. In the event of an armed conflict not of an international character occurring within the territory of one of the High Contracting Parties, each party to the conflict shall be bound to apply, as a

---

830 Ibid., para. 1065, p. 214.
831 Ibid., para. 1069, p. 214.

minimum, the provisions of the present Convention which relate to respect for cultural property.

2. The parties to the Conflict shall endeavour to bring into force, by means of special agreements, all or part of the other provisions of the present Convention.

3. The United Nations Educational, Scientific and Cultural Organization may offer its services to the parties to the conflict.

4. The application of the preceding provisions shall not affect the legal status of the parties to the conflict.

Paragraph 1

As in Article 3 of the Geneva Conventions, Article 19 does not define the conflict itself. The scope of application is the same as for Article 3. The situation is the same for Article 22 of the 1999 Second Protocol, where the Article states that '[t]his Protocol shall apply in the event of an armed conflict not of an international character, occurring within the territory of one of the Parties.' These words are therefore identical to Article 3 common to the 1949 Geneva Conventions, Article 19 of the 1954 Hague Convention, and Article 22 of the 1999 Second Protocol to the Hague Convention.

We have dealt extensively with the definition of non-international armed conflict in our 1996 Commentary on Article 19 of the Hague Convention[832] and shall return to it again in the commentary below on the first paragraph of Article 22.

Paragraph 2

As indicated in the 1996 Commentary, the second paragraph of Article 19, inspired by the corresponding paragraph of Article 3, opened up the possibility for parties to the conflict to widen the protection of cultural property. This provision and the commentary remain valid for parties to the conflict bound only by the Hague Convention.[833] As we shall see, the Second Protocol binding the States Parties to it went a step further: it ensures the application of all provisions of the Second Protocol to conflicts not of an international character.

---

832 Toman (1996), pp. 210–15.
833 Ibid., p. 216.

Paragraphs 3 and 4

Regarding these two paragraphs, which were included in the Second Protocol *expressis verbis*, we refer to the 1996 Commentary on Article 19 of the Convention[834] and to the corresponding paragraphs of Article 22 and its commentary.[835]

Practical application of the Hague Convention

During the application of the Convention, situations of internal conflict arose quite frequently, but the Convention had little or no effect on the protection of cultural property. All efforts for such protection were undertaken on an *ad hoc* basis by the Director-General, who often made appeals to the parties to the conflicts to respect cultural values – such as in the conflicts in Lebanon, Cambodia and Yugoslavia.

The first joint effort of States Parties to the Convention and UNESCO for the implementation of the Convention was the First Meeting of the High Contracting Parties, held at UNESCO from 16 to 25 July 1962.[836] The issue of internal conflict was not mentioned.

The legal experts who met in Vienna in 1983[837] considered that it would be useful for a meeting of the High Contracting Parties – if one were convened – to examine important developments in the practical application of the Convention, new developments in the nature of conflicts, the results of the reaffirmation and development of humanitarian international law between 1974 and 1977, and, above all, the adoption of two articles concerning the protection of cultural property in the context of the 1977 Additional Protocols to the Geneva Conventions. The adoption of Protocol II dealing with internal conflicts also demonstrated growing interest in the codification of international law in this area. But the advisability of convening a meeting of the High Contracting Parties in the near future was still ruled out. Instead, emphasis was placed on the importance of endeavours to raise the level of awareness of States about the application of the Convention and to promote ratification of and accession to this important instrument. An assessment of

---

834 Ibid., pp. 216–19.
835 See below, pp. 452-457.
836 Report of the meeting, document UNESCO/CUA/120 of 3 September 1962.
837 UNESCO, Meeting of Legal Experts on the Convention for the Protection of Cultural Property in the Event of Armed Conflict. Vienna, 17–19 October 1983. UNESCO doc. CLT-83/CONF. 641/1.

the current situation was also deemed necessary and States were encouraged to prepare for a meeting before one was actually convened,[838] so as to ensure its total success.

Beginning of the process of review of the Convention (1991–1999)

The UNESCO General Conference, at its 26th Session in 1991, reaffirmed its conviction 'that the preservation of the world cultural and natural heritage is of the utmost importance to all humankind' and called 'on all States to increase their effort [in that area] to achieve better implementation of the existing instruments and to reinforce UNESCO's action'.[839]

The document presented by the Netherlands to the UNESCO 1992 Executive Board 140th Session referred[840] to recent conflicts in the Middle East, the Gulf Wars, and conflict in the former Yugoslavia, particularly to the tragic events in Dubrovnik and Sarajevo. The document facilitated a first round of discussions at the Executive Board and presented points for debate by an informal group of experts. The relationship between the protection of cultural property and the two 1977 Additional Protocols was mentioned as a suggestion for the future debate.

To prepare the Executive Board to reach a decision and to give guidance to discussions of this topic, the Government of the Netherlands took the initiative, in close consultation with the Director-General of UNESCO, of convening a Meeting of Experts, which took place from 5 to 7 July 1993 in The Hague. The issues to be discussed at the meeting were included in the discussion paper.[841] Regarding non-international armed conflict,

---

838 See Toman (1984), pp. 60–62.
839 Resolution 26C/Resolution 3.9 Reinforcement of UNESCO's action for the protection of the world cultural heritage, adopted on 6 November 1991. http://unesdoc.unesco.org/images/0009/000904/090448e.pdf.
840 Review of the application of the Convention for the Protection of Cultural Property in the Event of Armed Conflict (The Hague, 14 May 1954), 140 EX/26.
841 Discussion paper, prepared for the Expert Meeting on the Application and Effectiveness of the 1954 Convention. The Hague, 29 June 1993. The following issues had to be discussed: a) scope of the Convention, to be enlarged to include the protection of the natural heritage; b) (special) protection regime; c) relation to other (multilateral) cultural protection instruments, mentioning in particular the 1970 Convention; d) the destruction of cultural property in times of armed conflict of a non-international character; e) institutional issues (in particular, the lack of institutional mechanism, possible relationship UNESCO-UN in this field – including UN peacekeeping activities, and possible role of NGOs). It was suggested that an organ could perhaps be modelled on the World Heritage Committee; f) Commissioners-General/Protecting Powers; g) dissemination, including assitance to Third World countries; h) procedural approaches including the following: i)

the discussion paper stated that during the discussion 'ways and means of improving the protection must be studied'. The 1993 Hague Expert Meeting considered that, ideally, protection in internal conflicts should not differ from that given in international conflicts, but several participants linked this question to respect for national sovereignty.

On 15 October 1993 the 142nd Session of the Executive Board adopted Decision 5.5.2, which welcomes the report of the Hague Meeting of Experts and expressed, *inter alia*, the opinion that the scope of the 1954 Convention should be maintained. It included paragraph 6.4.[842]

Paragraph 6.4: The destruction of cultural property in times of armed conflicts of a non-international character

The wish was expressed that, ideally, the protection afforded to cultural heritage in internal conflicts should not differ from that given in international conflicts. However, this question is linked to the issue of respect for national sovereignty, as several participants stressed. In this respect, mention was made of the possible role of the Security Council in ensuring the protection of cultural heritage in an internal conflict that poses a threat to international peace and security. However, some delegations expressed doubt about a possible role for the UN in the protection of cultural heritage, emphasizing the need for the consent of the host State and recalling the military necessity principle.

In any event the preparation in peacetime at the national level of appropriate lists of protected cultural properties could certainly improve their protection in the event of an internal conflict.

The 1994 Lauswolt Meeting of Experts, held in Lauswolt at the invitation of the Netherlands Government from 9 to 11 February 1994, drafted the first legal instrument constituting the beginning of the process of codification, which was completed by the adoption of the 1999 Second Protocol. The document is known as the 'Lauswolt document'. Its Chapter 3 was entitled 'The protection of cultural property in times of armed conflicts of a non-international character'. The chapter had only one article:

---

drafting of a new legally binding instrument; ii) formal amendment or revision; iii) recommendations/guidelines; iv) combination of (i) and (ii).

842 Report by the Director-General on the Reinforcement of UNESCO's Action for the Protection of World Cultural and Natural Heritage, UNESCO document 142 EX/15, Paris, 18 August 1993, Annex 6.4, p. 4. http://unesdoc.unesco.org/images/0009/000958/095820Eo.pdf

Article 12 Non-international armed conflicts[843]

1. The provisions of the Convention, its 1954 Protocol and this instrument, which relate to the protection of cultural property shall apply as a minimum in the event of an armed conflict not of an international character, occurring within the territory of one of the States Parties.

2. This instrument shall not apply to situations of internal disturbances and tensions, such as riots, isolated and sporadic acts of violence and other acts of a similar nature, as not being armed conflicts.

3. a. [The acts] referred to in Article[s] […] of this instrument are and shall remain prohibited at any time and any place whatsoever.
    b. In particular cultural property specially protected shall be respected and protected at all times.

4. Nothing in [this instrument] shall be invoked for the purpose of affecting the sovereignty of a State or the responsibility of the government, by all legitimate means, to maintain or re-establish law and order in the State or to defend the national unity and territorial integrity of the State.

5. Nothing in this instrument shall be invoked as a justification for intervening, directly or indirectly, for any reason whatever, in the armed conflict or in the internal or external affairs of the State Party in the territory in which that conflict occurs.

The Director-General informed the 145th Session of the Executive Board (1994) about the Lauswolt proposal and considered that there was a need for further discussion by technical, military and legal experts before any written proposal could be presented to the States Parties to the Convention for their consideration. He decided to organize at least one meeting of experts before the next session of the General Conference.[844] This meeting, the 1994 Paris Expert Meeting (28 December 1994),[845] was organized on the basis of an excellent working document, which the UNESCO Secretariat prepared using our 1996 Commentary on the Convention, Patrick Boylan's Report, and the

---

843 The following note was added to the Article: 'One participant questioned the appropriateness of the insertion of this Article in the text.'

844 UNESCO Executive Board, 145th session. Report by the Director-General on the review of the Convention for the Protection of Cultural Property in the Event of Armed Conflict, 145 EX/21, 20 July 1994, para. 4–6, p. 2.

845 Expert Meeting on the Review of the 1954 Hague Convention for the Protection of Cultural Property in the Event of Armed Conflict. Paris, UNESCO Headquarters, 28 November–2 December 1994. UNESCO document CLT/CH/94/608/2, *Final Report*.

Hague and the Lauswolt expert meetings, and which provided the Secretariat's comments on each issue.[846] In this document, UNESCO considered the provision on non-international armed conflict particularly important in view of recent experience in the territory of the former Yugoslavia. Discussion at the Expert Meeting was divided into two parts. The first – a kind of general debate – addressed the basic issues, whereas the second part was devoted to a study of new legal provisions. A number of interventions concerned the issue of internal conflict, and there was no clear consensus on this matter. A few participants stressed that Article 19 of the Convention was self-sufficient in this respect and questioned the appropriateness of Article 12 of the Lauswolt document.[847]

The 1996 *Summary of comments*[848] received from States Parties to the Hague Convention before the 1997 Expert Meeting included only Slovenia's proposal to replace Article 19 of the Convention with paragraphs 1, 4 and 5 of Article 12 of the Lauswolt document and Poland's proposal to mention non-international armed conflict in the Preamble.

The 1997 Government Expert Meeting did not make much progress in this area. It was pointed out that the overwhelming majority of cultural property destroyed since the adoption of the Hague Convention occurred in non-international armed conflicts. For this reason, the participants underscored the necessity of obtaining additional protection for cultural property in such conflicts. However, some participants were not in favour of adopting a more protective article and preferred to retain Article 19 of the Convention alone. They claimed that a new draft article might be used as a pretext for interference in internal affairs. India and Turkey asked for further examination of paragraph 1. Another argument raised during the discussion was that this draft Article tried to modify the notion of non-international armed conflict as embodied in Article 3 common to the four 1949 Geneva Conventions.

---

846 Expert Meeting on the Review of the 1954 Hague Convention for the Protection of Cultural Property in the Event of Armed Conflict. Paris, 28 November–2 December 1994. A working document prepared by the Secretariat, CLT/94/608/1 of 28 November 1994.

847 Expert Meeting on the Review of the 1954 Hague Convention for the Protection of cultural property in the Event of Armed Conflict. Paris, UNESCO Headquarters, 28 November–2 December 1994. UNESCO document CLT/CH/94/608/2, *Final Report*, p. 7.

848 UNESCO, Meeting of Governmental Experts. Summary of comments received from States Parties to the Hague Convention and from the International Council on Archives. UNESCO document CLT-96/CONF.603/INF.4, Paris, December 1996.

The revised Lauswolt document,[849] which was distributed on 27 March 1997 at the closure of the meeting of governmental experts, shed some light on the previous text, clarifying that it is intended to increase protection beyond that provided by Article 19, which mentions only 'respect'. The reference to the 1954 Convention and Protocol was maintained in this text. Paragraph 3 was omitted 'because it seems to have less support'.

The 1998 Vienna Governmental Expert Meeting (11–13 May 1998)[850] led to the elaboration of a *Preliminary Draft Second Protocol,*[851] which was sent to the Member States for comments. Various proposals were made: Norway feared that the bracketed paragraphs would weaken Article 19. China and Syria, by contrast, wanted these paragraphs retained. The ICRC suggested that the system of penal repression should be extended to violations committed in non-international armed conflicts.[852]

On this basis, the UNESCO Secretariat and the Government of the Netherlands drew up the final draft of the Second Protocol: *Draft Second Protocol to the 1954 Hague Convention for the Protection of Cultural Property in the Event of Armed Conflict* (UNESCO doc. HC/1999/1/Rev.1, February 1999).

The proposed Article 24 read as follows:

---

849 The text of the provision in the revised Lauswolt document:
   Article 12. Non-international armed conflicts
   1. *All the provisions of this instrument,* the provisions of the Convention and its 1954 Protocol which relate to *safeguarding of, and respect for,* cultural property shall apply in the event of an armed conflict not of an international character, occurring within the territory of one of the States Parties.
   [2. This instrument shall not apply to situations of internal disturbances and tensions, such as riots, isolated and sporadic acts of violence and other acts of a similar nature, *which are not* armed conflicts.]
   3. Omitted
   [4. Nothing in [this instrument shall be invoked for the purpose of affecting the sovereignty of a State or the responsibility of the government, by all legitimate means, to maintain or re-establish law and order in the State or to defend the national unity and territorial integrity of the State.]
   [5. Nothing in this instrument shall be invoked as a justification for intervening, directly or indirectly, for any reason whatever, in the armed conflict or in the internal or external affairs of the State Party, in the territory in which that conflict occurs.]
   (Draft provisions for the revision of the 1954 Hague Convention and commentary from UNESCO Secretariat. CLT-97/CONF.208/2, Paris, October 1997).
850 UNESCO, Meeting of Governmental Experts on the Revision of the Hague Convention for the Protection of Cultural Property in the Event of Armed Conflict of 1954. Vienna, 11–13 May 1998. UNESCO document Paris, May 1998, *Final Report.*
851 *Preliminary Draft Second Protocol to the 1954 Hague Convention.* UNESCO document HC/1999/1, October 1998 (English, French and Russian).
852 UNESCO, Meeting of Governmental Experts. Summary of comments received from States Parties to the Hague Convention, the International Committee of the Red Cross and the International Council on Archives. UNESCO document Paris, March 1998.

1. All the provisions of this Protocol [,which relate to the general and enhanced special protection of cultural property] shall apply in the event of an armed conflict not of an international character, occurring within the territory of one of the Parties.

[2. This Protocol shall not apply to situations of internal disturbances and tensions, such as riots, isolated and sporadic acts of violence and other acts of a similar nature.]

[3. Nothing in this Protocol shall be invoked for the purpose of affecting the sovereignty of a State or the responsibility of the government, by all legitimate means, to maintain or re-establish law and order in the State or to defend the national unity and territorial integrity of the State.]

[4. Nothing in this Protocol shall be invoked as a justification for intervening, directly or indirectly, for any reason whatever, in the armed conflict or in the internal or external affairs of the Party in the territory of which that conflict occurs.]

5. In conformity with Article 19 paragraph 3 of the Convention, UNESCO may offer its services to the parties to the conflict.

This draft formed the basis of discussion at the 1999 Hague Conference, where Chapter 5 was discussed by the Plenary Session of the Conference on 18 March 1999.

As in the preparatory stage, some States expressed their doubts about the applicability of Chapter 5;[853] others felt that the scope of the Article should be limited so that not all the provisions of the *Draft Second Protocol* would be applicable in the event of a non-international armed conflict.[854] Penal jurisdiction of the territorial State would be in force regardless of the extent and duration of the conflict.[855]

On the other hand, several views were expressed that Article 22, paragraphs 2–4 were inconsistent with the provisions of the Hague Convention and the spirit of some of the other provisions of the *Draft Second Protocol*.[856] While some States felt that Article 22, paragraphs 2 and 3 should be maintained,[857] others preferred to see them deleted. Some thought that paragraphs 1 and 5 should be removed, since they reflected the provisions of

---

853 1999 Hague Conference, Plenary Session, 18 March 1999, Lebanon, p. 195.
854 Ibid., Azerbaijan, India, p. 202.
855 Ibid., Turkey, p. 195.
856 Ibid., Armenia, Belgium, Bosnia and Herczegovina, Poland and Sweden, pp. 197–204.
857 Ibid., Azerbaijan, China, India, pp. 195–202.

Article 19 of the Hague Convention, and replaced with a paragraph stating that the provisions of Article 19 of the Hague Convention will be applicable in the event of a non-international armed conflict. However, these States were not opposed to the idea of placing non-international armed conflicts under the same regime as international armed conflicts, where cultural property is given 'enhanced special protection'.[858] With regard to Article 24(5), one State requested a clarification of the services that UNESCO could offer regarding cultural property in the event of a non-international armed conflict, and maintained that such services were already covered by the Convention.[859]

A large number of States welcomed the provisions of Chapter 5 as they stood, however, in view of the threat posed by non-international conflicts to peace and development. They contended that because the Second Protocol deals with cultural property representing a value to all humanity, non-international armed conflicts must be subject to the same regime as international conflicts.[860] The Polish delegate said that 'the same rules must govern both situations . . . Cultural heritage cannot be divided in two categories according to the character of the conflict'.[861]

Since such conflicts can be as violent as international conflicts, a large number of States were of the opinion that all provisions of the *Draft Second Protocol* relating to enhanced protection should be applicable. Some States suggested that these provisions be included under Article 2 on the scope of the *Draft Second Protocol*.

The delegates of Cameroon and the ICRC referred to the growing variety of conflicts, some of them having international implications.[862]

Some delegates asked that the Article be restructured.[863] Redrafting was proposed by Italy and Argentina. The Italian delegate, supported by Austria and Canada, made the following proposal: 'All the provisions of this Protocol, which relate to the general and enhanced special protection of cultural property shall apply *mutatis mutandis* in the event of an armed conflict not of an international character, occurring within the territory of one of the Parties.'[864]

---

858 Ibid., Ireland, Spain and Ukraine, pp. 198–205.
859 Ibid., Turkey, p. 195.
860 Ibid., Armenia, Belgium, Bosnia and Herczegovina, Poland and Sweden, pp. 197–204.
861 Ibid., p. 204.
862 Ibid., Cameroon, ICRC, pp. 199–205.
863 Ibid., Thailand, Macedonia, pp. 197–202.
864 Ibid., Italy, Austria, Canada, pp. 197–204.

Ariel Gonzales, the delegate of Argentina,[865] proposed the following text: 'Article 19 of the 1954 Convention will apply as appropriate to the present Protocol.' His proposal was supported by Azerbaijan, Cameroon, Colombia and India.[866] However, the addition of this text would do nothing to reduce the ambiguity that already characterizes Article 19.

Some delegates also remembered the difficulties of the codification of Protocol II during the 1974–77 Geneva Conference.[867]

The representative of the ICRC explained that non-international armed conflicts are very complex and that it is precisely because of this that they should fall under the same regime as international armed conflicts. Government forces in non-international conflicts are trained to respect certain obligations and those fighting against them should be subject to the same obligations:

> Attacks against cultural property and pillaging were already treated as war crimes recognized as such in Article 8(2)(e)(iv) and (v) of the Statute of the International Criminal Court. Therefore, she considered that it was important that the Protocol should not have a lower standard than other instruments which had recently been adopted. It would be possible, if the Conference chose to retain paragraphs (3) and (4), to have exactly the same notions in a much shorter form as has been done in Article 8 (3) of the ICCR Statute.[868]

Some delegates were in favour of the creation of a committee to investigate infringements.[869] The Swedish delegate pointed out the necessity of effective sanctions.[870]

The Chairman concluded by stating that Chapter 5 required some redrafting and that it had to be done bearing in mind the existing regime in the Hague Conventions. The text was further discussed by the Working Group,[871] chaired by Alpha Connelly, the delegate of Ireland. The Working Group was dealing with Chapters 1 and 5.

---

865 Ibid., p. 196.
866 Ibid., pp. 197–202.
867 Ibid., Argentina and Sweden, pp. 196–200.
868 Ibid., p. 205.
869 Ibid., Bosnia and Herzegovina, Macedonia, Panama, pp. 200–01.
870 Ibid., p. 205.
871 Diplomatic Conference on a *Draft Second Protocol to the 1954 Hague Convention for the Protection of Cultural Property in the Event of Armed Conflict*. The Hague, 15–26 March 1999. Working Group on

After extensive discussion, the Working Group agreed that the Protocol should apply in the event of an armed conflict of a non-international character occurring within the territory of one of the Parties to the Protocol. As the Chairperson said when introducing the report of the Working Group, no State was opposed to the application of the Protocol *per se* in the event of such a conflict.[872]

The divergences of views concerned the extent to which the provisions on serious violations of the Protocol should apply in such situations. In particular, China and India wished to provide for the exclusive jurisdiction of the State in which the armed conflict occurred over such violations. After discussion, it was agreed to rephrase and simplify paragraph 1: 'This Protocol shall apply in the event of an armed conflict not of an international character, occurring within the territory of one of the Parties.' To satisfy the delegations preoccupied with the exclusive jurisdiction of the territorial State, a new paragraph 4 was added:

> Nothing in this Protocol shall prejudice the primary jurisdiction of a Party in whose territory an armed conflict not of an international character occurs over the violations set forth in [the relevant Article on serious violations] of this Protocol.

The Working Group also agreed on the following modifications of the draft submitted to the Conference:

i) The brackets around paragraphs 2 and 4 of the Conference text should be removed as they mirrored comparable provisions in earlier international humanitarian law treaties, particularly Geneva Protocol II, and that paragraph 4 should be renumbered 5.

ii) A new paragraph 6 should be inserted along the lines of paragraph 4 of Article 19 of the Convention to read: 'The application of this Protocol to the situation referred to in paragraph 1 shall not affect the legal status of the parties to the conflict'.

iii) The phrase, 'In conformity with Article 19 paragraph 3 of the Convention', should be deleted from paragraph 5 of the Conference text, and paragraph 5 should be renumbered 7 and read: 'UNESCO may offer its services to the parties to the conflict'.

Chapter 1 and 5. Chair's Note on Meeting of 25 March 1999. Document HC/1999/5/rev.2 (English), HC/1999/5/rev. 6 and HC/1999/5/rev.5 (French).

872 1999 Hague Conference, Plenary Session, 25 March 1999, p. 68.

India, which had led opposition to the draft of the Additional Protocol II at the 1974–1977 Diplomatic Conference, expressed the view that, in the event of an armed conflict of a non-international character, there should be no role for a Protecting Power as envisaged by Chapter 8, but accepted that the 1949 Geneva Conventions allow for the appointment of Protecting Powers. India also observed that such Powers are rarely appointed.

The text presented by the Working Group was transmitted to the Drafting Committee.

In the final Plenary Session of the Conference the issue of the definition of 'Party' was raised. The use of the capital 'P' 'could give the impression, because of the definition that it only talks about the State Party and that perhaps one would only think of the governmental side'.[873] The German delegate added that 'there was the capital "P" in the first part of Article 22. It referred to the "State Party" and only in paragraphs 6 and 7 was it logical to continue with "the parties to the conflict" which would be the other entities engaged in conflict'.[874] The Chairman of the Drafting Committee confirmed that the basic rule of the Drafting Committee was as follows:

> in general the Protocol applied to the State Parties to the Protocol. Thus the Committee used the word 'Party' with a capital 'P' throughout the text. . . . He emphasized that the Committee considered that Article 22 provided that the Protocol apply in the event of armed conflict. This meant that it had to apply to all parties to the conflict because it was logical both in terms of Article 22 and the system set out in the Protocol. He stated that the Protocol should be understood in light of Article 22 which meant that when a provision is to be applied in a non-international armed conflict, the word 'party' to the conflict means 'party' with a small 'p', namely non-State party to the conflict.[875]

After the discussion of Articles 12 and 36 and a suggestion to add the explanation in the Final Act of the Conference, the Chairman concluded that, in the authentication of the six official languages, consistent use will be ensured and 'there should be no misunderstanding that sometimes the

---

873 The ICRC delegate raised this question at the 1999 Hague Conference, Plenary Session, 26 March 1999, p. 82
874 Ibid., German delegate, p. 82.
875 Ibid., 25 March 1999, p. 83.

reference to parties with a small "p" is appropriate.'[876] The word 'party' with a lowercase 'p' refers to insurgents and not to the third States that are not parties to the Second Protocol.[877]

The Plenary Session of the Conference adopted the text of Article 22.

---

876 Ibid., p. 88.

877 As the Summary report of the Conference indicates, 'the Chairman of the Drafting Committee made the fllowing statement: The Drafting Committee considered that the term "parties to a conflict" could also apply to non-State parties to a conflict by virtue of Article 22 which provides that the Second Protocol applies to non-international armed conflicts and that this Protocol is to be interpreted in that sense.' UNESCO, Diplomatic Conference on the Second Protocol to the Hague Convention for the Protection of Cultural Property in the Event of Armed Conflict. The Hague, 15–26 March 1999. Summary Report. Paris, June 1999, para. 36, pp. 7–8.

Article 22
ARMED CONFLICTS NOT OF AN INTERNATIONAL CHARACTER

1. *This Protocol shall apply in the event of an armed conflict not of an international character, occurring within the territory of one of the Parties.*
2. *This Protocol shall not apply to situations of internal disturbances and tensions, such as riots, isolated and sporadic acts of violence and other acts of a similar nature.*
3. *Nothing in this Protocol shall be invoked for the purpose of affecting the sovereignty of a State or the responsibility of the government, by all legitimate means, to maintain or re-establish law and order in the State or to defend the national unity and territorial integrity of the State.*
4. *Nothing in this Protocol shall prejudice the primary jurisdiction of a Party in whose territory an armed conflict not of an international character occurs over the violations set forth in Article 15.*
5. *Nothing in this Protocol shall be invoked as a justification for intervening, directly or indirectly, for any reason whatever, in the armed conflict or in the internal or external affairs of the Party in the territory of which that conflict occurs.*
6. *The application of this Protocol to the situation referred to in paragraph 1 shall not affect the legal status of the parties to the conflict.*
7. *UNESCO may offer its services to the parties to the conflict.*

Preparatory work

Discussion paper, prepared for the Expert Meeting on the Application and Effectiveness of the 1954 Convention. The Hague, 29 June 1993.

UNESCO, Executive Board, 142nd Session of the Executive Board, Report by the Director-General on the Reinforcement of UNESCO's action for the Protection of World Cultural and Natural Heritage. 142 EX/15, Paris, 18 August 1993, A2 EX/15, Annex: Meeting of experts on the application and effectiveness of the Convention for the Protection of Cultural Property in the Event of Armed Conflict (The Hague, 14 May 1954), The Hague, 5–7 July 1993. http://unesdoc.unesco.org/images/0009/000958/095820Eo.pdf

Expert meeting on the review of the 1954 Hague Convention for the Protection of Cultural Property in the Event of Armed Conflict. Paris, UNESCO Headquarters, 28 November–2 December 1994. UNESCO document CLT/CH/94/608/2, *Final Report.*

UNESCO document: A working document prepared by the Secretariat, CLT/94/608/1 of 28 November 1994.

Expert meeting on the review of the 1954 Hague Convention for the Protection of Cultural Property in the Event of Armed Conflict. Paris, UNESCO Headquarters, 28 November–2 December 1994. UNESCO document CLT/CH/94/608/2, *Final Report*, p. 7.

UNESCO, Meeting of Governmental Experts. Summary of comments received from States Parties to the Hague Convention and from the International Council on Archives. UNESCO document CLT-96/CONF.603/INF.4, Paris, December 1996.

Draft provisions for the revision of the 1954 Hague Convention and commentary from UNESCO Secretariat. UNESCO document CLT-97/CONF.208/2, Paris, October 1997.

UNESCO, Meeting of Governmental Experts on the Revision of the Hague Convention for the Protection of Cultural Property in the Event of Armed Conflict of 1954. Vienna, 11–13 May 1998. UNESCO document Paris, May 1998, *Final Report.*

Preliminary Draft Second Protocol to the 1954 Hague Convention. UNESCO document HC/1999/1, October 1998 (English, French and Russian).

UNESCO, Meeting of Governmental Experts. Summary of comments received from States Parties to the Hague Convention, the International Committee of the Red Cross and the International Council on Archives. UNESCO document Paris, March 1998.

Draft Second Protocol to the 1954 Hague Convention for the Protection of Cultural Property in the Event of Armed Conflict. UNESCO document HC/1999/1/rev.1, February 1999.

1999 Hague Conference: Plenary Session of the Conference, particularly 18 and 24 March 1999.

Bibliography

Chamberlain, K. 2004. *War and Cultural Heritage.* Leicester: Institute of Art and Law, pp. 217–19.

Desch, T. 1999. The Second Protocol to the 1954 Convention for the Protection of Cultural Property in the Event of Armed Conflict. *Yearbook of International Humanitarian Law*, Vol. 2, pp. 82–84.

Henckaerts, J.-M. 1999. New rules for the protection of cultural property in armed conflict: the significance of the Second Protocol to the 1954

Hague Convention for the Protection of Cultural Property in the Event of Armed Conflict. *IRRC*, No. 835, pp. 617–19.

Toman, J. 1996. *The Protection of Cultural Property in the Event of Armed Conflict: Commentary on the Hague Convention of 14 May 1954*. Aldershot: Dartmouth/Paris: UNESCO, pp. 207–20.

Sandoz, Y., Swiniarski, C. and Zimmermann, B. (eds.). 1987. *Commentary on the Additional Protocols of 8 June 1977 to the Geneva Conventions of 12 August 1949*. Geneva: ICRC, Martinus Nijhoff, pp. 1319–56.

PREPARATORY WORK

See the Introduction to Chapter 5 of this Commentary.

ANALYSIS OF THE TEXT

Paragraph 1

The drafts of this paragraph included the reference not only to the Protocol but also to the 1954 Hague Convention and the 1954 Protocol. Unfortunately, this broad definition disappeared in the final stage. Only the last draft Article submitted to the Conference, *Draft Second Protocol to the 1954 Hague Convention for the Protection of Cultural Property in the Event of Armed Conflict* (UNESCO doc. HC/1999/1/rev.1, February 1999), contained the reference to the Protocol. It is certainly regrettable, but it shows that the international community would not go much further on the route to codifying rules concerning internal conflict. The 1977 Additional Protocol was a lucky exception.

The only positive aspect of this reference is that, according to this paragraph, the Protocol applies *in toto*, that is, with all its provisions, to situations of non-international armed conflict.

It concerns in particular the provisions on enhanced protection. Article 19 of the 1954 Convention was limited to general protection (art. 4) and does not include special protection (art. 8).

The Protocol also applies to the provisions of Chapter 4 concerning criminal responsibility and jurisdiction – the most important increase in the application of prosecution and punishment for violations committed in non-international armed conflicts. As we indicated in Chapter 4 above, the 1977 Additional Protocol I established the repression of violations directed against cultural property, but only in situations of international armed conflict. No such provisions were contained in Additional Protocol II. According to the 1999 Second Protocol, criminal prosecution and punishment apply to both categories of conflict: international and non-international. Similarly, the Rome Statute of the International Criminal Court ensures penal repression in both categories of conflict.

As already mentioned in the introduction to this chapter, the scope of application of Article 22 (the situation in which the provisions should apply) is set forth in the first paragraph of this Article and is identical to the scope of application of Article 3 of the Geneva Conventions and Article 19 of the Hague Convention.

Since we already dealt extensively with the definition of non-international armed conflict in the 1996 Commentary on Article 19 of the Hague Convention,[878] we shall mostly refer back to that previous Commentary. Drawing on our previous conclusions, let us first characterize the words used in Article 3 of the 1949 Geneva Conventions, Article 19 of The Hague Convention and Article 22 of the 1999 Second Protocol.

Scope of application: the definition of 'Armed Conflict Not of an International Character'

When previously dealing with the scope of application of Article 3 of the Geneva Conventions, used in the wording of Articles 19 and 22, we had to refer to the Commentary on the Geneva Conventions. That Commentary noted[879] that this Article is one of the most important in the 1949 Conventions, for in it the whole spirit and substance of the Conventions were concentrated. It was called a 'mini-convention'.

What is meant by 'armed conflict not of an international character'? The determination of the scope of application was:

> the burning question which arose again and again at the Diplomatic Conference. The expression was so general, so vague, that many of the delegations feared that it might be taken to cover any act committed by force of arms – any form of anarchy, rebellion, or even plain banditry. For example, if a handful of individuals were to rise in rebellion against the State and attack a police station, would that suffice to bring into being an armed conflict within the meaning of the Article? In order to reply to questions of this sort, it was suggested that the term 'conflict'

---

878 Toman (1996), pp. 210–15.
879 Pictet (1952–1960), Vol. I, p. 38.

should be defined or, which would come to the same thing, that a certain number of conditions for the application of the Convention should be enumerated. The idea was finally abandoned.[880]

The ICRC Commentary provides a list of different proposals made during the Conference in relation to the definition of conflict situations. These criteria are not in any way binding, but are nevertheless helpful for gaining an understanding of the concept of 'armed conflict not of an international character':

(1) That the Party in revolt against the *de jure* Government possesses an organized military force, an authority responsible for its acts, acting within a determinate territory and having the means of respecting and ensuring respect for the Convention.

(2) That the legal Government is obliged to have recourse to the regular military forces against insurgents organized as military and in possession of a part of the national territory.

(3) (a) That the *de jure* Government has recognized the insurgents as belligerents; or

(b) that it has claimed for itself the rights of a belligerent; or

(c) that it has accorded the insurgents recognition as belligerents for the purposes only of the present Convention; or

(d) that the dispute has been admitted to the agenda of the Security Council or the General Assembly of the United Nations as being a threat to international peace, a breach of the peace, or an act of aggression.

(4) (a) That the insurgents have an organization purporting to have the characteristics of a State;

(b) That the insurgent civil authority exercises de facto authority over persons within a determinate territory;

(c) That the armed forces act under the direction of the organized civil authority and are prepared to observe the ordinary laws of war;

(d) That the insurgent civil authority agrees to be bound by the provisions of the Convention.'[881]

---

880 Final Record of the Diplomatic Conference of Geneva, 1949, Vol. II-B, p. 121.
881 Pictet (1952–1960), Vol. IV, pp. 35–36.

Does this mean that Article 3 is not applicable in cases where armed strife breaks out in a country, but does not fulfill any of the above conditions (which are not obligatory and are only mentioned as an indication)? We do not subscribe to this view. We think, on the contrary, that the Article should be applied as widely as possible. There can be no reason against this. For, contrary to what may have been thought, the Article in its reduced form does not in any way limit the right of a State to put down rebellion. Nor does it increase in the slightest the authority of the rebel party. It merely demands respect for certain rules, which were already recognized as essential in all civilized countries, and enacted in the municipal law of the States in question, long before the Convention was signed. What Government would dare to claim before the world, in a case of civil disturbances which could justly be described as mere acts of banditry, that, Article 3 not being applicable, it was entitled to leave the wounded uncared for, to inflict torture and mutilations and to take hostages? However useful, therefore, the various conditions stated above may be, they are not indispensable, since no Government can object to respecting, in its dealings with internal enemies, whatever the nature of the conflict between it and them, a few essential rules which it in fact respects daily, under its own laws, even when dealing with common criminals.[882]

In the 1996 Commentary we raised the question: Is it not in similar terms that the question of the protection of cultural property should be framed? After all, it is hardly imaginable that a government or an authority representing an insurrectional movement would justify the destruction of cultural property that, for any government or authority, represents values that are in most cases part of the ideas for which the fighting was begun on the grounds of uncertainty about the criteria for the definition of the conflict or some similar excuse.

By affording protection to cultural property, the government – like the rebel forces – is simply protecting national heritage, the expression of the historical and artistic traditions of the nation in support of which they are fighting. To allow this property to be destroyed would therefore be the negation of the very aims of their national struggle. Such will be our conclusion in conflicts where there is a unique culture for both government and rebels.

---

882 Ibid., p. 36.

But what happens when the country is divided by cultural, ethnic and religious barriers, as happened in recent conflicts in the former Yugoslavia?

As several past civil wars and internal conflicts have shown, the situation becomes very complex. The cultural values of religious, ethnic or racial minorities can become the objective of the war. In certain circumstances, they form part of the conflict itself and even a fundamental material objective for destruction of opposite values representing, for example, ethnic or other minorities. We have seen quite recently such situations in the conflict in Yugoslavia, where attacks on religious symbols formed part of the conflict and the objective of belligerents.

When we have

> to face the fact that, in a case of conflict between a majority and a minority, the protection of the minority is not ensured on an enforceable international legal basis we see that the majority in most cases is acting according to the same pattern: In order to prevent those conflicts to spread or to be repeated it is necessary to withdraw the moral and value basis of minorities. That means: minorities have to be forced with all means to give up their feeling of identity. This happens most effectively by depriving them of their right to an individual language, writing, religion, names, etc. This applies not only to the living but also the past generations. Therefore in a conflict the destruction of cemeteries, archives, libraries, katastars, marriage lists but also museums and monuments plays a vital role. [883]

The Commentary on the Geneva Conventions also concludes:

> speaking generally, it must be recognized that the conflicts referred to in Article 3 [common to the Geneva Conventions] are armed conflicts, with armed forces on either side engaged in hostilities – conflicts, in short, which are in many respects similar to an international war, but take place within the confines of a single country. In many cases, each of the Parties is in possession of a portion of the national territory, and there is often some sort of front.[884]

---

883 Habsburg-Lothringen (2002), p. 22.
884 Pictet (1952–1960), Vol. IV, p. 36.

It should be noted that both Article 3 and Additional Protocol II, when accepted by the government, become part of national law and, as such, are binding on both the government and national citizens, and therefore on insurrectional movements as well. It is also the duty of the government and of the leaders of insurrectional movements to ensure knowledge of the principles of the protection of cultural property, as is clear from the specific provisions relating to dissemination:

> The general principles of humanitarian law should be regarded as binding in any event. In the decades since 1954, general principles have advanced greatly in this area so that prohibitions of torture, for example, now apply generally, whether in peace or conflict. Similarly, it can be argued, that general principles of cultural protection law have developed, in particular international rules such as the Convention concerning the Protection of the World Cultural and Natural Heritage 1971, which is on the way to universal acceptance, which provides a general obligation to protect cultural heritage on a States' own territory, as well as that of other States.[885]

Paragraph 2

Article 3 of the 1949 Geneva Convention did not provide a specific definition of conflicts of a non-international character. Such determination was left to the parties or to the organizations involved.

The situation changed at the moment when a restrictive definition was included in Article 1, paragraph 1 of the 1977 Additional Protocol II. The States who agreed to this restrictive definition wanted to add a complement to it in order, quite clearly, to exclude from the definition all low-intensity conflicts and to provide States with assurance that international law would not intervene in their internal affairs beyond the restrictive definition provided. This was the will of the States participating in the 1974–1977 Geneva Diplomatic Conference.

The following paragraph reproduces exactly Article 1, paragraph 2 of the 1977 Additional Protocol II, which states:

---

885 UNESCO document Expert Meeting on the Review of the 1954 Hague Convention for the Protection of Cultural Property in the Event of Armed Conflict. Paris, 28 November–2 December 1994. A working document prepared by the Secretariat. CLT/94/608/1 of 28 November 1994, pp. 16–17.

> 2. This Protocol shall not apply to situations of internal disturbances
> and tensions, such as riots, isolated and sporadic acts of violence
> and other acts of a similar nature, as not being armed conflicts.

As in the case of this paragraph, paragraph 2 of Article 22 expressly excludes internal disturbances and tensions from the Protocol's scope of application. These are not considered to be armed conflicts.[886] In Article 1 of Additional Protocol II, the criteria laid down in paragraph 1, taken by themselves, are clearly sufficient to exclude internal disturbances and, *a fortiori*, internal tensions. This is not the case for Article 22, where internal conflict is defined in the same way as in Article 3 common to the Geneva Conventions.[887]

Regarding Article 1, the Federal Republic of Germany's delegation to the CDDH stated:

> This Article constitutes a compromise solution which was difficult to reach. An essential element of this compromise is the fact that the existing conditions of application of Article 3 common to the Geneva Conventions are not modified. This is clearly expressed in Article 1, paragraph 1, of Protocol II. It also applies to paragraph 2 of the same article. Consequently, the negative definition of the term armed conflict in paragraph 2 applies only to Protocol II, not to Article 3 common to the Geneva Conventions. This is the understanding of the Federal Republic of Germany as to the interpretation of Article 1 of Protocol II. It does not, however, intend to express any view, be it only by implication, on the meaning of the term armed conflict as used in Article 3 common to the Geneva Conventions.[888]

In this interpretation, the fact that the same provision as Article 1, paragraph 2 was included in paragraph 2 of Article 22 shows that in the Article of the 1999 Second Protocol the States went quite beyond the meaning of this provision in the context of international humanitarian law in general. Here

---

886 In Article 1 of the Additional Protocol, the English phrase 'as not being' is rendered in French as *qui ne sont pas considérés* (which are not considered to be). This has no effect on the meaning. This formulation is not used in Article 22.

887 This paragraph, taken from the ICRC draft, made sense in the context of the original draft article. Its purpose was to define the lower threshold of the concept of armed conflict, assuming that the scope of application of common Article 3 and the Protocol would be identical. The paragraph was not questioned and was retained and adopted without lengthy debates. (*Commentary on Additional Protocols of 8 June 1977*, para. 4473.)

888 See *Official Records of CDDH*, Vol. VII, pp. 7–80, CDDH/SR.49, Annex (FRG).

the definition of the conflict, identical to Article 3, is limited even more by the inclusion of paragraph 2, which restricts the meaning of non-international armed conflict, as originally intended. The limitations were going too far.

No definitions are given of the terms used in paragraph 2 of Article 22 (terms also included in paragraph 2 of Article 1 of the Second Additional Protocol). The ICRC Commentary says:

> The concept of internal disturbances and tensions may be illustrated by giving a list of examples of such situations without any attempt to be exhaustive: riots, such as demonstrations without a concerted plan from the outset; isolated and sporadic acts of violence, as opposed to military operations carried out by armed forces or armed groups; other acts of a similar nature, including, in particular, large scale arrests of people for their activities or opinions. As the ICRC has a legally recognized right of initiative to offer its services with a view to assisting and protecting the victims in such situations, it has for a long time been attempting to define them in order to better guide its activities. Originally drawn up for internal use, some definitions were submitted in particular to a group of government experts in 1970. On the basis of their comments the ICRC gave the following description of internal disturbances during the first session of the Conference of Government Experts in 1971:

> This involves situations in which there is no non-international armed conflict as such, but there exists a confrontation within the country, which is characterized by a certain seriousness or duration and which involves acts of violence. These latter can assume various forms, all the way from the spontaneous generation of acts of revolt to the struggle between more or less organized groups and the authorities in power. In these situations, which do not necessarily degenerate into open struggle, the authorities in power call upon extensive police forces, or even armed forces, to restore internal order. The high number of victims has made necessary the application of a minimum of humanitarian rules.[889]

---

889 CE/5b, p. 79, reproduced in *The ICRC, the League and the Report on the Re-Appraisal of the Role of the Red Cross* (Geneva: ICRC, 1979), pp. 24–25 (offprint first published in the *IRRC*, July–August 1978, pp. 210–11). See also *Commentary on the Additional Protocols of 8 June 1977 to the Geneva Conventions of 12 August 1949* (Geneva: ICRC, 1987), para. 4475, p. 1355.

As regards internal tensions, these could be said to include particular situations of serious tension (political, religious, racial, social, economic, etc.), but also the sequels to armed conflict or internal disturbances. Such situations have one or more of the following characteristics, if not all at the same time:

- large scale arrests;
- a large number of 'political' prisoners;
- the probable existence of ill-treatment or inhumane conditions of detention;
- the suspension of fundamental judicial guarantees, either as part of the promulgation of a state of emergency or simply as a matter of fact;
- allegations of disappearances.

In short, as stated above, there are internal disturbances, without being an armed conflict, when the State uses armed force to maintain order; there are internal tensions, without being internal disturbances, when force is used as a preventive measure to maintain respect for law and order.

These definitions are not contained in a convention but form part of ICRC doctrine. While designed for practical use, they may serve to shed some light on these terms, which appear in an international law instrument for the first time.

Internal disturbances and tensions are not at present within the field of application of international humanitarian law; the ICRC has carried out activities in this field on an ad hoc basis. However, this does not mean that there is no international legal protection applicable to such situations, as they are covered by universal and regional human rights instruments. It is not within the scope of this commentary, however, to go into that subject. [890]

This paragraph is not only a compromise but a real and additional concession given to States that were reluctant to go beyond the provision of Article 19 of the Hague Convention. It is an example of how difficult it was in the past and how difficult it remains in the present international community to agree on any provision that concerns such a highly political issue as internal conflict and the willingness of States and Governments to preserve their sovereignty. Nevertheless, two experts: Hans Peter Gasser from the ICRC, and Theodor Meron, former professor at New York University and former President of

---

890 Commentary on Additional Protocols of 8 June 1977, para. 4474–79, 1355–56.

the ICTY – have sought to draft minimum rules for low-intensity conflicts and to have them adopted in the form of resolutions by the United Nations Human Rights Commission or the General Assembly.[891]

In practice the ICRC has not limited its actions to conflicts of non-international character. Many interventions have taken place during internal disturbances and tensions, the ICRC basing its actions on its Statutes and, above all, on the courageous initiative of the Committee that 'must, any place where there is a civil war, revolution, coup d'état, dictatorship and everywhere where there are political prisoners, remember that the latter are often more unhappy than prisoners of war and deserve its attention and concern'.[892]

Like the ICRC, UNESCO may also find itself having to interpret and define situations of conflict in order to determine whether an international or internal conflict or some other type of low-key conflict is involved. However, the Organization would risk running counter to the provision in paragraph 3 of Article I of its Constitution, according to which 'the Organization is prohibited from intervening on matters which are essentially within their [States Members of the Organization] domestic jurisdiction'.[893] In order to avoid possible and even probable friction with its Member States, UNESCO has to refer to its general mandate for the protection of cultural property, a mandate that derives from Article I(2)(c) of its Constitution.[894] The following question should be raised in such situations: Is it more important to refrain from any action, thus avoiding a possible accusation of interference in internal affairs of Member States, or to save historical monuments or other cultural heritage?

The ICRC's position is unquestionably easier because it is a private organization, whose status is fully recognized and respected by the international community as a whole. Despite all the difficulties it may encounter, UNESCO must fulfill the responsibilities entrusted to it by its Constitution, but it must also comply with Article 19 of the Hague Convention. It must expect criticism, opposition and accusations of interference in the internal affairs of States. But, in acting as it does, UNESCO is simply carrying out its mandate

---

891 Declaration of Minimum Humanitarian Standards of 2 December 1990. Turku/Abo, Institute for Human Rights, 1991.

892 *ICRC Report*, quoted in Moreillon (1973), p. 95.

893 *Constitution of the United Nations Educational, Scientific and Cultural Organization*. Adopted in London on 16 November 1945 and amended by the General Conference at its 2nd, 3rd, 4th, 5th, 6th, 7th, 8th, 9th, 10th, 12th, 15th, 17th, 19th, 20th, 21st, 24th, 25th, 26th, 27th, 28th, 29th and 31st sessions. In UNESCO (2004), p. 9.

894 Ibid., p. 8.

and ensuring respect for what represents the higher interest: the protection of cultural property. Surely it is preferable to face up to these criticisms, criticisms reflecting only passing interests. In carrying out the duties assigned to it, UNESCO should be able to count on the understanding of all States. Public opinion and future generations will appreciate the courageous stand.

Paragraph 3

Two major reasons exists for this paragraph. On the one hand, it provides Parties to the Protocol with assurance of their sovereignty and their responsibility for the maintenance and establishment of law and order and defense of their national unity and integrity. On the other hand, by its specific wording ('nothing . . . shall be invoked') it excludes situations in which States and their governments and governmental representatives use and invoke sovereignty and exclusive responsibility as an excuse for the non-application of the Protocol.

This smart formulation provides a guarantee for both sides: the government and all those, including UNESCO, who seek to provide maximum protection for cultural values.

This paragraph is also inspired by Additional Protocol II, Article 3, paragraph 1 of which states:

> Article 3. Non-intervention
> 1. Nothing in this Protocol shall be invoked for the purpose of affecting the sovereignty of a State or the responsibility of the government, by all legitimate means, to maintain or re-establish law and order in the State or to defend the national unity and territorial integrity of the State.

The ICRC commentary made the following remarks:

> Article 3 is a response to the fear that Protocol II might be used as a pretext to violate the sovereignty of States and intervene in their internal or external affairs, i.e. that it might serve as a justification for intervention. Such fear became apparent at the Conference of Government Experts. Some of the experts would even have liked to include a clause in the Preamble to the effect that respect for national

sovereignty and for the principle of non-interference in internal affairs
was a pre-requisite for applying the Protocol.[895]

In view of this recurring concern, the ICRC had already included such a
provision in the draft submitted to the Diplomatic Conference. Although
it had the same tenor, the proposed provision was nevertheless more
succinct.[896]

This is a saving clause, which brings to mind the two complementary
principles of international law enshrined in the *United Nations Charter*:[897] the
principle of inviolability of national sovereignty and of non-intervention in
matters that are essentially within the domestic jurisdiction of a State.

The reference to legitimate means can be defined as the right of a State
to protect itself, but this right is not unlimited: 'the State is still required to
act in accordance with international law, including international humanitarian
law.'[898]

With specific reference to paragraph 1 of Article 3, the ICRC
commentary states:

> Paragraph 1 reaffirms the principle of the inviolability of the national
> sovereignty of States. The Protocol has a purely humanitarian aim.
> Consequently it does not affect the right of States to take appropriate
> measures for maintaining or restoring law and order, defending their
> national unity and territorial integrity. This is the responsibility of
> governments and is expressly recognized here. If the State's authority
> had been totally reserved, that would have risked depriving the Protocol
> of its substance and meaning; for this reason it was of paramount
> importance to specify that only legitimate means may be used. Thus
> imperative needs of State security may not be invoked to justify
> breaches of the rules of the Protocol. In ratifying or acceding to the
> Protocol, a State accepts its terms by the unfettered exercise of its
> sovereign powers. Consequently, the obligation to respect the rules
> contained in it cannot later be considered as an infringement of its

---

895 CE 1972, Report, Vol. I, p. 120, para. 2.534 and 2.539.
896 Draft art. 4.
897 *United Nations Charter*, art. 2, para. 1 and 7.
898 Chamberlain (2004), p. 218.

sovereignty, as the government's freedom of action is limited by the obligations it has itself freely agreed to.[899] [900]

Paragraph 4

If the preceding paragraph 3 provided satisfaction to both sides (governments and those who wish to protect cultural property), paragraph 4 is exclusively designed for the benefit of the State and its authorities. It resolves the primacy of jurisdiction in favour of the State in whose territory the internal conflict is taking place, over serious violations of the Protocol according to Article 15. It concerns not only the most serious violations specified in paragraphs (a), (b) and (c), but all violations, including those specified in paragraphs (d) and (e). This paragraph was included at the request of China and India.

Jean-Marie Henckearts rightly points out that when Parties to the Protocol exercise primary jurisdiction, there is no place for any additional judicial intervention. Justice is done. But if the Parties in whose territory the violations are taking place are not exercising jurisdiction, then 'jurisdiction may be exercised by other States or by international criminal tribunal with the competence to do so'.[901] The question of primacy and complementarity was raised with the appearance of the international tribunals. The problem arises only when one or several States may assert their jurisdiction over a specific crime on the legal grounds and principles of territoriality, active or passive nationality or universality. There is no general rule to help settle this problems, and this is why – regarding the international tribunals – the question had to be decided by the legal instruments by which the tribunals were constituted.

In the case of the ICTY and the ICTR, primacy was given to international tribunals. This was due to the conflicts that took place on the territory of the former Yugoslavia and the tensions among the ethnic and religious groups there, which precluded the possibility of national tribunals

---

899 On this question, see 'The SS Wimbledon case', Reports of the Permanent Court of International Justice, Series A, No. 1, 17 August 1923: 'The Court declines to see in the conclusion of any treaty by which a State undertakes to perform or refrain from performing a particular act an abandonment of its sovereignty. No doubt any Convention creating an obligation of this kind places a restriction upon the exercise of the sovereign rights of the State, in the sense that it requires them to be exercised in a certain way. But the right to enter into international engagements is an attribute of State sovereignty.' See also O.R. VIII, pp. 215–18, CDDH/I/SR.23, para. 1–19.

900 Commentary to Additional Protocols of 8 June 1977, para. 4500–1, pp. 1362–63.

901 Henckaerts (1999), p. 618.

conducting fair trials. In Rwanda, the national judicial system was not functioning. In the case of the ICC the principle of complementarity prevailed. The national courts have priority in the exercise of jurisdiction.[902]

This paragraph simply repeats the conclusion made at the 1999 Hague Conference concerning primary jurisdiction in relation to Article 15 discussed above.[903]

Paragraph 5

Paragraph 5 is another provision that aims to insure governments against intervention in their affairs. The Protocol, as with any treaty, cannot serve as a pretext or justification for direct or indirect intervention[904] in an armed conflict or in the internal or external affairs of the High Contracting Party concerned.

All these limiting provisions in favour of the States are a necessary price for the possible ratification or accession of States particularly sensitive to this matter.

The principle of non-intervention is an old principle of international law; it first emerged at the end of the 18th century and appears in the writing of Emer de Vattel.[905] In its most recent form, it is included in Article 2, paragraph 7 of the *Charter of the United Nations* and in its interpretation in the Declaration on Principles of International Law Concerning Friendly Relations and Co-operation among States in Accordance with the Charter of the United Nations:[906]

> No State or group of States has the right to intervene, directly or indirectly, for any reason whatever, in the internal or external affairs of any other State. Consequently, armed intervention and all other forms of interference or attempted threats against the personality of

---

902 For more information, see Cassese (2003), pp. 350 ff., and Holmes (2002).

903 See page 311 ff.

904 According to the ICRC Commentary to the Additional Protocols, one delegation at the Diplomatic Conference pointed out that a distinction is currently made between 'intervention' and 'interference': 'intervention' is applied to subversive or terrorist activities, whereas the word 'interference' may be used for ordinary *démarches* or protests. Official Records VIII, p. 300, CDDH/I/SR.30, para. 5. This remark is based on Resolution 2625 (XXV) of the United Nations on Principles of International Law concerning Friendly Relations and Co-operation among States, and Principle VI of the Final Act of Helsinki: 'Non-intervention'. See also on this point, Dupuy and Leonetti (1979), pp. 272–74.

905 Sahovic (1972), p. 224.

906 UN General Assembly Resolution 2625 (XXV) of 24 October 1970.

the State or against its political, economic and cultural elements, are in violation of international law.

The paragraph is not only inspired by but also copied from Article 3, paragraph 2 of Additional Protocol II, which states:

> Article 3. Non-intervention
> [. . .]
> 2. Nothing in this Protocol shall be invoked as a justification for intervening, directly or indirectly, for any reason whatever, in the armed conflict or in the internal or external affairs of the High Contracting Party in the territory of which that conflict occurs.

The ICRC Commentary on Article 3, paragraph 2 mentioned that 'the prohibition is ... addressed not only to States, but also to other bodies, international or non-governmental organizations, which might use the Protocol as a pretext for interfering in the affairs of the State in whose territory the armed conflict is taking place'.[907] But because some of the organizations have a mandate to offer their services, such an offer cannot be considered a hostile act.[908]

As Kevin Chamberlain rightly points out, the prohibition of intervention

> does not mean, however, that where a Party to the Protocol is in clear breach of its obligations under the Protocol, the other Parties to the Protocol or competent international organizations such as UNESCO or the ICRC are precluded from making diplomatic representations to

---

907 Commentary to Additional Protocols of 8 June 1977, p. 1363.
908 It should also be recalled here that common Article 3 provides that: 'An impartial humanitarian body, such as the International Committee of the Red Cross, may offer its services to the Parties to the conflict.' Such an offer of services, legitimate under common Article 3, cannot be considered a hostile act. Even in the absence of explicit reaffirmation, the position achieved in 1949 is not adversely affected by Protocol II, which, as specified in Article 1 (Material field of application), supplements and develops common Article 3 without modifying its conditions of application. Nor does it prohibit the offer by an impartial humanitarian organization, such as the ICRC, to provide assistance and protection to the victims of the armed conflict and to contribute to the implementation of the Protocol. This possibility is expressly provided for with regard to assistance for persons who have been deprived of their liberty and with regard to the organization of relief actions for the benefit of the civilian population. However, there is no obligation to accept assistance from such an organization. Parties remain free to accept or refuse assistance offered them, precisely in order to retain their complete freedom of judgment and so as not to be exposed to external interventions. (*Commentary to Additional Protocols of 8 June 1977*, p. 1363.)

that Party. All the Parties to the Protocol have an interest in ensuring its observance and consequently have the right to make representations to any other Party in breach of the Protocol. This right overrides any obligation that the Parties may have not to intervene in the domestic affairs of the Party in whose territory the conflict is taking place.[909]

Paragraph 6

Paragraph 6 is a repetition of Article 19, paragraph 4 of the Hague Convention, which itself was taken from Article 3 common to the Geneva Conventions.

If paragraph 4 of Article 19 is the last paragraph of Article 19, then paragraph 6 of Article 22 of the Protocol is placed more logically before the provision concerning UNESCO's offer of services. This represents an improvement in the order of paragraphs, in our view.

As we noted in the 1996 Commentary, this is an essential provision without which the very existence of Article 19 of the Hague Convention (and Article 3 of the Geneva Convention as well) would be impossible. It is a kind of guarantee that, in the event of a civil war, the application of the Convention, however limited in scope, will not interfere with a legal government and its efforts – deemed to be legitimate – to quell a rebellion, or confer a status of belligerency, which would add to an adversary's authority and power.

Regarding Article 3, this provision had already been suggested at the Conference of Government Experts convened by the ICRC in 1947.[910] It was reintroduced with very little change in all the succeeding drafts. It makes absolutely clear that the object of the Convention is purely humanitarian, that it is in no way concerned with the internal affairs of States, and that it merely ensures respect for the few essential rules of humanity that all civilized nations consider to be valid everywhere and under all circumstances and to be above and outside war itself:

> Consequently, the fact of applying Article 3 does not in itself constitute any recognition by the *de jure* Government that the adverse Party has authority of any kind; it does not limit in any way the Government's

---

909 Chamberlain (2004), p. 219.
910 See Report on the Work of the Conference of Government Experts for the Study of the Conventions for the Protection of War Victims (Geneva, 14–26 April, 1947), Geneva, 1947, p. 9.

right to suppress a rebellion using all the means – including arms – provided for under its own laws; it does not in any way affect its right to prosecute, try and sentence its adversaries for their crimes, according to its own laws. In the same way, the fact of the adverse Party applying Article does not give it any right to special protection or any immunity, whatever it may be and whatever title it may give itself or claim.[911]

Because the question of legal status was included in the common Article 3, it was not repeated again in Additional Protocol II. This was explained in the ICRC commentary:

> In fact, the ICRC draft contained yet another savings clause which recalled that the legal status of the parties to the conflict would not be affected by the application of the Protocol.[912] That Article was deleted by consensus during the final stage of the adoption of the Protocol.[913] On the one hand, its *raison d'être* had disappeared since all mention of parties to the conflict had been deleted from the text, precisely so as not to give any semblance of recognition to any sort of international status of the insurgent party;[914] on the other hand, such a clause is already contained in common Article 3, and therefore retains its full validity with regard to Protocol II.[915] Thus it is perfectly clear that the application of international humanitarian law in situations of non-international armed conflict has no effect whatever on the qualification of relations between the parties.[916]

The *raison d'être* of this paragraph is that the object of the Article is the protection of cultural property alone and that this in no way interferes with a State's domestic affairs. In addition, the fact that the legal government applies this Article in no way represents recognition of any status whatsoever of the opposing party. The purpose of the Article is confined to the protection of cultural property and in no way restricts actions the government may take in order to put down a rebellion as stated in paragraph 5.

---

911 Pictet (1952–1960), Vol. I, pp. 38–39.
912 Draft art. 3.
913 See Official Records VII, p. 86, CDDH/SR.50, para. 9.
914 See the introduction to this Part, supra, p. 1343.
915 Common art. 3, para. 4.
916 Commentary to Additional Protocols of 8 June 1977, para. 1497–99, p. 1362.

Similarly the application of the Article does not entitle the opposing party – whoever it may be and whatever qualification it may give itself or claim – to special status, special protection or immunity. What matters is that the mandate is carried out. All political considerations that are not relevant to the accomplishment of this task should be set aside.

Paragraph 7

As in Article 19 of the Hague Convention, Article 22 of the Second Protocol reintroduces the right of initiative in the same wording. It must also be read in conjunction with Article 23, paragraph 2 of the Convention, according to which '[the] Organization is authorized to make, on its own initiative, proposals on this matter to the High Contracting Parties'.[917]

Instead of using the full name of the Organization, the Second Protocol uses the abbreviation, which was introduced among the terms defined in Article 1 of the Protocol. Otherwise, the formulation is the same, including the use of the small 'p' in 'parties to the conflict', which confirms that all parties to the conflict are covered, including non-State Parties.

This paragraph concerning the right of initiative is placed as the last paragraph of the Article. The placement does not follow the examples of Article 19 of the Hague Convention and Article 3 common to the 1949 Geneva Conventions, where right of initiative is placed before the Article concerning legal status of the parties. This seems quite logical and constitutes – in our view – an editorial improvement that does not affect its substance.

Our present commentary on this does not differ from our 1996 Commentary on Article 19, paragraph 3. There we referred once again to the example of Article 3 of the Geneva Conventions, whence this provision was taken.[918]

The right of initiative conferred on UNESCO by paragraph 3 of Article 19 of the Hague Convention and by paragraph 7 of Article 22 of the 1999 Second Protocol is based on Article 3 of the Geneva Conventions, which grants the same right to an impartial humanitarian body, such as the ICRC. We have also indicated that in the French text of the Geneva Conventions, this offer is formulated in a stronger manner (*pourra*) than in

---

917 Chamberlain (2004, p. 219) considers that the 'provision goes somewhat further than Article 23 of the Convention, paragraph 2 of which authorizes UNESCO to make proposals on its own initiative. Article 23 only applies to making proposals to the Contracting Parties, whereas Article 19 of the Protocol gives UNESCO the right to offer its services to both sides in the conflict.'

918 Toman (1996), pp. 216–18.

Article 19 of the Hague Convention (*peut*). There is no such distinction in the Spanish or Russian texts. The offer of services may be made to all entities – whether States or not – when they are parties to an armed conflict of a non-international character.

The identical nature of this provision to Article 3 of the Geneva Conventions tells us that UNESCO should play a role in the protection of cultural property which should, *mutatis mutandis*, be similar to that of the ICRC for protection of victims of armed conflicts.

Since paragraph 3 of Article 19 of the Hague Convention and paragraph 7 of Article 22 of the 1999 Second Protocol have been copied from the Geneva Conventions, we may again refer to the conclusions of the ICRC commentary on Article 3:

> It is obvious that any organization can 'offer its services' to the Parties to a conflict at any time, just as any individual can. To offer one's services costs little and, what is more important, in no way binds the recipient of the offer, since the offer need not be accepted. The International Committee of the Red Cross, for its part, has not failed to offer its services for humanitarian purposes during various civil wars, whenever it considered that this was in the interests of those suffering as a result of hostilities, just as it has offered them when any international conflict has broken out. This paragraph may therefore appear at first sight to be merely decorative and without any real significance. Nevertheless, it is of great moral and practical value.[919]

UNESCO should do the same when cultural property is at risk.

The existence of provisions in a Convention is useful for putting an offer of services into effect:

> Although the International Committee of the Red Cross has been able to do a considerable amount of humanitarian work in certain civil wars, in others the doors have been churlishly closed against it, the mere offer of charitable services being regarded as an unfriendly act – an inadmissible attempt to interfere in the internal affairs of the State. The adoption of Article 3 has placed matters on a different footing, an impartial humanitarian organization now being legally entitled to offer its services. The parties to the conflict can, of course, decline the

---

919 Pictet (1952–1960), Vol. IV, p. 41.

offer if they can do without it. But they can no longer look upon it as an unfriendly act, nor resent the fact that the organization making the offer has tried to come to the aid of the victims of the conflict.[920]

It should also be pointed out that the offer of services is supplementary and that responsibility for the application of Articles 19 and 22 (as in the case of Article 3) lies first and foremost with the parties to the conflict and with the authorities of the countries that have been designated to supervise the protection of cultural property.

As noted above, the protection of cultural property is a complex subject and it may happen that a country is not able to ensure that protection by itself. Outside help offered by international organizations authorized by the community of States to provide such protection can be received only with satisfaction. The parties to the conflict can hardly refuse this aid without incurring full responsibility for any deterioration or even destruction of the cultural property.

We have already mentioned in the 1996 Commentary our view on the international body offering the services: the nature of the body offering its services is obviously very important. In the case of the ICRC, its character as a humanitarian and impartial body has been stressed. The legal basis offered to it by Article 2 is no more than confirmation of its practical and pragmatic role developed during the course of its history.[921]

The right of initiative introduced by Article 19 of the Hague Convention was not based on earlier experience, as was the case with the ICRC. This right in the case of armed conflicts of a non-international character has been transposed to the 1954 Convention: to turn to the ICRC as a reference for the purpose of developing this right in the area of cultural property therefore is not surprising. The transposition of this right was no doubt designed to ensure the effectiveness of protection but without any deep thought about consequences and practical possibilities.

In interpreting this provision we must be careful to avoid any automatic transfer based on ICRC experience. The profound difference between a private Swiss body (ICRC) and an intergovernmental organization (UNESCO) has to be borne in mind. UNESCO is well aware of this difference, and it is for that reason that it is seeking new modes of action to carry out its

---

920 Ibid., p. 41.
921 On the proposal of Gustave Moynier, the ICRC offered its good offices for the first time during the second Carlist War in Spain in 1872. For other examples, see in particular Moreillon (1973), pp. 24 ff.

mandate. The Director-General himself raised the problem in connection with the monuments of Angkor Vat: the Organization must be able to act independently of any but cultural considerations.[922]

Practical application

In the practical application of its mandate, UNESCO will be called upon to make contact with the authorities of the parties to the conflict. It will encourage them to take preventive measures and, if relevant, such measures as are necessary in the event of the partial destruction of cultural property. Drawing on ICRC experience, UNESCO will do well to keep its approaches confidential. It is only in the event of flagrant and exceptional violations that it will be entitled to make them public and seek the support of the international community. UNESCO could proceed by making a general appeal to the parties to the conflict. An illustration of the difficulty of the UNESCO mandate is the case of the civil war in Biafra in Nigeria. Whereas the humanitarian action of the ICRC and other humanitarian organizations has been seen on a considerable scale in this country, UNESCO's offer of services was refused, but the authorities gave the assurance that the provisions of the Convention would be observed.

There is a fundamental difference between the role of UNESCO and the ICRC. As we said in the 1996 Commentary to the 1954 Hague Convention:

> after the Second World War, it was quite natural that UNESCO should play a fundamental part in the protection of cultural property, as laid down in its Constitution. It therefore fell upon the Conference to determine the role it should play. In order to do this, the authors of the Convention took the Geneva Conventions as their model without, however, going as far as they had done. On the basis of its very Constitution, UNESCO was accordingly given a special task in the application of standards concerning the protection of cultural property. The 1954 Hague Convention developed this task and introduced a number of clarifications with regard to its implementation. However, while granting UNESCO certain powers, the authors failed to take into account the fundamental difference between the various institutions

---

922 Le patrimoine culturel de l'humanité : une responsabilité commune. Paris: UNESCO, May 1982, p. 212.

responsible for controlling the application of humanitarian law. In conferring certain rights and powers upon the ICRC, the authors of the Geneva Conventions took account of the particular and specific nature of that institution. The ICRC is, of course, a private Swiss body, an association governed by Article 60 et seq. of the Swiss Civil Code, and possessing legal personality. The special nature of the ICRC was recognized by the International Conferences of the Red Cross and by the Geneva Conventions. When the States assigned the ICRC certain rights and duties, they did so in full awareness of the special structure of the Committee but also of the principles that have governed its activities throughout its history, in particular the principles of humanity, impartiality, neutrality and independence. It was its character as an impartial humanitarian body that won the trust of the States when they asked the ICRC to assume certain functions in periods of armed conflict, stressing that it was its total structural independence that imposed on the ICRC, at least in its activities under the Convention, a correspondingly greater obligation to remain faithful to itself. UNESCO on the other hand, is an intergovernmental organization composed of States that form part of the international community. Its powers and competence are established, by decision of the Member States, in its Constitution (the instrument creating a United Nations Educational, Scientific and Cultural Organization, signed at London on 16 November 1945). The Organization's policy is laid down by its General Conferences, which reflect the points of view of all the States. For the Organization to play a role similar to that entrusted to the ICRC, the UNESCO Secretariat must be able to perform its functions in a way that conforms as closely as possible to the principles of humanitarian international law. For that, *States must first bear in mind and understand the functions that UNESCO has to perform in this area and give the Secretariat the fullest opportunity of carrying out those functions.*[923]

---

923 Toman (1996), pp. 257–58.

Chapter 6

INSTITUTIONAL ISSUES

INTRODUCTION

Institutional issues are characteristic elements that accompany many chapters of international law and develop into the specific branch of international law called the law of international institutions. Many international lawyers have devoted a great part of their writings to international organizations. Today, hardly any subject relating to international law exists without appropriate institutional support.

One international lawyer dealing with this subject is Sir Derek William Bowett. His book on international institutions, first published in 1962, became an acknowledged classic in this field. He started his first chapter by saying:

> The development of international organizations has been, in the main, a response to the evident need arising from international intercourse rather than to the philosophical or ideological appeal of the notion of world government. The growth of international intercourse, in the sense of the development of relations between different peoples, was a constant feature of maturing civilizations; advances in the mechanics of communications combined with the desire for trade to produce a degree of intercourse which ultimately called for regulation by institutional means.[924]

The protection of cultural property in the event of armed conflict requires the same institutional attention. From the very beginning of efforts for the protection of cultural property and the codification of this issue, the promoters of the new forms of codification paid attention to the institutional aspects. It was clear to them that a certain type of institutional framework was indispensible in order to ensure the implementation of the rules concerning protection.

---

924 Bowett (1982), p. 1. See also Sands and Klein (2001), p. 1.

Historical background

As we know, the first provisions for the protection of cultural property occurred in the national legislation of the US, in the Lieber Instructions of 1863: *Instructions for the Government of Armies of the United States in the Field, General Orders*, No. 100, War Department, Adjutant General's Office, Washington, 24 April 1863. Respect of the provisions concerning Articles 34 to 36 is ensured by the victorious army acting under the direction of its government (art. 31).[925] In short, it is the victorious army that is the protective institution.

Jean-Gaspar Bluntschli went a step further by limiting the power of the victorious army.[926] According to him, 'the victor is no longer recognized as having the right to appropriate buildings belonging to the national of the enemy State. . . . To take from a conquered enemy his money or other objects of value, however, is considered an unworthy act, contrary to the laws of warfare of civilized nations'.[927]

The Brussels Declaration in 1874 and the Hague regulations or other Hague conventions of 1899 and 1907 did not create any form of supervisory mechanism for the protection of cultural property.

The first step in the direction of protective institutions was undertaken during the First World War, particularly following the destruction of the cities of Rheims, Louvain and Arras, when additional efforts were made to reinforce the protection of cultural property. At a public meeting in Geneva in April 1913, Vetter from Berne and Mauriaud from Geneva suggested the establishment of an international body called 'the Golden Cross' (Croix d'Or). The idea, inspired by the Red Cross, gained ground.

A conference in Brussels in August 1915 prepared the broad outlines of a convention providing for the establishment of an international office for the protection of monuments in wartime. The failure of this conference led the Netherlands Archaeological Society (Nederlandsche Oudleidhundige Bond) to propose to the Queen of the Netherlands, in April 1918, the convening of another, international conference for the protection of monuments and historical and art objects against the perils of war. The report drawn up by

---

925 Schindler and Toman (2004), pp. 7–8.
926 J.-G. Bluntschli, Das moderne Völkerrecht des civilisierten Staaten als Rechtbuch dargestellt. In German in 1868, 1872, 1878. In French: *Le droit international codifié* (Paris: Librairie de Guillaumin, 1874).
927 Bluntschli (1874), pp. 43 and 45.

Van Eysinga envisaged control of the application of the rules by neutral States and the establishment of an office to implement such control.

The Hague Rules Concerning the Control of Wireless Telegraphy in Time of War and Air Warfare

The 1922 Washington Conference on the Limitation of Armaments adopted a resolution for the appointment of a Commission of Jurists charged with the preparation of rules relating to aerial warfare and rules concerning the use of radio in time of war. The Commission, presided over by John Bassett Moore, was composed of representatives of the US, Great Britain, France, Italy, Japan and the Netherlands. It had to report its conclusions to each of the governments of the six countries. The Commission met from December 1922 to February 1923 in The Hague. The Hague Rules Concerning the Control of Wireless Telegraphy in Time of War and Air Warfare, drafted by the Commission, were never adopted in legally binding form, but are of importance 'as an authoritative attempt to clarify and formulate rule of law governing the use of aircraft in war'.[928] The Hague Rules had considerable influence on future projects.

Article 26 of the Hague Rules deals with the protection of monuments of great historic value:

> Art. 26. The following special rules have been adopted to permit the States to ensure a more efficient protection of monuments of great historic value situated on their territory provided they are disposed to abstain from using for military purposes not only such monuments and also the area surrounding them and to accept a special system for control to this end.
>
> 1. A State, if it deems it suitable, may establish a protected area around such monuments situated on its territory. In time of war, such areas shall be sheltered form bombardments;
>
> 2. Monuments around which such area is to be established, shall already be, in time of peace, the object of a notification addressed to the other Powers through the diplomatic channel; the notification shall also state the limits of such areas. This notification cannot be revoked in time of war;

---

928 Oppenheim (1952), p. 519.

3. The protected area may include, in addition to the space occupied by the monument or the group of monuments, a surrounding zone, the width of which may not exceed 500 metres from the periphery of the said space;

4. Marks well visible from the aircraft, both by day and by night, shall be employed to enable the belligerent aeronauts to identify the limits of the areas;

5. The marks placed on the monuments themselves shall be those mentioned in Article 25.[929] The marks employed to indicate the areas surrounding the monuments shall be fixed by every State which accepts the provisions of this Article and shall be notified to the other Powers together with the list of the monuments and areas;

6. Every improper use of the marks referred to in paragraph 5 shall be considered an act of perfidy;

7. A State which accepts the provisions of this Article should abstain from making use of the historic monuments and the zone surrounding them for military purposes or for the benefit of its military organization in any manner whatsoever and should also abstain from committing, in the interior of such monument or within such zone, any act for military purposes;

8. A *commission of control*, composed of three neutral representatives accredited to the State which has accepted the provisions of the present Article, or of their delegates, shall be appointed for the purpose of ascertaining that no violation of the provisions of Paragraph 7 has been committed. One of the members of this commission of control shall be the representative, or his delegate, of the State which has been entrusted with the interests of the other belligerent.

---

929 Article 25.

In bombardments by aircraft, all necessary steps should be taken by the commander to spare, as far as possible, buildings dedicated to public worship, art, science and charitable purposes, historic monuments, hospital ships, hospitals and other places where the sick and wounded are gathered, provided that such buildings, objectives and places are not being used at the same time for military purposes. Such monuments, objects and places must be indicated, during the day, by signs visible from the aircraft. Using such signs to indicate buildings, objects or places other than those hereinbefore specified shall be considered a perfidious act. The signs of which the above mentioned use is to be made, shall be, in the case of buildings protected under the Geneva Convention, the red cross on a white ground and, in the case of the other protected buildings, a large rectangular panel divided diagonally into two triangles, the one white and the other black.

A belligerent who desired to ensure by night the protection of hospitals and other above mentioned privileged buildings, must take the necessary steps to make the aforesaid special signs sufficiently visible.

This is the first time that we encounter the proposal of the inspection committee. Three neutral representatives accredited to the State adopting the provisions of this article, or their delegates, shall be appointed for the purpose of ensuring that no violation is committed of the provisions of paragraph 7. One of the members of the commission of control shall be the representative (or his delegate) of the State to which has been entrusted the interests of the opposing belligerent. The idea of a neutral institution gained ground.

1935 Treaty of Washington – Roerich Pact

The 1935 Treaty of Washington – Roerich Pact did not provide for any control system and rested solely on the undertaking of the parties 'to adopt the measures of internal legislation necessary to ensure said protection and respect'.

Preliminary draft International Convention for the Protection of Historic Buildings and Works of Art in Time of War

The Hague Rules of 1922 inspired the project led by Charles de Visscher in 1936. In his report to the Director's Committee of the International Museums Office (OIM) in 1936, de Visscher suggested an elaborate system of control, which was then included in the 1938 Preliminary draft International Convention for the protection of historic buildings and works of art in time of war. Articles 11–13 of the draft Convention deal with protective institutions, and the roots of their system were adopted and substantially simplified in 1954 Hague Convention:

> Article 11
> 1. *International Commissions of Inspection* shall satisfy themselves while military operations are proceeding that no breach of the provisions of this Convention is committed.
> 2. Offences committed in breach of the provisions of this Convention shall be established by the International Commission of Inspection operating in the territory in which they were committed.
> 3. Details of the constitution and operation of these Commissions are laid down in the *Regulations for the execution* of this Convention.
>
> Article 12
> 1. The High Contraction Parties agree to meet from time to time in a *general conference* to decide conjointly upon measures for ensuring

the application of this Convention, and to review if necessary, the Regulations for its execution.

2. The General Conference shall appoint its *Standing Committee and Secretariat*, whose powers in the intervals between sessions of the Conference shall be defined by the Regulations for the execution of this Convention.

Article 13

In the event of disagreement between the belligerents as to the application of the provisions of this Convention, the *Contracting States entrusted with the interests of the belligerents* and the Standing Committee of the General Conference shall lend their good offices for the settlement of the dispute.

As we know, several issues elaborated in this Draft Convention inspired the drafters of the 1954 Hague Convention:

- The structure of the Convention was divided in two separate parts: the text of the Convention itself and the Regulations for its execution.
- The elaboration of the organizational details in the Regulations.
- The powers conferred upon the General Conference.
- The Contracting States entrusted with the interests of the belligerents (representatives for cultural property – Article 2(a) of the Regulation for the execution of the 1954 Hague Convention).

The Final Provisions of the Preliminary Draft include the Regulations for the Execution of the Convention:

FINAL PROVISIONS.

Regulations for the Execution of the Convention.

Article 1.

As soon as the Convention comes into force, there shall be drawn up an international list of commissioners to whom missions arising out of the execution of the Convention may be entrusted during the period of hostilities. This list shall consist of persons of acknowledged impartiality, selected by the Standing Committee of the General Conference on the nomination of qualified institutions in the contracting countries (Court of Justice, Government Departments, Academies, Universities and Museums).

Article 2.

1. As soon as the Convention has been ratified, each of the High Contracting Parties shall designate the refuges which are to enjoy in his territory the immunity provided for in Article 4 of the Convention, and the monuments which are to enjoy the special protection provided for in Article 5, paragraph 2.

2. Each High Contracting Party shall send to the Standing Committee of the Conference a list of the refuges and monuments designated, together with the written approval of the International Verification Commission referred to in Article 4 of these Regulations.

Article 3.

1. The International Verification Commission shall certify that the refuges and monuments designated satisfy the conditions laid down in Articles 4 and 5 of the Convention respectively. It may also give an opinion on the number of refuges and the material conditions in which they are fixed up.

2. In cases of countries with a dense population and small area, it shall rest with the Commission to decide what minimum distance may be allowed between the refuges and the danger points mentioned in Article 4, paragraph (a) of the Convention.

Article 4.

The International Verification Commission shall consist of:

    (a) a representative of the State in whose territory the refuges and monuments have been designated;

    (b) a commissioner on the international list appointed by the Standing Committee, who shall act as Chairman of the Commission;

    (c) a representative of each of such States as the Standing Committee may have named.

Article 5.

1. Applications for the appointment of a Verification Commission must be sent to the Standing Committee of the Conference, together with a list of the refuges and monuments designated. The Standing Committee shall immediately carry out the necessary consultations with a view to the definitive appointment of the Commission which shall meet at the invitation of the Government concerned and at such place as the latter may appoint.

2. The Commission's work of verification shall be conducted on the spot, and shall, if it thinks necessary, deal separately with each of the refuges and monuments designated.

3. The conclusions of the Verification Commission shall be delivered to the member of the Commission representing the Government concerned.

4. The conclusions of the Verification Commission must be unanimously agreed by the members present.

Article 6.

1. Each of the High Contracting Parties who has made the declaration referred to in Article 6 of the Convention shall forward to the Standing Committee of the General Conference, as soon as he thinks fit, a list of the monuments or groups of monuments for which he desires to secure immunity.

2. The Standing Committee shall communicate this list to each of the High Contracting Parties and shall lend them its good offices with a view to the conclusion on a reciprocal basis, of the immunity agreements as indicated in Article 6 of the Convention.

Article 7.

1. For each of the Contracting States involved in the conflict, an International Commission of Inspection, as provided in Article 11 of the Convention, shall be appointed by the Standing Commission immediately upon the outbreak of hostilities. It shall comprise a commissioner from a neutral country, selected from the international list and appointed by the Standing Committee to act as Chairman of the Commission; a representative of the State on whose territory the inspection is to be carried out; and a representative (or his delegate) of the State to which the interests of other belligerent in the same territory have been entrusted. This last-mentioned member may likewise be selected from among the commissioners on the international list belonging to neutral countries.

2. The Chairmen of International Commissions of Inspection or their delegates may at any time inspect refuges and monuments enjoying the special protection provided for in Article 5 of the Convention.

3. The Standing Committee may attach additional commissioners to the Chairman of the Commission, as the requirements of inspection may dictate.
4. The Chairmen of International Commissions of Inspection may consult experts whose advice seems to them necessary in the performance of the missions entrusted to them.
5. The conclusions of International Commissions of Inspection shall be adopted by majority vote. The representatives of the parties concerned shall have no vote.
6. The conclusions of International Commissions of Inspection shall be submitted to the Standing Committee, which shall communicate them to each of the High Contracting Parties, and shall decide whether they shall also be made public.
7. The Standing Committee shall decide upon the procedure to be followed for establishing breaches of or exceptions to the Convention for which no special provision has been made.

Article 8.
1. Works of art may not be transferred from one refuge to another unless this is necessary for their safety.
2. As soon as evacuation is completed, the protecting mark must be removed.
3. Exceptionally, should there be any obstacle to the transfer of works of art to a regular refuge, the responsible authorities shall decide what steps are to be taken to store them temporarily in a place of safety. Such temporary store may be shown by the protecting mark, which shall be affixed by the International Commission of Inspection, the latter having the sole right to affix it.
4. In occupied territories, any other exceptional measures that may be dictated by unforeseeable circumstances and by the necessity of preserving monuments and works of art must be taken with the agreement of the International Commission of Inspection.
5. In occupied territories, refuges and monuments enjoying special protection shall be under the supervision of the International Commission of Inspection of the occupying State.
6. The International. Commission of Inspection, jointly with the authorities of the occupying State, shall take all necessary steps for the preservation of any monuments which may be damaged. Such steps shall not, however, amount to more than temporary strengthening.

Article 9.

During military occupation, the national staff appointed to preserve and guard refuges, museums, or monuments must be retained in their employment unless there is any legitimate military reason for their dismissal. They shall however, be in the same position in relation to the military authorities of occupation as the civil population of the occupied territories.

Article 10.

In the event of the transfer of works of art to the territory of a foreign country as provided in Article 9 of the Convention, the following rules shall apply:

1. Transport shall be carried out in collaboration with the International Commission of Inspection, to which an inventory of the works to be transferred shall be delivered.
2. The International Commission of Inspection shall give notice of the proposed transfer to the Standing Committee of the General Conference, which shall inform the other belligerent or belligerents. Transport shall not take place until the latter have been so informed.
3. The convoy shall be covered by the protecting mark, and accompanied by a delegate of the International. Commission of Inspection, or by a neutral Commissioner appointed for the purpose by the Standing Committee.
4. For transport otherwise than by land, the Standing Committee shall lay down such additional rules as may be applicable in each particular case.

Article 11.

For the purposes of the application of Article 10 of the Convention, the Standing Committee of the Conference shall lend its good offices to the contending parties with a view to taking all necessary steps for the protection of monuments and works of art threatened by the operations.

Article 12.

1. The General Conference provided for in Article 12 of the Convention shall consist of one representative of each of the Contracting States.

2. The General Conference shall meet whenever necessary, but at least once in every five years. Any State may entrust its representation to another Contracting State, which shall in such case have as many votes as the number of States it represents.

3. The first session of the General Conference shall be held in the year following the entry into force of the Convention.

4. The Conference shall fix the number and the term of office of members of its Standing Committee, and shall designate the States from which they shall be drawn. Any State may entrust its representation to another State represented on the Standing Committee, and such State shall then have as many votes as the number of States it represents.

5. The General Conference shall decide all matters connected with the application and proper operation of the Convention, and in general all questions relating to the protection of the artistic and historic heritage of the international community in time of war.

6. The Standing Committee shall perform the functions assigned to it by the Convention.

7. In the intervals between sessions of the Conference, the Standing Committee shall settle all questions relating to the application of the Convention, except as the Conference may otherwise decide.

8. The Standing Committee shall meet whenever necessary, but at least once in each year.

9. The Standing Committee shall elect its Chairman and shall determine the powers to be vested in him and in the Secretariat of the Conference during the intervals between the Committee's sessions.

10. The chairmanship may not be held in time of war by a national of a belligerent country.

11. In time of war, any belligerent countries which are not represented on the Standing Committee shall appoint representatives, whose term of office shall come to an end as soon as their respective countries cease to be belligerents. If, however, it is impossible to balance the votes of the representatives of the belligerent countries on the Standing Committee, the voices of all of them shall become purely advisory. If the number of deliberative voices is thereby reduced to less than three, the Standing Committee may unanimously co-opt members belonging to neutral countries as substitutes for other Contracting States.

12. The decisions of the Conference and of the Standing Committee shall be taken by a two-thirds majority of the members present; but unanimity must be secured for decisions of the Conference involving the special interests of Contracting States.

13. Two-thirds of the members of the General Conference and of the Standing Committee shall form a quorum.

14. The General Conference and the Standing Committee shall themselves determine the venue of their meetings. Any State may invite the General Conference and the Standing Committee to hold their sessions in its territory.

15. In time of war, if the State in whose territory the Secretariat has its headquarters is a belligerent, the Standing Committee shall decide whether it shall be transferred to the territory of another State.

16. Any High Contracting Party may at any time call the attention of the Standing Committee to any circumstance affecting the application or proper operation of the measures contemplated by the Convention.

17. In the discharge of their duties under the Convention, members of International Commissions of Inspection, Commissioners entrusted with missions and members of the Standing Committee and the Secretariat shall enjoy all the privileges and immunities belonging to international agents.

As we have seen, Article 1 of the Preliminary Draft Convention of 1938 provided for the defense of monuments and works of art against the foreseeable effects of armed conflicts even in time of peace.

As for paragraph 2 of Article 2 of the Preliminary Draft, it envisaged the possibility that the administrations of the Contracting States would secure the technical collaboration of the International Museums Office (OIM) in organizing that defense which, in this draft text, was a synonym for safeguarding. This provision formed a nucleus that was substantially developed in the 1954 Convention.

It is probably appropriate to say that in the time between the two world wars experience with international organizations was limited. The 1938 draft is a product of great idealism and is very complex. It was not attached to any existing organization and was naturally totally independent from the League of Nations and any other institution. This is also why the structure of the proposed organization was very complex. It is also understandable that such a complicated structure had no chance of being adopted when submitted to the States. In a very simplified form, it inspired the drafters of the 1954 Hague Convention where a good part of its idealism remained but was adapted to the understanding of international institutions as they existed after the Second World War.

'Lieux de Genève' (Geneva Zones)

Another, much more modest institution was developed at nearly the same time. In 1931, the French Surgeon-General Georges Saint-Paul founded in Paris the 'Lieux de Genève Association', from which the present International Civil Defense Organization (ICDO)[930] originated. He envisaged the forming of neutralized zones in which certain categories of civilian population could seek refuge. In 1937, the Association was transferred from Paris to Geneva and became the International Association for the Protection of Civilian Populations and Historic Buildings in Wartime. Following the death of its founder, a friend of Georges Saint-Paul, Henri George, became the Secretary-General. The Association intervened between the belligerents in the Spanish Civil War (1936) and the Sino-Japanese conflict (1937). In 1943, during the Second World War, the Association envisaged the establishment of a commission composed of neutrals that was to be responsible, in wartime, for the supervision of duly notified non-transportable historic monuments and the zones around those monuments so as to ensure that no violation was committed.[931] When a convention was first mooted, the initial idea was to set up a permanent international body whose functions would have been similar to those of the ICRC. This project was abandoned so as to avoid adding to the number of international organizations, and it was decided to entrust the responsibility to an organization then in the process of being formed: UNESCO.

UNESCO's role in the protection of cultural property

It was only after the end of the Second World War, in the context of post-war enthusiasm for human rights and humanitarian law, that the first universal convention for the protection of cultural property was adopted. The 1954 Hague Convention gave a lot of hope to its drafters, who considered it an instrument 'of great importance for all peoples of the world'. However, they

---

930 For more about the International Civil Defense Organization, see www.icdo.org
931 Secrétariat Général des 'Lieux de Genève' (1943), p. 61 et seq.

were also conscious of the concessions made to the exigencies of a military nature, as expressed by the Netherlands Minister of Public Instruction, Art and Sciences, who considered that 'the law, supported by the views of various High Commands and military experts, had been more conservative than "prudent moderation" demanded'.[932]

That UNESCO should play a fundamental part in the protection of cultural property was quite natural and was laid down in its Constitution.

The *Constitution of UNESCO*, signed in London on 16 November 1945, gives to the Organization the mandate to take care 'of the conservation and protection of the universal inheritance of books, work of art and other monuments of historical or scientific interest, and by recommending to the peoples interested international conventions for this purpose'. UNESCO adopted many recommendations to carry out this mandate. It also adopted several conventions whose impact is also important for the protection of cultural property in period of war:

- Convention on the Means of Prohibiting and Preventing the Illicit Import, Export and Transfer of Ownership of Cultural Property, adopted by the General Conference at its 16th Session in Paris on 14 November 1970.
- Convention concerning the Protection of the World Cultural and Natural Heritage, adopted by the General Conference at its 17th Session in Paris, 16 November 1972.

However, while granting UNESCO certain powers, the authors failed to take into account the fundamental differences between the various institutions responsible for controlling the application of humanitarian law.

In conferring certain rights and powers upon the ICRC, the authors of the Geneva Conventions took account of the particular and specific nature of that institution. The ICRC is, of course, a private Swiss body, an association governed by Article 60 et seq. of the Swiss Civil Code, and possessing a legal personality. The special nature of the ICRC was recognized by the International Conferences of the Red Cross and by the Geneva Conventions. When the States assigned the ICRC certain rights and duties, they did so in full awareness of the special structure of the Committee but also of the principles that have governed its activities throughout its history, especially the principles of humanity, impartiality, neutrality and independence. It was its character as an impartial humanitarian body that won the trust of the States when they asked the ICRC to assume certain functions in periods of armed

---

932 CBC/INF/3, p. 2; quoted in Toman (1996), p. 23.

conflict, stressing that it was its total structural independence that imposed on the ICRC, at least in its activities under the Convention, a correspondingly greater obligation to remain faithful to itself.[933]

By contrast, UNESCO is an intergovernmental organization composed of States that form part of the international community. Its powers and competence are established, by decision of the Member States, in its Constitution. The Organization's policy is laid down by its General Conferences, which reflect the points of view of all Member States. In order to play a role similar to the ICRC, the UNESCO Secretariat should be able to perform its functions in a way that conforms as closely as possible to the principles of humanitarian international law. For UNESCO to do so, States must first bear in mind and understand the functions that UNESCO has to perform in this area and give the Secretariat the fullest opportunity of carrying out those functions.

The mandate of UNESCO is provided by its Constitution and its General Conferences. To serve the protection of cultural property in time of conflict and in accomplishing its mandate for the whole international community, UNESCO and its Secretariat must remain aloof from politics so as to avoid confrontations. It must act impartially and help to settle disputes between its members. Experience has shown that UNESCO is capable of fulfilling its mission and that the action it has taken to protect cultural property is credible.[934]

Implementation of UNESCO's mandate and application of the 1954 Hague Convention

The beginning of the life of the 1954 Hague Convention was not disappointing. It seems that the Convention satisfied the characteristic established by Charles de Visscher concerning the rules of international law:

> Every rule of positive international law thus presents two essential aspects for critical examination on different planes: the degree in which its content corresponds to social needs, and the accuracy of its formal expression compared with the practice of States. The rule of

---

933 Sandoz (1979), p. 362.
934 Toman (1996), p. 259.

international law retains its full force in application only insofar as it satisfies this double requirement.[935]

This was not surprising. The world had just emerged from the Second World War and was fully aware of the dangers which continued to threaten the post-war world. Thus, the 1954 Hague Convention fell within the frame of other very *progressive developments* in the field of human rights (1948 Universal Declaration of Human Rights) and humanitarian law (1949 Geneva Conventions).

Parties to the 1954 Hague Convention: signatures, ratifications and accessions

By the end of 1954, the Convention was signed by 21 developing States, 22 Western and 7 Eastern States. It entered into force on 7 August 1956, three months after the deposit of the fifth instrument of ratification.

During its first decade (1954–1964), 52 States became parties to the Convention: 26 developing countries, 16 Western and all Eastern countries (ten), undoubtedly still under the influence of the post-war period. Then came a slower period. From 1964–1974, only 12 States became parties; from 1974–1984 only six (an overall total of 70 States Parties). The years 1984–1994 were better: 15 States became parties. This was undoubtedly the influence of the end of the Cold War, followed by changes in Russia and the conflict in Yugoslavia. From 1994–2004, 28 States became parties because of the start of the new codification process. But from 2004 until now, only ten States have joined the Convention. Today, 123 States are parties to the Convention, including the US.

Practical implementation by use of control

The practical implementation of the Convention experienced at the very beginning the same dynamism as ratification and accession. If the post-war situation influenced the drafting of the text of Convention and the number of

---

935 Visscher (1957), p. 133. The original French text reads: *'Toute règle de droit international positif présente deux aspects essentiels qui, dans des plans différends, s'offrent à l'examen critique: le degré de correspondance de son contenu avec les besoins sociaux, l'exactitude de son expression formelle au regard de la pratique des Etats. La règle de droit international ne conserve sa pleine force d'application et, par conséquence toute sa positivité, que tant qu'elle satisfait à cette double exigence.'* (Visscher [1970], p. 164.)

the States that became parties to it, it also influenced the first practical steps of implementation and the development of its institutional mechanism.

The Middle East

The area of the Middle East seems predestined to deal with problems relating to the protection of cultural property. It is in this part of the world that the practical application of the Convention began. In 1956 and 1957, Professor Gerard Garitte of the University of Louvain carried out, at the request of the Member States of UNESCO, a mission in Egypt and Israel.[936]

The procedures prescribed by the Convention were coming into existence: Following the conflict of 1967 in the Middle East, the States concerned designated representatives for cultural property, as required by the 1954 Hague Convention. Moreover, they appointed the Commissioner-General, in accordance with the procedure stipulated in the Regulations, by using the good offices of Switzerland. Karl Brunner (Swiss) was designated by Jordan, Lebanon, Egypt and Syria; H. J. Reinink (Netherlands), by Israel. After the death of Karl Brunner, Gugliemo de Angelis d'Ossat (Italy) was named. The two Commissioner-Generals resigned in 1977. Unfortunately, the replacement procedure did not lead to the appointment of new Commissioners.

When civil war broke out in Lebanon in 1975, the persons in charge of cultural property, in particular the director of the National Museum of Beirut, undertook a large number of safeguarding measures, including the transfer of irreplaceable objects to the French Institute of Archaeology in Damascus. In 1982, a mission was sent to the archaeological site of the town of Tyre in Lebanon at the request of the State. In his call for the safeguarding of the site and in his decision to send a mission, the Director-General of UNESCO appealed to the provisions of the 1954 Hague Convention (in particular, art. 23), but also to a special mandate conferred by Resolution 4/13 adopted by the General Conference at its 21st session (Belgrade, 23 September–28 October 1980). As the site was occupied by the Israeli army, the Director-General asked the Israeli authorities to cooperate and transmitted to them the Lebanese request. This mission is an example of cooperation between governments, various authorities, the UN, and the local population. Indeed, the mission was characterized by the indissoluble bond at

---

936 On this occasion, he prepared a detailed report on the state of the Saint Catherine's Monastery (Sinai Peninsula) and made several suggestions for its protection.

Tyre: between the archaeological sites, relics of an often very distant past, and the inhabitants of a modern city, seeking to survive and prosper despite the numerous difficulties witnessed by the mission. The mission was constrained only by the absence of Lebanese archaeologists despite the steps taken by the Lebanese and Israeli authorities.[937]

First Meeting of the High Contracting Parties (1962)

During the years following the adoption of the 1954 Hague Convention, UNESCO's bodies and its Secretariat made an effort to improve the implementation of the Convention and the participation of States in its application. The first joint effort of the States Parties to the Convention and UNESCO was the *First Meeting of the High Contracting Parties*, which was held at UNESCO from 16 to 25 July 1962.[938] In this meeting 39 States Parties participated together with 18 States non-Parties to the Convention, which sent observers. If for no other reason than the broad participation of both Parties and non-Parties to the Convention, the meeting must be deemed a success.

No amendments were proposed to this first meeting, which confined its proceedings to the examination of problems concerning the application of the Convention. It considered that in order 'to encourage other States to become Parties to the Convention and to facilitate its application, it ought also to make some suggestions for future action'. Poland made the only institutional proposal. In the course of the discussion at this first meeting, the Polish Delegation found an opportunity to draw attention to certain aspects of the text of the Convention:

1. Should there be difficulties in interpreting the Convention and should the procedure it lays down for its application prove inadequate, the Committee whose establishment it recommended might have a useful part to play.

2. On the other hand, in the case of clauses likely to weaken the effectiveness of the Convention, such as the possibility of waiving special protection in the event of unavoidable military necessity, there would be no other means of remedying the matter than to contemplate

---

937 The report of the mission, impartial and objective, expressed several recommendations, several of which could be carried out without the assistance of UNESCO. Lebanese authorities were given 150 distinctive signs to mark the archeological sites and the monuments in Tyre.
938 Report of the meeting, document UNESCO/CUA/120 of 3 September 1962.

a review of the Convention, in the manner provided for the Convention itself.[939]

The meeting set up a group of experts to examine certain problems concerning the application of the Convention, and their report was annexed to the report of the meeting.

At the conclusion of the general discussion, the importance of the following points was stressed:

a) The desirability of ensuring that as many States as possible become Parties to the Convention.

b) The importance of action to be taken at the national level for the implementation of the Convention, such as the preparation of inventories, exchanges of information, etc.

c) The part that should be played, in compliance with Resolution II adopted by the Hague Conference, by the National Committees set up to advise on the implementation of the Convention.

Actions undertaken by UNESCO following the initiatives of the Director-General

Wars and armed conflicts changed their character over the decades that followed the adoption of Convention. It was thus necessary to resort to other, more flexible methods in order to ensure protection.

Given the impossibility of ensuring the adequate application of the Convention in the traditional manner, UNESCO explored the possibility of employing Article 23 (Assistance of UNESCO), as well as its cultural mandate, which is based on its Constitution. Article 1 (Purposes and functions) states the purpose of the Organization and the ways in which it can be realized: 'Maintain, increase and diffuse knowledge: by assuring the conservation and protection of the world's inheritance of books, works of art and other monuments of history and science, and recommending to the nations concerned the necessary international conventions'.[940] The World Conference on Cultural Policies, held in Mexico City in 1982, noted that in a world of conflicts which endanger the cultural values of civilizations, the Member States and the Secretariat of UNESCO must multiply their efforts intended to preserve these values and to look further into actions in favour of the development of humanity.

---

939 Report of the meeting, document UNESCO/CUA/120 of 3 September 1962, p. 5, para. 19.
940 Constitution of the UNESCO, art. 1, para. 2(c), in UNESCO (2004), p. 8.

An excellent example of an initiative of UNESCO dates back to 1969, when hostilities occurred between Honduras and El Salvador – the 'war of football'. The Director-General launched an appeal to the two governments and suggested that they become Parties to the Convention in order to ensure the protection of cultural property in their respective territories.

The Director-General established a practice of announcing to States their duties at the beginning of hostilities, particularly when these States were Contracting Parties to the Convention. Thus, such messages were sent in 1971 to India and Pakistan, in 1974 to Cyprus and Turkey at the time of the conflict in Cyprus, and in 1980 to Iraq and the Islamic Republic of Iran, both also Parties to the Convention. In the latter conflict, the authorities answered and declared their intention to respect their obligations.

Fact-finding missions were also undertaken in Cyprus before and after the *de facto* partition of the island in 1972, as were safeguarding measures in the historical Mediterranean city of Tyre following the Israeli occupation of South Lebanon in 1982, and more recently in Yugoslavia, especially in Dubrovnik.

The Director-General intervened many times, through diplomatic channels, public appeals and declarations at conferences, and especially at the UNESCO General Conference. A public appeal was even launched jointly with the Secretary-General of the UN. UNESCO continues to send personal observers, representatives and experts. The General Conference adopts resolutions reminding States of their obligations.

At the time of the internal conflict in Nigeria (1967–70), the Director-General, referring to Article 19, offered the services of UNESCO to the authorities of Nigeria. These services were not accepted, but the authorities responded by sending documentation to demonstrate their respect for the Convention.

1983 Meeting of Legal Experts on the Convention for the Protection of Cultural Property in the Event of Armed Conflict (The Hague, 1954)

Encouraged by some of these new forms of implementation, UNESCO decided to invite a group of high-level legal experts from 11 countries to meet in Vienna from 17–19 October 1983 to discuss ways of enhancing the impact of the 1954 Convention. These experts reaffirmed the importance of the Convention and made a number of suggestions of ways to renew and improve its application. The central difficulties were restated: the very complex, technical nature of the work and a corresponding lack of experts; the small number of countries that actually marked their monuments with the emblem of the Convention; the limited use of special protection; difficulties with the appointment of Commissioner-Generals and lengthy negotiations; and the fact that not all States wished to apply the system of international control. The experts were also aware of the problems relating to implementation in situations of international and non-international armed conflicts, insufficient technical implementation, and lack of interest in providing reports on peacetime actions.

The meetings discussed extensively the question of the right of initiative of UNESCO according to Articles 19 and 23. It was suggested that UNESCO should help States to draw up inventories of cultural property, which would warrant inscription in the International Register of Cultural Property under Special Protection. The connection with the World Heritage Convention was underlined. At that time, the experts considered it unnecessary to amend the Convention and preferred rather to concentrate on direct efforts to better apply the Convention in its present form.[941] The experts noted a lack of information on how States complied with their obligation to provide sanctions within their ordinary criminal jurisdiction. It was also recommended that UNESCO should provide assistance to accelerate the procedure of appointment of Commissioner-Generals.

A few remedies were proposed: the launching of an appeal by the Director-General, the adoption of a resolution by the General Conference, the establishment of high-level contacts in States, the preparation of an information campaign and the organization of training programmes. At the same time, it was considered essential that actions be taken in countries to promote awareness of the need to protect cultural heritage and one of the means of achieving this purpose was the establishment of national associations.[942] The possibility of a Conference of all Member States of UNESCO on the protection of the heritage was also mentioned.[943]

---

941 1983 Meeting of Legal Experts on the Convention for the Protection of Cultural Property in the Event of Armed Conflict (The Hague, 1954), Vienna, 17–19 October 1983, CLT-83/CONF.641/1, p. 10.

942 Ibid., p. 4.

943 The advisability of convening a meeting of the High Contracting Parties was ruled out: 'On the one hand, if such a meeting were convened, this would risk giving the impression that amendments were necessary to make the Convention more effective. In the present context and, in particular given the arms reduction talks, any amendment process risked leading to inconclusive results. In these circumstances, the experts considered that it was preferable to direct efforts towards a better application of the Convention in its present form. On the other hand, the interest of States which

My response at the time was to recommend that several measures be undertaken, mostly in the institutional field: the creation of national coordination bodies as well as non-governmental associations to support governmental bodies, the constitution of a technical advisory committee to UNESCO, the establishment of intervention teams, the setting-up of a fund for the protection of cultural property, the development of teaching and research on the Convention and the wider dissemination of the Convention.

In their conclusions, the experts, recognizing the importance of the Convention but also its insufficient effectiveness, recommended the organization of a conference for all Member States of the Organization. This conference was prepared with special care and was accompanied by a wide-ranging campaign to raise public awareness with the participation of the National Commissions for UNESCO and many other national and international organizations to encourage the establishment of national advisory committees as envisaged in Resolution II of the 1954 Hague Conference, as well as the creation of private associations whose help could be essential. The long-term programme covering the development of teaching and research would be part of the overall UNESCO programme in the field of culture. The legal experts also considered that it would be useful to examine important developments in the practical application of the Convention, as well as new developments in the nature of conflicts, the results of the reaffirmation and development of humanitarian international law between 1974 and 1977, and especially the adoption of two Articles concerning the protection of cultural property by the 1977 Additional Protocols to the Geneva Conventions.

The experts recommended the formation of a permanent technical advisory committee, such as that recommended at the meeting of the High Contracting Parties in 1962.[944]

At the 1983 Expert Meeting, the lack of interest characterizing the period following the enthusiasm of the post-war years was explained by the tense international political situation of the Cold War, which alongside rapid advances in military technology led to doubts as to whether the Convention

---

were not parties to the Convention could more appropriately be encouraged by convening a conference of all the Member States of UNESCO. Ibid., p. 10, para. 31.

944 'Such a committee could be established within UNESCO, which would not require a revision of the Convention. It would fall within the framework of the technical assistance foreseen in Article 23 of the Convention. The Committee could take the form of a committee of experts appointed by the Director-General in their personal capacity or of a subsidiary body of the Executive Board. . . . It was furthermore recalled that a proposal to establish a permanent council of representatives of High Contracting Parties had been made at The Hague Conference in 1954.' Ibid., p. 12.

could still be effective under these new conditions and circumstances.[945] They considered that the review process 'clearly reflected the evolution of international relations since the Second World War and that the noted ineffectiveness was essentially due to the lack of political will on the part of the governments to put into application all the protective measures foreseen'.[946]

New conflicts in the 1980s and 1990s

Iran-Iraq

Another example of UNESCO action occurred against the backdrop of the Iran-Iraq War in the 1980s. The UNESCO Executive Board and the Director-General expressed their concern regarding the threat the conflict posed to the protection of human lives, educational, scientific and cultural institutions and cultural and natural heritage. The President of the General Conference and the Director-General sent a joint telegram to the Foreign Ministers of the two Member States. From the resumption of the 'war of the cities', there were frequent contacts with the permanent delegates of these two countries. The Director-General stressed the importance of the provisions of the Hague Convention, proposing specific measures. The resolutions of the 23rd and 24th Sessions of the General Conference, as well as the decisions of the Executive Board, called upon both States to put an end to the war, to seek a peaceful solution and to observe international humanitarian principles, particularly those concerning the protection of cultural and natural heritage, the environment and educational, scientific and cultural institutions. The Director-General sent two personal representatives – Dr. Abdul-Aziz Abdulgani and Professor Raymond Lemaire – to the Islamic Republic of Iran (31 October–7 November 1985) and to Iraq (11–15 January 1986). They visited the sites and monuments that had suffered damage during the war and sites that the authorities of the two respective countries were willing to show them. In discussions with the authorities of the two States, both

---

945 Ibid., p. 3. At the signing ceremony of the Second Protocol to the Hague Convention for the Protection of Cultural Property in the Event of Armed Conflict in The Hague on 16 May 1999, Mr Colin Powers made the following statement: 'However, there was a period when the mechanism of the Hague Convention of 1954 were thoughts to have been superseded by technology: how could painting a sign on the roof of a museum to indicate a protected site be an adequate warning when the menace was an intercontinental ballistic missile? Thus little attention has been paid to the Convention in the 1970s and 1980s.' (Text as distributed at the signing ceremony, p. 3).
946 Ibid., p. 12.

affirmed their willingness to respect the provisions of Convention. The two governments committed themselves to examining the possibility of appointing a Commissioner-General for Cultural Property, but the war ended before the appointment could be made.

Yugoslavia

The war in former Yugoslavia represented a turning point in the systematic destruction of cultural heritage. It undoubtedly constituted an important persuasive element for the undertaking of more vigorous actions and led finally to the adoption of the 1999 Second Protocol. The destruction of the Old Bridge in Mostar or the bombardments of Dubrovnik, a historical city registered on the World Heritage List, became symbols of the total negligence of protection. The worst realization was the confirmation that such destruction was intentional and the objective of military actions. It was not a question of destroying the cultural object itself but of destroying the joint life, religion and peaceful cohabitation of the populations. The Yugoslav armed forces knew the provisions of the Convention as Yugoslavia was one of the most active States in the promotion of the Convention and in the dissemination of international humanitarian law. During the 1970s, it was very actively engaged in the process of reaffirming and developing humanitarian law. That highlights the fact that knowledge of the provisions in itself is insufficient: political goodwill is required. Since the beginning and following the declarations of independence of Slovenia and Croatia, the Director-General multiplied appeals for the respect of cultural property, based upon the Conventions of 1954 and 1972. UNESCO sent missions and the Director-General launched innumerable appeals together with the Secretary-General of the UN, the United Nations Impartial Commission of experts created by Resolution 780(1992) of the Security Council,[947] and the European Community. Later, UNESCO also established contacts with the ICTY, which has dealt with several cases concerning the destruction of cultural property.[948]

---

947 United Nations Security Council Resolution 780 (Establishing a Commission of Experts to Examine and Analyse Information Submitted Pursuant to Resolution 771), SC res. 780, UNSCOR at 36, UN Doc. S/RES/780 (1992), p. 1.
948 Meron (2005).

The first Gulf War of 1991

Immediately after Iraq's occupation of Kuwait, the Director of antiquities of Iraq came to Kuwait to recover the Sabah Collection and transport it to Baghdad. The collection remained in the cellars and was protected from bombardments. After the war, between 14 September and 20 October 1991, Iraq gave 25,082 objects from the Dar-Al-Athar Al-Islamiyya (DAI) and the Kuwait National Museum (KNM) to the representatives of Kuwait in Baghdad, under the supervision of the United Nations Return of Property Unit (UNROP), which carried out an inventory, inspection and evaluation of the damage. Once restored, experts were identified, thanks to the intervention of the UNDP and UNESCO, to repair the damaged objects. Thus, plundering did not take place at the outset of the war, but the Iraqis themselves seized antiquities.

The war itself caused damage. The operation 'Desert Storm' has sometimes been called a 'masterpiece of planning and execution at the strategic and tactical level'. The US soldiers focused their attention for military objectives, but collateral damage could not be avoided. The plundering of archaeological sites and museums was the principal concern. The Iraqis presented a list of some 4,000 disappeared objects. Thanks to UNESCO and many other agencies, information on the stolen objects was transmitted to customs, police officers and antique dealers. Although the trade in cultural objects was prohibited by the Security Council, Iraqi antiquities began to appear on the European and American markets. In 1997, it was said that the antiquities confiscated at the border with Jordan were sufficient to organize an exhibition at the National Museum of Baghdad.

To save them from bombardments, certain objects were placed in safety deposit. The sanctions which followed the war prevented a serious evaluation of losses and delayed or blocked international assistance. From 1998 onwards, UNESCO provided assistance enabling the restoration of the museum of Baghdad, which was opened again to the public in April 2000.

Afghanistan

At the time of the combat that followed the Soviets' departure from Kabul in 1988, the National Museum of Afghanistan was emptied of its contents, 70 percent of which disappeared. Those objects that remained were later destroyed on the orders of the Taliban. The ensuing years were characterized by conflicts of many kinds – the civil war, the occupation and fundamentalist extremism of the Taliban – resulting in massive destruction symbolized by the loss of the Bamiyan Buddhas and the plundering of the country's treasures, in particular those of the National Museum in Kabul and the museums of Ghazni and Herat. The destruction was also followed by negligence. The end of the Taliban regime did not prevent plundering and traffic, stripping Afghanistan of its historical treasures. UNESCO established relationships with Afghan and foreign institutions to preserve the country's heritage. The International Coordination Committee for the Safeguarding of Afghanistan's Cultural Heritage was created and took preventive measures against the illicit excavations and illegal export of cultural property, but also in favour of the restoration of a series of monuments.

The invasion of Iraq by the armed forces of the United States and the coalition (2003)

In 2003 the invasion of Iraq by the troops of the coalition, directed by the US Army, put all the aforementioned efforts to the test, particularly those relating to the dissemination of humanitarian law and the protection of cultural property. The US Army's *Field Manual 27-10* contains clear provisions that refer to the Hague Regulations, the Roerich Pact, and customary international law. At the time of the invasion in 2003, the US was not bound by the 1954 Hague Convention. The news media provided broad coverage of what actually occurred. It is impossible to describe the negligence of those who permitted the plundering to take place and their incapacity to prevent the subsequent destruction. Articles and books have been, and still more undoubtedly will be, devoted to this subject.[949] The armed forces were well informed and forewarned. McGuire Gibson, professor at the Institute of Eastern Studies of the University of Chicago, took part in the preparation of lists containing several thousands of names of archaeological sites. The National and international organizations provided necessary information and voiced warnings stressing that Iraq is universally known to have a particularly rich cultural heritage – the country often being described as the 'cradle of civilization'. The Director-General of UNESCO intervened with the US observer, recalling the plundering that occurred during the Gulf War. The US authorities answered that they had taken note of international concerns. But the army demonstrated total negligence, permitting the plundering and ransacking of the Iraq National Museum in Baghdad, the Iraq National

---

949 Flandrin (2004); Rothfield (2008); Stone and Farchakh Bajjaly (2008).

Library and Archive (INLA) and its related files, and the library of Awqatfs. Plundering started immediately after the seizure of Baghdad, on 9 April 2003, and it seems that two distinct groups were involved: professional robbers (who took objects from the Uruk and Akkadien periods – those most sought by collectors) and ordinary robbers. Only on 16 April did American tanks arrive at the Iraq National Museum in Baghdad. According to Mounir Bouchenaki, UNESCO Assistant Director-General for Culture, the Americans were not concerned in the least for the well-being of cultural heritage, whether in Baghdad or elsewhere, and are responsible for what took place. Their military concern was to obtain a foothold in specific strategic places, safeguarding in particular the Ministries of Oil and the Interior, situated 2–3 kilometres from the National Museum. This constitutes a notorious failure on the part of the US Army. UNESCO sent experts and missions to investigate the situation, and organized meetings and rescue projects. Many international organizations and main roads were mobilized to provide assistance. Interpol, the FBI, the US military and the Italian Carabinieri dispatched agents to the spot. Three White House cultural advisers resigned in protest over the failure of the armed forces to prepare the invasion in this respect. On this subject, the Security Council adopted the following resolutions: Resolution 1483, adopted on 22 May 2003, section 7 of which concerned the protection of Iraqi cultural objects, and prohibited international trade in Iraqi cultural property illegally removed from the national museum, national library and other places,[950] and Resolution 1546, adopted by the Council on 8 June 2004, which stressed 'the need for all parties to respect and protect Iraq's archaeological, istorical, cultural, and religious heritage'. ICOM urgently published a red list to allow customs officers, police officers and antiquities dealers to identify objects coming from Iraq, stressing that all such antiquities must be viewed with precaution. Following these tragic failures, US authorities took measures intended to save face. They proceeded to appoint a consultant to the provisional authority, to send missions, experts and advisers, and to make equipment available for the museum to the Iraqi authorities.

---

950 '7. Decides that all Member States shall take appropriate steps to facilitate the safe return to Iraqi institutions, of Iraqi cultural property and other items of archaeological, historical, cultural, rare scientific, and religious importance illegally removed from the Iraq National Museum, the National Library, and other locations in Iraq since the adoption of Resolution 661 (1990) of 2 August 1990, including by establishing a prohibition on trade in or transfer of such items and items with respect to which reasonable suspicion exists that they have been illegally removed, and calls upon the United Nations Educational, Scientific, and Cultural Organization, Interpol, and other international organizations, as appropriate, to assist in the implementation of this paragraph.'

These recent events in Iraq, but also those of Yugoslavia and other places around the globe, demonstrate the points at which an implementation mechanism is indispensible.

New approach during the 1990s

UNESCO was aware of these difficulties and the insufficiencies of protection. After several ad hoc measures, the decision was taken to improve the text of the Convention and reinforce the measures for implementation. The following were considered as the main insufficiencies:

- Lack of adequate preparation in times of peace was recognized as a central problem.
- Only a very limited number of States had sought recourse to special protection and registration of cultural property on the list established and administered by UNESCO. Reasons for this included the clause of military necessity, political obstacles to registration on the list, and finally the unrealistic conditions required for inscription.
- The reference to non-international conflicts needed greater precision and required clarification.
- The system of control, even if original in its concept, proved to be completely inadequate in practice, and had to be adapted to the new conditions of the international community, particularly to the activities of international organizations dealing with the protection of and respect for human rights.
- The need to reinforce the reporting system, which should then contribute to the improvement of the protection of cultural property.
- The lack of adequate sanctions for all those who violate the provisions relating to protection of cultural property. There was thus a disproportionate gap between the provisions of the Convention and the new provisions concerning sanctions introduced by the 1977 Additional Protocols, the ICTY Statute and the Articles of the ICC Statute.
- Institutionally speaking, the separation of the Secretariat of the World Heritage Convention from other treaties, including the 1954 Convention, had – in our view – a negative impact on protection in time of war.

Codification of institutional issues – preparatory work, 1991–1998: new efforts undertaken at the beginning of 1990s

At its 26th session in 1991, the UNESCO General Conference reaffirmed its conviction 'that the preservation of the world's cultural and natural heritage is of the utmost importance to all humankind' and called 'on all States to increase their efforts [in that area] to achieve better implementation of the existing instruments and to reinforce UNESCO's action'.[951] In his report to the 1992 Executive Board's 140th session the Director-General indicated[952] that the 1954 Hague Convention no longer met current requirements, citing the slow ratification process and unsatisfactory geographical distribution, the small number of entries in the International Register of Cultural Property under Special Protection, cumbersome procedures, the lack of account of the current state of 'military science', complex procedures for the appointment of Commissioner-Generals and weak UNESCO assistance.

It was then, nearly ten years after the 1983 Vienna Legal Experts Meeting, that the UNESCO Secretariat and the Netherlands Government asked Professor Patrick Boylan to prepare an in-depth analysis of the issues and to present a set of recommendations to the members of the Executive Board.[953] His study presented the results of the operation of the Hague Convention and its Protocol and included proposals on how to improve the Convention's and the Protocol's application and effectiveness. It also responded to the question of whether a review of the Convention was needed.

From the institutional point of view, Boylan's study included the following key affirmation and proposal:

18.6. There are currently serious problems in relation to the procedures for the appointment of Commissioner-Generals for Cultural Property, both in general and particularly in relation to situations where there are no nominated Protecting Powers. Changes in this area are needed, with the aim of making the Commissioner-General provisions enforceable on both parties to an armed conflict. However, achieving this would require solutions to difficult problems of international law, and the matter therefore needs to be considered by appropriate experts in international law.

---

951 Resolution 26C/Res. 3.9, adopted on 6 November 1991.
952 Report by the Director-General on the reinforcement of UNESCO's action for the Protection of the World Cultural and Natural Heritage, 140 EX/13 and Corr.
953 Boylan (1993).

18.7. In order to improve the understanding and application of The Hague Convention there is a need for it to be supported by an Intergovernmental Advisory Committee on the Protection of Cultural Property in the Event of Armed Conflict, modeled on the World Heritage Committee. The proposed terms of reference and composition are outlined in Appendix X of this Report.[954]

Boylan recommended to UNESCO that it establish such a committee on the basis of a resolution. The committee would follow the model of the World Heritage Committee, but without executive power. Its role should be to keep under review the effectiveness and implementation of the Convention; advise the Director-General, the General Conference, States Parties and also non-signatory States; and receive, review and formally publish periodic reports.[955] As Chamberlain rightly notes, Articles 23–29 of the Second Protocol 'are in line with the Boylan proposal for the establishment of a standing committee'.[956] The supervisory function was then conferred on two bodies: a Meeting of the Parties (art. 23) and a Committee (art. 24–29).

On the basis of these proposals, and others included in his report, the Netherlands Government, in close cooperation with the UNESCO Secretariat, organized an informal, open-ended information session in Paris (9 February 1993), where Patrick Boylan presented his preliminary views on certain fundamental issues, including the institutional mechanism.

The Netherlands Government accordingly convened a Meeting of Experts on 5–7 July 1993 in The Hague. Among the issues discussed at the meeting included two that were particularly important:

- Institutional issues (in particular the lack of an institutional mechanism, and the possible UNESCO-UN relationship in this field – including UN peacekeeping activities and the possible role of NGOs). It was suggested that an organ could perhaps be modelled on the World Heritage Committee.
- Commissioners-General/Protecting Powers.

The final report of the 1993 Hague Meeting of Experts made several proposals concerning an institutional mechanism:

- '[An] organ modelled along the lines of the World Heritage Committee could contribute to the more effective application of the

---

954 Boylan (1993), para. 18.6 and 18.7, p. 144. Appendix X of the Report is reproduced in the comments on Article 24 (see pp. 526-527 below).
955 For more information, see p. 525 ff.
956 Chamberlain (2004), p. 221.

1954 Convention. In this connection the meeting took note of the recommendations of Professor Boylan (Appendix X of his report)[957] concerning the appropriateness of establishing a committee, and identified various tasks and functions, such as monitoring, supervising, education and advising which could be undertaken by such an organ. This needed further elaboration, however.'[958]

- An 'institutional mechanism could perform important functions with respect to evaluating requests for (new) entries in the International Register of Cultural Property under Special Protection' and the reporting system. And 'the establishment of an organ could . . . raise awareness among States and its citizens of the objective and purpose of the 1954 Convention'.[959]

- 'Some participants noted, whilst acknowledging the appropriateness and urgency of establishing some sort of institutional mechanism, the need for administrative and secretarial support. Various options for servicing an institutional mechanism and their financial consequences were discussed. There was a general feeling that the UNESCO Secretariat, because of its experience and expertise, could perform an important role in this connection. Some delegations raised important issues relating to the more procedural aspects of the establishment of such an organ. These issues were not discussed in detail, although it was pointed out by many experts that here the practice of the World Heritage Committee and the 1970 Convention on measures against illicit traffic in cultural property could provide guidance on how to approach this matter.'[960]

- The experts recognized the failure of the Commissioner-General and the Protecting Powers' system but were hesitant to propose its abolition and the deletion of provisions thereon. It was observed that this was partly the result of benign neglect of the 1954 Convention, however States were also extremely hesitant about admitting that they were involved in armed conflict. The role of the ICRC and International

957 See p. 526-527 under the comment on Article 24.
958 UNESCO, Executive Board, 142th Session, Report by the Director-General on the Reinforcement of UNESCO's action for the Protection of the World Cultural and Natural Heriatge. 142 EX/15, Paris, 18 August 1993. Annex. Meeting of experts on the application and effectiveness of the Convention for the Protection of Cultural Property in the Event of Armed Conflict (The Hague, 14 May 1954), The Hague, 5-7 July 1993, p. 4. http://unesdoc.unesco.org/images/0009/000958/095820Eo.pdf
959 Ibid.
960 Ibid.

Fact-Finding Commission (Article 90 of the 1977 Additional Protocol I) were discussed. In addition, the importance of developing a flexible and simplified regime involving UNESCO representatives and NGOs in operational and preventive activities was stressed. Some delegations referred to the possibility of adding to the 1954 Convention a provision along the lines of the common Articles 9/10 (Activities of ICRC or any other impartial humanitarian organization) and 10/11 (Substitutes for Protecting Powers) of the Geneva Conventions.

The 142nd Session of the Executive Board adopted on 15 October 1993 Decision 5.5.2, which welcomed the report of the Hague Meeting of Experts and expressed, *inter alia*, the opinion that the scope of the 1954 Convention should be maintained. The Board made a series of recommendations to the 27th Session of the General Conference, which met in Paris in October and November 1993. In Resolution 3.5, adopted on the report of Commission IV at the 28th plenary meeting on 13 November 1993, the General Conference endorsed the proposals of the Executive Board and reaffirmed in particular that 'the fundamental principles of protecting and preserving cultural property in the event of armed conflict could be considered part of international customary law'. It invited the High Contracting Parties to the 1954 Hague Convention to consider:

> (b) the need for an institutional mechanism under the 1954 Hague Convention that could perform both advisory and operational functions, taking into account the functions performed by the existing organs established under other UNESCO instruments for the protection of cultural property.

Another meeting of experts was held in Lauswolt on 9–11 February 1994 at the invitation of the Netherlands Government. In this small Netherlands town was drafted a legal instrument that initiated the process of codification that ended with the adoption of the 1999 Second Protocol. The document is known as the 'Lauswolt document'.[961] The meeting drafted the legal instrument in the form of a protocol to the Hague Convention, Chapters 4 and 5 of which were structured as follows:

Chapter 4: Commissioners-General/Protecting Powers
* Article 13. Substitute for the organization of control

---

961 The Second Expert Meeting on the 1954 Hague Convention for the Protection of Cultural Property in the Event of Armed Conflict. Lauswolt, The Netherlands, 9–11 February, 1994.

Chapter 5: Institutional issues
- Article 14. Committee
- Article 15. Terms of office
- Article 16. Rules of procedure
- Article 17. Functions
- Article 18. Secretariat

It was at this Lauswolt meeting that the structure of Chapter 6 (on institutional issues) was established, a structure that was maintained in its final form adopted in the 1999 Second Protocol.

The Director-General informed the 145th Session of the Executive Board (1994) of the proposals of the Lauswolt meeting and stated that these proposals 'need to be further discussed by technical, military and legal experts before any written proposal could be presented to the States Parties to the Convention for their consideration'. Thus, he decided to organize at least one meeting of experts before the next session of the General Conference. He also began researching the possibility of increasing the Secretariat's staff and the financial resources allocated to it. In his report to the Executive Board, the Director-General also expressed his intention to convene a meeting of representatives of States Parties to the Convention to be held at the time of the 28th Session of the General Conference.[962]

On the basis of the previous studies and reports and the numerous expert meetings, the UNESCO Secretariat prepared an excellent working document for the next expert session to be held in Paris in November–December 1994. This document made use of our 1996 Commentary on the Convention, Patrick Boylan's Report, and the reports of the Hague and the Lauswolt expert meetings, and provided the UNESCO Secretariat's comments on each issue.[963] The discussion at the 1994 Paris Expert Meeting was devoted to a study of new legal provisions and concentrated on a few major issues, including the following:

- Creation of an advisory or executive body that would be given specific functions. The Secretariat considered the various advantages of creating a bureau or an advisory committee composed of the representatives of ICOM, ICOMOS and ICCROM: lower costs and speedy actions were seen as the main advantages. The author of these lines made a

---

962 UNESCO Executive Board, 145th session. Report by the Director-General on the review of the Convention for the Protection of Cultural Property in the Event of Armed Conflict, 145 EX/21, 20 July 1994, para. 4–6, p. 2.
963 UNESCO document: a working document prepared by the Secretariat, CLT/94/608/1 of 28 November 1994.

comparison with the ICRC, which has a rather large Secretariat, and this idea was also reflected in the report.[964] In addition, it was pointed out that the Secretariat should be reinforced.

* A general meeting of all States Parties could also be held on a regular (biennial) basis.

The Second Meeting of the High Contracting Parties to the 1954 Convention was convened by the Director-General at UNESCO Headquarters on Monday, 13 November 1995,[965] on the occasion of the 28th Session of the General Conference, in conformity with Decision 5.5.5, which the Executive Board adopted at its 145th Session in October–November 1994. The participants considered it indispensible to create a supervisory body in the form of an intergovernmental committee or an advisory body. Issues concerning the role of UN peacekeeping forces in the implementation of the Convention, the role of NGOs, the protection of documentary heritage, the notion of military necessity and control systems were discussed. A majority of participants were in favour of adopting an additional protocol.

The 149th Session of the Executive Board approved the Director-General's proposal to invite 20 States to appoint one expert to participate in the 1997 Governmental Experts Meeting.[966] The Secretariat submitted to the meeting the 1996 *Summary of comments* received from States Parties to the Hague Convention and from the ICA.[967] The experts also received an Information Note that suggested points on which they might focus

964 UNESCO Executive Board, 145th session. Report by the Director-General on the review of the Convention for the Protection of Cultural Property in the Event of Armed Conflict, 145 EX/21, 20 July 1994, p. 5.

965 UNESCO, Second Meeting of the High Contracting Parties to the Convention for the Protection of Cultural Property in the Event of Armed Conflict (The Hague, 1954), UNESCO House, Paris, 13 November 1995. *Final Report.* CLT-95/CONF.009/5, November 1995. See also Hladík (1996).

966 UNESCO, Meeting of Governmental Experts on the Review of the 1954 Hague Convention for the Protection of Cultural Property in the Event of Armed Conflict 1954, UNESCO Headquarters, Paris, 24–27 March 1997. *Final Report.* UNESCO document CLT-96/CONF.603/5, Paris, 30 April 1997.

967 UNESCO, Meeting of Governmental Experts. Summary of comments received from States Parties to the Hague Convention and from the International Council on Archives. UNESCO document: CLT-96/CONF.603/INF.4, Paris, December 1996. As at 28 November 1996, the Secretariat has received replies from nine States of the total number of 88 States Parties to the Convention.

their work,[968] the provisional agenda[969] and the provisional rules of procedure.[970]

Institutional issues formed an important part of the discussion (draft Articles 14–17), but the experts could not reach a consensus on the form of a body – committee or bureau – as discussed above. It was proposed to set up a fund to allocate financial resources. The role of NGOs was also welcomed.

The Second Meeting of the High Contracting Parties in 1995 invited the Director-General to convene another meeting – the Third Meeting of the High Contracting Parties – during the 29th Session of the UNESCO General Conference.[971] This third meeting took place at UNESCO Headquarters on 13 November 1997 with the participation of 65 Parties, six observers, and the representatives of six international organizations. Twenty Parties, one observer and two representatives of international organizations participated in the general debate, which clarified certain points; regarding institutional issues, the majority of speakers were in favour of creating a permanent intergovernmental committee. The final resolution invited States Parties to provide comments on the draft provisions by 1 February 1998 and convene a Preparatory Meeting of Government Experts in Vienna on 11–13 May 1998.[972] Here again the majority of delegates were in favour of the creation of

---

968 Information note, UNESCO document: CLT-96/CONF.603/INF.3, Paris, November 1996.
  The following points were relating to the institutional issues:
  15. When discussing the improvement of the Convention, the Governmental experts may wish to focus their work on the following points: [...]
  - the replacement of the existing control system of the Convention by a more flexible and efficient structure, the form that such alternative system could take; [...]
  - the desirability of setting up a supervisory body which would monitor the implementation of the Convention and the form that such a body could take (intergovernmental, advisory or expert body) and its functions; [...]
  - the growing role of non-governmental organizations in the preservation and protection of cultural heritage in the event of armed conflict and how they could participate in the implementation of the Convention;
  - the opportunity for adopting new international norms reflecting the results and discussions of the above and the procedure to adopt these norms;
  - either by amendments to the Convention;
  - or by the adoption of a Protocol to the Convention;
  - or by a new Convention.
969 UNESCO document CLT-96/CONF.603/1.
970 UNESCO document CLT/96/CONF.603/3.
971 UNESCO, Third Meeting of the High Contracting Parties to the Convention for the Protection of Cultural Property in the Event of Armed Conflict (The Hague, 1954), UNESCO House, Paris, 13 November 1997. *Final Report*. CLT-97/CONF.208/3, Paris, November 1997. See also Hladík (1998b).
972 UNESCO, Meeting of Governmental Experts on the Revision of the Hague Convention for the Protection of Cultural Property in the Event of Armed Conflict of 1954. Vienna, 11–13 May 1998. UNESCO document: Paris, May 1998, *Final Report*.

an intergovernmental committee. The experts asked the UNESCO Secretariat to prepare a comprehensive working document to be distributed well in advance of the Diplomatic Conference, which the Netherlands generously proposed to hold in The Hague from 14 to 26 March 1999.

The UNESCO Secretariat prepared the *Preliminary Draft Second Protocol* based upon the previous meetings of government experts, and particularly on the discussions that took place at the May 1998 Vienna Meeting. [973] The Protocol was sent to the Member States of UNESCO and the UN, and selected international organizations with requests for comments, which would be taken into account in the preparation of a final draft for the Diplomatic Conference to be held in The Hague from 15 to 26 March 1999.

On this basis, the UNESCO Secretariat and the Government of the Netherlands drew up the final draft of the Second Protocol: *Draft Second Protocol to the 1954 Hague Convention for the Protection of Cultural Property in the Event of Armed Conflict* (UNESCO doc. HC/1999/1/rev.1, February 1999). The Diplomatic Conference on the Second Protocol to the Hague Convention of 1954 for the Protection of Cultural Property in the Event of Armed Conflict took place in The Hague from 15 to 26 March 1999.

We shall follow the discussion at the Diplomatic Conference of each article relating to institutional issues. But before entering into the discussion of the articles of Chapter 6, it is useful to underline the fact that most of these provisions were inspired or even copied from one of the most successful conventions concerning the protection of cultural property: the 1972 Convention concerning the Protection of the World Cultural and Natural Heritage. The articles of this convention provided a very useful guide for the drafting of the new protocol.

But a question remains: even if it is self-evidently easy to copy an instrument, is it actually possible to do so? Are the circumstances relating to the use of the original instrument the same as those that necessitated the new instrument? The 1972 World Heritage Convention was successful thanks to the peaceful environment at the time and the interest of different members of the international community. All States, whether from the West, the East or the North-South countries, were interested in the protection of cultural property.

But when armed conflicts arise, whether international or non-international, the circumstances are fundamentally different. We have

---

973 *Preliminary Draft Second Protocol to the 1954 Hague Convention.* UNESCO document HC/1999/1, October 1998 (English, French and Russian).

seen the extent to which the conflicts arising during the Cold War period constituted an obstacle to the implementation of the 1954 Convention. Whatever future instrument will deal with conflict situations, it must take into consideration such different environments.

Even if this basic difference seems obvious, it was not often raised in discussions at the experts meetings and the 1999 Hague Conference. This was also quite natural. The 1990s was a time of hope: the Cold War was over and the final form of humanity's socio-cultural evolution began with an affirmation of 'the end of the history'. But we know that the contrary was in fact the case: Yugoslavia, Rwanda and periods of terrorism were not changing world history; they were its continuation.

At the Plenary Session of the Diplomatic Conference on 17 March 1999, the Argentine delegate was alone in basing his evaluation of the circumstances on three 'rational' criteria:[974] the financial situation, functions to be accomplished, and especially the scope of the object. A distinction should be made between the universal and permanent scope of protection within the framework of the World Heritage Convention of 1972 and more specific protection during armed conflict when an institutional scheme would be needed to regulate and protect.

Here we recall the basic distinction of two branches of international law: the laws of peace and the laws of war. Even if in the light of present international law we must continue to affirm the wrongness of this distinction in view of the prohibition of the threat and use of force, it is always good to remember the words of Lassa Oppenheim:

> As within the boundaries of the modern State an armed contention between two or more citizens is illegal, public opinion has become convinced that armed contests between citizens are inconsistent with Municipal Law. Influenced by this fact, as well as by the recent abolition of the right of war as an instrument of national policy, many persons frequently consider war and law inconsistent. Such a view ignores the fact that as States are sovereign, and as consequently no central authority exists above them able to enforce compliance with International Law, war cannot, under the existing conditions. always be avoided. International Law recognizes this fact, but at the same time

---

974 1999 Hague Conference, Plenary Session, 17 March 1999: Argentine delegate, p. 143. His idea was supported by other delegates: Israel, ibid., p. 145 (insisting on equitable representation); US, ibid., p. 149; Austria, ibid., p. 153.

contains obligations limiting the right to resort to war and provides regulations with which belligerents have customarily, or by special conventions, agreed to comply in case war breaks out between them. Accordingly, although with the outbreak of war peaceable relations between the belligerents cease, there remain certain mutual legal obligations and duties. Thus conceived, war is not inconsistent with, but a condition regulated by, International Law.[975]

Finally it is important to underline that Chapter 6 (on institutional issues) is only complementary to the provisions of the regime of international control established by the 1954 Hague Convention and the Regulations for its Execution. This is mentioned in Article 2 of the Second Protocol, which states that the Protocol only supplements the Convention and only in relations between Parties to the Protocol. The participants at the 1999 Hague Conference took this decision in order to keep obligations according to the Convention and the Regulations alive for eventual future use where appropriate. According to Article 34 of the Protocol, the 'Protocol shall be applied with the co-operation of the Protecting Powers responsible for safeguarding the interests of the Parties to the conflict'.

---

975 Oppenheim (1952), pp. 201–2.

Article 23
MEETING OF THE PARTIES

1. *The Meeting of the Parties shall be convened at the same time as the General Conference of UNESCO, and in co-ordination with the Meeting of the High Contracting Parties, if such a meeting has been called by the Director-General.*
2. *The Meeting of the Parties shall adopt its Rules of Procedure.*
3. *The Meeting of the Parties shall have the following functions:*
   (a) to elect the Members of the Committee, in accordance with Article 24 paragraph 1;
   (b) to endorse the Guidelines developed by the Committee in accordance with Article 27 sub-paragraph 1(a);
   (c) to provide guidelines for, and to supervise the use of the Fund by the Committee;
   (d) to consider the report submitted by the Committee in accordance with Article 27 sub-paragraph 1(d);
   (e) to discuss any problem related to the application of this Protocol, and to make recommendations, as appropriate.
4. *At the request of at least one-fifth of the Parties, the Director-General shall convene an Extraordinary Meeting of the Parties.*

Preparatory work

Second Expert meeting on the 1954 Hague Convention for the Protection of Cultural Property in the Event of Armed Conflict. Lauswolt, The Netherlands, 9–11 February 1994.

Expert meeting on the review of the 1954 Hague Convention for the Protection of cultural property in the Event of Armed Conflict. Paris, UNESCO Headquarters, 28 November–2 December 1994. UNESCO document CLT/CH/94/608/2, *Final Report.*

UNESCO document: a working document prepared by the Secretariat, CLT/94/608/1 of 28 November 1994.

Expert meeting on the review of the 1954 Hague Convention for the Protection of Cultural Property in the Event of Armed Conflict. Paris, UNESCO Headquarters, 28 November–2 December 1994. UNESCO document CLT/CH/94/608/2, *Final Report*, p. 7.

UNESCO, Second Meeting of the High Contracting Parties to the Convention for the Protection of Cultural Property in the Event of Armed

Conflict (The Hague, 1954), UNESCO House, Paris, 13 November 1995, *Final Report.* CLT-95/CONF.009/5, November 1995.

UNESCO, Meeting of Governmental Experts. Summary of comments received from States Parties to the Hague Convention and from the International Council on Archives. UNESCO document: CLT-96/CONF.603/INF.4, Paris, December 1996.

UNESCO, Third Meeting of the High Contracting Parties to the Convention for the Protection of Cultural Property in the Event of Armed Conflict (The Hague, 1954), UNESCO House, Paris, 13 November 1997, *Final Report.* CLT-97/CONF.208/3, Paris, November 1997, p. 3.

Draft provisions for the revision of the 1954 Hague Convention and commentary from UNESCO Secretariat. CLT-97/CONF.208/2, Paris, October 1997

UNESCO, Meeting of Governmental Experts on the Review of the Hague Convention for the Protection of Cultural Property in the Event of Armed Conflict of 1954. Vienna, 11–13 May 1998. UNESCO document: Paris, May 1998, *Final Report.*

Preliminary Draft Second Protocol to the 1954 Hague Convention. UNESCO document HC/1999/1, October 1998 (English, French and Russian).

UNESCO, Meeting of Governmental Experts. Summary of comments received from States Parties to the Hague Convention, the International Committee of the Red Cross and the International Council on Archives. UNESCO document: Paris, March 1998.

Draft Second Protocol to the 1954 Hague Convention for the Protection of Cultural Property in the Event of Armed Conflict. UNESCO document HC/1999/1/rev.1, February 1999.

UNESCO, Synoptic report of comments on the Preliminary Draft Second Protocol to the 1954 Hague Convention received from High Contracting Parties to the Hague Convention for the Protection of Cultural Property in the Event of Armed Conflict 1954, other UNESCO Member States and international organizations, Paris, 15 January 1999.

1999 Hague Conference, Plenary Session, particularly 18 and 24 March 1999.

Bibliography

Chamberlain. K. 2004. *War and Cultural Heritage.* Leicester: Institute of Art and Law, pp. 221–22.

Desch, T. 1999. The Second Protocol to the 1954 Convention for the Protection of Cultural Property in the Event of Armed Conflict. *Yearbook of International Humanitarian Law*, Vol. 2, pp. 84–85.

Government of the Netherlands. 1961. *Records of the Conference convened by the United Nations Educational, Scientific and Cultural Organization and held at The Hague from 21 April to 14 May 1954*. The Hague: Staatsdrukkerij en Uitgeverijbedrijf, p. 314.

Hladík, J. 1996. Meeting of the High Contracting Parties to the Hague Convention for the Protection of Cultural Property in the Event of Armed Conflict of 1954. *International Journal of Cultural Property*, Vol. 5, No. 2, pp. 339–41.

Hladík, J. 1998b. The Third Meeting of the High Contracting Parties to the Hague Convention for the Protection of Cultural Property in the Event of Armed Conflict of 1954 (Paris, November 13, 1997). *International Journal of Cultural Property*, Vol. 7, No. 1, pp. 268–71.

O'Keefe, R. 2006. *The Protection of Cultural Property in Armed Conflict*. Cambridge: Cambridge University Press, pp. 293–94.

UNESCO. 1983. Meeting of Legal Experts on the Convention for the Protection of Cultural Property in the Event of Armed Conflict (The Hague, 1954), Vienna, 17–19 October 1983, *Final Report*, Paris, p. 10, para. 31 (CLT-83/CONF.641 /1).

PREPARATORY WORK

The importance and responsibility of Contracting Parties was mentioned in the very beginnings of the codification of rules concerning the protection of cultural property. The 1938 Preliminary Draft International Convention for the Protection of Historic Buildings and Works of Art in Time of War, prepared by a group of experts under the direction of Charles de Visscher, stated in Article 12:

Article 12

1. The High Contraction Parties agree to meet from time to time in *general conference* to decide conjointly upon measures for ensuring the application of this Convention, and to review if necessary, the Regulations for its execution.

2. The General Conference shall appoint its *Standing Committee and Secretariat,* whose powers in the intervals between sessions of the

Conference shall be defined by the Regulations for the execution
of this Convention.

This Article not only referred to the role of the General Conference in the
enforcement of the Convention but also envisaged the appointment of
the Standing Committee and the Secretariat. We have to keep in mind
that the envisaged Convention had to be independent of any international
organization, which is why the institutional mechanism had to be so carefully
planned.

It is obvious that the drafters of the 1954 Convention were inspired by
the work of the 1936 Committee of experts and the 1938 Preliminary Draft.
During the preparation of the 1954 Convention, the UNESCO Secretariat
expressed the following view on the role of meetings of High Contracting
Parties, which was certainly known to the drafters of Article 23 of the 1999
Second Protocol:

> If the Convention is to remain effective and if its application is to
> be gradually extended and improved, it is highly desirable that the
> States Parties to it should maintain direct contact with each other,
> otherwise than through the inter-communication of reports by means
> of UNESCO. This can only be achieved by exchanges of views between
> the States in question. As a result of such exchanges, it may be found
> that the Convention or the Regulations for its Execution stand in need
> of revision in certain respects.
>
> How should this periodical conference discharge its function? It
> was considered desirable to avoid swelling the number of standing
> committees equipped with secretariats and involving fresh expense, and
> also to avoid overlapping. It was noted, in this respect, that there were
> already bodies like UNESCO, the International Council of Museums
> and the International Committee on Monuments, which had made
> and published studies constituting a substantial source of information.
> A second source of useful information, for the purpose of adapting and
> improving the Convention, derives from the obligation, undertaken
> by the signatory States, to furnish reports on the measures taken by
> them with a view to applying the Convention.
>
> No permanent body, therefore, was deemed necessary; and a reasonable
> and economical solution for this problem appeared to be that the
> periodical meeting proposed should be held, in principle, every four

years, preferably at the same time as a session of the General Conference of UNESCO, from which it would remain independent.[976]

At the 1954 Conference itself, the role of periodic meetings was extensively discussed and a number of amendments were proposed. France proposed that the procedure for the appointment of Commissioners-General be linked to the institution of 'Periodic Meetings' by entrusting them, for example, with the establishment of a nominal list of Commissioners-General.[977] The UK asked for the article to be deleted, whereas Italy wanted to make the meetings more useful by proposing that they also be entrusted with problems that might arise in connection with inscription in the International Register.[978]

The 1954 Hague Convention included Article 27 on the Meetings of High Contracting Parties:

Article 27. Meetings

1. The Director-General of the United Nations Educational, Scientific and Cultural Organization may, with the approval of the Executive Board, convene meetings of representatives of the High Contracting Parties. He must convene such a meeting if at least one-fifth of the High Contracting Parties so request.

2. Without prejudice to any other functions which have been conferred on it by the present Convention or the Regulations for its execution, the purpose of the meeting will be to study problems concerning the application of the Convention and of the Regulations for its execution, and to formulate recommendations in respect thereof.

3. The meeting may further undertake a revision of the Convention or the Regulations for its execution if the majority of the High Contracting Parties are represented, and in accordance with the provisions of Article 39.

The practical implementation of this Article was very limited. Until the meeting of the Parties for the adoption of the 1999 Second Protocol, only one meeting of High Contracting Parties had taken place. It was held at UNESCO Headquarters on 16–25 July 1962[979] and participation was excellent: 39 States participated and 18 States non-Parties to the Convention

---

976 *Records*/Government of the Netherlands (1961), p. 314.
977 Ibid., p. 322.
978 Ibid., para. 1133–36, pp. 219, 344.
979 Report of the meeting, document UNESCO/CUA/120 of 3 September 1962.

sent observers. This first meeting had no proposed amendments before it. It confined its proceedings to the examination of problems concerning the application of the Convention and encouraging other States to become Parties to the Convention and to facilitate its application, and sought also to make suggestions for future action.

In 1970 an attempt was made to organize a second meeting of the High Contracting Parties. At the request of the Executive Board, the Director-General of UNESCO consulted the States Parties to the Convention on the advisability of convening a new meeting. Of the 23 States that replied, 19 were in favour, with various qualifications, and four against. The results of this consultation could not be interpreted as an express request on the part of at least one-fifth of the High Contracting Parties. After examining the replies received and taking budget resources into account, the Executive Board endorsed the Director-General's viewpoint and decided that it would not be advisable to convene a meeting 'in the present circumstances'.[980] This decision was taken at a critical time for the Convention, when it indeed would have been appropriate to take more vigorous measures for its promotion and to examine important developments in its practical application, alongside new developments in relation to the results of the process of reaffirmation and development of humanitarian international law between 1974 and 1977, and especially the adoption of two articles concerning the protection of cultural property in the context of the Additional Protocols to the Geneva Conventions.

Unfortunately, the Meeting of Legal Experts in Vienna in 1983 also advised against convening a meeting of the High Contracting Parties in the near future for several reasons:

> On the one hand, if such a meeting were convened, this would risk giving the impression that amendments were necessary to make the Convention more effective. In the present context and, in particular given the arms reduction talks, any amendment process risked leading to inconclusive results. In these circumstances, the experts considered that it was preferable to direct efforts towards a better application of the Convention in its present form. On the other hand, the interest of States which were not parties to the Convention could more

---

980 UNESCO document 87 EX/32 Draft, item 4.4.1.

appropriately be encouraged by convening a conference of all the Member States of UNESCO.[981]

In 1988 the permanent delegate of the Islamic Republic of Iran, Reza Feiz, informed the Executive Board of UNESCO that he had asked the Director-General to convene a meeting of the High Contracting Parties to the Hague Convention. This information did not elicit any response from the members of the Board.[982] It was therefore necessary to wait until the new process of codification, which started in 1993.

The second meeting of the High Contracting Parties to the 1954 Convention was convened by the Director-General at UNESCO Headquarters on Monday, 13 November 1995,[983] on the occasion of the 28th Session of the General Conference, in conformity with Decision 5.5.5, which the Executive Board adopted at its 145th Session in October–November 1994. In the Information Note of June 1995,[984] the Director-General expressed the desire to learn the views of States Parties on whether new provisions should be adopted, the existing text revised, or an additional protocol drawn up.

The meeting was attended by 69 High Contracting Parties, eight observers, the representative of the UN, and four NGOs. There was a consensus among participants regarding the necessity for improving implementation of the Convention. A number of participants expressed the need for the creation of a supervisory body in the form of an intergovernmental committee or an advisory body. Issues concerning the role of the UN peacekeeping forces in the implementation of the Convention, the role of NGOs, the protection of documentary heritage, the notion of military necessity and the control system were also discussed. A majority of participants were in favour of adopting an additional protocol.

The resolution adopted at the meeting, *inter alia*, invited the Parties to submit to the Secretariat written comments on the substantive proposals by 1 September 1996. The resolution also endorsed the initiatives taken by the Director-General to send his personal representatives, encouraged him to

---

981 Meeting of Legal Experts on the Convention for the Protection of Cultural Property in the Event of Armed Conflict (The Hague, 1954), Vienna, 17–19 October 1983, *Final Report*, Paris, UNESCO, 1983, p. 10, para. 31 (CLT-83/CONF.641/1).

982 Toman (1996), p. 289.

983 UNESCO, Second Meeting of the High Contracting Parties to the Convention for the Protection of Cultural Property in the Event of Armed Conflict (The Hague, 1954), UNESCO House, Paris, 13 November 1995, *Final Report*. CLT-95/CONF.009/5, November 1995. See also Hladík (1996).

984 Information note, CLT-95/CONF.009/INF.1.

improve cooperation with the UN peacekeeping forces, and requested him to provide the means necessary to develop dissemination activities. Furthermore, the participants emphasized the importance of organizing a meeting of a limited number of governmental experts and invited the Director-General to convene another meeting of the High Contracting Parties during the 29th Session of the UNESCO General Conference.

This third meeting took place at UNESCO Headquarters on 13 November 1997[985] with the participation of 65 Parties, six observers, and the representatives of six international organizations. The Meeting of the High Contracting Parties was informed of the results of the four previous expert meetings (Hague 1993, Lauswolt 1994, Paris 1994, Paris 1997) and of the conclusions of the Second Meeting of the High Contracting Parties (November 1995).

The general debate, in which participated 20 Parties, one observer, and two representatives of international organizations, clarified certain points discussed at the expert meetings and favoured the adoption of a new instrument. The participants also asked the Director-General to convene a fourth meeting of the High Contracting Parties during the 30th Session of the General Conference.

The fourth meeting of the High Contracting Parties to the 1954 Convention took on 18 November 1999, after the adoption of the 1999 Second Protocol. Its main role was to encourage High Contracting Parties to sign, ratify or accede to the Second Protocol. The fifth, sixth and seventh meetings followed in 2001, 2005 and 2007, respectively.[986]

New codification

As we mentioned in the introduction to this chapter, it was at the Lauswolt Meeting of Experts (9–11 February 1994) that the legal instrument known as the 'Lauswolt document' was drafted.[987] This document contains quite an elaborate project for a committee, though – curiously – this committee was to be attached not to the Parties of the future protocol but to UNESCO

---

985 UNESCO, Third Meeting of the High Contracting Parties to the Convention for the Protection of Cultural Property in the Event of Armed Conflict (The Hague, 1954), UNESCO House, Paris, 13 November 1997, *Final Report*. CLT-97/CONF.208/3, Paris, November 1997. See also Hladík (1998b).

986 See UNESCO, Meetings and conferences: http://portal.unesco.org/culture/en/ev.php-URL_ID=36651&URL_DO=DO_TOPIC&URL_SECTION=201.html.

987 The Second Expert Meeting on the 1954 Hague Convention for the Protection of Cultural Property in the Event of Armed Conflict. Lauswolt, The Netherlands, 9–11 February 1994.

itself. The 'States Parties to this instrument . . . shall be elected during the ordinary session of the General Conference of UNESCO in accordance with the Rules of Procedure as referred to in Article [...] of this instrument.'[988] There is no mention of the meeting of High Contracting Parties (to the Convention) or Parties to the future instrument, as the present Protocol was called at that stage. It is rather odd to find no reference to either the Parties to the Convention or to the Protocol.

On the basis of the previous studies and reports and the numerous expert meetings, the UNESCO Secretariat prepared an excellent working document for the next expert session to be held in Paris in November–December 1994. This document made use of our manuscript of the Commentary on the Convention, Patrick Boylan's Report, and the reports of the Hague and the Lauswolt expert meetings, and provided the UNESCO Secretariat's comments on each issue.[989] The Secretariat proposed an alternative: 'Since there was a strong feeling among the experts that there should be some body representing the States Parties to assist UNESCO in the implementation of the Convention, it is proposed that a Bureau and an Advisory Committee be established.' The document describes in details this proposal and concludes that 'a bureau could be elected by a meeting of States Parties called at the same time as the General Conference'.[990]

The discussion at the Paris Expert Meeting (28 November–2 December 1994)[991] concentrated on a few major issues, including:

- Creation of an advisory or executive body that would be given specific functions. There were different views as to the form such a body would take. The Secretariat considered the various advantages of creating a bureau or an advisory committee composed of the representatives of ICOM, ICOMOS and ICCROM: lower costs and speedy actions were seen as the main advantages. The author of these lines made a comparison with the ICRC, which has a rather large Secretariat, and this idea was also reflected in the report.[992] In addition, it was pointed out that the Secretariat should be reinforced.

---

988 Ibid., art. 14.

989 UNESCO document: a working document prepared by the Secretariat, CLT/94/608/1 of 28 November 1994.

990 Alternative Article 14. Ibid., pp. 21–22.

991 Expert meeting on the review of the 1954 Hague Convention for the Protection of Cultural Property in the Event of Armed Conflict. Paris, UNESCO Headquarters, 28 November–2 December 1994. UNESCO document CLT/CH/94/608/2, *Final Report*.

992 Ibid., p. 5.

- A general meeting of all States Parties could also be held on a regular (biennial) basis.

In the meetings that followed, all discussion concentrated on the form of the future committee and a preference for the creation of an intergovernmental committee started to prevail even if some delegates 'opposed this concept, invoking the cost of such a Committee, the existing mandate of UNESCO and the need to prevent overlaps between the activities of the various units of UNESCO'.[993]

Another Governmental Expert Meeting on the Review of the Hague Convention for the Protection of Cultural Property in the Event of Armed Conflict 1954 was approved by the 149th Session of the Executive Board and met at UNESCO Headquarters on 24–27 March 1997.[994] A total of 18 States of the 20 invited participated in the meeting. In addition, 50 UNESCO Member States and two States with observer status took part in the proceedings, as did the representatives of six international organizations. The discussion was based on the Lauswolt document, and attention was paid to the comments presented by nine States. The drafting group was composed of representatives of Ghana, Lebanon, the Netherlands and Thailand. The group expanded upon the revised version of the Lauswolt document, which was important for future codification work. At the conclusion of the meeting, Estelle Appiah, Chairperson of the drafting group, proposed the redrafted articles. The Secretariat was charged with preparing a working document,[995] known as the 'revised Lauswolt document'. Option I of this document contains the revised Article 14, which states:

> A Committee is hereby established within UNESCO. It shall be composed of [...] States Parties to this instrument which shall be elected *by the States Parties* during the ordinary session of the General Conference of UNESCO in accordance with the Rules of Procedure as referred to in Article [...] of this instrument.[996]

---

993 UNESCO, Third Meeting of the High Contracting Parties to the Convention for the Protection of Cultural Property in the Event of Armed Conflict (The Hague, 1954), UNESCO House, Paris, 13 November 1997, *Final Report*. CLT-97/CONF.208/3, Paris, November 1997, p. 3

994 UNESCO, Meeting of Governmental Experts on the Review of the 1954 Hague Convention for the Protection of Cultural Property in the Event of Armed Conflict 1954, UNESCO Headquarters, Paris, 24–27 March 1997, *Final Report*. UNESCO document CLT-96/CONF.603/5, Paris, 30 April 1997.

995 *Draft provisions for the revision of the 1954 Hague Convention and commentary from the UNESCO Secretariat*. CLT-97/CONF.208/2, Paris, October 1997. The document included the text of the 'revised Lauwolt document'.

996 Ibid., art. 14, p. 9 (in boldface in the original text).

The document refers to election by States Parties without mentioning the meeting of the States Parties, which was probably in the mind of the drafters. Option II referred to the creation of the Bureau and was much clearer. According to Article 14 of Option 2:

(a) The Director-General will call a meeting of States Parties to the Convention to be held at the same time as the General Conference of UNESCO.

(b) The meeting shall elect a Bureau, consisting of 6 States party to the Convention, with due regard to equitable representation of the different regions and cultures of the world. It shall elect a President and Rapporteur.

The 1998 Vienna Governmental Experts Meeting on the revision of the Hague Convention for the Protection of Cultural Property in the Event of Armed Conflict of 1954 (11–13 May 1998)[997] valorized Option I of the revised Lauswolt document, as mentioned above.

The UNESCO Secretariat prepared the document based on several meetings of Government experts, and particularly on the discussions that took place at the May 1998 Vienna Meeting.[998] The text was sent to the Member States of UNESCO and the UN, and selected international organizations with requests for comments, which would be taken into account in the preparation of a final draft for the Diplomatic Conference to be held at The Hague from 14 to 26 March 1999. This document includes two provisions relating to the present Article. Chapter 6 (on institutional issues) includes Article 17, entitled 'General Assembly of States Parties':

1. The General Assembly shall consist of the representatives of the States Parties to this Protocol. It shall meet at the same time as the General Conference of UNESCO.

2. States parties to the Convention which are not party to the present Protocol may send observers to the meeting of the General Assembly.[999]

---

997 UNESCO, Meeting of Governmental Experts on the Revision of the Hague Convention for the Protection of Cultural Property in the Event of Armed Conflict of 1954. Vienna, 11–13 May 1998. UNESCO document: Paris, May 1998, *Final Report*, p. 4.

998 *Preliminary Draft Second Protocol to the 1954 Hague Convention*. UNESCO document HC/1999/1, October 1998 (English, French and Russian).

999 Ibid., p. 7 (inconsistency in the use of capital letters.)

The Draft includes another article, Article 34, entitled 'Meetings':

1. The Director-General of UNESCO may, with the approval of the Executive Board, convene meetings of representatives of the States Parties. He must convene such a meeting if at least one-fifth of the States Parties so request.
2. Without prejudice to any other functions which have been conferred on it by the present Protocol, the purpose of the meeting will be to study problems concerning the application of the Protocol, and to formulate recommendations in respect thereof.
[3. The meeting may further undertake a revision of the Protocol if it so decides.]

By 15 January 1999, the Secretariat had received comments from the High Contracting Parties to the Convention.[1000] China proposed to add three paragraphs covering the adoption of rules of procedure by the General Assembly both for the Assembly and the Committee, that decisions and quorum be based on a majority, and that the General Assembly study problems concerning the application of the Protocol and formulate recommendations in respect thereof, also providing that it may further undertake a revision of the protocol if it so decides. Israel considered that the General Assembly of States Parties was an unnecessary duplication of Article 27 of the Convention and contradicts the basic aim of the Convention, which is to establish a uniform regime to protect cultural property in the event of armed conflict.[1001]

George H. Aldrich, who submitted the comments and analysis to the Preliminary Draft Second Protocol, mentioned as precedents other multilateral conventions, such as the 1982 UN Convention on the Law of the Sea, which established the Assembly of the International Sea-Bed Authority. He also suggested that it would be helpful if the Director-General of UNESCO would act as Chairman of the General Assembly.[1002]

Regarding Article 34, China wished to delete it. Turkey wished to give it a new title: 'Meetings of States Parties'. Norway questioned the relationship between the meetings under this Article and the General Assembly of States

---

1000   UNESCO, Synoptic report of comments on the Preliminary Draft Second Protocol to the 1954 Hague Convention received from High Contracting Parties to the Hague Convention for the Protection of Cultural Property in the Event of Armed Conflict 1954, other UNESCO Member States and international organizations, Paris, 15 January 1999.

1001   Ibid., p. 9

1002   Aldrich (1998), p. 14.

Parties. Regarding paragraph 1, Turkey wished to insert the word 'UNESCO' before the word 'Executive'. Regarding paragraph 3, Norway proposed to amend the paragraph in line with Article 27(3) of the Convention. Switzerland and Turkey wished to delete the square brackets.[1003]

In February 1999 a revised draft was sent to the States and organizations participating at the Conference, which met one month later in The Hague. The revised draft contains the revised articles:[1004]

Chapter 6. Institutional Issues
Article 25. General Assembly of Parties
1. The General Assembly shall consist of the representatives of the Parties. It shall meet at the same time as the General Conference of UNESCO.
2. A meeting of the General Assembly shall be convened if a least one-fifth of the Parties so request.
3. The General Assembly shall adopt its own Rules of Procedure.
4. High Contracting Parties which are not party to the present Protocol may send observers to the meeting of the General Assembly.[1005]

Chapter 8. Execution of this Protocol
Article 42. Meetings
1. The Director-General may, in consultation with the Chairman of the Committee [Bureau], convene the General Assembly of Parties. She/He will notify the Executive Board of UNESCO of any such action. The purpose of the meeting will be to study problems concerning the application of this Protocol, and to formulate recommendations in respect thereof.
[2. The meeting may further undertake a revision of this Protocol if it so decides.]

A Diplomatic Conference met in The Hague on 14–26 March 1999. It was on 17 March that the question of the intergovernmental committee or bureau was discussed.[1006] During the discussion of institutional issues, the delegate

---

1003   Ibid., p. 12.
1004   Draft Second Protocol to the 1954 Hague Convention for the Protection of Cultural Property in the Event of Armed Conflict, UNESCO doc. HC/1999/1/rev.1, February 1999.
1005   Ibid., p. 16.
1006   See pp. 497, 544 ff.

of Argentina, Ariel Gonzalez, also raised the issue of the General Assembly and the Meeting as mentioned in the draft:

> Keeping in mind the supplementary nature of the draft, the creation of a General Assembly of Parties by Article 25 could create difficulties with respect to the meetings regulated by Article 27 of the Convention. There was a risk of their being two parallel systems of meetings, firstly the meeting of States Parties to the Convention, and secondly, the General Assembly of States Parties to the Protocol. A more rational approach would be, on the basis of Article 27, to revitalize and reinforce the systems of meetings without creating, denaturing or amending that system.[1007]

In the general discussion, his argument received the support of the delegate of Israel.[1008] Canada required the harmonization of the bodies keeping in mind the existing structure created by the Convention.[1009] W. Hays Parks, the US delegate, was in agreement with the Argentine delegate, considering that a body of intergovernmental character should be as light as possible. He stated that the supervision of the implementation of the Protocol should be the responsibility of States and that this provision could instead refer to 'the Committee or the Bureau assisting Parties in monitoring or supervising implementation of the Protocol'.[1010] The German delegate, R. Hilger, considered that Article 25 should read 'Meeting of the States Parties' and not 'General Assembly', the latter being reserved already for another institution. 'Article 27 of the Convention spoke of "Meeting of representatives of High Contracting Parties". If the name "Meeting of the Parties" was also in the main instrument, then the same name should appear throughout the Second Protocol.'[1011] Other delegates preferred that 'General Assembly' be maintained.[1012] Creusen, the Belgian delegate and rapporteur, concluded this first debate on institutional issues by suggesting that all institutional issues be grouped under Chapter 6 to avoid repetitions and contradictions in the text, since Article 25 concerns the 'Assembly of the Parties' and Article 42 concerns the 'Meeting of the Parties'.[1013]

1007   1999 Hague Conference, Plenary Session, 17 March 1999: Ariel Gonzalez, p. 144.
1008   Ibid., p. 145.
1009   Ibid., p. 148.
1010   Ibid., p. 149.
1011   Ibid., R. Hilger, p. 152.
1012   Ibid., Spanish delegate, p. 144.
1013   Ibid., p. 158

The Chairman concluded the session by announcing that János Jelen (Hungary) had agreed to Chair an informal Working Group to work on the provisions of Chapter 6.[1014] Two days of the Conference, 22 and 23 March, were reserved for working groups. At the Plenary Session on 24 March, the Chairman of this informal Working Group submitted to the delegates the revised text (HC/1999/5/Add.6), which represented a compromise between the two propositions for an institutional body present in the original UNESCO draft of the Second Protocol.[1015]

The report on the results of the Working Group on Chapter 6, presented by Ambassador Jelen, chairman of the Working Group, affirmed that the concern of delegations was 'to co-ordinate relationships between the meeting of the High Contracting Parties and the members of this Protocol and also with the General Conference of UNESCO'[1016] and to establish 'proper relationships between the meeting of the Parties to the Protocol, the Committee and all other institutional arrangements'.[1017] The document of the Working Group[1018] included the following text of Article 25:

Article 25. Meeting of the Parties
1. The Meeting of the Parties to this Protocol shall be convened at the same time as the General Conference of UNESCO, and in coordination with the Meeting of the High Contracting Parties, if such a meeting has been called by the Director-General of UNESCO.
2. The Meeting of the Parties to this Protocol shall adopt its own Rules of Procedure.
3. The Meeting of the Parties to this Protocol shall have the following functions:
   (a) to elect the Members of the Bureau, in accordance with Article 26 para. 1;

1014   Diplomatic Conference on a Draft Second Protocol to the 1954 Hague Convention for the Protection of Cultural Property in the Event of Armed Conflict. Précis, Wednesday 17 March 1999, Addendum, p. 2.
1015   Diplomatic Conference on a Draft Second Protocol to the 1954 Hague Convention for the Protection of Cultural Property in the Event of Armed Conflict. Précis, Wednesday 24 March 1999, p. 2.
1016   Conference document: Report on the results of the Working Group on Chapter 6 (Institutional isssues), presented by H. E. Ambassador János Jelen, chairman of the Working Group, [n.d.], p. 1.
1017   1999 Hague Conference, Plenary Session, 24 March 1999, p. 2.
1018   HC/1999/5/Add.6, 23 March 1999. Original: English, p. 1.

(b) to endorse the Guidelines developed by the Bureau in accordance with Article 29. para. I. a.;

(c) to provide guidelines for, and to supervise the use of the Fund by the Bureau;

(d) to consider the report submitted by the Bureau in accordance with Article 29 para. 1 d.;

(e) to discuss any problem related to the application of the present Protocol, and to make recommendations, as appropriate.

4. At the request of at least one-fifth of the Parties, the Director-Generalshall convene an Extraordinary Meeting of the Parties.

During discussion of the report of the Working Group in the Plenary Session, no comments were made on Articles 25 and 42. The text of the Working Group's proposal was transmitted to the Drafting Committee of the Conference.[1019]

With very few formal modifications, such as the replacement of the word 'Bureau' with the word 'Committee', the text proposed by the Working Group was included in the final text of the Second Protocol.

ANALYSIS OF THE TEXT

Paragraph 1

The first paragraph of this Article requires that the meeting of the Parties to the Protocol be convened at the same time as the General Conference of UNESCO:

1. The Meeting of the Parties shall be convened at the same time as the General Conference of UNESCO, and in co-ordination with the Meeting of the High Contracting Parties, if such a meeting has been called by the Director-General.

Since the General Conference must meet in ordinary session every two years, the meeting of Parties to the Protocol must also take place every two years. According to this provision, if the General Conference meets for an

---

1019   1999 Hague Conference, Plenary Session, 24 March 1999, pp. 9–10.

extraordinary session, a meeting of the Parties to the Protocol should also take place.[1020]

The meeting of the Parties to the Second Protocol has to be coordinated with the meeting of the High Contracting Parties to the Convention. The convocation of such a meeting is left to the discretion of the Director-General, who may arrange it with the approval of the Executive Board (Article 27 of the Convention), although it is probable that the meeting of the High Contracting Parties will take place at the same time.[1021]

The texts incorporate logical guidelines concerning the organization of the two meetings at the same time as the General Conference of UNESCO, for which representatives of the States of these two bodies will be present. This economic and efficient measure was welcomed by the States involved. It is the responsibility of the Director-General to proceed to the convocation of such meetings.

To date, two meetings of the Parties to the Second Protocol have taken place:

- First Meeting of the Parties, UNESCO Headquarters, Paris, 26 October 2005; and
- Second Meeting of the Parties, UNESCO Headquarters, Paris, 20 December 2007.
- The third Meeting of the Parties is foreseen for November 2009.

Paragraph 2

The Meeting of the Parties shall adopt its Rules of Procedure.

The meeting of the Parties to the Second Protocol adopted the Rules of Procedure.[1022]

1020   The meetings of the General Conference of UNESCO are regulated by Article IV, paragraph 9(a) of the Constitution of UNESCO: 'The General Conference shall meet in ordinary session every two years. It may meet in extraordinary session if it decides to do so itself or if summoned by the Executive Board, or on the demand of at least one-third of the Member States.'

1021   Chamberlain (2004, p. 221) explains that given the fact 'that the Contracting Parties to the Convention have an interest in the application of the Protocol than it would make practical sense for meeting of the Parties to the Protocol to be held in conjunction with meetings of the Partiesd to the Convention. As more States become Parties to the Protocol then the greater need arises for the two meetings to be held together'.

1022   Rules of procedure. Adopted at the first meeting of the Parties to the Second Protocol (Paris, 26 October 2005).

Paragraph 3

> 3. The Meeting of the Parties shall have the following functions:
> (a) to elect the Members of the Committee, in accordance with Article 24 paragraph 1;
> (b) to endorse the Guidelines developed by the Committee in accordance with Article 27 sub-paragraph 1(a);
> (c) to provide guidelines for, and to supervise the use of the Fund by the Committee;
> (d) to consider the report submitted by the Committee in accordance with Article 27 sub-paragraph 1(d);
> (e) to discuss any problem related to the application of this Protocol, and to make recommendations, as appropriate.

This paragraph is self-explanatory. One of the major preoccupations of the Working Group was to ensure an appropriate balance between Chapter 3 (Enhanced protection) and Chapter 6 (Institutional issues).[1023] According to the rapporteur, there was a need for close cooperation with the Working Group on Chapter 3, and an agreement was reached between two Groups. 'Equipped with a better understanding of the functions of the future body, the necessity arose to define the functions of the meeting of the Parties to the Protocol. This was done in a new Article, namely Article 25(3)'.[1024]

The meeting will exercise a leading role especially regarding supervision of the Committee, which is supposed to follow guidelines for implementation of the Protocol and make recommendations – in other words, to undertake more concrete work that it will be able to accomplish only in cooperation with the Secretariat.

Paragraph 4

> 4. At the request of at least one-fifth of the Parties, the Director-General shall convene an Extraordinary Meeting of the Parties.

This provision is self-explanatory and is inspired by the similar provision of Article 27 of the Convention, which obliges the Director-General to convene

---

1023   1999 Hague Conference, Plenary Session, 24 March 1999: Rapporteur (Chairman of the working group), pp. 1–2, Mr. Berezovsky (Austria), p. 3.
1024   Ibid., p. 2.

a meeting of the High Contracting Parties if at least one-fifth of these Parties so request. This obligation was not termed 'extraordinary' in the Convention, but was in fact so. This provision has not yet been used in practice.

Article 24

COMMITTEE FOR THE PROTECTION OF CULTURAL PROPERTY IN THE EVENT OF ARMED CONFLICT

1. *The Committee for the Protection of Cultural Property in the Event of Armed Conflict is hereby established. It shall be composed of twelve Parties which shall be elected by the Meeting of the Parties.*
2. *The Committee shall meet once a year in ordinary session and in extra-ordinary sessions whenever it deems necessary.*
3. *In determining membership of the Committee, Parties shall seek to ensure an equitable representation of the different regions and cultures of the world.*
4. *Parties members of the Committee shall choose as their representatives persons qualified in the fields of cultural heritage, defense or international law, and they shall endeavour, in consultation with one another, to ensure that the Committee as a whole contains adequate expertise in all these fields.*

Preparatory work

UNESCO, Executive Board, 142nd Session, Report by the Director-General on the Reinforcement of UNESCO's action for the Protection of the World Cultural and Natural Heritage. 142 EX/15, Paris, 18 August 1993. Annex. Meeting of experts on the application and effectiveness of the Convention for the Protection of Cultural Property in the Event of Armed Conflict (The Hague, 14 May 1954), The Hague, 5–7 July 1993, p. 4. http://unesdoc.unesco.org/images/0009/000958/095820Eo.pdf

UNESCO. The Second Expert Meeting on the 1954 Hague Convention for the Protection of Cultural Property in the Event of Armed Conflict. Lauswolt, The Netherlands, 9–11 February 1994.

UNESCO Executive Board, 145th Session. Report by the Director-General on the review of the Convention for the Protection of Cultural Property in the Event of Armed Conflict, 145 EX/21, 20 July 1994.

UNESCO. Expert meeting on the review of the 1954 Hague Convention for the Protection of Cultural Property in the Event of Armed Conflict. Paris, UNESCO Headquarters, 28 November–2 December 1994. UNESCO document CLT/CH/94/608/2, *Final Report.*

UNESCO document: a working document prepared by the Secretariat, CLT/94/608/1 of 28 November 1994.

UNESCO, Second Meeting of the High Contracting Parties to the Convention for the Protection of Cultural Property in the Event of Armed Conflict (The Hague, 1954), UNESCO House, Paris, 13 November 1995, *Final Report*. CLT-95/CONF.009/5, November 1995.

UNESCO, Meeting of Governmental Experts. Summary of comments received from States Parties to the Hague Convention and from the International Council on Archives. UNESCO document: CLT-96/CONF.603/INF.4, Paris, December 1996.

UNESCO, Meeting of Governmental Experts on the Review of the 1954 Hague Convention for the Protection of Cultural Property in the Event of Armed Conflict 1954, UNESCO Headquarters, Paris, 24–27 March 1997, *Final Report*. UNESCO document CLT-96/CONF.603/5, Paris, 30 April 1997.

UNESCO, Third Meeting of the High Contracting Parties to the Convention for the Protection of Cultural Property in the Event of Armed Conflict (The Hague, 1954), UNESCO House, Paris, 13 November 1997, *Final Report*. CLT-97/CONF.208/3, Paris, November 1997, p. 3

Draft provisions for the revision of the 1954 Hague Convention and commentary from UNESCO Secretariat. CLT-97/CONF.208/2, Paris, October 1997.

UNESCO, Meeting of Governmental Experts on the Review of the Hague Convention for the Protection of Cultural Property in the Event of Armed Conflict of 1954. Vienna, 11–13 May 1998. UNESCO document: Paris, May 1998, *Final Report*.

Preliminary Draft Second Protocol to the 1954 Hague Convention. UNESCO document HC/1999/1, October 1998 (English, French and Russian).

UNESCO, Meeting of Governmental Experts. Summary of comments received from States Parties to the Hague Convention, the International Committee of the Red Cross and the International Council on Archives. UNESCO document: Paris, March 1998.

Draft Second Protocol to the 1954 Hague Convention for the Protection of Cultural Property in the Event of Armed Conflict. UNESCO document HC/1999/1/rev.1, February 1999.

UNESCO, Synoptic report of comments on the Preliminary Draft Second Protocol to the 1954 Hague Convention received from High Contracting Parties to the Hague Convention for the Protection of Cultural Property in the Event of Armed Conflict 1954, other UNESCO Member States and international organizations, Paris, 15 January 1999.

Addendum to the Synoptic report of comments on the Preliminary Draft Second Protocol to the 1954 Hague Convention received from High Contracting Parties to the Hague Convention for the Protection of Cultural Property in the Event of Armed Conflict 1954, other UNESCO Member States and international organizations. Paris, March 1999, HC/1999/4.

1999 Hague Conference: Plenary Session of the Conference, in particular the 17, 18 and 24 March 1999.

Bibliography

Aldrich, G. H. 1998. *Analysis of the Preliminary Draft Second Protocol to the 1954 Hague Convention.* Mimeographed manuscript of 9 December, p. 15.

Boylan, P. J. 1993. *Review of the Convention for the Protection of Cultural Property in the Event of Armed Conflict (The Hague Convention of 1954).* Paris: UNESCO

Chamberlain. K. 2004. *War and Cultural Heritage.* Leicester: Institute of Art and Law, pp. 221–22.

Desch, T. 1999. The Second Protocol to the 1954 Convention for the Protection of Cultural Property in the Event of Armed Conflict. *Yearbook of International Humanitarian Law,* Vol. 2, pp. 84–85.

Government of the Netherlands. 1961. *Records of the Conference convened by the United Nations Educational, Scientific and Cultural Organization and held at The Hague from 21 April to 14 May 1954.* The Hague: Staatsdrukkerij en Uitgeverijbedrijf, pp. 224–25.

Hladík, J. 1996. Meeting of the High Contracting Parties to the Hague Convention for the Protection of Cultural Property in the Event of Armed Conflict of 1954. *International Journal of Cultural Property,* Vol. 5, No. 2, pp. 339–41.

Hladík, J. 1998b. The Third Meeting of the High Contracting Parties to the Hague Convention for the Protection of Cultural Property in the Event of Armed Conflict of 1954 (Paris, November 13, 1997). *International Journal of Cultural Property,* Vol. 7, No. 1, pp. 268–71.

Hladík, J. 1998a. The review process of the 1954 Hague Convention for the Protection of Cultural Property in the Event of Armed Conflict and its impact on international humanitarian law. *Yearbook of International Humanitarian Law,* Vol. 1, pp. 313–22.

UNESCO. 1983. Meeting of Legal Experts on the Convention for the Protection of Cultural Property in the Event of Armed Conflict (The

Hague, 1954), Vienna, 17–19 October 1983, *Final Report*, Paris, p. 10, para. 31 (CLT-83/CONF.641 /1).

Toman, J. 1983. *Le Mandat de l'UNESCO dans la mise en oeuvre de la Convention de La Haye pour la protection des biens culturels en cas de conflit armé.* Paris: UNESCO, p. 78 et seq.

The Hague Conference of 1954

Following on from previous efforts to create a supervisory body, mentioned in the introduction to this chapter,[1025] the Hague Diplomatic Conference in 1954 also considered the possibility of a permanent committee with the aim of ensuring the protection of cultural property in the event of armed conflict. It may be instructive to include here the discussion of this issue at the Conference.

During the discussion of Article 4 of the Regulations for the Execution of the Convention (Appointment of the Commissioner-General), Mr. Nyns, the Belgian delegate, reminded the meeting of the general remarks his government had submitted during the UNESCO consultation on the Draft Project (CBC/4):

> As regards the Regulations for the Execution of the Convention it must be pointed out that the control arrangements set out in Chapter I still do not ensure either a full degree of effectiveness or speed desirable. Supervision of the way in which the Convention is carried out is of primary importance. It is essential that it should enter into force at the very beginning of hostilities. In fact this is the period in which major damage to cultural property is chiefly to be feared. Article 4 calls for joint agreement between Parties in conflict on the appointment of a Commissioner-General for Cultural Property. It is to be feared that such agreement will be neither easy nor rapid. The Parties in conflict will give priority to many other measures just as urgent and it may be in the interest of the Aggressor Power to keep its hands free and delay any agreement. At a later stage, the task of the Commissioner-General, inspectors and experts could also be hampered by delay on the part of the Power to which they were accredited in paying their remuneration and expenses as prescribed in Article 10.

1025 See p. 489 ff.

'This being so, it seems wise to consider whether the appointment of the Commissioner-General and the immediate institution of supervision should not be entrusted to a permanent independent body set up in peace time and with a sufficient minima of financial resources for use if needed, the authority of which would be accepted by all Contracting Parties. Appointments by this body could, if preferred, be provisional only and subject to any later agreement within a specific period between the interested parties.'

He stressed the fact that action at the very beginning of hostilities was essential. A small permanent committee of five to seven members could be employed with the power to appoint a Commissioner-General from the list deposited with UNESCO. The Netherlands and France made the same point. The Italian amendment (CBC/DR/129), which had been submitted and dealt with the establishment of a Permanent Council, could be coordinated with the others. A single body with extensive powers could be set up, as referred to in the Italian plan. The Conference should be consulted on the question.

1200. The CHAIRMAN (E) – wondered whether, if the amendments to Article 26 of the Convention (CBC/DR/129 and 130) were adopted, Article 4 of the Regulations would have to be altered He asked the Italian delegate for his views on that point.

1201. Mr. MATIEUCCI (Italy) (F) – explained that the Italian amendment had been conceived to ensure coordination in the execution of the Convention. Most multilateral conventions, for example, the Red Cross Convention and the Universal Convention for the Protection of Copyright, referred to the establishment of a permanent committee to ensure the application of the convention. No qualified body for such a task existed within UNESCO, and it was from this fact that the idea arose of establishing within the UNESCO framework, a body ensuring the application of the Convention which would make it possible for recourse to a complicated arbitration procedure be avoided.

The choice of property to be placed under general protection had been left to each country. He asked how their number could be reduced if the list submitted by every country was too long. While in cases of disagreement, recourse might be had to the objection procedure the latter was unpleasant and to avoid it, required preliminary control by a body comprising the main Contracting Parties to the Convention.

That body would have other duties, such as the choice of Commissioners-General and other permanent tasks. The meetings referred to in Article 26 of the Draft would thus be more frequent. The name, whether council, coordinating committee or permanent bureau, was of little importance. What was important was that such a body should be representative of the Governments and would enjoy some discretion in the compilation of the lists of property falling under general protection. While an exchange of such lists was essential – it was also provided for in the Washington Pact – a general examination with the object of making recommendations to those Governments that had submitted lists which were too long was also necessary. [1026] The Italian amendment was rejected by thirty votes to five with one abstention.[1027]

Even though the Conference abandoned the idea of a committee, it was not completely forgotten. The Secretary-General of the Belgian National Commission for UNESCO later suggested the establishment of a consultative committee responsible for monitoring the execution of the Convention and for interpreting it. Such a committee might be composed of two delegates from the International Committee for Monuments and the International Council of Museums, together with two jurists (modelled on the Universal Copyright Convention).[1028]

1962 Meeting of the High Contracting Parties

The first meeting of the High Contracting Parties in 1962 considered, *inter alia*, the possibility of 'setting up an ad hoc body in the form of an advisory committee consisting of experts on the different matters covered by the Convention'.[1029]

In the course of the discussion at this first meeting of the Contracting Parties' reports, the Polish delegation drew attention to certain points in the text of the Convention: '(1) Should there be difficulties in interpreting the Convention and should the procedure which it lays down for its application prove inadequate, the Committee which it was recommended to set up might prove to have a useful part to play.'[1030]

1026   *Records*/Government of the Netherlands (1961), para. 1199–201, pp. 223–25.
1027   Ibid., para. 1214, p. 225.
1028   Toman (1983), p. 285
1029   For more information on the committee, see CUA/120, p. 3 et seq. See also Toman (1983), p. 78 et seq.
1030   Report of the meeting, document UNESCO/CUA/120 of 3 September 1962, p. 5, para. 19.

The meeting set up a group of experts to examine certain problems concerning the application of the Convention, and their report was appended to the report of the meeting, but without providing further details about the proposal of the committee.

1983 Meeting of Legal Experts on the Convention for the Protection of Cultural Property in the Event of Armed Conflict (The Hague, 1954)

Encouraged by some of these new forms of implementation, UNESCO decided to invite a group of high-level legal experts from 11 countries to meet in Vienna on 17–19 October 1983 to discuss ways of enhancing the impact of the 1954 Convention.

As we have seen, here again the idea of the committee appeared in the discussion. Among the possible remedies, the idea of a Conference of all Member States of UNESCO on the protection of heritage was mentioned,[1031] in addition to the formation of a technical advisory committee to UNESCO. The experts recommended setting up a permanent technical advisory committee, such as the one recommended at the meeting of the High Contracting Parties in 1962.[1032]

At the 1983 Expert Meeting, the lack of interest characterizing the period following the enthusiasm of the post-war years was explained by the tense international political situation of the Cold War, which alongside rapid advances in military technology led to doubts as to whether the Convention could still be effective under these new conditions and circumstances.[1033] They considered that the review process 'clearly reflected the evolution of the international relations since the Second World War and that the

---

1031   See Note 946.

1032   'Such a committee could be established within UNESCO, which would not require a revision of the Convention. It would fall within the framework of the technical assistance foreseen in Article 23 of the Convention. The Committee could take the form of a committee of experts appointed by the Director-General in their personal capacity or of a subsidiary body of the Executive Board. . . . It was furthermore recalled that a proposal to establish a permanent council of representatives of High Contracting Parties had been made at The Hague Conference in 1954.' Ibid., p. 12

1033   Ibid., p. 3. At the signing ceremony of the Second Protocol to the Hague Convention for the Protection of Cultural Property in the Event of Armed Conflict at The Hague on 16 May 1999, Mr. Colin Powers made the following statement: 'However, there was a period when the mechanism of the Hague Convention of 1954 were thoughts to have been superseded by technology: how could painting a sign on the roof of a museum to indicate a protected site be an adequate warning when the menace was an intercontinental ballistic missile? Thus little attention has been paid to the Convention in the 1970s and 1980s.' (Text as distributed at the signing ceremony, p. 3).

noted ineffectiveness was essentially due to the lack of political will on the part of the governments to put into application all the protective measures foreseen.'[1034]

No other attempts were made until the beginning of the new codifications efforts undertaken in the 1990s.

New codification process in the 1990s

At its 26th Session in 1991, the UNESCO General Conference reaffirmed its conviction 'that the preservation of the world cultural and natural heritage is of the utmost importance to all humankind' and called 'on all States to increase their efforts [in that area] to achieve better implementation of the existing instruments and to reinforce UNESCO's action'.[1035] In his report to the 1992 Executive Board's 140th Session, the Director-General indicated[1036] that the 1954 Hague Convention no longer met current requirements, citing slow ratification and unsatisfactory geographical distribution, the small number of entries in the International Register of Cultural Property under Special Protection, cumbersome procedures, the lack of account of the current state of 'military science', complex procedures for the appointment of the Commissioners-General and weak UNESCO assistance.

Patrick Boylan was asked by the UNESCO Secretariat and the Netherlands Government to prepare an in-depth analysis of these issues and to present a set of recommendations to the members of the Executive Board.[1037] His study presented the objectives and results of the operation of the Hague Convention and its Protocol and included proposals and recommendations on how to improve the Convention's and the Protocol's application and effectiveness. The study also contained a chapter on amendments that might be made to the Hague Convention in the event that a decision was taken to revise it. One of the main proposals included in his report was the creation of an intergovernmental committee:

18.7. In order to improve the understanding and application of The Hague Convention there is a need for it to be supported by an Intergovernmental Advisory Committee on the Protection of Cultural

---

1034 Ibid., p. 12.
1035 Resolution 26C/Res. 3.9, adopted on 6 November 1991.
1036 Report by the Director-General on the reinforcement of UNESCO's action for the Protection of the World Cultural and Natural Heritage, 140 EX/13 and Corr.
1037 Boylan (1993).

Property in the Event of Armed Conflict, modelled on the World Heritage Committee. The proposed terms of reference and composition are outlined in Appendix X of this Report.[1038]

To understand the substance of his proposal, we should examine Appendix X. In view of the importance of this proposal, we included here its full text to aid understanding of the future evolution of this draft:

> *APPENDIX X: Outline of recommended composition and role of the proposed Intergovernmental Advisory Committee on the Protection of Cultural Property in the Event of Armed Conflict*
>
> 1. An Intergovernmental Advisory Committee for the Protection of Cultural Property in the Event of Armed Conflict should be established within UNESCO, constituted initially under Category 11 (Articles 18–20) of the UNESCO Regulations for the general classification of the various categories of meetings convened by UNESCO.[1039] In the longer term the Committee might be re-constituted under specific powers in an updated text of the 1954 Hague Convention and Protocol, or by a new Additional Protocol, in either case incorporating appropriate arrangements for financial contributions from High Contracting Parties to meet the necessary expenses of the Committee and its Secretariat.
>
> 2. The Committee should follow in general terms the model of the World Heritage Committee,[1040] though it would not have executive powers.
>
> 3. The main purpose would be keep under review the effectiveness and implementation of the 1954 Convention and Protocol, to advise the Director General, the General Conference, States Party to the Convention, as well as non-signatory sovereign states, on appropriate practice in relation to all aspects of the implementation of the Convention and more generally on the Protection of Cultural Property in times of Armed Conflict.
>
> 4. The Intergovernmental Advisory Committee would in particular receive, review and formally publish the periodic reports of High

---

1038   Boylan (1993), para. 18.6 and 18.7, p. 144.
1039   Regulations adopted at the 14th, 18th and 25th sessions of the UNESCO General Conference. In UNESCO (1992), pp. 120–22.
1040   UNESCO, 1972. Convention concerning the Protection of the World Cultural and Natural Heritage. Chapter III, Articles 8–10.

Contracting Parties specified Article 26(2) of the 1954 Convention, and would assist the Director General in relation to the training and education programs referred to below.

5. The Committee should be composed of eleven States who shall be High Contracting Parties to the Hague Convention elected with due regard to an equitable representation of the different regions and cultures of the world at a meeting in general assembly of States Parties to the Convention held during the ordinary session of each UNESCO General Conference. The number of States members of the Committee shall be increased to fifteen States following the entry into force of the Convention for at least 100 States, and to twenty-one when the number of States Parties reaches 130.

6. The membership of States Parties to the Convention shall be rotated in accordance with the practice of the World Heritage Committee, under rules to be made by the general assembly of High Contracting Parties, based on those in Article 9 of the World Heritage Convention.

7. In addition, the following international organizations with special interest and expertise relevant to the application of the Convention may be invited by the periodic general assemblies of the High Contracting Parties to attend the meetings of the Committee in an advisory capacity: International Centre for the Study of the Preservation and Restoration of Cultural Property (ICCROM): International Committee of the Red Cross; International Council of Monuments and Sites (ICOMOS); International Council of Museums (ICOM); International Federation of Library Associations and Institutions (IFLA); International Council on Archives (ICA).[1041]

On the basis of this proposal, and several others included in Boylan's report, the Netherlands Government, in close cooperation with the UNESCO Secretariat, organized an informal, open-ended information session in Paris (9 February 1993), where Boylan presented his preliminary views on certain fundamental issues, including the proposal of the intergovernmental committee.

The Netherlands Government took the initiative, in close consultation with the Director-General of UNESCO, of convening a Meeting of Experts

---

1041   Boylan (1993), pp. 219–20.

on 5 to 7 July 1993 at The Hague. The participants examined Boylan's report and discussed the application of the Convention, including – among others – two important points:
- Institutional issues (in particular the lack of an institutional mechanism, and the possible UNESCO-UN relationship in this field – including UN peacekeeping activities and the possible role of NGOs). It was suggested that an organ could perhaps be modelled on the World Heritage Committee.
- Commissioners-General/Protecting Powers.

The final report of this meeting included several proposals concerning the proposed institutional mechanism. Concerning the future committee, the delegates

> concluded that an organ modelled along the lines of the World Heritage Committee could contribute to the more effective application of the Convention. In this connection the meeting took note of the recommendations of Professor Boylan (Appendix X of his report) concerning the appropriateness of establishing a committee, and identified various tasks and functions, such as monitoring, supervising, education and advising which could be undertaken by such an organ. This needed further elaboration, however. . . . Some delegations raised important issues relating to the more procedural aspects of the establishment of such an organ. These issues were not discussed in detail, although it was pointed out by many experts that here the practice of the World Heritage Committee and the 1970 Convention on measures against illicit traffic in cultural property could provide guidance on how to approach this matter.[1042]

On 15 October 1993, the 142nd Session of the Executive Board adopted Decision 5.5.2, which welcomed the report of the Hague Meeting of Experts and expressed, *inter alia*, the opinion that the scope of the 1954 Convention should be maintained. The Board made a series of recommendations to the 27th Session of the General Conference, which met in Paris in October

---

1042 UNESCO, Executive Board, 142th Session, Report by the Director-General on the Reinforcement of UNESCO's action for the Protection of the World Cultural and Natural Heritage. 142 EX/15, Paris, 18 August 1993. Annex. Meeting of experts on the application and effectiveness of the Convention for the Protection of Cultural Property in the Event of Armed Conflict (The Hague, 14 May 1954), The Hague, 5–7 July 1993, p. 4. http://unesdoc.unesco.org/images/0009/000958/095820Eo.pdf

and November 1993.[1043] With Resolution 3.5, adopted on the report of Commission IV at the 28th plenary meeting on 13 November 1993, the General Conference endorsed the proposals of the Executive Board and reaffirmed that 'the fundamental principles of protecting and preserving cultural property in the event of armed conflict could be considered part of international customary law'.[1044] It invited the High Contracting Parties to the 1954 Hague Convention to consider:

> (b) the need for an institutional mechanism under the 1954 Hague Convention that could perform both advisory and operational functions, taking into account the functions performed by the existing organs established under other UNESCO instruments for the protection of cultural property.[1045]

Another meeting of experts was held at Lauswolt at the invitation of the Netherlands Government on 9–11 February 1994. In this small Netherlands town was drafted the first legal instrument constituting the beginning of the process of codification that ended with the adoption of the 1999 Second Protocol. The 'Lauswolt document',[1046] as it is usually called, established the structure of Chapter 6 of the 1999 Second Protocol. It is in this document that the first version of an Article devoted to a Committee appeared. Article 14 of the Lauswolt document stated:

> Article 14. Committee[1047]
> 1. A Committee is hereby established within UNESCO. It shall be composed of [...] States Parties to this instrument which shall be elected during the ordinary session of the General Conference of

---

1043 UNESCO, Executive Board, 142th Session, Report by the Director-General on the Reinforcement of UNESCO's action for the Protection of the World Cultural and Natural Heritage. 142 EX/15, Paris, 18 August 1993, p. 4. http://unesdoc.unesco.org/images/0009/000958/095820Eo.pdf

1044 3.5. Convention for the Protection of Cultural Property in the Event of Armed Conflict (The Hague, 1954). Resolution adopted on the report of Commission IV at the 28th plenary meeting, on 13 November 1993. Records of the General Conference, 27th session, Paris, 25.10.–16.11.1993. Vol. 1, Resolutions, p. 40.

1045 Ibid., p. 40.

1046 The Second Expert Meeting on the 1954 Hague Convention for the Protection of Cultural Property in the Event of Armed Conflict. Lauswolt, The Netherlands, 9–11 February 1994.

1047 Note in the Lauswolt draft: 'The proposed provisions on the establishment of a Committee assisted by a Secretariat appointed by the Director-General of UNESCO should not be considered as reflecting the official position of UNESCO. Further consultations have to be held at UNESCO on this institutional issue.'

UNESCO in accordance with the Rules of Procedure as referred to in Article [...] of this instrument.

2. Election of members of the Committee shall ensure an equitable representation of the different regions and cultures of the world.

3. Representatives of intergovernmental or non-governmental organizations may attend the meetings of the Committee in an advisory capacity upon invitation of the Committee.

The Director-General informed the 145th Session of the Executive Board (1994) of the proposals of the Lauswolt meeting and envisaged a further meeting of technical, military and legal experts before submission of written proposals to the States Parties to the Convention. Thus, he decided to organize at least one meeting of experts before the next session of the General Conference. In his report to the Executive Board, the Director-General also expressed his intention to convene a meeting of representatives of States Parties to the Convention to be held during the 28th Session of the General Conference.[1048]

On the basis of previous studies and reports and numerous expert meetings, the UNESCO Secretariat prepared an excellent working document for the next expert session to be held in Paris in November–December 1994. This document made use of our 1996 Commentary on the Convention, Patrick Boylan's Report, and the reports of the Hague and the Lauswolt expert meetings, and provided the UNESCO Secretariat's comments on each issue.[1049] The comments of the Secretariat pertaining to the role of the committee and other institutional issues were of particular importance.

The first problem arose in relation to draft Article 13, according to which 'the States Parties are invited to encourage the Director-General of UNESCO to perform the mission of control according to the Regulations for the execution of the Convention in coordination with the Committee', and sub-paragraph 2, which stated: 'The Committee may also invite the Director-General of UNESCO to fulfill those functions'.

The Secretariat's comments were clear:

1048   UNESCO Executive Board, 145th session. Report by the Director-General on the review of the Convention for the Protection of Cultural Property in the Event of Armed Conflict, 145 EX/21, 20 July 1994, para. 4–6, p. 2.

1049   UNESCO document: a working document prepared by the Secretariat, CLT/94/608/1 of 28 November 1994.

The Secretariat approves this decision which strengthens the legal basis of the action of the Director-General. However, a slight ambiguity remains concerning the meaning, in actual practice, of the words 'in coordination with the Committee'. The 'Committee' is the body proposed by the Lauswolt experts in Article 14 concerning institutional issues. Considering that one criticism made of the present system of Commissioners-General is its unwieldiness, there is clearly a danger that the involvement of a 'Committee' will make this control procedure even more cumbersome. Is there not a case to be made for considering that the Director-General – in view of the fact that, as the head of an intergovernmental body, he is empowered to represent its views as with one voice – has more scope and room for manoeuvre in situations of conflict between states than a committee made up of representatives of states?[1050]

The Secretariat preferred to leave the role of encouragement to the meeting of the State Parties.

The Secretariat drew attention to the fact that it was Patrick Boylan and the 1993 Hague meeting that made the proposal concerning the committee, for which the Lauswolt meeting of experts reserved five articles. The UNESCO Secretariat's comments are extremely relevant to present questions on the committee's role, and therefore it seems worthwhile to reproduce them here *in toto*:

The UNESCO Secretariat has carefully considered these proposals but has some hesitation about their adoption. It is true that such a committee would be likely to attract more interest in the Convention and could perhaps give more publicity to breaches of its provisions. However there are several difficulties with the proposal.

 (i) The Hague Convention, which applies in time of conflict, usually becomes relevant in very tense political situations (recent examples, the Gulf conflict, and the present conflict in ex-Yugoslavia). States Parties to the Convention may not wish to invest such a Committee, on which it is only intermittently represented, with executive powers over a conflict in which it is engaged.

 (ii) The servicing of an Intergovernmental Committee requires considerable financial resources. Each Committee, if held at

---

1050 Ibid., p. 19 ff. (italics in original)

Headquarters in the two working languages (as is the World Heritage Committee), for 20 members for 4 days, would cost US$20,000. If held in 5 languages (as is the Intergovernmental Committee for Promoting the Return of Cultural Property to its Countries of Origin or its Restitution in case of Illicit Appropriation), each Committee would cost US$45,000. Since the Executive Board has determined that there should be no increase in the budget of UNESCO, it would have to decide from what part of the programme the additional funds to finance the Committee could be taken;

(iii) The need to call together a Committee, in an urgent situation, could considerably slow down the procedures which could be applied in cases of urgency.

The **World Heritage Committee** is financed from the **World Heritage Fund**, set up under the World Heritage Convention. It might be argued that **Parties to the Hague Convention 1954** should themselves contribute pro *rata funds* for the activities of the Committee. However such a provision may deter many States from becoming Party to the Convention, many States which it would be particularly important to have participate.

UNESCO wishes to propose an alternative. Since there was a strong feeling among the experts that there should be some body representing the States Parties to assist UNESCO in the implementation of the Convention, it is proposed that a Bureau and an Advisory Committee be established. These should be cheaper and able to act more quickly than an intergovernmental committee, while able to contribute substantially to the work of the Convention.

(i) A bureau could be elected by a meeting of States Parties called at the same time as the General Conference (as will be done for the first time in 1995). The Bureau could consist of a President, 4 Vice-Presidents and a Rapporteur, elected with due regard to geographical distribution which could be called on at any time by the Director-General. Alternatively, the Bureau could meet regularly (e.g. in the year when the General Conference is not held) in order to take up any questions of particular importance which members may wish to raise.

(ii) An advisory committee (Category V) could be made up of representatives of ICOM, ICOMOS and ICCROM which could be constantly consulted by the Director-General and called into session in emergencies. The advantage of this procedure would be its speed, as these bodies (two in Paris, one in Rome) could meet within hours if necessary. As these bodies also receive information from their own national sections and contacts, they could usefully exchange information with the UNESCO Secretariat. The majority of expert consultants sent out under the Convention are also likely to be members of these bodies, and they have a useful store of expertise in emergency action. (A committee of the three chief executives of these bodies is under consideration as the 'International Committee of the Blue Shield (ICBS)' which would liaise with UNESCO and national emergency Blue Shield societies for emergency care of cultural property.)

The institution of these two bodies would give the Convention a new support structure and would provide additional assistance to the Director-General who could call on the ICBS in emergencies and the elected Bureau in situations which call for a statement of position on behalf of the States Parties to the Convention or at any other appropriate time.

Accordingly, UNESCO proposes the following two articles:

Alternative Article 14

   (a) The Director-General will call a meeting of States Parties to the Convention to be held at the same time as the General Conference of UNESCO.
   (b) The meeting shall elect a Bureau, consisting of 6 States Parties to the Convention, with due regard to equitable representation of the different regions and cultures of the world. It shall elect a President and a Rapporteur.
   (c) The Bureau shall hold office for two years and shall hold at least one meeting each year. The Director-General of UNESCO may call the Bureau into session at any other time as he considers necessary.
   (d) The Bureau shall adopt its own rules of procedure.

(d) [A representative of ICOMOS (the International Council of Monuments and Sites), a representative of ICOM (International Council of Museums) and a representative of the International Centre for the Study of the Preservation and Restoration of Cultural Property (Rome Centre) (ICCROM)] [Representatives of the International Committee of the Blue Shield] may attend the meetings of the Bureau in an advisory capacity.[1051]

Alternative Article 15
The Director of ICOMOS, the Secretary-General of ICOM and the Director of ICCROM shall constitute the International Committee of the Blue Shield (ICBS). ICBS shall maintain a network of cultural experts willing to act in emergencies and shall provide advice to the Director-General of UNESCO in any emergency concerning cultural property.

Article 16 (Rules of Procedure) and 17 (Functions) of the **Lauswolt document** would then be suppressed.[1052]

The next Paris Expert Meeting of legal and cultural experts and military professionals met at UNESCO Headquarters from 28 November to 2 December 1994. The second part of the meeting was devoted to a study of new legal provisions and gave rise to a broad range of differing views among the participants, particularly from those who had helped in the preparation of the Lauswolt document, among others, and included the Secretariat's proposal of a Bureau of States Parties and the proposal of an advisory committee, as mentioned above. The advantage of the second proposal was the lower cost and the potential for rapid response so necessary in emergencies. The author of these lines made a comparison with the ICRC, which has a rather large Secretariat, and this idea was also reflected in the report.[1053] In addition, it was pointed out that the Secretariat should be reinforced. A general meeting of all States Parties could also be held on a regular (biennial) basis.

The Second Meeting of the High Contracting Parties to the 1954 Convention was convened by the Director-General at UNESCO

1051   The second paragraph (d) is an alternative provision as marked in the original.
1052   Ibid., pp. 20–22 (italics and boldface in the original text).
1053   UNESCO, Expert Meeting on the Review of the 1954 Hague Convention for the Protection of Cultural Property in the Event of Armed Conflict. Paris, UNESCO Headquarters, 28 November–2 December 1994, document CLT/CH/94/2, *Final Report*, p. 5.

Headquarters on Monday, 13 November 1995,[1054] on the occasion of the 28th Session of the General Conference, in conformity with Decision 5.5.5, which the Executive Board adopted at its 145th session in October–November 1994.

> [A] number of participants expressed the need for the creation of a supervisory body which would monitor the implementation of the Convention. However, it was pointed out that such a body should be flexible and able to act in case of necessity; its nature and composition are yet to be determined. Some countries pointed out that such a body might be an intergovernmental committee which would be analogous to the World Heritage Committee. This proposal, however, did not receive unanimous support as some delegates expressed their concern about additional expense caused by its creation and its activities. An alternative would be to create an advisory body composed of experts and representatives of non-governmental organizations.[1055]

The 149th Session of the Executive Board approved the Director-General's proposal to invite 20 States to appoint one expert to participate in the 1997 Governmental Experts Meeting.[1056] The Secretariat submitted to the meeting the 1996 *Summary of comments* received from States Parties to the Hague Convention and the ICA.[1057] Several States presenting their comments agreed on the need for a supervisory body without expressing a preference for a proposed form for this body, and the Secretariat in its comments summarized the present state of proposals.[1058]

1054 UNESCO, Second Meeting of the High Contracting Parties to the Convention for the Protection of Cultural Property in the Event of Armed Conflict (The Hague, 1954), UNESCO House, Paris, 13 November 1995, *Final Report*. CLT-95/CONF.009/5, November 1995. See also Hladík (1996).

1055 Ibid., p. 3.

1056 UNESCO, Meeting of Governmental Experts on the Review of the 1954 Hague Convention for the Protection of Cultural Property in the Event of Armed Conflict 1954, UNESCO Headquarters, Paris, 24–27 March 1997, *Final Report*. UNESCO document CLT-96/CONF.603/5, Paris, 30 April 1997.

1057 UNESCO, Meeting of Governmental Experts. Summary of comments received from States Parties to the Hague Convention and from the International Council on Archives. UNESCO document: CLT-96/CONF.603/INF.4, Paris, December 1996. As of 28 November 1996, the Secretariat had received replies from nine States of the total number of 88 States Parties to the Convention.

1058 UNESCO, Meeting of Governmental Experts. Summary of comments received from States Parties to the Hague Convention and from the International Council on Archives. UNESCO document: CLT-96/CONF.603/INF.4, Paris, December 1996, pp. 8–9.

The Meeting of Governmental Experts on the Review of the 1954 Hague Convention for the Protection of Cultural Property in the Event of Armed Conflict 1954 met at UNESCO Headquarters on 24–27 March 1997. The experts also received an Information Note suggesting points on which they might focus their work,[1059] the provisional agenda,[1060] and the provisional rules of procedure.[1061] Institutional issues formed an important part of the discussion (draft Articles 14–17), but the experts could not reach a consensus on the form of such a body: committee or bureau, as discussed above. It was also proposed to set up a fund that could allocate financial resources.

> Some States were in favour of establishing an intergovernmental committee, others preferred to elect a six-member Bureau during the meeting of States Parties convened on the occasion of the General Conference. Option I of the redrafted Articles establishes the Intergovernmental Committee, Option II creates the Bureau of States Parties.

1059 *Information Note*, UNESCO document: CLT-96/CONF.603/INF.3, Paris, November 1996. The following points were suggested:

15. When discussing the improvement of the Convention, the Governmental experts may wish to focus their work on the following points:

- the reconsideration of the whole concept of Special Protection and of criteria for inscription in the *International Register of Cultural Property under Special Protection* of the Convention and its functioning;
- the replacement of the existing control system of the Convention by a more flexible and efficient structure, the form that such alternative system could take;
- the notion of 'military necessity';
- the reinforcement of sanctions for violation of the Convention;
- individual and state criminal responsibility;
- the improvement of the implementation of the Convention in conflicts not of an international character;
- the desirability of setting up a supervisory body which would monitor the implementation of the Convention and the form that such a body could take (intergovernmental, advisory or expert body) and its functions;
- the enhancement of the potential role of the United Nations peacekeeping forces in the implementation of the Convention;
- the growing role of non-governmental organizations in the preservation and protection of cultural heritage in the event of armed conflict and how they could participate in the implementation of the Convention;
- the opportunity for adopting new international norms reflecting the results and discussions of the above and the procedure to adopt these norms;
- either by amendments to the Convention;
- or by the adoption of a Protocol to the Convention;
- or by a new Convention.

1060 UNESCO document CLT-96/CONF.603/1.

1061 UNESCO document CLT/96/CONF.603/3.

22. One delegate noted that his country strongly opposed the creation of new intergovernmental committees. The majority of participants, however, stressed the advantages of having an Intergovernmental Committee which would give more weight to the practical implementation of the Convention and would involve States more closely in it implementation. It would, therefore, not only ensure a better application of a new instrument but it would also enhance awareness of the world public opinion on the destruction of cultural property. The principal tasks of the Committee would be to grant special protection, to monitor the implementation of the new instrument and to carry out technical assistance. It was also proposed to set up a trust Fund which could allocate financial resources on projects for the protection of cultural heritage in the event of armed conflict.

23. The creation of the Bureau would have certain financial and operational advantages. The Bureau would include a President and a Rapporteur and could be called on at any time by the Director-General. If necessary, the Bureau could meet regularly (e.g. in the year when the General Conference is not held) to take up an important questions which members may wish to raise. The Bureau would be assisted by the International Committee of the Blue Shield and ICCROM.[1062]

The results of the discussions that took place at the 1997 Paris Meeting of Experts were included in the 'revised Lauswolt document', which was distributed on 27 March 1997 at the closure of the meeting. This document presented a new version of the articles, reflecting the discussions at this and previous expert meetings.

As there was no unanimous agreement among experts regarding whether to give preference to an intergovernmental committee or a bureau (with an advisory board), the following two options were both included within the revised Lauwolt document:

> OPTION 1: Article 14 Committee
> Article 15 Term of office
> Article 16 Rules of procedure

[1062] UNESCO, Meeting of Governmental Experts on the Review of the 1954 Hague Convention for the Protection of Cultural Property in the Event of Armed Conflict 1954, UNESCO Headquarters, Paris, 24–27 March 1997, *Final Report*. UNESCO document CLT-96/ CONF.603/5, Paris, 30 April 1997, p. 4.

Article 17 Functions
Article 17a The Fund

OPTION 2: Article 1 Bureau
Article 15 The International Committee of the Blue Shield
Article 16 Rules of Procedure (no text)
Article 17 Functions (no text)
Article 18 Secretariat

We reproduce here the draft Articles concerning 'Option 1: Committee' and 'Option 2: Bureau', as well as Article 15, 'The International Committee of the Blue Shield'. Other draft articles relating to these two options (concerning the term of office, rules of procedure, functions and the fund), will be reproduced below under the commentary on Articles 25–29.

OPTION 1: Article 14 Committee[1063]
1. A Committee is hereby established within UNESCO. It shall be composed of . . . States Parties to this instrument which shall be elected *by the States Parties*[1064] during the ordinary session of the General Conference of UNESCO in accordance with the Rules of Procedure as referred to in Article . . . of this instrument.
2. Election of members of the Committee shall ensure an equitable representation of the different regions and cultures of the world.
[3. States members of the Committee shall choose as their representatives persons qualified in the fields of defense, international law and culture.][1065]

1063 Revised Lauswolt document. 27 March 1997. Mimeographed text established by the Secretariat (boldface in the original). See also UNESCO, *Draft provisions for the revision of the 1954 Hague Convention and commentary from the UNESCO Secretariat*. CLT-97/CONF.208/2, Paris, October 1997, p. 18.

1064 The Secretariat explained that the phrase 'by the States Parties' was included in paragraph 1 in order to make clear that it is the States Parties, not the General Conference of UNESCO, which will elect the Committee. UNESCO, *Draft provisions for the revision of the 1954 Hague Convention and commentary from the UNESCO Secretariat*. CLT-97/CONF.208/2, Paris, October 1997, p. 21.

1065 Paragraph 3 introduces a new element on the profile of the members of the Committee. UNESCO, *Draft provisions for the revision of the 1954 Hague Convention and commentary from the UNESCO Secretariat*. CLT-97/CONF.208/2, Paris, October 1997, p. 21.

4. Representatives of intergovernmental or non-governmental organizations may attend the meeting of the Committee in an advisory capacity upon invitation of the Committee.[1066]

OPTION 2: Article 14 Bureau[1067] [1068]

(a) The Director-General will call a meeting of States Parties to the Convention to be held at the same time as the General Conference of UNESCO.

(b) The meeting shall elect a Bureau, consisting of 6 States party to the Convention, with due regard to equitable representation of the different regions and cultures of the world. It shall elect a President and Rapporteur.

(c) The Bureau shall hold office for two years and shall hold at least one meeting each year. The Director-General of UNESCO may call the Bureau into session at any other time as he considers necessary.

(d) The Bureau shall adopt its own rules of procedure.

(e) Representatives of the International Committee of the Blue Shield (ICBS) shall attend the Bureau in an advisory capacity. A representative of the International Centre for the Study of the Preservation and Restoration of Cultural Property (Rome Centre) (ICOROM)] shall also be invited to attend.[1069]

1066 Revised Lauswolt document, 27 March 1997. Mimeographed text established by the Secretariat (boldface text in the original). See also UNESCO, *Draft provisions for the revision of the 1954 Hague Convention and commentary from the UNESCO Secretariat.* CLT-97/CONF.208/2, Paris, October 1997, p. 18.

1067 Revised Lauswolt document. 27 March 1997. Roneographed text established by the Secretariat. See also UNESCO, *Draft provisions for the revision of the 1954 Hague Convention and commentary from the UNESCO Secretariat.* CLT-97/CONF.208/2, Paris, October 1997, p. 18.

1068 Note in the Revised Lauswolt document: 'These provisions would be further developed if a decision was taken to select this option.' The Secretariat explained in the document UNESCO, *Draft provisions for the revision of the 1954 Hague Convention and commentary from the UNESCO Secretariat.* CLT-97/CONF.208/2, Paris, October 1997, pp. 23–24, the reasons for this provision, which was not in the original Laudwolt document: 'Option II proposed by the Secretariat in the working papers for the expert meeting in November – December 1994 in Paris (UNESCO document CLT/94/608/1 of 28 November 1994, pp. 21–22) fundamentally differs from Option I by proposing an *ad hoc* body – a Bureau of States Parties to the Convention – which would be convened on the occasion of the General Conference and would not have a permanent character. This body would be more flexible than a permanent intergovernmental committee and would also have certain financial advantages. However, as the meeting has not reached unanimity on either option, the institutional question will be subject to further negotiation. If Option II is chosen, these provisions will need to be substantially supplemented.'

1069 Ibid. The International Committee of the Blue Shield proposed to modify paragraph (e) of Article 14 as indicated in the following footnotes in relation to Article 15 (Option II).

Article 15. The International Committee of the Blue Shield
The ICBS shall maintain a network of experts willing to act in
emergencies and shall provide advice to the Director-General of
UNESCO in any emergency concerning cultural property.[1070]

The UNESCO Secretariat reprinted the 'revised Lauswolt document' of 1997
with several terminological proposals along with the Secretariat's comments
comparing the original provisions of the Lauswolt document (prepared
in February 1994) with the revised provisions of 1997. In this document,
such comments are entitled 'Reasons for change'. The Secretariat has also
summarized the main points raised in the discussion in the section 'Main
points of discussion'.[1071]

This document was submitted to the Third Meeting of the High
Contracting Parties, which met during the 29th Session of the UNESCO
General Conference.[1072] This meeting took place at UNESCO Headquarters
on 13 November 1997. A majority of speakers at this meeting were in favour
of creating a permanent intergovernmental committee that would be vested
with large responsibilities as reflected in Option I of the March 1997 Expert
Meeting. Some delegates opposed this concept, invoking the costs of such
a committee, the existing mandate of UNESCO, and the need to prevent
overlaps between activities of the various units of UNESCO.[1073]

The final resolution invited States Parties to provide comments on the
draft provisions by 1 February 1998 and convened a preparatory meeting of

---

1070   Ibid. The International Committee of the Blue Shield proposed to modify Article 15 (Option II)
       as follows: 'Representatives of the International Committee of the Blue Shield (ICBS) established
       by the International Council on Archives (ICA), the International Council of Monuments and
       Sites (ICOMOS) and the International Federation of Library Associations (IFLA) shall attend
       the Committee in an advisory capacity. A representative of the International Centre for the Study
       of the Preservation and Restoration of Cultural Property (Rome Centre) (ICCROM) shall also
       be invited to participate.' UNESCO, *Draft provisions for the revision of the 1954 Hague Convention
       and commentary from the UNESCO Secretariat.* CLT-97/CONF.208/2, Paris, October 1997,
       p. 22.
1071   Ibid. It was indicated in the footnote that this document should be read together with the final
       report of the March 1997 meeting of government experts in the review of the Hague Convention
       1954 (UNESCO document CLT-96/CONF.603/5).
1072   UNESCO, Third Meeting of the High Contracting Parties to the Convention for the Protection
       of Cultural Property in the Event of Armed Conflict (The Hague, 1954), UNESCO House,
       Paris, 13 November 1997, *Final Report.* CLT-97/CONF.208/3, Paris, November 1997. See also
       Hladík (1998b).
1073   UNESCO, Third Meeting of the High Contracting Parties to the Convention for the Protection
       of Cultural Property in the Event of Armed Conflict (The Hague, 1954), UNESCO House,
       Paris, 13 November 1997, *Final Report.* CLT-97/CONF.208/3, Paris, November 1997, p. 3.

Government Experts in Vienna on 11–13 May 1998.[1074] In the comments, no unanimity was reached on the choice between the two options.[1075]

At the 1998 Vienna Meeting of Governmental Experts on the Revision of the Hague Convention for the Protection of Cultural Property in the Event of Armed Conflict of 1954:

> the participants considered the two options contained in the revised Lauswolt document as well as a fact sheet prepared by UNESCO on the practical, staffing and financial implications. All the speakers emphasized the necessity of elaborating an efficient institutional framework. Although several delegates spoke in favour of Option II (election of a non-permanent bureau of States Parties), most delegates were in favour of the creation of an intergovernmental committee inspired by the proposal contained in Option I of the revised Lauswolt document. A number of important concerns were expressed regarding the composition, the function and the financial implications of such a Committee. It was considered that it should not have more than twelve members and that it should be based on an equitable geographical distribution. Reference was also made to the useful precedent of Article 90 (International Fact-Finding Commission) of Protocol I to the Geneva Conventions. The professional expertise of specialized international non-governmental organizations was recognized and it was unanimously felt important that their role be clearly mentioned in the text of Option I. Two particular concerns were expressed: first that the functions of the Committee should be further elaborated and second that careful attention be given to financial implications in order to allow the Committee to perform its functions.[1076]

The experts asked the UNESCO Secretariat to prepare a comprehensive working document to be distributed well in advance of the Diplomatic

---

1074 Ibid., Annex.
1075 UNESCO, Meeting of Governmental Experts on the Revision of the Hague Convention for the Protection of Cultural Property in the Event of Armed Conflict, Vienna, 11–13 May 1998. Summary of comments received from States Parties to the Hague Convention, the International Committee of the Red Cross and the International Council on Archives, Paris, March 1998, p. 7.
1076 UNESCO, Meeting of Governmental Experts on the Revision of the Hague Convention for the Protection of Cultural Property in the Event of Armed Conflict of 1954, Vienna, 11–13 May 1998. UNESCO document: Paris, May 1998, *Final Report*, p. 4.

Conference, which the Netherlands proposed generously to hold in The Hague from 14 to 26 March 1999.[1077]

Following the May 1998 Vienna meeting on the revision of the Hague Convention for the Protection of Cultural Property in the Event of Armed Conflict 1954, the authorities of the Netherlands, with the assistance of the UNESCO Secretariat, elaborated a *Preliminary Draft Second Protocol to the 1954 Hague Convention*.[1078] This draft was submitted for consideration to the High Contracting Parties to the Convention and for information to other Member States of UNESCO and the UN and selected international organizations. By 15 January 1999, the Secretariat had received substantive replies from 15 High Contracting Parties to the Convention, which were included in the Synoptic report of comments.[1079] On the basis of these comments,[1080] the UNESCO Secretariat and the Government of the Netherlands drew up the final draft of the Second Protocol: the *Draft Second Protocol to the 1954 Hague Convention for the Protection of Cultural Property in the Event of Armed Conflict* (UNESCO doc. HC/1999/1/rev.1, February 1999),[1081] which was submitted to the Diplomatic Conference in March 1999.

We present here the text of the Articles on 'Committee' and 'Bureau' proposed to the Diplomatic Conference. The Articles concerning other institutional issues (term of office, rules of procedure, functions and the fund) will be presented below in our commentary on Articles 25–29.[1082]

1077   The Report was also transmitted to the 155th UNESCO Executive Board, 155 EX/51, Paris, 17 August 1998.

1078   *Preliminary Draft Second Protocol to the 1954 Hague Convention.* UNESCO document HC/1999/1, October 1998 (English, French and Russian).

1079   UNESCO, Synoptic report of comments on the Preliminary Draft Second Protocol to the 1954 Hague Convention received from High Contracting Parties to the Hague Convention for the Protection of Cultural Property in the Event of Armed Conflict 1954, other UNESCO Member States and international organizations. Paris, 15 January 1999, Original: English. See also Addendum to the Synoptic report of comments on the Preliminary Draft Second Protocol to the 1954 Hague Convention received from High Contracting Parties to the Hague Convention for the Protection of Cultural Property in the Event of Armed Conflict 1954, other UNESCO Member States and international organizations. Paris, March 1999, HC/1999/4.

1080   In these comments, Armenia, China, Finland, France, Georgia, Israel, Italy, Turkey (with 18 Members) and Switzerland favoured the Committee. Germany and Spain preferred a Bureau of States Parties. Other comments are included under the other Articles of Chapter 6.

1081   Draft Second Protocol to the 1954 Hague Convention for the Protection of Cultural Property in the Event of Armed Conflict. UNESCO doc. HC/1999/1/rev.1, February 1999 (English, French and Russian).

1082   The following explanatory note was included in the document HC/1999/1/rev.1: 'Articles 26–30 deal with a new administrative body which has been proposed: the Committee. An alternative scheme for a Bureau only will be found in square brackets and in italics below Article 30.'

Chapter 6. Institutional issues

Article 25. General Assembly of Parties[1083]

Article 26. Committee

1. A Committee is hereby established. It shall be composed of 12 Parties which shall be elected by the General Assembly of Parties.
2. The Committee shall meet once every two years in ordinary session. If deemed necessary by the Bureau the Committee may meet in extra-ordinary session in between regular Committee meetings.
3. Election of Members of the Committee shall ensure an equitable representation of the different regions and cultures of the world.
4. Parties Members of the Committee shall choose as their representatives persons qualified in the fields of defence, international law or cultural administration.
5. From its midst the Committee shall choose a Bureau consisting of 3 Members. It shall elect a Chairperson and a Rapporteur. The Bureau shall meet at least once a year (between regular Committee meetings.)

Article 27. Terms of office[1084]

Article 28. Rules of Procedure[1085]

Article 29. Functions[1086]

Article 30. Procedure before the Committee relating to enhanced special protection[1087]

[Alternative Articles 26–29 for a lighter administrative structure][1088]

1083   See our comments under Article 23 below.
1084   See our comments under Article 25 below.
1085   See our comment under Article 26 below.
1086   See our comments under Article 27 below.
1087   See Chapter 3 on enhanced protection, p. 175 ff.
1088   Option II: alternative Articles 26–29 are printed in italics in the original.

Article 26. Bureau

1. *A Bureau of Parties is hereby established. It shall be composed of six Parties to this Protocol which shall be elected by the General Assembly of Parties in accordance with the Rules of Procedure established by that General Assembly.*

2. *The Bureau shall meet once a year in ordinary session and in extra-ordinary sessions whenever the Bureau deems such sessions necessary.*

3. *Election of Members of the Bureau shall ensure an equitable representation of the different regions and cultures of the world.*

4. *Each Member of the Bureau shall be represented by a person notified to the Director-General who is qualified in one or more of the following fields: defence, international law, or cultural administration. Each Member may also designate several alternate representatives similarly qualified.*

5. *From its Members, the Bureau shall elect a President and a Rapporteur.*

Article 27. Terms of office[1089]

Article 28. Rules of Procedure[1090]

Article 29. Functions[1091]

The Diplomatic Conference on the Second Protocol to the Hague Convention of 1954 for the Protection of Cultural Property in the Event of Armed Conflict took place in The Hague from 15 to 26 March 1999. Discussion of institutional issues began in the latter part of the afternoon session on Wednesday, 17 March 1999, and the early part of the morning session of Thursday, 18 March, in the Plenary Session. The discussion was based

---

1089   The specific Articles on the terms of office, rules of procedure and functions of the Bureau are also included under the specific articles. See our comments under Article 25 below.

1090   The specific Articles on the terms of office, rules of procedure and functions of the Bureau are also included under the specific articles. See our comments under Article 26 below.

1091   The specific Articles on the terms of office, rules of procedure and functions of the Bureau are also included under the specific articles. See our comments under Article 27 below. There is no draft Article 30 (Procedure before the Committee relating to enhanced special protection) in the alternative draft articles.

on Chapter 6 of the Draft Second Protocol (5HC/1999/1/rev.1, February 1999).[1092]

First part of the discussion on institutional issues (17–18 March 1999)

The decision concerning a monitoring institution was present throughout the whole period of preparatory work: should the choice be an intergovernmental committee or a bureau accomplishing more practical daily work concerning the implementation of the Convention and the new Protocol?

The representative of the Secretariat, Lyndel Prott, expressed the view of the Director-General of UNESCO. According to him, it would be more in line with present policies in international administration not to expand unduly the administration. But if the members of the Conference felt that the intergovernmental committee was the more appropriate way to go, 'he would try and see that the right resources were available'.[1093]

Several delegations questioned the argument that an intergovernmental body was the best forum to take such fundamental decisions relating to the protection of cultural property. The delegates were afraid that such a body would create enormous bureaucracy[1094] and would constitute a great financial burden.[1095] It might also lead to unnecessary politicization of any decisions that had to be reached, which might prove particularly difficult in situations of conflict.[1096] Many delegates suggested that an impartial and expert body would be better able to assume the responsibility of taking such decisions and nominating cultural property for inclusion on the list of cultural property. They preferred a body of a light bureaucratic nature, modest and flexible, composed of maximum of 12 representatives. [1097]

The delegates of Australia and Thailand went even further by proposing a third option: the creation of a body that would be composed of individuals independent of their governments.[1098]

1092 Draft Second Protocol to the 1954 Hague Convention for the Protection of Cultural Property in the Event of Armed Conflict, UNESCO doc. HC/1999/1/rev.1, February 1999 (English, French and Russian).

1093 1999 Hague Conference, Plenary Session of the Conference, 17 March 1999, p. 140.

1094 Ibid., Lebanese delegate, p. 141.

1095 Ibid., Spanish delegate, p. 144.

1096 Ibid., delegate of Australia suported by the delegate of Thailand, p. 142, 144.

1097 Ibid., Canada, p. 148.

1098 Ibid., p. 142. The delegate gave the example of a fact-finding commission or related body such as the International Narcotics Control Board.

The delegate of Argentina, Ariel Gonzalez, based his evaluation on three criteria for a rational approach:[1099]

> The financial situation of the organization: even if the Director-General is willing to provide financial resources, he will be obliged to follow the decisions of the Conference and the Executive Board. UNESCO already has several Committees. 'The multiplication of institutional mechanisms should therefore be avoided.'
>
> The scope of the object: the distinction should be made between the universal and permanent scope of protection in the framework of World Heritage Convention of 1972 and the more specific protection required during armed conflict when an institutional scheme would be needed to regulate and protect.
>
> The functions to be accomplished require a lighter administrative structure and for this reason a Bureau is preferable.

Other delegations held a different view, believing that decisions concerning cultural property should only be taken within the context of an intergovernmental committee because of the potential political implications of such decisions. Some States felt that such a committee could fairly reflect the cultural diversity of the States Parties[1100] and that an intergovernmental body was essential to the implementation not only of the Draft Second Protocol but also of the Hague Convention.[1101] The preference for a committee was expressed by the delegates of Italy,[1102] the Netherlands,[1103] Turkey and China (but both Turkey and China requiring a larger number of members, between 18 and 24), India,[1104] Greece[1105] and Belgium.[1106] The US delegate was also in favour of it, but on the condition that it be 'as light as possible'.[1107] The need for sufficient financial means was stressed by China, considering that 'if contributions were compulsory, it may damage the universality of the present Protocol'.[1108]

1099 Ibid., Argentine delegate, p. 143. His idea was supported by other delegates: Israel, ibid., p. 145 (insisting on equitable representation); US, p. 149; Austria, p. 153.
1100 Ibid., French delegate, p. 150.
1101 Ibid., delegates of France and the Netherlands, pp. 150, 153.
1102 Ibid., p. 147.
1103 Ibid., p. 153.
1104 Ibid., p. 154.
1105 Ibid., p. 155.
1106 Ibid., p. 158.
1107 Ibid., US delegate, p. 149.
1108 Ibid., Chinese delegate, p. 155.

Even those who did not express a preference for one form of body or another considered that it should be different from the World Heritage Committee.[1109] Such a body should be composed of qualified members – representatives, persons qualified in the fields of defense, international law or cultural affairs – and 'they should endeavour, in consultation with one another, to ensure that the Committee or the Bureau as a whole contains adequate expertise in all these fields'.[1110] This idea was expressed in the end of paragraph 4.

Some States felt that all the articles of the Draft Second Protocol relating to the responsibilities of the intergovernmental committee should fall under Chapter 6 and that the chapter should therefore be reformulated to include certain provisions of Articles 12, 16 and 17. The view was also expressed that the reformulation of Chapter 6 should clearly define the respective roles of the intergovernmental committee, and those of the advisory bodies.

With respect to Article 25, the view was expressed that since the Draft Second Protocol is a supplementary document, it should revitalize the meetings provided for in Article 27 of the Hague Convention, rather than making provision for new meetings (Draft Second Protocol, art. 25(2)).

The view was stated that the functions of the intergovernmental committee should include the monitoring of provisions of the Hague Convention; this would further extend the role of the committee from simply monitoring 'enhanced special protection' to that of monitoring both this higher level of protection and general protection. Some delegations felt that there was a need for Article 19(d) to be clarified in order to reflect the reason for and intended use of the Fund, and that Article 29(g) should include a provision obliging the Committee to report on the use of the Fund.

Many States seemed to favour the idea that only voluntary contributions should be made to the Fund (art. 32). Other States felt that contributions should be compulsory to ensure the viability of the Fund.

The Chairman concluded the session by announcing that János Jelen (Hungary) had agreed to chair an informal Working Group to work on the provisions of Chapter 6.

1109   Ibid., Swedish delegate, ibid., p. 151.
1110   Ibid., p. 152. Supported by the delegate of Germany and Greece, pp. 153, 155.

Working Group[1111]

In the comments on Article 24, we shall deal only with the issues relating to the committee or bureau. All other issues concerning Chapter 6 (Institutional issues) will be discussed below under each of the Articles 25–29.

The Working Group on Chapter 6 was mandated to produce a consensus text on the institutional issues relating to the implementation of the Second Protocol to the 1954 Convention. The basis for discussions was the draft text in document HC/1999/rev.1, with the debate in the plenary sessions to take place on 17 March 1999. The only open question that remained to be decided by the future plenary session was the title of the new institution to be created after the ratification of the Second Protocol by the requested number of States Parties to that Protocol.

During deliberations on the draft text, the Working Group devoted most of its time to discussing the following issues:

- The functions of the new institution to be established.
- The relationship among the statutory bodies of the Convention and the Protocol, including a special emphasis on the Director-General and the Secretariat of UNESCO.
- The establishment of the new fund (to be discussed under Article 29).
- The title of the new body.
- The definition of the NGOs and their role in the functioning of the new institution.
- The role of the guidelines for the operation of the new body and the use of the funds made available for the new body.

Because the Working Group's report is the only available description of the deliberations, it is reproduced here in full:[1112]

> The text emerged as a result of 10 hours of intensive debate between Delegations with widely different attitudes about the future role, functions and resources for establishing a new intergovernmental body for managing the implementation of the Second Protocol. The long debate about the title of the new body was actually related to the differences among the Delegations regarding the interpretation of

---

1111   Report of the results of the Working Group on Chapter 6 (Institutional issues). H.E. Ambassador János Jelen, chairman of the Working Group. Mimeographed text distributed at the Plenary Session.

1112   Ibid.

the functions of the new institution. Most Delegations favoured the political weight and representative character of an Intergovernmental Committee. Some delegations doubted whether an intergovernmental body because of its political character was the best forum for taking decisions on the protection of cultural property of importance to all humankind and would have preferred an impartial, expert body. As a result of the debate most, if not all, proposals regarding the distribution of functions for implementing this Protocol where carefully distributed among the Meeting of the Parties (Article 23(3)), the Committee (Article 27) and the Secretariat (Article 28).

The co-ordination of the relationship between meetings of the High Contracting Parties and the members to this Protocol as well as the General Conference of UNESCO was also a concern of the Delegations. The carefully designed balance is an achievement that should be maintained, as was emphasized, to secure a smooth operation without creating further complications when the Secretariat of UNESCO decides upon the fulfillment of its duties and responsibilities relating to the Second Protocol (Article 28) to the Hague Convention, the Convention itself (Article 23(1)), and the World Heritage Convention. The flexibility of the Director-General of UNESCO to co-ordinate among its different responsibilities was secured within this Chapter, it was believed, through Article 23(1).

A particularly difficult issue was the establishment of the Fund for the protection of cultural property in the event of armed conflict. Despite the fact that an obligatory contribution was not acceptable for the majority of Delegations to generate the necessary financial resources, a major effort was made to create a framework that could maintain a stable and flexible base for all interested parties (Article 29 (4)) to find a way to support the work of the Committee. It was the clear understanding of the Delegations that the Fund is only for purposes as the Committee shall decide in accordance with the guidelines as defined in Article 23 sub-para. 3(c).

The number of Parties to be elected as members of the Committee for the Protection of Cultural Property in the Event of Armed Conflict (6 or 12 or 21 or more), as well the debate on the title of the Committee (Committee, Bureau, Commission) were not resolved within the Working Group, however, the text enabled this question to be easily resolved by the Plenary, since the clear definition of functions and relationship among the different statutory organs made the issue secondary. The approved number of 12 members for the Committee was a compromise between those who wanted to minimize and those who thought to broaden the activities of the new body.

An important debate for the future interpretation of the text developed within the WG about the necessary guidelines for the work of the Committee and the use of the resources provided through the Fund. In accordance with Article 27 the Committee shall develop Guidelines for the implementation of this Protocol (para. 1(a)), and the Guidelines shall be endorsed by the Meeting of the Parties (Article 23 3(a)).

The final draft of the Working Group[1113] submitted to the Plenary Session read as follows:

Article 26. Bureau for the Protection of Cultural Property in the Event of Armed Conflict

1. Bureau for the Protection of Cultural Property in the Event of Armed Conflict is hereby established. It shall be composed of 12 Parties which shall be elected by the Meeting of the Parties to this Protocol.

2. The Bureau shall meet once every year in ordinary session and in extra-ordinary sessions whenever it deems such sessions necessary.

3. In determining membership[1114] of the Bureau States Parties to this Protocol shall seek to ensure[1115] an equitable representation of the different regions and cultures of the world.

4. Parties Members of the Bureau shall choose as their representatives persons qualified in the fields of cultural heritage, defense or international law, and they shall endeavour, in consultation with one another, to ensure that the Bureau as a whole contains adequate expertise in all these fields.

1113   HC/1999/5/Add.6, 23 March 1999. Original: English. Registered time 12.33.

1114   1999 Hague Conference, Plenary Session, 24 March 1999: The delegate of Thailand suggested the use of the words 'In electing members of the Committee', p. 4.

1115   Ibid. The delegate of Thailand suggested the use of the words 'shall ensure', using the wording of the World Heritage Committee. The delegate of India expressed his concern 'that there may be not all regions represented at the intial stage of the Protocol which could cause a problem with regard to the term "ensuring"'. He suggested leaving this issue to the Rules of Procedure of the Committee rather than diluting the principles as contained in the Protocol. Therefore, he suggested keeping the words 'shall ensure'. Ibid., p. 8.

Article 27 Term of Office (Reproduced under Article 25)

Article 28 Rules of Procedure (Reproduced under Article 26)

Article 29 Functions (Reproduced under Article 27)

Article 30 Secretariat (Reproduced under Article 28)

Article 31 The Fund for the Protection of Cultural Property in the Event of Armed Conflict (Reproduced under Article 29).

Second part of discussion on institutional issues (24 March 1999)

The Chairman of the informal Working Group for Chapter 6 informed the Plenary Session of the manner in which they had reached the revised text (HC/1999/5/Add.6), which represented a compromise between the two propositions for an institutional body presented in the original UNESCO draft for the Second Protocol.[1116] The group had, however, not been able to reach an agreement on a name for this body. They had agreed that Article 30 would be better situated in Chapter 3 because, although its provisions relate to matters of procedure, they are also of importance regarding matters of substance.

As no agreement was reached on the title of the body, some delegates expressed a preference for 'Committee' instead of 'Bureau'.[1117] Other delegates still preferred 'Bureau' mainly because this appellation expressed better the need for structural flexibility.[1118] At the last Plenary Session dealing with Chapter 6, the title of the institution was still undecided, so it was suggested that 'the Chairman continue these discussions in an informal manner to look for an appropriate name'.[1119] The Italian delegate also proposed that the Committee, by its composition, should provide broad geographic representation.[1120] He suggested the adoption of measures providing immediate intervention in cases of emergency. In cases where the composition of the Committee will be

---

1116   Ibid., p. 2.
1117   Ibid., delegates of Thailand, Italy, France, pp. 4, 6, 9.
1118   Ibid., Argentine delegate, p. 5.
1119   Ibid., p. 10.
1120   Ibid., p. 6.

enlarged from 12 to 15 members, a Bureau composed of five members should be created, and this Bureau should be able to take emergency decisions and create an efficient mechanism.[1121]

The new text of Chapter 6 includes a clear enumeration of the functions of the institutional body and guidelines for the use of the Fund, which no longer comprises compulsory contributions. Furthermore, the definition of NGOs has been clarified so as not to exclude the participation of specialist NGOs and IGOs other than those mentioned in the draft.[1122]

Most of the Delegations expressed their satisfaction with the results of the informal Working Group.[1123] Some delegates required clarification of the functions of the institutional body with the reformulation of provisions related to the Fund. The delegate of Nigeria was concerned that there was no longer provision for compulsory contributions to the Fund.[1124]

Some felt that the functions of the institutional body should be more in line with those of its corresponding body under the World Heritage Convention. The geographical distribution of the institutional body ((26(3) of HC/1999/6/Add.6) should be equitable.[1125] One view held was that the institutional body should have the possibility of giving assistance to developing countries to protect their cultural property. With regard to the type of institutional body that was required, some States still felt that it should be an Intergovernmental Committee, though the majority were happy with the compromise reached.

The revised document was sent to the Drafting Committee[1126] and, after its approval, was submitted to the Plenary Session of the Conference on 26 March 1999 and became part of the 1999 Second Protocol.

ANALYSIS OF THE TEXT

As we have already indicated, the proposal of the creation of an Intergovernmental Committee was based on the example of the Intergovernmental Committee for the Protection of the Cultural and Natural Heritage of Outstanding Universal Value, otherwise known as the 'World

---

1121   Ibid., p. 7
1122   Ibid., Austrian delegate, p. 3.
1123   In particular, the delegates of Austria, Argentina, Cameroon, France, Italy, Nigeria and Thailand. Ibid., pp. 3–8.
1124   Ibid., p. 7
1125   Ibid., Indian delegate, p. 7.
1126   Ibid., p. 10.

Heritage Committee'.[1127] The World Heritage Committee was created by the Convention Concerning the Protection of the World Cultural and Natural Heritage, adopted by the General Conference of UNESCO at its 17th session in Paris, on 16 November 1972.[1128]

The World Heritage Committee is first mentioned in the Convention in Article 8, which states:

Article 8

1. An Intergovernmental Committee for the Protection of the Cultural and Natural Heritage of Outstanding Universal Value, called 'the *World Heritage Committee*', is hereby established within the United Nations Educational, Scientific and Cultural Organization. It shall be composed of 15 States Parties to the Convention, elected by States Parties to the Convention meeting in general assembly during the ordinary session of the General Conference of the United Nations Educational, Scientific and Cultural Organization. The number of States members of the Committee shall be increased to 21 as from the date of the ordinary session of the General Conference following the entry into force of this Convention for at least 40 States.

2. Election of members of the Committee shall ensure an equitable representation of the different regions and cultures of the world.

3. A representative of the International Centre for the Study of the Preservation and Restoration of Cultural Property (*ICCROM*), a representative of the International Council of Monuments and Sites (*ICOMOS*) and a representative of the International Union for Conservation of Nature and Natural Resources (*IUCN*), to whom may be added, at the request of States Parties to the Convention meeting in general assembly during the ordinary sessions of the General Conference of the United Nations Educational, Scientific and Cultural Organization, representatives of other intergovernmental or non-governmental organizations, with similar objectives, may attend the meetings of the Committee in an advisory capacity.

1127   See pp. 526-527.
1128   UNESCO, Convention Concerning the Protection of the World Cultural and Natural Heritage, 23 November 1972. http://whc.unesco.org/en/conventiontext

The first two paragraphs of this Article 8 are reflected in the two paragraphs of Article 14 of the revised Lauswolt document and also the final text of Article 24 of the 1999 Second Protocol. Paragraph 3 of this Article 8 is reflected in Article 27, paragraph 3 of the 1999 Second Protocol.

Paragraph 1

> The Committee for the Protection of Cultural Property in the Event of Armed Conflict is hereby established. It shall be composed of twelve Parties which shall be elected by the Meeting of the Parties.

The Committee for the Protection of Cultural Property in the Event of Armed Conflict is copied from Article 8, paragraph 1 of the World Heritage Convention, except that the Committee is not established *within* UNESCO. The new Committee is mostly attached and dependent on the Parties to the Protocol and is not directly attached to UNESCO, contrary to original attempts. This fundamental point has important financial implications.

The World Heritage Convention, the World Heritage Committee and the World Heritage Centre are attached directly to the Organization itself, and benefit from its attention and cooperation. The 1954 Convention and the 1954 and 1999 Protocols are attached to the High Contracting Parties or the Parties to these instruments only.

On the other hand, the independence of the World Heritage Committee is limited by the fact that only representatives of the States Parties to the World Heritage Convention can be elected as Members of the World Heritage Committee.

As in the case of the World Heritage Committee, the Committee for the Protection of Cultural Property in the Event of Armed Conflict is composed of individuals who act not in their personal capacity but as representatives of States by which they are appointed. This also means that the State, which is elected as a Member of the Committee, may change the individual who is representing its interests in the Committee. Each State will be responsible for the cost of its representative.[1129]

During the discussion on the representative body (Committee or Bureau), a proposal was made to have the organ composed of individuals in a form similar to the Human Rights Committee – the highly successful organ created for the protection of civil and political rights by the 1966

1129   Ibid.

International Covenant on Civil and Political Rights. However, this proposal was not accepted.

George Aldrich also raised an interesting question, whether the State should be represented by only one or by several persons.[1130]

In the case of the World Heritage Committee, the number of States represented was increased from 15 to 21 after the entry into force of the Convention for at least 40 States. An attempt to increase the membership of the Committee for the Protection of Cultural Property in the Event of Armed Conflict was not successful. It is interesting to note that the ratio between States Members of the World Heritage Committee and States Parties to the World Heritage Convention has decreased from initial theoretical 0.75 (15/20, 20 being the number of parties required for the entry into force of the Convention) to 0.114 (21/184).[1131] The ratio of the Committee for the Protection of Cultural Property in the Event of Armed Conflict is actually the following: 12 Member States of the Committee versus 55 States Parties to the 1999 Second Protocol (at 1st October 2009. Ratio 0.2181).

The Committee for the Protection of Cultural Property in the Event of Armed Conflict does not possess a Secretariat in the form of that of the World Heritage Centre. In some ways it follows the older tradition of the Secretariat of the 1954 Convention and its original Protocol, which were constituted by one person – and sometimes none.

The Rules of Procedure for the election of the World Heritage Committee include details on the presentation of candidates and elections: Rules 13 and 14.[1132]

1130   Aldrich (1998), p. 15.
1131   Scovazzi (2008), p. 150.
1132   Rules 13 and 14 read as follows:
Rule 13. Procedures for the presentation of candidatures to the World Heritage Committee
13.1 The Secretariat shall ask all States Parties, at least three months prior to the opening of the General Assembly, whether they intend to stand for election to the World Heritage Committee. If so, its candidature should be sent to the Secretariat at least six weeks prior to the opening of the General Assembly.
13.2 At least four weeks prior to the opening of the General Assembly the Secretariat shall send to all States Parties the provisional list of States Parties candidates. The Secretariat will also provide information on the status of all compulsory and voluntary contributions to the World Heritage Fund made by each of the candidates. This list of candidatures will be revised as necessary.
13.3 This list of candidatures shall be finalised 48 hours before the opening of the General Assembly. No other candidatures nor payments of compulsory and voluntary contributions to the World Heritage Fund (for the purpose of presenting a candidature to the Committee) will be accepted in the 48-hour period prior to the opening of the General Assembly.
Rule 14. Election of members of the World Heritage Committee

Paragraph 2

The Committee shall meet once a year in ordinary session and in extra-ordinary sessions whenever it deems necessary.

Up until now, the Committee has meetings in regular ordinary sessions. The following meetings have taken place:
- First and second sessions of the First Meeting of the Committee (UNESCO Headquarters, 26 October 2006 and 11 June 2007, respectively).
- Second Meeting of the Committee (UNESCO Headquarters, Paris, 17–19 December 2007).

14.1 The election of members of the World Heritage Committee shall be conducted by secret ballot whenever five or more delegations having the right to vote so request, or if the Chairperson so decides.

A certain number of seats may be reserved for States Parties who do not have sites on the World Heritage List, upon decision of the World Heritage Committee at the session that precedes the General Assembly. Such a ballot for reserved seats would precede the open ballot for the remaining seats to be filled. Unsuccessful candidates in the reserved ballot would be eligible to stand in the open ballot.

14.2 Before the election begins, the Chairperson shall appoint two tellers from among the delegates present; he/she shall hand to them the list of States entitled to vote and the list of States candidates. He/She shall announce the number of seats to be filled.

14.3 The Secretariat shall distribute to the delegations a voting paper in the form of a list of all the States which are candidates.

14.4 Each delegation shall cast its vote by encircling the names of those States for which it desires to vote.

14.5 The tellers shall collect from each delegation their voting paper and shall proceed to count the votes, under the supervision of the Chairperson.

14.6 Voting papers on which all names of States have been circled shall be considered to be abstentions.

14.7 Voting papers on which more names have been circled than there are seats to be filled shall be considered invalid.

14.8 Those States obtaining in the first ballot the required majority shall be elected, unless the number of States obtaining that majority is greater than the number of seats to be filled. In that case, the States obtaining the greatest number of votes, up to the number of seats to be filled, shall be declared elected. If the number of States obtaining the majority required is less than the number of seats to be filled, there shall be a second ballot. If the number of States obtaining the majority required is still less than the number of seats to be filled, there shall be a third and, if necessary, a fourth ballot, to fill the remaining seats. For the third and fourth ballots, the voting shall be restricted to the States obtaining the greatest number of votes in the previous ballot, up to a number twice that of the seats remaining to be filled.

14.9 After the fourth ballot, the candidates obtaining to the greatest number of votes, up to the number of seats to be filled, shall be declared elected.

14.10 If, in the fifth ballot, two or more candidates obtain the same number of votes, the Chairperson shall decide between them by drawing lots.

14.11 The Chairperson shall announce the results of the election.

- Third Meeting of the Committee (UNESCO Headquarters, 4–6 June 2008).
- Fourth Meeting of the Committee (UNESCO Headquarters, 27–29 May 2009).

At the fourth meeting the Committee decided to hold an extraordinary session on 2 September 2009.

This also means that the Members of the Committee as a whole meet four times during the entire period of their function as Members of the Committee (with the exception of those Committee Members whose term of office expired at the end of the second Meeting of the Parties in accordance with Article 25(2) of the Second Protocol). This situation may affect their personal involvement in the work of the Committee and their engagement for the cause of cultural property.

Paragraph 3

> In determining membership of the Committee, Parties shall seek to ensure an equitable representation of the different regions and cultures of the world.

The requirement of equitable representation was present in Patrick Boylan's 'Outline of recommended composition and role of the proposed Intergovernmental Advisory Committee on the Protection of Cultural Property in the Event of Armed Conflict'. It was also mentioned in all drafts submitted to expert meetings and underlined by the States delegates at the Diplomatic Conference.[1133]

The same request was expressed in Article 8, paragraph 2 of the World Heritage Convention; it is interesting to note how this representation was realized within the World Heritage Committee, which endeavours to encourage States Parties to nominate sites for inscription in the World Heritage List. For example, paragraph 22 of the Operational Guidelines states that 'a certain number of seats may be reserved for States Parties who do not have a property on the World Heritage List, upon decision of the Committee at the session that precedes the General Assembly.'[1134] In 2007, the World Heritage Committee decided to reserve for such a State one seat

---

1133 See p. 525.
1134 Operational Guidelines for the Implementation of the World Heritage Convention, WHC.08/01, January 2008.

in the World Heritage Committee.[1135] A sum was allocated to cover the participation of representatives of developing countries, 'but only for persons who are experts in cultural or natural heritage'.[1136] This was an important requirement, demanding that members of the Committee be personally engaged and efficient.

A similar provision is found in Article V, paragraph 3 of UNESCO's Constitution concerning the election of the Executive Board. Chamberlain rightly points out that it is easier to achieve balanced cultural and geographical representation in the UNESCO Executive Board, which is composed of 58 members, than in the Committee, which has just 12 members.[1137]

As mentioned under paragraph 1, George Aldrich raised the interesting question of whether the State should be represented by only one or by several persons.[1138] This question is interesting also in relation to the appropriate representation of different cultures. To date, the vast majority of Committee Members were represented at meetings by more than one representative.

Paragraph 4

> Parties members of the Committee shall choose as their representatives persons qualified in the fields of cultural heritage, defense or international law, and they shall endeavour, in consultation with one another, to ensure that the Committee as a whole contains adequate expertise in all these fields.

As mentioned above, it is the responsibility of States Parties to the Protocol to choose their representative in the Committee. The representative should be a person qualified in one of the three areas mentioned in this paragraph: cultural heritage, defense or international law. It is advisable that the States undertake a preliminary consultation regarding the persons they envisage sending to the Committee. It is their collective responsibility to ensure that they will be appropriately represented. This is not an easy task as the movement of representatives will be relatively frequent, as we shall see under the following article.

1135   Decision 31 COM 6.
1136   WHC Rules of Procedure, Rule 5.4.
1137   Chamberlain (2004), p. 223.
1138   Aldrich (1998), p. 15.

George Aldrich's query regarding representation by only one or by several persons[1139] is of interest in connection with the matter of appropriate representation of all three fields – in particular, when representation of one of the three fields will not be adequately performed and one of the States Members of the Committee may provide such an expertise. The commentary on the World Heritage Convention is quite strict with regard to choice of State representatives:

> Persons having more general competence, such as diplomats or politicians, are in principle excluded from the World Heritage Committee (WHC). States members of the WHC must transmit to the Secretariat in writing the names, designations and qualifications of their representatives. However, it seems very difficult, if not practically impossible, for a State Party to challenge the margin of discretion that a WHC member state has in choosing its own representatives. WHC member states are strongly encouraged to include in their delegation persons qualified in both the cultural and natural field. This is facilitated by the fact that the delegate may be assisted by alternates, advisors and experts.[1140]

1139   Ibid.
1140   Scovazzi (2008), p. 155.

Article 25
TERM OF OFFICE

1. *A Party shall be elected to the Committee for four years and shall be eligible for immediate re-election only once.*
2. *Notwithstanding the provisions of paragraph 1, the term of office of half of the members chosen at the time of the first election shall cease at the end of the first ordinary session of the Meeting of the Parties following that at which they were elected. These members shall be chosen by lot by the President of this Meeting after the first election.*

Preparatory work

The Second Expert meeting on the 1954 Hague Convention for the Protection of Cultural Property in the Event of Armed Conflict. Lauswolt, The Netherlands, 9–11 February 1994.

Draft provisions for the revision of the 1954 Hague Convention and commentary from UNESCO Secretariat. CLT-97/CONF.208/2, Paris, October 1997

Revised Lauswolt Document. 27 March 1997. Mimeographed text established by the Secretariat.

UNESCO, Third Meeting of the High Contracting Parties to the Convention for the Protection of Cultural Property in the Event of Armed Conflict (The Hague, 1954), UNESCO House, Paris, 13 November 1997, *Final Report.* CLT-97/CONF.208/3, Paris, November 1997.

UNESCO, Meeting of Governmental Experts on the Review of the Hague Convention for the Protection of Cultural Property in the Event of Armed Conflict of 1954. Vienna, 11–13 May 1998. UNESCO document: Paris, May 1998, *Final Report.*

Preliminary Draft Second Protocol to the 1954 Hague Convention. UNESCO document HC/1999/1, October 1998 (English, French and Russian).

Draft Second Protocol to the 1954 Hague Convention for the Protection of Cultural Property in the Event of Armed Conflict. UNESCO document HC/1999/1/rev.1, February 1999.

UNESCO, Synoptic report of comments on the Preliminary Draft Second Protocol to the 1954 Hague Convention received from High Contracting Parties to the Hague Convention for the Protection of Cultural Property in the Event of Armed Conflict 1954, other UNESCO Member States and international organizations, Paris, 15 January 1999.

Addendum to the Synoptic report of comments on the Preliminary Draft Second Protocol to the 1954 Hague Convention received from High Contracting parties to the Hague Convention for the Protection of Cultural Property in the Event of Armed Conflict 1954, other UNESCO Member States and international organizations. Paris, March 1999, HC/1999/4.

1999 Hague Conference, Plenary Session, particularly 18 and 24 March 1999.

Bibliography

Chamberlain. K. 2004. *War and Cultural Heritage*. Leicester: Institute of Art and Law, pp. 221–22.

Desch, T. 1999. The Second Protocol to the 1954 Convention for the Protection of Cultural Property in the Event of Armed Conflict. *Yearbook of International Humanitarian Law*, Vol. 2, pp. 84–85.

Hladík, J. 1996. Meeting of the High Contracting Parties to the Hague Convention for the Protection of Cultural Property in the Event of Armed Conflict of 1954. *International Journal of Cultural Property*, Vol. 5, No. 2, pp. 339–41.

Hladík, J. 1998b. The Third Meeting of the High Contracting Parties to the Hague Convention for the Protection of Cultural Property in the Event of Armed Conflict of 1954 (Paris, November 13, 1997). *International Journal of Cultural Property*, Vol. 7, No. 1, pp. 268–71.

As we mentioned in the commentary on Article 24, the Meeting of Experts, held at Lauswolt at the invitation of the Netherlands Government from 9 to 11 February 1994,[1141] established the basic structure of Chapter 6 and also provided the first draft of the articles for this chapter. This is also the case for Article 25, which deals with the term of office of the Committee.

Article (15) of the Lauswolt document stated:

Article 15. Term of office
1. The term of office of States Parties members of the Committee shall extend from the end of the ordinary session of the General Conference during which they are elected until the end of its [...]

1141 The Second Expert meeting on the 1954 Hague Convention for the Protection of Cultural Property in the Event of Armed Conflict. Lauswolt, The Netherlands, 9–11 February 1994.

subsequent ordinary session. The term of office of members can be renewed once.

2. The term of office of one-third of the members designated at the time of the first election shall, however, cease at the end of the [...] ordinary session of the General Conference following that at which they were elected; and the term of office of a further third of the members designated at the same time shall cease at the end of the [...] ordinary session of the General Conference following that at which they were elected. The names of these members shall be chosen by lot by the President of the General Conference of UNESCO after the first election.[1142]

No decision was made at the different meetings of experts and High Contracting Parties regarding which of the two possible forms the supervisory body could take: committee or bureau. The situation remained the same at the Meeting of Governmental Experts on the Review of the 1954 Hague Convention for the Protection of Cultural Property in the Event of Armed Conflict 1954, which met at UNESCO Headquarters in Paris on 24–27 March 1997. The results of this meeting of experts were integrated in the 'revised Lauswolt document' of 27 March 1997, which included two options: Option I (Intergovernmental committee) and Option II (Bureau with an advisory board). Option I included a draft version of Article 15, entitled 'Terms of office', which was practically identical to the aforementioned text with the exception of paragraph 1:

1. The term of office of States Parties members of the Committee shall extend from the end of the ordinary session of the General Conference during which they are elected until the end of its [...] subsequent ordinary session. The term of office of members *may* be renewed once.[1143]

The UNESCO Secretariat reprinted the 'revised Lauswolt document' of 1997 with several terminological proposals along with the Secretariat's comments comparing the original provisions of the Lauswolt document (prepared in

---

1142   Ibid., p. 8.

1143   Revised Lauswolt document, 27 March 1997. Mimeographed text established by the Secretariat. Italics in the original, replacing 'can' in the previous text. See also UNESCO, Draft provisions for the revision of the 1954 Hague Convention and commentary from the UNESCO Secretariat. CLT-97/CONF.208/2, Paris, October 1997, p. 18.

February 1994) with the revised provisions of 1997.[1144] This document was submitted to the Third Meeting of the High Contracting Parties, which met during the 29th Session of the UNESCO General Conference on 13 November 1997. [1145] The final resolution invited States Parties to provide comments on the draft provisions by 1 February 1998 and convened a preparatory Meeting of Government Experts in Vienna.[1146]

At the Meeting of Governmental Experts on the Revision of the Hague Convention for the Protection of Cultural Property in the Event of Armed Conflict of 1954 in Vienna on 11–13 May 1998:

> the participants considered the two options contained in the revised Lauswolt document as well as a fact sheet prepared by UNESCO on the practical, staffing and financial implications. The experts asked the UNESCO Secretariat to prepare a comprehensive working document to be distributed well in advance before the Diplomatic Conference, which the Netherlands proposed generously to hold in The Hague from 14 to 26 March 1999.[1147]

Following the May 1998 Vienna meeting, the authorities of the Netherlands, with the assistance of the UNESCO Secretariat, elaborated a Preliminary Draft Second Protocol to the 1954 Hague Convention.[1148] This draft was submitted for consideration to the High Contracting Parties to the Convention and for information to other Member States of UNESCO and the UN and selected international organizations. By 15 January 1999, the Secretariat had received substantive replies from 15 High Contracting Parties to the

---

1144 UNESCO, *Draft provisions for the revision of the 1954 Hague Convention and commentary from the UNESCO Secretariat.* CLT-97/CONF.208/2, Paris, October 1997. It was indicated in the footnote that this document should be read together with the final report of the March 1997 meeting of government experts in the review of the Hague Convention 1954 (UNESCO document CLT-96/CONF.603/5).

1145 UNESCO, Third Meeting of the High Contracting Parties to the Convention for the Protection of Cultural Property in the Event of Armed Conflict (The Hague, 1954), UNESCO House, Paris, 13 November 1997, *Final Report.* CLT-97/CONF.208/3, Paris, November 1997. See also Hladík (1998b).

1146 UNESCO, Third Meeting of the High Contracting Parties to the Convention for the Protection of Cultural Property in the Event of Armed Conflict (The Hague, 1954), UNESCO House, Paris, 13 November 1997, *Final Report.* CLT-97/CONF.208/3, Paris, November 1997, Annex.

1147 The Report was also transmitted to the 155th UNESCO Executive Board, 155 EX/51, Paris, 17 August 1998.

1148 *Preliminary Draft Second Protocol to the 1954 Hague Convention.* UNESCO document HC/1999/1, October 1998 (English, French and Russian).

Convention, which were included in the Synoptic report of comments.[1149] On the basis of these comments, the UNESCO Secretariat and the Government of the Netherlands drew up the final draft of the Second Protocol: the *Draft Second Protocol to the 1954 Hague Convention for the Protection of Cultural Property in the Event of Armed Conflict* (UNESCO doc. HC/1999/1/rev.1, February 1999),[1150] which was submitted to the Diplomatic Conference in March 1999. In our comments on Article 24 above, we have seen the draft articles concerning the Committee (Option I) and Bureau (Option II). As the delegates of the States Parties had not yet decided which option they preferred, the Draft Second Protocol included two provisions of the article concerning 'Term of office': one for Option I and one for Option II:

OPTION I. Committee
Draft Article 27 Term of office
1. A Party shall be elected Member of the Committee for four years. A serving Member shall be eligible for re-election only once.
2. Notwithstanding the provisions of paragraph 1 above, the term of office of half of the Members designated[1151] at the time of the first election shall cease at the end of the first ordinary session of the General Assembly following that at which they were elected. The names of these Members shall be chosen by lot by the President of the General Assembly after the first election.

OPTION II. Bureau
Draft Article 27 Term of office
1. A Party shall be elected Member of the Bureau for a term of two years.
2. A serving Member is eligible for re-election only once.[1152]

1149 UNESCO, Synoptic report of comments on the Preliminary Draft Second Protocol to the 1954 Hague Convention received from High Contracting Parties to the Hague Convention for the Protection of Cultural Property in the Event of Armed Conflict 1954, other UNESCO Member States and international organizations. Paris, 15 January 1999, Original: English. See also Addendum to the Synoptic report of comments on the Preliminary Draft Second Protocol to the 1954 Hague Convention received from High Contracting Parties to the Hague Convention for the Protection of Cultural Property in the Event of Armed Conflict 1954, other UNESCO Member States and international organizations. Paris, March 1999, HC/1999/4.
1150 Draft Second Protocol to the 1954 Hague Convention for the Protection of Cultural Property in the Event of Armed Conflict, UNESCO doc. HC/1999/1/Rev.1, February 1999 (English, French and Russian).
1151 The delegate of Thailand proposed to replace this word by 'elected'. Plenary Session of 24 March 1999, p. 4.
1152 In italics in the Draft.

Most of the issues concerning Chapter 6 on Institutional Issues were discussed during the Plenary Session of 17 and 18 March 1999. However, the question of Term of Office was not mentioned during the discussions. At the end of the Plenary Session of 18 March, the Chairman concluded the session by announcing that János Jelen (Hungary) had agreed to chair an informal Working Group to work on the provisions of Chapter 6. The Working Group on Chapter 6 was mandated to produce a consensus text on the institutional issues related to the implementation of the Second Protocol to the 1954 Convention. The basis for discussions was the draft text in document HC/1999/rev.1 and the debate in the plenary sessions that took place on 17 and 18 March 1999. The Working Group adopted the text of the Article, which is almost identical to the text of the Option I above, and was adopted as the final text of the Second Protocol.

ANALYSIS OF THE TEXT

The formulation of this Article is fully inspired by the World Heritage Convention, not only in its content but also in its form. Article 9 of the World Heritage Convention states:

1. The term of office of States members of the World Heritage Committee shall extend from the end of the ordinary session of the General Conference during which they are elected until the end of its third subsequent ordinary session.
2. The term of office of one-third of the members designated at the time of the first election shall, however, cease at the end of the first ordinary session of the General Conference following that at which they were elected; and the term of office of a further third of the members designated at the same time shall cease at the end of the second ordinary session of the General Conference following that at which they were elected. The names of these members shall be chosen by lot by the President of the General Conference of the United Nations Educational, Scientific and Cultural Organization after the first election.
3. States Members of the Committee shall choose as their representatives persons qualified in the field of the cultural or natural heritage.

Paragraph 1

> 1. A Party shall be elected to the Committee for four years and shall be eligible for immediate re-election only once.

This paragraph clearly indicates the length of membership of the Committee with the exception expressed in paragraph 2. Once elected, the Member State may be immediately re-elected for another term of four years, but only once. This does not mean that following a period of non-membership, a former Committee member could not be re-elected again.

Membership of the World Heritage Committee is longer – six years. This seems more appropriate to ensure better continuity with regard to the exercise of functions and better involvement in the accomplishment of functions as members of the Committee.

Paragraph 2

> Notwithstanding the provisions of paragraph 1, the term of office of half of the members chosen at the time of the first election shall cease at the end of the first ordinary session of the Meeting of the Parties following that at which they were elected. These members shall be chosen by lot by the President of this Meeting after the first election.

It is quite general practice in many other elected bodies to subdivide the elected body into two or three terms. This avoids sudden changes of all members of the body instead of maintaining at least a part of the members. This is why the term of office of half of the members elected the first time, at the moment of the constitution of the Committee, expires at the end of the first ordinary session of the Meeting of the Parties following that at which they were elected – in other words, two years after their election.

The Meeting of the Parties takes place at the same time as the UNESCO General Conference, that is, every second year. This also means that the term of office of half of the members of the Committee will expire after two years in office instead of four years, the period to which they would normally be elected.

As a consequence, this electoral system ensures that half of the members of the Committee will remain in office at least for two additional years, prior to the election of the half.

The choice of which Members, elected at the first session, will exercise their mandate for half of the first term (i.e. two years) is left to the President of the first Meeting, who determines the selection by lot.[1153]

This procedure does not alter State representation. As indicated, each State chooses its representatives after consultation with other members. In the event of a change of representative, it is advisable to proceed with a new consultation to ensure that the three fields required for the activity of the Committee (culture, defense and international law) are fully respected.

1153 'Lot' in the abstract sense: 'The casting or drawing of lots, or the use of any equivalent process to obtain a decision. Chiefly in phr. By lot (occas. by lots).' *Oxford English Dictionary*, Vol. VI L–M, p. 454.

Article 26

RULES OF PROCEDURE

1. *The Committee shall adopt its Rules of Procedure.*[1154]
2. *A majority of the members shall constitute a quorum. Decisions of the Committee shall be taken by a majority of two-thirds of its members voting.*
3. *Members shall not participate in the voting on any decisions relating to cultural property affected by an armed conflict to which they are parties.*

Preparatory work

The Second Expert meeting on the 1954 Hague Convention for the Protection of Cultural Property in the Event of Armed Conflict. Lauswolt, The Netherlands, 9–11 February 1994.

Expert meeting on the review of the 1954 Hague Convention for the Protection of cultural property in the Event of Armed Conflict. Paris, UNESCO Headquarters, 28 November–2 December 1994. UNESCO document CLT/CH/94/608/2, *Final Report.*

UNESCO document: a working document prepared by the Secretariat, CLT/94/608/1 of 28 November 1994.

UNESCO, Third Meeting of the High Contracting Parties to the Convention for the Protection of Cultural Property in the Event of Armed Conflict (The Hague, 1954), UNESCO House, Paris, 13 November 1997, *Final Report.* CLT-97/CONF.208/3, Paris, November 1997, p. 3.

Draft provisions for the revision of the 1954 Hague Convention and commentary from UNESCO Secretariat. CLT-97/CONF.208/2, Paris, October 1997.

Preliminary Draft Second Protocol to the 1954 Hague Convention. UNESCO document HC/1999/1, October 1998 (English, French and Russian).

Draft Second Protocol to the 1954 Hague Convention for the Protection of Cultural Property in the Event of Armed Conflict. UNESCO document HC/1999/1/rev.1, February 1999.

UNESCO, Synoptic report of comments on the Preliminary Draft Second Protocol to the 1954 Hague Convention received from High Contracting Parties to the Hague Convention for the Protection of Cultural Property

---

1154   Rules of Procedure were adopted at the first session of the first meeting of the Committee for the Protection of Cultural Property in the Event of Armed Conflict (Paris, 26 October 2006). See pp. 551–564.

in the Event of Armed Conflict 1954, other UNESCO Member States and international organizations, Paris, 15 January 1999.

Addendum to the Synoptic report of comments on the Preliminary Draft Second Protocol to the 1954 Hague Convention received from High Contracting parties to the Hague Convention for the Protection of Cultural Property in the Event of Armed Conflict 1954, other UNESCO Member States and international organizations. Paris, March 1999, HC/1999/4.

1999 Hague Conference: Plenary session of the Conference, in particular the 18 and 24 March 1999.

Bibliography

Aldrich, G. H. 1998. *Analysis of the Preliminary Draft Second Protocol to the 1954 Hague Convention.* Mimeographed manuscript of 9 December, p. 15.

Chamberlain. K. 2004. *War and Cultural Heritage.* Leicester: Institute of Art and Law, pp. 221–22.

Desch, T. 1999. The Second Protocol to the 1954 Convention for the Protection of Cultural Property in the Event of Armed Conflict. *Yearbook of International Humanitarian Law,* Vol. 2, pp. 84–85.

Hladík, J. 1996. Meeting of the High Contracting Parties to the Hague Convention for the Protection of Cultural Property in the Event of Armed Conflict of 1954. *International Journal of Cultural Property,* Vol. 5, No. 2, pp. 339–41.

Hladík, J. 1998b. The Third Meeting of the High Contracting Parties to the Hague Convention for the Protection of Cultural Property in the Event of Armed Conflict of 1954 (Paris, November 13, 1997). *International Journal of Cultural Property,* Vol. 7, No. 1, pp. 268–71.

As mentioned above in our commentary on Article 24, the Meeting of Experts, held at Lauswolt at the invitation of the Netherlands Government from 9 to 11 February 1994,[1155] established the basic structure of Chapter 6 and also provided the first draft of articles of this Chapter. This is also the case for Article 26, which deals with the rules of procedures of the Committee.

1155 The Second Expert meeting on the 1954 Hague Convention for the Protection of Cultural Property in the Event of Armed Conflict. Lauswolt, The Netherlands, 9–11 February 1994.

Article (16) of the first Lauswolt document stated:

Article 16 Rules of procedure
1. The Committee shall adopt its Rules of Procedure.
2. Decisions of the Committee shall be taken by a majority of two-thirds of its members present and voting. A majority of the members of the Committee shall constitute a quorum.[1156]

As we have noted above, the Secretariat of UNESCO prepared an excellent working document for the next session of experts, held in Paris in November–December 1994, which included an innovative proposal that had as its consequence the elimination of this draft Article.[1157]

No decision was made at the different meetings of experts and High Contracting Parties concerning the two possible options for a supervisory body: committee or bureau. The situation remained the same at the Meeting of Governmental Experts on the Review of the 1954 Hague Convention for the Protection of Cultural Property in the Event of Armed Conflict 1954, which met at the UNESCO Headquarters in Paris on 24–27 March 1997. The results of this meeting of experts were integrated in the 'revised Lauswolt document' of 27 March 1997, which again included two options: Option I (Intergovernmental committee) and Option II (Bureau with an advisory board). Option I included the draft Article 16, entitled 'Rules of procedure', which is identical to the aforementioned text.[1158]

The Secretariat of UNESCO reprinted the 'revised Lauswolt document' of 1997 with several terminological proposals and the comments of the Secretariat comparing the original provisions of the Lauswolt document (prepared in February 1994) with the revised provisions of 1997.[1159] This document was submitted to the Third Meeting of the High Contracting Parties, which met during the 29th Session of the UNESCO General

---

1156 Ibid., p. 8.
1157 UNESCO document: a working document prepared by the Secretariat, CLT/94/608/1, 28 November 1994, p. 22.
1158 UNESCO, Draft provisions for the revision of the 1954 Hague Convention and commentary from the UNESCO Secretariat. CLT-97/CONF.208/2, Paris, October 1997, p. 19.
1159 UNESCO, *Draft provisions for the revision of the 1954 Hague Convention and commentary from the UNESCO Secretariat.* CLT-97/CONF.208/2, Paris, October 1997. It was indicated in the footnote that this document should be read together with the final report of the March 1997 meeting of government experts in the review of the Hague Convention 1954 (UNESCO document CLT-96/CONF.603/5).

Conference on 13 November 1997.[1160] The final resolution invited States Parties to provide comments on the draft provisions by 1 February 1998 and convened a preparatory Meeting of Government Experts in Vienna.[1161] At the Meeting of Governmental Experts on the Revision of The Hague Convention for the Protection of Cultural Property in the Event of Armed Conflict of 1954 in Vienna on 11–13 May 1998,

> the participants considered the two options contained in the revised Lauswolt document as well as a fact sheet prepared by UNESCO on the practical, staffing and financial implications. The experts asked the UNESCO Secretariat to prepare a comprehensive working document to be distributed well in advance before the Diplomatic Conference, which the Netherlands proposed generously to hold in The Hague from 14 to 26 March 1999.[1162]

Following the May 1998 Vienna meeting, the authorities of the Netherlands, with the assistance of the UNESCO Secretariat, elaborated a *Preliminary Draft Second Protocol to the 1954 Hague Convention*.[1163] This draft was submitted for consideration to the High Contracting Parties to the Convention and for information to other Member States of UNESCO and the UN and selected international organizations. By 15 January 1999, the Secretariat had received substantive replies from 15 High Contracting Parties to the Convention, which were included in the Synoptic report of comments.[1164] On the basis of these comments, the UNESCO Secretariat and the Government of the

---

1160   UNESCO, Third Meeting of the High Contracting Parties to the Convention for the Protection of Cultural Property in the Event of Armed Conflict (The Hague, 1954), UNESCO House, Paris, 13 November 1997, *Final Report*. CLT-97/CONF.208/3, Paris, November 1997. See also Hladík (1998).

1161   UNESCO, Third Meeting of the High Contracting Parties to the Convention for the Protection of Cultural Property in the Event of Armed Conflict (The Hague, 1954), UNESCO House, Paris, 13 November 1997, *Final Report*. CLT-97/CONF.208/3, Paris, November 1997, Annex.

1162   The Report was also transmitted to the 155th UNESCO Executive Board, 155 EX/51, Paris, 17 August 1998.

1163   *Preliminary Draft Second Protocol to the 1954 Hague Convention*. UNESCO document HC/1999/1, October 1998 (English, French and Russian). In the comments to the Rules of Procedure, George H. Aldrich (1998, p. 15) reminded that as '[presumably] the Rules of Procedure to be established by the General Assembly [sic!] will determine how the common costs of the Committee, e.g. offices, utilities, staff, if any, translation and communications, are to be funded, as such decision seems unlikely to be left to the Committee itself.'

1164   UNESCO, Synoptic report of comments on the Preliminary Draft Second Protocol to the 1954 Hague Convention received from High Contracting parties to the Hague Convention for the Protection of Cultural Property in the Event of Armed Conflict 1954, other UNESCO Member States and international organizations. Paris, 15 January 1999, Original: English.

Netherlands drew up the final draft of the Second Protocol: *Draft Second Protocol to the 1954 Hague Convention for the Protection of Cultural Property in the Event of Armed Conflict* (UNESCO doc. HC/1999/1/rev.1, February 1999),[1165] which was submitted to the Diplomatic Conference in March 1999. In the comments under Article 24 we have seen the draft articles concerning the Committee (Option I) and Bureau (Option II). As the delegates of the States Parties had not yet decided whether they preferred Option I or II, the Draft Second Protocol included two provisions of the Article concerning the 'Rules of procedure': one for Option I and another for Option II.

OPTION I. Committee

Article 28 Rules of procedure

1. The Committee shall adopt its own Rules of Procedure.
2. Decisions of the Committee shall be taken by a majority of two-thirds of its Members present and voting. A majority of the members of the Committee shall Constitute a quorum.
3. Members of the Committee shall recuse themselves from voting on any decisions relating to cultural property affected by an armed conflict to which they are parties.

OPTION II. Bureau[1166]

Article 28 Rules of procedure

1. *The Bureau shall adopt its Rules of Procedure which shall ensure that four Members shall constitute a quorum and that all decisions by the Bureau shall be taken by a majority of two-thirds of the Members [present and] voting.*
[2. *A decision may be taken without meeting if the Bureau deems it appropriate to poll the Members and if no more than three Members request a meeting.]*
3. *Members of the Bureau shall recuse themselves from voting on any decisions relating to cultural property affected by an armed conflict to which they are parties.*

Most of the issues concerning Chapter 6 (Institutional issues) were discussed during the Plenary Session of the Conference on 17 and 18 March 1999.

1165   Draft Second Protocol to the 1954 Hague Convention for the Protection of Cultural Property in the Event of Armed Conflict. UNESCO doc. HC/1999/1/rev.1, February 1999 (English, French and Russian).
1166   In italics in the Draft.

However, the question of Rules of Procedure was not mentioned in the discussion. At the end of the Plenary Session of 18 March, the Chairman concluded the session by announcing that János Jelen (Hungary) had agreed to chair an informal Working Group to work on the provisions of Chapter 6. The Working Group on Chapter 6 was mandated to produce a consensus text on the institutional issues related to the implementation of the Second Protocol to the 1954 Convention. The basis for discussions was the draft text in document HC/1999/rev.1 and the debate in the plenary sessions, which took place on 17 and 18 March 1999. The Working Group adopted the text of the Article:

> Article 28 Rules of procedure
> 1. The Bureau shall adopt its own Rules of Procedure.
> 2. A majority of the Members of the Bureau shall constitute a quorum. Decisions of the Bureau shall be taken by a majority of two-thirds of its Members voting.
> 3. Members of the Bureau shall not vote on any decisions relating to cultural property affected by an armed conflict to which they are parties.

In the final text of the Second Protocol, the word 'Bureau' was replaced by the word 'Committee'.

ANALYSIS OF THE TEXT

Article 10 of the World Heritage Convention also deals with Rules of Procedure, but in more detail than Article 26 of the 1999 Second Protocol.[1167]

Paragraph 1

> The Committee shall adopt its Rules of Procedure.

1167 Article 10:
   1. The World Heritage Committee shall adopt its Rules of Procedure.
   2. The Committee may at any time invite public or private organizations or individuals to participate in its meetings for consultation on particular problems.
   3. The Committee may create such consultative bodies as it deems necessary for the performance of its functions.

Article 26 of the 1999 Second Protocol as well as Article 10 of the World Heritage Convention refer to the Rules of Procedure.

The Rules of Procedure of the Committee for the Protection of Cultural Property in the Event of Armed Conflict were adopted at the first session of the first meeting of the Committee in Paris on 26 October 2006.[1168]

The text of the Second Protocol does not include provisions concerning the invitation of public or private organizations or individuals to participate in its meetings for consultation on particular problems, nor concerning the creation of consultative bodies which it deems necessary for the performance of its functions. These issues were included in the Rules of Procedure of the World Heritage Committee, particularly Rules 6–8.

Paragraph 2

> A majority of the members shall constitute a quorum. Decisions of the Committee shall be taken by a majority of two-thirds of its members voting.

A majority of the members constitute a quorum: 'an assembly of the number of members entitled to vote who must be present in order that business can be legally transacted. The quorum refers to the number of such members present, not to the number of actually voting on a particular question'.[1169] This is also defined by the Rules of Procedure in Rule 20:

> *Rule 20. Quorum*
> 20.1 A quorum shall consist of a majority of the States members of the Committee.
> 20.2 The Committee shall not decide on any matter unless a quorum is present. [1170]

The quorum therefore requires the presence of a majority of States members. If a majority is not present, the Committee is not able to proceed with any decision.

1168   See pp. 557-544.
1169   *Robert's rules of order newly revised.* Scott, Foresman and Company, 1981, para. 39, p. 293.
1170   UNESCO, *Committee for the Protection of Cultural Property in the Event of Armed Conflict. Rules of Procedure.* Adopted at the first session of the first meeting of the Committee in Paris on 26 October 2006, Rule 20.

The decisions of the Committee shall be taken by a majority of two-thirds of its voting members. Rule 35 of the Rules of Procedure provides details on voting:

Rule 35. Voting

35.1 Each State member of the Committee shall have one vote in the Committee.

35.2 All decisions of the Committee shall be taken by a majority of two-thirds of its members present and voting, with the exception of the election of the Bureau of the Committee under Rule 15 and of procedural motions under Rule 28 above, which shall require a majority of the States members present and voting, and issues related to enhanced protection covered by Article 11, paragraph 9, of the Second Protocol, which shall require a four-fifths majority. The States members shall not participate in the voting on any decisions relating to cultural property affected by an armed conflict to which they are parties.

35.3 For the purpose of the present Rules, the expression 'States members present and voting' shall mean States members casting an affirmative or negative vote. States members abstaining from voting shall be regarded as not voting.

35.4 Voting shall normally be by a show of hands.

35.5 When the result of a vote by a show of hands is in doubt, the presiding officer may take a second vote by a roll-call. A vote by a roll-call shall also be taken if it is requested by not less than two States members before the voting takes place.

35.6 A decision shall be voted on by secret ballot whenever two or more States members shall so request or if the Chairperson so decides. [1171]

In the case of Committee decisions regarding enhanced protection (art. 11, para. 5 and 9), a four-fifths majority of Committee members present and voting is required. In the event that all members of the Committee are present and voting, the decision must be taken by ten votes out of twelve members in favour of the proposal. For all other decisions the majority required is eight votes out of twelve. When not all Members are present and voting the four-fifth majority has to be calculated proportionally.

1171   Ibid., Rule 35.

Paragraph 3

> Members shall not participate in the voting on any decisions relating to cultural property affected by an armed conflict to which they are parties.

As we have seen, Rule 35.2 of the Rules of Procedure includes this provision: 'The States members shall not participate in the voting on any decisions relating to cultural property affected by an armed conflict to which they are parties.'[1172]

1172   Ibid., Rule 35.2.

UNITED NATIONS EDUCATIONAL, SCIENTIFIC AND CULTURAL ORGANIZATION COMMITTEE FOR THE PROTECTION OF CULTURAL PROPERTY IN THE EVENT OF ARMED CONFLICT

RULES OF PROCEDURE[1173]

I. Membership

Rule 1. The Committee

The Committee for the Protection of Cultural Property in the Event of Armed Conflict (hereinafter referred to as the 'Committee') is composed of twelve States Parties to the Second Protocol to the Hague Convention of 1954 for the Protection of Cultural Property in the Event of Armed Conflict (hereinafter referred to as the 'Second Protocol') elected in accordance with Article 24 of the Second Protocol.

II. Sessions

Rule 2. Ordinary and Extraordinary Sessions

2.1   The Committee shall meet once a year in ordinary session.

2.2   The Committee shall meet in extraordinary session whenever it deems necessary in accordance with the procedure defined below in this Rule.

2.3   Requests for an extraordinary session of the Committee may be submitted to the Secretariat of the Committee in writing at any time by: (1) any member of the Committee, (2) any State Party to the Second Protocol not represented on the Committee and (3) the Director-General of UNESCO (hereinafter referred to as 'the Director-General').

2.4   Requests for extraordinary sessions shall give details on the proposed urgent matters relevant to the Committee's responsibilities to be considered, and shall be communicated by the Secretariat to the members of the Committee in writing.

1173   Adopted at the first session of the first meeting of the Committee for the Protection of Cultural Property in the Event of Armed Conflict (Paris, 26 October 2006).

2.5   The requested extraordinary session shall be convened if the proposal is approved in writing by a two-thirds majority of the members of the Committee.

Rule 3. Convocation

3.1   The first session of the Committee shall be convened by the Director-General.

3.2   Subsequent sessions shall be convened by the Chairperson of the Committee in consultation with the Director-General.

3.3   The Director-General shall notify the States members of the Committee, the date, place and provisional agenda of each session, not less than sixty days in advance in the case of an ordinary session and, so far as possible, not less than thirty days in advance in the case of an extraordinary session. However, in cases of special urgency, such as an armed conflict involving the territory of one or more States Parties to the Second Protocol or the imminent threat of such a conflict, the Committee may agree by a two-thirds majority to meet in extraordinary session with a shorter notice.

3.4   The Director-General shall, at the same time, notify to the States, organizations and individuals mentioned in Rules 6, 7 and 8 below, the date, place and provisional agenda of each session.

Rule 4. Date and Place

4.1   The Committee shall determine at each session, in consultation with the Director-General, the date and the place of the next session. The date and/or place may be modified, if necessary, by the Chairperson/the Bureau, in consultation with the members of the Committee and the Director-General.

4.2   Any State member of the Committee may invite the Committee to hold a session on its territory.

III. Participants

Rule 5. Delegations

5.1   Each State member of the Committee shall be represented by one delegate, who may be assisted by alternates, advisers or experts. It shall bear the expense of participation of its representatives in the sessions of the

Committee and of any subsidiary bodies or subcommittees created by the Committee.

5.2   States members of the Committee shall choose as their representatives persons qualified in the fields of cultural heritage (which term for the purposes of the Second Protocol includes archives, libraries, monuments and sites, and museums), defence or international law, and they shall endeavour, in consultation with one another, to ensure that the Committee as a whole contains adequate expertise in all these three fields.

Rule 6. Organizations attending in an advisory capacity

6.1   To assist in the implementation of its functions, in accordance with Article 27, paragraph 3, of the Second Protocol, the Committee may invite to its meetings, in an advisory capacity, eminent professional organizations such as those which have formal relations with UNESCO, including the International Committee of the Blue Shield (ICBS) and its constituent bodies such as the International Council on Archives (ICA), the International Federation of Library Associations and Institutions (IFLA), the International Council of Monuments and Sites (ICOMOS), and the International Council of Museums (ICOM). Representatives of the International Centre for the Study of the Preservation and Restoration of Cultural Property (ICCROM) and of the International Committee of the Red Cross (ICRC) may also be invited to attend in an advisory capacity. They shall not have the right to vote.

6.2   The above-mentioned organizations shall bear the expense of participation of their representatives in the sessions of the Committee and participation in any subsidiary body or subcommittee created by the Committee.

Rule 7. Invitations for consultation

The Committee may at any time invite public or private organizations or qualified individuals to participate in its sessions for consultation on particular problems.

Rule 8. Observers

8.1   States Parties to the Second Protocol which are not members of the Committee, States non-Parties to the Second Protocol which are Parties to the 1954 Hague Convention, and other States which are Member States of UNESCO or of the United Nations may attend the sessions of the Committee as observers. They shall bear the expense of participation of their representatives in the sessions of the Committee and of any subcommittee created by the Committee. Those States shall not have the right to vote.

8.2   The United Nations and organizations of the United Nations system, may attend the sessions of the Committee as observers. They shall bear the expense of their participation in the sessions of the Committee and of any subsidiary body or subcommittee created by the Committee. They shall not have the right to vote.

8.3   The Director-General may provisionally invite any organization referred to in Rule 6.1 subject to subsequent confirmation by the Committee.

IV. Functions

Rule 9. Functions of the Committee

9.1   In accordance with Article 27 of the Second Protocol, the Committee shall have the following functions:

a) to develop Guidelines for the implementation of the Second Protocol;

b) to grant, suspend or cancel enhanced protection for cultural property and to establish, maintain and promote the List of Cultural Property under Enhanced Protection;

c) to monitor and supervise the implementation of the Second Protocol and promote the identification of cultural property under enhanced protection;

d) to consider and comment on reports of the States Parties, to seek clarifications as required, and prepare its own report on the implementation of the Second Protocol for the Meeting of the Parties;

e) to receive and consider requests for international assistance under Article 32 of the Second Protocol;

f) to determine the use of the Fund for the Protection of Cultural Property in the Event of Armed Conflict to be established in accordance with Article 29 of the Second Protocol;

g) to perform any other function which may be assigned to it by the Meeting of the Parties to the Protocol.

9.2   Pursuant to Article 27, paragraph 2, of the Second Protocol, the functions of the Committee shall be performed in co-operation with the Director-General.

V. Subsidiary Bodies and Ad Hoc Subcommittees

Rule 10. Subsidiary bodies

10.1   The Committee may establish such subsidiary bodies as it deems necessary for the conduct of its work, within the limits of the technical facilities available.

10.2   The composition and the terms of reference (including mandate and duration of office) of such subsidiary bodies shall be defined by the Committee at the time of their creation. These bodies can only be constituted from amongst States members of the Committee.

10.3.   These Rules shall be applicable *mutatis mutandis* to the subsidiary bodies, unless otherwise decided by the Committee.

10.4   Each subsidiary body shall itself elect its Chairperson and, if necessary, its Rapporteur.

10.5   In appointing members of subsidiary bodies, due regard shall be given to the need to ensure an equitable representation of the different regions and cultures of the world.

Rule 11. Subcommittees

11.1   The Committee may set up *ad hoc* subcommittees for the study of specific problems related to its activities, as described in Chapter IV of the present Rules of Procedure. Membership of such subcommittees may also be open to States Parties to the Second Protocol which are not represented in the Committee without the right to vote.

11.2   The composition and terms of reference (including mandate and duration of the office) of the *ad hoc* subcommittees shall be defined by the Committee at the time of their creation.

11.3   The *ad hoc* subcommittees shall meet in accordance with the decision of the Committee and shall elect their Chairperson, Vice-Chairperson and, if necessary, a Rapporteur.

VI. Agenda

Rule 12. Provisional Agenda

12.1 The provisional agenda of the sessions of the Committee shall be prepared by the Director-General.

12.2 The provisional agenda of an ordinary session of the Committee shall include:

- all questions, the inclusion of which has been decided by the Committee at previous sessions;
- all questions proposed by members of the Committee;
- all questions proposed by States Parties to the Second Protocol not members of the Committee;
- all recommendations made under Article 11, paragraph 3, of the Second Protocol by the International Committee of the Blue Shield (ICBS), and other international nongovernmental organizations with relevant expertise, for the inclusion of specific cultural property in the List of Cultural Property under Enhanced Protection;
- all questions proposed by the Director-General.

12.3 The provisional agenda of an extraordinary session shall include only those questions for the consideration of which the session has been convened.

Rule 13. Adoption of the Agenda

The Committee shall adopt its agenda at the beginning of each session.

Rule 14. Amendments, deletions and new items

The Committee may amend, delete or add items to the agenda so adopted if so decided by a two-thirds majority of the members present and voting.

VII. Bureau

Rule 15. Bureau

15.1 The Bureau of the Committee shall consist of the Chairperson, the four Vice-Chairpersons and the Rapporteur. The Bureau shall co-ordinate the work of the Committee and fix the dates, hours and order of business of meetings. The Vice-Chairpersons and the Rapporteur shall assist the Chairperson in carrying out his/her duties.

15.2   The Bureau shall meet during the sessions of the Committee as frequently as deemed necessary.

Rule 16. Elections

16.1   The Committee, at the beginning of each ordinary session, shall elect, from amongst those members whose term continues until the election of the Bureau at the next ordinary session, a Chairperson, four Vice-Chairpersons and a Rapporteur.

16.2   The Chairperson, the Vice-Chairpersons and the Rapporteur shall be eligible for immediate re-election for one additional term of office.

16.3   In electing the Bureau, due regard shall be given to the need to ensure an equitable representation of the different regions and cultures of the world.

Rule 17. Duties of the Chairperson

17.1   In addition to exercising the powers which are conferred upon him/her elsewhere by the present Rules, the Chairperson shall open and close each plenary meeting of the Committee. He/she shall direct the discussions, ensure observance of these Rules, accord the right to speak, put questions to the vote and announce decisions. He/she shall rule on points of order and, subject to the present Rules, shall control the proceedings and the maintenance of order. He/she shall not vote, but he/she may instruct another member of his/her delegation to vote on his/her behalf. He/she shall exercise all other functions given to him by the Committee.

17.2   A Vice-Chairperson acting as Chairperson shall have the same powers and duties as the Chairperson.

Rule 18. Replacement of the Chairperson

18.1   If the Chairperson is unable to act at any session of the Committee or Bureau, or part thereof, his/her functions shall be exercised by a Vice-Chairperson, in the English alphabetical order of States members of the Committee commencing with the country of the Chairperson.

18.2   If the Chairperson ceases to represent a State member of the Committee or is for any reason unable to complete his term of office, he/she is replaced by a Vice-Chairperson, in the English alphabetical order of States members of the Committee commencing with the country of the Chairperson, for the remainder of the term of office.

18.3   The Chairperson shall abstain from exercising his/her functions for all issues relating to a property situated on the territory of the State Party of which he/she is a national.

Rule 19. Replacement of the Rapporteur

19.1   If the Rapporteur is unable to act at any session of the Committee or the Bureau, or part thereof, his/her functions shall be exercised by a Vice-Chairperson in the English alphabetical order of States members of the Bureau commencing with the country of the Rapporteur.

19.2   If the Rapporteur ceases to represent a State member of the Committee or if he/she is for any reason unable to complete his/her term of office, he/she is replaced by a Vice-Chairperson, in the English alphabetical order of States members of the Bureau, for the remainder of the term of office.

VIII. Conduct of Business

Rule 20. Quorum

20.1   A quorum shall consist of a majority of the States members of the Committee.

20.2   The Committee shall not decide on any matter unless a quorum is present.

Rule 21. Public meetings

Meetings shall be held in public unless decided otherwise by the Committee or by the subcommittee concerned.

Rule 22. Private meetings

22.1   When in exceptional circumstances, the Committee decides to hold a private meeting; it shall determine the persons who, in addition to the representatives of States members, shall be present.

22.2   Any decision taken by the Committee at a private meeting shall be presented in written form at a subsequent public meeting.

22.3   At each private meeting, the Committee shall decide whether the working documents of that meeting shall be published. Documents resulting from private meetings shall be made public after a period of twenty years.

Rule 23. Order and time-limit of speeches

23.1   The Chairperson shall call upon speakers in the order in which they signify their wish to speak.

23.2   The Chairperson may limit the time allowed to each speaker if the circumstances make this desirable.

23.3   The representatives of the Director-General, of organizations, individuals and observers referred to in Rules 6, 7 and 8, may address the meeting with the prior consent of the Chairperson.

Rule 24. Voting on amendments

24.1   When an amendment to a proposal is moved, the amendment shall be voted on first. When two or more amendments to a proposal are moved, the Committee shall first vote on the amendment deemed by the presiding officer to be furthest removed in substance from the original proposal, and then on the amendment next furthest removed therefrom and so on, until all the amendments have been put to the vote.

24.2   If one or more amendments are adopted, the amended proposal shall then be voted upon as a whole.

24.3   A motion is considered an amendment to a proposal if it merely adds to, deletes from or revises part of that proposal.

Rule 25. Voting on proposals

If two or more proposals relate to the same question, the Committee shall, unless it decides otherwise, vote on the proposals in the order in which they have been submitted. The Committee may, after each vote on a proposal, decide whether to vote on the next proposal.

Rule 26. Withdrawal of proposals

A proposal may be withdrawn by its proposer at any time before voting on it has begun, provided that the proposal has not been amended. A proposal withdrawn may be reintroduced by any State member of the Committee.

Rule 27. Points of order

27.1   During a discussion, any State member may raise a point of order concerning procedural matters; such point of order shall be immediately decided upon by the Chairperson.

27.2   An appeal may be made against the ruling of the Chairperson. Such appeal shall be put to the vote immediately and the Chairperson's ruling shall stand unless overruled.

Rule 28. Procedural motions

During the discussion on any matter, a member of the Committee may propose a procedural motion: suspension or adjournment of the meeting, adjournment of the debate or closure of the debate.

Rule 29. Suspension or adjournment of the meeting

During the discussion of any matter, any State member of the Committee may move the suspension or adjournment of the meeting. Such motions shall not be debated but shall be immediately put to the vote.

Rule 30. Adjournment of debate

During the discussion of any matter, any State member of the Committee may move the adjournment of the debate on the item under discussion. On moving the adjournment the State member shall indicate whether he moves the adjournment *sine die* or to a particular time which he shall specify. In addition to the proposer of the motion, one speaker may speak in favour of, and one against, the motion.

Rule 31. Closure of debate

A State member of the Committee may at any time move the closure of the debate; whether or not any other speaker has signified his/her wish to take part in the discussion. If application is made for permission to speak against the closure, it may be accorded to not more than two speakers. The Chairperson shall then put to the vote the motion for closure and, if the Committee is in favour of the motion, he/she shall declare the closure of the debate.

Rule 32. Order of procedural motions

Subject to Rule 27 the following motions shall have precedence in the following order over all other proposals or motions before the meeting:
- suspension of the meeting;
- adjournment of the meeting;
- adjournment of the debate on the question under discussion;
- closure of the debate on the question under discussion.

Rule 33. Working languages

33.1   The working languages of the Committee shall be Arabic, Chinese, English, French, Russian and Spanish.
33.2   Speeches made at a meeting of the Committee in one of the working languages shall be interpreted into the other working languages.
33.3   Speakers may, however, speak in any other language, provided they make their own arrangements for interpretation of their speeches into one of the working languages.
33.4   The documents of the Committee shall be issued in Arabic, Chinese, English, French, Russian and Spanish.

Rule 34. Deadline for distribution of documents

The documents relating to the items on the provisional agenda of each session of the Committee shall be distributed at the latest six weeks before the beginning of the session in the working languages to the members of the Committee, to the organizations attending the meetings in an advisory capacity. They shall also be made available to States Parties non-members of the Committee and to all other observers in electronic format.

Rule 35. Voting

35.1 Each State member of the Committee shall have one vote in the Committee.

35.2 All decisions of the Committee shall be taken by a majority of two-thirds of its members present and voting, with the exception of the election of the Bureau of the Committee under Rule 15 and of procedural motions under Rule 28 above, which shall require a majority of the States members present and voting, and issues related to enhanced protection covered by Article 11, paragraph 9, of the Second Protocol, which shall require a four-fifths majority. The States members shall not participate in the voting on any decisions relating to cultural property affected by an armed conflict to which they are parties.

35.3 For the purpose of the present Rules, the expression 'States members present and voting' shall mean States members casting an affirmative or negative vote. States members abstaining from voting shall be regarded as not voting.

35.4 Voting shall normally be by a show of hands.

35.5 When the result of a vote by a show of hands is in doubt, the presiding officer may take a second vote by a roll-call. A vote by a roll-call shall also be taken if it is requested by not less than two States members before the voting takes place.

35.6 A decision shall be voted on by secret ballot whenever two or more States members shall so request or if the Chairperson so decides.

Rule 36. Decisions and Recommendations

36.1 The Committee shall adopt such decisions and recommendations as it may deem appropriate.

36.2 The Committee shall maintain and publish in any way that is considered appropriate, including electronic publication, the List of Cultural Property under Enhanced Protection in accordance with Articles 10 and 11 of the Second Protocol.

36.3 In accordance with Article 11, paragraph 11, of the Second Protocol, the Director-General shall, without delay, send to the Secretary-General of the United Nations and to all Parties notification of any decision of the Committee to include cultural property on the List of Cultural Property under Enhanced Protection, or to suspend or cancel the enhanced protection of cultural property.

IX. Secretariat of the Committee

Rule 37. The Secretariat

37.1   The Committee shall be assisted by a Secretariat appointed by the Director-General.

37.2   The Director-General, after any appropriate consultation with the International Committee of the Blue Shield (ICBS) and of its constituent bodies, the International Centre for the Study of the Preservation and Restoration of Cultural Property (ICCROM) and the International Committee of the Red Cross (ICRC) in their respective specialised areas of competence and expertise, shall prepare the Committee's documentation and shall have the responsibility for the implementation of its decisions.

37.3   The Director-General or his/her representative shall participate in the work of the Committee, its subsidiary bodies and subcommittees without the right to vote. He/She may at any time make either oral or written statements on any question under consideration.

37.4   The Director-General shall appoint an official of the Secretariat of UNESCO to act as Secretary to the Committee, and other officials who shall together constitute the Secretariat of the Committee.

37.5   The Secretariat shall receive, translate and distribute all official documents of the Committee and shall arrange for the interpretation of the discussions as provided under Rule 33.2.

37.6   The Secretariat shall perform all other duties necessary for the proper conduct of the work of the Committee.

X. Reports

Rule 38. Reports to the Meeting of the States Parties

38.1   The Committee shall submit a report on its activities at each ordinary session of the Meeting of the States Parties to the Second Protocol, and may also offer to report to each periodic meeting of the High Contracting Parties to the 1954 Hague Convention.

38.2   The Committee may authorise its Chairperson to submit such reports on its behalf.

38.3   Copies of this report shall be sent to all States Parties to the Second Protocol.

XI. Adoption, Amendment and Suspension of the Rules of Procedure

Rule 39. Adoption

The Committee shall adopt its Rules of Procedure by a decision taken in a plenary meeting by a two-thirds majority of the States members present and voting. These Rules shall be communicated to all States Parties to the Second Protocol, and reported to the next ordinary session of the Meeting of the States Parties.

Rule 40. Amendment

The Committee may amend these Rules of Procedure except when they reproduce provisions of the Second Protocol by a decision taken in plenary meeting by a two-thirds majority of the States members present and voting, provided the proposal has been included in the agenda of the session in accordance with Rules 12 and 13. Amendments shall be communicated to all States Parties, and reported to the next ordinary session of the Meeting of the States Parties.

Rule 41. Suspension

The Committee may suspend during one of its sessions the application of any of these Rules, except when they reproduce provisions of the Protocol, by a decision taken in plenary meeting by a two-thirds majority of the States members present and voting.

Article 27
FUNCTIONS

1. *The Committee shall have the following functions:*
   a. *to develop Guidelines for the implementation of this Protocol;*
   b. *to grant, suspend or cancel enhanced protection for cultural property and to establish, maintain and promote the List of Cultural Property under Enhanced Protection;*
   c. *to monitor and supervise the implementation of this Protocol and promote the identification of cultural property under enhanced protection;*
   d. *to consider and comment on reports of the Parties, to seek clarifications as required, and prepare its own report on the implementation of this Protocol for the Meeting of the Parties;*
   e. *to receive and consider requests for international assistance under Article 32;*
   f. *to determine the use of the Fund;*
   g. *to perform any other function which may be assigned to it by the Meeting of the Parties.*
2. *The functions of the Committee shall be performed in co-operation with the Director-General.*
3. *The Committee shall co-operate with international and national governmental and non-governmental organizations having objectives similar to those of the Convention, its First Protocol and this Protocol. To assist in the implementation of its functions, the Committee may invite to its meetings, in an advisory capacity, eminent professional organizations such as those which have formal relations with UNESCO, including the International Committee of the Blue Shield (ICBS) and its constituent bodies. Representatives of the International Centre for the Study of the Preservation and Restoration of Cultural Property (Rome Centre) (ICCROM) and of the International Committee of the Red Cross (ICRC) may also be invited to attend in an advisory capacity.*

Preparatory work

The Second Expert meeting on the 1954 Hague Convention for the Protection of Cultural Property in the Event of Armed Conflict. Lauswolt, The Netherlands, 9–11 February 1994.

UNESCO document: a working document prepared by the Secretariat, CLT/94/608/1 of 28 November 1994.

UNESCO, Meeting of Governmental Experts on the Review of the 1954 Hague Convention for the Protection of Cultural Property in the Event of Armed Conflict 1954. UNESCO Headquarters, Paris, 24–27 March 1997.

UNESCO, Third Meeting of the High Contracting Parties to the Convention for the Protection of Cultural Property in the Event of Armed Conflict (The Hague, 1954), UNESCO House, Paris, 13 November 1997, *Final Report*. CLT-97/CONF.208/3, Paris, November 1997, p. 3.

Draft provisions for the revision of the 1954 Hague Convention and commentary from UNESCO Secretariat. CLT-97/CONF.208/2, Paris, October 1997.

UNESCO, Meeting of Governmental Experts on the Review of the Hague Convention for the Protection of Cultural Property in the Event of Armed Conflict of 1954. Vienna, 11–13 May 1998. UNESCO document: Paris, May 1998, *Final Report*.

Preliminary Draft Second Protocol to the 1954 Hague Convention. UNESCO document HC/1999/1, October 1998 (English, French and Russian).

Draft Second Protocol to the 1954 Hague Convention for the Protection of Cultural Property in the Event of Armed Conflict. UNESCO document HC/1999/1/rev.1, February 1999.

UNESCO, Synoptic report of comments on the Preliminary Draft Second Protocol to the 1954 Hague Convention received from High Contracting Parties to the Hague Convention for the Protection of Cultural Property in the Event of Armed Conflict 1954, other UNESCO Member States and international organizations, Paris, 15 January 1999.

Addendum to the Synoptic report of comments on the Preliminary Draft Second Protocol to the 1954 Hague Convention received from High Contracting parties to the Hague Convention for the Protection of Cultural Property in the Event of Armed Conflict 1954, other UNESCO Member States and international organizations. Paris, March 1999, HC/1999/4.

1999 Hague Conference, Plenary Session, particularly 17, 18 and 24 March 1999.

Bibliography

Aldrich, G. H. 1998. *Analysis of the Preliminary Draft Second Protocol to the 1954 Hague Convention*. Mimeographed manuscript of 9 December, p. 15.

Chamberlain. K. 2004. *War and Cultural Heritage*. Leicester: Institute of Art and Law, pp. 221–22.

Desch, T. 1999. The Second Protocol to the 1954 Convention for the Protection of Cultural Property in the Event of Armed Conflict. *Yearbook of International Humanitarian Law*, Vol. 2, pp. 84–85.

Hladík, J. 1996. Meeting of the High Contracting Parties to the Hague Convention for the Protection of Cultural Property in the Event of Armed Conflict of 1954. *International Journal of Cultural Property*, Vol. 5, No. 2, pp. 339–41.

Hladík, J. 1998b. The Third Meeting of the High Contracting Parties to the Hague Convention for the Protection of Cultural Property in the Event of Armed Conflict of 1954 (Paris, November 13, 1997). *International Journal of Cultural Property*, Vol. 7, No. 1, pp. 268–71.

As mentioned in the commentary on the previous Articles of this chapter, the Meeting of Experts, held at Lauswolt at the invitation of the Netherlands Government from 9 to 11 February 1994,[1174] established the basic structure of Chapter 6 of the 1999 Second Protocol and also provided the first draft of the articles of this chapter. This also holds of Article 27, one of the most important in this context, dealing with the functions of the Committee.

Article (17) of the Lauswolt document stated:[1175]

Article 17. Functions
1. Without prejudice to UNESCO's competence to offer its services under Article 19 of the Convention, and to take initiative to make proposals under Article 23 of the Convention, the Committee shall have the following functions and tasks:
   (a) to identify and formulate criteria on the basis of which cultural property will be specially protected.
   (b) to receive requests from States Parties for the entry into the Register established in accordance with Article [...] of this instrument cultural property (protected by the Convention) (as defined in Article 1 of the Convention), situated in its territory and suitable for inclusion in the Register provided for

---

1174 The Second Expert meeting on the 1954 Hague Convention for the Protection of Cultural Property in the Event of Armed Conflict. Lauswolt, The Netherlands, 9–11 February 1994.
1175 Ibid.

in Article [...] of this Instrument.[1176] This request shall include information and documentation about the exact location, significance and nature of the cultural property.

(c) to monitor and supervise the implementation of this instrument;[1177]

(d) to cooperate with the Director-General of UNESCO in fulfilling the functions provided for in Article [...] of this instrument;

[(e) to decide on the use of the resources of the [Fund] established in accordance with Article [...] of this instrument;]

(f) to establish, keep up to date, publish, and distribute every two years a list of cultural property specially protected by this instrument.

(g) to perform any other function which, may be attributed to it under this instrument or by the States Parties.[1178]

[(h) to receive and study requests for international assistance formulated by States Parties under Article [...] of this instrument with respect to ....]

[(i) to decide on the action to be taken with regard to requests for international assistance under Article [...] of this instrument, determine where appropriate, the nature and extent of its assistance, and authorize the conclusion, on its behalf, of the necessary arrangements with the government concerned;]

[(j) to draw up, keep up to date and publicize a list of projects and programmes under Article [...] of this instrument for which international assistance has been granted;]

[(k) to define the procedure by which requests to it for international assistance shall be considered.]

2. The Committee shall cooperate with international and national governmental and non-governmental organizations having

---

1176   Regarding the Register, George H. Aldrich (1998, p. 16) revealed that 'the Draft Second Protocol does not indicate that its Register is separate from the Register under the Convention, that may be well desired. This question needs to be clarified. Even if there are to be separate Registers, however, I see no reason why the Director-General could not manage both, even if decisions as to special protection are to be made by the Committee or the Bureau.'

1177   Note in the Lauswolt draft: 'The exercise of this function needs further elaboration since it is one of the more important functions.'

1178   Aldrich (1998, p. 16) considered this function ambiguous 'as to whether additional functions may be attributed to it by a single State Party or only by all States Parties.'

objectives similar to those of the Convention, its 1954 Protocol and
this instrument and also may call upon individual experts.

As noted above, the UNESCO Secretariat prepared an excellent working
document for the next session of experts held in Paris in November–December
1994, and made an innovative proposal, of which one of the consequences
was the elimination of this draft Article.[1179]

But the situation did not change. No decision was made at the different
meetings of experts and High Contracting Parties between the two possible
options for a supervisory body. The situation remained the same at the Meeting
of Governmental Experts on the Review of the 1954 Hague Convention for
the Protection of Cultural Property in the Event of Armed Conflict 1954,
which met at UNESCO Headquarters in Paris on 24–27 March 1997. Here,
too, the experts could not reach a consensus on the eventual form of the
supervisory body, and both alternatives remained: committee and bureau.
The results of this meeting of experts were integrated within the 'revised
Lauswolt document' of 27 March 1997, which included two options: Option
I (Intergovernmental committee) and Option II (Bureau with an advisory
board). Option I included draft Article 17, entitled 'Functions', which would
remain in the event that the decision was taken to adopt a Committee. Few
changes were made in this draft Article; some paragraphs were renumbered
and some were added:

Article 17 Functions

1. *The Committee shall have the following functions and tasks without
   limiting* UNESCO's competence to offer its services under Article
   19 of the Convention and to initiate proposals under Article 23 of
   the Convention:
   *(a)   to identify and formulate criteria on the basis of which cultural
   property will be specially protected.*
   (b)   to receive requests from States Parties for the entry into the
   Register established in accordance with Article [...] of this
   instrument cultural property (protected by the Convention)
   (as defined in Article 1 of the Convention), situated in its
   territory and suitable for inclusion in the Register provided
   for in Article [...] of this instrument. This request shall include

---

1179   UNESCO document: a working document prepared by the Secretariat, CLT/94/608/1 of 28
       November 1994, p. 22.

information and documentation about the exact location, significance and nature of the cultural property;

(c) to establish, keep up to date, publish, and distribute every two years *the Register*;

(d) to monitor and supervise the implementation of this instrument;[1180]

(e) to cooperate with the Director-General of UNESCO in fulfilling the functions provided for in Article [...] of this instrument *and in his performance of the mission of control according to the Regulations for the execution of the Convention*;[1181]

[(f) to decide on the use of the resources of the [Fund] established in accordance with Article [...] of this instrument;]

(g) to perform any other function which, may be attributed to it under this instrument or by the States Parties;

[(h) to receive and study requests for international assistance formulated by States Parties under Article [...] of this instrument with. respect to [...];

[(i) to decide on the action to be taken with regard to requests for international assistance under Article [...] of this instrument, determine where appropriate, the nature and extent of its assistance, and authorize the conclusion, on its behalf, of the necessary arrangements with the government concerned;]

[(j) to draw up, keep up to date and publicize a list of projects and programmes under Article [...] of this instrument for which international assistance has been granted;]

[(k) to define the procedure by which requests to it for international assistance shall be considered;]

(l) *to submit to the General Conference of UNESCO at each of the ordinary sessions a report on its activities*;[1182]

1180   Note in the Lauswolt draft: 'The exercise of this function needs further elaboration since it is one of the more important functions.'

1181   The Secretariat explained that the phrase in italics was 'included to strenghten the role of the Director-General in the implementation of the Convention, thus combining the scope of the Committee's activities with the Director-General's prerogatives under the Regulations for the Execution of the Hague Convention. This provision needs, however, further clarification with respect of the compatibility of the new instrument with the provisions of the Hague Convention'. UNESCO, *Draft provisions for the revision of the 1954 Hague Convention and commentary from the UNESCO Secretariat.* CLT-97/CONF.208/2, Paris, October 1997, p. 21.

1182   The Secretariat indicated that this phrase was inserted in order 'to improve the reporting system under the Hague Convention (Article 26(2)) in order to raise public awarness of the need for implementation of this instrument.' UNESCO, *Draft provisions for the revision of the 1954 Hague*

2. The Committee shall cooperate with international and national governmental and non-governmental organizations having objectives similar to those of the Convention, its 1954 Protocol and this instrument and also may call upon individual experts.

[2. Representatives of the International Committee of the Blue Shield (ICBS) shall attend the Committee in an advisory capacity. A representative of the International Centre for the Study of the Preservation and Restoration of Cultural Property (Rome Centre) (ICCROM) shall also be invited to attend.][1183]

The Secretariat of UNESCO reprinted the 'revised Lauswolt document' of 1997 with several terminological proposals and the comments of the Secretariat comparing the original provisions of the Lauswolt document (prepared in February 1994) with the revised provisions of 1997.[1184] This document was submitted to the Third Meeting of the High Contracting Parties, which met during the 29th session of the UNESCO General Conference on 13 November 1997. [1185] The final resolution invited States Parties to provide comments on the draft provisions by 1 February 1998 and convened a preparatory Meeting of Government Experts in Vienna.[1186] At the Meeting of Governmental Experts on the Revision of the Hague Convention for the Protection of Cultural Property in the Event of Armed Conflict of 1954 in Vienna (11–13 May 1998),

---

Convention and commentary from the UNESCO Secretariat. CLT-97/CONF.208/2, Paris, October 1997, p. 21.

1183 The International Committee of the Blue Shield proposed to modify paragraph 2 of Article 17 as follows: 'Representatives of the International Committee of the Blue Shield (ICBS) established by the International Council of Archives (ICA), the International Council of Monuments and Sites (ICOMOS) and the International Federation of Library Associations (IFLA) shall attend the Committee in an advisory capacity. A representative of the International Centre for the Study of the Preservation and Restoration of Cultural Property (Rome Centre) (ICCROM) shall also be invited to participate.' UNESCO, *Draft provisions for the revision of the 1954 Hague Convention and commentary from the UNESCO Secretariat.* CLT-97/CONF.208/2, Paris, October 1997, p. 22.

1184 Ibid. It was indicated in the footnote that this document should be read together with the final report of the March 1997 meeting of government experts in the review of the Hague Convention 1954 (UNESCO document CLT-96/CONF.603/5).

1185 UNESCO, Third Meeting of the High Contracting Parties to the Convention for the Protection of Cultural Property in the Event of Armed Conflict (The Hague, 1954), UNESCO House, Paris, 13 November 1997, *Final Report.* CLT-97/CONF.208/3, Paris, November 1997. See also Hladík (1998).

1186 UNESCO, Third Meeting of the High Contracting Parties to the Convention for the Protection of Cultural Property in the Event of Armed Conflict (The Hague, 1954), UNESCO House, Paris, 13 November 1997, *Final Report.* CLT-97/CONF.208/3, Paris, November 1997, Annex.

the participants considered the two options contained in the revised Lauswolt document as well as a fact sheet prepared by UNESCO on the practical, staffing and financial implications. The experts asked the UNESCO Secretariat to prepare a comprehensive working document to be distributed well in advance before the Diplomatic Conference, which the Netherlands proposed generously to hold in The Hague from 14 to 26 March 1999.[1187]

Following the May 1998 Vienna meeting on the revision of the Hague Convention for the Protection of Cultural Property in the Event of Armed Conflict 1954, the authorities of the Netherlands, with the assistance of the UNESCO Secretariat, elaborated a Preliminary Draft Second Protocol to the 1954 Hague Convention.[1188] This draft was submitted for consideration to the High Contracting Parties to the Convention and for information to other Member States of UNESCO and the UN and selected international organizations. By 15 January 1999, the Secretariat had received substantive replies from 15 High Contracting Parties to the Convention, which were included in the Synoptic report of comments.[1189] On the basis of these comments, the UNESCO Secretariat and the Government of the Netherlands drew up the final draft of the Second Protocol: *Draft Second Protocol to the 1954 Hague Convention for the Protection of Cultural Property in the Event of Armed Conflict* (UNESCO doc. HC/1999/1/rev.1, February 1999),[1190] which was submitted to the Diplomatic Conference in March 1999. In the comments under Article 24 we have seen the draft Articles concerning the Committee (Option I) and Bureau (Option II). As the delegates of the States Parties had not yet decided whether they preferred Option I or Option II, the Draft Second Protocol included two provisions of the Article concerning the Rules of Procedure: one for Option I and another for Option II.

1187   The Report was also transmitted to the 155th Session of the UNESCO Executive Board, 155 EX/51, Paris, 17 August 1998.

1188   *Preliminary Draft Second Protocol to the 1954 Hague Convention.* UNESCO document HC/1999/1, October 1998 (English, French and Russian).

1189   UNESCO, Synoptic report of comments on the Preliminary Draft Second Protocol to the 1954 Hague Convention received from High Contracting Parties to the Hague Convention for the Protection of Cultural Property in the Event of Armed Conflict 1954, other UNESCO Member States and international organizations. Paris, 15 January 1999, Original: English.

1190   Draft Second Protocol to the 1954 Hague Convention for the Protection of Cultural Property in the Event of Armed Conflict. UNESCO doc. HC/1999/1/rev.1, February 1999 (English, French and Russian).

OPTION I. Committee:[1191]

Draft Article 29 Functions

1. The Committee shall have the following functions and tasks:
   a. to grant cultural property enhanced special protection upon the request of a Party or determine its suspension or cancellation in accordance with this Protocol;
   b. to establish, update and publish the List;
   c. to cooperate with the Director-General in fulfilling the functions provided for in Chapter 8 and Article 36 of this Protocol and in his performance of the mission of control according to the Regulations for the Execution of the Convention;
   d. to determine the use of the resources of the Fund established in accordance with Article 32 of this Protocol;
   e. to receive and study requests for international assistance formulated by Parties under Article 35 and to determine the action to be taken with regard to requests for international assistance, including, where appropriate, the nature and extent of its assistance, and to authorize the conclusion, on its behalf, of the necessary arrangements with the government concerned;
   f. to monitor and supervise[1192] the implementation of this Protocol;[1193]
   g. to submit to the General Assembly of Parties and to General Conference of UNESCO at each of the ordinary sessions a report on its activities;[1194]
   h. to perform any other function which may be attributed to it under this Protocol or by the Parties.[1195]

1191 During the discussion at the Diplomatic Conference in March 1999, the State represenatives made comments on this draft and these comments are included in the footnotes to this document.

1192 1999 Hague Conference, Plenary Session, 17 March 1999, p. 154: the Turkish delegate proposed the deletion of the supervisory function.

1193 Ibid., p. 145: the Israeli delegate wanted to add the words 'as amended according to the procedure approved by the General Assembly of the States Parties to the Convention as amended'.

1194 Ibid.: the Israeli delegate wanted to add the words 'and when appropriate to make suggestions and general recommendations based on such examination'. Ibid., p. 149: the US delegate preferred a reference to 'the Committee or the Bureau assisting Parties in monitoring and supervising implementation of the Protocol'.

1195 Ibid., p. 154: the Turkish delegate considered this paragraph open to interpretation. 'It should be clarified who attributed the functions and what the functions were.'

2. The Committee may
   a. propose rules to promote the identification of cultural property under enhanced special protection;
   b. at its discretion receive information from Parties concerned about the effective implementation of the present Protocol.[1196]
3. The functions of the Committee set forth in paragraphs 1 and 2 are without prejudice to the role of UNESCO in conformity with its mandate for the protection of cultural property under its Constitution and standard-setting instruments. All functions of the Committee shall be performed in close co-operation with the Director-General.
4. The Committee shall cooperate with international and national governmental and non-governmental organizations having objectives similar to those of the Convention, its First Protocol and this Protocol[1197] and also may call upon individual experts.[1198]
5. Representatives of the International Committee of the Blue Shield (ICES) shall be invited to attend the Committee in an advisory capacity and shall maintain a list of experts willing to act in emergencies. Representatives of the International Centre for the Study of the Preservation and Restoration of Cultural Property (Rome Centre) (ICCROM) and of the International Committee of the Red Cross (ICRC) shall also be invited to attend in an advisory capacity.[1199]

OPTION II. Bureau[1200]
Draft Article 29 Functions
1. The Bureau shall have the following functions:
   a. to grant cultural property enhanced special protection upon the request of a Party or determine its suspension or cancellation in accordance with this Protocol;
   b. *to establish, update and publish the List;*

1196   Ibid., p. 155: the Indian delegate expressed doubts about the expression 'at its discretion' and suggested deleting this provision.
1197   Ibid., 24 March 1999, p. 4: the Thai delegate proposed to replace these words with a reference to the 'objectives similar to those of the Convention' only.
1198   In the cases of paragraphs 4 and 5, discretion should be given to the Committee or Bureau rather than to the organizations listed. Ibid., 17 March 1999, p. 149: US delegate.
1199   Ibid., p. 154: the Turkish delegate preferred that members of NGOs and the ICRC be invited as observers instead of in an advisory capacity.
1200   Italics in original.

c. *to cooperate with the Director-General in fulfilling the functions provided for in* Chapter and Article 36 of this Protocol and in her/his performance of the mission of control according to the Regulations for the Execution of the Convention;

d. to determine the use of the resources of the Fund established in accordance with Article 32 of this Protocol;

e. *to receive and study requests for international assistance formulated by Parties* under Article 35, to determine the action to be taken with regard to requests for international assistance, including, where appropriate, the nature and extent of such assistance, and to authorize the conclusion, on its behalf, of the necessary arrangements with the government concerned;

f. to monitor and supervise the implementation of this Protocol;

g. *to submit a report on its activities to the General Assembly and to the General Conference* of UNESCO at each of the ordinary sessions;

h. to perform any other function attributed to it under this Protocol or by the Parties.

2. *The functions of the Bureau set forth in paragraph 1 are without prejudice to the* role of UNESCO in conformity with its mandate for the protection of cultural property under its Constitution and standard-setting instruments. All functions of the Bureau shall be performed in close cooperation with the Director-General.

3. *The Bureau shall cooperate with international and national governmental and non-governmental organizations* having objectives similar to those of the Convention, its 1954 Protocol and this Protocol. The Bureau may also call upon individual experts.

4. *Representatives of the International Committee of the Blue Shield (ICBS) shall be* invited to attend the Bureau in an advisory capacity and shall maintain a list of experts willing to act in emergencies. Representatives of the International Centre for the Study of the Preservation and Restoration of Cultural Property (Rome Centre) (ICCROM) and of the International Committee of the Red Cross (ICRC) shall also be invited to attend in an advisory capacity.][1201]

1201 There is no draft Article 30 (Procedure before the Committee relating to enhanced special protection) in the alternative draft articles.

The Diplomatic Conference on the Second Protocol to the Hague Convention of 1954 for the Protection of Cultural Property in the Event of Armed Conflict took place in The Hague from 15 to 26 March 1999. Discussion of institutional issues began in the latter part of the afternoon session on Wednesday, 17 March 1999, and the early part of the morning session of Thursday, 18 March, in the Plenary Session. The discussion was based on Chapter 6 of the Draft Second Protocol (5HC/1999/1/rev.1, February 1999).[1202] The delegates favoured the creation of an Intergovernmental Committee. France considered that the function of the Committee should be more precise, for example, requiring that the Committee provide an orientation for the implementation of the Protocol and Convention.[1203] Some States insisted on the maintenance of the reporting obligation and the need for the chosen body to study reports and provide recommendations.[1204] The body should be able to provide expertise and be engaged in protection in situations where it is endangered.[1205] At the end of the Plenary Session of 18 March, the Chairman concluded the session by announcing that János Jelen (Hungary) had agreed to chair an informal Working Group to work on the provisions of Chapter 6. The Working Group on Chapter 6 was mandated to produce a consensus text on institutional issues related to the implementation of the Second Protocol to the 1954 Convention. The basis for discussion was the draft text in document HC/1999/rev.1 and the debate in the plenary sessions which had taken place on 17 and 18 March 1999. The Working Group adopted the following text of the Article with a few changes; however, the text is almost identical to that of Option I above:

Article 29 Functions
1. The Bureau shall have the following functions:
   a. to develop Guidelines for the implementation of this Protocol;[1206]

1202 *Draft Second Protocol to the 1954 Hague Convention for the Protection of Cultural Property in the Event of Armed Conflict.* UNESCO doc. HC/1999/1/rev.1, February 1999 (English, French and Russian). The comments and proposals of the State representatives are also included in the footnotes of this draft.

1203 1999 Hague Conference, Plenary Session, 17 March 1999: delegates of France and Belgium, p. 151, 158.

1204 Ibid., Greek delegate, p. 155.

1205 Ibid., Swedish delegate, p. 151.

1206 According to the French delegate, the Committee (Bureau) 'should elaborate the guidelines not only for the application of the Protocol, but also, for the application of the Convention and submit them to the Meeting of the Parties.' Ibid., 24 March 1999, p. 8.

b. to grant, suspend or cancel enhanced protection for cultural property and to establish; maintain and promote the List of Cultural Property under Enhanced Protection;

c. to monitor and supervise the implementation of this Protocol and to promote the identification of cultural property under enhanced protection according to the procedure given by the Parties to this Protocol;

d. to consider and comment on reports of the Parties, to seek clarifications as required, and prepare its own report on the implementation of this Protocol for the Meeting of the Parties to this Protocol;

e. to receive and study requests for international assistance according to Article 35;

f. to determine the use of the Fund for the Protection of Cultural Property;[1207]

g. to perform any other function which may be assigned by the Meeting of the Parties to this Protocol.

2. The functions of the Bureau will be performed in co-operation with the Director-General of UNESCO.

3. The Bureau shall co-operate with international and national governmental and non-governmental organizations having objectives similar to those of the Convention, its First Protocol and this Protocol. To assist in the implementation of its functions, the Bureau may invite to attend, in an advisory capacity, pre-eminent professional organizations such as those who have formal relations with UNESCO, including the International Committee of the Blue Shield (ICBS) and its constituent bodies. Representatives. of the International Centre for the Study of the Preservation and Restoration of Cultural Property (Rome Centre) (ICCROM) and of the International Committee of the Red Cross (ICRC) may also be invited to attend in an advisory capacity.

Not many comments were raised during the second Plenary Session of 24 March 1999, which discussed the text adopted by the Working Group. The Austrian delegate expressed satisfaction about the way in which civil society had been accommodated in the text:

1207   Ibid., p. 3.

in particular the inclusion of the International Committee of the Blue Shield which had a decade-long history of cooperation with UNESCO and had been estimated in cooperating in the implementation of the Convention. This redrafted text provided also for the invitation of other relevant non-governmental organizations which are active and successful in this field, to assist the international community and UNESCO in the implementation process.[1208]

The French delegate considered that the Committee should exercise broader functions than actually stated and should concentrate on the general protection of cultural property.[1209] In response to his remark mentioned under Article 29, paragraph 1(a), the rapporteur explained that the Working Group 'tried to avoid assigning directly any tasks to the Committee. This question also depends upon the structure of the Committee and whether the Fund was voluntary or compulsory.' [1210]

The delegate of Cameroon considered that the function in the field of general safeguarding and assistance to developing countries was missing in the text.[1211]

With minor editorial changes, the text prepared by the Working Group was included as final in the Second Protocol.

ANALYSIS OF THE TEXT

Paragraph 1

1. The Committee shall have the following functions:
    a. to develop Guidelines for the implementation of this Protocol;
    b. to grant, suspend or cancel enhanced protection for cultural property and to establish, maintain and promote the List of Cultural Property under Enhanced Protection;
    c. to monitor and supervise the implementation of this Protocol and promote the identification of cultural property under enhanced protection;

1208   Ibid.
1209   Ibid., p. 8.
1210   Ibid., p. 9.
1211   Ibid., delegate of Cameroon, pp. 5–6.

d. to consider and comment on reports of the Parties, to seek clarifications as required, and prepare its own report on the implementation of this Protocol for the Meeting of the Parties;

e. to receive and consider requests for international assistance under Article 32;

f. to determine the use of the Fund;

g. to perform any other function which may be assigned to it by the Meeting of the Parties.

It was relatively easy to draw inspiration from the World Heritage Convention for certain institutional issues, but more difficult to do so with relation to the functions of the Committee, as these functions depend greatly on a substantive part of the Second Protocol.

According to the paragraph 1 of this Article 27, the Committee for the Protection of Cultural Property in the Event of Armed Conflict will accomplish the following categories of function:

* Guidelines
* Enhanced protection
* Comments on the reports
* Requests for international assistance
* Use of the Fund
* Other functions.

Guidelines

a. to develop Guidelines for the implementation of this Protocol.

The first function was inspired by the practical application of the World Heritage Convention. Development of these Guidelines began in 1977, and it is thanks to them that provisions of the text of the Convention have been amplified. The Guidelines were adopted for the first time by the World Heritage Committee on 30 June 1977 and have been revised and completed several times since. The most recent text stems from January 2008.[1212] The Guidelines are not specifically mandated by the Convention and are an

---

1212 The Operational Guidelines for the Implementation of the World Heritage Convention: http://whc.unesco.org/en/guidelines

expression of the requirement found in Article 11, paragraph 5 of the World Heritage Convention:

> The Committee shall define the criteria on the basis of which a property belonging to the cultural or natural heritage may be included in either of the lists mentioned in paragraphs 2 and 4 of this article.

The Guidelines do not constitute a legally binding instrument, but rather perform a valuable policy function in guiding the implementation of the Convention and serving the States and all institutions involved.[1213]

Given the importance of the Guidelines in the practical implementation of the World Heritage Convention, it is not surprising that reference was made to them in the final stage of the drafting of the functions of the Committee for the Protection of Cultural Property in the Event of Armed Conflict.[1214] The French delegate even stated in the final Plenary Session of the Conference on 24 March 1999 that the Committee (Bureau) 'should elaborate the guidelines not only for the application of the Protocol, but also, for the application of the Convention and submit them to the Meeting of the Parties'. [1215]

It was at the very first meeting of the Committee for the Protection of Cultural Property in the Event of Armed Conflict that the Committee referred to the issue of the Draft Guidelines:

> 4. In view of the late submission by the Secretariat of the Draft Guidelines and the subsequent need for Committee Members and observers to consider it in depth, the Committee Members decided to suspend the meeting after having adopted final recommendations. Those recommendations invited Committee Members and other States Parties to the Second Protocol and Member States of UNESCO not party to the Second Protocol as well as entities referred to under Article 27(3) to provide in writing to the Secretariat their submissions on the Draft Guidelines by the end of February 2007. They also invited the Secretariat to convene a second session of the Committee's meeting in Paris

---

1213 Redgwell (2008), p. 67.
1214 It started to be formulated in the same way as it was in Article 11, paragraph 5 of the World Heritage Convention. Reference was made to the first Lauswolt document which gave to the Committee as its first function to 'to identify and formulate criteria on the basis of which cultural property will be specially protected' (see p. 4). The reference to the Guidelines is naturally easier and practical.
1215 1999 Hague Convention, Plenary Session, 24 March 1999, p. 8.

by the beginning of June 2007 to revise, in light of the written comments received, the Draft Guidelines which will be submitted to the next meeting of the Committee in October 2007.[1216]

The Second Meeting of the Committee, in Paris on 17–19 December 2007, was mostly devoted to examination of the Draft Guidelines. Dr. Christoph Bazil, Chairperson of the Committee, informed the meeting of the work of the Bureau by referring to the outcome of its August 2007 Vienna informal working meeting and the subsequent October 2007 Paris informal working meeting. He introduced the main tenets of the new draft of the Guidelines. After a chapter-by-chapter detailed discussion of the Draft Guidelines,[1217] the Committee developed Chapters 1, 2 and 3 of the Draft and recommended the endorsement of the Draft Guidelines by the Extraordinary Meeting of the Parties to the Second Protocol, to be held in 2008.[1218]

At the Third Meeting of the Committee, discussion continued on Chapter 4 (Dissemination), Chapter 5 (Monitoring the implementation of the Second Protocol) and Chapter 6 (International assistance).[1219]

The Guidelines required the endorsement of the Meeting of the Parties under sub-paragraph 1(b) of Article 23. From the moment they are endorsed by the Meeting of Parties, the Guidelines have considerable authority with regard to interpretation of the Protocol itself. Kevin Chamberlain rightly points out that the Guidelines 'will constitute subsequent practice in the application of the Protocol establishing the agreement of the Parties regarding its interpretation'.[1220] Article 31, paragraph 3 and in particular subparagraph (b) of the 1969 Vienna Convention on the Law of Treaties states:

3. There shall be taken into account, together with the context:
   (a) any subsequent agreement between the parties regarding the interpretation of the treaty or the application of its provisions;

1216   UNESCO, First Meeting of the Committee for the Protection of Cultural Property in the Event of Armed Conflict, Paris, 11 June 2007, CLT-07/CONF/210/3, Paris 20 June 2007, p. 1.

1217   Second Meeting of the Committee for the Protection of Cultural Property in the Event of Armed Conflict, Paris, 17–19 December 2007, CLT-07/CONF/212/4, Paris, 4 April 2008, pp. 2–4.

1218   Ibid., p. 4.

1219   Third Meeting of the Committee for the Protection of Cultural Property in the Event of Armed Conflict, Paris, 4–6 June 2008, CLT-07/CONF/204/4, Paris, 15 September 2008, pp. 2–5.

1220   Chamberlain (2004), p. 226.

(b) any subsequent practice in the application of the treaty which establishes the agreement of the parties regarding its interpretation;

(c) any relevant rules of international law applicable in the relations between the parties.

The Guidelines endorsed by the Meeting of the Parties constitute such an agreement of the Parties.

Chamberlain also mentions 'the reports of the Parties and their consideration by the Meeting of the Parties when receiving the report of the Committee',[1221] but only if such reports constitute the agreement regarding interpretation.

At the opening of the Third Session of the Committee, the Director-General 'underlined the fact that adopting the Guidelines was not an end in itself but, on the contrary, was a means of enabling the Committee to be fully effective. It was thus important to be able to rely on the commitment of all States Parties to the Second Protocol.'[1222]

Enhanced protection

b. to grant, suspend or cancel enhanced protection for cultural property and to establish, maintain and promote the List of Cultural Property under Enhanced Protection;

c. to monitor and supervise the implementation of this Protocol and promote the identification of cultural property under enhanced protection.

See the comments on Article 11 of the Second Protocol.

Reports of the Parties

d. to consider and comment on reports of the Parties, to seek clarifications as required, and prepare its own report on the implementation of this Protocol for the Meeting of the Parties.

1221 Ibid., p. 226.

1222 Third Meeting of the Committee for the Protection of Cultural Property in the Event of Armed Conflict, Paris, 4–6 June 2008, CLT-07/CONF/204/4, Paris, 15 September 2008, p. 1.

See the comments on Article 37, paragraph 2.

International assistance

> e. to receive and consider requests for international assistance under Article 32.

See Article 32 of the Second Protocol.

Fund

> f. to determine the use of the Fund.

See Article 29 of the Second Protocol.

Other functions

> g. to perform any other function which may be assigned to it by the Meeting of the Parties.

The Meeting of the Parties, the highest body in the protective system created by the Second Protocol, has the authority to assign to the Committee other functions that were not included in this Article.

Paragraph 2

> 2. The functions of the Committee shall be performed in co-operation with the Director-General.

There are two possible interpretations of the text of this paragraph:
- The Director-General will provide the activities of the Committee with the necessary prestige and professional assistance. As we have seen, the Director-General participated, for example, personally at the opening of the Second and Third Meetings of the Committee in 2007 and 2008 and provided the members of the Committee with encouragement for their work.
- The second practical understanding is linked to the following Article 28, that is, providing the Committee with necessary personnel

and programme resources and a Secretariat; both are indispensible for the accomplishment of the aims of the Second Protocol.[1223]

To understand how this paragraph appeared in the Article, we must compare successive preparatory texts. The first and second Lauswolt document of 1994 and 1997, respectively, did not include this paragraph. It appears for the first time in the draft submitted to the Diplomatic Conference in 1999 in the following form:

> 3. The functions of the Committee set forth in paragraphs 1 and 2 are without prejudice to the role of UNESCO in conformity with its mandate for the protection of cultural property under its Constitution and standard-setting instruments. All functions of the Committee shall be performed in close co-operation with the Director-General.[1224]

It was the Working Group at the Plenary Session of the Conference that modified the text and gave it its present form:

> 2. The functions of the Bureau will be performed in co-operation with the Director-General of UNESCO.[1225]

Paragraph 3

> 3. The Committee shall co-operate with international and national governmental and non-governmental organizations having objectives similar to those of the Convention, its First Protocol and this Protocol. To assist in the implementation of its functions, the Committee may invite to its meetings, in an advisory capacity, eminent professional organizations such as those which have formal relations with UNESCO, including the International Committee of

---

1223   At the Second Meeting in Paris in 2007, 'the Director-General informed the Committee members and observers of his decision to transfer the management of the 1954 Hague Convention and its two (1954 and 1999) Protocols to the Division of Cultural Objects and Intangible Heritage, with the corresponding personnel and programme resources'. Second Meeting of the Committee for the Protection of Cultural Property in the Event of Armed Conflict, Paris, 17–19 December 2007, CLT-07/CONF/212/4, Paris, 4 April 2008, p. 2.

1224   Draft Second Protocol to the 1954 Hague Convention for the Protection of Cultural Property in the Event of Armed Conflict. UNESCO doc. HC/1999/1/rev.1, February 1999.

1225   Conference document of 23 March 1999, HC/1999/5/Add.6, p.3

the Blue Shield (ICBS) and its constituent bodies. Representatives of the International Centre for the Study of the Preservation and Restoration of Cultural Property (Rome Centre) (ICCROM) and of the International Committee of the Red Cross (ICRC) may also be invited to attend in an advisory capacity.

The idea for the third paragraph of the present Article also has its origin in Article 8 of the World Heritage Convention, even if it has been slightly reformulated:

A representative of the International Centre for the Study of the Preservation and Restoration of Cultural Property (*ICCROM*), a representative of the International Council of Monuments and Sites (*ICOMOS*) and a representative of the International Union for Conservation of Nature and Natural Resources (*IUCN*), to whom may be added, at the request of States Parties to the Convention meeting in general assembly during the ordinary sessions of the General Conference of the United Nations Educational, Scientific and Cultural Organization, representatives of other intergovernmental or non-governmental organizations, with similar objectives, may attend the meetings of the Committee in an advisory capacity.

During the elaboration of this paragraph different options were presented to the expert meetings, as we have seen above.

The final text of this paragraph refers generally to governmental and non-governmental organizations, but only to those that have similar objectives to the 1954 Conventions and both Protocols. It was transferred from the end of the third paragraph of Article 8 of the World Heritage Convention to the beginning of paragraph 3 of the Article 27, which is more logical.

Three organizations are mentioned in this paragraph:
- International Committee of the Blue Shield (ICBS) and its constituent bodies:
    - International Council on Archives (ICA),
    - International Council of Museums (ICOM),
    - International Council of Monuments and Sites (ICOMOS),
    - International Federation of Library Associations and Institutions (IFLA),
    - Co-ordinating Council of Audiovisual Archives Associations (CCAAA) (as from 2005),

- International Centre for the Study of the Preservation and Restoration of Cultural Property (Rome Centre) (ICCROM), and
- International Committee of the Red Cross (ICRC).

Article 28
SECRETARIAT

The Committee shall be assisted by the Secretariat of UNESCO which shall prepare the Committee's documentation and the agenda for its meetings and shall have the responsibility for the implementation of its decisions.

Preparatory work

The Second Expert meeting on the 1954 Hague Convention for the Protection of Cultural Property in the Event of Armed Conflict. Lauswolt, The Netherlands, 9–11 February 1994.

UNESCO document: a working document prepared by the Secretariat, CLT/94/608/1 of 28 November 1994.

UNESCO, Meeting of Governmental Experts on the Review of the 1954 Hague Convention for the Protection of Cultural Property in the Event of Armed Conflict 1954, UNESCO Headquarters, Paris, 24–27 March 1997, *Final Report*. UNESCO document CLT-96/CONF.603/5, Paris, 30 April 1997.

Draft provisions for the revision of the 1954 Hague Convention and commentary from UNESCO Secretariat. CLT-97/CONF.208/2, Paris, October 1997.

Preliminary Draft Second Protocol to the 1954 Hague Convention. UNESCO document HC/1999/1, October 1998 (English, French and Russian).

Draft Second Protocol to the 1954 Hague Convention for the Protection of Cultural Property in the Event of Armed Conflict. UNESCO document HC/1999/1/rev.1, February 1999.

UNESCO, Synoptic report of comments on the Preliminary Draft Second Protocol to the 1954 Hague Convention received from High Contracting Parties to the Hague Convention for the Protection of Cultural Property in the Event of Armed Conflict 1954, other UNESCO Member States and international organizations, Paris, 15 January 1999.

Addendum to the Synoptic report of comments on the Preliminary Draft Second Protocol to the 1954 Hague Convention received from High Contracting Parties to the Hague Convention for the Protection of Cultural Property in the Event of Armed Conflict 1954, other UNESCO Member States and international organizations, Paris, March 1999, HC/1999/4.

1999 Hague Conference, Plenary Session, particularly 18 and 24 March 1999.

Bibliography

Desch, T. 1999. The Second Protocol to the 1954 Convention for the Protection of Cultural Property in the Event of Armed Conflict. *Yearbook of International Humanitarian Law*, Vol. 2, pp. 84–85.

Hladík, J. 1996. Meeting of the High Contracting Parties to the Hague Convention for the Protection of Cultural Property in the Event of Armed Conflict of 1954. *International Journal of Cultural Property*, Vol. 5, No. 2, pp. 339–41.

Hladík, J. 1998b. The Third Meeting of the High Contracting Parties to the Hague Convention for the Protection of Cultural Property in the Event of Armed Conflict of 1954 (Paris, November 13, 1997). *International Journal of Cultural Property*, Vol. 7, No. 1, pp. 268–71.

Vrdoljak, A. F. 2008. Article 14, the Secretariat and support of the World Heritage Committee. F. Francioni and F. Lenzerini (eds.), *The 1972 World Heritage Convention: A Commentary*. Oxford: Oxford University Press, p. 244.

As we have mentioned in the commentary to the previous articles, the Meeting of experts, held at Lauswolt at the invitation of the Netherlands Government from 9 to 11 February 1994,[1226] established the basic structure of Chapter 6 of the 1999 Second Protocol and also provided the first draft of articles for this chapter. This is also the case of Article 28, dealing with the Secretariat.

Article (18) of the Lauswolt document stated:

Article 18 Secretariat[1227]

1. The Committee shall be assisted by a Secretariat [appointed by the Director-General of UNESCO].

UNESCO, utilizing to the fullest extent possible its services in their respective areas of competence and capability, shall prepare the

---

1226   The Second Expert Meeting on the 1954 Hague Convention for the Protection of Cultural Property in the Event of Armed Conflict. Lauswolt, The Netherlands, 9–11 February 1994.

1227   It is understood that the administrative support and servicing of such a mechanism should have sufficient human and financial resources in order to perform its tasks with all the necessary rapidity, efficiency and flexibility.

Committee's documentation and the agenda for its meetings and shall have the responsibility for the implementation of its decisions.

On the basis of the previous studies and reports and numerous expert meetings, the UNESCO Secretariat prepared an excellent working document for the next expert session to be held in Paris in November–December 1994. This document made use of our 1996 Commentary on the Convention, Patrick Boylan's Report, and the reports of the Hague and the Lauswolt expert meetings, and provided the UNESCO Secretariat's comments on each issue.[1228]

Regarding this draft Article, the Secretariat noted only that 'UNESCO agrees that it should provide the Secretariat for whatever executive or advisory body is created.'[1229]

The discussion at the Paris Expert meeting of legal and cultural experts and military professionals met at the UNESCO Headquarters from 28 November to 2 December. The second part of the meeting was devoted to a study of new legal provisions and demonstrated differing views between the participants, particularly on the part of those who had helped in the preparation of the Lauswolt document, among others, and included the Secretariat proposal of a Bureau of States Parties and the proposal of an advisory committee, as mentioned above. The advantage of the second proposal was the lower cost and the potential for rapid response so necessary in emergencies. The author of these lines made a comparison with the ICRC, which has a rather large Secretariat, and this idea was also reflected in the report.[1230] In addition, it was pointed out that the Secretariat should be reinforced. A general meeting of all States Parties could also be held on a regular (biennial) basis.

At the Meeting of Governmental Experts on the Review of the 1954 Hague Convention for the Protection of Cultural Property in the Event of Armed Conflict 1954, which met at UNESCO Headquarters in Paris from 24–27 March 1997, the experts could not reach a consensus on the eventual form of the supervisory body and both alternatives remained: committee and bureau, as discussed above. The results of this meeting of experts were

---

1228 UNESCO document: a working document prepared by the Secretariat, CLT/94/608/1 of 28 November 1994.

1229 Ibid., p. 22.

1230 UNESCO, Expert Meeting on the Review of the 1954 Hague Convention for the Protection of Cultural Property in the Event of Armed Conflict. Paris, UNESCO Headquarters, 28 November–2 December 1994, document CLT/CH/94/2, *Final Report*, p. 5.

integrated within the 'revised Lauswolt document' of 27 March 1997. This document presents a new version of the draft Articles reflecting the discussion at this and previous expert meetings. Since no unanimous agreement was reached between the experts regarding whether to give preference to an Intergovernmental Committee or a Bureau with an Advisory Board, two options were included in this revised Lauwolt document:

> *OPTION I*: Article 14 Committee
> Article 15 Term of office
> Article 16 Rules of procedure
> Article 17 Functions
> Article 17a The Fund

> *OPTION 2*: Article 14 Bureau
> Article 15 The International Committee of the Blue Shield
> Article 16 Rules of Procedure (no text)
> Article 17 Functions (no text)
> Article 18 Secretariat

The Article concerning the Secretariat remained the same, with references to the Committee or Bureau:

> Article 18. Secretariat
> 1. The Committee [*the Bureau*] shall be assisted by a Secretariat [appointed by the Director-General of UNESCO].
> 2. UNESCO, utilizing to the fullest extent possible its services in their respective areas of competence and capability, shall prepare the Committee's [*the Bureau*] documentation and the agenda for its meetings and shall have the responsibility for the implementation of its decisions.[1231]

The same wording used in the draft Article 18 was included in the *Draft Second Protocol to the 1954 Hague Convention for the Protection of Cultural*

1231   Revised Lauswolt document, 27 March 1997. Mimeographed text established by the Secretariat. Italic text in the original. The Secretariat explained in the comments on this Article that '[n]o decision has been taken yet with regard to a form of the institutional body responsible for administering the new instrument. For this reason, the drafting group used two terms 'the Committee' and 'the Bureau'. UNESCO, *Draft provisions for the revision of the 1954 Hague Convention and commentary from the UNESCO Secretariat.* CLT-97/CONF.208/2, Paris, October 1997, p. 26.

Property in the Event of Armed Conflict (UNESCO doc. HC/1999/1/rev.1, February 1999),[1232] which was submitted to the Diplomatic Conference in March 1999.

The Diplomatic Conference on the Second Protocol to the Hague Convention of 1954 for the Protection of Cultural Property in the Event of Armed Conflict took place in The Hague from 15 to 26 March 1999. Discussion of institutional issues began in the latter part of the afternoon session on Wednesday, 17 March 1999, and the early part of the morning session of Thursday, 18 March, in the Plenary Session. The discussion was based on Chapter 6 of the Draft Second Protocol (5HC/1999/1/rev.1, February 1999).[1233] An interesting approach was suggested by the Italian delegate, who proposed the unification of UNESCO's secretarial services for all main Conventions in the cultural field, in particular including the World Heritage Centre, which actually deals only with the 1972 Convention. This would favour the coordination and unification of all financial, technical and human resources.[1234]

At the end of the Plenary Session of 18 March, the Chairman concluded the session by announcing that János Jelen (Hungary) had agreed to chair an informal Working Group to work on the provisions of Chapter 6. The Working Group on Chapter 6 was mandated to produce a consensus text on the institutional issues related to implementation of the Second Protocol to the 1954 Convention. The basis for discussion was the draft text in document HC/1999/rev.1 and the debate in the plenary sessions, which had taken place on 17 and 18 March 1999. The Working Group adopted the following text of the Article, which is almost identical to the text of Option I above, and this was adopted as the final text of the Second Protocol.

> Article 30 Secretariat
> The Bureau shall be assisted by the Secretariat of UNESCO which shall prepare the Bureau's documentation and the agenda for its meetings and shall have the responsibility for the implementation of its decisions.

1232 Draft Second Protocol to the 1954 Hague Convention for the Protection of Cultural Property in the Event of Armed Conflict. UNESCO doc. HC/1999/1/rev.1, February 1999 (English, French and Russian).
1233 Ibid.
1234 1999 Hague Conference, Plenary Session, 17 March 1999, p. 148: the Italian delegate.

During the Plenary Session of 24 March 1999, the delegates of Thailand and India considered that 'it should not be the responsibility of the Secretariat to implement the decisions of the Committee, but rather the Bureau or Committee itself.'[1235] The rapporteur acknowledged the usefulness of this remark and noted that it would be taken into account by the Drafting Committee.[1236]

With the replacement of the word 'Bureau' by the word 'Committee', the text of this Article was included as final in the text of the Second Protocol.

ANALYSIS OF THE TEXT

Once again, an article was inspired by the 1972 World Heritage Convention, in this case Article 14:

1. The World Heritage Committee shall be assisted by a Secretariat appointed by the Director-General of the United Nations Educational, Scientific and Cultural Organization.

2. The Director-General of the United Nations Educational, Scientific and Cultural Organization, utilizing to the fullest extent possible the services of the International Centre for the Study of the Preservation and the Restoration of Cultural Property (the Rome Centre), the International Council of Monuments and Sites (ICOMOS) and the International Union for Conservation of Nature and Natural Resources (IUCN) in their respective areas of competence and capability, shall prepare the Committee's documentation and the agenda of its meetings and shall have the responsibility for the implementation of its decisions.

The institutional framework of the World Heritage Convention is similar to the institutional framework created by the 1999 Second Protocol: a General Assembly of the States Parties, the World Heritage Committee and the Secretariat. According to the aforementioned Article 14, the Secretariat is intended to facilitate the work of the Committee: to prepare the Committee's documentation and the agenda of its meetings and to bear the responsibility for

---

1235 1999 Hague Conference, Plenary Session, 24 March 1999: delegates of Thailand and India, pp. 5 and 8.
1236 Ibid., p. 9.

implementation of its decisions. The same role is assigned to the Committee for the Protection of Cultural Property in the Event of Armed Conflict created by the 1999 Second Protocol.

It is interesting to note that, aside from the success of the Secretariat of the World Heritage Convention, its original formulation was criticized for being vague[1237] and leaving its role to other instruments: resolutions, decisions of the General Assembly and Committee and the Operational Guidelines. These critics apparently had no influence on the transmission of the same vagueness to the text of the Second Protocol and its Article 28. The role of the Secretariat of World Heritage Convention was originally proposed by the US, which suggested

> that the Secretariat should prepare the Committee's agenda and documentation for its meetings and ensure implementation of its decisions; it would provide information to all interested parties on the Committee's programme of operation and its priorities, and secure financial assistance; and it would act on the Committee's behalf to provide services to States Parties (or non-parties) if grave danger threatens a site or monument on their territory which was of universal importance and for which the State has not requested international protection.[1238]

The reality was different; the role attributed to the Secretariat in the final text of the Convention was 'to assist'.

The vagueness of Article 14 of the World Heritage Convention 'led to significant difficulties in the articulation of the inter-relationship between the Secretariat of the World Heritage Committee, the UNESCO Secretariat and its other organs'.[1239]

The Secretariat of the World Heritage Committee was very successful in practice. On the occasion of the 20th anniversary of the Convention, the Director-General of UNESCO announced the creation of the World Heritage Centre,[1240] which carried out the functions that the Convention entrusted to the Director-General and took the Convention 'to new heights, and for this it will have all the autonomy necessary within the Organization'.[1241]

1237   Vrdoljak (2008), p. 244.
1238   SHC/MD/17, Annex II, 5–6; quoted in Vrdoljak (2008), p. 250.
1239   Ibid.
1240   DG/Note/92/13 (13 April 1992).
1241   DG/92/27, 2.

The Secretariat of the Committee for the Protection of Cultural Property in the Event of Armed Conflict was far less successful in terms of secretarial assistance. It usually consisted of just one person in charge of administration of the 1954 Convention, often as a part-time occupation. Under such limitations, it says much about the devotion of the person in charge that the activity required was accomplished.

As we have just seen, the expert meetings that prepared the 1999 Second Protocol did not actively engage in discussions concerning the role of Secretariat. Moreover, it is not an exaggeration to say that almost nobody among the States delegates at the Conference understood the work of international institutions. Unfortunately, very little attention was paid to the proposed Article at the plenary sessions of the Diplomatic Conference. What is the reason for this negligence?

One reason perhaps was the exclusive importance given to the body composed of States representatives. The States and their representatives can provide the ideas and orientation, but they cannot accomplish real groundwork, which is absolutely necessary.

This was also the reason behind the comparison with the ICRC, which holds a very special position as an institution benefiting from neutrality, independence and a solid legal basis in the 1949 Geneva Convention. Even if it is very difficult to compare it with the position of IGOs dominated by the wills of States Parties, the ICRC is a very good example of the *sui generis* structure, which gives it a special position in situations of armed conflict. The strength of the ICRC lies in its principles. The word 'Committee' means much more than a group composed of a few humanitarian leaders: it comprises the Assembly, composed of approximately 25 personalities drawn from the Swiss economic and social structure, which determines doctrine and provides general orientation and supervision; the Executive Counsel, which is responsible for daily activities, organization and administration; and the vital Swiss and multinational staff of hundreds of employees. It is thanks to these principles, its specific structure and recognition of its *sui generis* role in international relations that the ICRC can accomplish its difficult mission in the field of armed conflicts.[1242]

It would have been preferable if the drafters of the Protocol had drawn more inspiration from this body, which has more than 150 years of experience in dealing with greater responsibilities concerning the protection of victims of war. Ultimately, however, in armed conflict, cultural property is also a victim.

1242   Pictet (1985).

Article 29
THE FUND FOR THE PROTECTION OF CULTURAL PROPERTY IN THE EVENT OF ARMED CONFLICT

1. *A Fund is hereby established for the following purposes:*
   a. *to provide financial or other assistance in support of preparatory or other measures to be taken in peacetime in accordance with,* inter alia, *Article 5, Article 10 sub-paragraph (b) and Article 30; and*
   b. *to provide financial or other assistance in relation to emergency, provisional or other measures to be taken in order to protect cultural property during periods of armed conflict or of immediate recovery after the end of hostilities in accordance with,* inter alia, *Article 8 sub-paragraph (a).*
2. *The Fund shall constitute a trust fund, in conformity with the provisions of the financial regulations of UNESCO.*
3. *Disbursements from the Fund shall be used only for such purposes as the Committee shall decide in accordance with the guidelines as defined in Article 23 sub-paragraph 3(c). The Committee may accept contributions to be used only for a certain programme or project, provided that the Committee shall have decided on the implementation of such programme or project.*
4. *Resources of the Fund shall consist of:*
   (a) voluntary contributions made by the Parties;
   (b) contributions, gifts or bequests made by:
      (i)   other States;
      (ii) UNESCO or other organizations of the United Nations system;
      (iii) other intergovernmental or non-governmental organizations; and
      (iv) public or private bodies or individuals;
   (c) any interest accruing on the Fund;
   (d) funds raised by collections and receipts from events organized for the benefit of the Fund; and
   (e) all other resources authorized by the guidelines applicable to the Fund.

Preparatory work

The Second Expert Meeting on the 1954 Hague Convention for the Protection of Cultural Property in the Event of Armed Conflict. Lauswolt, The Netherlands, 9–11 February 1994.

UNESCO document: a working document prepared by the Secretariat, CLT/94/608/1 of 28 November 1994.

UNESCO, Third Meeting of the High Contracting Parties to the Convention for the Protection of Cultural Property in the Event of Armed Conflict (The Hague, 1954), UNESCO House, Paris, 13 November 1997, *Final Report*. CLT-97/CONF.208/3, Paris, November 1997, p. 3

Draft provisions for the revision of the 1954 Hague Convention and commentary from UNESCO Secretariat. CLT-97/CONF.208/2, Paris, October 1997.

UNESCO, Meeting of Governmental Experts on the Review of the Hague Convention for the Protection of Cultural Property in the Event of Armed Conflict of 1954. Vienna, 11–13 May 1998. UNESCO document: Paris, May 1998, *Final Report*.

Preliminary Draft Second Protocol to the 1954 Hague Convention. UNESCO document HC/1999/1, October 1998 (English, French and Russian).

Draft Second Protocol to the 1954 Hague Convention for the Protection of Cultural Property in the Event of Armed Conflict. UNESCO document HC/1999/1/rev.1, February 1999.

UNESCO, Synoptic report of comments on the Preliminary Draft Second Protocol to the 1954 Hague Convention received from High Contracting Parties to the Hague Convention for the Protection of Cultural Property in the Event of Armed Conflict 1954, other UNESCO Member States and international organizations, Paris, 15 January 1999.

1999 Hague Conference, Plenary Session, particularly 18 and 24 March 1999.

Bibliography

Chamberlain, K. 2004. *War and Cultural Heritage*. Leicester: Institute of Art and Law, pp. 227–28.

Desch, T. 1999. The Second Protocol to the 1954 Convention for the Protection of Cultural Property in the Event of Armed Conflict. *Yearbook of International Humanitarian Law*, Vol. 2, pp. 84–85.

Hladík, J. 1996. Meeting of the High Contracting Parties to the Hague Convention for the Protection of Cultural Property in the Event of Armed Conflict of 1954. *International Journal of Cultural Property*, Vol. 5, No. 2, pp. 339–41.

Hladík, J. 1998b. The Third Meeting of the High Contracting Parties to the Hague Convention for the Protection of Cultural Property in the Event of Armed Conflict of 1954 (Paris, November 13, 1997). *International Journal of Cultural Property*, Vol. 7, No. 1, pp. 268–71.

The financing of safeguarding measures was the preoccupation of States that became Party to the 1954 Convention. Several States earmarked funds for this purpose (Germany, both the Democratic Republic and the Federal Republic of Germany, Italy and Switzerland). [1243]

Within the framework of the 1954 Convention, the financial aspect inherent in safeguarding measures would no doubt constitute an obstacle for countries with limited resources, such as developing countries. For this reason, the creation of an international fund enabling aid to be provided to countries exposed to the risk of conflicts and disasters was considered highly desirable. The establishment of such a fund was proposed by Spain during the preparatory work on the Hague Convention, but its proposal was not adopted. [1244]

As mentioned in the commentary on the previous articles, the Meeting of Experts, held in Lauswolt at the invitation of the Netherlands Government from 9 to 11 February 1994,[1245] established the basic structure of Chapter 6 of the 1999 Second Protocol. This meeting also provided the first draft of articles of Chapter 6 on Institutional issues, except for Article 29 on the Fund for the Protection of Cultural Property. The idea for this fund was nevertheless present in the minds of the experts in Lauswolt, even if the provision was not yet drafted. We can easily deduce this from the fact that the Fund was mentioned among the functions of the Committee according to the draft Article 17 of the Lauswolt draft:

> 1. Without prejudice to UNESCO's competence to offer its services under Article 19 of the Convention, and to take initiative to make proposals under Article 23 of the Convention, the Committee shall have the following functions and tasks:
> [(e) to decide on the use of the resources of the [Fund] established in accordance with Article [...] of this instrument;]

Another step in the evolution towards the creation of the Fund was reached at the Meeting of Governmental Experts on the Review of the 1954 Hague Convention for the Protection of Cultural Property in the Event of Armed Conflict 1954, which met at UNESCO Headquarters in Paris on 24–27 March 1997. It was at this meeting that a proposal was made to set up a

---

1243   Toman (1996), p. 63.
1244   Ibid., p. 64.
1245   The Second Expert Meeting on the 1954 Hague Convention for the Protection of Cultural Property in the Event of Armed Conflict. Lauswolt, The Netherlands, 9–11 February 1994.

Fund that could allocate financial resources on projects for the protection of cultural heritage in the event of armed conflict.[1246] The results of this meeting of experts were integrated into the 'revised Lauswolt document' of 27 March 1997. This document revised the functions of the eventual Intergovernmental Committee and kept the same reference to the Fund as mentioned above in the first Lauswolt document.

In the event that Option I (the Intergovernmental Committee) was adopted, it included a draft Article 17a concerning the Fund:

> Article 17a The Fund[1247]
> (i) A Fund is hereby established for the protection of cultural property in the event of armed conflict.
> (ii) The Fund shall constitute a trust fund, in conformity with the provisions of the Financial Regulations of UNESCO.[1248]

Regarding this Article, the Secretariat indicated that it

> is a fundamentally new provision, neither included in the Hague Convention nor in the Lauswolt document, which should assure the Committee's capability to act in case of armed conflict and its ability to provide technical assistance. It is, however, necessary to determine the source of contribution to this Fund (e.g. voluntary, governmental, non-governmental or individual contribution). Further elaboration can take place when it has been decided whether to establish the Fund or not.[1249]

A much more developed version of this draft Article was included in *The Draft Second Protocol to the 1954 Hague Convention for the Protection of Cultural Property in the Event of Armed Conflict* (UNESCO doc. HC/1999/1/rev.1,

---

1246 UNESCO, Meeting of Governmental Experts on the Review of the 1954 Hague Convention for the Protection of Cultural Property in the Event of Armed Conflict 1954, UNESCO Headquarters, Paris, 24–27 March 1997, *Final Report.* UNESCO document CLT-96/CONF.603/5, Paris, 30 April 1997, p. 4.

1247 Revised Lauswolt document, 27 March 1997. Mimeographed text established by the Secretariat. The use of the capital letters and italic in original, p. 11. See also UNESCO, *Draft provisions for the revision of the 1954 Hague Convention and commentary from the UNESCO Secretariat.* CLT-97/CONF.208/2, Paris, October 1997, p. 20.

1248 Note in the revised Lauswolt document: 'The provisions of the Fund will be further developed if a decision is taken to establish it.'

1249 UNESCO, Draft provisions for the revision of the 1954 Hague Convention and commentary from the UNESCO Secretariat. CLT-97/CONF.208/2, Paris, October 1997, p. 21.

February 1999),[1250] which was submitted to the Diplomatic Conference in March 1999. Here is the text of this draft Article, which in its draft form has the number 32:

> Article 32 The Fund
> 1. A Fund is hereby established for the protection of cultural property in the event of armed conflict.
> 2. The Fund shall constitute a trust fund in conformity with the provisions of the Financial Regulations of UNESCO.[1251]
> 3. The resources of the Fund shall consist of:
>   a. [compulsory[1252] and] voluntary contributions made by the Parties;
>   b. contributions, gifts or bequests made by:
>   i.   other States;
>   ii. UNESCO, other organizations of the United Nations system or other intergovernmental or non-governmental organizations;
>   iii. public or private bodies or individuals;
>   c. any interest due to the resources of the Fund;
>   d. funds raised by collections and receipts from events organized for the benefit of the Fund;[1253]
>   e. all other resources received.

The Diplomatic Conference on the Second Protocol to the Hague Convention of 1954 for the Protection of Cultural Property in the Event of Armed Conflict took place in The Hague from 15 to 26 March 1999. Discussion of institutional issues began in the latter part of the afternoon session on

---

1250 Draft Second Protocol to the 1954 Hague Convention for the Protection of Cultural Property in the Event of Armed Conflict. UNESCO doc. HC/1999/1/rev.1, February 1999 (English, French and Russian).

1251 George H. Aldrich (1998, p. 17) rightly pointed out that the text of the draft Article 'is drawn from Article 15 of the 1972 Paris Convention. While one of the functions of the Committee is stated in Article 21 to be deciding upon the use of the Fund, it seems necessary to state here who is responsible for managing, investing, and accounting for the Fund. If, as stated in paragraph 2, it is to be a trust fund in conformity with the Financial Regulations of UNESCO, then it would seem that the text should state that the Fund will be managed by UNESCO.'

1252 Aldrich (1998, p. 17) raised the question: 'Are there to be compulsory contributions? If so, paragraph 4 is ambiguous in its 1 per cent limit on compulsory contributions. Is it a *total* of 1 per cent of UNESCO's Regular Budget, or is it 1 per cent of each State Party's annual contribution to UNESCO? Moreover, is it an annual limit, or is there a different budgetary period? Is it possible that a Party to the Protocol may not be a Member of UNESCO?'

1253 For Aldrich (1998, p. 17), this sub-paragraph seems unnecessary as all contributions are already covered by (a) and (b).

Wednesday, 17 March 1999, and the early part of the morning session of Thursday, 18 March, in the Plenary Session. The discussion was based on Chapter 6 of the Draft Second Protocol (5HC/1999/1/rev.1, February 1999).[1254]

During this first Plenary Session, the question of the Fund was mentioned several times. The first speaker, the delegate of Lebanon, was surprised that the objective and utility of the Fund was not mentioned. He also indicated that the Committee should report to the Assembly of the States Parties concerning the use of the Fund.[1255] The delegate of Argentina underlined the voluntary contribution character of the Fund, similar to the fund created within the framework of the 1970 Convention on Illicit Expert and Import of Cultural Property. He also highlighted the difficult process of implementation in the case of the World Heritage Fund.[1256] The idea of the Fund was well accepted by some delegates[1257] and the delegates insisted on its voluntary character.[1258] Some delegates were not sure whether such a fund was really necessary[1259] and insisted on the need to clarify the use of the Fund.[1260]

At the end of the Plenary Session of 18 March, the Chairman concluded the session by announcing that János Jelen (Hungary) had agreed to chair an informal Working Group to work on the provisions of Chapter 6. The Working Group on Chapter 6 was mandated to produce a consensus text on the institutional issues related to the implementation of the Second Protocol to the 1954 Convention. The basis for discussion was the draft text in document HC/1999/Rev.1 and the debate in the plenary sessions which had taken place on 17 and 18 March 1999.

As we have seen in the report on discussions in the Working Group, the following text was included concerning discussion on the Fund:

A particularly difficult issue was the establishment of the Fund for the protection of cultural property in the event of armed conflict. Despite

---

1254 Draft Second Protocol to the 1954 Hague Convention for the Protection of Cultural Property in the Event of Armed Conflict. UNESCO doc. HC/1999/1/rev.1, February 1999 (English, French and Russian).
1255 1999 Hague Conference, Plenary Session, 17 March 1999, p. 141.
1256 Ibid., Argentine delegate, p. 144.
1257 Ibid., delegates of Spain, Italy, Sweden, pp. 144, 148, 152.
1258 Ibid., delegates of Israel, Italy, Canada, US, France, Sweden, Turkey, India and China, pp. 145, 148, 149, 151, 152, 154, 155.
1259 Ibid., delegates of Canada, France, Germany, pp. 148, 151, 153.
1260 Ibid., delegates of France, Sweden, India, pp. 151, 152, 155.

the fact that an obligatory contribution was not acceptable for the majority of Delegations to generate the necessary financial resources, a major effort was made to create a framework that could maintain a stable and flexible base for all interested parties (Article 29 (4)) to find the way for supporting the work of the Committee. It was the clear understanding of the Delegations that the Fund is only for purposes as the Committee shall decide in accordance with the guidelines as defined in Article 23 sub-para. 3(c). [1261]

The Working Group adopted the following text of the Article, which is almost identical to that of the text of Option I above, and was adopted as the final text of the Second Protocol:

Article 31 The Fund for the Protection of Cultural Property in the Event of Armed Conflict
1. A Fund is hereby established for the following purposes:
   a. to provide financial or other assistance in support of preparatory or other measures to be taken in peacetime in accordance with, inter alia, Article 5, Article 10 sub-paragraph (b) and Article 30;[1262] and
   b. to provide financial or other assistance in relation to emergency, provisional or other measures to be taken in order to protect cultural property during periods of armed conflict or of immediate recovery after the end of hostilities in accordance with, inter alia, Article 8 sub-paragraph (a).
2. The Fund shall constitute a trust fund, in conformity with the provisions of the financial regulations of UNESCO.
3. From the Fund shall be used only for such purposes as the Committee shall decide in accordance with the guidelines as defined in Article 23 sub-paragraph 3(c). The Committee may accept contributions to be used only for a certain programme or project, provided that the Committee shall have decided on the implementation of such programme or project.

1261 Report of the results of the Working Group on Chapter 6 (Institutional Issues). H.E. Ambassador János Jelen, Chairman of the Working Group. Mimeographed text distributed at the Plenary Session.
1262 According to the French delegate, the reference to these articles reduces unnecessarily the attribution of this body. Ibid., 24 March 1999, p. 8.

4. The resources of the Fund shall consist of:
   (a) voluntary contributions made by the Parties;
   (b) contributions, gifts or bequests made by:
      (i)   other States;
      (ii)   UNESCO or other organizations of the United Nations system;
      (iii) [other] intergovernmental or non-governmental organizations; and
      (iv)   public or private bodies or individuals;
   (c) any interest accruing on the Fund;
   (d) funds raised by collections and receipts from events organized for the benefit of the Fund; and
   (e) all other resources authorized by the guidelines applicable to the Fund.

During the discussion at the second part of the plenary meeting of 24 March 1999 on the result of the Working Group draft, the delegates welcomed the greater precision in the provisions on the Fund, including its role and objectives:

> The functioning of the Fund would, in the view of Austrian delegate, depend on the question of what the Fund could realistically do. In relation to further defining the functions of the Fund, he suggested studying the World Heritage system which offered assistance in their world countries to protect their property. This Fund functioned very well, because the functions had been clearly defined.[1263]

The delegate of Cameroon drew attention to the need for the establishment of inventories in developing countries and activities concerning Article 3 of the draft Protocol.[1264]

The delegate of Nigeria regretted that the word 'compulsory' had been removed from the text and that the Committee could rely only upon voluntary contributions, stating that this would lead to a lack of finances.[1265] The rapporteur explained that there was insufficient support in the Working Group to make a final decision and it was difficult for him to judge the real

---

1263 Ibid., pp. 3–4.
1264 Ibid., p. 6. The Chairperson observed in this relation that some assistance for the inventory and aid is already available through the World Heritage Convention.
1265 Ibid., p. 7

balance of interest among the different participants. He referred this issue to the Plenary Session.[1266] The delegate of Nigeria also explained that the intervention of his delegation regarding compulsory contributions was actually the position of the African Group and requested that it be taken into account by the Drafting Committee.[1267]

With changes of references to other articles, a few editorial changes and the replacement of the 'Bureau' by 'Committee', the Article was included as final in the text of the Second Protocol.

ANALYSIS OF THE TEXT

The reason for the establishment of the Fund is probably very similar to that of the establishment of the World Heritage Fund. The obligations imposed on States by the 1954 Hague Convention and by the protocols require expenses, whether for measures to be taken in peacetime or in time of hostilities. This is particularly relevant in the case of countries with limited financial resources.

The drafting of the present Article is based again on the usual model, Article 15 of the 1972 World Heritage Convention. The entirety of Chapter IV of this Convention is reserved for the Fund, but only Article 15 served as a model for the 1999 Second Protocol, Article 29. The reason for this is that Article 16 of Chapter IV of the World Heritage Convention deals with compulsory contributions, which were not accepted by the Plenary Session of the 1999 Diplomatic Conference.

> IV. FUND FOR THE PROTECTION OF THE WORLD CULTURAL AND NATURAL HERITAGE
>
> Article 15
> 1. A Fund for the Protection of the World Cultural and Natural Heritage of Outstanding Universal Value, called 'the World Heritage Fund', is hereby established.
> 2. The Fund shall constitute a trust fund, in conformity with the provisions of the Financial Regulations of the United Nations Educational, Scientific and Cultural Organization.

1266   Ibid. p. 9.
1267   Ibid., p. 10.

3. The resources of the Fund shall consist of:
   (a) compulsory and voluntary contributions made by States Parties to this Convention,
   (b) contributions, gifts or bequests which may be made by:
      (i) other States;
      (ii) the United Nations Educational, Scientific and Cultural Organization, other organizations of the United Nations system, particularly the United Nations Development Programme or other intergovernmental organizations;
      (iii) public or private bodies or individuals;
   (c) any interest due on the resources of the Fund;
   (d) funds raised by collections and receipts from events organized for the benefit of the fund; and
   (e) all other resources authorized by the Fund's regulations, as drawn up by the World Heritage Committee.
4. Contributions to the Fund and other forms of assistance made available to the Committee may be used only for such purposes as the Committee shall define. The Committee may accept contributions to be used only for a certain programme or project, provided that the Committee shall have decided on the implementation of such programme or project. No political conditions may be attached to contributions made to the Fund.

When the World Heritage Fund was created, we expressed in our 1996 Commentary the hope that it could be enlarged to include the financing of safeguarding measures provided by Article 3 of the 1954 Hague Convention,[1268] but unfortunately this was not the case.

The Commentary to the Fund characterizes it as having an 'operational' dimension

> which probably constitutes one of the main reasons for the huge success of the Convention since its entry into force. In fact – although the Fund falls greatly short of covering the whole cost of implementing the Convention – the availability of resources necessary for the Convention to function does not rely (at least in part) on the 'lunatic' willingness of States Parties to provide them voluntarily, but may count on a reserve of funds 'inherently produced' by the system of the Convention itself.

1268   Toman, (1996), p. 64.

In addition, the existence of the Fund is one of the elements making the ratification of the Convention particularly attractive for (most) states, on account of the fact that, through accessing the Convention, they not only have the chance of obtaining international recognition for their own cultural and/or natural heritage, but also tangible economic assistance for its preservation.[1269]

We have seen that in the 1999 Diplomatic Conference, the issue of the Fund provoked significant discussions. While the developed states insisted from the very beginning on the exclusivity of the voluntary character of the contributions, the developing countries – and particularly the African countries – favoured compulsory contributions.[1270]

Paragraph 1

1. A Fund is hereby established for the following purposes:
   a. to provide financial or other assistance in support of preparatory or other measures to be taken in peacetime in accordance with, *inter alia*, Article 5, Article 10 sub-paragraph (b) and Article 30; and
   b. to provide financial or other assistance in relation to emergency, provisional or other measures to be taken in order to protect cultural property during periods of armed conflict or of immediate recovery after the end of hostilities in accordance with, *inter alia*, Article 8 sub-paragraph (a).

Article 15 of the World Heritage Fund does not include details on the purposes of the Fund; these are covered by other articles of the World Heritage Convention. It is quite obvious that the main purpose of this Fund is to support States Parties to the World Heritage Convention in need of international assistance.[1271]

1269　Lenzerini (2008), p. 271.
1270　In the case of the World Heritage Fund, the compulsory contributions cover about 60 percent of the total resources of the Fund. Voluntary contributions represent 40 percent.
1271　The 'Financial Regulations for the World Heritage Fund', established by the UNESCO Director-General, state that '[the] purpose of this Fund shall be to receive contributions from the sources indicated in 3.1 below and to make payments therefrom, to assist in the protection of properties forming part of the World Cultural and Natural Heritage of Outstanding Universal Value in accordance with the terms of the Convention and of the present Regulations (1.1).'

By contrast, the present paragraph of the 1999 Second Protocol is quite explicit about the purposes of the Fund. Sub-paragraph (a) deals with the preparatory and other measures to be taken in peacetime, and presents the following as an example of financial and other assistance:

Article 5 Safeguarding of cultural property
Article 10, sub-paragraph (b) Enhanced protection
Article 30 Dissemination

Sub-paragraph (b) refers to financial and other forms of assistance in situations of emergency: expenses related to provisional and other measures that have to be taken in order to protect cultural property during periods of armed conflict; expenses relating to immediate recovery following the end of hostilities, referring in particular to Article 8, sub-paragraph (a) the removal of movable cultural property from the vicinity of military objectives; or providing for adequate *in situ* protection.

These examples are naturally not exhaustive. Other assistance can be provided in accordance with the guidelines to be established under the Article 23(3)(b).

Paragraph 2

2. The Fund shall constitute a trust fund, in conformity with the provisions of the financial regulations of UNESCO.

As in the case of the World Heritage Fund,[1272] the Fund for the Protection of Cultural Property in the Event of Armed Conflict is a 'trust fund', managed as a 'Special account' in conformity with UNESCO financial regulations.

Paragraph 3

3. Disbursements from the Fund shall be used only for such purposes as the Committee shall decide in accordance with the guidelines as defined in Article 23 sub-paragraph 3(c). The Committee may accept contributions to be used only for a certain programme or

---

1272 The World Heritage Fund is governed by special financial regulations, called 'Financial Regulations for the World Heritage Fund', established by the UNESCO Director-General in accordance with Regulation 6.7 of the Financial Regulations of the Organization. See http://unesco.org/en/financialregualtions

project, provided that the Committee shall have decided on the implementation of such programme or project.

The present paragraph is also based on Article 15, paragraph 4 of the World Heritage Convention. Management and use of the Fund rests in the hands of the World Heritage Committee, which takes into account the urgency of the requests. Article 22 of the World Heritage Convention deals with international assistance and provides details on the forms of such assistance.[1273] The following categories could be covered:

- Preparatory assistance
- Training assistance
- Technical cooperation (professional and material support)
- Emergency assistance
- Promotional and educational assistance.[1274]

These categories of assistance will resemble the implementation of international assistance according to Article 32 of the 1999 Second Protocol:

1. A Party may request from the Committee international assistance for cultural property under enhanced protection as well as assistance with respect to the preparation, development or implementation of the laws, administrative provisions and measures referred to in Article 10.

2. A party to the conflict, which is not a Party to this Protocol but which accepts and applies provisions in accordance with Article 3, paragraph 2, may request appropriate international assistance from the Committee.

1273   Article 22 states: 'Assistance granted by the World Heritage Committee may take the following forms:
   1. studies concerning the artistic, scientific and technical problems raised by the protection, conservation, presentation and rehabilitation of the cultural and natural heritage, as defined in paragraphs 2 and 4 of Article 11 of this Convention;
   2. provisions of experts, technicians and skilled labor to ensure that the approved work is correctly carried out;
   3. training of staff and specialists at all levels in the field of identification, protection, conservation, presentation and rehabilitation of the cultural and natural heritage;
   4. supply of equipment which the State concerned does not possess or is not in a position to acquire;
   5. low-interest or interest-free loans which might be repayable on a long-term basis;
   6. the granting, in exceptional cases and for special reasons, of non-repayable subsidies.'
1274   Lenzerini (2008), p. 285.

3. The Committee shall adopt rules for the submission of requests for international assistance and shall define the forms the international assistance may take.

4. Parties are encouraged to give technical assistance of all kinds, through the Committee, to those Parties or parties to the conflict who request it.

Chamberlain rightly points out that 'assistance from the Fund is not confined to Parties to the Protocol: assistance can be granted to any State, subject to the agreement of the Committee and the guidelines established under Article 23(3)(c).'[1275]

Paragraph 4

4. The resources of the Fund shall consist of:

(a) voluntary contributions made by the Parties;
(b) contributions, gifts or bequests made by:
   (i)   other States;
   (ii) or other organizations of the United Nations system;
   (iii) other intergovernmental or non-governmental organizations; and
   (iv) public or private bodies or individuals;
(c) any interest accruing on the Fund;
(d) funds raised by collections and receipts from events organized for the benefit of the Fund; and
(e) all other resources authorized by the guidelines applicable to the Fund.

Let us compare this paragraph with Article 15, paragraph 3 of the World Heritage Convention, which states:

The resources of the Fund shall consist of:
(a) compulsory and voluntary contributions made by States Parties to this Convention,
(b) contributions, gifts or bequests which may be made by:
   (i)   other States;

1275   Chamberlain (2004), p. 228.

(ii) the United Nations Educational, Scientific and Cultural Organization, other organizations of the United Nations system, particularly the United Nations Development Programme or other intergovernmental organizations;

(iii) public or private bodies or individuals;

(c) any interest due on the resources of the Fund;

(d) funds raised by collections and receipts from events organized for the benefit of the fund; and

(e) all other resources authorized by the Fund's regulations, as drawn up by the World Heritage Committee.

Sub-paragraph (a) of paragraph 4

The texts covering resources of the Fund are also formulated in a way similar to those concerning the resources of Article 15, paragraph 3 of the World Heritage Convention. The only major category that was excluded from their formulation in the 1999 Second Protocol was compulsory contributions, which were not accepted in the Plenary Session of the Conference.[1276]

Voluntary contributions of the States Parties constitute the basic form of resources of the Fund for the Protection of Cultural Property in the Event of Armed Conflict. In the case of the World Heritage Fund, these contributions constitute 40 percent of the income of the Fund.[1277]

Sub-paragraph (b) of the paragraph 4

In this category of resources, the Fund for the Protection of Cultural Property in the Event of Armed Conflict can benefit from contributions, gifts or bequests from the following sources:

i) Other States, namely States that are not party to the Protocol. By way of comparison, it is interesting to note that in the case of World Heritage Fund these contributions constituted an important source of funding, but only in the very beginning of the Fund. This income was progressively reduced since almost all countries of the international

---

1276 See p. 627 ff.

1277 Doc. WHC-06/30.COM/15 of 29 June 2006, p. 2 noted that 'receipts for voluntary contributions have reached [in the biennium 2004–2005] the highest level ever since the creation of the Fund'. Quoted in Lenzerini (2008), p. 279.

community became parties to the World Heritage Convention and became ordinary contributors under category (a).[1278]

ii)   UNESCO or other organizations of the UN system; Article 15 of the World Heritage Convention also mentioned 'particularly the United Nations Development Programme or other intergovernmental organizations'. In the case of the Fund for the Protection of Cultural Property in the Event of Armed Conflict, a special category (iii) was created for IGOs and NGOs.

iii) Other IGOs or NGOs.

iv)   Public or private bodies or individuals.

Sub-paragraph (c), (d) and (e) of paragraph 4

These categories are self-explanatory and will be developed in the Guidelines.

1278   Ibid.

Chapter 7

DISSEMINATION OF INFORMATION AND INTERNATIONAL ASSISTANCE

INTRODUCTION

In the 1954 Hague Convention, dissemination of the Convention (art. 25) and UNESCO assistance (art. 23) were included in Chapter 7 concerning execution of the Convention. In 1999, the legislators took a different approach, devoting a separate chapter to the issues of dissemination, cooperation and assistance, despite the views of certain experts present at the Conference that these issues do not belong together.[1279] There was little discussion of these issues at the 1999 Hague Conference and no dedicated Working Group was set up.

These issues are fundamental for implementation of the Convention and Protocols. Lack of appropriate knowledge and assistance constitutes one of the fundamental gaps for implementation of the provisions concerning protection of cultural property in the event of armed conflict. This was one of the shortcomings of the 1954 Convention, and one reason why it remains overshadowed by the Geneva Conventions.

The following issues are included in this chapter:

- Dissemination (Article 30)
- International Cooperation (Article 31)
- International Assistance (Article 32)
- Assistance of UNESCO (Article 33).

1279 Desch (1999), p. 85. The 1977 Additional Protocol I included dissemination and cooperation among its provisions concerning execution of the Protocol (art. 83 and 89).

Article 30
DISSEMINATION

1. *The Parties shall endeavour by appropriate means, and in particular by educational and information programmes, to strengthen appreciation and respect for cultural property by their entire population.*
2. *The Parties shall disseminate this Protocol as widely as possible, both in time of peace and in time of armed conflict.*
3. *Any military or civilian authorities who, in time of armed conflict, assume responsibilities with respect to the application of this Protocol, shall be fully acquainted with the text thereof. To this end the Parties shall, as appropriate:*
   (a) incorporate guidelines and instructions on the protection of cultural property in their military regulations;
   (b) develop and implement, in cooperation with UNESCO and relevant governmental and non-governmental organizations, peacetime training and educational programmes;
   (c) communicate to one another, through the Director-General, information on the laws, administrative provisions and measures taken under sub-paragraphs (a) and (b);
   (d) communicate to one another, as soon as possible, through the Director-General, the laws and administrative provisions which they may adopt to ensure the application of this Protocol.

Preparatory works

Meeting of Legal Experts on the Convention for the Protection of Cultural Property in the Event of Armed Conflict (The Hague, 1954), Vienna, 17–19 October 1983. *Final Report*, Paris, UNESCO, 1983, pp. 10, 14, para. 32 and 45 (CLT-83/CONF.641/1).

Report by the Director-General on the reinforcement of UNESCO's action for the Protection of the World Cultural and Natural Heritage, 140 EX/13, para. 3, p. 2.

Review of the application of the Convention for the Protection of Cultural Property in the Event of Armed Conflict (The Hague, 14 May 1954), 140 EX/26, part VII, p. 5.

Convention on the Protection of Cultural Property in the Event of Armed Conflict (The Hague, 1954). Discussion paper, prepared for the Expert Meeting on the Application and Effectiveness of the 1954 Convention. The Hague, 29 June 1993.

The Hague Meeting of Experts on the application and effectiveness of the Convention for the Protection of Cultural Property in the Event of Armed Conflict (The Hague, 5, 6 and 7 July 1993), *Final Report*, p. 6.

UNESCO document: a working document prepared by the Secretariat, CLT/94/608/1 of 28 November 1994, pp. 23–24.

Expert Meeting on the review of the 1954 Hague Convention for the Protection of Cultural Property in the Event of Armed Conflict. Paris, UNESCO Headquarters, 28 November–2 December 1994. UNESCO document CLT/CH/94/608/2, *Final Report*, pp. 4–5.

UNESCO, Meeting of Governmental Experts on the Review of the 1954 Hague Convention for the Protection of Cultural Property in the Event of Armed Conflict 1954, UNESCO Headquarters, Paris, 24–27 March 1997, *Final Report*, UNESCO document CLT-96/CONF.603/5, Paris, 30 April 1997, p. 5.

UNESCO, Meeting of Governmental Experts on the Revision of the Hague Convention for the Protection of Cultural Property in the Event of Armed Conflict of 1954. Vienna, 11–13 May 1998. UNESCO document: Paris, May 1998, *Final Report*.

Meeting of Legal Experts on the Convention for the Protection of Cultural Property in the Event of Armed Conflict (The Hague, 1954), Vienna, 17–19 October 1983, *Final Report*, Paris, UNESCO, 1983, pp. 10, 14, para. 32 and 45 (CLT-83/CONF.641/1).

Preliminary Draft Second Protocol to the 1954 Hague Convention. UNESCO document HC/1999/1, October 1998 (English, French and Russian).

Draft Second Protocol to the 1954 Hague Convention for the Protection of Cultural Property in the Event of Armed Conflict. UNESCO document HC/1999/1/rev.1, February 1999.

Bibliography

Chamberlain, K. 2004. *War and Cultural Heritage.* Leicester: Institute of Art and Law, p. 229.

Desch, T. 1999. The Second Protocol to the 1954 Convention for the Protection of Cultural Property in the Event of Armed Conflict. *Yearbook of International Humanitarian Law*, Vol. 2, pp. 63–90.

PREPARATORY WORK

Dissemination of law

As stated by the ICRC Commentary on the Geneva Conventions, 'knowledge of law is an essential condition for its effective application. One of the worst enemies of the Geneva Conventions is ignorance'.[1280]

The necessity for appropriate legal knowledge was stated at the very beginning of the codification process, in 1880, in the *Oxford Manual, The Laws of War on Land*. Written by Gustave Moynier, a co-founder of the Red Cross and President of the ICRC, the Preface to the Manual stated:

> it is not sufficient for sovereigns to promulgate new laws. It is essential, too, that they make these laws known among all people, so that when a war is declared, the men called upon to take up arms to defend the causes of the belligerent States, may be thoroughly impregnated with the special rights and duties attached to the execution of such a command.[1281]

All the Geneva Conventions that followed and the 1977 Additional Protocols included a provision requiring dissemination of the text of the Convention as widely as possible 'in their respective countries'.[1282]

The 1938 Preliminary Draft International Convention for the Protection of Historic Buildings and Works of Art in Time of War requested

---

1280 Pictet (1952–1960), Vol. I, p. 348.
1281 Schindler and Toman (2004), p. 30. The application of these rules requires in fact a rapid, spontaneous, almost immediate response, which means that the official, officer or ordinary soldier has little time available for interpreting them or taking a decision. He must therefore be familiar with the rules well before becoming involved in military action.
1282 The relevant provisions read as follow:
  • 1906 Geneva Convention, art. 26: 'The signatory governments shall take the necessary steps to acquaint their troops, and particularly the protected personnel, with the provisions of this convention and to make them known to the people at large.'
  • The 1949 Conventions included the common Article 47/48/127/144, which reads: 'The High Contracting Parties undertake, in time of peace as in time of war, to disseminate the text of the present Convention as widely as possible in their respective countries, and, in particular, to include the study thereof in their programmes of military and, if possible, civil instruction, so that the principles thereof may become known to the entire population, in particular to the armed fighting forces, the medical personnel and the chaplains.'
  • The 1977 Additional Protocol I states in Article 83:
    1. The High Contracting Parties undertake, in time of peace as in time of armed conflict, to disseminate the Conventions and this Protocol as widely as possible in their respective countries and, in particular, to include the study thereof in their programmes of military instruction and to encourage the study thereof by the civilian population, so that those instruments may become known to the armed forces and to the civilian population.

that governments and military high commands take steps to impress upon their troops the idea of respect for cultural property with a view to involving them in the protection of monuments and works of art (art. 3, para. 2).

Dissemination under Article 25 of the 1954 Hague Convention

At the 1954 Hague Conference, both the UNESCO Draft and the Conference debate demonstrated that legislators recognized the importance and necessity of disseminating the provisions of the Convention. As on many other occasions, the Hague Conference took inspiration from the provisions of the Red Cross Conventions and included in the text of Article 25 of the 1954 Hague Convention, based on these precedents:

> The High Contracting Parties undertake, in time of peace as in time of armed conflict, to disseminate the text of the present Convention and the Regulations for its execution as widely as possible in their respective countries. They undertake, in particular, to include the study thereof in their programmes of military and, if possible, civilian training, so that its principles are made known to the whole population, especially the armed forces and personnel engaged in the protection of cultural property.

This provision applies both in time of peace and time of war, and concerns civilian as well as military training. The inclusion of study of the Convention in civilian training programmes is, however, qualified by the words 'if possible'. The same formula was used in Articles 47/48/127/144 common to the Geneva Conventions. According to the Commentary on the Geneva Conventions, these words by no means imply that civilian training is less important than military training. The only reason for their inclusion is that 'education comes under the provincial authorities in certain countries with federal constitutions, and not under the central government. Constitutional scruples, the propriety of which is open to question, led some delegations to safeguard the freedom of

---

2. Any military or civilian authorities who, in time of armed conflict, assume responsibilities in respect of the application of the Conventions and this Protocol shall be fully acquainted with the text thereof.

• The Fourth Hague Convention of 1907 does not contain any provision relating to dissemination.

• The 1977 Additional Protocol II states in Article 19: 'This Protocol shall be disseminated as widely as possible.'

provincial decisions.'[1283] Nevertheless, the general character of the provision did not encourage the inclusion of training in civilian programmes.

In acceding to the Convention, States Parties undertook an engagement to disseminate the provisions of the Convention. The Report of the First Meeting of the High Contracting Parties (UNESCO/CUA/120 of 3 September 1962) stressed the importance of measures at the national level with a view to applying the Convention, such as the drawing up of inventories and the exchange of information (concerning dissemination methods employed in different countries).

Details of some forms of dissemination can be found in the reports by States – addressed more or less regularly – to the Director-General of UNESCO.[1284] Some indicate that study of the Convention has been incorporated in the training programmes of military academies or armed forces and that handbooks, brochures and guides have been distributed, together with press articles, to the general public and, especially, schoolchildren. Similarly, conferences, exhibitions and special courses have been organized for museum personnel.[1285]

The ICRC has long experience with the dissemination of humanitarian law. The development of the 1954 Hague Convention drew on close ties to the 1949 Geneva Conventions, and it even became known for a while as the 'Red Cross Treaty on Cultural Property'. In recent years, this has led to cooperation between UNESCO and the ICRC in the field of training. The ICRC regularly included protection of cultural property in its seminars, and many joint UNESCO-ICRC seminars on cultural property and humanitarian law have been organized in different parts of the world (e.g. Uzbekistan, Egypt, Cambodia and Argentina).

Knowledge and familiarity with the Convention is first and foremost the duty of members of the armed forces:

> Within the armed forces, the main effort of instruction should be directed to privates, who are in the majority and who go into action on the battlefield; they should be the first to receive instruction. When teaching privates, consideration should be given to the most favourable circumstances, when the fighting man, almost or entirely alone, suddenly has to face the unexpected: an enemy who surrenders,

---

1283   Pictet (1952–1960), Vol. I, p. 349.
1284   Reports submitted in particular in 1962, 1967, 1970, 1979, 1984 and 1995.
1285   See Toman (1984), p. 150 et seq.

a wounded soldier lying across his path, a civilian who moves into his line of fire just as he is about to squeeze the trigger, an objective which is found during an attack to be marked with a red cross, and so on. Such situations demand a response which should not only be immediate, but should be above all correct and in conformity with the law of war. These responses should be as automatic to every soldier as is his use of weapons.[1286]

Training begins at the rank-and-file level, where the ordinary soldier is taught a few basic principles. Knowledge of the Conventions must be adapted to the various categories and ranks of the armed forces. Whereas the training for privates and NCOs should be restricted to the essentials, training intended for the ranks of lieutenant to captain and especially for commanding officers should be more thorough. Commanders-in-chief are supposed to have in-depth knowledge of the humanitarian conventions, including the 1954 Hague Convention. It is they, above all, who bear the responsibility of command.

No less important are the authorities – police, paramilitary bodies and law-enforcement agencies – that might assume certain responsibilities in the event of armed conflict, especially in connection with the administration of an occupied territory. They too should be familiar with the principles of the Convention. It is interesting to note that at the 1954 Hague Conference itself, the French delegate drew attention to the need to disseminate the provisions of the Convention among police forces.[1287] This was said at a time when general dissemination of the Geneva Conventions to police forces was practically unknown.

Article 82 of the 1977 Additional Protocol I provides for the obligation to ensure that legal advisers are available to the armed forces. These advisers have both peacetime tasks (consultation on dissemination for the armed forces) and wartime duties (specific advice for military commanders who have to prepare or take decisions during hostilities). Obviously, they also need to be thoroughly trained in the protection of cultural property.

UNESCO is also aware of the need to train those who bear considerable responsibility for the protection of cultural property, particularly those

---

1286 Mulinen (1978). For example, the German military manual, *Humanitarian Law in Armed Conflicts – Manual*, edited by the Federal Ministry of Defence of the Federal Republic of Germany, VR II 3, August 1992, includes chap. 9, para. 901–36, which deals entirely with the protection of cultural property.
1287 *Records*, para. 1123, p. 218.

concerned with the safeguarding and administration of cultural property in time of peace: curators of museums and art galleries, keepers of historic monuments and buildings, attendants, and so forth. A programme for mid-level personnel and senior specialists, organized at national, regional and international level, should include courses on protection of cultural property.[1288] Provision has also been made to offer training for government officials, at the university level, as well as for the general public.

Review process of the 1954 Hague Convention

The meeting of legal experts in Vienna on 17–19 October 1983 drew attention to military and civilian training programmes and suggested that UNESCO organize such programmes covering the various aspects of protection of cultural property.[1289]

From the very beginning of the review process, the need for knowledge of the Convention's provisions was made a priority issue. In his report to the 1992 Executive Board's 140th session, the Director-General mentioned training as an essential feature of the Hague Convention.[1290] Training was also mentioned in the document presented by the Netherlands to the UNESCO Executive Board.[1291] The discussion paper prepared for the Hague Expert Meeting in July 1993 asked the experts to 'indicate how a better understanding of, and respect for, the cultural heritage can be disseminated among the armed forces' and what 'measures should be taken at both national and international level to achieve this goal? How can UNESCO assist Third World countries in this respect?'[1292] The 1993 Hague Meeting of Experts on the Application and Effectiveness of the Convention for the Protection of Cultural Property in the Event of Armed Conflict, in The Hague on 5–7 July 1993, responded to these questions by underlining the need for education at both public and military

---

1288   The Cultural Heritage of Humanity: A Shared Responsibility, Paris, UNESCO, 1982 (CLT-82/WS/27).

1289   Meeting of Legal Experts on the Convention for the Protection of Cultural Property in the Event of Armed Conflict (The Hague, 1954), Vienna, 17–19 October 1983. *Final Report*, Paris, UNESCO, 1983, pp. 10, 14, para. 32 and 45 (CLT-83/CONF.641/1).

1290   Report by the Director-General on the reinforcement of UNESCO's action for the Protection of the World Cultural and Natural Heritage, 140 EX/13, para. 3, p. 2.

1291   Review of the Application of the Convention for the Protection of Cultural Property in the Event of Armed Conflict (The Hague, 14 May 1954), 140 EX/26, part VII, p. 5.

1292   *Convention on the Protection of Cultural Property in the Event of Armed Conflict (The Hague, 1954).* Discussion paper, prepared for the Expert Meeting on the Application and Effectiveness of the 1954 Convention, The Hague 29 June 1993.

levels, preparation of training schemes, and peacetime preparation.[1293] On the basis of the Executive Board recommendations, the 27th Session of the General Conference in Paris (October–November 1993) reaffirmed, among other things, that 'better dissemination of information on the 1954 Hague Convention to the military and the public at large is important' (Resolution 3.5).

It was at the Expert Meeting held in Lauswolt, The Netherlands (9–11 February 1994), that a specific article on dissemination was adopted: Article 19.[1294] While most of the draft Articles of the Lauswolt Expert Meetings underwent modification, this was not the case for Article 19. It remained practically unchanged throughout the entire review process of the 1954 Hague Convention. Those changes that were introduced were of a purely editorial character (e.g. replacing the word 'instrument' by 'Protocol'). The only substantial modification was made in the paragraph 3(d), where the wording 'official translations of the Protocol' was deleted from the Article because it was already present in Article 37 of the Protocol.[1295]

The provision included in the Lauswolt meeting found the full support of the meetings that followed, particularly at the Government Expert Meeting

---

1293 Report by the Director-General on the reinforcement of UNESCO's action for the Protection of the World Cultural and Natural Heritage. UNESCO document 142 EX/15, Annex: Hague Meeting of Experts on the Application and Effectiveness of the Convention for the Protection of Cultural Property in the Event of Armed Conflict (The Hague, 5, 6 and 7 July 1993), *Final Report*, p. 6. http://unesdoc.unesco.org/images/0009/000958/095820Eo.pdf
See also recommendation of Patrick Boylan (1993), D.4, p. 14.

1294 The Second Expert Meeting on the 1954 Hague Convention for the Protection of Cultural Property in the Event of Armed Conflict. Lauswolt, The Netherlands, 9–11 February 1994.

1295 Article 19 of the Lauswolt document (with modifications in relation to the final text in square brackets) reads:
1. The [States] Parties shall endeavour by appropriate means, and in particular by educational and information programmes, to strengthen appreciation and respect for cultural property by their entire population.
2. The [States] Parties shall disseminate this Protocol as widely as possible, both in time of peace and in time of armed conflict.
3. Any military or civilian authorities who, in time of armed conflict, assume responsibilities with respect to the application of this instrument [Protocol], shall be fully acquainted with the text thereof. To this end the Parties shall, as appropriate:
(a) incorporate guidelines and instructions on the protection of cultural property in their military regulations [manuals];
(b) develop and implement, in cooperation with UNESCO and relevant governmental and non-governmental organizations, peacetime training and educational programmes;
(c) communicate to one another, through the Director-General [of UNESCO], information on the laws, administrative provisions and measures taken under sub-paragraphs (a) and (b);
(d) communicate to one another, as soon as possible, through the Director-General [of UNESCO], [their official translations of this instrument as well as] the laws and administrative provisions which they may adopt to ensure [its] [the] application [of this Protocol].

held in Paris at UNESCO Headquarters on 24–27 March 1997.[1296] No government comments were made concerning the Article on dissemination, and it was included as number 25 of the Preliminary Draft Second Protocol to the 1954 Hague Convention, October 1998 (HC/1999/1) and then as number 33 of the Draft Second Protocol (HC/1999/1/rev.1) and submitted to the Hague Conference.

The issues of Chapter 7 were not discussed by a special Working Group at the 1999 Hague Conference, and insufficient time was reserved for in-depth discussion. But dissemination was one of the issues mentioned at the first Plenary Meeting of the Conference. At the Plenary Session on 18 March, the UNESCO and ICRC representatives and the Austrian delegate stressed the importance of dissemination, noting that its lack constituted one of the unfortunate experiences of the previous decade.[1297] Whereas the Lebanese delegate considered Article 33(1) so general that it had no place in Chapter 7, the delegate of Israel 'considered that the provisions of the Convention on dissemination were sufficient and that there was no need to add it to this document'.[1298] The UK delegate considered the provision ambitious and comparable to Article 83 of the 1977 Additional Protocol I. It was the Argentine delegate who proposed mentioning the UN peacekeeping forces in the context of Articles 33(3), 34 and 37. The Secretariat prepared a new draft based on the discussion at the Plenary Session. Paragraph 2 of Article 33 was redrafted as follows:

> 2. The Parties shall disseminate this Protocol as widely as possible, both in time of peace and in time of armed conflict, including all necessary measures to disseminate the provisions of the present Protocol within their military contingents which take part in the United Nations operations.[1299]

Another solution was proposed by the Chairperson, which consisted of the adoption of an additional fourth paragraph to Article 33, replacing the final part of the current paragraph 2 of Article 33:

1296 UNESCO, Meeting of Governmental Experts on the Review of the 1954 Hague Convention for the Protection of Cultural Property in the Event of Armed Conflict 1954, UNESCO Headquarters, Paris, 24–27 March 1997. *Final Report.* UNESCO document CLT-96/CONF.603/5, Paris, 30 April 1997, p. 5.
1297 1999 Hague Conference, Plenary Session, 18 March 1999: Lyndel Prott, p. 206. See also pp. 209 and 213.
1298 Ibid., p. 207.
1299 Conference document HC/1999/5/Add.2.

4. Dissemination efforts shall extend to military forces taking part in operations under the auspices of international organizations.[1300]

In respect of the Secretariat's draft, one view was that information on listed cultural property might need to be considered as classified, except in the event of a conflict, because of the threat (for example from terrorists) that could be posed to such property in times of peace. Other States expressed concern about the provision of the new Article 33(2), feeling that it was unnecessary to specifically include a provision for the dissemination of information regarding the Second Protocol to soldiers who form part of a UN force, when the earlier part of the sub-paragraph has already provided for its dissemination within the context of their national forces. Others questioned the introduction of a provision, which is not reflected in the Hague Convention. The Chairperson replied that there was no reason not to include a provision which does not exist under the regime of the Hague Convention since the Second Protocol is a supplementary document, and that the new Article 33(2) would be re-examined in order to address the concerns expressed with regard to this sub-paragraph.[1301]

The two above-mentioned texts were submitted to the Drafting Committee which asked the Plenary Session for a decision. The Chairman of the Conference considered that '[in] all circumstances military personnel need to respect the rules in order to achieve that the authorities of each Party need to disseminate the rules to the maximum extent. The beginning of the phrase said everything, and he did not believe that it would add much to include a provision on the United Nations Forces'.[1302] His conclusion was supported by the majority of delegates and the Argentinean delegate withdrew his proposal.[1303]

ANALYSIS OF THE TEXT

Paragraph 1

The formulation used in this Article is stronger than Article 25 of the Convention. If Article 25 favours that dissemination be carried out 'as widely as possible', leaving the decision to local authorities, the Second Protocol refers to the 'entire population'. In this respect, it is covering all segments

---

1300 Conference document HC/1999/5/Add.2/1.
1301 See 1999 Hague Conference, Plenary Session, 22 March 1999, Précis.
1302 Ibid., 26 March 1999, p. 90.
1303 Ibid., delegates of Thailand, Germany, the US, Lebanon, Austria, Turkey, pp. 91–92.

of the population. The decision on the form of dissemination is left to State authorities, who should undertake it 'by appropriate means'. The Italian delegation at the Plenary Session of the Conference finally withdrew the additional phrase to paragraph 1. The Italian delegation was particularly concerned by the words 'shall endeavour by appropriate means', which meant that it was up to States Parties themselves to decide what the appropriate means were.[1304]

Paragraph 2

Paragraph 2 repeats the provision of Article 25 of the Convention, leaving to State authorities the decision relating to the scale of dissemination ('as widely as possible'), and reiterates the reference to the time of peace and time of armed conflict.

The UNESCO Secretariat[1305] made a useful proposal to include a reference to the 1954 Hague Protocol, which does not include a reference to dissemination. This could have been effected by placing the word 'protocol' in plural instead of singular. But this was not done and a duty to disseminate the 1954 Protocol was therefore not included.

Paragraph 3

Sub-paragraph (a) parallels Article 7, paragraph 1 of the Convention, which already engaged High Contracting Parties 'to introduce in time of peace into their military regulations or instructions such provisions as may ensure observance of the present Convention, and to foster in the members of their armed forces a spirit of respect for the culture and cultural property of all peoples.'

Only paragraphs (b), (c) and (d) are new, even if the information on laws and administrative provisions are partially dealt with in the publication of national reports. As many countries do not submit such reports, the repetition of this obligation – at least to the Parties to the Second Protocol – is very useful. The UNESCO Secretariat fully supported these three paragraphs.[1306]

1304 1999 Hague Conference, Plenary Session, 22 March 1999: Chairperson, p. 246.

1305 UNESCO document: A working document prepared by the Secretariat, CLT/94/608/1 of 28 November 1994, pp. 23–24.

1306 UNESCO document: A working document prepared by the Secretariat, CLT/94/608/1 of 28 November 1994.

Sub-paragraph (b) concentrates on peacetime training, part of the indispensible preparatory measures undertaken in times without tension, which is usually provoked by situations of conflict. This is the role, not only of governmental organizations, but should also exploit the potential of civil society.

Sub-paragraph (c) creates an information chain concerning the laws, administrative provisions and measures taken under sub-paragraphs (a) and (b). This was the purpose of the reporting system, and if such a system worked systematically, all these documents would be readily available. The problem stems from the causal and limited responses of States. We can hope that the new system will be substantially more efficient. The important part of this paragraph is the reference to the intermediary: the Director-General of UNESCO. The efficiency of this new system will very much depend on the capacity of UNESCO to respond to this role.

Sub-paragraph (d) is related to sub-paragraph (c) and concerns the laws and administrative provisions for the application of the Second Protocol.

Some experts present at the Conference considered that '[the] last part of Article 30, however, appears to be systematically misplaced as it contains an obligation of States Parties to communicate to one another the laws and administrative provisions which they may adopt to ensure the application of the Protocol, a provision which would have been better placed in Chapter 8 on the execution of the Protocol.'[1307]

1307   Desch (1999), p. 86.

Article 31
INTERNATIONAL COOPERATION

In situations of serious violations of this Protocol, the Parties undertake to act, jointly through the Committee, or individually, in cooperation with UNESCO and the United Nations and in conformity with the Charter of the United Nations.

Preparatory works

UNESCO document: A working document prepared by the Secretariat, CLT/94/608/1 of 28 November 1994, p. 24.

Expert Meeting on the review of the 1954 Hague Convention for the Protection of Cultural Property in the Event of Armed Conflict. Paris, UNESCO Headquarters, 28 November–2 December 1994. UNESCO document CLT/CH/94/608/2 *Final Report*, p. 7.

CLT-96/CONF.603/5 of 27 March 1997 and Draft provisions for the revision of the 1954 Hague Convention and commentary from the UNESCO Secretariat CLT-97/CONF.208/2.

Preliminary Draft Second Protocol to the 1954 Hague Convention. UNESCO document HC/1999/1, October 1998 (English, French and Russian), pp. 4, 11.

UNESCO Synoptic report of comments on the Preliminary Draft Second Protocol, Paris, 15 January 1999, p. 11.

Addendum to the Synoptic report of comments on the Preliminary Draft Second Protocol, Paris, March 1999, HC/1999/4, p. 4.

Draft Second Protocol to the 1954 Hague Convention for the Protection of Cultural Property in the Event of Armed Conflict. UNESCO document HC/1999/1/rev.1, February 1999.

Bibliography

Chamberlain, K. 2004. *War and Cultural Heritage*. Leicester: Institute of Art and Law, p. 230.

Desch, T. 1999. The Second Protocol to the 1954 Convention for the Protection of Cultural Property in the Event of Armed Conflict. *Yearbook of International Humanitarian Law*, Vol. 2, p. 86

'International cooperation' is a misleading title for this Article, in the context suggesting a follow-up on implementation of the Protocol, rather than a provision on serious violations. As such, the provision, inspired by Article 89 of the 1977 Additional Protocol I, is misplaced.

Article 89 was closely linked to provisions concerning sanctions, directly following Article 88 on mutual assistance in criminal matters. The present Article, on the contrary, appears in the chapter on dissemination and international assistance, which has nothing to do with criminal matters and violations. The Article would have been better placed at the end of Chapter 4 on criminal responsibility and jurisdiction.

Article 89 of the 1977 Additional Protocol resulted from a discussion concerning reprisals, and provided a useful remedy on their avoidance:

> together with other Articles of the Conventions and of the Protocol, it should help to make reprisals unnecessary, even in situations where they are not explicitly prohibited. Like provisions concerned with the individual and collective responsibility of the Contracting Parties, the mechanisms for execution and supervision, fact-finding and repression, this Article actually has as its purpose the ensuring of respect for the law, and more especially, the prevention of breaches being answered by further breaches.[1308]

The text was adopted by the Conference by a 50-3-40 vote, but the delegations regretted that the provision was not discussed in greater detail.

Article 89 addresses State responsibility for violations, and despite the general heading 'Cooperation', it refers only to cooperation with the UN. It constitutes an addition to other forms of cooperation between Contracting Parties, such as Article 1, Article 7 and provisions on repression of breaches.[1309]

The ICRC Commentary considered the wording of Article 89 to follow *mutatis mutandis* Article 56 of the Charter of the United Nations,[1310] which is aimed at cooperation towards the achievement of universal respect for, and observance of, human rights and fundamental freedoms.

1308 Commentary on the Additional Protocols of 8 June 1977, para. 3585, p. 1032.
1309 Ibid., para 3586, p. 1032.
1310 Article 56 of the Charter: 'All Members pledge themselves to take joint and separate action in co-operation with the Organization for the achievement of the purposes set forth in Article 55.' (*Commentary on the Additional Protocols of 8 June 1977*, para. 3595–96, p. 1034.)

PREPARATORY WORK

The Article appeared for the first time in the draft prepared by the Lauswolt Expert Meeting in February 1994. Already there, it was placed in Chapter 6 on 'Dissemination of information and international assistance' as Article 20, entitled 'Cooperation'.[1311] The Article remained essentially unchanged from the time of the Lauswolt meeting, with only the last part of the Article dropped.

The Secretariat of UNESCO supported this Article[1312] at the following Expert Meeting[1313] and it appeared unchanged in the revised Lauswolt document, again as Article 20.[1314] In the Preliminary Draft Second Protocol of October 1998, it appeared in completed form, referring to the final parts of Article 10 (Grave breaches) and 11 (Other violations) under the title 'International Cooperation'.[1315]

In the comments submitted before the Conference,[1316] only a few remarks were made regarding this draft provision. The remark of Israel is interesting, proposing consultation 'with the Party involved in the situation of serious violations and obtaining its approval for any proposed action to be taken against it'. Norway proposed an alternative wording, suggesting that 'undertake . . . to act' be substituted with the less strict 'should act' or 'should consider acting', and referred to Article 14 concerning the duty to provide reparations. Armenia proposed the addition of the following words at the end of the sentence: 'by creating special groups of neutral experts in case of the request of the State Party'.[1317]

1311   Article 20 Cooperation: 'In situations of serious violations of this instrument, the States Parties undertake to act, jointly, through the Committee or individually, in cooperation with UNESCO and the United Nations and in conformity with the United Nations Charter, with a view to halting and preventing [the acts] enumerated in Article[s] of this instrument.'

1312   UNESCO document: A working document prepared by the Secretariat, CLT/94/608/1 of 28 November 1994, p. 24.

1313   Expert Meeting on the review of the 1954 Hague Convention for the Protection of Cultural Property in the Event of Armed Conflict. Paris, UNESCO Headquarters, 28 November–2 December 1994. UNESCO document CLT/CH/94/608/2 *Final Report*, p. 7.

1314   CLT-96/CONF.603/5 of 27 March 1997 and Draft provisions for the revision of the 1954 Hague Convention and commentary from the UNESCO Secretariat CLT-97/CONF.208/2.

1315   *Preliminary Draft Second Protocol to the 1954 Hague Convention.* UNESCO document HC/1999/1, October 1998 (English, French and Russian), pp. 4, 11.

1316   UNESCO Synoptic report of comments on the Preliminary Draft Second Protocol, Paris, 15 January 1999, p. 11.

1317   Addendum to the Synoptic report of comments on the on the Preliminary Draft Second Protocol, Paris, March 1999, HC/1999/4, p. 4.

The same text as that found in the Preliminary Draft Second Protocol of October 1998 (art. 34) was included in the final draft submitted to the Conference, with references respectively to Articles 18 and 19.[1318] The proposals made by States were not included. As previously mentioned, the Article was not submitted to a Working Group for consideration. The draft text went directly to the Plenary Sessions of the Conference, where it was included in the final text without modification.

ANALYSIS OF THE TEXT

As mentioned above, this Article refers to serious violations, that is, violations according to Article 15 of the Second Protocol, and as such, it logically belongs in Chapter 4 of the Protocol. However, as the Article was placed elsewhere, it is unclear whether the term 'serious violations' has a different meaning than its usage in Article 15:

> Although Article 15 may serve as a guideline for what the drafters of the Second Protocol considered to be violations of such a character, States Parties are free to also consider other violations of the Second Protocol as serious in the sense of Article 31, such as, for example, the systematic and widespread use of cultural property in violation of the 1954 Convention or the Second Protocol, the illicit removal of cultural property from occupied territory, in particular when committed as a part of a plan or policy, or the (continuous) violation by a State Party of its obligation to either try or extradite the alleged offender of a serious violation of the Second Protocol.[1319]

But as the text exists in its present form and at its present position, we can only stress that it concerns serious violations of the Protocol, and not of the Convention. This is logical, as the Article concerns international cooperation between States Parties to the Second Protocol. Therefore, only Parties to the Second Protocol have a duty to ensure cooperation. The Convention has no provision of this kind.

In the event that serious violations arise, the Parties can respond in two ways:

1318   Draft Second Protocol to the 1954 Hague Convention, HC/1999/1/rev.1.
1319   Desch (1999), pp. 86–87.

a) *'Undertake to act, jointly through the Committee'*: The model, Article 89 of the 1977 Additional Protocol I, also uses the word 'jointly', meaning the mutual action of States Parties to the Protocol. This simple formulation is understandable and may prove a practical way of reacting to serious violations. How this will be done 'through the Committee' is less evident and far less practical. By definition, not all Parties will be members of the Committee. How will they submit their request to the Committee? Perhaps, not all members of the Committee will agree with the attitude of other States. It seems that the experts who favoured the creation of the Committee were willing to provide it with an additional role without looking too closely at the practical side of the question.

b) *'undertake to act [...] individually' 'in cooperation with UNESCO and the United Nations and in conformity with the Charter of the United Nations'.*

In both situations, according to our view, the Parties will act 'in cooperation with UNESCO and the United Nations and in conformity with the Charter of the United Nations'. Whether they act through the Committee, or individually, they should cooperate with UNESCO or the UN. The choice of option is theirs, but may also be dictated by the situation. As we have seen, in certain conflict situations, the UN may be better placed to provide the necessary resources to resolve the situation.

The Charter of the United Nations constitutes the framework in which international relations take place. Today, practically all States, which constitute the international community, are members of the UN, and as such should act in full conformity with its Charter.[1320]

It is also important to note that according to Article 103 of the Charter, '[in] the event of a conflict between the obligations of the Members of the UN under the present Charter and their obligations under any other international agreement, their obligations under the [present] Charter shall prevail.'

What form of cooperation may UNESCO or the UN provide to assist the individual actions of States? The ICRC commentary considers that the actions.

1320   The ICRC commentary on Article 89 rightly pointed out that even if not a member of the United Nations, such States will be exposed to the influence of other Members of the United Nations, who have an obligation to ensure that States that are not Members act in accordance with the principles laid down in Article 2 of the Charter. It should be noted that at the moment when the Commentary was written, in 1984, States such as the Republic of Korea and Switzerland were not members of the United Nations. See *Commentary on the Additional Protocols of 8 June 1977*, para. 3594, p. 1034.

to which Article 89 refers may therefore consist of issuing an appeal to respect humanitarian law, just as well as, for example, setting up enquiries on compliance with the Conventions and the Protocol and even, where appropriate, of coercive actions which may include the use of armed force.[1321] United Nations actions may also take the form of assistance in terms of material or personnel, given to Protecting Powers, their substitutes or to humanitarian organizations.[1322]

The ICRC Commentary also rightly points out that this Article does not create a new law and leaves intact the rights of States to collective and individual self-defense. The same can be said for UNESCO, which can issue appeals or establish investigation commissions in cases of violations. As Kevin Chamberlain rightly pointed out, it is a weak provision leaving it to 'UNESCO and/or the UN to decide what should be done'.[1323]

As the provision was copied rather mechanically from Article 89 of the 1977 Additional Protocol I, UNESCO was added to the UN in consideration of the fact that protection of cultural property falls within the competence of this specialized agency. However, it appears that the drafters of this Article did not exert much effort in establishing exactly what UNESCO's role might be.

1321 The ICRC notes refer to the following Article of the Charter: 'Relevant Articles of the Charter: (a) General Assembly: 10, 11 (paras. 2 and 3), 12, 14 and 15; (b) Security Council: 24, 39–51. In addition, the General Assembly, in its Resolution 377(V) of 1950 ('Uniting for Peace'), confirmed its competence to recommend collective measures, including the use of armed force when necessary, if the Security Council because of lack of unanimity fails to act where there appears to be a threat to the peace, breach of the peace, or act of aggression'. *Commentary on the Additional Protocols of 8 June 1977*, p. 1035, n. 21.

1322 Ibid., para. 3597, p. 1035.

1323 Chamberlain (2004), p. 230.

Article 32
INTERNATIONAL ASSISTANCE

1. *A Party may request from the Committee international assistance for cultural property under enhanced protection as well as assistance with respect to the preparation, development or implementation of the laws, administrative provisions and measures referred to in Article 10.*
2. *A party to the conflict, which is not a Party to this Protocol but which accepts and applies provisions in accordance with Article 3, paragraph 2, may request appropriate international assistance from the Committee.*
3. *The Committee shall adopt rules for the submission of requests for international assistance and shall define the forms the international assistance may take.*
4. *Parties are encouraged to give technical assistance of all kinds, through the Committee, to those Parties or parties to the conflict who request it.*

Preparatory works

The Second Expert Meeting on the 1954 Hague Convention for the Protection of Cultural Property in the Event of Armed Conflict. Lauswolt, The Netherlands, 9–11 February 1994, p. 11.

UNESCO document: A working document prepared by the Secretariat, CLT/94/608/1 of 28 November 1994, part 10, p. 25.

Draft provisions for the revision of the 1954 Hague Convention and commentary from the UNESCO Secretariat. CLT-97/CONF.208/2, Paris, October 1997. The document included the text of the 'revised Lauswolt document'.

Preliminary Draft Second Protocol to the 1954 Hague Convention. UNESCO document HC/1999/1, October 1998 (English, French and Russian), pp. 4, 11.

UNESCO, Summary of comments on Preliminary Draft Second Protocol to the 1954 Hague Convention received from High Contracting Parties to the Hague Convention for the Protection of Cultural Property in the Event of Armed Conflict 1954, other UNESCO Member States and international organizations, Paris, 15 January 1999.

Draft Second Protocol to the 1954 Hague Convention for the Protection of Cultural Property in the Event of Armed Conflict. UNESCO document HC/1999/1/rev.1, February 1999.

Bibliography

Chamberlain, K. 2004. *War and Cultural Heritage*. Leicester: Institute of Art and Law, pp. 230–31.

Desch, T. 1999. The Second Protocol to the 1954 Convention for the Protection of Cultural Property in the Event of Armed Conflict. *Yearbook of International Humanitarian Law*, Vol. 2, pp. 63–90.

Article 32 is a complement to Article 23 of the Convention, 'Assistance of UNESCO'. The latter Article was also included in Article 33 of the Second Protocol.

To understand the motivations of the drafters who elaborated this additional Article on international assistance, these two provisions need to be reconciled. Perhaps the preparatory work for the Protocol may help us understand their intentions.

PREPARATORY WORK

This Article appears in its first form in the Lauswolt document, adopted by the Second Expert Meeting on the 1954 Hague Convention.[1324] Article 21 of this document is entitled 'International assistance' and consists of one paragraph:

> Without prejudice to the Convention any State Party to the Convention may request *the Committee international assistance for cultural property* specially protected as well as assistance with respect to the preparation, development or implementation of the laws, administrative provisions and measures referred to in Article [...] of this instrument.[1325]

The basis of this Article is already present, while other elements were added during the development of the Protocol. It is interesting to note that, at this stage, in 1994, the draft Article already speaks of the Committee; as we know, the decision to create the Committee came at a much later stage. Two forms of assistance are already envisaged:

1. Assistance concerned with special protection, which later became 'enhanced protection', and

---

1324 The Second Expert Meeting on the 1954 Hague Convention for the Protection of Cultural Property in the Event of Armed Conflict. Lauswolt, The Netherlands, 9–11 February 1994, p. 11.

1325 The emphasized text is maintained in Article 32 of the Second Protocol.

2. Assistance with respect to the preparation, development or implementation of laws, administrative provisions and measures referred to in Article [...].

The comments of the UNESCO Secretariat – included in the commentary on the preparatory work, included in the Lauswolt document[1326] – make for interesting reading. In our view, the experts would have been wise to pay more attention to the following suggestion of the Secretariat:

> UNESCO considers that this Article may create confusion. It is important that, in an emergency situation, a State which needs assistance should have no doubt as to the correct place to seek assistance. Article 23 of the Convention already provides for application for assistance to UNESCO. UNESCO would, of course, apply to the ICBS or the Bureau (or Committee) in the appropriate circumstances. Accordingly, UNESCO does not support this article.[1327]

The comments of States presented to the subsequent Expert Meetings and the Expert Meetings themselves paid no attention to this provision. Instead, they were mostly preoccupied with the decision concerning the creation of the body that would implement the new instrument, whether a Bureau or an Intergovernmental Committee. The revised Lauswolt document left the provision on international assistance unchanged.[1328]

The *Preliminary Draft Second Protocol to the 1954 Hague Convention* from October 1998[1329] included the same provision under number 27 with one additional paragraph 2, which we find now with slight modification as paragraph 3 of Article 32 of the Second Protocol:

> The Committee shall adopt rules of procedure for the submission of requests for international assistance and shall define the forms the international assistance may take.

1326 UNESCO document: A working document prepared by the Secretariat, CLT/94/608/1 of 28 November 1994.

1327 Ibid., part 10, p. 25.

1328 *Draft provisions for the revision of the 1954 Hague Convention and commentary from the UNESCO Secretariat.* CLT-97/CONF.208/2, Paris, October 1997. The document included the text of the 'revised Lauswolt document'.

1329 *Preliminary Draft Second Protocol to the 1954 Hague Convention.* UNESCO document HC/1999/1, October 1998 (English, French and Russian), pp. 4, 11.

This Article on 'International assistance' was followed in the Preliminary Draft by Article 28, which repeated the provision of Article 23 of the Convention and is identical to it:[1330]

> Article 28 Assistance of UNESCO
> 1. The States [High Contracting] Parties may call upon UNESCO [the United Nations Educational, Scientific and Cultural Organization] for technical assistance in organizing the protection of their cultural property, or in connection with any other problem arising out of the application of the present Protocol [Convention or the Regulations for its execution]. UNESCO [The Organization] shall accord such assistance within the limits fixed by its programme and by its resources.
> 2. UNESCO [The Organization] is authorized to make, on its own initiative, proposals on this matter to the States [High Contracting] Parties.

Only a few comments were made on the Preliminary Draft.[1331] China proposed to delete the words 'rules of' in paragraph 2. Concerning Article 28 (repetition of Article 23 from the Convention), Austria requested that the paragraph be reconsidered and Turkey wished to delete paragraph 2.

The draft submitted to the Conference included Article 35, its text almost identical to that finally adopted,[1332] and also Article 36, 'Assistance of UNESCO', which repeated Article 23 of the Convention with only minor editorial changes, as indicated above.

1330   The minor editorial changes, in comparison with Article 23, are indicated by square brackets.

1331   UNESCO, Summary of comments on Preliminary Draft Second Protocol to the 1954 Hague Convention received from High Contracting Parties to the Hague Convention for the Protection of Cultural Property in the Event of Armed Conflict 1954, other UNESCO Member States and international organizations, Paris, 15 January 1999.

1332   Article 35 International assistance
1. A Party may request the Committee [*Bureau*] for international assistance for cultural property under enhanced protection as well as assistance with respect to the preparation, development or implementation of the laws, administrative provisions and measures referred to in *Article 11 of this Protocol.*
2. A party to the conflict, which is not a Party to this Protocol but which notified its intention to comply [accepts and applies] with the provisions of this Protocol in accordance with *Article 2,* paragraph 2, may request appropriate international assistance from the Committee [*Bureau*].
3. The Committee [*Bureau*] shall adopt rules for the submission of requests for international assistance and shall define the forms the international assistance may take.
4. Parties are encouraged to give technical assistance of all kinds, through the Committee [*Bureau*], to those Parties or parties to the conflict who request it.

Little attention was paid to this Article at the Conference. The representative of the Secretariat explained that some countries 'would not be able to give adequate protection to their cultural heritage unless they were aided by the international community'.[1333] This is why these provisions were included. Several delegates expressed their opinion on this Article, and their comments will be dealt with in the following section.

ANALYSIS OF THE TEXT

Here we are again confronted with a misplaced text, demonstrating that Chapter 7 serves more or less as a depository for articles relating to different issues. The provisions of this Article have no connection to the subject at hand. It is tempting to speculate that the delegates, pressed for time, added to this chapter articles that were supposed to be placed in other chapters of the Protocol. The present Article is a good example: it deals with an issue that falls within the competence of the Committee and should therefore have been placed in Chapter 6 on institutional matters.

Paragraph 1

1. A Party may request from the Committee international assistance for cultural property under enhanced protection as well as assistance with respect to the preparation, development or implementation of the laws, administrative provisions and measures referred to in Article 10.

At the Plenary Session, the delegate of Cameroon considered that technical assistance with inventories would be necessary for his country, but expressed doubt about the need for assistance with the preparation of texts.[1334]

The major problem, extensively discussed at the Plenary Session, was the reference not only to enhanced protection under Article 10 but also to general protection under Article 5. The Nigerian delegate, supported by several delegates of developing countries proposed a modification to Article 32, paragraph 1 ('A Party may request from the Committee international assistance for cultural property under enhanced protection as well as assistance with respect to the preparation, development or implementation'), and the

---

1333   1999 Hague Conference, Plenary Session, 18 March 1999: Lyndel Prott, p. 206.
1334   Ibid., p. 208.

deletion of the wording 'of the laws, administrative provisions and' and substitute 'of measures referred to in Articles 5 and 10'.[1335]

These changes were opposed by the rapporteur (Chairman of the Working Group on Chapters 6 and 7), who considered that:

> Chapter 6, including the Fund was designed mainly to help and provide international assistance for cultural property under enhanced protection, as was also the case in Article 32(1). The Article in its current form already incorporated the notion of 'preparation', together with assistance for the preparation of sites for nomination whether they are under the general or special protection regimes of the Convention.[1336]

This explanation was opposed by the Ethiopian delegate, who stated that paragraph 1 'did not go far enough and would exclude cultural property under general protection which was of particularly great importance to developing countries where the general protection regime would predominantly apply'.[1337] As no other countries intervened, the Chairman interpreted the silence to mean a lack of support for the Nigerian delegate's proposal, which was ultimately withdrawn.[1338]

In our view, the proposal of the developing countries, and of Nigeria in particular, gave much more sense to this provision than the text has in its present form. This was another example of how the lack of time for the discussion of issues resulted in the adoption of a confusing provision. The attitude of the Chairman of the Working Group on Chapters 6 and 7 is difficult to understand.

Interesting in this connection is the paragraph of the resolution adopted by the 1999 Hague Diplomatic Conference, which refers to the needs of developing countries regarding the implementation of instruments concerning cultural property:

> *Recognising* that a number of developing countries may have difficulty in fully implementing the provisions of The Hague Convention, its First Protocol and the present Protocol.

1335   Ibid., 26 March 1999, Nigerian delegate, pp. 93–94.
1336   Ibid., Ethiopian delegate, supported by the delegate of Senegal, p. 94.
1337   Ibid., p. 94.
1338   Ibid., p. 97.

Nevertheless, it is doubtful that the drafting of the laws, administrative provisions and measures will be particularly helpful, and these will not require mention in major legal instruments.

The Article is concerned only with international assistance provided through the Committee. It may be theoretically good and just, but we should not forget that such assistance will often be provided in bilateral form, which cannot be excluded and will necessarily be based on political considerations. It would also, in our view, be preferable to cover international assistance addressing both enhanced protection and general protection.

However, we should not forget the main reason for this provision, which is closely related to Article 10, paragraph (b). It acts as an executive provision for the paragraph, enabling the Committee to replace the requirement of paragraph (b) and help the Party obtain enhanced protection. This was probably the understanding of the silent majority of the delegates. Another commentator observed that:

> where a State is unable to meet the requirements of Article 10, sub-paragraph (b), enhanced protection may be granted where the other conditions of Article 10 are fulfilled, provided a request for assistance is made under Article 32. Since the Fund established under Article 29 is competent *inter alia* to provide assistance to enable a party to fulfill its obligations under Article 10, sub-paragraph (b), then the resources of the Fund could be used to provide international assistance under Article 32.[1339]

As one of the delegates, Thomas Desch, stated, 'this right to request assistance applies in peacetime as well as in times of armed conflicts'.[1340]

Paragraph 2

> 2. A party to the conflict, which is not a Party to this Protocol but which accepts and applies provisions in accordance with Article 3, paragraph 2, may request appropriate international assistance from the Committee.

1339 Chamberlain (2004), pp. 230–31.
1340 Desch (1999), p. 87.

This is a necessary provision with respect to Article 3, paragraph 2, in order to maintain the same level of protection and attention for all Parties. It is a consequence of the decision to open up the application of the Protocol to States who then become *de facto* Party to it. It is also consistent with the Fund's being available not only to Parties to the Protocol.

Paragraph 3

> 3. The Committee shall adopt rules for the submission of requests for international assistance and shall define the forms the international assistance may take.

This paragraph appears first in the *Preliminary Draft Second Protocol to the 1954 Hague Convention* (UNESCO document HC/1999/1, October 1998). Paragraph 2 of this Article referred to the rule of procedure for submission. The words 'of procedure' were deleted in the final text.

The preparation of such rules for submission will be one of the Committee's tasks. The experience of the World Heritage Committee will be of great assistance in this respect.[1341]

Paragraph 4

> 4. Parties are encouraged to give technical assistance of all kinds, through the Committee, to those Parties or parties to the conflict who request it.

The Australian delegate said that this paragraph provides

> that Parties are encouraged to give technical assistance of all kinds through the Committee to those Parties or parties to a conflict who request it, seemed to read as though it would be the only channel for technical assistance while the vast majority of technical assistance would in fact be given bilaterally. He suggested redrafting this

---

1341 See Operational Guidelines for the Implementation of the World Heritage Convention. UNESCO, Intergovernmental Committee for the Protection of World Cultural and Natural Heritage, World Heritage Centre, WHC.05/2, 2 February 2005, pp 63–66. See, in particular, Annex 8 International Assistance Request Form, pp. 129–38. Evaluation criteria of the Advisory Bodies for International Assistance Requests are in preparation and will be included as Annex 9 to the Operational Guidelines.

provision to ensure that it would not preclude the Parties' ability to assist other parties to implement the Convention other than through the Committee.[1342]

By contrast, the Argentine delegate was in favour of the assistance provided by the new institutional scheme.[1343]

These two proposals demonstrate a realistic and an idealistic attitude. It seems likely that States will always prefer to provide assistance to States on a bilateral basis. This was also recognized by the Protocol itself in Article 33, paragraph 2, which refers to bilateral and multilateral assistance. This was also expressed in the resolution adopted by the 1999 Hague Diplomatic Conference, which stated that it '*Urges* all States party to the present Protocol to give careful consideration to requests from developing countries either at bilateral level or within the framework of intergovernmental organizations'.

As the paragraph refers to 'parties' (lower case), the technical assistance might be provided to insurgent forces in cases of non-international armed conflict.

1342   1999 Hague Conference, Plenary Session, 18 March 1999, p. 209.
1343   The Argentine delegate was opposed to Article 36 on assistance of UNESCO and declared this Article to be inappropriate 'for the reason that the Second Protocol established an institutional scheme and possibly a Fund. He preferred that the international assistance therefore be provided within that institutional scheme' (ibid., p. 210).

Article 33
ASSISTANCE OF UNESCO

1. *A Party may call upon UNESCO for technical assistance in organizing the protection of its cultural property, such as preparatory action to safeguard cultural property, preventive and organizational measures for emergency situations and compilation of national inventories of cultural property, or in connection with any other problem arising out of the application of this Protocol. UNESCO shall accord such assistance within the limits fixed by its programme and by its resources.*
2. *Parties are encouraged to provide technical assistance at bilateral or multilateral level.*
3. *UNESCO is authorized to make, on its own initiative, proposals on these matters to the Parties.*

Preparatory works

UNESCO document: A working document prepared by the Secretariat, CLT/94/608/1 of 28 November 1994, p. 24.

Expert Meeting on the review of the 1954 Hague Convention for the Protection of Cultural Property in the Event of Armed Conflict. Paris, UNESCO Headquarters, 28 November–2 December 1994. UNESCO document CLT/CH/94/608/2 *Final Report*, p. 7.

Preliminary Draft Second Protocol to the 1954 Hague Convention. UNESCO document HC/1999/1, October 1998 (English, French and Russian), pp. 4, 11.

Draft Second Protocol to the 1954 Hague Convention for the Protection of Cultural Property in the Event of Armed Conflict. UNESCO document HC/1999/1/rev.1, February 1999.

Bibliography

Chamberlain, K. 2004. *War and Cultural Heritage.* Leicester: Institute of Art and Law, p. 230.

Desch, T. 1999. The Second Protocol to the 1954 Convention for the Protection of Cultural Property in the Event of Armed Conflict. *Yearbook of International Humanitarian Law*, Vol. 2, pp. 63–90.

Article 33 is an important complement to Article 23 of the Convention entitled 'Assistance of UNESCO'. As mentioned in the commentary on Article 23 above, this constitutes one of the fundamental provisions, one on which the entire edifice of the present state of cultural property is built. Furthermore, it stressed the institutional framework for protection. Article 23 of the 1954 Hague Convention reads:

> Article 23 Assistance of UNESCO
> 1. The High Contracting Parties may call upon the United Nations Educational, Scientific and Cultural Organization for technical assistance in organizing the protection of their cultural property, or in connexion with any other problem arising out of the application of the present Convention or the Regulations for its execution. The Organization shall accord such assistance within the limits fixed by its programme and by its resources.
> 2. The Organization is authorized to make, on its own initiative, proposals on this matter to the High Contracting Parties.

In our 1996 Commentary on this Article, we indicated that protection of cultural property not only is based on the 1954 Hague Convention but is also included in the Constitution of UNESCO, giving the Organization a general mandate 'to maintain, increase and diffuse knowledge: by assuring the conservation and protection of the world's inheritance of books, works of art and monuments of history and science, and recommending to the nations concerned the necessary international conventions'.[1344] In our 1996 Commentary, we made the following observations:

> In order to carry out this mandate in peacetime, UNESCO has adopted numerous recommendations and conventions, in particular the Convention on the Means of Prohibiting and Preventing the Illicit Import, Export and Transfer of Ownership of Cultural Property adopted by the General Conference at its session in Paris on 14 November 1970, and the Convention concerning the Protection of the World Cultural and Natural Heritage, approved by the General Conference at its seventeenth session in Paris on 16 November 1972. In giving UNESCO this mandate, the States thereby recognized that the protection of cultural property was no longer an internal affair but

---

1344   UNTS, Vol. 4, p. 276 et seq.

a question of concern to the whole of humanity and the international community in general. As we noted in connection with Article 19 [of the Convention], States can no longer cite paragraph 3 of Article 1 of UNESCO's Constitution and refuse any initiative on the pretext that it is an internal matter in which UNESCO has no right to intervene. It should also be noted that the World Conference on Cultural Policies, held in Mexico City from 26 July to 6 August 1982, concluded that 'in a world torn by dissensions which imperil the cultural values of the different civilizations, the Member States and Secretariat of the United Nations Educational, Scientific and Cultural Organization must increase their efforts to preserve such values and take more intensive action to further the development of mankind. The establishment of a lasting peace is essential to the very existence of human culture.' Moreover, under this same mandate, the international community also gave UNESCO the right to take cultural initiatives, such as formulating recommendations, adopting international conventions, offering its services, making proposals and giving advice, not only in situations of armed conflict but also in other exceptional situations, such as internal strife, natural disasters, and so on. Without that right, UNESCO would certainly not be able to carry out this mandate. To perform the mission entrusted to it, UNESCO must remain faithful to its objective and work exclusively for its realization. In order to serve cultural property and hence the whole of the international community, it must remain aloof from politics so as to avoid confrontations. It must also act impartially and help to settle disputes between its members. Experience has shown that UNESCO is capable of fulfilling its mission, and that the action it has taken to protect cultural property is credible.[1345]

In one of the previous studies, we also mentioned

how great is the responsibility placed upon UNESCO in connection with the application of the [...] Convention. This responsibility, together with its right of initiative, provides UNESCO with numerous possibilities for action. The example of ICRC shows that this initiative can be carried very far, without being scrupulously confined to the letter of the legal provisions. This no doubt leaves UNESCO exposed

---

1345   Toman (1996), pp. 258–59.

to criticism from those whose intentions are not always in keeping with the spirit of the Convention.[1346]

PREPARATORY WORK

As we have seen, an Article entitled 'Substitute for the organization of control' already appeared in the Lauswolt document.[1347] Article 13 stated:

1. In addition to the provisions of the Convention, the States Parties are invited to encourage the Director-General of UNESCO to perform the mission of control according to the Regulations for the execution of the Convention in coordination with the Committee.
2. The Committee may also invite the Director-General of UNESCO to fulfill these functions.

It is obvious that the UNESCO Secretariat placed great emphasis on the future role of the Organization.[1348] It referred to the previous work of UNESCO on the basis of both the 'general right of cultural initiatives' and its Constitution. The Secretariat also quoted the text of our 1996 Commentary on the Convention, and mentioned Patrick Boylan's proposals, who 'too found that UNESCO could accomplish far more on the basis of the existing texts, provided that it is given the necessary means'. Boylan proposed a series of initiatives and activities, some of which the Secretariat has since carried out, despite meagre funding. In particular, they have organized regional workshops on the Convention, conducted campaigns to increase the number of ratifications by States, engaged in closer cooperation with the Red Cross, initiated negotiations with the UN to send advisers to protect cultural heritage in war zones, sent requests to Member States that have sites on the World Heritage List to explore the possibility of including these in the Register of Property Enjoying Special Protection, and launched programmes to teach tolerance or to train military personnel. Boylan does not in fact recommend

---

1346 UNESCO document: A working document prepared by the Secretariat, CLT/94/608/1 of 28 November 1994, p. 17.

1347 The Second Expert Meeting on the 1954 Hague Convention for the Protection of Cultural Property in the Event of Armed Conflict. Lauswolt, The Netherlands, 9–11 February 1994, p. 7.

1348 UNESCO document: A working document prepared by the Secretariat, CLT/94/608/1 of 28 November 1994, pp. 17–19.

making any formal amendments to the Convention;[1349] instead he feels that priority should be given to effective application of the provisions of the existing text.[1350]

The Secretariat considered that

> the Lauswolt experts therefore desired, by means of Article 13 of the *Lauswolt document*, to invite the Director-General UNESCO to perform such missions of control, although not to the exclusion of the present system. Accordingly, the system of control provided for in the *Regulations for the Execution of the Convention* would remain in force conjointly with the new practice.
>
> The Secretariat approves this decision which strengthens the legal basis of the action of the Director-General. However, a slight ambiguity remains concerning the meaning, in actual practice, of the words 'in coordination with the Committee'. The 'Committee', is the body proposed by the Lauswolt experts in Article 14 concerning institutional issues. Considering that one criticism made of the present system of Commissioners-General is its unwieldiness, there is clearly a danger that the involvement of a 'Committee', will make this control procedure even more cumbersome. Is there not a case to be made for considering that the Director-General – in view of the fact that, as the head of an intergovernmental body, he is empowered to represent its views as with one voice – has more scope and room for manoeuvre in situations of conflict between states than a committee made up of representatives of states?
>
> The Secretariat wishes to point out, however, that it is not absolutely essential to amend the texts for the purpose of investing the Director-General with such power of control concurrently with the present system in the Regulations for the Execution of the Convention. An alternative solution might well be envisaged, i.e. a meeting of the States Parties convened in accordance with Article 27 of the Convention could address a recommendation to the Director-General endorsing the practice of sending personal representatives, and the significant political role of that practice. The Regulations for the Execution of the Convention would continue to organize control as they have

---

1349   Boylan (1993), p. 7, para. A.4.
1350   Ibid., p. 18.

always done: however, in case of their failure to function, the personal representatives of the Director-General would be operational.[1351]

Article 13(1) of the Lauswolt document was reconfirmed at the Paris Expert Meeting in 1994.[1352] In the subsequent meetings and documents, the role of UNESCO was not reiterated since the experts' attention was focused primarily on the creation of the special committee. In Article 18 of the revised Lauswolt document, UNESCO appears more in the role of the Secretariat of the Committee and its specific role is not mentioned:

Article 18 Secretariat
1. The Committee [the Bureau] shall be assisted by a Secretariat [appointed by the Director-General of UNESCO].
2. UNESCO, utilizing to the fullest extent possible its services in their respective areas of competence and capability, shall prepare the Committee's [the Bureau's] documentation and the agenda for its meetings and shall have the responsibility for the implementation of its decisions.

The Article appears in the *Preliminary Draft Second Protocol to the 1954 Hague Convention* from October 1998.[1353] Renamed Article 28, it follows the provision on international assistance. It is identical to Article 23 of the Convention:[1354]

Article 28 Assistance of UNESCO
1. The States [High Contracting] Parties may call upon UNESCO [the United Nations Educational, Scientific and Cultural Organization] for technical assistance in organizing the protection of their cultural property, or in connection with any other problem arising out of the application of the present Protocol [Convention or the Regulations for its execution]. UNESCO [The Organization] shall accord

---

1351 UNESCO document: A working document prepared by the Secretariat, CLT/94/608/1 of 28 November 1994, p. 19.
1352 Expert Meeting on the review of the 1954 Hague Convention for the Protection of Cultural Property in the Event of Armed Conflict. Paris, UNESCO Headquarters, 28 November– 2 December 1994. UNESCO document CLT/CH/94/608/2, *Final Report*, p. 7.
1353 *Preliminary Draft Second Protocol to the 1954 Hague Convention*. UNESCO document HC/1999/1, October 1998 (English, French and Russian), pp. 4, and 11.
1354 The few editorial changes – in comparison with Article 23 – are indicated by square brackets.

> such assistance within the limits fixed by its programme and by
> its resources.
> 2. UNESCO [The Organization] is authorized to make, on its own
>   initiative, proposals on this matter to the States [High Contracting]
>   Parties.

Only a few comments were submitted regarding this Article before 15 January 1999: Austria wanted this Article to be reconsidered and Turkey wished to delete paragraph 2.

The draft submitted to the Conference included 'Assistance of UNESCO' as Article 36, repeating Article 23 of the Convention with only minor editorial changes, as indicated above. The Article was seldom mentioned during the discussion at the Conference. The final text submitted to the Drafting Committee was formulated by the Secretariat and included few additions in comparison with the text of the Draft submitted to the Conference.[1355] This text, proposed by the UNESCO Secretariat under number 36, was included in the final text of the Second Protocol to become Article 33.

ANALYSIS OF THE TEXT

Article 33 deals with assistance provided to States Parties in peacetime, paragraph 1 of which refers to preparatory and preventive actions.

Paragraph 1

> 1. A Party may call upon UNESCO for technical assistance in
>   organizing the protection of its cultural property . . . UNESCO
>   shall accord such assistance within the limits fixed by its programme
>   and by its resources.

As mentioned above, the text finally adopted by the Conference was reformulated by the Secretariat.[1356] This new formulation included a new middle section containing examples of technical assistance: 'preparatory action to safeguard cultural property, preventive and organizational measures for

---

1355   Draft Second Protocol to the 1954 Hague Convention for the Protection of Cultural Property in the Event of Armed Conflict. UNESCO document HC/1999/1/rev.1, February 1999 (original: English).

1356   HC/1999/5/Add. 2.

emergency situations and compilation of national inventories of cultural property'. This text was most likely inspired by Article 5 on the safeguarding of cultural property in time of peace, which completed the Convention provision by the addition of examples of safeguarding measures. It was also probably a response to the requirements of delegates from developing countries.

Paragraph 2

> 2. Parties are encouraged to provide technical assistance at bilateral or multilateral level.

This paragraph, included by the Secretariat, was a response to the discussion in the Plenary Session concerning assistance independent of the decision of the Committee. The Australian delegate, in particular, insisted on the existence of practical measures concerning bilateral assistance, independent of the decision of Committee.[1357]

Paragraph 3

> 3. UNESCO is authorized to make, on its own initiative, proposals on these matters to the Parties.

This provision was simply taken from Article 23 of the Convention.[1358]

1357 The Australian delegate noted that this paragraph (art. 32, para. 4), which provides 'that Parties are encouraged to give technical assistance of all kinds through the Committee to those Parties or parties to a conflict who request it, seemed to read as though it would be the only channel for technical assistance while the vast majority of technical assistance would in fact be given bilaterally. He suggested redrafting this provision to ensure that it would not preclude the Parties' ability to assist other parties to implement the Convention other than through the Committee' (1999 Hague Conference, Plenary Session, 18 March 1999, p. 209).

1358 See Toman (1996), pp. 262–64.

Chapter 8
EXECUTION OF THIS PROTOCOL

INTRODUCTION

Before dealing with the technical issues included in the final clauses, the conventions of international humanitarian law devote substantial space to provisions concerning the execution and the implementation of the conventions. This is the aim of the provisions which follow in this chapter 8:

- Protecting Powers (art. 34)
- Conciliation procedure (art. 35)
- Conciliation in absence of Protecting Powers (art. 36)
- Translations and reports (art. 37)
- State responsibility (art. 38).

The issues of dissemination and cooperation, which the humanitarian convention usually places in this chapter, were however in this case already included in Chapter 7 of the Second Protocol. We should also point out that, due to the specific nature of the conventions concerning protection for victims of war, the chapter on the execution of the conventions was placed before the final or general clauses. This was already the case for Chapter 7 of the revised Geneva Convention of 1906, the 'Convention for the Amelioration of the Condition of the Wounded and Sick in Armies in the Field' (signed in Geneva on 6 July 1906), entitled 'Application and Execution of the Convention'.[1359] A similar chapter was included in the two Geneva Convention of 1929 and the four Geneva Conventions of 1949 and in the Additional Protocol I of 1977.

1359 This chapter included a clause on applicability among Contracting Parties, dissemination, and also an interesting provision on the 'duty of commanders in chief of the belligerent armies to provide for the details of execution of the foregoing articles, as well as for unforeseen cases, in accordance with the instructions of their respective governments, and conformably to the general principles of this convention' (art. 25).

Article 34
PROTECTING POWERS

This Protocol shall be applied with the co-operation of the Protecting Powers responsible for safeguarding the interests of the Parties to the conflict.

Preparatory works

Convention on the Protection of Cultural Property in the Event of Armed Conflict (The Hague, 1954). Discussion paper, prepared for the Expert Meeting on the Application and Effectiveness of the 1954 Convention. The Hague 29 June 1993.

Report by the Director-General on the reinforcement of UNESCO's action for the Protection of the World Cultural and Natural Heritage. UNESCO document 142 EX/15, Annex: Hague Meeting of Experts on the application and effectiveness of the Convention for the Protection of Cultural Property in the Event of Armed Conflict (The Hague, 14 May 1954), *Final Report.* http://unesdoc.unesco.org/images/0009/000958/095820Eo.pdf

Preliminary Draft Second Protocol to the 1954 Hague Convention. UNESCO document HC/1999/1, October 1998 (English, French and Russian).

UNESCO, Summary of comments on Preliminary Draft Second Protocol to the 1954 Hague Convention received from High Contracting Parties to the Hague Convention for the Protection of Cultural Property in the Event of Armed Conflict 1954, other UNESCO Member States and international organizations, Paris, 15 January 1999; Article 30.

Draft Second Protocol to the 1954 Hague Convention for the Protection of Cultural Property in the Event of Armed Conflict. UNESCO document HC/1999/1/ rev.1, February 1999, art. 38.

Bibliography

Chamberlain, K. 2004. *War and Cultural Heritage.* Leicester: Institute of Art and Law, p. 232.

Desch, T. 1999. The Second Protocol to the 1954 Convention for the Protection of Cultural Property in the Event of Armed Conflict. *Yearbook of International Humanitarian Law*, Vol. 2, pp. 63–90.

ANALYSIS OF THE TEXT

The issue of the control of the application of international law remains a major area in need of improvement, and this is equally the case for the application of the 1954 Hague Convention.

In his study, Patrick Boylan also mentioned the need for improvement of the procedures for the appointment of Commissioners-General where there are no nominated Protecting Powers.[1360]

A discussion paper submitted to the Expert Meeting in 1993[1361] also stated that '[neither] the Commissioner-General nor the Protection Power provisions seem to have been very effective. The Expert Meeting should consider ways and means to improve the 1954 Conventions in this respect, in the light of the suggestions referred to under (e).' The point (e) referred to different proposals concerning the institutional mechanisms we discussed in our commentary on Chapter 6 above.[1362] At the Expert Meeting, there was

> general agreement that neither the mechanism of the Commissioners-General nor that of the Protecting Powers had worked, but there was some hesitation about abolishing the systems laid down and about deleting the provisions from the 1954 Convention and its Regulations at a future stage of the revision process. It was observed that this was partly the result of benign neglect of the 1954 Convention, but States were also extremely hesitant about admitting that they were involved in armed conflicts.
>
> The meeting discussed various modalities which could be developed to improve the 1954 Convention in this respect. Some delegations referred to a possible role for the ICRC, which could act as a neutral intermediary in the event of conflict, but others opined that this might result in a conflict of interest for that organization, whilst the primary task of the ICRC seemed to be directed to the saving of human life. It was observed that the Fact-Finding Commission established under Article 90 of Additional Protocol I could also play a role, although it was pointed out that the number of States having accepted the

---

1360   Boylan (1993), p. 17, paragraph G.7.
1361   *Convention on the Protection of Cultural Property in the Event of Armed Conflict (The Hague, 1954).* Discussion paper, prepared for the Expert Meeting on the Application and Effectiveness of the 1954 Convention, The Hague 29 June 1993, p. 8.
1362   See p. 489 ff.

competence of the Fact-Finding Commission did not coincide with the number of ratifications of Additional Protocol I.

The meeting stressed the importance of developing a flexible and simplified regime which would involve representatives of UNESCO and non-governmental organizations in performing certain operational and preventive activities. In this respect the creation of some kind of 'Blue Shield' organization which could operate in emergency situations or in situations where UNESCO's involvement proved difficult was mentioned. Some delegations referred to the possibility of adding to the 1954 Convention a provision along the lines of Articles 9 and 10 of Geneva Conventions I–III and Articles 10 and 11 of Geneva Convention IV. Some delegations pointed out that a future institutional mechanism could play a role in providing UNESCO and/or non-governmental organizations and parties to a conflict with relevant documentation and information on the cultural heritage.[1363]

The subsequent Lauswolt meeting and the draft elaborated there concentrated more on institutional issues, in other words, on the Committee. No reference to Protecting Power was made until the *Preliminary Draft Second Protocol to the 1954 Hague Convention*, which was based on the previous meetings of governmental experts and was submitted to the Parties to the Hague Convention for comment.[1364] Article 30 of this document simply reproduced Article 21 of the 1954 Hague Convention, replacing the reference to the Convention and the Regulations with a reference to the 'present Protocol'. Turkey was the only country to respond to Article 30, proposing 'to replace the word "Parties" by the words "States Parties" with a view to harmonizing the terminology of the Protocol and to refer to Geneva Protocol I (Art. 2, c)) for the meaning of "Protecting Powers".'[1365]

The *Draft Second Protocol to the 1954 Hague Convention for the Protection of Cultural Property in the Event of Armed Conflict* (UNESCO doc. HC/1999/1/

1363   Report by the Director-General on the Reinforcement of UNESCO's action for the Protection of the World Cultural and Natural Heritage. UNESCO document 142 EX/15, Annex: Hague Meeting of Experts on the application and effectiveness of the Convention for the Protection of Cultural Property in the Event of Armed Conflict (The Hague, 14 May 1954), *Final Report*, p. 5. http://unesdoc.unesco.org/images/0009/000958/095820Eo.pdf

1364   Preliminary Draft Second Protocol to the 1954 Hague Convention. UNESCO document HC/1999/1, October 1998, p. 12, art. 30.

1365   UNESCO, Summary of comments on Preliminary Draft Second Protocol to the 1954 Hague Convention received from High Contracting Parties to the Hague Convention for the Protection of Cultural Property in the Event of Armed Conflict 1954, other UNESCO Member States and international organizations, Paris, 15 January 1999, p. 11.

Rev.1, February 1999), prepared by UNESCO and the Government of the Netherlands, made only one significant change, the replacement in Article 38 of the word 'Parties' with the word 'parties' in lower case – in other words, envisaging the cooperation of the Protecting Powers not only in international but also in non-international armed conflicts. No reference to Additional Protocol I, suggested by Turkey, was made.

As previously mentioned, no special Working Group was set up to deal with these Articles at the Plenary Session of the Conference.

Chapter 8 of the Protocol was discussed at the Plenary Session on 19 March 1999. With regard to this Article [38] and also Article [39], some delegates (Lebanon,[1366] Cameroon and the UK)[1367] questioned the need for making provision for protection by Protecting Powers in the Draft Second Protocol, when protection already existed in the forms of Articles 21 and 22 of the Hague Convention. The representative of the Secretariat defended this provision, stating that 'the protecting powers system had been well understood and worked well in this kind of conflict in World War II. Therefore the feeling was that this system should not be jettisoned particularly if such a conflict occurred again.'[1368]

A suggestion was made that if indeed a State had to be Party to the Convention before becoming Party to the Second Protocol, then Articles 38 and 39 of the Draft Second Protocol should be removed and replaced with another Article stating simply that Articles 21 and 22 of the Hague Convention shall apply also to situations covered by the Second Protocol.

Some delegates (Italy and Israel) wondered whether the notion of Protecting Powers might not be difficult to apply in non-international armed conflicts, and preferred to limit the use of 'Protecting Powers' to the same scope as in Article 22 of the Convention.[1369]

The contribution of the ICRC delegate saved this Article. She provided the Conference with precedents for the inclusion of the provision on Protecting Powers in the Draft Second Protocol: Article 8 of the first three Geneva Conventions, Article 9 of the fourth Geneva Convention on the protection of civilians, and also Article 5 of Additional Protocol I:

1366 The delegate of Lebanon also suggested that the definition to be included be based on the 'texts of the Red Cross' (1999 Hague Conference, Plenary Session, 19 March 1999, p. 215).
1367 Ibid., p. 222.
1368 Ibid., p. 216.
1369 Ibid., pp. 220–21.

The idea was that during an armed conflict the Parties should either have the same or different protecting powers which were basically a neutral State vis-à-vis that armed conflict. They would be there to look after the interests of the Parties to the conflict with a view to ensuring that the law is properly implemented. The specific duties of the protecting powers were most obvious in the case of the protection of prisoners of war and civilian internees, as indicated in Geneva Conventions III and IV. The use of protecting powers however, had unfortunately been extremely rare since the Second World War and the vast majority of cases had not witnessed their creation. In reality, the International Committee of the Red Cross cared for prisoners of war and civilian internees because it has the right to do so within the terms of the Geneva Conventions. There would be no harm in leaving the provision of protecting powers in the Protocol. However, she warned that the system should not be relied on too heavily and that if there was a desire to carefully follow-up and supervise, then another system ought to be established. She stated that care must be taken in the drafting of a substitutive system because it would in reality, probably be the normal system.[1370]

For more information about the Protecting Powers system, refer to our 1996 Commentary on Article 21 of the Convention[1371] and the ICRC *Commentary on the Additional Protocols of 8 June 1977.*[1372]

1370   Ibid., pp. 217–18.
1371   Toman (1996), pp. 222–26.
1372   *Commentary on the Additional Protocols of 8 June 1977*, pp. 75–89

Article 35
CONCILIATION PROCEDURE

1. *The Protecting Powers shall lend their good offices in all cases where they may deem it useful in the interests of cultural property, particularly if there is disagreement between the Parties to the conflict as to the application or interpretation of the provisions of this Protocol.*

2. *For this purpose, each of the Protecting Powers may, either at the invitation of one Party, of the Director-General, or on its own initiative, propose to the Parties to the conflict a meeting of their representatives, and in particular of the authorities responsible for the protection of cultural property, if considered appropriate, on the territory of a State not party to the conflict. The Parties to the conflict shall be bound to give effect to the proposals for meeting made to them. The Protecting Powers shall propose for approval by the Parties to the conflict a person belonging to a State not party to the conflict or a person presented by the Director-General, which person shall be invited to take part in such a meeting in the capacity of Chairman.*

Preparatory works

Convention on the Protection of Cultural Property in the Event of Armed Conflict (The Hague, 1954). Discussion paper, prepared for the Expert Meeting on the Application and Effectiveness of the 1954 Convention. The Hague 29 June 1993.

Report by the Director-General on the reinforcement of UNESCO's action for the Protection of the World Cultural and Natural Heritage. UNESCO document 142 EX/15, Annex: Hague Meeting of Experts on the application and effectiveness of the Convention for the Protection of Cultural Property in the Event of Armed Conflict (The Hague, 14 May 1954), *Final Report.* http://unesdoc.unesco.org/images/0009/000958/095820Eo.pdf

Preliminary Draft Second Protocol to the 1954 Hague Convention. UNESCO document HC/1999/1, October 1998 (English, French and Russian).

UNESCO, Summary of comments on Preliminary Draft Second Protocol to the 1954 Hague Convention received from High Contracting Parties to the Hague Convention for the Protection of Cultural Property in the Event of Armed Conflict 1954, other UNESCO Member States and international organizations, Paris, 15 January 1999; Article 30.

Draft Second Protocol to the 1954 Hague Convention for the Protection of Cultural Property in the Event of Armed Conflict. UNESCO document HC/1999/1/rev.1, February 1999, art. 38.

Bibliography

Chamberlain, K. 2004. *War and Cultural Heritage*. Leicester: Institute of Art and Law, p. 232.

Desch, T. 1999. The Second Protocol to the 1954 Convention for the Protection of Cultural Property in the Event of Armed Conflict. *Yearbook of International Humanitarian Law*, Vol. 2, pp. 63–90.

ANALYSIS OF THE TEXT

Article 35 of the Second Protocol is almost identical to Article 22 of the Hague Convention.[1373] And as we have seen, Article 22 itself was inspired by the 1929 and 1949 Geneva Conventions. In our 1996 Commentary to the 1954 Hague Convention, we said:

> Article 22 describes the good offices functions of the Protecting Power in almost identical terms to those of Article 11/11/11/12 common to the Geneva Conventions.
>
> As far as the Geneva Conventions are concerned, this Article was not entirely new. It was based on a similar text which appeared in Articles 83, paragraph 3, and 87 of the 1929 Geneva Convention

---

1373　The modifications are indicated in the following text. The parts of the text of Article 22 that were replaced are enclosed in brackets and the new text is italicized:

　　1. The Protecting Powers shall lend their good offices in all cases where they may deem it useful in the interests of cultural property, particularly if there is disagreement between the Parties to the conflict as to the application or interpretation of the provisions of [the present Convention or the Regulations for its Execution] *of this Protocol*.

　　2. For this purpose, each of the Protecting Powers may, either at the invitation of one Party, of the Director-General [of the United Nations Educational, Scientific and Cultural Organization], or on its own initiative, propose to the Parties to the conflict a meeting of their representatives, and in particular of the authorities responsible for the protection of cultural property, if considered appropriate, [on suitably chosen neutral territory] *on the territory of a State not party to the conflict*. The Parties to the conflict shall be bound to give effect to the proposals for meeting made to them. The Protecting Powers shall propose for approval by the Parties to the conflict a person belonging [to a neutral Power] *to a State not party to the conflict* or a person presented by the Director-General [of the United Nations Educational, Scientific and Cultural Organization], which person shall be invited to take part in such a meeting in the capacity of Chairman.

relative to the treatment of prisoners of war. The Article was adopted by the Diplomatic Conference of 1949 without much discussion. Nor should it be forgotten that the 1938 Preliminary Draft Convention also raised the question of possible disagreement between belligerents; its Article 13 accordingly provided that, in this case, 'the Contracting States entrusted with the interests of the belligerents and the Standing Committee of the General Conference shall lend their good offices for the settlement of -the dispute. It is immediately clear that the application of this provision depends on the appointment of Protecting Powers. Indeed, if in a conflict Protecting Powers are not appointed, this provision ceases to have any practical effect.[1374]

During the preparatory phase of the Second Protocol, the conciliation procedure was not mentioned, having been overshadowed by the discussion of Protecting Powers. It was introduced only in the final draft submitted to the States by the UNESCO Secretariat under Article [31]. This text was identical to Article 22 of the Convention, the sole modification being the use of the abbreviation UNESCO in place of the Organization's full name.[1375] Turkey was the only country to propose a modification, requesting that the words 'of the Director General of UNESCO' be deleted from paragraph 2 of the proposed Article 31.[1376]

The *Draft Second Protocol to the 1954 Hague Convention for the Protection of Cultural Property in the Event of Armed Conflict* (UNESCO doc. HC/1999/1/rev.1, February 1999), prepared by UNESCO and the Government of the Netherlands, made no changes to the text apart from deleting the reference to the Organization, considering mention of the Director-General sufficient in itself.

As we have already mentioned, no special Working Group was set up to deal with these Articles at the Plenary Session of the Conference.

Chapter 8 of the Protocol was discussed at the Plenary Session on 19 March 1999. As indicated in the commentary on Article 34 above, with regard to Articles [38] and [39], some delegates (Lebanon,[1377] Cameroon

---

1374 Toman (1996), p. 251.
1375 Preliminary Draft Second Protocol to the 1954 Hague Convention. UNESCO document HC/1999/1, October 1998, p. 12, art. 31.
1376 UNESCO, Summary of comments on Preliminary Draft Second Protocol to the 1954 Hague Convention received from High Contracting Parties to the Hague Convention for the Protection of Cultural Property in the Event of Armed Conflict 1954, other UNESCO Member States and international organizations, Paris, 15 January 1999, p. 11.
1377 See note 88.

and the UK)[1378] questioned the need for making provision for protection by Protecting Powers in the Draft Second Protocol.[1379] This Plenary Session also dealt with the maintenance of the provision of Article [39], which concerned conciliation procedures.

A suggestion was made that if indeed a State had to be Party to the Convention before becoming Party to the Second Protocol, then Articles [38] and [39] of the draft Second Protocol should be removed and replaced with another Article that stated simply that Articles 21 and 22 of the Hague Convention shall apply also to situations covered by the Second Protocol.

The Austrian delegate proposed replacing the words 'neutral territory' and 'neutral Power' with alternative wording. This was done in the final text where the Article refers to 'the territory of a State not party to the conflict' and 'a State not party to the conflict'.

For more information on the conciliation procedure, see our 1996 Commentary on Article 22 of the Convention[1380] and the ICRC Commentary on the Additional Protocols of 8 June 1977.[1381]

1378   See note 89.
1379   See note 90.
1380   Toman (1996), pp. 250–54.
1381   *Commentary on the Additional Protocols of 8 June 1977*, pp. 75–89.

Article 36
CONCILIATION IN ABSENCE OF PROTECTING POWERS

1. *In a conflict where no Protecting Powers are appointed the Director-General may lend good offices or act by any other form of conciliation or mediation, with a view to settling the disagreement.*

2. *At the invitation of one Party or of the Director-General, the Chairman of the Committee may propose to the Parties to the conflict a meeting of their representatives, and in particular of the authorities responsible for the protection of cultural property, if considered appropriate, on the territory of a State not party to the conflict.*

Preparatory works

Preliminary Draft Second Protocol to the 1954 Hague Convention. UNESCO document HC/1999/1, October 1998 (English, French and Russian).

UNESCO, Summary of comments on Preliminary Draft Second Protocol to the 1954 Hague Convention received from High Contracting Parties to the Hague Convention for the Protection of Cultural Property in the Event of Armed Conflict 1954, other UNESCO Member States and international organizations, Paris, 15 January 1999; Article 31.

Draft Second Protocol to the 1954 Hague Convention for the Protection of Cultural Property in the Event of Armed Conflict. UNESCO document HC/1999/1/rev.1, February 1999, art. 38.

Bibliography

Chamberlain, K. 2004. *War and Cultural Heritage.* Leicester: Institute of Art and Law, p. 233.

Desch, T. 1999. The Second Protocol to the 1954 Convention for the Protection of Cultural Property in the Event of Armed Conflict. *Yearbook of International Humanitarian Law*, Vol. 2, pp. 63–90.

ANALYSIS OF THE TEXT

The 1999 Second Protocol sought new alternatives for situations in which no Protecting Power has been appointed. As mentioned in Article 36:

a) One way is to give to the Director-General the initiative to *'lend good offices or act by any other form of conciliation or mediation, with a view to settling the disagreement.'*

b) Another way is to give the initiative to the newly constituted Committee, and to its Chairman in particular, at the invitation of one Party or of the Director-General. In such cases, *'the Chairman of the Committee may propose to the Parties to the conflict a meeting of their representatives, and in particular of the authorities responsible for the protection of cultural property, if considered appropriate, on the territory of a State not party to the conflict.'*

Aware of the inexistence of Protecting Powers in present armed conflicts,[1382] the UNESCO Secretariat looked for practical ways to settle conflicts and frictions between States Parties to conflicts.

The provisions of Articles 34 and 35 were introduced very late in the Protocol's preparation, as was Article 36, which was in some ways a response to negative expectations concerning the practical impact of Articles 34 and 35. The representative of the UNESCO Secretariat introduced the draft Article to the Plenary Session of the Conference as follows:

> therefore it was felt necessary to include a provision on [...] conciliation in absence of protecting powers. The Director-General of UNESCO had done his best, from his constitutional mandate for the protection of cultural property, to remedy this situation by appointing special representatives for cultural property in those countries which had problems. She thought that it might also be appropriate to provide in Article 42 that the Chairman of the Committee have a role in the conciliation procedure.[1383]

The delegate of Cameroon considered that the competence of the Director-General in the field of conciliation is subsidiary. In case of the existence

---

1382   Naturally, we should not forget that the moment the institution of Protecting Power was included in international treaties it ceased to function. The last massive use of the Protecting Power system took place during the Second World War. After 1945 and after the 1949 Geneva Conventions, the Protecting Powers system was used in very few conflicts: Suez, Goa and Bangladesh. The reasons that are sometimes mentioned are: fear that the designation will be seen as recognition of the other Party; unwillingness to admit that an armed conflict exists; maintenance of diplomatic relations between belligerents; the pace of events in some wars; and, finally, the difficulty of finding neutral States acceptable to both parties and able and willing to act in this capacity. See Sandoz (1995), p. 16.

1383   1999 Hague Conference, Plenary Session, 19 March 1999, p. 214.

of Protecting Power, its role is totally replaced by the Protecting Power. The fact that the Protecting Power is not appointed should not negate the role of the Director-General.[1384] The representative of the Secretariat explained the need for such an alternative, but also underlined the point that according to paragraph 2, the Committee will play a role.[1385] Even so, the Director-General can continue to exercise his mandate independently of the Convention and the Protocol based on constitutional rights conferred by UNESCO's Constitution, as he has done in many cases.

The Israeli delegate considered that

> with regard to Article 40 on conciliation in absence of protecting powers, her view was that a conciliation procedure should only be made at the initiative of the Parties to the conflict, and therefore she was against the inclusion of the phrase 'at the invitation of the Director-General of UNESCO'. However, the Parties could apply to the Director-General if they so desire, but not vice versa. She also opposed the involvement of the Committee in this respect and asked to omit Article 42.[1386]

The final text of the Article clearly refers to the 'Parties to the conflict', using the uppercase. It therefore concerns only situations of international armed conflicts. Kevin Chamberlain considers the situation to be unclear and concludes that

> it would certainly be in the spirit of Article 36 for there to be power for the Director-General or Chairman of the Committee to be able to propose a meeting of the parties to the conflict in an internal conflict. But even if Article 36 cannot be interpreted to include internal conflicts, it would appear in any event that the Director-General or Chairman of the Committee would have inherent power under the Protocol to take an initiative of this kind in an internal conflict.[1387]

The Austrian delegate, Thomas Desch, raised another issue in his article on the Protocol:

1384   Ibid., pp. 216, 219.
1385   Ibid., p. 217.
1386   Ibid., p. 221.
1387   Chamberlain (2004), p. 233.

It is not clear from the wording of this provision whether it applies in case of disagreement about the appointment of delegates of Protecting Powers only, or whether it provides a general dispute settlement procedure for any disagreement among States Parties on the application or interpretation of the Second Protocol. As the Final Clauses of the Second Protocol do not contain a provision on the settlement of disputes, it seems as if Article 36 was intended to serve as a general dispute settlement clause. Its wording, however, limits its applicability to situations of armed conflict.[1388]

This interpretation seems to go too far. It is very difficult to imagine that the present Article will constitute a general settlement disputes clause when nothing like it can be deduced from the text, nor from the intention of the States that participated in the Conference. This provision was included in the final stage of the Conference by the Secretariat.

1388   Desch (1999), p. 88.

Article 37
TRANSLATIONS AND REPORTS

1. *The Parties shall translate this Protocol into their official languages and shall communicate these official translations to the Director-General.*
2. *The Parties shall submit to the Committee, every four years, a report on the implementation of this Protocol.*

Preparatory works

Preliminary Draft Second Protocol to the 1954 Hague Convention. UNESCO document HC/1999/1, October 1998 (English, French and Russian), art. 33, p. 13.

UNESCO, Summary of comments on Preliminary Draft Second Protocol to the 1954 Hague Convention received from High Contracting Parties to the Hague Convention for the Protection of Cultural Property in the Event of Armed Conflict 1954, other UNESCO Member States and international organizations, Paris, 15 January 1999, art. 33.

Draft Second Protocol to the 1954 Hague Convention for the Protection of Cultural Property in the Event of Armed Conflict. UNESCO document HC/1999/1/rev.1, February 1999, art. 33.

Bibliography

Chamberlain, K. 2004. *War and Cultural Heritage*. Leicester: Institute of Art and Law, p. 233.

Desch, T. 1999. The Second Protocol to the 1954 Convention for the Protection of Cultural Property in the Event of Armed Conflict. *Yearbook of International Humanitarian Law*, Vol. 2, p. 88.

Hladík, J. 2000. Reporting system under the 1954 Convention for the Protection of Cultural Property in the Event of Armed Conflict. *IRRC*, No. 840, pp. 1001–16

ANALYSIS OF THE TEXT

The present Article is a modified version of Article 26 of the Convention. This version of the text was proposed by the UNESCO Secretariat in the last phase of the preparatory work of the Protocol.

The Article was proposed as Article [33] of the *Preliminary Draft Second Protocol* of October 1998.[1389] The Secretariat's version was based on Article 26 of the Convention, though simplified; it also differed slightly from the final text:

1. The States Parties shall communicate to one another, through the Director-General of UNESCO official translations of the present Protocol.
2. States Parties shall submit to the Committee, every four years, a report on the implementation of this Protocol.

This text was submitted to States for comment, but Syria was the only State to propose a change, namely to delete paragraph 1. The text submitted to the Conference maintained paragraph 1, but in a different version:[1390]

1. The Parties shall provide for the translation of this Protocol into the languages that exist in their countries and shall communicate these official translations to the Director-General of UNESCO.
2. The Parties shall submit to the Committee [Bureau], every four years, a report on the implementation of this Protocol.

Surprisingly enough, this provision provoked a great deal of discussion in the Plenary Session of the Conference. The Turkish delegate suggested deleting the words 'into the languages that exist in their countries' and proposed the following version: 'The Parties shall provide the official translations of this Protocol and shall communicate these official languages to the Director-General of UNESCO'. The Chinese delegate proposed to include the word 'official' in the first line of the text proposed by the Secretariat and the Government of the Netherlands.[1391] The Chairperson proposed to deal with the issue of languages in the next chapter, noting that the Conference might address it following completion of the discussion of Chapter 8. The Argentine

---

1389   *Preliminary Draft Second Protocol to the 1954 Hague Convention.* UNESCO document HC/1999/1, October 1998 (English, French and Russian), art. 33, p. 13.
1390   Draft Second Protocol to the 1954 Hague Convention for the Protection of Cultural Property in the Event of Armed Conflict. UNESCO document HC/1999/1/rev.1, February 1999 (original: English), art. 33.
1391   1999 Hague Conference, Plenary Session, 19 March 1999, p. 221.

delegate noted that it should be made explicit which languages would be considered 'authentic', and which would constitute the official texts:

> All countries should be encouraged to translate the Protocol into their own languages in order to disseminate it, although this may be different to having it translated into their official language. For example, two countries may share a common language and they could provide UNESCO with different versions of the text. He stressed therefore, that the word 'official' should be used with great care'[1392]

On this basis the text went to the Drafting Committee which adopted the final version, retaining the word 'official'.

A distinction must be drawn between the authentic languages of the Protocol and so-called official national texts, where differences will certainly appear unless States coordinate these texts on a bilateral basis. Because the communicated text will be 'official', UNESCO cannot really play a role in the coordination of these texts.

Such coordination may be difficult, and it was proposed that 'whenever possible in the preparation of documents, multilateral drafting should be preferred over subsequent translation into required languages, thus ensuring early interaction of the various language versions'.[1393]

Paragraph 2

The representative of the Secretariat of UNESCO explained that the reason for introducing this paragraph was based on the disappointing results of the reporting procedure. Because the maximum number of reports the Secretariat received was 23 of a possible total number of 95 States Parties, 'it seemed appropriate that the Committee include in its mandate the question of reporting.'[1394] The UK delegate suggested that States be encouraged to combine their reports on the Convention and the Protocol.[1395]

1392   Ibid., p. 222.
1393   Tabory (1980), p. 231.
1394   1999 Hague Conference, Plenary Session, 19 March 1999, p. 215.
1395   Ibid., p. 222.

Article 38
STATE RESPONSIBILITY

No provision in this Protocol relating to individual criminal responsibility shall affect the responsibility of States under international law, including the duty to provide reparation.

Preparatory works

UNESCO document: A working document prepared by the Secretariat, CLT/94/608/1 of 28 November 1994.

Expert Meeting on the review of the 1954 Hague Convention for the Protection of Cultural Property in the Event of Armed Conflict. Paris, UNESCO Headquarters, 28 November–2 December 1994. UNESCO document CLT/CH/94/608/2, *Final Report*, p. 5.

UNESCO, Meeting of Governmental Experts on the Review of the 1954 Hague Convention for the Protection of Cultural Property in the Event of Armed Conflict 1954, UNESCO Headquarters, Paris, 24–27 March 1997. *Final Report*. UNESCO document CLT-96/CONF.603/5, Paris, 30 April 1997, p. 3.

UNESCO, Meeting of Governmental Experts on the Revision of the Hague Convention for the Protection of Cultural Property in the Event of Armed Conflict of 1954. Vienna (Austria) 11 – 13 May 1998. *Summary of comments received from States Parties to the Hague Convention, the International Committee of the Red Cross and the International Council on Archives.* UNESCO document: Paris, March 1998. Original: English [no number].

UNESCO, Meeting of Governmental Experts on the Revision of the Hague Convention for the Protection of Cultural Property in the Event of Armed Conflict of 1954. Vienna, 11–13 May 1998. UNESCO document: Paris, May 1998, *Final Report*.

Preliminary Draft Second Protocol to the 1954 Hague Convention. UNESCO document HC/1999/1, October 1998 (English, French and Russian).

UNESCO, Summary of comments on Preliminary Draft Second Protocol to the 1954 Hague Convention received from High Contracting Parties to the Hague Convention for the Protection of Cultural Property in the Event of Armed Conflict 1954, other UNESCO Member States and international organizations, Paris, 15 January 1999, art. 30.

Draft Second Protocol to the 1954 Hague Convention for the Protection of Cultural Property in the Event of Armed Conflict. UNESCO document HC/1999/1/rev.1, February 1999, art. 38.

Bibliography

Chamberlain, K. 2004. *War and Cultural Heritage*. Leicester: Institute of Art and Law, p. 232.

Desch, T. 1999. The Second Protocol to the 1954 Convention for the Protection of Cultural Property in the Event of Armed Conflict. *Yearbook of International Humanitarian Law*, Vol. 2, pp. 63–90.

ANALYSIS OF THE TEXT

Responsibility for violations of protection of cultural property, within the wider framework of improving protection, was one of the main issues of the 1999 Hague Conference. The first provision on responsibility appears in the document adopted by the Second Expert Meeting, held in Lauswolt at the invitation of the Netherlands Government, on 9–11 February 1994. The draft elaborated by this meeting included Chapter 2 on 'Jurisdiction and responsibility' and dealt mostly with individual criminal responsibility. It nevertheless included Article 7, which states:

> Article 7. Responsibility of states
> 1. States Parties are responsible for serious violations of the provisions of this instrument, which are attributable to a State under international law.
> 2. Prosecution of an individual for [a grave breach] [an act] under Article[s]- […] of this instrument: does not relieve a State Party of any responsibility under international law for an act or omission attributable to it.

The first paragraph of this Article was certainly inspired by Article 3 of the 1907 Hague Convention Concerning the Laws and Customs of War on Land and the rules of customary international law. It constituted a sanction for violations of the Hague Regulations, which are part of this Convention. This provision also corresponded to international rules on the responsibility of States.

The 1949 Geneva Conventions also included a provision on the 'Responsibility of Contracting Parties' (common Articles 51/52/131/148), which states:

> No High Contracting Party shall be allowed to absolve itself or any other High Contracting Party of any liability incurred by itself or by another High Contracting Party in respect of breaches referred to in the preceding Article.

Article 91 of the 1977 Additional Protocol I was the most direct source used by the framers of the 1999 Second Protocol, but the text was formulated in a simpler form; compensation received no mentioned in this Article:

> Article 91 Responsibility
> A Party to the conflict which violates the provisions of the Conventions or of this Protocol shall, if the case demands, be liable to pay compensation. It shall be responsible for all acts committed by persons forming part of its armed forces.

At the 1994 Paris Expert Meeting on the review of the 1954 Hague Convention for the Protection of Cultural Property in the Event of Armed Conflict:

> It was also acknowledged that, in accordance with international law, the resposibility of States could be considered from the legal and financial point of view (restitution and compensation), but not from the political standpoint. It was important that the State itself take responsibility for compliance with the Convention; it was not sufficient if it punished individuals after a violation occurred.[1396]

The UNESCO Secretariat commented on the second paragraph of Article 7 as follows:

> This provision goes further than the relevant Article in *Protocol I* which provides only that a *breach* by a subordinate does not absolve

---

1396 Expert Meeting on the review of the 1954 Hague Convention for the Protection of Cultural Property in the Event of Armed Conflict. Paris, UNESCO Headquarters, 28 November–2 December 1994. UNESCO document CLT/CH/94/608/2 Final Report, p. 5.

his superiors from penal or disciplinary responsibility 'if they knew, or had information which should have enabled them to conclude in the circumstances at the time, that he was committing or was going to commit such a breach and if they did not take all feasible measures within their power to prevent or repress the breach.'[1397]

In addition to the duty to prosecute and impose penal and disciplinary sanctions according to Article 28, the 1954 Hague Convention places the following responsibilities on States:

(i)   to plan for the contingency of conflict to protect their own cultural property (Art. 3);

(ii)   to respect the cultural property on their own territory as well as on that of other Contracting Parties (Art. 4);

(iii)   to support authorities in territories occupied by its forces in the protection of cultural property (Art. 5);

(iv)   to train its military forces in the principles of the Convention and to establish special units of protection (Art. 7);

(v)   to respect transport under special protection (Art. 12); and transport in urgent cases (Art. 13);

(vi)   to respect the personnel engaged in the protection of cultural property (Art. 15);

(vii)   to disseminate the Convention (Art. 25);

(viii) to provide translations and reports on their activities implementing the Convention (Art. 26).

During the drafting of this provision, the experts and the UNESCO Secretariat closely followed the work of the ILC, which, at that time, in 1995, was completing its first reading of draft Articles on the responsibility of States.[1398]

At the meeting of governmental experts in Paris in 1997, several participants reiterated the necessity for holding States responsible for violations of norms of international humanitarian law, thus strengthening respect for the protection of cultural property in the event of armed conflicts,

---

1397   UNESCO document: A working document prepared by the Secretariat, CLT/94/608/1 of 28 November 1994, p. 13 (in boldface in the original).

1398   International Law Commission. Report to United Nations General Assembly, Official Records of the General Assembly, 49th session, Supplement No. 10.

and emphasized the importance of the work of the ILC on the responsibility of States.[1399]

The revised Lauswolt document of 27 March 1997[1400] included the new provision in its Article 8 (formerly Article 7):

1. States Parties are responsible for any violation of their obligations under this instrument.
2. States Parties are responsible for any [serious] violation of a provision of this instrument which is attributable to a State under international law.
[3. This responsibility entails the duty to provide reparation in accordance. with international law, including i.a. compensation and restitution, as the case may be.]

The Secretariat's comments indicated that the original version was reworded to make clear that States are liable for any violation of their direct responsibility and also for violations by persons or bodies whose actions they are responsible for. The drafting group was not clear whether the experts wished to make States liable for every violation or only for serious violations, as indicated in the brackets. The new Article was also completed by a provision corresponding to the aforementioned Article 91 of Additional Protocol I, 'namely to be responsible for wrongful acts and to be obliged to provide full reparation in the form of restitution in kind, compensation, satisfaction and assurances and guarantees of non-repetition, either singly or in combination'.[1401]

1399 UNESCO, Meeting of Governmental Experts on the Review of the 1954 Hague Convention for the Protection of Cultural Property in the Event of Armed Conflict 1954, UNESCO Headquarters, Paris, 24–27 March 1997. *Final Report*. UNESCO document CLT-96/CONF.603/5, Paris, 30 April 1997, p. 3.

1400 *Draft provisions for the revision of the 1954 Hague Convention and commentary from the UNESCO Secretariat*. CLT-97/CONF.208/2, Paris, October 1997. The document included the text of the 'revised Lauwolt document'. Draft Articles are followed by the Secretariat's comments comparing the original provisions of the Lauswolt document with the revised provisions resulting from the deliberation of participants. Such comments are entitled 'Reasons for change'. The Secretariat has also summarized the main points raised in the discussions in the sections entitled 'Main points of discussion'. Some parts of the revised Lauswolt document were placed within square brackets because the discussion did not reveal unanimity on these issues. These were subject to further negotiation.

1401 Ibid., p. 11. This is referring to the Draft Articles on State Responsibility, art. 42(1), p. 141. International Law Commission. Report to United Nations General Assembly. Official Records of the General Assembly, 48th session, Supplement No. 10 (A/51/10).

In the comments the Secretariat received before the Vienna Expert Meeting in 1998,[1402] only the ICRC proposed a redrafted text for this article.[1403]

At the 1998 Vienna Governmental Expert Meeting on the revision of the Hague Convention for the Protection of Cultural Property in the Event of Armed Conflict of 1954,[1404] several delegations preferred to avoid explicit mention of State responsibility in the new instrument on the grounds that it was already found in international customary law and was undergoing codification by the ILC. Other delegations countered that a number of international legal instruments already mentioned responsibility of States and, on this basis, it should be mentioned in the instrument.[1405]

The draft elaborated by the Secretariat in October 1998 on the basis of previous meetings,[1406] included in Chapter 4 on Jurisdiction and Responsibility a short Article 14:

1. States Parties are responsible for any violation of their obligations under this Protocol.

2. This responsibility entails the duty to provide reparation in accordance with international law.

This draft was sent to the Member States of UNESCO, the UN and selected international organizations, with requests for comments, which would be taken into account in the preparation of a final draft for the Diplomatic Conference to be held at The Hague from 14 to 26 March 1999. By 15

1402 UNESCO, Meeting of Governmental Experts. Summary of comments received from States Parties to the Hague Convention, the International Committee of the Red Cross and the International Council on Archives. UNESCO document: Paris, March 1998.

1403 The ICRC proposes to redraft the present version as follows:
1. States Parties are responsible for those violations of this instrument [or the Convention], whether by act or omission, which are attributable to it under international law.
2. This responsibility entails the duty to provide reparation in accordance with international law, including *inter alia* compensation and restitution, as the case may be.
3. Prosecution of an individual for a breach of this instrument shall not relieve a State Party of any such responsibility for a violation of this instrument [or the Convention], whether by act or omission, which is attributable to it under international law.

1404 UNESCO, Meeting of Governmental Experts on the Revision of the Hague Convention for the Protection of Cultural Property in the Event of Armed Conflict of 1954. Vienna, 11–13 May 1998. UNESCO document: Paris, May 1998, *Final Report*.

1405 Ibid., p. 4.

1406 *Preliminary Draft Second Protocol to the 1954 Hague Convention*. UNESCO document HC/1999/1, October 1998 (English, French and Russian), art. 14.

January 1999, the Secretariat had received substantial replies. The following were the comments on Article 14:[1407]

> *Australia* would like discussion of the responsibility of States towards rebel groups. It also questions who will make an order for compensation and whether the violations take into account the military necessity exception. *France* wishes to harmonize this Article with the Rome Statute of the International Criminal Court. *Germany* suggests deleting this Article in view of the current work of the International Law Commission on this subject. *Italy* supports this Article. *Norway* questions the clarity of this Article and proposes a no-prejudice clause such as 'Nothing in this Protocol affects state responsibility in accordance with international law'. *Slovenia* wishes to define in detail the responsibility of States Parties. *Switzerland* proposes to include the notion of omission in paragraph 1. *ICRC* proposes to redraft this Article.[1408]

In the final draft submitted to the Conference, the title of the Article [22] has changed and the text appears in a more simplified form:

> Article 22 Responsibility of parties to a conflict
> 1. Parties to a conflict are responsible for any violation of their obligations under this Protocol.
> 2. This responsibility entails the duty to provide reparation.

At the Diplomatic Conference, Article 22 was discussed in the context of Chapter 4 on 'Jurisdiction and responsibility'. Several States welcomed this provision, which reflects the generally accepted rules of customary international law and constitutes a good supplement to Article 28 of the Convention, which does not mention responsibility of States. Some States (Germany, Italy, Greece, the UK, Egypt and Peru) preferred to delete the provision because they contended that it already formed part of customary international law and was presently under discussion by the ILC. For the same reason, the Israeli delegate proposed to delete paragraph 1 and considered that

---

1407   UNESCO, Summary of comments on Preliminary Draft Second Protocol to the 1954 Hague Convention received from High Contracting Parties to the Hague Convention for the Protection of Cultural Property in the Event of Armed Conflict 1954, other UNESCO Member States and international organizations, Paris, 15 January 1999, p. 8.
1408   Ibid., pp. 8–9 (in boldface in the original text).

the 'phrasing of paragraph (2) was not consistent with current requirements of international law'.[1409] The French delegate questioned the need to mention this traditional rule of international law, which was repeated in Article 91 of Additional Protocol I. Because of the different nature of responsibility of States and responsibility of individuals, he proposed transferring this Article to another chapter of the Protocol.[1410] The representative of the ICRC 'suggested inserting what was reflected in Article 91 of Additional Protocol I, namely that "a State shall be responsible for all acts committed by persons forming part of its armed forces."'[1411]

The Working Group on Chapter 4 proposed the following text: 'No provision in this Protocol relating to individual criminal responsibility shall affect the responsibility of States under international law, including the duty to provide reparation'.[1412] This compromise text was produced by the delegations of Egypt and Argentina, and the Working Group proposed that the Article on 'State responsibility' be transferred to another chapter of the Protocol. The final text, approved by the Drafting Committee, was included in this form in the final text of the Protocol as Article 38.

As we have seen – and as many delegates indicated – the discussion of State responsibility took place during the preparatory works and at the start of the second reading process by the ILC, which was undertaken over four sessions of the Commission from 1998 to 2001.[1413] The articles adopted by the ILC were transmitted to the UN General Assembly. The General Assembly, in Resolution 59/35 of 2 December 2004, again commended the articles on responsibility of States for internationally wrongful acts and requested that the Secretary-General invite governments to submit written comments on any future action regarding these articles. It also requested the Secretary-General to prepare an initial compilation of decisions of international courts, tribunals and other bodies referring to the articles, and to invite governments to submit information on their practice in this regard. It further requested that the Secretary-General submit this material well in advance of the 62nd session and decided to include in the provisional agenda of its 62nd session (2007) an item entitled 'Responsibility of States for internationally wrongful acts'.

1409 1999 Hague Conference, Plenary Session, 18 March 1999, p. 181.
1410 Ibid., p. 178.
1411 Ibid., p. 188
1412 Horst Fischer, Chairman of the Working Group, proposed a simplified version of the article: 'This Protocol is without prejudice to responsibility of states and the duty to provide reparations under international law.'
1413 Crawford (2002), pp. 25–26.

Whereas Article 38 of the Second Protocol states that 'no provision in this Protocol relating to individual criminal responsibility shall affect the responsibility of States under international law, including the duty to provide reparation', the articles adopted by the ILC include a provision on individual responsibility:

> Article 58 Individual responsibility
> These Articles are without prejudice to any question of the individual responsibility under international law of any person acting on behalf of a State.

The ILC provided the following comment on this Article:

(1) Article 58 makes clear that the Articles as a whole do not address any question of the individual responsibility under international law of any person acting on behalf of a State. It clarifies a matter which could be inferred in any case from the fact that the Articles only address issues relating to the responsibility of States.

(2) The principle that individuals, including State officials, may be responsible under international law was established in the aftermath of World War II. It was included in the London Charter of 1945 which established the Nuremberg Tribunal[1414] and was subsequently endorsed by the General Assembly.[1415] It underpins more recent developments in the field of international criminal law, including the two *ad hoc* tribunals and the Rome Statute of the International Criminal Court.[1416] So far this principle has operated in the field of criminal responsibility, but it is not excluded that developments may occur in the field of individual civil responsibility.[1417] As a saving clause Article 58 is not intended to exclude that possibility; hence the use of the general term 'individual responsibility'.

1414 Agreement for the Prosecution and Punishment of Major War Criminals of the European Axis, and Establishing the Charter of the International Military Tribunal, London, 8 August 1945, UNTS, Vol. 82, p. 279.

1415 G.A. Res. 95(1) of 11 December 1946. See also the International Law Commission's Principles of International Law Recognized in the Charter of the Nuremberg Tribunal and in the Judgment of the Tribunal, *Yearbook of the International Law Commission 1950*, Vol. II, p. 374.

1416 See Commentary to Part 2, Chapter 3, para. 6.

1417 See, e.g., the Convention against Torture and Other Cruel, Inhuman or Degrading Treatment or Punishment, 10 December 1984, UNTS, Vol. 1465, p. 112, art. 14, dealing with compensation for victims of torture.

(3) Where crimes against international law are committed by State officials, it will often be the case that the State itself is responsible for the acts in question or for failure to prevent or punish them. In certain cases, in particular aggression, the State will by definition be involved. Even so, the question of individual responsibility is in principle distinct from the question of State responsibility.[1418] The State is not exempted from its own responsibility for internationally wrongful conduct by the prosecution and punishment of the State officials who carried it out.[1419] Nor may those officials hide behind the State in respect of their own responsibility for conduct of theirs which is contrary to rules of international law which are applicable to them. The former principle is reflected, for example, in Article 25(4) of the Rome Statute, which provides that '[no] provision in this Statute relating to individual criminal responsibility shall affect the responsibility of States under international law.' The latter is reflected, for example, in the well-established principle that official position does not excuse a person from individual criminal responsibility under international law.[1420]

(4) Article 58 reflects this situation, making it clear that the Articles do not address the question of the individual responsibility under international law of any person acting on behalf of a State. The term 'individual responsibility' has acquired an accepted meaning in light of the Rome Statute and other instruments; it refers to the responsibility of individual persons, including State officials, under certain rules of international law for conduct such as genocide, war crimes and crimes against humanity.'[1421]

Many of the Articles relate to the provision which was included in the 1999 Second Protocol. The comments on these Articles are beyond the scope of

---

1418 See, e.g., Streletz, Kessler & Krenz v. Germany (Applications Nos. 34044/96, 35532/97 and 44801/98), European Court of Human Rights, judgment of 22 March 2001, at para. 104 ('If the GDR still existed, it would be responsible from the viewpoint of international law for the acts concerned. It remains to be established that alongside that State responsibility the applicants individually bore criminal responsibility at the material time').

1419 Prosecution and punishment of responsible State officials may be relevant to reparation, especially satisfaction: see commentary on art. 36, para. 5.

1420 See, e.g., the International Law Commission's Principles of International Law Recognized in the Charter of the Nuremberg Tribunal and in the Judgment of the Tribunal, Principle III (*Yearbook of the International Law Commission 1950*, Vol. II, p. 375); Rome Statute of the International Criminal Court, 17 July 1998, A/CONF.183/9, art. 27.

1421 Crawford (2002), pp. 312–13.

our objective in this commentary and we refer the reader of this comment to the Articles adopted by the International Law Commission and to its commentary.[1422]

1422   Ibid., p. 387.

Chapter 9

FINAL CLAUSES

INTRODUCTION

Preparatory works

The Second Expert Meeting on the 1954 Hague Convention for the Protection of Cultural Property in the Event of Armed Conflict. Lauswolt, The Netherlands, 9–11 February 1994, p. 11. (The final clauses were mentioned only *P.M. Pro Memoria.*)

UNESCO document: A working document prepared by the Secretariat, CLT/94/608/1 of 28 November 1994, p. 26. (The document mentioned the form of instrument.)

Expert Meeting on the review of the 1954 Hague Convention for the Protection of Cultural Property in the Event of Armed Conflict. Paris, UNESCO Headquarters, 28 November–2 December 1994. UNESCO document CLT/CH/94/608/2, *Final Report*, p. 7.

UNESCO, Meeting of the States Parties to the 1954 Hague Convention for the Protection of Cultural Property in the Event of Armed Conflict (Paris, 13 November 1995). *Information Note.* CLT-95/CONF.009/INF.1, Paris, June 1995, p. 3. (The note requested the views of States concerning the form of improvement of the Convention.)

UNESCO, Second Meeting of the High Contracting Parties to the Convention for the Protection of Cultural Property in the Event of Armed Conflict (The Hague, 1954), UNESCO House, Paris, 13 November 1995, *Final Report*, CLT-95/CONF.009/5, November 1995, p. 3.

UNESCO, Meeting of Governmental Experts. Summary of comments received from States Parties to the Hague Convention and from International Council on Archives. UNESCO document: CLT-96/CONF.603/INF.4, Paris, December 1996, p. 10.

Draft provisions for the revision of the 1954 Hague Convention and commentary from the UNESCO Secretariat. CLT-97/CONF.208/2, Paris, October 1997. (The document included the text of the 'revised Lauwolt document'.)

UNESCO, Third Meeting of the High Contracting Parties to the Convention for the Protection of Cultural Property in the Event of Armed Conflict

(The Hague, 1954), UNESCO House, Paris, 13 November 1997, *Final Report*, CLT-97/CONF.208/3, Paris, November 1997, p. 2.

UNESCO, Meeting of Governmental Experts on the Revision of the Hague Convention for the Protection of Cultural Property in the Event of Armed Conflict of 1954. Vienna, 11–13 May 1998. UNESCO document: Paris, May 1998, *Final Report*, p. 2.

Preliminary Draft Second Protocol to the 1954 Hague Convention. UNESCO document HC/1999/1, October 1998 (English, French and Russian). (This Preliminary Draft includes the first version of the final clauses.)

Preliminary Draft Second Protocol to the 1954 Hague Convention. Revised. UNESCO document. No number. December 1998 (original: English). Key to source of proposed changes: G: Germany; LM: Leiden meeting; N: Norway. (This is the slightly modified Preliminary Draft which includes the final clauses.)

UNESCO, Summary of comments on Preliminary Draft Second Protocol to the 1954 Hague Convention received from High Contracting Parties to the Hague Convention for the Protection of Cultural Property in the Event of Armed Conflict 1954, other UNESCO Member States and international organizations, Paris, 15 January 1999.

Draft Second Protocol to the 1954 Hague Convention for the Protection of Cultural Property in the Event of Armed Conflict. UNESCO document HC/1999/1/rev.1, February 1999. (The draft includes the final clauses as they were submitted to the 1999 Hague Conference.)

It is clear that the formulation of the final clauses was considered at the very end of the drafting of the Protocol. The Lauswolt draft Protocol includes no such provisions: it mentions only the need for preparation of such clauses using the abbreviation 'P.M.' (Pro Memoria).[1423]

In its comments on the Lauswolt draft, the Secretariat 'considers it wise to embody any agreed new provisions in a Protocol to the Convention, rather than attempt a revision of the text of the Hague Convention 1954'.[1424] This proposal was discussed at the 1994 Paris Expert Meeting on the review of the 1954 Hague Convention for the Protection of Cultural Property in the Event of Armed Conflict, held in Paris, at UNESCO Headquarters, from

---

1423 The Second Expert Meeting on the 1954 Hague Convention for the Protection of Cultural Property in the Event of Armed Conflict. Lauswolt, The Netherlands, 9–11 February 1994, p. 11.

1424 UNESCO document: A working document prepared by the Secretariat, CLT/94/608/1 of 28 November 1994, p. 26.

28 November to 2 December 1994. The question of an amendment to the Convention or a supplementary Protocol remained undecided. Some views expressed 'the desirability of excluding accessions to the original text once the new provisions had been accepted. However, the meeting made no decision on the matter which – as it was agreed – needs further discussion.'[1425]

It was only at the second meeting of the High Contracting Parties on 13 November 1995 that

> a majority of participants were in favour of adopting an additional Protocol which would supplement the provisions of the Convention and, at the same time, allow the States not Parties to the Convention to become party to it. Two points of view were expressed: some delegations were in favour of holding a diplomatic conference which would elaborate and adopt the protocol, others preferred to convene an Expert Meeting for drafting such instrument before its subsequent adoption by the High Contracting Parties.[1426]

In the comments presented in view of the meeting of governmental experts in 1997, Belgium, Ecuador and the ICA recommended 'that the amendment of the Convention be in the form of an additional Protocol'.[1427] The UNESCO Secretariat was also in favour of this proposal, as being simpler than amending the existing Convention.

At the conclusion of the meeting of governmental experts in March 1997, redrafted Articles were proposed by the Chairperson of the drafting group, Estelle Appiah. The Secretariat was charged with preparing a working document,[1428] known as the revised Lauswolt document. This document

---

1425 Expert Meeting on the review of the 1954 Hague Convention for the Protection of Cultural Property in the Event of Armed Conflict. Paris, UNESCO Headquarters, 28 November–2 December 1994. UNESCO document CLT/CH/94/608/2, *Final Report*, p. 7.

1426 UNESCO, Second Meeting of the High Contracting Parties to the Convention for the Protection of Cultural Property in the Event of Armed Conflict (The Hague, 1954), UNESCO House, Paris, 13 November 1995, *Final Report*, CLT-95/CONF.009/5, November 1995, p. 3. See also Hladík (1996), p. 339.

1427 UNESCO, Meeting of Governmental Experts. Summary of comments received from States Parties to the Hague Convention and from the International Council on Archives. UNESCO document: CLT-96/CONF.603/INF.4, Paris, December 1996, p. 10.

1428 *Draft provisions for the revision of the 1954 Hague Convention and commentary from the UNESCO Secretariat*. CLT-97/CONF.208/2, Paris, October 1997. The document included the text of the 'revised Lauwolt document'. Draft Articles are followed by the Secretariat's comments comparing the original provisions of the Lauswolt document with the revised provisions resulting from the deliberation of participants. Such comments are entitled 'Reasons for change'. The Secretariat also summarized the main points raised in the discussions in the sections entitled 'Main points of

offered no detailed proposals for the final clauses; it only included the Secretariat's note, stating that:

> the new instrument should include a provision on the relation between this instrument and the Hague Convention, as some of its provisions, if implemented, may contradict those of the Hague Convention. Such provision was inspired by Article 36 of the Hague Convention. In conformity with the 1969 Vienna Convention on the Law of Treaties (quoting Article 19 of the Vienna Convention) and customary international law, it is proposed that the new instrument could also include a provision on reservations in order to exclude the States Parties' possibility of minimizing protection under this instrument in order to maintain a 'hard core of obligation' of the instrument which would be legally binding for all States Parties.[1429]

The desirability of adopting a new instrument supplementing the Hague Convention was also favoured by the third meeting of the High Contracting Parties in November 1997:

> Delegates were in favour of adopting a new instrument which would bridge the existing gaps in the Hague Convention, thus reinforcing the protection of cultural heritage before and during hostilities. They pointed out, however, that the present draft provisions for its revision elaborated at the meeting of government experts last March are not yet sufficiently final for adoption by a Diplomatic Conference and, consequently, a further Expert Meeting is required.[1430]

It was only at the 1998 Vienna Governmental Experts Meeting on the revision of the Hague Convention for the Protection of Cultural Property in the Event of Armed Conflict of 1954, held in Vienna, 11–13 May 1998, that progress was made:

---

discussion'. Some parts of the revised Lauswolt document were placed within square brackets because the discussion did not reveal unanimity on these issues. These were subject to further negotiation.

1429 Draft provisions for the revision of the 1954 Hague Convention and commentary from the UNESCO Secretariat. CLT-97/CONF.208/2, Paris, October 1997, pp. 28–29.

1430 UNESCO, Third Meeting of the High Contracting Parties to the Convention for the Protection of Cultural Property in the Event of Armed Conflict (The Hague, 1954), UNESCO House, Paris, 13 November 1997, *Final Report*, CLT-97/CONF.208/3, Paris, November 1997, p. 2. See also Hladík (1998b).

8. The Expert Meeting considered three options regarding the form of the new instrument. First, a new convention supersedes the 1954 Hague Convention; second, an optional Protocol supplementing the provisions of the Hague Convention and finally, an instrument revising the Hague Convention in accordance with its Art. 39.

9. It was agreed that the relationship between the new instrument and the Hague Convention requires careful consideration, and that a flexible solution should be sought. Some delegations interpreted Art. 39 of the Hague Convention as providing the only possibility for supplementing the Convention. They felt that applying Art. 39 would be desirable in order to guarantee a uniform protection regime. Most delegations, however, held the view that it is not obligatory to follow the procedure outlined in Art. 39, but that the general rules of international treaty law, including Art. 41 of the Vienna Convention on the Law of Treaties should be applied. The latter approach would enable States to agree on an improved protection regime between themselves without the formal acceptance of all States Parties to the Hague Convention.

10. Most delegations expressed the view that the Hague Convention 1954 should be retained as the basis for the protection of cultural property in the event of armed conflict. They shared the assessment that the Hague Convention enjoys a high reputation and wide acceptance in the international community and that States willing to accede to the Hague Convention should not be precluded from doing so. The majority of delegations felt that an optional Protocol would be the best choice for the format of the new instrument.[1431]

The UNESCO Secretariat prepared the document based on several meetings of government experts, and particularly on the discussions that took place at the May 1998 Vienna Meeting: the *Preliminary Draft Second Protocol*.[1432] It is

---

1431 UNESCO, Meeting of Governmental Experts on the Revision of the Hague Convention for the Protection of Cultural Property in the Event of Armed Conflict of 1954. Vienna, 11–13 May 1998. UNESCO document: Paris, May 1998, *Final Report*, p. 2. See also the summary of comments received from States Parties to the Hague Convention, the International Committee of the Red Cross and the International Council on Archives, prepared for that meeting by the UNESCO Secretariat, Paris, March 1998, p. 8.

1432 *Preliminary Draft Second Protocol to the 1954 Hague Convention*. UNESCO document HC/1999/1, October 1998 (English, French and Russian).

in this Preliminary Draft that we find the first versions of the 'Final clauses'. Later versions of these clauses are examined under the final articles.

The *Preliminary Draft Protocol* was sent to the Member States of UNESCO, the UN, and selected international organizations, with requests for comments, which would be taken into account in the preparation of a final draft for the Diplomatic Conference to be held at The Hague from 14 to 26 March 1999. The comments of various governments are also included under the different articles.[1433]

On this basis, the UNESCO Secretariat and the Government of the Netherlands drew up the final draft of the Second Protocol: *Draft Second Protocol to the 1954 Hague Convention for the Protection of Cultural Property in the Event of Armed Conflict* (UNESCO doc. HC/1999/1/rev.1, February 1999).

Reservations concerning the 1999 Protocol

The first proposal of the final clauses prepared by the UNESCO Secretariat[1434] included, *inter alia*, the following proposal:

> Article 44 Reservations
> No reservations may be made to this Protocol.

In the 14th Plenary Meeting of the Conference, on 25 March 1999, the Chairman of the Conference, Adriaan Bos, opened the discussion of the question of reservations concerning the treaty, in particular concerning Chapter 9, Article 44 as quoted in document HC/1999/rev.1, and asked whether such a clause was necessary. 'He pointed out that the existing

---

1433   UNESCO, Summary of comments on Preliminary Draft Second Protocol to the 1954 Hague Convention received from High Contracting Parties to the Hague Convention for the Protection of Cultural Property in the Event of Armed Conflict 1954, other UNESCO Member States and international organizations, Paris, 15 January 1999.

1434   *Preliminary Draft Second Protocol to the 1954 Hague Convention.* UNESCO document HC/1999/1, October 1998 (English, French and Russian). The same text is also reproduced in the following documents: *Preliminary Draft Second Protocol to the 1954 Hague Convention.* Revised UNESCO document. No number. December 1998 (original: English). Key to source of proposed changes: G: Germany; LM: Leiden meeting; N: Norway. (This document refers to the Leiden Meeting – LM.) Another document, entitled 'Revised Draft Second Protocol to the 1954 Hague Convention', circulated at the Conference on 8 December 1998, keeps the same text and the same number. *Draft Second Protocol to the 1954 Hague Convention for the Protection of Cultural Property in the Event of Armed Conflict.* UNESCO doc. HC/1999/1/rev.1, February 1999. (This retains the same text and the same number 44 as the Preliminary Draft of October 1998.)

practice with regard to reservations under applicable international law was pertinent.'[1435]

Several delegates took the floor, starting with Shukri (Syrian Arab Republic). He supported the Chairperson's proposal to delete this Article[1436] and recalled the previous debate, wherein the majority of participants preferred to delete the provision based on reservations in the light of Article 19 of the Vienna Convention on the Law of Treaties. The Austrian delegate, Brezovszky, also supported the Chairperson's proposal, as did the UK delegate. Article 19 of the Vienna Convention, to which the delegates referred, reads as follows:

> Article 19 Formulation of reservations
>
> A State may, when signing, ratifying, accepting, approving or acceding to a treaty, formulate a reservation unless:
>
> (a) the reservation is prohibited by the treaty;
> (b) the treaty provides that only specified reservations, which do not include the reservation in question, may be made; or
> (c) in cases not falling under sub-paragraphs (a) and (b), the reservation is incompatible with the object and purpose of the treaty.

By contrast, another group of delegates was in favour of maintaining Article 44 as proposed by the UNESCO Secretariat. Wågnert, the Swedish delegate, and his delegation

> preferred not to use the Vienna regime because the wording 'incompatible with the object and purpose of this treaty' was vague and there was the risk that different reservations would create different regimes on the battlefield. He stated that his first preference was to maintain Article 44 in the UNESCO draft. However, in the spirit of compromise his second option was to discuss which type of reservations would be acceptable. Reservations to Chapter 2 and 3 should not be allowed. Reservations to Chapter 4 could be contemplated.[1437]

He was also supported by the delegates of Finland and Greece.

1435   1999 Hague Conference, Plenary Session, 25 March 1999, p. 63.
1436   This proposal was also included in the written preliminary remarks of the Syrian Arab Republic, submitted to the UNESCO Secretariat on 13 December 1998, p. 6.
1437   1999 Hague Conference, Plenary Session, 25 March 1999, p. 64.

The UK delegate[1438] opposed the procedure suggested by Sweden. 'He considered that it was much better to rely upon the general rule of public international law, even though there may be difficulties in interpreting whether a particular reservation is or is not compatible with the treaty'.[1439] His proposal, that no provision on the prohibition of reservations be included in the Protocol, was supported by the Chairman, as well as by the delegates of France, Germany and Turkey.[1440]

The Conference finally adopted the Chairman's proposal to rely on the regime of the Vienna Convention and not to include the provision on reservation. The Swedish delegate withdrew his proposal.[1441]

The discussion at the Conference reflected two different prevailing tendencies in the international community in relation to reservations to humanitarian conventions. One of these tendencies, corresponding to the views of the Swedish, Finnish and Greek delegates at the 1999 Hague Conference, found practical application in the ICC Statute. Article 120 of the Statute simply states: 'No reservations may be made to this Statute'. As a participant in the 1998 Rome Conference reflected,[1442]

> it was widely agreed during the informal consultation that, if the statute provided for automatic jurisdiction, allowing states to reserve on the core of the crimes would be self-defeating. There were also strong concerns about allowing reservations to the provisions obligating state parties to co-operate with the court. At the same time, there was sympathy for the view that reservations could be permitted to other aspects of the statute, especially more procedural questions, to take account of different legal systems. This possibility was considered in the informal consultations, but ultimately no easy distinction could be found between essential and other provisions of the statute. Given

---

1438 The UK had already expressed doubts about the prohibition on reservations in the written comments, 'given the State practice in relation to other instruments relating to the conduct of hostilities, such a prohibition might not in fact discourgage States from adhering to the Protocol'. Letter of P. H. B. Baker, Security Policy Department, Foreign & Commonwealth Office, 14 December 1998, p. 2.

1439 1999 Hague Conference, Plenary Session, 25 March 1999, p. 64.

1440 Turkey had already proposed a more flexible approach to reservations in its written remarks. Comments and suggestions by the Turkish Government on the Preliminary Draft Second Protocol to the 1954 Hague Convention for the Protection of Cultural Property in the Event of Armed Conflict, [n.d.], p. 7.

1441 Ibid., p. 66.

1442 Philippe Kirsch served as the Chairman of the Committee of the Whole of the United Nations Diplomatic Conference of Plenipotentiaries on the Establishment of an International Criminal Court.

this situation, the Bureau concluded it had to include a provision that reservations to the statute were not permitted.[1443]

This decision was taken on the last day of the Conference.[1444]

But the provision of Article 120 has not prevented some States from making 'declarations' at the time of ratifications. Several States did so.[1445] The writings about the Statute discuss the character of these declarations, which can be assimilated to genuine reservations. This was, for example, the case of the territorial declaration of Denmark or the reference to the Constitution by Uruguay, objected to by Denmark, Ireland, Germany, Norway, the Netherlands and the UK.[1446]

Another tendency prevailed at the 1974–77 Geneva Conference, which adopted the Additional Protocol to the Geneva Conventions. The draft of Additional Protocol I contained an Article on reservations, composed of two paragraphs: the first listed the articles to which no reservation could be made, and the second provided that any reservation would lose effect five years after it had been formulated, failing renewal by means of a declaration addressed to the depositary. Although it proposed this solution, the ICRC

1443   Kirsch and Holmes (2004), p. 33. The option to leave reservations to the regime of the Vienna Convention was also debated, but 'some insisted that it could lead to an unseemly confusion: some States exercised their right to object to other State's reservations while others failed to act'. See Neroni Slade and Clark (2002), p. 432.

1444   This was also one of the negative arguments used by the US delegation in presenting the Statute to the US Senate: 'Finally, we were confronted on 17 July with a provision stipulating that no reservations to the treaty would be allowed. We had long argued against such a prohibition and many countries had joined us in that concern. We believed that as a minimum there were certain provisions of the treaty, particularly in the field of state cooperation with the court, where domestic constitutional requirements and national judicial procedures might require a reasonable opportunity for reservations that did not defeat the intent or purpose of the treaty'. Statement of David J. Scheffer, Ambassador-at-Large for War Crimes Issues and Head of the US Delegation to the UN Diplomatic Conference on the Establishment of a Permanent International Criminal Court. 'Is a UN International Criminal Court in the US Interests?' Hearing before the Subcommittee on Foreign Operations of the Committee on Foreign Relations, US Senate. 105th Congress. 2nd session. July 23, 1998, p. 15.

1445   Schabas (2007), pp. 470–86.

1446   Ibid., pp. 372–73. William Schabas also recalled that the Rome Statute itself makes its own exception to the prohibition of reservations by allowing States to forumulate a kind of reservation to Article 8. 'For a seven-year period, States may ratify the Statute but escape jurisdiction over war crimes' (ibid., p. 374). Article 124 (Transitional provision) states: 'Notwithstanding Article 12, paragraphs 1 and 2, a State, on becoming a party to this Statute, may declare that, for a period of seven years after the entry into force of this Statute for the State concerned, it does not accept the jurisdiction of the Court with respect to the category of crimes referred to in Article 8 when a crime is alleged to have been committed by its nationals or on its territory. A declaration under this Article may be withdrawn at any time. The provisions of this Article shall be reviewed at the Review Conference convened in accordance with Article 123, paragraph 1.'

was nevertheless ready to support a view in favour of deleting any provision on reservations and consequently to leave this matter to be governed by general international law. This ultimately happened, and the 1977 Protocol has no Article prohibiting reservations. Reservations are thus subject to the rules of general international law as codified in the Vienna Convention. The hope expressed by the ICRC commentary in this connection can be also applied to the 1999 Second Protocol, which adopted the same solution – not to have any provision on reservations:

(a) that the possibility of making reservations will facilitate the universal acceptance of the Protocol without adversely affecting its object and purpose, which is to improve the protection provided by the Conventions to the victims of international armed conflicts;

(b) that any objections that may be raised to a reservation should not involve a refusal to enter into treaty relations with the State making the reservation;

(c) that States will not only study with the greatest caution the need to make a reservation but will regularly re-examine the need to maintain that reservation.[1447]

Thus far these hopes have been fully satisfied; to date, no State that has become Party to the Second Protocol has made a reservation. Only Canada and the Islamic Republic of Iran provided interpretative declarations.

In 1998, during its preparation of the draft provision on reservations, the UNESCO Secretariat had to make a choice between these two tendencies. The draft was assembled during a period that also saw preparatory discussions for the ICC and so it is not surprising that the Secretariat's choice was influenced by the recent discussions on reservations at the Rome Conference. But the delegates at the Hague Conference instead turned to the example provided by the 1977 Additional Protocol. The recent evolution in the accession of States to the Protocol demonstrated that their choice was a good one.

The ICRC Commentary on the 1977 Additional Protocols included a useful evaluation of the situation regarding reservations according to the Vienna Convention. Since the 1999 Second Protocol adopted the same position on reservations, it may be useful to reprint this evaluation here:

1447 Commentary on the Additional Protocols of 8 June 1977, pp. 1064–65.

The rules on reservations

1. Principle

The Vienna Convention provides that when a State signs, ratifies or accedes to a treaty, it may formulate a reservation unless 'the reservation is incompatible with the object and purpose of the treaty' (Article 19).

Reservations must be formulated in writing and communicated to the Contracting States and other States entitled to become Parties to the treaty (Article 23, paragraph 1). A reservation formulated at the time a treaty is signed subject to ratification, must, in order to be valid, be formally confirmed when the treaty is ratified by the State which formulated the reservation (Article 23, paragraph 2).

Just as it is the responsibility of every other State concerned to determine whether any particular declaration does or does not constitute a reservation, so every State determines individually whether a reservation formulated by another State is or is not compatible with the object and purpose of the treaty.

2. Acceptance and objection

A State may 'accept' the reservation formulated by another State either explicitly or tacitly. Acceptance of the reservation by a Contracting State allows the treaty to enter into force between that State and the State which had made the reservation. The treaty applies between these two States as modified by the reservation (Article 20, paragraph 4(a) and (c), and paragraph 5; Article 21, paragraph 1(a) and (b); Article 23, paragraphs 1 and 3).

A State may make an 'objection' to a reservation made by another State. Unless the State which formulated the objection clearly expressed its intention to the contrary, an objection by a Contracting State does not prevent the treaty from entering into force, as soon as at least one other Contracting State has accepted the reservation, between the State formulating the objection and the State which made the reservation; however, 'the provisions to which the reservation relates do not apply as between the two States to the extent of the reservation' (Article 20, paragraph 4(b) and (c); Article 21, paragraph 3; Article 23, paragraphs 1 and 3).

Thus, it is necessary for the objecting State clearly to express its intention for the treaty not to enter into force, as modified by the reservation, between itself and the State which had made the reservation once at least one other Contracting State has accepted a reservation. Otherwise, the State accepting a reservation and that objecting to it may find themselves in the same situation, depending on the specific object of the reservation.

It should be emphasized that a reservation only applies as between the State making it and other States bound by the treaty. The reservation does not modify the provisions of the treaty for the other Parties to the treaty 'inter se' (Article 21, paragraph 2).

As we saw with regard to objections, the Vienna Convention provides that a ratification or accession containing a reservation is effective only if at least one other Contracting State has accepted the reservation. The twelve-month period laid down for tacit acceptance by States which had previously consented to be bound by the treaty may be longer than the periods laid down by certain treaties for their entry into force for a State after depositing its instrument of ratification or accession. This requires two comments. Although, as we have seen, the Vienna Convention codified customary law, this period of twelve months may, on the other hand, be seen as a new norm, strictly applicable only between States bound by the Vienna Convention at the time of concluding a particular treaty. In any event, the uncertainty which may exist, as to whether a State making a reservation has the status of a Contracting State, is relative in view of the fact that the risk is slight that a reservation will not be accepted by any other Contracting State, either explicitly or tacitly, whether the expression of that State's consent to be bound by the treaty is given either before or after that of the State making the reservation.

3. Withdrawal of reservations and objections

A reservation or an objection to a reservation may be withdrawn at any time, in writing. The withdrawal of a reservation becomes operative in relation to all other Contracting States when they have received notice thereof; the withdrawal of an objection becomes operative when notice thereof has been received by the State which formulated the reservation (Article 22 and Article 23, paragraph 4).[1448]

1448   Commentary on the Additional Protocols of 8 June 1977, pp. 1061–63 (reproduced without footnotes).

Revision of the Protocol

The 1954 Hague Convention included an Article 39 entitled 'Revision of the Convention and of the Regulations for its Execution'. Several drafts prepared for the 1999 Hague Conference included a *pro memoria* (P.M.) reference to a possible article concerning revision of the Protocol. Such an article was not included in the Protocol, since the Protocol was already undergoing revision. It probably would be considered an expression of great pessimism to speak already – at this phase – about the possibility of revising the Second Protocol.

Declarations and Reservations

The following declarations or reservations were deposited as of 9 May 2008:

Iran: 'Accession of the Islamic Republic of Iran to this Protocol shall not mean the recognition of any country it does not recognize, neither shall it give rise to any commitment toward such states or governments.' Annexed to the instrument was the following explanatory declaration:

> *Considering* the special importance of protecting cultural heritage of nations against damages caused by war,
> *Bearing* in mind the fact that cultural heritage of nations is deemed as part of cultural heritage of humanity,
> *Considering* that full protection of cultural heritage against damages caused by armed conflicts needs the protections more than that which is provided for in the present Protocol,
> The Islamic Republic of Iran regards the conclusion of bilateral and multilateral supplementary agreements to the present Protocol as necessary and states its readiness to conclude such agreements. These agreements shall entail the granting of privileges and providing more possibilities for protection of cultural heritage of nations and shall also articulate the rules stipulated in the Protocol including customary rules of international law, in a way that solely include the rules that are not protested by the Government of the Islamic Republic of Iran and as well as explain more clearly the modality for the implementation of provisions of section 4 of this Protocol.

Canada: The statement of understanding reproduced below was annexed to the instrument of accession:

> STATEMENT OF UNDERSTANDING
>
> 1. It is the understanding of the Government of Canada that the definition of a military objective in Article 2(f) is to be interpreted the same way as Article 52(2) of Additional Protocol I to the Geneva Conventions of 1949.
> 2. It is the understanding of the Government of Canada that in relation to Article 6(a)(ii), 6(b), 7(a), 7(b), 8, 13(2)(a) and 13(2)(b) the word 'feasible' means that which is practicable or practically possible, taking into account all circumstances ruling at the time, including humanitarian and military considerations.
> 3. It is the understanding of the Government of Canada that in relation to Article 6(a)(ii), 6(b), 7(c) and 7(d)(ii) that the military advantage anticipated from an attack is intended to refer to the advantage anticipated from the attack considered as a whole and not from isolated or particular parts of the attack.
> 4. It is the understanding of the Government of Canada that any cultural property that becomes a military objective may be attacked in accordance with a waiver of imperative military necessity pursuant to Article 4(2) of the Convention.
> 5. It is the understanding of the Government of Canada that a decision to invoke imperative military necessity pursuant to Article 6(c) of this Protocol may be taken by an officer commanding a force smaller than the equivalent of a battalion in size in circumstances where the cultural property becomes a military objective and the circumstances ruling at the time relating to force protection are such that it is not feasible to require the decision to be made by an officer commanding a force the equivalent of a battalion in size or larger.
> 6. It is the understanding of the Government of Canada that under Article 6(a)(i), cultural property can be made into a military objective because of its nature, location, purpose or use.

Article 39
LANGUAGES

This Protocol is drawn up in Arabic, Chinese, English, French, Russian and Spanish, the six texts being equally authentic.

Preparatory work

Preliminary Draft Second Protocol to the 1954 Hague Convention. UNESCO document HC/1999/1, October 1998 (English, French and Russian). (This Preliminary Draft includes the first version of the final clauses.)

Preliminary Draft Second Protocol to the 1954 Hague Convention. Revised. UNESCO document. No number. December 1998 (original: English). Key to source of proposed changes: G: Germany; LM: Leiden meeting; N: Norway. (This is a slightly modified Preliminary Draft which includes the final clauses.)

UNESCO, Summary of comments on Preliminary Draft Second Protocol to the 1954 Hague Convention received from High Contracting Parties to the Hague Convention for the Protection of Cultural Property in the Event of Armed Conflict 1954, other UNESCO Member States and international organizations, Paris, 15 January 1999.

Draft Second Protocol to the 1954 Hague Convention for the Protection of Cultural Property in the Event of Armed Conflict. UNESCO document HC/1999/1/rev.1, February 1999.

ANALYSIS OF THE TEXT

The first draft of the final clauses prepared by the UNESCO Secretariat[1449] included the following proposal:

1449   *Preliminary Draft Second Protocol to the 1954 Hague Convention.* UNESCO document HC/1999/1, October 1998 (English, French and Russian). The same text is also reproduced in the following documents: *Preliminary Draft Second Protocol to the 1954 Hague Convention.* Revised. UNESCO document. No number. December 1998 (original: English). Key to source of proposed changes: G: Germany; LM: Leiden meeting; N Norway (this is a slightly modified Preliminary Draft which includes the final clauses). *Draft Second Protocol to the 1954 Hague Convention for the Protection of Cultural Property in the Event of Armed Conflict.* UNESCO doc. HC/1999/1/rev.1, February 1999.

Article 35 Languages

1. The present Protocol is drawn up in English and French, the two texts being equally authoritative.

2. Official texts of this Protocol shall be established by the Director-General of UNESCO in Arabic, Chinese, Russian and Spanish.

The Secretariat's proposal was based on practice before the Second World War (of the League of Nations) to have only a few – in fact, two – authentic texts.

Even if this was, in our personal view, a reasonable and economical proposal, it did not conform to the practice established in the UN or correspond to Article 29 of the Hague Convention, which considered as 'authoritative' the following four languages: English, French, Russian and Spanish. In practical terms, it was therefore impossible to limit the number of authentic languages.

There can be no doubt that the multiplicity of authentic texts creates difficulties for the process of interpretation. As noted in our Commentary on the 1954 Hague Convention, UNESCO drew up a list of discrepancies found in the translations of authentic texts of the Convention.

But the prevalent tendency towards a multiplicity of languages in the post-1945 world led to a different approach. Not surprisingly, several comments were formulated on this issue. The Syrian Arab Republic proposed the inclusion of Arabic, Chinese, Russian and Spanish among the languages.[1450] Turkey also proposed that the terminology refer not to 'authoritative' but rather 'authentic' languages, which also conforms to the terminology used by the 1969 Vienna Convention on the Law of Treaties (Article 86 of the Vienna Convention).[1451]

However, the next draft, prepared by the UNESCO Secretariat and the Government of the Netherlands,[1452] effected no changes to the Preliminary Draft.

At the Diplomatic Conference, the issue of languages (draft Article 43) was discussed at a Plenary Session on 25 March 1999. In the meantime, the original draft was modified and a reference to several equally authentic texts

---

1450   Preliminary remarks of the Syrian Arab Republic of 13 December 1998.

1451   Comments and suggestions by the Turkish Government on the Preliminary Draft Second Protocol to the 1954 Hague Convention for the Protection of Cultural Property in the Event of Armed Conflict, [n.d.], p. 6.

1452   Draft Second Protocol to the 1954 Hague Convention for the Protection of Cultural Property in the Event of Armed Conflict. UNESCO doc. HC/1999/1/rev.1, February 1999.

included: Arabic, Chinese, English, French, Russia and Spanish.[1453] The Argentine delegate, Ariel Gonzalez, expressed his satisfaction, considering 'the situation […] at the beginning of the Conference somewhat abnormal'. Several other delegates (Russia, Syria, China and Libya) were satisfied with the new formula.

The requirement was requested by Fattal of Lebanon. According to him, all conferences drafting international instruments should use six languages in order to avoid this kind of problem, that is, discussion on reduction in the number of authentic languages. The representative of the Secretariat stressed the issue of the cost of these translations and the Chairperson of the Conference proposed leaving the decision to the UNESCO Executive Board. The Secretariat was required only to report on this question orally to the next session of the General Conference.[1454]

Following this short discussion, the text was sent to the Drafting Committee. It was then included without further modifications in the final text of the Protocol.

Moreover, the Secretariat of UNESCO will maintain a database containing the other available texts, as it did for the text of the 1954 Hague Convention.

1453   A new version of the 43 was formulated in document HC/1999/5/Add.10.
1454   Plenary Session of the Conference, 26 March 1999, pp. 48–50.

Article 40
SIGNATURE

This Protocol shall bear the date of 26 March 1999. It shall be opened for signature by all High Contracting Parties at The Hague from 17 May 1999 until 31 December 1999.

Preparatory work

Preliminary Draft Second Protocol to the 1954 Hague Convention. UNESCO document HC/1999/1, October 1998 (English, French and Russian). (This Preliminary Draft includes the first version of the final clauses.)

Preliminary Draft Second Protocol to the 1954 Hague Convention. Revised. UNESCO document. No number. December 1998 (original: English). Key to source of proposed changes: G: Germany; LM: Leiden meeting; N: Norway. (This slightly modified Preliminary Draft includes the final clauses.)

UNESCO, Summary of comments on Preliminary Draft Second Protocol to the 1954 Hague Convention received from High Contracting Parties to the Hague Convention for the Protection of Cultural Property in the Event of Armed Conflict 1954, other UNESCO Member States and international organizations, Paris, 15 January 1999.

Draft Second Protocol to the 1954 Hague Convention for the Protection of Cultural Property in the Event of Armed Conflict. UNESCO document HC/1999/1/rev.1, February 1999.

ANALYSIS OF THE TEXT

The formalities of adoption for the Protocol conformed to standard practice for international treaties in the present international community (the system established by the 1969 Vienna Convention). In the Preliminary Draft,[1455] Article 37 concerning signatures was formulated in a similar way to the final text of the Hague Convention, but with modified dates:

1455   *Preliminary Draft Second Protocol to the 1954 Hague Convention.* UNESCO document HC/1999/1, October 1998 (English, French and Russian). The same text is also reproduced in the following documents: *Preliminary Draft Second Protocol to the 1954 Hague Convention.* Revised. UNESCO document. No number. December 1998 (original: English). Key to source of proposed changes: G: Germany; LM: Leiden meeting; N: Norway. (This slightly modified Preliminary Draft includes the final clauses.)

Article 37

The present Protocol shall bear the date of ... May 1999 and, until the date of 31 December 1999, it shall remain open for signature by all States Parties to the Convention.

The final date of the Conference, 26 March 1999, was chosen as the date of the Protocol by the Drafting Committee. For practical reasons relating to the establishment of the final text in six languages and verification of the translations, the actual date of signature was 17 May 1999, several weeks after the end of the Conference.

The final text of Article 40 was modified in the *Draft Second Protocol* (HC/1999/1/rev.1 of February 1999)[1456] and submitted to the Conference. The section of text proposed in the Preliminary Draft of October 1998 referring to 'all States Parties to the Convention' was modified and replaced with a reference to the 'High Contracting Parties', following the definition in Article 1(d): '"High Contracting Party" means a State Party to the Convention'.

The following point made in the Commentary to the 1977 Additional Protocols to the Geneva Conventions applies equally here: 'the Protocol might be considered as a "restricted" treaty, since, only specific States may become Parties to it; in fact, it is open-ended since, like the 1949 Conventions, it is intended to be universally applicable'.[1457]

By 31 December 2009, the Second Protocol has been signed by the following States:

Albania	26 March 1999
Armenia	22 October 1999
Austria	26 March 1999
Belarus	26 March 1999
Belgium	26 March 1999
Bulgaria	15 September 1999
Cambodia	26 March 1999
Colombia	31 December 1999
Côte d'Ivoire	26 March 1999
Croatia	26 March 1999

1456   Draft Second Protocol to the 1954 Hague Convention for the Protection of Cultural Property in the Event of Armed Conflict. UNESCO doc. HC/1999/1/rev.1, February 1999, p. 30.

1457   Commentary on the Additional Protocols of 8 June 1977, p. 1059.

Cyprus	19 August 1999
Ecuador	29 December 1999
Egypt	9 October 1999
Estonia	26 March 1999
Finland	26 March 1999
Germany	26 March 1999
Ghana	26 March 1999
Greece	26 March 1999
Holy See	26 March 1999
Hungary	26 March 1999
Indonesia	26 March 1999
Italy	26 March 1999
Luxembourg	26 March 1999
Madagascar	26 March 1999
Morocco	21 December 1999
Netherlands	26 March 1999
Nigeria	26 March 1999
Oman	30 June 1999
Pakistan	26 March 1999
Peru	13 July 1999
Qatar	26 March 1999
Romania	8 November 1999
Slovak Republic	22 December 1999
Spain	26 March 1999
Sweden	26 March 1999
Switzerland	26 March 1999
Syria	26 March 1999
Yemen	26 March 1999

Most of the signatories also assumed their obligations according to Article 18 of the 1969 Vienna Convention, thereby ensuring that the object and purpose of the treaty would not be defeated prior to its entry into force.

Article 41
RATIFICATION, ACCEPTANCE OR APPROVAL

1. *This Protocol shall be subject to ratification, acceptance or approval by High Contracting Parties which have signed this Protocol, in accordance with their respective constitutional procedures.*
2. *The instruments of ratification, acceptance or approval shall be deposited with the Director-General.*

Preparatory work

Preliminary Draft Second Protocol to the 1954 Hague Convention. UNESCO document HC/1999/1, October 1998 (English, French and Russian). (This Preliminary Draft includes the first version of the final clauses.)

Preliminary Draft Second Protocol to the 1954 Hague Convention. Revised. UNESCO document. No number. December 1998 (original: English). Key to source of proposed changes: G: Germany; LM: Leiden meeting; N: Norway. (This slightly modified Preliminary Draft includes the final clauses.)

UNESCO, Summary of comments on Preliminary Draft Second Protocol to the 1954 Hague Convention received from High Contracting Parties to the Hague Convention for the Protection of Cultural Property in the Event of Armed Conflict 1954, other UNESCO Member States and international organizations, Paris, 15 January 1999.

Draft Second Protocol to the 1954 Hague Convention for the Protection of Cultural Property in the Event of Armed Conflict. UNESCO document HC/1999/1/rev.1, February 1999.

ANALYSIS OF THE TEXT

In the Preliminary Draft,[1458] Article 38 concerning ratification was formulated in a similar way to the final text of the Hague Convention:

1458 *Preliminary Draft Second Protocol to the 1954 Hague Convention.* UNESCO document HC/1999/1, October 1998 (English, French and Russian). The same text is also reproduced in the following documents: *Preliminary Draft Second Protocol to the 1954 Hague Convention.* Revised. UNESCO document. No number. December 1998 (original: English). Key to source of proposed changes: G: Germany; LM: Leiden meeting; N: Norway. (This slightly modified Preliminary Draft includes the final clauses.). In the *Draft Second Protocol to the 1954 Hague Convention for the Protection of Cultural Property in the Event of Armed Conflict* (UNESCO doc. HC/1999/1/rev.1,

Article 38

1. The present Protocol shall be subject to ratification by States Parties to the Convention, in accordance with their respective constitutional procedures.
2. The instrument of ratification shall be deposited with the Director-General of UNESCO.

The model for this Article was the 1954 Hague Convention, formulated under the classic system of customary international law, which regulated the law of treaties. As Lord McNair stated, ratification was essential to bring the treaty into force.[1459] In the following decades, the regulation of the law of treaties was subject to important developments; in particular, the 1969 Vienna Convention on the Law of Treaties[1460] was an important step in the development of this area of international law, and today 109 States are Parties to this Convention.

It was therefore not surprising that several States recommended following the procedure adopted by the Vienna Convention for the conclusion of treaties, particularly the use of new terminology, which retained adoption of treaties by ratification but also included new ways by which a state could express its consent to be bound by an international treaty. Ratification is defined by the Vienna Convention as 'the international act so named whereby a State establishes on the international plane its consent to be bound by a treaty' (Article 2(1)(b)). According to Article 14(2) of that Convention, the consent to be bound can be expressed by 'acceptance' or 'approval' under conditions similar to those which apply to ratification:

February 1999), the formulation of this Article was only slightly modified: it was given the number 46, replaced 'States Parties' with 'High Contracting Parties', and referred only to the 'Director-General', as this term was defined in another provision. The section of text proposed in the Preliminary Draft of October 1998 referring to 'all States Parties to the Convention' was modified and replaced with a reference to the 'High Contracting Parties' following the definition in Article 1(d): "'High Contracting Party" means a State Party to the Convention'. The text stating that instruments of ratification 'shall be deposited with the Director-General *of UNESCO'* was altered, since Article 1, paragraph (i) had already defined the term 'Director-General' to mean '*Director-General of UNESCO'*. The modified text read as follows: '*Article 46. 1. The present Protocol shall be subject to ratification by High Contracting Parties which have signed the Protocol, in accordance with their respective constitutional procedures. 2. The instrument of ratification shall be deposited with the Director-General.*' These modifications were included in the final text together with the newly introduced reference to 'acceptance' or 'approval'.

1459   McNair (1961), p. 130.
1460   The Vienna Convention on the Law of Treaties was adopted on 22 May 1969 and opened for signature on 23 May 1969 by the United Nations Conference on the Law of Treaties. It entered into force on 27 January 1980, in accordance with Article 84(1). (United Nations, *Treaty Series*, Vol. 1155, p. 331.) As of 5 May 2008, 108 States are Parties to this Convention.

There is no substantive difference between signature subject to acceptance or approval and signature subject to ratification. It is now common for multilateral treaties (though not the Convention itself) to provide that they shall be 'subject to ratification, acceptance or approval'. The use of acceptance or approval was developed in order to enable some states to avoid constitutional requirements to obtain parliamentary authority to ratify, particularly when the parliamentary process was described as 'ratification', and no clear distinction was drawn by the parliament or the constitution between that process and ratification on the international plane.[1461]

This new formulation was used by the Drafting Committee of the 1999 Second Protocol. The brackets around the words 'acceptance and approval' were deleted as stated by the Chairperson of the Conference on the last day of the Conference (i.e. 26 March 1999).[1462]

1461   Aust (2000), p. 87.
1462   1999 Hague Conference, Plenary Session, 26 May 1999, pp. 102–3.

Article 42
ACCESSION

1. This Protocol shall be open for accession by other High Contracting Parties from 1 January 2000.

2. Accession shall be effected by the deposit of an instrument of accession with the Director-General.

Preparatory work

Preliminary Draft Second Protocol to the 1954 Hague Convention. UNESCO document HC/1999/1, October 1998 (English, French and Russian). (This Preliminary Draft includes the first version of the final clauses.)

Preliminary Draft Second Protocol to the 1954 Hague Convention. Revised. UNESCO document. No number. December 1998 (original: English). Key to source of proposed changes: G: Germany; LM: Leiden meeting; N: Norway. (This slightly modified Preliminary Draft which includes the final clauses.)

UNESCO, Summary of comments on Preliminary Draft Second Protocol to the 1954 Hague Convention received from High Contracting Parties to the Hague Convention for the Protection of Cultural Property in the Event of Armed Conflict 1954, other UNESCO Member States and international organizations, Paris, 15 January 1999.

Draft Second Protocol to the 1954 Hague Convention for the Protection of Cultural Property in the Event of Armed Conflict. UNESCO document HC/1999/1/rev.1, February 1999.

ANALYSIS OF THE TEXT

In the Preliminary Draft,[1463] Article 39 concerning accession was formulated as follows:

Article 39. Accession

1463   *Preliminary Draft Second Protocol to the 1954 Hague Convention.* UNESCO document HC/1999/1, October 1998 (English, French and Russian). The same text is also reproduced in the following document: *Preliminary Draft Second Protocol to the 1954 Hague Convention.* Revised. UNESCO document. No number. December 1998 (original: English). Key to source of proposed changes: G: Germany; LM: Leiden meeting; N: Norway.

1. From the date of its entry into force, the present Protocol shall be open for accession by all States Parties to the Convention.
2. Accession shall be effected by the deposit of an instrument of accession with the Director-General of UNESCO.

The formulation of this Article was modified in the *Draft Second Protocol to the 1954 Hague Convention for the Protection of Cultural Property in the Event of Armed Conflict* (UNESCO doc. HC/1999/1/rev.1, February 1999). The Article was given the number 47, the words 'States Parties' were replaced by the words 'High Contracting Parties', and the date specified for the opening for accession was introduced as 1 January 2000. As in the case of ratification, the reference to 'High Contracting Parties' eliminated the need to repeat 'States Parties to the Convention', as a result of the definition given in Article 1(d). The text stating that instruments of ratification 'shall be deposited with the Director-General of UNESCO' was also altered, deleting 'of UNESCO', since Article 1(i) had already defined the term 'Director-General' to mean *'Director-General of UNESCO'*.

The 1954 Hague Convention required in Article 32 that accession to the Convention was possible only after its entry into force. The reference to 'entry into force' before accession was also eliminated from the final text of the Protocol, the adoption of the Vienna Convention having rendered this condition unnecessary. Article 15 of the Vienna Convention provides that accession is a means by which a State can consent to be bound by a treaty if:

a) the treaty so provides;
b) it is otherwise established that the negotiating states were agreed that consent could be so expressed; or
c) all the parties have subsequently agreed that a state may express its consent by such means.

The Article read as follows:

Article 47.
1. The present Protocol shall be open for accession by all other High Contracting Parties from 1 January 2000.
2. Accession shall be effected by the deposit of an instrument of accession with the Director-General.

This new formulation was included in the final text of the Protocol.

Article 43
ENTRY INTO FORCE

1. *This Protocol shall enter into force three months after twenty instruments of ratification, acceptance, approval or accession have been deposited.*
2. *Thereafter, it shall enter into force, for each Party, three months after the deposit of its instrument of ratification, acceptance, approval or accession.*

Preparatory work

Preliminary Draft Second Protocol to the 1954 Hague Convention. UNESCO document HC/1999/1, October 1998 (English, French and Russian). (This Preliminary Draft includes the first version of the final clauses.)

Preliminary Draft Second Protocol to the 1954 Hague Convention. Revised. UNESCO document. No number. December 1998 (original: English). Key to source of proposed changes: G: Germany; LM: Leiden meeting; N: Norway. (This slightly modified Preliminary Draft includes the final clauses.)

UNESCO, Summary of comments on Preliminary Draft Second Protocol to the 1954 Hague Convention received from High Contracting Parties to the Hague Convention for the Protection of Cultural Property in the Event of Armed Conflict 1954, other UNESCO Member States and international organizations, Paris, 15 January 1999.

Draft Second Protocol to the 1954 Hague Convention for the Protection of Cultural Property in the Event of Armed Conflict. UNESCO document HC/1999/1/rev.1, February 1999.

ANALYSIS OF THE TEXT

During the drafting of the provision on entry into force of the Protocol to the Hague Convention by the UNESCO Secretariat, the point of departure for the formulation of the final clauses was the text of these final clauses as they were included in the 1954 Hague Convention itself.[1464] In the Preliminary

---

1464   The 1954 Hague Convention for the Protection of Cultural Property in the Event of Armed Conflict with Regulations for the Execution of the Convention 1954
Article 33 Entry into force:
1.   The present Convention shall enter into force three months after five instruments of ratification have been deposited.
2.   Thereafter, it shall enter into force, for each High Contracting Party, three months after the deposit of its instrument of ratification or accession.

Draft of the Second Protocol,[1465] Article 40 concerning entry into force was formulated as follows:

Article 40 Entry into force

1. The present Convention shall enter into force ... months after ... instruments of ratification have been deposited.

2. Thereafter, it shall enter into force, for each State Party, ... months after the deposit of its instrument of ratification or accession.

3. The situations referred to in Articles 18 and 19 of the Convention (Article ... of this Protocol) shall give immediate effect to ratifications or accessions deposited by the Parties to the conflict either before or after the beginning of hostilities or occupation. In such cases the Director-General of UNESCO shall transmit the communications referred to in Article 38 of the Convention (Article ... of this Protocol) by the speediest method.

The *Draft Second Protocol to the 1954 Hague Convention for the Protection of Cultural Property in the Event of Armed Conflict* (UNESCO doc. HC/1999/1/ rev.1, February 1999), which was submitted to the Hague Conference in 1999, contains a different formulation of this provision. The provision on entry into force was divided into two separate articles: Article 48, which contains the two paragraphs of the previous proposal of Article 40 without any changes, and the separate Article 49:

Article 49 Entry into force in situations of armed conflict

The situations referred to in Articles 18 and 19 of the Convention shall give immediate effect to ratifications or accessions to this Protocol deposited by the parties to the conflict either before or after the beginning of hostilities or occupation. In such cases the Director-

---

3. The situations referred to in Articles 18 and 19 shall give immediate effect to ratifications or accessions deposited by the Parties to the conflict either before or after the beginning of hostilities or occupation. In such cases the Director-General of the United Nations Educational, Scientific and Cultural Organization shall transmit the communications referred to in Article 38 by the speediest method.

1465 *Preliminary Draft Second Protocol to the 1954 Hague Convention.* UNESCO document HC/1999/1, October 1998 (English, French and Russian). The same text is also reproduced in the following document: *Preliminary Draft Second Protocol to the 1954 Hague Convention.* Revised. UNESCO document. No number. December 1998 (original: English). Key to source of proposed changes: G: Germany; LM: Leiden meeting; N: Norway.

General shall transmit the communications referred to in Article 51 of this Protocol by the speediest method.

This new formulation reflected the advanced stage of codification reached in the Conference.[1466] Article 49 was enumerated in the final text and given the number 44 in the final text of the Protocol. Only one minor change was made in comparison with Article 40 of the Preliminary Draft.[1467] The separation of the provisions was wisely maintained in the final text of the 1999 Protocol.

As indicated in our 1996 Commentary on Article 33 of the 1954 Hague Convention, these Articles were inspired by the common Articles 62/61/141/153 of the Geneva Conventions. As with Article 33 of the 1954 Hague Convention, this Article gives immediate effect to ratifications and accessions to the Protocol deposited by parties to the conflict either before or after the beginning of hostilities or occupation.[1468]

Regarding general entry into force, the 1954 Hague Convention required the deposit of five instrument of ratification. The 1977 Additional Protocols to the Geneva Conventions limited this number further: only two ratifications were required. One probable reason for the 1999 Second Protocol proceeding in a different fashion was that the 12 States needed to constitute the Committee had to be elected by the Meeting of the Parties to the Protocol. Accordingly, the Meeting needed to include a suitable number of Parties. The Syrian Arab Republic proposed 30 instruments of ratification to be submitted for entry into force of the Protocol.[1469]

The 1999 Second Protocol entered into force on 9 March 2004, in accordance with its Article 43(1).

1466   Turkey alone proposed the deletion of paragraph 3 of Article 40, considering that 'as international legal instruments are based on the free will of participating States, it may not be appropriate to impose upon the States Parties the procedure outlined in Art. 40/3'. Comments and suggestions by the Turkish Government on the Preliminary *Draft Second Protocol to the 1954 Hague Convention for the Protection of Cultural Property in the Event of Armed Conflict*, [n.d.], p. 7.

1467   Replacement of the 'Director-General of UNESCO', by 'Director-General' as defined in Article 1(i) of the Protocol.

1468   Toman (1996), pp. 311–12.

1469   Preliminary remarks of the Syrian Arab Republic, 13 December 1998, p. 6.

Article 44
ENTRY INTO FORCE IN SITUATIONS OF ARMED CONFLICT

The situations referred to in Articles 18 and 19 of the Convention shall give immediate effect to ratifications, acceptances or approvals of or accessions to this Protocol deposited by the parties to the conflict either before or after the beginning of hostilities or occupation. In such cases the Director-General shall transmit the communications referred to in Article 46 by the speediest method.

For the comments on this article, see the comments on Article 43 above.

Article 45
DENUNCIATION

1. *Each Party may denounce this Protocol.*
2. *The denunciation shall be notified by an instrument in writing, deposited with the Director-General.*
3. *The denunciation shall take effect one year after the receipt of the instrument of denunciation. However, if, on the expiry of this period, the denouncing Party is involved in an armed conflict, the denunciation shall not take effect until the end of hostilities, or until the operations of repatriating cultural property are completed, whichever is the later.*

Preparatory work

Preliminary Draft Second Protocol to the 1954 Hague Convention. UNESCO document HC/1999/1, October 1998 (English, French and Russian). (This Preliminary Draft includes the first version of the final clauses.)

Preliminary Draft Second Protocol to the 1954 Hague Convention. Revised. UNESCO document. No number. December 1998 (original: English). Key to source of proposed changes: G: Germany; LM: Leiden meeting; N: Norway. (This slightly modified Preliminary Draft includes the final clauses.)

UNESCO, Summary of comments on Preliminary Draft Second Protocol to the 1954 Hague Convention received from High Contracting Parties to the Hague Convention for the Protection of Cultural Property in the Event of Armed Conflict 1954, other UNESCO Member States and international organizations, Paris, 15 January 1999.

Draft Second Protocol to the 1954 Hague Convention for the Protection of Cultural Property in the Event of Armed Conflict. UNESCO document HC/1999/1/ rev.1, February 1999.

ANALYSIS OF THE TEXT

During the drafting of the final provisions of the Protocol to the Hague Convention by the UNESCO Secretariat, the point of departure for the formulation of the final clauses was the text of these clauses as it was included in the 1954 Hague Convention itself.[1470] In the Preliminary Draft,[1471] Article 41 concerning denunciation was formulated as follows:

Article 41 Denunciation
1. Each High Contracting Party may denounce the present Protocol.
2. The denunciation shall be notified by an instrument in writing, deposited with the Director-General of UNESCO.
3. The denunciation shall take effect one year after the receipt of the instrument of denunciation. However, if, on the expiry of this period, the denouncing Party is involved in an armed conflict, the denunciation shall not take effect until the end of hostilities, or until the operations of repatriating cultural property are completed, whichever is the later.

This provision is almost identical to the text of Article 37 of the Convention. The first paragraph was obviously shortened and the phrase 'on its own behalf, or on behalf of any territory for whose international relations it is responsible' was eliminated. The Soviet Union opposed this phrase at the time and made a proposal to delete it.[1472] The Soviet Union no longer existed in 1999, but the international situation and the attitude of the international community towards the trusteeship system and colonialism had altered so much that the elimination of this phrase was quite self-evident.

The *Draft Second Protocol to the 1954 Hague Convention for the Protection of Cultural Property in the Event of Armed Conflict* (UNESCO

1470 The 1954 Hague Convention for the Protection of Cultural Property in the Event of Armed Conflict with Regulations for the Execution of the Convention 1954
Article 37 Denunciation
1. Each High Contracting Party may denounce the present Convention, on its own behalf, or on behalf of any territory for whose international relations it is responsible.
2. The denunciation shall be notified by an instrument in writing, deposited with the Director-General of the United Nations Educational, Scientific and Cultural Organization.
3. The denunciation shall take effect one year after the receipt of the instrument of denunciation. However, if, on the expiry of this period, the denouncing Party is involved in an armed conflict, the denunciation shall not take effect until the end of hostilities, or until the operations of repatriating cultural property are completed, whichever is the later.
1471 *Preliminary Draft Second Protocol to the 1954 Hague Convention.* UNESCO document HC/1999/1, October 1998 (English, French and Russian). The same text is also reproduced in the following document: *Preliminary Draft Second Protocol to the 1954 Hague Convention.* Revised. UNESCO document. No number. December 1998 (original: English). Key to source of proposed changes: G: Germany; LM: Leiden meeting; N: Norway.
1472 Toman (1996), p. 322.

doc. HC/1999/1/rev.1, February 1999), which was submitted to the Hague Conference in 1999, only slightly simplified the text of paragraphs 1 and 2: replacing the words '*Each High Contracting Party*' with '*A Party*' in the first paragraph, and the reference to the '*Director-General*' omitted the mention of UNESCO.[1473] Paragraph 3 remains unchanged.[1474] Turkey suggested a different wording for paragraph 3.[1475] As we noted in our 1996 Commentary on the Convention,

> The denunciation does not have immediate effect. In normal circumstances – in peacetime – it is to take effect one year after the receipt of the instrument of denunciation. However, if, on the expiry of this period, the denouncing Party is involved in an armed conflict, the denunciation shall not take effect until the end of hostilities, or until the operations of repatriating cultural property are completed, whichever is the later. This second sentence was introduced to cover the case in which a Power, on the point of engaging in hostilities or expecting to become involved, might want to free itself as speedily as possible from the obligations imposed upon it by the Convention. Therefore, for a denouncing Power involved in an armed conflict on the expiry of the year following its denunciation, the denunciation will not take effect until the end of hostilities or possibly even later, namely

---

1473   Article 1 of the Second Protocol states: "'Director-General' means the Director-General of UNESCO'.

1474   A short terminological discussion took place at the final Plenary Session (26 March 1999). The Syrian delegate suggested the replacement of the term 'denunciation' in Article 46 with 'withdrawal' already present in the written statement (Preliminary remarks of the Syrian Arab Republic, 13 December 1998, p. 6) as 'used in the Vienna Convention on the Law of Treaties and Geneva system'. Following explanations by the delegates of Argentina, the UK and France, the Syrian delegate withdrew the proposed amendment. Mr. Eaton, the UK delegate, said that Article 56 of the Vienna Convention talked about 'denunciation of or withdrawal from any treaty containing no provision regarding termination, denunciation or withdrawal'. He said that it recognized various terms for describing the same kind of action, namely when a Party does not wish to be bound by a treaty. In his view it was a technical term without any negative connotation. He was in favour of keeping the text as it was which followed the terminology of the 1954 Convention. (1999 Hague Conference, Plenary Session, 26 March 1999, p. 102.)

1475   'Art. 41/3, which reads: "However, if, on the expiry of this period" be replaced with "However, if before or shortly after the expiry of this period". Turkey explained that "[according] to the present wording of Art. 41/3, if a denouncing party is involved in an armed conflict, on or shortly after the expiry of the one year period, 'the denunciation shall not take effect until the end of hostilities'. This precludes the possibility that a State Party/Parties may get involved in an armed conflict on or shortly after the expiry of the one year period, due to compelling and/or unforeseen reasons. Therefore, Art. 41/3 should be paraphrased accordingly)."' Comments and suggestions by the Turkish Government on the Preliminary Draft Second Protocol to the 1954 Hague Convention for the Protection of Cultural Property in the Event of Armed Conflict, [n.d.], p. 7.

until the operations of repatriating cultural property are completed. Such restitution may be required under the peace treaty, but most actually be put into effect.[1476]

In our 1996 Commentary on the Convention, we noted that even if a State withdraws from the Convention, it remains bound by the principles and customary rules of international law. The Preamble of the Protocol is clear on this issue and includes the affirmation 'that the rules of customary international law will continue to govern questions not regulated by the provisions of this Protocol'.[1477] As Jean Pictet stated,

> These principles exist independently of the Convention and are not limited to the field covered by it. The clause shows clearly [...] that a Power which denounced the Convention would nevertheless remain bound by the principles contained in it insofar as they are the expression of inalienable and universal rules of customary international law.[1478]

1476 Toman (1996), pp. 322–23.
1477 See also the Additional Comments on this issue concerning paragraph 4 of the UNESCO draft of the 1954 Convention. Toman (1996), pp. 322–23.
1478 Pictet (1952–56), Vol. I, p. 413.

Article 46
NOTIFICATIONS

The Director-General shall inform all High Contracting Parties as well as the United Nations, of the deposit of all the instruments of ratification, acceptance, approval or accession provided for in Articles 41 and 42 and of denunciations provided for Article 45.

Preparatory work

Preliminary Draft Second Protocol to the 1954 Hague Convention. UNESCO document HC/1999/1, October 1998 (English, French and Russian). (This Preliminary Draft includes the first version of the final clauses.)

Preliminary Draft Second Protocol to the 1954 Hague Convention. Revised. UNESCO document. No number. December 1998 (original: English). Key to source of proposed changes: G: Germany; LM: Leiden meeting; N: Norway. (This slightly modified Preliminary Draft includes the final clauses.)

UNESCO, Summary of comments on Preliminary Draft Second Protocol to the 1954 Hague Convention received from High Contracting Parties to the Hague Convention for the Protection of Cultural Property in the Event of Armed Conflict 1954, other UNESCO Member States and international organizations, Paris, 15 January 1999.

Draft Second Protocol to the 1954 Hague Convention for the Protection of Cultural Property in the Event of Armed Conflict. UNESCO document HC/1999/1/rev.1, February 1999.

ANALYSIS OF THE TEXT

During the drafting of the final provisions of the Protocol to the Hague Convention by the UNESCO Secretariat, the point of departure for the formulation of the final clauses were the text of these clauses as it was included in the 1954 Hague Convention itself. This was also the case for the Article on notifications.[1479] In the Preliminary Draft,[1480] Article 42 concerning notifications was formulated as follows:

Article 42 Notifications

The Director-General of UNESCO shall inform the States referred to in Articles ... and ... , as well as the United Nations, of the deposit of all the instruments of ratification, accession or acceptance provided for in Articles ... and ... and of the notifications and denunciations provided for respectively in Articles ... and ...

The *Draft Second Protocol to the 1954 Hague Convention for the Protection of Cultural Property in the Event of Armed Conflict*, UNESCO doc. HC/1999/1/Rev.1, February 1999, which was submitted to the Hague Conference in 1999, simplified the text, replacing the word 'States' with '*High Contracting Parties*'. The reference to the '*Director-General*' omitted the mention of UNESCO.[1481]

The final text adopted by the Conference inserted the missing Article numbers.

1479 The 1954 Hague Convention for the Protection of Cultural Property in the Event of Armed Conflict with Regulations for the Execution of the Convention of 1954.
Article 38. Notifications
The Director-General of the United Nations Educational, Scientific and Cultural Organization shall inform the States referred to in Articles 30 and 32, as well as the United Nations, of the deposit of all the instruments of ratification, accession or acceptance provided for in Articles 31, 32 and 39 and of the notifications and denunciations provided for respectively in Articles 35, 37 and 39.

1480 *Preliminary Draft Second Protocol to the 1954 Hague Convention.* UNESCO document HC/1999/1, October 1998 (English, French and Russian). The same text is also reproduced in the following document: *Preliminary Draft Second Protocol to the 1954 Hague Convention.* Revised. UNESCO document. No number. December 1998 (original: English). Key to source of proposed changes: G: Germany; LM: Leiden meeting; N: Norway.

1481 Article 1(i) of the Second Protocol states: "Director-General" means the Director-General of UNESCO'.

Article 47
REGISTRATION WITH THE UNITED NATIONS

In conformity with Article 102 of the Charter of the United Nations, this Protocol shall be registered with the Secretariat of the United Nations at the request of the Director-General.

Preparatory work

Preliminary Draft Second Protocol to the 1954 Hague Convention. UNESCO document HC/1999/1, October 1998 (English, French and Russian). (This Preliminary Draft includes the first version of the final clauses.)

Preliminary Draft Second Protocol to the 1954 Hague Convention. Revised. UNESCO document. No number. December 1998 (original: English). Key to source of proposed changes: G: Germany; LM: Leiden meeting; N: Norway. (This slightly modified Preliminary Draft includes the final clauses.)

UNESCO, Summary of comments on Preliminary Draft Second Protocol to the 1954 Hague Convention received from High Contracting Parties to the Hague Convention for the Protection of Cultural Property in the Event of Armed Conflict 1954, other UNESCO Member States and international organizations, Paris, 15 January 1999.

Draft Second Protocol to the 1954 Hague Convention for the Protection of Cultural Property in the Event of Armed Conflict. UNESCO document HC/1999/1/ rev.1, February 1999.

ANALYSIS OF THE TEXT

During the drafting of the final provisions of the Protocol to the Hague Convention by the UNESCO Secretariat, the point of departure for the formulation of the final clauses was the text which is in the 1954 Hague Convention itself. This was also the case for the Article on registration with the UN.[1482] In the Preliminary

---

1482   The 1954 Hague Convention for the Protection of Cultural Property in the Event of Armed Conflict with Regulations for the Execution of the Convention of 1954.
Article 40 Registration
In accordance with Article 102 of the Charter of the United Nations, the present Convention shall be registered with the Secretariat of the United Nations at the request of the Director-General of the United Nations Educational, Scientific and Cultural Organization.

Draft,[1483] the Article on registration was not mentioned. A reminder concerning this issue was issued in the comments of the Federal Republic of Germany[1484] and the Syrian Arab Republic.[1485] The Article was included for the first time in the *Draft Second Protocol to the 1954 Hague Convention for the Protection of Cultural Property in the Event of Armed Conflict* (UNESCO doc. HC/1999/1/rev.1, February 1999), which was submitted to the Conference. It was given the number 52 and was formulated as follows:

> Article 52 Registration with the United Nations
> In conformity with Article 102 of the Charter of the United Nations, this Protocol shall be registered with the Secretariat of the United Nations at the request of the Director-General

The Article was included in the final text of the Protocol without any modification.

The 1999 Second Protocol to the 1954 Hague Convention was registered with the United Nations: *Registration at the UN*: 5 May 2004, No. 3511.

1483 *Preliminary Draft Second Protocol to the 1954 Hague Convention.* UNESCO document HC/1999/1, October 1998 (English, French and Russian). Nor was it included in the *Preliminary Draft Second Protocol to the 1954 Hague Convention.* Revised. UNESCO document. No number. December 1998 (original: English). Key to source of proposed changes: G: Germany; LM: Leiden meeting; N: Norway.

1484 Comments of the Federal Republic of Germany on the Preliminary Draft Second Protocol to the 1954 Hague Convention, Bonn, 14 December 1998, p. 6.

1485 Preliminary remarks of the Syrian Arab Republic, 13 December 1998, p. 6.

PART II
FINAL ACT AND RESOLUTION OF THE 1999 HAGUE CONFERENCE. SUMMARY REPORT OF THE 1999 HAGUE CONFERENCE

1. The Final Act and Resolution Adopted by the March 1999 Hague Diplomatic Conference on the Second Protocol
2. Declarations of two States Parties to the 1954 Hague Convention: Belgium and Israel
3. United Nations Educational, Scientific and Cultural Organization Diplomatic Conference on the Second Protocol to The Hague Convention for the Protection of Cultural Property in the Event of Armed Conflict. (The Hague, 15–26 March 1999). Summary Report.

1. THE FINAL ACT AND RESOLUTION ADOPTED BY THE MARCH 1999 HAGUE DIPLOMATIC CONFERENCE ON THE SECOND PROTOCOL

In this chapter we shall include the official texts of the Final Act, the Resolution, and the Declaration of two States: Belgium and Israel. We also include the Summary Report prepared by the Secretariat of UNESCO after the Conference. Only very few comments are made since most of these documents are self-explanatory.

FINAL ACT OF THE DIPLOMATIC CONFERENCE ON THE SECOND PROTOCOL TO THE HAGUE CONVENTION FOR THE PROTECTION OF CULTURAL PROPERTY IN THE EVENT OF ARMED CONFLICT (THE HAGUE, 15–26 MARCH 1999)

1. The Diplomatic Conference convened by the Government of the Netherlands and the United Nations Educational, Scientific and Cultural Organization on the Second Protocol to the Hague Convention for the Protection of Cultural Property in the Event of Armed Conflict was held at The Hague, at the invitation of the Government of the Netherlands, from 15 to 26 March 1999 and deliberated on the basis of a draft prepared jointly by the Government of the Netherlands and the United Nations Educational, Scientific and Cultural Organization.
2. Altogether 93 States, Members of UNESCO or the United Nations, took part in the Conference. Representatives of 74 States Parties to the Hague Convention for the Protection of Cultural Property in the Event of Armed Conflict participated in the Conference, namely representatives of: Albania, Argentina, Armenia, Australia, Austria, Azerbaijan, Belarus, Belgium, Bosnia and Herzegovina, Bulgaria, Cambodia, Cameroon, Canada, Colombia, Côte d'Ivoire, Croatia, Cuba, Cyprus, Czech Republic, the Democratic Republic of the Congo, Egypt, Estonia, Finland, France, Georgia, Germany, Ghana, Greece, Guatemala, Holy See, Hungary, India, Indonesia, Islamic Republic of Iran, Israel, Italy, Jordan, Kuwait, Lebanon, Libyan Arab Jamahiriya, Luxembourg, Mali, Malaysia, Mongolia, Morocco, Netherlands, Niger, Nigeria, Norway, Oman, Pakistan, Panama, Peru, Poland, Qatar, Romania, Russian Federation, Saudi Arabia, Senegal, Slovakia, Slovenia, Spain, Sudan, Sweden, Switzerland, Syrian Arab Republic, Tajikistan, Thailand, the former Yugoslav Republic of Macedonia, Tunisia, Turkey, Ukraine, Uzbekistan and Yemen.

3. 19 non-States Parties were represented at the Conference, namely: Algeria, Botswana, Chile, China, Denmark, Ethiopia, Ireland, Japan, Philippines, Portugal, Republic of Korea, South Africa, Suriname, Tonga, Turkmenistan, United Kingdom, United States of America, Uruguay and Vietnam. The observer delegation of Palestine was also represented.

4. The International Committee of the Red Cross (ICRC) was represented as an observer at the Conference.

5. The following international non-governmental Organization was represented by observers at the Conference: International Committee of the Blue Shield (ICES). Its representative spoke on behalf of the four following constituent bodies of this Committee – International Council on Archives (ICA), International Council of Museums (ICOM), International Council on Monuments and Sites (ICOMOS) and International Federation of Library Associations and Institutions (IFLA).

6. The Conference elected Mr. A. Bos (the Netherlands) as President.

7. The Conference elected as Vice-Presidents the following countries:
Argentina
Senegal
Syrian Arab Republic
Thailand.

8. The Conference also elected Mr. Jelen (Hungary) as Rapporteur.

9. The following subsidiary bodies were set up by the Conference:
Credentials Committee:
Chair: Mr. R. Hilger (Germany)
Members: Islamic Republic of Iran and the Russian Federation
Drafting Committee:
Chair: Mr. Ch. Held (Switzerland)
Members: Australia, Cameroon, China, Egypt, France, the Russian Federation, Spain and the United Kingdom.

10. The basic working documents used by the Conference and its organs were the Draft Second Protocol to the Hague Convention for the Protection of Cultural Property in the Event of Armed Conflict (HC/1999/1/rev. 1) with reference document to this draft (HC/1999/INF/1) together with its Addendum (HC/1999/INF. 1/Add. 1) as well as the Synoptic report with its Addendum of comments of States party to the Convention, other States not party to the Convention and international organizations (HC/1999/4 and Add.). The Conference and its subsidiary bodies also considered proposals and comments by Governments and international organizations on the Draft.

11. The Conference established working groups on Chapters 1 and 5 (chaired by Ms A. M. Connelly, Ireland), Chapter 2 (chaired by Mr. T. Desch, Austria), Chapter 3 (chaired by Ms. Terrillon-McKay, Canada), Chapter 4 (chaired by Prof. H. Fischer, Germany) and Chapter 6 (chaired by Mr. J. Jelen, Hungary) in order to develop a compromise text, taking account of the views expressed in the Plenary, for redrafted provisions of the text.

The Chairperson of the working group on Chapters 1 and 5 noted the clarification provided by the working group that the word 'supplements' in Article 2 signifies that the Protocol does not affect the rights and obligations of States Parties to the Convention.

The Chairperson of the working group on Chapter 4 made the following interpretative statement with regard to Article 16 (Jurisdiction):

> Nothing in this Protocol, including Article 16, in any way limits the State's ability to legislate, criminalize or otherwise deal with any substantive offences including conduct addressed in this Protocol. Nothing in Article 16(2)(b) should be interpreted as in any way affecting the application of Article 16(1)(a).

12. The Conference assigned to the Drafting Committee the 1st Reading of the Draft text as amended in discussions and accepted in the Plenary in the English and French versions. The Conference assigned to the Drafting Committee the authentication of the texts in Arabic, Chinese, Russian and Spanish.

13. On the basis of the deliberations of the Conference, the Conference drew up the Second Protocol to the Hague Convention for the Protection of Cultural Property in the Event of Armed Conflict. The Second Protocol, the text of which was established in English and French, is attached to the present Act.

14. The Chairman noted the agreement of the delegates to adopt Article 43 subject to the provision of official versions in Arabic, Chinese, Russian and Spanish which will be provided by UNESCO and authenticated before the day of signature.

In witness whereof the undersigned have signed the present Final Act.

The Conference further adopted a resolution which is also attached to the present Act.

Done at The Hague, this twenty-sixth day of March, 1999.

In attachment to this document is the English and French text of the Second Protocol.

DIPLOMATIC CONFERENCE ON THE SECOND PROTOCOL TO THE HAGUE CONVENTION FOR THE PROTECTION OF CULTURAL PROPERTY IN THE EVENT OF ARMED CONFLICT

Resolution

The Diplomatic Conference on the Second Protocol to the Hague Convention for the Protection of Cultural Properly in the Event of Armed Conflict,

Reiterating the importance of adoption and implementation of adequate legal standards to protect cultural property within the framework of national culture heritage protection policy,

Stressing that safeguarding measures such as the compilation of national inventories of cultural property, taken in peacetime, are essential in preventing foreseeable effects of armed conflicts.

Noting with appreciation the positive results reached by the use of resources of the Fund for the Protection of the World Cultural and Natural Heritage of Outstanding Universal Value established under the UNESCO Convention concerning the Protection of the World Cultural and Natural Heritage of 1972 and the successful application of AFRICOM documentation standards for museum collections in African countries as well as similar co-operative developments for libraries and archives,

Recognizing that a number of developing countries may have difficulty in fully implementing the provisions of The Hague Convention, its First Protocol and the present Protocol,

Urges all States party to the present Protocol to give careful consideration to requests from developing countries either at bilateral level or within the framework of intergovernmental organizations.

COMMENTS

First paragraph of the Resolution

It is in the spirit of Article 3 of the Convention that the drafters of this resolution decided to include this precise provision expressing the wish that the States adopt the legal measures and develop the national legislation for the protection of cultural property. It is well known that many States adopted such national legal standards and informed UNESCO in their reports about it.

Second paragraph of the Resolution

This paragraph develops the provision of Article 3 of the Convention and includes more precise wording as it is now included in the Article 5 of the Second Protocol. This concerns in particular the preparation of inventories, which, according to our previous commentary, could mean: 'survey, identification, classification and registration of moveable and immovable property, drawing up of lists, publication of maps, preparation of indexes'.[1486] We should read this paragraph in the light of Article 11, paragraph 1 of the World Heritage Convention of 1972, which states:

> Every State Party to this Convention shall, insofar as possible, submit to the World Heritage Committee an inventory of property forming part of the cultural and natural heritage, situated in its territory and suitable for inclusion in the list provided for in paragraph 2 of this Article. This inventory, which shall not be considered exhaustive, shall include documentation about the location of the property in question and its significance.

The inventories will be larger than those that were eventually included on the list, and it is one of the aims of the Global Strategy[1487] to encourage and facilitate States Parties' efforts to prepare and submit the Tentative Lists and it is envisaged that this in turn would encourage States Parties which are under-represented and unrepresented on the World Heritage List to nominate properties for inscription and widen the types of properties on the List.[1488] States Parties are encouraged to review and resubmit their tentative list every ten years.[1489] As Francesco Francioni indicated,

> an ideal inventory of all the treasures of the world would have been too difficult, unrealistic, and even misleading' and it is why in the later stage there was a shift to the development of a dynamic interpretation of 'universality', which takes into account the evolving knowledge about

---

1486   Toman (1996), p. 64.
1487   Global Strategy for a Balanced, Representative, and Credible World Heritage List, adopted by the World Heritage Committee in 1994. See 2005 Operational Guidelines for the Implementation of the World Heritage Convention, para. 54–58; http://whc.unesco.org/en/guidelines
1488   Vrdoljak (2008), p. 267.
1489   2005 Operational Guidelines, para. 65.

the contribution that different cultural have made at different times to the world heritage.[1490]

Interestingly a similar suggestion of the need for the preparation of inventories was made already in 1962 by the First Meeting of the High Contracting Parties[1491] and also at the 1983 Meeting of Legal Experts.[1492]

Third paragraph of the Resolution

This paragraph is just a compliment to the action of the Fund for the Protection of the World Cultural and Natural Heritage of Outstanding Universal Value established under the UNESCO Convention concerning the Protection of the World Cultural and Natural Heritage of 1972.[1493] The Fund was an example for the preparation of the Fund created on the basis of Article 29 of the 1999 Second Protocol. As several African countries felt disappointed by the decision of the 1999 Hague Conference not to include the compulsory contributions to the Fund, the resolution is undergoing another important action undertaken by the World Heritage Fund: the successful application of AFRICOM documentation standards for museum collections in African countries, as well as similar co-operative developments for libraries and archives.[1494]

Fourth paragraph of the Resolution

The present paragraph underlines the need to provide assistance to developing countries that 'may have difficulty in fully implementing the provisions of The Hague Convention, its First Protocol and the present Protocol'. We also hope that the present commentary, as well as previous commentaries to the 1954 Hague Convention and 1954 First Protocol, will be helpful for the developing and developed countries in their efforts to gain a better understanding of

---

1490   Francioni (2008), p. 20.
1491   Report of the meeting, document UNESCO/CUA/120 of 3 September 1962.
1492   1983 Meeting of Legal Experts on the Convention for the Protection of Cultural Property in the Event of Armed Conflict (The Hague, 1954), Vienna 17–19 October 1983, CLT-83/CONF.641/1, p. 10.
1493   Lenzerini (2008), pp. 269–87; Patchett (2008), pp. 289–304.
1494   Standardization of collections inventories in Africa. *Handbook of Standards*. 2nd version. January 1995: http://icom.museum/africom/standards.html; http://www.africom.mil/pdfFiles/AFRICOM%20Engagement%20with%20Industry.pdf

the provisions of these important instruments for the protection of cultural property in the event of armed conflict.

Fifth paragraph of the Resolution

In response to the previous paragraph mentioning the possible difficulties of developing countries to fully implement the provisions of the Hague Convention, its First Protocol and the present Protocol, the fifth paragraph of the Resolution 'urges all States party to the present Protocol to give careful consideration to requests from developing countries either at bilateral level or within the framework of intergovernmental organizations.' This appeal is also a reaction to the final phase of the discussion at the Plenary Session of the Conference on 24 March 1999 when the Plenary Session refused to adopt the compulsory contribution to the Fund for the Protection of Cultural Property in the Event of Armed Conflict and when the Nigerian delegate mentioned that the proposal to keep the compulsory contribution was made on behalf of the African group of States participating at the Conference.[1495]

1495   See p. 629.

2. DECLARATIONS OF TWO STATES PARTIES TO THE 1954 HAGUE CONVENTION

Belgium and Israel made the following declarations:[1496]

Belgium

The Belgian Delegation is delighted that the Representatives of States wishing to protect cultural property in the event of armed conflict have satisfactorily conducted their work and, therefore, will be able to sign the Final Act of the Conference dealing with this matter.

The Draft Second Protocol to the Convention for the Protection of Cultural Property in the Event of Armed Conflict concerns matters which, to a large extent, fall in Belgium within the competence of the Communities and Regions in conformity with the Constitution and laws.

Federal authorities are authorized to undertake international obligations within the limits of their competence. Moreover, they are duly represented in the Belgian Delegation.

The Kingdom of Belgium shall take the necessary steps that if it signs the Second Protocol, the above-mentioned competence of the Communities and Regions to undertake international obligations shall be formalized in an appropriate manner.

Israel

It should be noted that some delegations were of the opinion that the provisions of Article 39(5) of the 1954 Hague Convention should have been applied in relation to the adoption of this Protocol.[1497]

1496   No comments are necessary or appropriate here. We simply reproduce Article 39(5) of the Hague Convention in the next note.

1497   Article 39. Revision of the convention and of the regulations for its execution.

   4. The Director-General shall convene a Conference of the High Contracting Parties to consider the proposed amendment if requested to do so by more than one-third of the High Contracting Parties.

   5. Amendments to the Convention or to the Regulations for its execution, dealt with under the provisions of the preceding paragraph, shall enter into force only after they have been unanimously adopted by the High Contracting Parties represented at the Conference and accepted by each of the High Contracting Parties.

3. UNITED NATIONS EDUCATIONAL, SCIENTIFIC AND CULTURAL ORGANIZATION DIPLOMATIC CONFERENCE ON THE SECOND PROTOCOL TO THE HAGUE CONVENTION FOR THE PROTECTION OF CULTURAL PROPERTY IN THE EVENT OF ARMED CONFLICT[1498]

(THE HAGUE, 15–26 MARCH 1999)

Summary Report

1. The Diplomatic Conference convened jointly by the Netherlands and UNESCO on the Second Protocol to the Hague Convention for the Protection of Cultural Property in the Event of Aimed Conflict was held at The Hague. at the invitation of the Government of the Netherlands, from 15 to 26 March 1999.

2. Of the current 95 States Parties, 74 participated in the Conference. Nineteen States not party to the Convention as well as Palestine were represented as Observers at the Conference of international organizations the International Committee of the Red Cross (ICRC) and the International Committee of the Blue Shield (ICBS), a four-member international non-governmental organization (International Council on Archives (ICA), International Council of Museums (ICOM), International Council on Monuments and Sites (ICOMOS) and International Federation of Library Associations and Institutions (IFLA)) were represented.

3. The Conference was opened by Mr. J. J. Van Aartsen, Minister of Foreign Affairs of the Neth F. Van Der Ploeg, Secretary of State of the Netherlands for Culture and Dr. Federico Mayor, Director-General of UNESCO. They summarised reasons for the review of the Convention which resulted in the elaboration of the Draft Second Protocol and the need for a new concept for the protection of cultural heritage during hostilities in the contemporary world. The link with the First Hague Peace Conference in 1899 was noted for the development of international law, international relations and humanitarian law.

1498   The current report reflects the main issues of the March 1999 Hague Diplomatic Conference on the Second Protocol to the Hague Convention. The full proceedings will be published at a later date.

4. The Conference elected by consensus Mr. Adriaan Bos (the Netherlands) as Chairperson. On his proposal, the Conference decided to proceed as far as possible on the basis of consensus. It then elected its Bureau, consisting of Mr. J. Jelen (Hungary) Rapporteur, and Argentina, Senegal, Syrian Arab Republic and Thailand as Vice-Presidents, and adopted its agenda. It further elected the Credentials Committee (Germany, Islamic Republic of Iran and the Russian Federation) chaired by Mr. R. Hilger (Germany), and the Drafting Committee chaired by Mr. Ch. Held (Switzerland) and composed of representatives of Australia, Cameroon, China, Egypt, France, the Russian Federation, Spain, Switzerland and the United Kingdom.

5. The Chairperson then opened general discussion. Some delegates thought that the Draft Second Protocol represented an amendment to the Convention and consequently that the procedure under Article 39 of the Convention should be applied; others were in favour of adopting a new Convention and yet others preferred the adoption of an Optional Second Protocol. Several States stressed that the adoption of the Second Protocol should not affect the rights and obligations of States Parties to the Convention which might decline to be bound by the Second Protocol.

6. The deficiencies of the current rules on 'special protection' and the need for an improved system were mentioned. Also noted was the need to strike a balance between military interest and the interest in the protection of human life, and in the protection of cultural property. The importance of provisions on 'military necessity' was also stressed. Some States thought that other instruments of international humanitarian law were not sufficiently reflected in the Draft Second Protocol. Another view expressed the importance of a clear, coherent instrument that could realistically be accepted.

7. Considerable interest was expressed in the important issues of criminal responsibility and international jurisdiction for enforcement and in legal co-operation. Some participants thought that the penal sanctions should exactly reflect those in Additional Protocol I to the Geneva Conventions. As to individual criminal responsibility, some States felt that the Second Protocol should establish a different legal regime from that which already exists in the 1998 Statute of the International Criminal Court, but others felt that it should follow it, since the concept of individual criminal responsibility and that of State responsibility had already been embraced by the international community in those instruments.

8. The establishment of an Intergovernmental Committee was preferred by some Delegations but an alternative structure also received some support. One State mentioned the importance of the draft provisions on occupied

territory, and another doubted the wisdom of compulsory contributions to a fund. Five States (China, Denmark, Ireland, the United Kingdom and United States of America) announced progress towards their participation in the Hague Convention.

9. The Chapter-by-Chapter discussions began with substantive issues raised by Chapter 2 (General protection of cultural property) of the Draft, discussion on Chapter 1 being postponed until these had been dealt with. With respect to the Standard of general protection of cultural property (draft Article 4), a few States wanted significant changes to the description of cultural property, considering that the draft weakened the provisions of the Hague Convention and was contrary to the provisions of Additional Protocol I to the Geneva Convention.

10. As to the Loss of general protection, some States felt that draft Article 5 should be reformulated to coincide with the relevant provisions of Additional Protocol I to the Geneva Convention. Others wanted a redraft to remove possible justification for attacks on cultural property.

11. When considering draft Article 6 on Conditions for military operations and its relation to the provision of Article 4(2) of the Convention on the notion of 'imperative military necessity', some States wanted a more precise and limited definition, outlining the conditions under which the concept could be invoked to better regulate the conduct of States. Others felt there should be more reliance on the provisions already existing in other instruments of international humanitarian law, notably Additional Protocol I to the Geneva Conventions while yet others doubted that the Draft made provision both for the attacker and the attacked. It was proposed that the authorisation for attack against cultural property (Article 6(a)) should be modified: some States wanted a higher level of approval and others wanted more flexibility.

12. There were two views on draft Article 7 (Precautions against attack) as to the provision or not of a waiver where urgent circumstances required. On the Protection of cultural property in occupied territory (draft Article 10) there was disagreement as to whether an occupying State should be permitted to excavate in occupied territories; e.g. to protect a damaged site. The terms 'integrity' and 'authenticity' and the term 'illicit' were said to need clarification and the language of Chapter 2 changed to better reflect its supplementary relationship to the Convention. Finally, some States expressed the need to avoid any changes that might lead to ambiguity, especially at the operational level.

13. Mr. T. Desch (Austria) chaired an informal Working Group on draft Articles 4–9 and reported back to the Plenary. Draft Article 3 raised little

discussion. The new draft Article 4 (Respect for cultural property) was intended to clarify 'imperative military necessity' in Article 4(2) of the Convention, by specifying situations where this might be invoked as well as inserting restrictions against its abuse. In determining that cultural property is a military objective, the use of cultural property for military purposes is significant. Two new draft Articles were formulated: Article 5 (Precautions in attack), based on Article 57 of Additional Protocol I, and Article 6 (Precautions against the effects of hostilities), inspired by Article 58 of Additional Protocol I. A new draft Article 7 (old draft Article 10) on the Protection of cultural property in occupied territory allowed the Occupying Power to carry out archaeological excavations but only in close co-operation with the national authorities of the occupied territory. In the Plenary one delegate expressed his strong opposition to the new Article 9(2) on archaeological excavations in occupied territory by pointing out that in some occupied territories, activities of national institutions are curtailed or even subjected to closure. The Chairperson pointed out that this Article, as well as the remainder of Chapter 2, was reached by consensus and on his appeal to accept the redrafted version, the delegate agreed.

14. A number of States supported what they considered to be the new level of protection contained in Chapter 3 (Enhanced special protection). Certain States felt that 'enhanced special protection' should be extended to include the surroundings of cultural property. A few States felt there was no need for the new level of protection proposed but others felt that, since the provisions of the Convention had been unsuccessful, these supplementary provisions were essential.

15. Many States felt that the provisions of draft Article 11 on Enhanced special protection should reflect those of Chapter 2 of the Convention and better distinguish the higher level of protection this Article provides; for example it should reflect Article 8 of the Convention which requires that specially protected cultural property must not be near a military objective nor used for military purposes. A substantial majority of the Delegations felt that the provisions of Article 11(a) should be revised to refer to 'humankind' as opposed to 'all peoples'; emphasizing the common interest in safeguarding important cultural heritage. One State felt that the text should reflect the right of a country to protect its cultural property as a human right. With regard to Article 11(b) and (c), some felt that making the granting of 'enhanced special protection' dependent on legislative and administrative actions taken at the national level, removed the superior level of this type of protection as accorded in Article 11(a) of the Draft Second Protocol, to a level no higher than the protection provisions of Article 8 of the Convention. Others felt

that sub-paragraphs (b) and (c) did not take into consideration the difficulties that could arise in a federal State, nor the difficulty that poorer countries could have in implementing these provisions, especially without international technical assistance.

16. Some States thought that the provisions of Article 12 on The granting of enhanced special protection should be moved to Chapter 6 (Institutional issues) since they concerned procedural matters under the responsibility of the Committee. Others felt that this draft Article should better clarify the relationship between special protection under the Convention, and 'enhanced special protection' under the Draft Second Protocol. One State proposed that Article 12(2) should allow Parties from one State to request inscription on the International List of Cultural Property under Enhanced Special Protection of cultural property located in a second State, in order to protect the cultural property of minorities. Two Delegates suggested amending Article 12(3) to clarify that a recommendation of a non-governmental organization had no effect without a request by a State (Article 12(2)) and a decision by the Committee. While some States welcomed Article 12(5), permitting objections to the inclusion of cultural property in the List, others felt that a belligerent State should abstain when a vote is taken; while yet others wanted the provision clarified to show that the Committee could overrule objections. While it was considered that Article 12(6) on emergency measures should remain unchanged, some States felt a need for the process to be simplified.

17. A request was made to restructure draft Article 13 on the Immunity of cultural property under enhanced special protection to clarify when immunity could be lost. Another view was that this draft Article should clearly indicate 'Party' in a singular sense in order to prevent any interpretation to include collective action.

18. Many States wanted to clarify conditions for the Loss of enhanced special protection under Article 14. Some argued for closing any possible loophole by making the conditions for loss 'direct and indirect support of military operations'. Others felt that the wording of Article 14 gave an unacceptable advantage to the side using such cultural property. Some participants were in favour of reconsidering phrases such as 'other than its normal function' and 'significant and direct support'. The ICRC Representative pointed out that, in Additional Protocol I to the Geneva Conventions, protection is no longer limited to only a few unique objects: attack is now allowed only on military objectives, all other objects being protected. The protection accorded to these significant items should therefore be substantially higher than the general protection.

19. As to draft Article 15 (Conditions for military operations), the view was expressed that Article 15(a) was not practical at an operational level and that such responsibility should either be accorded to the highest level of operational command, or a proviso such as 'where circumstances permit' added. The ICRC Representative stated that 'enhanced special protection' would apply only to supremely important cultural property and, since any attack on such objects would have very significant political implications, it should only be authorised at the highest political level.

20. Some States wanted to reformulate draft Article 16 on the Suspension of immunity of cultural property under enhanced special protection to include informing a State whose cultural property has had its 'enhanced special protection' removed.

21. Ms. L. Terrillon-McKay (Canada) chaired an informal Working Group on draft Articles 11–17 and reported back to the Plenary. The use of the term 'enhanced protection' instead of 'enhanced special protection' was recommended, sub-paragraphs (b) and (c) were amalgamated into sub-paragraph (b) and a new sub-paragraph (c) in Article 11 inserted on the obligation not to use cultural property under enhanced protection for military purposes or to shield military objectives. Draft Article 12 on The granting of enhanced protection was redrafted to include procedural elements of draft Article 30 on Procedure before the Committee relating to enhanced special protection. The redrafted Article 14 on the Loss of immunity of cultural property under enhanced protection, made use of elements of Article 57 of Additional Protocol I to the Geneva Conventions with emphasis on the use of cultural property for military purposes.

22. In Plenary the use of 'P' and 'p' for Parties throughout the text was discussed. With regard to the new Article 13(1)(b), one Delegate was in favour of seeing the compromise word use replaced by the word 'function' when defining the conditions under which immunity of property under enhanced protection could be lost thus bringing Chapter 3 in conformity with the relevant provisions of Chapter 2. The majority stressed that the different wording marked the distinction between the different levels of protection in each Chapter. In a spirit of compromise, the State concerned agreed to withdraw its objections.

23. Discussion of Chapter 6 (Institutional Issues) revealed two options for Parties to the new Protocol: an Intergovernmental Committee or a Bureau. Some doubted that whether an intergovernmental body because of its political character was the best forum for taking decisions on the protection of cultural property of importance to all humankind and preferred an impartial, expert

body. Others favoured the political weight and representative character of an Intergovernmental Committee for such decisions. The financial and institutional implications for the administration of the new Protocol made others prefer a Bureau, perhaps with some simplification of its functions.

24. In view of the linkage between the functions of the Committee and Chapter 3 (Enhanced Special Protection) it was proposed that Chapter 6 be reformulated to include certain provisions of draft Articles 12, 16 and 17 as well as to define clearly the respective roles of the Intergovernmental Committee and those of the advisory bodies. Some Delegations were in favour of granting the Committee the responsibility of monitoring of the provisions of the Convention. Other Delegations wished to clarify draft Article 29(1)(d) on the use of the resources of the Fund and to insert a provision obliging the Committee to report on the use of the Fund in draft Article 29(1)(g). While many States were in favour of making contributions for The Fund (Article 32) voluntary, others felt that contributions should be compulsory to ensure its viability.

25. Most States stressed that Chapter 4 (Jurisdiction and Responsibility), together with Chapter 3 (Enhanced special protection), constituted the core of the Draft Second Protocol and would determine its success, since they remedied the Convention on special protection and enforcement of sanctions and illustrated its supplementary character. One Delegate wished to clarify whether the sanctions under Chapter 4 should be of a more general nature as in Article 28 of the Convention, or whether they should be more specific as they are in the Draft Second Protocol, feeling that difficulties might arise if some States were obliged to adopt new national legislation.

26. With regard to draft Article 18 on Grave breaches: many States expressed their appreciation of the distinction between grave breaches and other violations which they felt reflected the approach of Additional Protocol I to the Geneva Conventions (particularly its Article 85(4)(d)) and of the Statute of the International Criminal Court, thus avoiding the creation of a new category of crimes and ensuring a large participation of the international community. Another view was that this draft Article introduced new categories of offences and crimes and this should be avoided in a supplementary instrument. Yet others accepted the draft Article in its present form since draft Articles 18(a) and (b) were applicable only to cultural property under 'enhanced special protection'. Draft Articles 18(c), (d) and (e), on the other hand, provided that, if violations against generally protected cultural property were of a systematic nature, were unlawful or wanton, thus creating extensive damage, or cultural property was the victim of reprisals, such violations would also be considered

as grave breaches. The ICRC representative noted that in its enumeration of grave breaches, this draft Article did not include either intentional attack or pillage, both of which were now accepted as war crimes in the Statute of the International Criminal Court.

27. As to draft Article 19 on Other violations, guidelines were proposed for introduction into 19(1) to indicate the type of national legislation to be adopted. Some Delegations wanted the obligation to enact legislation at national level (Article 19(2)) only for breaches enumerated in draft Article 18. One State noted the difficulty for some developing countries to enact the necessary legislation, since they often lacked adequate records of their cultural property. Finally, while some felt that the second paragraph could be moved to draft Article 21 since it dealt more with matters of jurisdiction, others felt that this paragraph should not only be separate, but also apply to Articles 18 and 19 of the Draft Second Protocol.

28. There was general satisfaction at the inclusion of the notion of Individual criminal responsibility (draft Article 20). Some States wished to harmonize the definition with other existing instruments of international humanitarian law such as Additional Protocol I to the Geneva Conventions or the Statute of the International Criminal Court and to avoid the inclusion of ancillary crimes such as those in draft Article 20(2). Opinions were divided on the criminalisation of attempts. Some were in favour of clarifying draft Article 20(4) and making it applicable only to grave crimes. In respect of draft Article 20(6) on superior orders, some States wished to follow the provisions of Article 33 of the Statute of the International Criminal Court because, at the operational level, the soldier would be more constrained by his obligation to obey a higher grade officer.

29. Speaking on draft Article 21 on Jurisdiction, the ICRC representative noted that the notion of international jurisdiction was already reflected in existing instruments of international humanitarian law, such as Article 8(a) of the Statute of the International Criminal Court. The experience of ICRC was that a two-tier system tended to heighten the difficulty of persuading States to enact national legislation. To adopt clear guidelines on international criminal jurisdiction, there must be a specific list of grave breaches as well as of acts creating criminal responsibility, both generally accepted as falling under international jurisdiction. Another view was that it was not appropriate to deal with international criminal law in a supplementary instrument.

30. Some States supported draft Article 22 on the Responsibility of parties to a conflict because, in their view, it reflected generally accepted rules of customary international law. Others referred to existing work in the United

Nations International Law Commission, and wished to delete it. The ICRC representative noted that Article 91 of Additional Protocol I to the Geneva Conventions provided for the responsibility of States for all acts committed by persons forming part of their armed forces.

31. Draft Article 23 on Mutual assistance in criminal matters was welcomed by some States as necessary for effective enforcement, others considered that it differed from provisions already existing in other instruments of international humanitarian law. Some Delegates argued for its retention unchanged because existing provisions in international humanitarian law were too vague, especially on the issues of extradition and co-operation.

32. Mr. H. Fischer (Germany) agreed to chair an informal Working Group to work on the reformulation of the provisions of Chapter 4 in the light of all these observations. Reporting back to the Plenary, the Chairman stated that the redraft had succeeded in reaching a balance between the rights of the attacker and those of the defender. The redraft provided for enforcement machinery not provided in the Convention.

33. Chapter 5 (The protection of cultural property in armed conflicts of a non-international character) containing one draft Article 24 (Non-international armed conflicts) elicited diverging views. Some States doubted its applicability and others wished to limit its scope, yet others wanted clarification. Some thought that draft Articles 24(2) to (4) were inconsistent with the provisions of Article 19 of the Convention and some of the other provisions of the Draft Second Protocol. However, in view of the loss of cultural heritage in recent non-international armed conflicts, a large number of States welcomed the provisions of Chapter 5. Some States suggested that these provisions should be included under Article 2 on the scope of the Draft Second Protocol.

34. The ICRC representative explained that non-international armed conflicts are very complex and that was precisely why they should be under the same regime as international armed conflicts. Government forces in non-international conflicts are trained to respect certain obligations and those fighting against them should be subject to the same obligations.

35. Ms. A. Connelly (Ireland) agreed to chair an informal Working Group to work on draft Article 24 together with Chapter 1 of the Draft. This Group considered and redrafted the provisions and reported to the Plenary. General agreement was reached on the applicability of the Second Protocol to non-international armed conflicts, occurring within the territory of one of the Parties. There being divergent views on the extent to which the provisions on serious violations of the Protocol should apply in such situations, this Chapter had been redrafted.

36. In Plenary the ICRC representative questioned the clarity of the use of the word 'Party' in the redrafted Article 22 and proposed to add the term 'to the conflict' at the end of Article 22(1). However, a number of States opposed this as it could lead to difficulties in interpretation because the word 'Parties ' in this instance refers both to Parties to the Protocol and Parties to the conflict. Finally, this proposal was not accepted. In this context, the Chairman of the Drafting Committee made the following statement: The Drafting Committee considered that the term 'parties to a conflict' could also apply to non-State Parties to a conflict by virtue of Article 22 which provides that the Second Protocol applies to non-international armed conflicts and that this Protocol is to be interpreted in that sense.

37. Mr. J. Jelen (Hungary) agreed to chair an informal Working Group to work on the provisions of Chapter 6. This Group reported back to the Plenary that the revised text of Chapter 6 represented a compromise between the two options proposed. The Plenary meeting decided that this body should be called an intergovernmental committee. The new text of Chapter 6 included a clear enumeration of the functions of the supervisory body, and guidelines for the use of the Fund, which no longer has compulsory contributions. The Working Group also added other professional non-governmental organizations which might advise the new supervisory body. A resolution was discussed and amended concerning the Fund and received no opposition.

38. As to Chapter 7 (Dissemination of Information and International Assistance), some delegates thought that means of Dissemination (draft Article 33) should not be limited to the provisions of 33(3)(b) to (d). Others considered it more ambitious than Article 25 of the Convention and the relevant provisions of Additional Protocol I to the Geneva Conventions and wished to modify or delete it.

39. When discussing draft Article 34 on the International Co-operation, some Delegations wished to refer to Articles 18 and 19 of the Draft Second Protocol in order to prevent confusion or subjective interpretation. Others preferred to replace the term 'serious violations' by the term 'grave breaches' with a view to harmonizing the terminology of the new Protocol.

40. In Plenary, one State felt that Article 32(1) of the redraft relating to International Assistance (former draft Article 35) was inconsistent with redrafted Articles 27(1) and 29(1)(a) related to the administration of the Fund; it would also include the notion of international assistance for the preparation of sites for enhanced protection and refer to Article 5 of the Second Protocol. The Chairman of the Working Group pointed out that the current version of the text took into account many differing interests and

ensured the cohesion between Chapters 6 and 7. Finally, the Chairman of the Conference referred to a draft resolution to be adopted by the Conference and asked whether the draft resolution would not solve this problem. This compromise was then accepted.

41. As to draft Article 37 on the Protection of international and national members of the Blue Shield Organisation and other persons, some Delegations wished to extend this protection to other NGOs and international workers. One State thought 'shall protect' was too heavy an obligation while the ICRC Representative suggested a version based on Article 71 of Additional Protocol I to the Geneva Conventions. Certain Delegates proposed that protection be withdrawn from Blue Shield workers if they involved themselves in the hostilities. Furthermore. it was felt that the provisions of paragraph 1(a) needed to be more specific. Following a discussion in Plenary draft Article 37 was deleted on the basis that the relevant provisions of the Convention and Additional Protocol I sufficed.

42. Considering Chapter 8 (Execution of this Protocol), some wanted deletion of draft Articles 38 on the Protecting Powers and 39 on Conciliation procedure, on the basis that Articles 21 and 22 of the Hague Convention sufficed. Responding to doubts as to the applicability of the system of Protecting Powers in non-international armed conflicts, the ICRC Representative stressed the importance of maintaining this notion, mentioning existing precedents in the Geneva Conventions. Some States felt that the use of the word 'neutral' in draft Article 39(2) could be confusing. Others felt that draft Articles 39 and 40 (Conciliation in absence of Protecting Powers) should be reformulated in order not to exclude the intervention of the Director-General of UNESCO even where Protecting Powers had been appointed.

43. During the discussion of draft Article 42 on Meetings some States enquired why the Director-General should report on the General Assembly of Parties to the Executive Board. Others queried the relationship between the General Assembly of Parties and the new supervisory body. With regard to paragraph 2 two options were proposed: to redraft it in conformity with Article 39 of the Convention or to delete it.

44. In discussing Chapter 9 (Final clauses), and especially draft Article 43 on Languages, some felt that all the language versions of the Second Protocol should be equally authentic. One State suggested that this draft Article should reflect the corresponding ones in the Convention, while another pointed out that Article 33(2) of the Vienna Convention on the Law of Treaties 1969 provides for authoritative versions of a treaty in languages in which it was not negotiated. Another view was that all 'authentic' texts had to be negotiated at

the Conference. It was decided that the Second Protocol would be prepared in six authentic languages (Arabic, Chinese, English, French, Russian and Spanish) and that the translations in all these languages would be sent to the Drafting Committee with a view of harmonising terminology and verifying the texts.

45. As to draft Article 44 on Reservations, some States thought a 'no reservations' clause without precedent in international humanitarian law and that it might prevent universal acceptance of the Second Protocol and preferred following the relevant provisions of the 1969 Vienna Convention on the Law of Treaties. Other States, arguing for its retention, stressed that the provisions of the Draft Second Protocol were of fundamental importance and deserved special legal status, urging that these were very detailed provisions on a specific topic and that a no-reservations principle was therefore permissible (as a precedent, the Convention on the Prohibition of the Use, Stockpiling, Production and Transfer of Anti-personnel Mines and on their Destruction 1997). Finally, a consensus was developed that Article 19 of the 1969 Vienna Convention sufficiently covered the case and, therefore, the draft Article was deleted.

46. The Secretariat provided a redraft of Chapter 9 (Final Clauses) based on the different views and suggestions made during the discussions. In Plenary, the terminology of Articles 42–46 was harmonized in conformity with the 1969 Vienna Convention.

47. The meeting then turned to the discussion of Chapter 1 (Introduction). Following discussion of draft Article 1 on Definitions in the Plenary, the final decision of the Plenary was that this Article was adequate, subject to two modifications related to the definition of 'military objective' and 'illicit'.

48. With respect to draft Article 2 on Relation to the Convention, questions were raised as to the status of States not party to the Convention and whether the Draft Second Protocol was supplementary or an amendment. This Chapter was considered further with Chapter 5 in the Working Group chaired by Ms. Connelly. On return to Plenary, it was proposed to divide draft Article 2 on the Relation to the Convention into three separate Articles, one on the general relationship of the Second Protocol to the Convention, a second on the scope of application of the Second Protocol, and a third on the relationship between Chapter 3 (Enhanced Protection) and other provisions of the Convention and of the Second Protocol. Most States thought the new Protocol should be supplementary to the Convention and could be validly adopted by the Diplomatic Conference. However, three States were in favour of applying Article 39(5) of the Convention. The redrafted provision on the

scope of application, a new paragraph related to the relationship between new Chapter 3 (Enhanced Protection) and other provisions of the Convention and of the Second Protocol were adopted.

49. The Plenary continued its work by discussing the Preamble. Several small modifications were proposed. A new paragraph stipulated expressly that issues not regulated by the Second Protocol would be governed by the rules of customary international law.

50. The whole text having been reviewed by the Drafting Committee, the Conference finished its work by adopting, by acclamation, the Second Protocol to the Hague Convention for the Protection of Cultural Property in the Event of Armed Conflict 1954 together with the Final Act of the Conference and a resolution. Copies appear as Annex 1 and 2 to this report. Two States made declarations (Annex 3).

51. Closing the Plenary meeting, the Chairperson congratulated the participants and observers for their efforts, diligence and spirit of consensus allowing the Conference to reach by compromise a final text, acceptable to States parties to the Convention. He expressed the hope that the Second Protocol would meet with wide acceptance.

PART III
INTERNATIONAL CRIMINAL LAW AND THE PROTECTION OF CULTURAL PROPERTY IN THE EVENT OF ARMED CONFLICT

Statute of the International Criminal Tribunal for the former Yugoslavia and the Relevant Case-Law (Article 3(d) of the Statute)

1999 Rome Statute of the International Criminal Court and the Relevant Case-Law (Articles 8(2)(b)(ix) and 8(2)(e)(iv))

Cambodian law on the establishment of Extraordinary Chambers in the courts of Cambodia for the prosecution of crimes committed during the period of Democratic Kampuchea, Article 7 on the responsibility for destruction of cultural property during armed conflict.

Statute of the International Tribunal for the Prosecution of Persons Responsible for Serious Violations of International Humanitarian Law Committed in the Territory of the former Yugoslavia and the Relevant Case-law (Article 3(d) of the statute)

The International Tribunal for the Prosecution of Persons Responsible for Serious Violations of International Humanitarian Law Committed in the Territory of the former Yugoslavia since 1991, more commonly referred to as the International Criminal Tribunal for the former Yugoslavia or ICTY, is an organ of the United Nations that was established for the prosecution of the serious crimes committed during the wars in the countries of the former Yugoslavia.

While the draft Statute of an international criminal court was under consideration by the ILC, the war in the territory of Yugoslavia was ongoing. The Security Council established a Commission of Experts charged with identifying war crimes and crimes against the humanity. The Commission urged the establishment of an international criminal tribunal:

> The Commission is shocked by the high level of victimization and the manner in which these crimes were committed, as are the populations of all the parties to the conflict. The difference is that each side sees only its own victimization, and not what their side has done to others.
>
> It is particularly striking to note the victims' high expectations that this Commission will establish the truth and that the International Tribunal will provide justice. All sides expect this. Thus, the conclusion is inescapable that peace in the future requires justice, and that justice starts with establishing the truth. The Commission would be remiss if it did not emphasize the high expectation of justice conveyed by the parties to the conflict, as well as by victims, intergovernmental organizations, non-governmental organizations, the media and world public opinion. Consequently, the International Tribunal must be given the necessary resources and support to meet these expectations and accomplish its task. Furthermore, popular expectations of a new world order based on the international rule of law require no less than effective and permanent institutions of international justice. The

International Tribunal for the Prosecution of Persons Responsible for Serious Violation of International Humanitarian Law Committed in the Territory of the Former Yugoslavia since 1991 must, therefore, be given the opportunity to produce the momentum for this future evolution.[1499]

The Report of the Commission included a substantive report on the destruction of cultural property:

J. Destruction of cultural property
In determining the extent of the destruction of cultural property in the former Yugoslavia, the Commission proceeded under its overall plan of work and made use more particularly of its database and reports by international organizations, including the United Nations Educational, Scientific and Cultural Organization (UNESCO), the Parliamentary Assembly of the Council of Europe and other intergovernmental sources and non-governmental organizations.

The Commission has received extensive information on destruction of cultural property, but it was not in a position to investigate all these allegations. In particular, it could not verify allegations that all Catholic churches and mosques in Serb-occupied territories of Bosnia had been systematically destroyed or damaged. Since the Commission could not consider, let alone investigate, all allegations of damage to cultural property, it has selected two examples which are typical of such breaches.

The two examples chosen by the Commission were the battle of Dubrovnik and the destruction of the Mostar Bridge.

In the autumn of 1991, the region of Dubrovnik was surrounded and besieged by the Yugoslav National Army. After a few weeks, Dubrovnik itself was cut off by land and sea by the forces of the former Yugoslavia. This situation continued up to the autumn of 1992, when the district of Dubrovnik was recognized as forming part of the Republic of Croatia. The military occupation of the district of Dubrovnik captured international attention because of the cultural and historical significance of the region and the town. Dubrovnik is

---

1499 United Nations Security Council, S/1994/674 - 27 May 1994. *Final Report of the Commission of Experts.* Established Pursuant to Security Council Resolution 780 (1992). http://www.his. com/~twarrick/commxyu1.htm

now known as an old town which has suffered great damage as a result of the Serbian attacks. In 1979, the old town had been included in UNESCO's list of the world's cultural heritage.

The attacks on Dubrovnik started with the Serbian paramilitary forces, supported by Yugoslavia's regular army, in June and August. On 1 October 1991 the Yugoslav Army invaded the district of Dubrovnik and laid siege to the town. It may be affirmed that there was virtually no defence of Dubrovnik and the surrounding area against the Yugoslav forces. Thus the destruction could on no account be justified as a military necessity.

The siege of Dubrovnik lasted from October until December. The first shelling began on 1 October and continued sporadically until 24 October 1991. After a short lull, the shelling started up again on 30 October and continued into December. The shelling on 6 December 1991 was especially intensive. The shelling was selective and deliberately aimed at the buildings in the old town and there is no doubt that the destruction of cultural property was intentional. However, the people doing the firing did not only hit the old town. The new town was also hit.

According to estimates, 55.9 per cent of the buildings of the old town were affected, either by fires or by damage to the structures and special elements or to the facades and roofs. Several palaces had their roofs either destroyed or burned, including the Festival Palace, whose archives were completely destroyed, and a number of monuments whose roofs caved in. Other examples are St. Blaise's Church, the Franciscan Cathedral and Convent, the Dominican Convent, St. Clair's Convent and the Fountain of Onofrio; and, of course, there was the destruction of the roofs of the old town. In this respect, the local authorities list 336 direct hits and 254 cases of partial destruction of roofs by shell fragments.

From the UNESCO experts' assessment, the total damaged roof areas can be estimated at 56,747 m². To this visible damage, the experts of the Commission have added damage resulting from vibrations, which may appear later, as well as the damage which simply could not be detected at the time the UNESCO experts were carrying out their work.

Thus, in respect of the statute of the International Tribunal, the offences in Dubrovnik can be said to concern extensive destruction and appropriation of property not justified by military necessity and seizure or destruction and damage to religious institutions dedicated to charity, education, the arts and sciences as well as historic monuments and artistic and scientific works.

The concept of a military objective should also be considered in this connection in order to shed light on the crimes committed. Indeed, it seems quite clear that this destruction of cultural property did not in any way contribute to the military action and could in no way be considered necessary in terms of the military objectives pursued. Nor is there any way that the perpetrators of these crimes can claim to have been utilizing the monuments for military purposes. In the Commission's view, other concepts in addition to military objectives should be applied: the concepts of undefended place or object, of proportionality and of neutrality.

At 10.16 am on 9 November 1993, Mostar Bridge was destroyed. In this connection, the Institute for the Protection of the Historic and Natural Cultural Heritage of Bosnia and Herzegovina has accused the Croatian Defence Council and the Croatian Army in a letter to UNESCO dated 10 November 1993. This letter and other documents attached to the present report describe the history of the bridge, which was built between 1557 and 1566 according to the plans of the Turkish architect Aerudin. It is a monument which, unfortunately, did not appear in the UNESCO list. However, this bridge was well known to the population in the region, whether Serbian, Croatian or Muslim. Moreover, the bridge was a symbol of Bosnia and Herzegovina which connected the gap between the Muslim and Croat communities. It embodied the links which united these peoples in spite of their religious differences and the circumstances of the present war. There can be no doubt, however, that it was of greater value to the Muslims.

Admittedly, before it was destroyed, the bridge had already suffered a certain amount of damage. Indeed, damage had already been done to its northern parapets. But, all things considered, the damage had been minor. The initial objective, it would seem, had been to discourage people from using it. Thus, prior to November 1993, the primary target had been the parapet, forcing anyone who might be tempted to cross the bridge to refrain from doing so. However, the shelling on 8 November 1993 clearly aimed at destroying the bridge. This destruction was carried out by tanks belonging apparently to the Croatian forces. On 9 November, the shelling continued. It was then that the supporting arch of the southern end of the bridge was hit and collapsed. It would seem that this incident was filmed by Folio Productions (a British production company).

The same criminal characterization which applies to the battle of Dubrovnik also applies to the destruction of Mostar Bridge, which was also devoid of any military significance. It would seem that the Croats were at the origin of the destruction of Mostar Bridge. A Mostar district military tribunal reportedly interrogated three Croatian Defence Council soldiers, who allegedly acted, according to a statement by the tribunal, "on their own initiative, without orders from their superiors". Clearly, these are questions of fact which have to be decided judicially to determine both individual responsibility and command responsibility.

K. Dubrovnik investigation

The Commission sent an investigative team of Canadian and Norwegian military lawyers and a French art historian to Dubrovnik for the period 20 October to 4 November 1993. The objective of the investigation was to prepare a law of armed conflict study of the battle of Dubrovnik which would attempt, among other things:

- To determine whether and when indiscriminate attacks or deliberate attacks on civilian persons or civilian objects occurred;
- To quantify the loss of civilian life, injury to civilian persons, and damage to civilian property, including cultural property;
- To attribute responsibility for apparent violations of the law of armed conflict.

On the basis of this investigation, the Commission finds that at least 82, and possibly as many as 88, civilians were killed as a result of JNA military operations in the district of Dubrovnik during the period from September 1991 until December 1992, inclusive, and that most of these persons were killed in 1991. Thirteen civilians were killed during the St. Nicholas Day bombardment of 6 December 1991. The Institute for the Restoration of Dubrovnik has completed a study of damage to housing in the district of Dubrovnik, which the Commission accepts. The Institute estimates that the cost of reconstructing housing alone will be DM 69,000,000, while the cost of complete reinstallation of families will be DM 480,000,000 (prices on 31 December 1990). Detailed reports on damage to cultural property have been prepared by UNESCO, the Institute for the Protection of Cultural Monuments and the Natural Environment of Dubrovnik and the Parliamentary

Assembly of the Council of Europe which the Commission has accepted as a basis for their investigation. These reports indicate in particular that a substantial amount of damage was caused to cultural property in the old town of Dubrovnik, mostly during the St. Nicholas Day bombardment.

It is the finding of the Commission that the St. Nicholas Day bombardment of 6 December 1991 was a deliberate attack on civilian persons and on civilian objects, including cultural property. It is the finding of the Commission that it is possible to determine the precise identity and status of persons killed or injured during the bombardment and to confirm the extent of civilian property damaged during the bombardment, the unit responsible for the bombardment, the identity of the unit commander and the identity and position in the chain of command of more senior officers responsible for the bombardment.

It is the view of the Commission that it is possible to develop prima facie cases directed against one or more officers responsible for the St. Nicholas Day bombardment and that it may be possible to develop cases concerning other incidents in the district of Dubrovnik.[1500]

The recommendation of the Commission of Experts addressed to the Security Council was followed by proposals from Lord Owen, Cyrus Vence, Robert Badinter and the German Foreign Minister Klaus Kinkel. The recommendation of the Commission was also endorsed by the United Nations General Assembly in December 1992. On 22 February 1993, the Security Council decided to establish a tribunal to prosecute 'persons responsible for serious violations of international humanitarian law committee in the territory of the former Yugoslavia since 1991'[1501] and adopted the draft proposed by the Secretary-General on 25 May 1993, Resolution of the Security Council 827 (1993):

> The Security Council, [...]
> *Having considered* the report of the Secretary-General (S/25704 and Add.1) pursuant to paragraph 2 of resolution 808 (1993), [...]
> *'Acting* under Chapter VII of the Charter of the United Nations,
> 1. *Approves* the report of the Secretary-General;

1500   Ibid., parts J and K of the Report. Footnotes not reprinted.
1501   Security Council Resolution 808 (1993).

2. *Decides* hereby to establish an international tribunal for the sole purpose of prosecuting persons responsible for serious violations of international humanitarian law committed in the territory of the former Yugoslavia between 1 January 1991 and a date to be determined by the Security Council upon the restoration of peace and to this end to adopt the Statute of the International Tribunal annexed to the above-mentioned report.[1502]

STATUTE OF THE INTERNATIONAL TRIBUNAL FOR THE PROSECUTION OF PERSONS RESPONSIBLE FOR SERIOUS VIOLATIONS OF INTERNATIONAL HUMANITARIAN LAW COMMITTED IN THE TERRITORY OF THE FORMER YUGOSLAVIA SINCE 1991

The draft submitted by the Secretary-General in the UN document S/25704[1503] was adopted without modifications by the Security Council. The tribunal was called to apply rules of international humanitarian law that are 'beyond doubt part of customary law'. It was based also on the previous work done by the ILC.

Article 3 of the Statute provided the definition of the crimes to be prosecuted:

Article 3. Violations of the laws or customs of war

The International Tribunal shall have the power to prosecute persons violating the laws or customs of war. Such violations shall include, but not be limited to:
  (a) employment of poisonous weapons or other weapons calculated to cause unnecessary suffering;
  (b) wanton destruction of cities, towns or villages, or devastation not justified by military necessity;

1502   Security Council Resolution 827 (1993), adopted on 25 May 1993. (S/RES/827 (1993)); Statute of the International Tribunal for the Prosecution of Persons Responsible for Serious Violations of International Humanitarian Law Committed in the Territory of the Former Yugoslavia since 1991, UN Doc. S/25704 at 36, annex (1993) and S/25704/Add.1 (1993), adopted by Security Council on 25 May 1993, UN Doc. S/RES/827 (1993). The Statute was amended by several resolutions of the Security Council and in particular by the Resolution 1166 (1998) of 13 May 1998 and 1329 (2000) of 30 November 2000.

1503   http://daccessdds.un.org/doc/UNDOC/GEN/N93/248/35/IMG/N9324835. pdf?OpenElement

(c) attack, or bombardment, by whatever means, of undefended towns, villages, dwellings, or buildings;

(d) seizure of, destruction or willful damage done to institutions dedicated to religion, charity and education, the arts and sciences, historic monuments and works of art and science;

(e) plunder of public or private property.

The most important provision concerning the protection of cultural property is paragraph (d).

Theodor Meron, former President of the Tribunal, indicated that '[this] Article requires that the acts prohibited under it have to be closely related to an armed conflict'.[1504] In elaborating this requirement, the Appeals Chamber of the Tribunal explained:

> What ultimately distinguishes a war crime from a purely domestic offence is that a war crime is shaped by or dependent upon the environment – the armed conflict – in which it is committed. . . . The armed conflict need not have been causal to the commission of the crime, but the existence of an armed conflict must, at a minimum, have played a substantial part in the perpetrator's ability to commit it, his decision to commit it, the manner in which it was committed or the purpose for which it was committed.[1505]

This requirement needs to be compared with the requirement of Article 18.1 of the Convention for the Protection of Cultural Property in the Event of Armed Conflict.[1506] Article 18.1 states, in part of relevance here, that the Convention 'shall apply in the event of declared war or of any other armed conflict which may arise between two or more of the High Contracting Parties.' While Article 18.1 applies only to international armed conflicts, Article 3 of the Tribunal's Statute has been interpreted in the Tribunal's case-law to apply to both international and national armed conflicts.[1507] [1508] Article 3 also states that the list of these crimes is not necessarily exhaustive.

1504   See, e.g. *Prosecutor* v. *Tadić*, IT-94-1-AR72, Decision on the Defence Motion for Interlocutory Appeal on Jurisdiction, 2 October 1995, para. 70.

1505   *Prosecutor* v. *Kunarac*, IT-96-23 & IT-96-23/1-A, Judgment, 12 June 2002, para. 58.

1506   Convention for the Protection of Cultural Property in the Event of Armed Conflict, signed 14 May 1954, 249 UNTS 240 [hereinafter 1954 Hague Convention].

1507   *Prosecutor* v. *Tadić*, IT-94-1-AR72, Decision on the Defence Motion for Interlocutory Appeal on Jurisdiction, 2 October 1995, para. 137.

1508   Meron (2005).

The text of paragraph (d) of Article 3 of the Statute reproduces the core of Articles 27 and 56 of the Hague Regulations annexed to the Fourth Hague Convention of 1907.[1509] The terms used in the Hague Regulations cover most of the objects that we today refer to under the global term 'cultural property'.

Professor Meron also explained the important relations between Article 2 of the Statute[1510] and Article 3, paragraph (d), which prohibits 'extensive destruction and appropriation of property not justified by military necessity and carried out unlawfully and wantonly.' The text of this Article would suggest that it may, in appropriate cases, serve as another statutory source of protection of cultural property:

> The practice of our Tribunal, to which I will turn in a moment, has been to use Article 3, Section D as the statutory provision under which to punish destruction of cultural property. None of the cases decided so far has done so under Section D of Article 2. The reason for this practice is likely two-fold. First, Article 3, Section D is a more specific provision than Article 2, Section D, because it expressly describes the kind of property whose destruction is punishable under the Statute. This property is described as 'institutions dedicated to religion, charity and education', and to 'the arts'; the provision also punishes destruction of 'historical monuments and works of art'. Section D of Article 2, by contrast, refers only to 'property', and provides no elaboration of the term. Second, as I already explained, under the jurisprudence of the Tribunal, Article 3, which concerns violations of laws or customs of war, applies both to international and internal armed conflict. By contrast, Article 2, which relates only to grave breaches of the Geneva Conventions of 1949, applies only to armed conflicts of

---

1509   Hague Convention No. IV of 18 October 1907, Respecting the Laws and Customs of War on Land, 36 Stat. 2227, TS 539 [hereinafter 1907 Hague Convention], and the annex thereto, embodying the Regulations Respecting the Laws and Customs of War on Land, 36 Stat. 2295 [hereinafter Hague Regulations].

1510   Article 2 Grave breaches of the Geneva Conventions of 1949.
The International Tribunal shall have the power to prosecute persons committing or ordering to be committed grave breaches of the Geneva Conventions of 12 August 1949, namely the following acts against persons or property protected under the provisions of the relevant Geneva Convention:
(a) willful killing; (b) torture or inhuman treatment, including biological experiments; (c) willfully causing great suffering or serious injury to body or health; (d) extensive destruction and appropriation of property, not justified by military necessity and carried out unlawfully and wantonly; (e) compelling a prisoner of war or a civilian to serve in the forces of a hostile power; (f) willfully depriving a prisoner of war or a civilian of the rights of fair and regular trial; (g) unlawful deportation or transfer or unlawful confinement of a civilian; (h) taking civilians as hostages.

international character. Given the nature of the armed conflict in the former Yugoslavia, which had both international and internal elements, Article 3 covers a broader swath of conduct than Article 2. The preference exhibited by the Trial Chambers of our Tribunal for Article 3 may, therefore, be viewed as a welcome development from the standpoint of safeguarding cultural property, because it affords that property a higher degree of protection.[1511]

It is also important to mention Article 5 of the Statute,[1512] and particularly its paragraph (h) concerning 'persecutions on political, racial and religious grounds', as these crimes against humanity cover a great number of offences punishable in international and internal conflicts. As we shall see below, the case-law of the Tribunal has explained that to be prohibited by this provision of the Statute, the proscribed act must form part of a widespread or systematic attack on the civilian population, and the perpetrator must know about the attack and that his/her acts form a part of that attack.[1513] 'While this provision does not mention cultural property (or even property in general) . . . it has been used by Trial Chambers of the Tribunal to hold individuals who committed destruction of cultural property responsible for their acts.'[1514] In this way, the Tribunal was able to strengthen the applicability of the Convention in times not only of war but also of peace.

EXAMPLES OF CASE-LAW

In this part we shall refer to several cases from the practice of the Tribunal that illustrate the Tribunal's contribution to the prosecution of violations against cultural property committed in the States of the former Yugoslavia. As most of the cases of the International Tribunal for the Prosecution of Persons Responsible for Serious Violations of International Humanitarian Law Committed in the Territory of the former Yugoslavia since 1991 were

---

1511   Meron (2005), pp. 43–45.
1512   Article 5 Crimes against humanity
The International Tribunal shall have the power to prosecute persons responsible for the following crimes when committed in armed conflict, whether international or internal in character, and directed against any civilian population: (a) murder; (b) extermination; (c) enslavement; (d) deportation; (e) imprisonment; (f) torture; (g) rape; (h) persecutions on political, racial and religious grounds; (i) other inhumane acts.
1513   See, e.g., *Prosecutor* v. *Krstić*, IT-98-33-A, Judgment, 19 April 2004, para. 223; see also *Prosecutor* v. *Kunarac*, IT-96-23 & IT-96-23/1-A, Judgment, 12 June 2002, para. 85, 96, 102.
1514   Meron (2005), p. 45.

presented at the Symposium organized by UNESCO on the occasion of the 50th anniversary of the 1954 Hague Convention, our presentation of the case law is based on the presentation of former President of the Tribunal, Professor Theodor Meron. No one else is more competent to provide this information.[1515]

A. The Prosecutor v. Tihomir Blaškić[1516]

Tihomir Blaškić was a Croatian general, convicted in March 2000 for offences that included violations of law and customs of war under Article 3 of the Statute.[1517] Among these violations was a conviction for the destruction of institutions dedicated to religion or education in 12 towns and villages located in the Lašva Valley in the central part of Bosnia and Herzegovina. In rendering a conviction for this offence, the Trial Chamber specified that, to be punishable under Article 3, Section (d), '[the] damage or destruction must have been committed intentionally to institutions which may clearly be identified as dedicated to religion or education and which were not being used for military purposes at the time of the acts.'[1518] The Trial Chamber also stated that, to constitute violations of international laws or customs of war, 'the institutions must not have been in the immediate vicinity of military objectives.'[1519] The Trial Chamber did not explain the rationale for this limiting requirement, but one can speculate that it might have been due to a concern regarding the difficulty of determining when the religious or educational institutions located in the immediate vicinity of military action served no military purpose, or whether the damage caused to these institutions could be seen as legitimate collateral damage.

Perhaps more interestingly, General Blaškić was also convicted for persecution as a crime against humanity. This conviction was premised, *inter alia*, on his participation in the destruction or willful damage of 'institutions dedicated to religion or education'.[1520] The Trial Chamber concluded that the destruction of such institutions can provide support for a charge that the defendant intended to persecute on statutorily enumerated grounds, such as those of race, religion or politics. The Chamber stated that:

1515   See ibid. See also Mettraux (2005), pp. 94–96.
1516   Meron (2005), pp. 45–47.
1517   *The Prosecutor* v. *Blaškić*, IT-95-14-T, Judgment, 3 March 2000.
1518   Ibid., para. 185.
1519   Ibid.
1520   *Prosecutor* v. *Blaškić*, IT-95-14-PT, Second Amended Indictment, 25 April 1997.

persecution may take forms other than injury to the human person, in particular those acts rendered serious not by their apparent cruelty but by the discrimination they seek to instill within humankind. [Persecution] may thus take the form of confiscation or destruction of private dwellings or businesses, symbolic buildings or means of subsistence belonging to the Muslim population of Bosnia-Herzegovina.[1521]

The Trial Chamber's reference, in the passage just quoted, to 'symbolic buildings' makes clear that it viewed the intentional destruction of religious (and perhaps other cultural) institutions, when committed with a prohibited discriminatory intent, as an act directed, in the final analysis, at the individual for whom these objects of patrimony exemplified his own religion or culture. As such, the wanton destruction of these institutions was punishable not only by virtue of the specific prohibition in Article 3 of the Statute but also as an indirect persecution of the individuals who associated with these institutions on the grounds of religion, race or politics. The destruction of property has been in this way equated with injury to human beings.

The Blaškić Appeals Judgment did not directly consider the extent to which destruction of cultural property can be considered a crime of persecution under Article 5 of the Statute.[1522] The Appeals Chamber noted that whether an attack on civilian property constitutes persecution 'may depend on the type of property involved' such that 'certain types of property whose destruction may not have a severe enough impact on the victim as to constitute a crime against humanity, *even if such destruction is perpetrated on discriminatory grounds.*'[1523] The Appeals Chamber noted that the destruction of property that 'constitutes an indispensable and vital asset to the owner' could be a crime against humanity, but did not discuss how cultural property or other 'symbolic buildings' would be treated under the test.[1524]

1521 Ibid., para. 227.

1522 *Prosecutor v. Blaškić*, IT-95-14-A, Judgment, 29 July 2004 ('Blaškić Appeals Judgment').

1523 Blaškić Appeals Judgment, para. 146, citing Kupreskić Trial Judgment, para. 631.

1524 Blaškić Appeals Judgment, para. 138, 146. The Appeals Chamber also emphasized that 'acts of persecutions, considered separately or together, should reach the level of gravity of other crimes listed in Article 5 of the Statute. Underlying acts are not rendered sufficiently grave only because they are committed with a discriminatory intent.'

B. The Prosecutor v. Dario Kordić and Mario Čerkez[1525]

The defendants Dario Kordić and Mario Čerkez[1526] were, respectively, a political and a military leader of the Croatian Defence Council, an organization responsible for military operations in Bosnia and Herzegovina in 1993. In the Trial Judgment, rendered in February 2001, both defendants were convicted for, among other crimes, the war crime of destroying or willfully damaging institutions dedicated to religion or education. This was a conviction under Article 3, Section D of the Statute. The Trial Chamber found that Kordić and Čerkez deliberately targeted Muslim mosques and other religious and cultural institutions in the course of the military campaign.

The relevant analysis of the Trial Chamber was much more detailed than that of the Trial Chamber in *Blaškić.* The Trial Chamber expressly noted that the former Yugoslavia ratified the 1954 Convention for the Protection of Cultural Property in 1956, and that the Convention continued to apply to both the Republic of Croatia and Republic of Bosnia-Herzegovina after their declarations of independence.[1527] The Trial Chamber then surveyed the types of cultural property protected under Article 1 of the Convention, such as 'movable or immovable property of great importance to the cultural heritage of every people', 'buildings whose main and effective purpose is to preserve or exhibit the movable cultural property,' and 'centres containing a large amount of cultural property'.[1528] The Trial Chamber then concluded, applying this definition to the case before it, that 'educational institutions are undoubtedly immovable property of great importance to the cultural heritage of peoples in that they are without exception centres of learning, arts, and sciences, with their valuable collections of books and works of arts and sciences.'[1529]

The Kordić Appeal Judgment identified two types of protection for cultural, historical and religious monuments: general and special.[1530] Discussing, *inter alia*, Article 52 of Additional Protocol I, the Appeals Chamber noted that protection is provided to a building or monument, including schools and places of worship, such that it 'cannot be destroyed

---

1525   Meron (2005), pp. 47–48.
1526   *Prosecutor* v. *Kordić and Čerkez*, IT-95-14/2-T, Judgment, 26 February 2001 ('Kordić Trial Judgment'); *Prosecutor v. Kordić and Cerkez*, IT-95-14/2-A, Judgment, 17 December 2004, para. 85–92 ('Kordić Appeal Judgment').
1527   Kordić Trial Judgment, para. 359.
1528   Ibid. (quoting Article 1 of the 1954 Convention for the Protection of Cultural Property in the Event of Armed Conflict).
1529   Ibid., para. 360.
1530   Ibid., para. 89, 90.

unless it has turned into a military object by offering the attacking side 'a definite military advantage' at the time of the attack.'[1531] Article 53 of the Additional Protocol I provides special protection to 'three categories of objects: historic monuments, works of art, and places of worship, provided they constitute the cultural or spiritual heritage of peoples', against which it is prohibited to direct any act of hostility.[1532] The Kordić and Čerkez Appeals Chamber found the Trial Chamber erred when it considered all educational institutions were subject to special protection afforded to cultural property.

The Kordić and Čerkez Trial Chamber also clarified the scope of Section D of Article 3. The Chamber noted that the offence of destroying religious or education institutions overlaps to a certain extent with the offence of unlawfully attacking civilian objects in general. In commenting on this overlap, the Trial Chamber observed that the offence with which Article 3, Section D is concerned has a more specific scope, because it is concerned solely with acts directed against 'cultural heritage'.[1533]

Also of interest is the Kordić and Čerkez Trial Chamber's rejection of the argument, put forward by the Defence, that the special protection provided by the 1954 Convention applied only to property registered under the International Register of Cultural Property. The Defence argued that in the absence of such registration, religious or educational institutions receive only ordinary protection and therefore could be destroyed or damaged in cases of military necessity regardless of whether they were occupied or used for military purposes.[1534] The Trial Chamber responded by observing that special protection under Article 8(1) of the 1954 Convention was a special measure provided for 'a limited number of refuges intended to shelter movable cultural property' and that 'this special protection would be lost if the refuges were used for military purposes.'[1535] The Trial Chamber concluded from this that there was 'little difference between the conditions for the according of general protection and those for the provision of special protection.'[1536] Consequently, the fundamental principle, in the Trial Chamber's view, was that 'protection of whatever type will be lost if cultural property, including educational institutions, is used for military purpose', a principle that the Trial Chamber found consistent with the custom codified in Article 27 of the

---

1531 Ibid., para. 89.
1532 Ibid., para. 90.
1533 Ibid., para. 361.
1534 See ibid., para. 357.
1535 Ibid., para. 361.
1536 Ibid.

Hague Regulations.[1537] The Kordić Appeals Judgment endorsed this holding by finding that special protection for educational institutions applied *qua* custom.[1538]

In addition to the conviction under Article 3, the Trial Chamber convicted both defendants for persecution as a crime against humanity. The rationale was similar to that adopted by the Trial Chamber in *Blaškić*, but considerably more developed. The Kordić and Čerkez Trial Chamber noted that the case-law of the Nuremberg Tribunal and the 1991 Report of the International Law Commission have singled out the destruction of religious buildings as 'a clear case of persecution as a crime against humanity'.[1539] The Trial Chamber commented that this destruction, 'when perpetrated with the requisite discriminatory intent, amounts to an attack on the very religious identity of a people. As such, it manifests a nearly pure expression of the notion of "crimes against humanity", for all of humanity is indeed injured by the destruction of a unique religious culture and its concomitant cultural objects'.[1540]

The Kordić Appeal Judgment considered that in order for the destruction of civilian property to amount to a crime of persecution as a crime against humanity the act must constitute 'a denial of or infringement upon a fundamental right laid down in international customary or treaty law'.[1541] According to the Kordić Appeals Judgment, deliberate attacks against civilian objects could constitute persecutions if the act, in isolation or in conjunction with other acts, was of gravity equal to the other crimes listed in Article 5 of the ICTY Statute.[1542]

1537   Ibid.

1538   Ibid., para. 92.

1539   Ibid., para. 206 (citing Nuremberg Judgment, pp. 248, 302; 1991 ILC Report, p. 268: persecution may take the form of the 'systematic destruction of monuments or buildings representative of a particular social, religious, cultural or other group').

1540   Kordić Appeals Judgment, para. 207.

1541   Ibid., para. 103.

1542   Ibid., para. 104–5. Under the heading, 'Crimes Against Humanity', Article 5 of the Statute states, 'The International Tribunal shall have the power to prosecute persons responsible for the following crimes when committed in armed conflict, whether international or internal in character, and directed against any civilian population:
(a) murder; (b) extermination; (c) enslavement; (d) deportation; (e) imprisonment; (f) torture; (g) rape; (h) persecutions on political, racial and religious grounds; (i) other inhumane acts'.

C. The Prosecutor v. Biljana Plavšić[1543]

The next case where the accused was convicted for the destruction of cultural property under Article 3, Section D, was the case of the former Serbian President Biljana Plavšić, which was decided in February 2003.[1544] Plavšić was convicted for persecution as a crime against humanity, and this conviction was based on, *inter alia*, the destruction of several cultural monuments and religious sites in the Foca, Visegrad and Zvornik municipalities. The Trial Chamber emphasized that these monuments, some of which dated from the Middle Ages, were 'culturally, historically and regionally significant sites', and described one of them, the Alidza mosque in Foca, as a 'pearl amongst the cultural heritage in the [Balkan] part of Europe'.[1545] Because the conviction was based on the defendant's guilty plea, however, the Trial Chamber's judgment did not contain any extensive discussion of the applicable law, and so it is of limited use to students of the Tribunal's jurisprudence on the protection of cultural property.

D. The Prosecutor v. Mladen Naletilić and Vinko Nartinović[1546]

The next case which raised the issue of cultural property, and which followed on the heels of *Plavšić*, was that of Mladen Naletilić and Vinko Nartinović, decided in March 2003.[1547] The two defendants were convicted, under Article 3, Section D, for ordering the destruction of a mosque in the village of Dosanj in Croatia. In entering the conviction, the Trial Chamber reiterated the requirement, first announced in *Blaškić*, that, to be punishable as a violation of the laws or customs of war, the institutions of religion or education which were damaged or destroyed must not have been used for military purposes at the time at issue.[1548] What is most noteworthy about the judgment in *Naletilić and Nartinović*, however, is that it expressly rejected *Blaškić*'s requirement that the institutions targeted need to be located outside of the immediate vicinity of military objectives. Relying on Article 27 of the Hague Regulations, the Trial Chamber concluded instead that the mere fact that a given institution is in the immediate vicinity of military objective does not justify its destruction.[1549]

1543   Meron (2005), p. 49.
1544   *Prosecutor* v. *Plavšić*, IT-00-39&40/1, Sentencing Judgment, 27 February 2003.
1545   Ibid., para. 31.
1546   Meron (2005), p. 49.
1547   *Prosecutor* v. *Naletilić and Nartinović*, IT-98-34-T, Judgment, 31 March 2003.
1548   Ibid., para. 603.
1549   Ibid., para. 604.

E. The Prosecutor v. Milomir Stakić[1550]

The next decision, in the case of Milomir Stakić, was issued a few months later, in July 2003.[1551] The defendant was convicted for having played a leading role in the destruction or willful damage of seven mosques and two Catholic churches located in the city of Prijedor, in the central part of Bosnia and Herzegovina, and in nearby villages. The Trial Chamber described these buildings as both religious and cultural institutions. Stakić was not charged under Article 3, Section D, so he was convicted only for persecution as a crime against humanity. The Trial Chamber's reasoning followed closely that of *Kordić and Čerkez*, on which it relied. The Trial Chamber cited both the case-law of the Nuremberg Tribunal and the 1991 Report of the International Law Commission in support of its conclusion that the destruction of religious buildings can amount to persecution as a crime against humanity.[1552] Quoting the decision in *Kordić and Čerkez*, the Trial Chamber stated that '[this] act, when perpetrated with the requisite discriminatory intent, amounts to an attack on the very religious identity of a people'.[1553] The Trial Chamber's finding of persecution is currently under Appeal on the grounds that the Trial Chamber erroneously found that the attack was widespread.[1554]

The Appellant denied that the attacks were systematic and submitted instead that they were isolated 'sporadic, random and uncontrollable, or committed by unrelated third parties'. The Appellant had failed to demonstrate to the Appeals Chamber how the Trial Chamber's findings of the existence of a systematic attack were unreasonable in light of all the evidence. Therefore, the Appeals Chamber found that there was no basis on which to overturn the finding by the Trial Chamber that the attack was systematic. Having found that the Trial Chamber did not err in concluding that a systematic attack occurred, the Appeals Chamber found that, for reasons of judicial economy, it was not necessary to address whether such an attack was also widespread. The related submissions were accordingly dismissed.[1555]

1550   Meron (2005), pp. 49–50.

1551   *Prosecutor v. Stakić*, IT-97-24-T, Judgment, 31 July 2003.

1552   Ibid., para. 766.

1553   Ibid., para. 767 (quoting *Kordić* Trial Judgment, para. 207) (internal quotation marks omitted).

1554   *Prosecutor v. Stakić*, IT-97-24-A, Milomar Stakić's Brief in Reply, 20 May 2004, para. 88–94.

1555   *Prosecutor v. Stakic*, IT-97-24-A, Summary of appeals judgment for Milomir Stakić, 22 March 2006.

F. The Old Town Dubrovnik Cases: Miodrag Jokić and Pavle Strugar[1556]

The next decision was characterized by Professor Meron as 'perhaps the most interesting': the cases against Miodrag Jokić and Pavle Strugar. These cases are particularly significant to the issue of the protection of cultural property because they concern the shelling of the Old Town of Dubrovnik in Croatia. In 1975, the entire Old Town was declared a UNESCO World Cultural Heritage site pursuant to the 1972 Convention for the Protection of the World Cultural and Natural Heritage.

The decision in the case of Miograd Jokić was issued in March 2004,[1557] and the sentence is currently under appeal.[1558] The defendant pleaded guilty to the charge, made under Article 3, Section D of the Statute, of having destroyed or willfully damaged institutions dedicated to religious, charity, education, and the arts and sciences, as well as historic monuments and works of art and science located in Dubrovnik. The indictment contained a detailed list of many historical buildings in the Old Town that had either been destroyed or damaged. Jokić was at the time commander of the Ninth Naval Sector of the Bosnian Serb Army, and, alongside others, he conducted the military campaign aimed at Dubrovnik.

In particular, Jokić admitted that, on 6 December 1991, the Yugoslavian forces under his command fired hundreds of shells upon the Old Town of Dubrovnik as part of their military campaign. Jokić also admitted that, at the time of these actions, he was aware of the protected status that the Old Town enjoyed as a UNESCO World Cultural Heritage site and of the fact that a number of buildings in the Old Town, as well as the Old Town's walls, were marked with the symbols mandated by the 1954 Hague Convention for the Protection of Cultural Property.

In applying Section D of Article 3 to these circumstances, the Trial Chamber noted that the protection of cultural property reflected in that provision of the Statute of the International Tribunal had a long history in international law. The Chamber emphasized Articles 27 and 56 of the Hague Regulations (annexed to the 1907 Fourth Hague Convention Respecting the Laws and Customs of War on Land) and Article 5 of the 1907 Hague

---

1556   Meron (2005), pp. 50–54.
1557   *Prosecutor v. Jokić*, IT-01-42/1-S, Sentencing Judgment, 18 March 2004.
1558   Prosecutor v. Jokić, IT-01-42/1-A, 30 August 2005. Mr. Jokić appealed the sentencing judgment, but his sentence of seven years' imprisonment was affirmed.

Convention Concerning Bombardment by Naval Forces in Time of War.[1559] The Trial Chamber stressed, however, that it was the 1954 Convention for the Protection of Cultural Property that strengthened the safeguards for cultural property in times of armed conflict.[1560] In particular, the Trial Chamber explained that the Convention's requirement of 'general protection' (as opposed to 'special protection', accorded to heritage listed in the International Register) imposed duties to safeguard and respect cultural property.

The Trial Chamber then turned to more recent international instruments concerned with the protection of cultural property. The Chamber discussed the Preamble to the 1972 UNESCO World Heritage Convention, which provides that the 'deterioration or disappearance of any item of the cultural or natural heritage *constitutes a harmful impoverishment of the heritage of all the nations of the world*.[1561] The 1972 Convention was of relevance because, as the Trial Chamber noted, the Old Town of Dubrovnik was listed as a World Heritage site.[1562] The Jokić Chamber also cited Article 53 of the 1977 Additional Protocol I and Article 16 of the Additional Protocol II to the Geneva Conventions of 1949. These articles, the Trial Chamber explained, reiterated the duty to protect cultural property and expanded the scope of the protection by outlawing 'any acts of hostility directed against the historic monuments, works of art or places of worship which constitute the cultural or spiritual heritage of peoples'.[1563] The Trial Chamber also explained that, under the Additional Protocols, direct attacks against protected heritage were prohibited irrespective of whether they resulted in actual damage.[1564]

Turning to the facts of the case, the Trial Chamber emphasized that the entire Old Town of Dubrovnik was considered, at the time at issue, 'an especially important part of the world cultural heritage. It was, among other things, an outstanding architectural ensemble illustrating a significant stage in human history'.[1565] The Chamber therefore concluded that '[the] shelling attack on the Old Town was an attack not only against the history and heritage of the region, but also against the cultural heritage of humankind.'[1566] Notably, the Trial Chamber explained that the protection

---

1559   Ibid., para. 47.
1560   Ibid., para. 48.
1561   Ibid., para. 49 (quoting the 1972 UNESCO World Heritage Convention) (internal quotation marks omitted) (emphasis added by the Jokić Trial Chamber).
1562   Ibid.
1563   Ibid., para. 50.
1564   Ibid. (citing ICRC Commentary to Additional Protocol I, para. 2067, 2069–72).
1565   Ibid., para. 51.
1566   Ibid.

accorded to Dubrovnik was not limited to individual buildings identified as having particular historical value. Rather, the fact that the Old Town received protected status in its entirety reflected the concern of the international community with the preservation of Dubrovnik as a living historical and cultural artefact. As the Trial Chamber stated, 'the Old Town was a "living city" . . . and the existence of its population was intimately intertwined with its ancient heritage. Residential buildings within the city also formed part of the World Cultural Heritage site, and were thus protected'.[1567]

Also of note is the Trial Chamber's apt reminder that the possibility of restoring the damaged historical buildings does not mitigate the gravity of the conduct directed at their destruction: 'Restoration of buildings of this kind, when possible, can never return the buildings to their state prior to the attack because a certain amount of original, historically authentic material will have been destroyed, thus affecting the inherent value of the buildings'.[1568]

In its conclusion, the Trial Chamber addressed the issue of what bearing Dubrovnik's status as a specially protected World Heritage site had on the criminality of the defendant's conduct. The Trial Chamber concluded that 'since it is a serious violation of international humanitarian law to attack civilian buildings, it is a crime of even greater seriousness to direct an attack on an especially protected site, such as the Old Town, constituted of civilian buildings and resulting in extensive destruction within the site'.[1569] In addition, the Trial Chamber stressed that the extent of effected destruction must be taken into account in assessing the gravity of the defendant's criminal act. As the Chamber explained, 'the attack on the Old Town was particularly destructive. Damage was caused to more than 100 buildings, including various segments of the Old Town's walls, ranging from complete destruction to damage to non-structural parts.'[1570] For these two reasons, the Trial Chamber concluded, '[the] unlawful attack on the Old Town must therefore be viewed as especially wrongful conduct'.[1571]

The Judgment in the *Pavle Strugar* case was issued on 31 January 2005.[1572] Strugar was convicted, *inter alia*, of the charge, made under Article 3, Section D of the Statute, of destruction or willful damage done to institutions

---

1567 Ibid.
1568 Ibid., para. 52.
1569 Ibid., para. 53.
1570 Ibid.
1571 Ibid.
1572 *Prosecutor v. Strugar*, IT-01-42-T, Judgment, 31 January 2005 [hereinafter Strugar Trial Judgment].

dedicated to religion, charity and education, the arts and sciences, historic monuments and works of art and science.[1573]

The Accused's culpability arose out of the position he then held as commander of the Second Operational Group. According to the Trial Chamber Judgment, forces of the 3rd Battalion of the 472nd Motorised Brigade (3/472 mtbr), under the command of Captain Vladimir Kovačević, unlawfully shelled the Old Town on 6 December 1991. The battalion commanded by Captain Kovačević was at the time directly subordinated to the Ninth Military Naval Sector, commanded by Admiral Miodrag Jokić, and the Ninth Military Naval Sector, in turn, was a component of the Second Operational Group, commanded by the Accused. Pavle Strugar was charged under Article 3(d) of the Statute with causing the damage to or destruction of 116 buildings and structures during the attack of the Old Town of Dubrovnik on 6 December 1991.[1574]

Early in the trial of the case, the Accused challenged the jurisdiction of the Tribunal over the offences on the grounds that the Additional Protocols that formed the basis of the Prosecution's charges did not apply to the parties of the conflict at the relevant time.[1575] Rather than addressing the application of the Additional Protocols as conventional law, the Appeals Chamber held that the principles prohibiting attacks on civilians and unlawful attacks on civilian objects articulated in Articles 51 and 52 of Additional Protocol I and Article 13 of Additional Protocol II to the Geneva Conventions were customary international law at the time of the alleged conduct. The Appeals Chamber noted that these articles of the Additional Protocols are a 'reaffirmation and reformulation' of the 'norms of customary international law designed to prohibit attacks on civilians and civilian objects'.[1576] As such, these articles do not contain new principles, but instead they codify principles found in earlier law.[1577] Significantly, the Appeals Chamber held that those principles constitute a customary law basis for charging and jurisdiction under

---

1573 *Prosecutor v. Strugar*, IT-01-42-PT, Third Amended Indictment, 10 December 2003.

1574 See *Prosecutor v. Strugar*, IT-01-42-T, Decision on Rule 98*bis* Motion on Acquittal, 21 June 2004 (substantially reducing the original list of 450 buildings listed in Schedule II to the Indictment).

1575 *Prosecutor v. Pavle Strugar, et. al,* IT-01-42-PT, Decision on Defense Preliminary Motion Challenging Jurisdiction, 7 July 2002, para. 17–22 ('Strugar Trial Decision on Jurisdiction'), para. 4.

1576 *Prosecutor v. Pavle Strugar, et. al,* IT-01-42-PT, Decision on Defense Preliminary Motion Challenging Jurisdiction, 7 July 2002, para. 17–22 ('Strugar Trial Decision on Jurisdiction').

1577 *Strugar* Trial Decision on Jurisdiction, paras. 17–19.

Article 3 of the Statute.[1578] This Decision permits the Prosecution not to plead an independent basis in conventional law for the offence under Article 3, Section D of the Statute on the grounds that the offence was recognized in customary international law at the relevant time.[1579]

To determine the elements of the offence under Article 3, Section D, the Trial Chamber in *Strugar* examined the sources of that provision in international customary and treaty law, including Article 27 of the Hague Regulations, the 1954 Hague Convention, Article 53 of Additional Protocol I, and Article 16 of Additional Protocol II. The Trial Chamber found that the property that is subject to Article 3(d) protection is property protected by all of the aforementioned instruments, although there may be precise differences in the terminology used in the Hague Convention of 1954 and the Additional Protocols.[1580] The Trial Chamber considered this property cumulatively to be the 'cultural property' subject to protection under Article 3(d) of the Statute.[1581]

Examining the *actus reus* of the offence under Article 3(d) of the Statute, the Trial Chamber determined that it necessarily involves an act of hostility directed against cultural property, which under the terms of the Statute must result in actual damage to, or destruction of the protected property.[1582] The Trial Judgment discussed the conventional law treatment of an exception for cultural property used for military purposes and noted that the Hague Regulations protect cultural property unless it is used for military purposes,[1583] the 1954 Hague Convention provides protection but with a 'waiver' from the Convention's obligations, though only when 'military necessity imperatively requires such a waiver',[1584] and the Additional Protocols to the Geneva Conventions that prohibit acts of hostility against cultural property but 'make no explicit reference to military necessity'.[1585] The Trial Chamber speculated that the Additional Protocols might not permit

---

1578   *Prosecutor v. Pavle Strugar, et. al,* IT-01-42-PT, Decision on Interlocutory Appeal, 22 November 2002, para. 9, 13 ('Strugar Interlocutory Appeal Decision').

1579   See also *Prosecutor v. Hadžihasanović,* IT-01-47-AR73.3, Decision on Joint Defence Interlocutory Appeal of Trial Chamber Decision on Rule 98*Bis* Motions for Acquittal, 11 March 2005.

1580   Compare Hague Convention of 1954 (protecting property 'of great importance to the cultural heritage of every people') with Additional Protocols (applying to 'historic monuments, works of art or places of worship which constitute the cultural or spiritual heritage of peoples').

1581   Strugar Trial Judgment, para. 307.

1582   Ibid., para. 308.

1583   Ibid. (noting Article 27 of the 1907 Hague Regulations, which reads in part: 'provided they are not being used at the time for military purposes').

1584   Ibid., para 309 (quoting Article 4, para. 1 of 1954 Hague Convention).

1585   Ibid., para. 309.

a military necessity exception, but ultimately concluded that the established jurisprudence of the Tribunal confirmed the 'military purposes' exception, such that 'the protection accorded to cultural property is lost where such property is used for military purposes'.[1586] In the *Strugar* case, the Trial Chamber concluded that the facts of the case indicated that the shelling of Old Town Dubrovnik could not have been premised on military necessity, and therefore the Trial Chamber did not need to determine whether the exception to the rule of protection applied.

The Strugar Trial Chamber examined the difference between the Blaškić Trial Judgment and the Naletilić Trial Judgment regarding the use of the immediate surroundings of cultural property for military purposes, and endorsed the Naletilić Trial Judgment conclusion that it is 'the use of the cultural property and not its immediate surroundings that determines whether and when the cultural property would lose its protection'.[1587] However, the Trial Chamber noted that in cases in which military activities or installations are in the immediate vicinity of the cultural property 'the practical result may be that it cannot be established that the acts which caused destruction of or damage to the cultural property were "directed against" that cultural property,' rather than the legitimate military objectives in its immediate vicinity.[1588]

The Trial Chamber concurred with previous jurisprudence of the Tribunal that the necessary *mens rea* of the offence under Article 3(d) is that the perpetrator must have acted with 'a direct intent to damage or destroy the property in question', but the Trial Chamber questioned, without deciding, whether indirect intent was sufficient *mens rea* for this crime.[1589]

Applying the law to the facts of the case, the Trial Chamber found that all the elements of the offence of willful damage of cultural property were established in the case. There was an artillery attack by the Yugoslav Peoples' Army (JNA) forces under the command of Pavle Strugar on the Old Town of Dubrovnik on 6 December 1991, and 52 of the 116 buildings and structures alleged to have sustained damage were in fact damaged during the 6 December shelling by the JNA.[1590] Six of these buildings were destroyed. The Trial Chamber noted that because the Old Town of Dubrovnik had been entered onto the World Heritage List in 1979, every building of the

---

1586   Ibid., para. 310.
1587   Ibid. (finding support in Article 27 of the 1907 Hague Regulations, Article 16 of the Second Protocol of the 1954 Hague Convention, and Naletilić Trial Judgment, para. 604).
1588   Ibid., para. 310.
1589   Ibid., para. 311.
1590   Kordić Trial Judgment, para. 317.

Old Town, including its walls, are properly described as cultural property. The Trial Chamber found that there were no military objectives in the immediate vicinity of the 52 buildings and structures destroyed or damaged on 6 December 1991, nor were any of the buildings being used for military purposes, therefore the destruction or damage was not justified by military necessity.

Regarding the criminal responsibility of Pavle Strugar, the Trial Chamber examined whether he was personally responsible or responsible as the commander of the Second Operational Group for the conduct of the JNA forces that actually perpetrated the offences. The Trial Chamber found that all of the JNA forces involved were subject to Ninth Military Naval Sector command, which was under the operational command of the Second Operational Group, therefore Strugar had both legal and effective control of the JNA forces that shelled the Old Town of Dubrovnik. The Trial Chamber found that at about 0700 on 6 December, Strugar was put on notice that his JNA artillery was shelling the Old Town by a communication from Admiral Jokić, but he failed to order the attacks stopped at that time. The Trial Chamber found that no steps were taken by Strugar to ensure the attacks were stopped until 1115, when he issued an order to stop the attack to some, but not all of the JNA artillery units. The Trial Chamber therefore found sufficient evidence that Strugar bore command responsibility under Article 7(3) of the Statute for the destruction of cultural property.

In its Appeal Judgment of 17 July 2008, the Tribunal indicated among others in relation to the destruction of cultural property the following:

> (b) Destruction or Willful Damage of Cultural Property (Count 6)
>
> 277. The crime of destruction or willful damage of cultural property under Article 3(d) of the Statute is *lex specialis* with respect to the offence of unlawful attacks on civilian objects. The *mens rea* requirement of this crime is therefore also met if the acts of destruction or damage were willfully (i.e. either deliberately or through recklessness) directed against such 'cultural property'.
>
> 278. The Trial Chamber held that 'a perpetrator must act with a direct intent to damage or destroy the property in question' and that the issue as to whether 'indirect intent' could also be sufficient for this crime did not arise in the circumstances of the case.
>
> 279. On the basis of the fact that the entire Old Town of Dubrovnik was added to the World Heritage List in 1979, the Trial Chamber concluded that each structure or building in the Old Town fell within

the scope of Article 3(d) of the Statute. The Trial Chamber also noted that the protective UNESCO emblems were visible from the JNA positions on Žarkovica and elsewhere. Strugar does not allege that any of these findings are erroneous. Hence, the Trial Chamber reasonably concluded that the direct perpetrators of the crime were aware of the protected status of the cultural property in the Old Town and that the attack on this cultural property was deliberate and not justified by any military necessity. Consequently, his submission that the Trial Chamber's findings on the *mens rea* of the direct perpetrators of the crime do not meet the standard of direct intent must fail.

280. In light of the foregoing, Strugar's challenges with respect to the Trial Chamber's findings on the required form of *mens rea* for the crimes of attacks on civilians and destruction or wilful damage to cultural property are dismissed in their entirety.[1591]

G. The Prosecutor v. Radoslav Brđanin[1592]

The last decision mentioned in the Theodor Meron's presentation was the case against Radoslav Brđanin, who was charged with 'the destruction of, or willful damage to, Bosnian Muslim and Bosnian Croat religious and cultural buildings' as an offence under Article 3(d) of the Statute.[1593] The Trial Chamber found that 'Muslim and Roman Catholic institutions dedicated to religion' in the Serb-controlled region of Bosnia known as the Autonomous Region of Krajina (ARK) 'were targeted and suffered severe damage during the summer months of 1992'.[1594] At that time, Brđanin 'held key leadership positions', including the position of President of the ARK Crisis Staff, and 'was situated near the highest echelons of the Bosnian Serb leadership and wielded great power in the ARK'.[1595]

The Trial Chamber noted that institutions dedicated to religion are protected under customary international law, Articles 27 and 56 of the Hague Regulations, Article 53 of Additional Protocol I and Article 16 of Additional

---

1591 *Prosecutor v. Pavle Strugar.* Appeal Trial Judgment of 17 July 2008, IT-01-42-A, p. 104, para. 277–280. (No footnotes reprinted.)

1592 Meron (2005), pp. 54–55.

1593 *Prosecutor v. Brđanin*, IT-99-36-PT, Sixth Amended Indictment, 9 December 2003, para. 47(3)(b).

1594 *Prosecutor v.Brđanin*, IT-99-36-T, Judgment, 1 September 2004 ('Brdanin Trial Judgment'), para. 1022.

1595 Brđanin Trial Judgment, para. 286, pp. 291–92.

Protocol II to the Geneva Conventions.[1596] Religious institutions, the Trial Chamber discussed, are presumed to have a civilian character and therefore share general prohibitions against attacks on civilian objects.[1597] The Brđanin Trial Judgment notes that civilian objects can only be attacked when they become a military objective, such that they 'by their nature, location, purpose or use make an effective contribution to military action and whose total or partial destruction, capture or neutralization, in the circumstances ruling the time, offers a definite military advantage'.[1598]

The Brđanin Trial Chamber held that because religious institutions 'enjoy the minimum protection afforded to civilian objects' the requisite *mens rea* for the offence 'should be equivalent to that required for the destruction or damage of property under Article 3(b)', which must have been either intentional, 'with the knowledge and will of the proscribed result or in reckless disregard of the substantial likelihood of the destruction of the destruction or damage'.[1599] Although there was no evidence to establish that the Accused had ordered or instigated the attacks on religious institutions, the Trial Chamber found that he was aware of the Bosnian Serb attacks on non-Serb areas, including Muslim and Catholic institutions, and, through his leadership roles, aided and abetted the physical perpetrators of the destruction.[1600]

The Trial Chamber found that willful damage done to both Muslim and Roman Catholic religious buildings and institutions ('Religious Buildings') was committed by Bosnian Serb forces, and that the Religious Buildings were not used for military purposes and stated that Bosnian Serb forces were responsible for such acts in specific locations. In the Appeal judgement, the Tribunal stated:

> 337. Turning now to the question of whether Religious Buildings had not been used for military purposes, the Appeals Chamber recalls that the Prosecution must establish that the destruction in question was not justified by military necessity; this cannot be presumed. Determining whether the Prosecution has fulfilled its burden of proof in a particular case necessarily requires that the trier of fact, considering all direct and circumstantial evidence, assess the factual context within which

---

1596 Ibid., para. 596.
1597 Ibid., para. 596 (discussing the general prohibition on attacks against civilians and civilian objects in Article 53 of Additional Protocol I).
1598 Ibid., para. 596 (citing Article 52 (2) of Additional Protocol I, and noting the article's status as customary international law).
1599 Ibid., para. 599.
1600 Ibid., para. 674–76.

the destruction occurred. Determining whether destruction occurred pursuant to military necessity involves a determination of what constitutes a military objective. Article 52 of Additional Protocol I contains a widely acknowledged definition of military objectives as being limited to 'those objects which by their nature, location, purpose or use make an effective contribution to military action and whose total or partial destruction, capture or neutralization, in the circumstances ruling at the time, offers a definite military advantage'.[1601]

The Appeal Chamber came to the conclusion that 'there is evidence that these sites were destroyed as part of the campaign to ethnically cleanse the area of its Muslim and Croat citizens'.[1602]

341. The various methods employed in damaging or destroying the institutions dedicated to religion in the various locations include: being targeted by a hand-held rocket launcher; mining, or destruction by explosives; shelling and arson; and the use of heavy machinery. The very manner in which many of the sites were damaged or destroyed, including the time required to mine churches, mosques, and minarets and to blow them up (or to set them on fire), suggests that these installations contained no military threat, but were instead systematically destroyed because of their religious significance to the ethnicities targeted. There is nothing to suggest that their destruction provided any kind of advantage in weakening the military forces opposing the Bosnian Serbs, favoured the Bosnian Serb position, or was otherwise justified by military necessity.[1603]

The Appeal Chamber concluded 'that the Trial Chamber did not err in finding Brianin responsible beyond reasonable doubt for aiding and abetting the crimes of (1) wanton destruction of cities, towns, and villages or devastation not justified by military necessity; and (2) destruction or willful damage done to religious institutions'.[1604]

1601   *Prosecutor v. Radoslav Brdanin*, Appeal Judgment, IT-99-36-A. 3 April 2007, p. 103, para. 337 (no footnotes reproduced).

1602   Ibid., p. 104, para. 340.

1603   Ibid., p. 105, para. 341. (No footnotes reproduced.)

1604   Ibid., p. 108, para. 351.

FUTURE CASES

In his article on the Tribunal decisions, Theodor Meron indicated the variety of indictments currently pending before the Yugoslavia Tribunal which contain allegations of damage or destruction inflicted upon cultural property. Some of these cases are currently at trial, while others are only at a pre-trial stage. Some of the indictments charge offences against cultural property are both violations of laws and customs of war under Article 3, Section D and persecution as a crime against humanity under Article 5.

Meron mentioned the following indictments: Vojislav Šešelj, Milan Martić,[1605] Paško Ljubičić, and the indictment against Slobodan Milošević with respect to Croatia.

The second group of indictments charge these offences only as persecution as a crime against humanity: indictments against Slobodan Milošević with respect to Kosovo, and the indictments against Goran Hadžić,[1606] Jadranko Prlić et al.,[1607] Nikola Šainović, Dragoljub Ojdanić and Momcilo Krajišnik.

Given the number of indictments that raise the issue of the protection of cultural property, and given the fact that many of these indictments contain detailed charges of alleged offences against cultural property, Professor Meron considered with some confidence that there is a real potential for a development of a rich and sophisticated jurisprudence on this issue in the Yugoslav Tribunal.[1608]

Conclusion of Professor Theodor Meron

In conclusion, I would like to observe that, most importantly, the case-law of the Yugoslavia Tribunal with respect to the protection of cultural property

---

1605 For example, Milan Martić was convicted among others of the crime of destruction or willful damage done to institutions dedicated to education or religion as violation of the laws and customs of war. Chamber I of the Yugoslav Tribunal, Judgment IT-95-11-T of 12 June 2007, pp. 36–37, 173, para. 96–98, 480.

1606 *Prosecutor v. Goran Hadzis*, Case No. IT-04-75-I. Indictment of 21 May 2004 against Goran Hadzic: 'This intentional and wanton destruction and plunder included the plunder and destruction of homes and religious and cultural buildings, and took place in the following towns and villages: Dalj, Dalj Planina, Celija, Vukovar, Erdut, Erdut Planina, Aljmas, Lovas, Sarengrad, Bapska and Tovarnik.'

1607 *Prosecutor v. Jadranko Prlic* et al, Indictment 2 March 2004, Count 21: destruction or wilful damage done to institutions dedicated to religion or education, a violation of the laws or customs of war, punishable under Statute Articles 3(d), 7(1) and 7(3) (as alleged in para. 15–17, 39, 53, 68, 83, 84, 97, 116, 152, 162, 163, 165, 166 and 179–81).

1608 Meron (2005), p. 55.

shows that provisions in international legal instruments designed to safeguard our historical and cultural heritage can be effectively enforced by the courts. The 1954 Convention, whose anniversary we commemorate today, is of particular importance in this regard. It reaffirmed the importance of protecting cultural property in wartime, and it considerably strengthened that protection. The norms elaborated by the Convention played an important role in several of the decisions which I described to you today. By firmly placing the offences against cultural property not only among wrongs leading to state responsibility but also among crimes punishable by international law as affecting the interests of the world community, and by holding individuals responsible for them accountable, our Tribunal has made a significant contribution to the protection of cultural property in armed conflicts. The prominence which this issue has achieved in our jurisprudence should help to prevent the commission of these crimes in the future.

In terms of the doctrinal contribution which our Tribunal has made to the international law protecting cultural property during the times of military conflicts, I would single out the notion, elaborated in the several cases I have discussed, that the destruction of institutions dedicated to religion or education can, if committed with the requisite discriminatory intent, amount to persecution as a crime against humanity. (Of course, where this intent is absent, the destruction can still amount to a war crime.) One may perhaps object to this crime against humanity approach on the ground that it tends to diminish the importance of protecting cultural property *per se*, viewing attacks on this property mainly as a form of a discriminatory attack directed against individuals. I would argue, however, that the characterization of such attacks against cultural or religious institutions as crimes against humanity is simply recognition of the importance of these institutions to the identity and the development of an individual. Without the protection of our cultural or religious patrimony the link with our heritage is severed, and with it is severed our ability to define our identity. By protecting our cultural heritage, the 1954 Convention protects the autonomy of the individual and the diversity of humankind, and the jurisprudence of our Tribunal has been faithful to these noble ideals.

It deserves mentioning that under the Statute adopted by the Security Council, our Tribunal has jurisdiction over crimes against humanity only if they were committed in the course of the armed conflict in the former Yugoslavia.[1609] As our Appeals Chamber has explained, however, this is

---

1609   *See Prosecutor* v. *Tadić*, IT-94-1-AR72, Decision on the Defence Motion for Interlocutory Appeal on Jurisdiction, 2 October 1995, para. 141.

a jurisdictional limitation specific to our Tribunal, and not a requirement mandated by customary international law.[1610] Under customary law, crimes against humanity can be committed in times of peace as well as in times of war. The doctrinal contribution that our Tribunal made to the law protecting cultural property from wanton destruction, by characterizing this destruction as a crime against humanity and not only as a war crime, can therefore be applied by other courts to criminalize the destruction of cultural property in time of peace. This is particularly relevant in today's world where terrorist and other attacks by non-governmental armed groups are unfortunately common, and where the line between armed conflicts and discriminatory attacks against a civilian population is often difficult to draw. By viewing the destruction of cultural property as a crime directed against individuals, our Tribunal has pointed to a potentially new way of enhancing the reach and the thrust of the 1954 Convention.

1610 Ibid.

1998 Rome Statute of the International Criminal Court and the Relevant Case-law (Articles 8(2)(b) (ix)) and 8(2)(e)(iv)

The road to the establishment of the International Criminal Court (ICC) has been long. Several attempts to establish it were made at different points in history. One of the first codifications of the laws of war, Francis Lieber's *Instructions for the Government of Armies of the United States in the Field*, stated that the inhuman treatment of civilians, pillage, abuse of prisoners and other atrocities are proscribed, and would be followed by sanctions in national courts.[1611]

The unsuccessful Leipzig Trials after the First World War were followed by an effort to create an international criminal court within the League of Nations by adoption of the Convention for the Creation of an International Criminal Court,[1612] which never came into force. Such experiences led the Allies during the Second World War to send a warning to Nazis leaders in the form of the Moscow Declaration of 1 November 1943, the creation of the United Nations Commission for the Investigation of War Crimes, and finally the adoption of the Charter of the International Military Tribunal annexed to the Agreement for the Prosecution and Punishment of Major War Criminals of the European Axis.[1613] In December 1945, the four Allied powers adopted the Control Council Law No. 10 which provided the legal basis for trials before military tribunals.[1614] The International Military Tribunal for the Far East (Tokyo 1948) was established by a special proclamation of General MacArthur as the Supreme Commander in the Far East for the Allied Powers.

The ILC prepared the Principles of International Law Recognized by the Charter of the Nuremberg Tribunal, which were adopted by Resolution 95(I) of the United Nations General Assembly at its first session on 11 December 1946.[1615] The ILC started to work on the 'Code of Crimes Against the Peace and Security of Mankind' and the General Assembly created a committee charged with drafting the statute of the international criminal

---

1611   General Order No. 100, 24 April 1863.
1612   League of Nations, Official Journal, Special Supplement, No. 156 (1936), LN Doc. C.547 (I).M.384(I).1937.V (1938)
1613   United Nations Treaty Series, Vol. 82, pp. 280–311.
1614   Control Council Law No. 10, Punishment of Persons Guilty of War Crimes, Crimes Against Peace and Against Humanity, 20 December 1945, *Official Gazette of the Control Council for Germany*, No. 3, 31 January 1946, pp. 50–55.
1615   United Nations Resolutions adopted by the General Assembly during the second part of its first session from 23 October to 15 December 1946, Lake Success, New York, 1947, p. 188.

court. In 1996, the Commission adopted the final draft of the Code which played an important role in the preparation of the Statute of the International Criminal Court. Two ad hoc tribunals were created in 1993 and 1994.

In this short chapter, we shall concentrate on the ICC Statute, which, subject to ratification, acceptance or approval, was adopted by the United Nations Conference of Plenipotentiaries on the Establishment of an International Criminal Court on 17 July 1998 and opened for signature on 17 July 1998, in accordance with its provisions, until 17 October 1998 at the Ministry of Foreign Affairs of Italy and, subsequently, until 31 December 2000, at UN Headquarters in New York. The same instrument was also opened for accession in accordance with its provisions. The Conference also decided to create a Preparatory Commission for the International Criminal Court, which had to prepare proposals for practical arrangements for the establishment and coming into operation of the Court, including in particular the draft texts of Elements of Crimes.

The Rome Statute includes two important provisions concerning the protection of cultural property. The Elements of Crimes, provided for in Article 9 of the Rome Statute,[1616] elaborate the definitions of offences in Articles 6, 7 and 8 of the Statute.

ARTICLES 8(2)(B)(IX) AND 8(2)(E)(IV) OF THE ROME STATUTE

Article 8. War crimes

1. The Court shall have jurisdiction in respect of war crimes in particular when committed as a part of a plan or policy or as part of a large scale commission of such crimes.

2. For the purpose of this Statute, 'war crimes' means:

   (a) Grave breaches of the Geneva Conventions of 12 August 1949, namely, any of the following acts against persons or property protected under the provisions of the relevant Geneva Convention:

   [...]

1616 Article 9 Elements of Crimes

1. Elements of Crimes shall assist the Court in the interpretation and application of Articles 6, 7 and 8. They shall be adopted by a two-thirds majority of the members of the Assembly of States Parties.

2. Amendments to the Elements of Crimes may be proposed by: (a) Any State Party; (b) The judges acting by an absolute majority; (c) The Prosecutor. Such amendments shall be adopted by a two-thirds majority of the members of the Assembly of States Parties.

3. The Elements of Crimes and amendments thereto shall be consistent with this Statute.

(b) Other serious violations of the laws and customs applicable in international armed conflict, within the established framework of international law, namely, any of the following acts:

[...]

(ix) Intentionally directing attacks against buildings dedicated to religion, education, art, science or charitable purposes, historic monuments, hospitals and places where the sick and wounded are collected, provided they are not military objectives;

[...]

(c) In the case of an armed conflict not of an international character, serious violations of Article 3 common to the four Geneva Conventions of 12 August 1949, namely, any of the following acts committed against persons taking no active part in the hostilities, including members of armed forces who have laid down their arms and those placed *hors de combat* by sickness, wounds, detention or any other cause:

[...]

(d) Paragraph 2(c) applies to armed conflicts not of an international character and thus does not apply to situations of internal disturbances and tensions, such as riots, isolated and sporadic acts of violence or other acts of a similar nature.

(e) Other serious violations of the laws and customs applicable in armed conflicts not of an international character, within the established framework of international law, namely, any of the following acts:

[...]

(iv) Intentionally directing attacks against buildings dedicated to religion, education, art, science or charitable purposes, historic monuments, hospitals and places where the sick and wounded are collected, provided they are not military objectives;

[...]

(f) Paragraph 2(e) applies to armed conflicts not of an international character and thus does not apply to situations of internal disturbances and tensions, such as riots, isolated and sporadic acts of violence or other acts of a similar nature. It applies to armed conflicts that take place in the territory of a State when there is protracted armed conflict between governmental authorities and organized armed groups or between such groups.

3. Nothing in paragraphs 2(c) and (d) shall affect the responsibility of a Government to maintain or re-establish law and order in the State or to defend the unity and territorial integrity of the State, by all legitimate means.

ELEMENTS OF CRIMES[1617]

Article 8(2)(b)(ix)

(ix) Intentionally directing attacks against buildings dedicated to religion, education, art, science or charitable purposes, historic monuments, hospitals and places where the sick and wounded are collected, provided they are not military objectives;

Text adopted by PrepCom[1618]

War crime of attacking protected objects[1619]

1. The perpetrator directed an attack.
2. The object of the attack was one or more buildings dedicated to religion, education, art, science or charitable purposes, historic

---

1617   As we indicated above, the Elements of Crimes are defined in Article 9 of the Rome Statute:
Article 9 Elements of Crimes
1. Elements of Crimes shall assist the Court in the interpretation and application of Articles 6, 7 and 8. They shall be adopted by a two-thirds majority of the members of the Assembly of States Parties.
2. Amendments to the Elements of Crimes may be proposed by: (a) Any State Party; (b) The judges acting by an absolute majority; (c) The Prosecutor. Such amendments shall be adopted by a two-thirds majority of the members of the Assembly of States Parties.
1618   In the following text we shall use the abbreviations:
AP: Additional Protocol
GC: Geneva Conventions
ICTY: The International Criminal Tribunal for the former Yugoslavia
PrepCom: Preparatory Committee.
1619   The presence in the locality of persons specially protected under the Geneva Conventions of 1949 or of police forces retained for the sole purpose of maintaining law and order does not by itself render the locality a military objective.

      monuments, hospitals or places where the sick and wounded are collected, which were not military objectives.

3. The perpetrator intended such building or buildings dedicated to religion, education, art, science or charitable purposes, historic monuments, hospitals or places where the sick and wounded are collected, which were not military objectives, to be the object of the attack.

4. The conduct took place in the context of and was associated with an international armed conflict.

5. The perpetrator was aware of factual circumstances that established the existence of an armed conflict.

Commentary[1620]

Travaux préparatoires/Understandings of the PrepCom

As in the case of all war crimes involving certain unlawful attacks, the PrepCom discussed whether this form of war crime required as a result actual damage to the objects mentioned. The majority of delegations were against a result requirement and this was eventually accepted. The material elements largely reproduce statutory language and were not controversial. The only addition to the statutory language is contained in a footnote, which is largely built upon the substance of Article 59(3) AP I. Given that Article 59 AP I applies to non-defended localities, some delegations questioned the relevance of that provision for this war crime. Nevertheless, the PrepCom eventually agreed to include the footnote. It was emphasized that the insertion of this footnote would not allow for an *a contrario* conclusion, that with regard to other crimes where the footnote is not included, the presence of persons specially protected under the Geneva Conventions of 1949 or of police forces retained for the sole purpose of maintaining law and order renders a locality a military objective. On the basis of this understanding, the footnote was acceptable.

      With regard to the interpretation of 'intentionally directing attacks against', see comments made under section Article 8(2)(b)(i), subsection '*Travaux préparatoires/ Understandings of the PrepCom*'.[1621]

1620 We reproduce the commentary from Dörmann et al. (2003), pp. 215–28.
1621 Ibid., pp. 130–47.

Legal basis of the war crime

The term 'intentionally directing attacks against buildings dedicated to religion, education, art, science or charitable purposes, historic monuments, hospitals and places where the sick and wounded are collected, provided they are not military objectives' is derived to a large extent from Articles 27 and 56 of the 1907 Hague Regulations and numerous provisions of the GC on the protection of hospitals and places where the sick and wounded are collected.

Remarks concerning the material element

In its judgment in the *Kordic and Cerkez* case the ICTY did not explicitly define the material elements. It did, however, make reference to Article 27 of the 1907 Hague Regulations, Article 53 AP I and Article 1 of the 1954 Cultural Property Convention, as well as to the Roerich Pact.[1622] In addition, it considered this crime to be a *lex specialis* with regard to attacks against civilian objects.[1623]

Attack

The term 'attack' is defined in Article 49(1) AP I as a 'means acts of violence against the adversary, whether in offence or in defense'.

As pointed out above, the concept of attack as defined in this provision refers to the use of armed force to carry out a military operation during the course of an armed conflict. Therefore, the terms 'offence' and 'defense' must be understood independently from the meaning attributed to them by the law regulating the recourse to force under the UN Charter.

Buildings dedicated to religion, education, art, science or charitable purposes, historic monuments

(a) General protection

The ICTY Prosecution defined the elements of the offence 'destruction or wilful damage to institutions dedicated to religion or education' under the ICTY Statute in the following terms:

1622   ICTY Judgment, *Prosecutor v. Dario Kordic and Mario Cerkez*, IT-95-14/2-T, para. 359 ff.
1623   Ibid., para. 361.

1. Institutions dedicated to religion or education were destroyed;
[...]
3. institutions destroyed or wilfully damaged were protected under international humanitarian law.[1624]

In one post-Second World War trial – the *Weizsacker and Others* case – the Military Tribunal referred to Article 56(2) of the 1907 Hague Regulations:

> All *seizure* of, destruction or wilful damage done to institutions of this character [religious and charitable], historic monuments, works of art and science, is forbidden, and should be made the subject of legal proceedings.[1625]

This general rule is still valid under customary international law and must be read in connection with Article 27 of the Hague Regulations:

> In sieges and bombardments all necessary steps must be taken to spare, as far as possible, buildings, dedicated to religion, art, science or charitable purposes, historic monuments, hospitals, and places where the sick and wounded are collected, provided they are not being used at the time for military purposes.
> It is the duty of the besieged to indicate the presence of such buildings or places by distinctive and visible signs, which shall be notified to the enemy beforehand.

However, a number of rules giving specific protection to specific objects have developed since then.

(b) Specific protections: cultural or religious objects

The following provision of AP I contains specific rules on historic monuments, works of art or places of worship:

> Art. 53:
> Without prejudice to the provisions of the Hague Convention for the Protection of Cultural Property in the Event of Aimed Conflict

---

1624 ICTY, Prosecutor's Pre-trial Brief, *The Prosecutor v. Dario Kordic and Mario* Cerkez, IT-95-14 / 2-PT, p. 49.
1625 In 16 AD 344 at 357.

of 14 May 1954, and of other relevant international instruments, it is prohibited:

> (a) to commit any acts of hostility directed against the historic monuments, works of art or places of worship which constitute the cultural or spiritual heritage of peoples;[1626]
>
> (b) to use such objects in support of the military effort;
>
> (c) to make such objects the object of reprisals.

As pointed out in the ICRC Commentary on this provision,

[the] protection laid down in this article is accorded 'without prejudice' to the provisions of other relevant international instruments. From the beginning of the discussions regarding Article 53 it was agreed that there was no need to revise the existing rules on the subject, but that the protection and respect for cultural objects should be confirmed. It was therefore necessary to state at the beginning of the article that it did not modify the relevant existing instruments. For example, this means that in case of a contradiction between this article and a rule of the 1954 Convention the latter is applicable, though of course only insofar as the Parties concerned are bound by that Convention. If one of the Parties is not bound by the Convention, Article 53 applies. Moreover, Article 53 applies even if all the Parties concerned are bound by another international instrument insofar as it supplements the rules of that instrument.

The Diplomatic Conference adopted Resolution 20, which stresses the fundamental importance of the Hague Convention of 1954, and states that the adoption of Article 53 will not detract from the application of that Convention in any way; moreover, it urges States which have not yet done so to become Parties to it.[1627]

1626　With regard to the phrase 'cultural or spiritual heritage of peoples' the ICRC Commentary states:
It was stated that the cultural or spiritual heritage covers objects whose value transcends geographical boundaries, and which are unique in character and are intimately associated with the history and culture of a people.
In general the adjective 'cultural' applies to historic monuments and works of art, while the adjective 'spiritual' applies to places of worship. However, this should not stop a temple from being attributed with a cultural value, or a historic monument or work of art from having a spiritual value. The discussions in the Diplomatic Conference confirmed this. However, whatever the case may be, the expression remains rather subjective. In case of doubt, reference should be made in the first place to the value or veneration ascribed to the object by the people whose heritage it is.
Thus all objects of sufficient artistic or religious importance to constitute the heritage of peoples are protected. See Wenger (1987), no. 2064 ff.

1627　Ibid., no. 2046 ff.

With regard to other instruments, especially the above-cited general rules as contained in the Hague Regulations, the Commentary points out:

> Even for States Parties to the Hague Convention of 1954 these provisions remain applicable to cultural property not covered by the more recent Convention.[1628]

Cultural Property

The Hague Convention of 1954 for the Protection of Cultural Property defines cultural property in Article 1 as follows:

> For the purposes of the present Convention, the term 'cultural property' shall cover, irrespective of origin or ownership:
> (a) movable or immovable property of great importance to the cultural heritage of every people, such as monuments of architecture, art or history, whether religious or secular; archaeological sites; groups of buildings which, as a whole, are of historical or artistic interest; works of art; manuscripts, books and other objects of artistic, historical or archaeological interest; as well as scientific collections and important collections of books or archives or of reproductions of the property defined above;
> (b) buildings whose main and effective purpose is to preserve or exhibit the movable cultural property defined in sub-paragraph (a) such as museums, large libraries and depositories of archives, and refuges intended to shelter, in the event of armed conflict, the movable cultural property defined in sub-paragraph (a);
> (c) centres containing a large amount of cultural property as defined in sub-paragraphs (a) and (b), to be known as 'centres containing monuments'.

A further indication, especially Article 4, which reads as follows:

> 1. The High Contracting Parties undertake to respect cultural property situated within their own territory as well as within the territory of other High Contracting Parties by refraining from

---

1628   Ibid., no. 2060.

any use of the property and its immediate surroundings or of the appliances in use for its protection for purposes which are likely to expose it to destruction or damage in the event of armed conflict; and by refraining from any act of hostility directed against such property.

2. The obligations mentioned in paragraph 1 of the present Article may be waived only in cases where military necessity imperatively requires such a waiver.

NB: The recently adopted Second Protocol to the Hague Convention of 1954 for the Protection of Cultural Property[1629] explains further the latter paragraph as follows:

> Article 6 Respect for cultural property
> With the goal of ensuring respect for cultural property in accordance with Article 4 of the Convention:
> (a) a waiver on the basis of imperative military necessity pursuant to Article 4 paragraph 2 of the Convention may only be invoked to direct an act of hostility against cultural property when and for as long as:
> (i) that cultural property has, by its function, been made into a military objective; and
> (ii) there is no feasible alternative available to obtain a similar military advantage to that offered by directing an act of hostility against that objective;
> (b) a waiver on the basis of imperative military necessity pursuant to Article 4 paragraph 2 of the Convention may only be invoked to use cultural property for purposes which are likely to expose it to destruction or damage when and for as long as no choice is possible between such use of the cultural property and another feasible method for obtaining a similar military advantage;

A special case is dealt with in Article 12:

> Immunity of cultural property under enhanced protection

1629 Second Protocol to the Hague Convention of 1954 for the Protection of Cultural Property in the Event of Armed Conflict adopted on 26 March 1999 (The Hague).

The Parties to a conflict shall ensure the immunity of cultural property under enhanced protection by refraining from making such property the object of attack or from any use of the property or its immediate surroundings in support of military action.

The AP I and the Second Protocol to the Hague Convention of 1954 for the Protection of Cultural Property contain specific criminality clauses: Article 85(4)(d) AP I states that

making the clearly recognized historic monuments, works of art or places of worship which constitute the cultural or spiritual heritage of peoples and to which special protection has been given by special arrangement, for example, within the framework of a competent international organization, the object of attack, causing as a result extensive destruction thereof, where there is no evidence of the violation by the adverse Party of Article 53, sub-paragraph (b) to use such objects in support of the military actions], and when such historic monuments, works of art and places of worship are not located in the immediate proximity of military objectives is a grave breach. Thereby it goes beyond the requirements of the 'normal' war crime derived from the Hague Regulations, making it a particularly serious war crime.

Article 15(1) of the Second Protocol to the Hague Convention of 1954 on the Protection of Cultural Property defines serious violations of this Protocol as follows:

1. Any person commits an offence within the meaning of this Protocol if that person intentionally and in violation of the Convention or this Protocol commits any of the following acts:
   (a) making cultural property under enhanced protection the object of attack;
   (b) using cultural property under enhanced protection or its immediate surroundings in support of military action;
   (c) extensive destruction or appropriation of cultural property protected under the Convention and this Protocol;
   (d) making cultural property protected under the Convention and this Protocol the object of attack;
   (e) theft, pillage or misappropriation of, or acts of vandalism directed against, cultural property protected under the Convention.

Para. (a) to (c) are in effect defined as grave breaches, since they result in mandatory universal jurisdiction (see Article 16(1) of the Protocol). Paras. (b) and (c) were seen by negotiators as new treaty rules, while para. (a) reflects Article 85(4) AP I. Paras. (d) and (e) were drafted as normal war crimes, reflecting existing customary international law.

Religious objects

Religious objects may fall under the above-cited protections defined in AP I or the Hague Convention of 1954 on the Protection of Cultural Property if they 'constitute the cultural or spiritual heritage of peoples' (AP I) or fulfil the conditions set forth in Article 1 of the Hague Conventions. However, it has to be indicated that they remain protected under customary international law without these additional qualifications in accordance with the general rules derived from the Hague Regulations.

Objects dedicated to education and science

These objects may also fall under the above-cited protections defined in AP I or the Hague Convention of 1954 on the Protection of Cultural Property if they 'constitute the cultural or spiritual heritage of peoples' (AP I) or fulfil the conditions set forth in Article 1 of the 1954 Hague Convention. However, if they do not fall under those definitions, they are protected under customary international law in accordance with the general rules derived from the Hague Regulations and the rules on the protection of civilian objects.

In the *Kordic and Cerkez* case the ICTY held that:

> The Trial Chamber notes that educational institutions are undoubtedly immovable property of great importance to the cultural heritage of peoples (in the sense of Art. 1 of the 1954 Hague Convention) in that they are without exception centres of learning, arts, and sciences, with their valuable collections of books and works of arts and science. The Trial Chamber also notes one international treaty which requires respect and protection to be accorded to educational institutions in time of peace as well as in war (i.e. the Roerich Pact) .[1630]

1630   ICTY, Judgment, *The Prosecutor* V. *Dario Kordic and Mario Cerkez*. IT-95-14/2-T, para. 360.

Hospitals and places where the sick and wounded are collected

The following rules accord protection for hospitals and places where the sick and wounded are collected (rules on hospital ships and aircraft are included on the assumption that the ordinary meaning of the term 'place' could cover those objects):

Article 19 GC I
Fixed establishments and mobile medical units of the Medical Service may in no circumstances be attacked, but shall at all times be respected and protected by the Parties to the conflict.[1631]

Article 20 GC I
Hospital ships entitled to the protection of the Geneva Convention for the Amelioration of the Condition of Wounded, Sick and Shipwrecked Members of Armed Forces at Sea of 12 August 1949, shall not be attacked from the land.

Article 21 GC I
The protection to which fixed establishments and mobile medical units of the Medical Service are entitled shall not cease unless they are used to commit, outside their humanitarian duties, acts harmful to the enemy. Protection may, however, cease only after a due ˉwarning has been given, naming, in all appropriate cases, a reasonable time limit, and after such warning has remained unheeded.

Article 22 GC I
The following conditions shall not be considered as depriving a medical unit or establishment of the protection guaranteed by Article 19: (1) That the personnel of the unit or establishment are armed, and that they use the arms in their own defence, or in that of the wounded and sick in their charge. (2) That in the absence of armed orderlies, the unit or establishment is protected by a picket or by sentries or by an escort. (3) That small arms and ammunition taken from the wounded and sick and not yet handed to the proper service, are found in the unit or establishment. (4) That personnel and material of the veterinary service are found in the unit or establishment, without forming an

---

1631   See also Article 21 AP I.

integral part thereof. (5) That the humanitarian activities of medical units and establishments or of their personnel extend to the care of civilian wounded or sick.

Article 23 GC I

In time of peace, the High Contracting Parties and, after the outbreak of hostilities, the Parties thereto, may establish in their own territory and, if the need arises, in occupied areas, hospital zones and localities so organized as to protect the wounded and sick from the effects of war [...]

Upon the outbreak and during the course of hostilities, the Parties concerned may conclude agreements on mutual recognition of the hospital zones and localities they have created. They may for this purpose implement the provisions of the Draft Agreement annexed to the present Convention,[1632] with such amendments as they may consider necessary.

Article 14 GC IV and Annex I to that Convention establish a similar regime for hospital and safety zones and localities.

Article 22 GC II

Military hospital ships, that is to say, ships built or equipped by the Powers specially and solely with a view to assisting the wounded, sick and shipwrecked, to treating them and to transporting them, may in no circumstances be attacked [...] on condition that their names and

---

1632   Annex I. Draft Agreement Relating to Hospital Zones and Localities:
Article 11
In no circumstances may hospital zones be the object of attack. They shall be protected and respected at all times by the Parties to the conflict.
Article 4
Hospital zones shall fulfil the following conditions:
(a) They shall comprise only a small part of the territory governed by the Power which has established them.
(b) They shall be thinly populated in relation to the possibilities of accommodation.
(c) They shall be far removed and free from all military objectives, or large industrial or administrative establishments.
(d) They shall not be situated in areas which, according to every probability may become important for the conduct of the war.
Article 5
Hospital zones shall be subject to the following obligations:
(a) The lines of communication and means of transport which they possess shall not be used for the transport of military personnel or material, even in transit.
(b) They shall in no case be defended by militant means.

descriptions have been notified to the Parties to the conflict ten days before those ships are employed.[1633]

Article 23 GC II

Establishments ashore entitled to the protection of the Geneva Convention for the Amelioration of the Condition of the Wounded and Sick in Armed Forces in the Field of August 12, 1949 shall be protected from bombardment or attack from the sea.

Article 34 GC 11

The protection to which hospital ships and sick-bays are entitled shall not cease unless they are used to commit, outside their humanitarian duties, acts harmful to the enemy. Protection may, however, cease only after due warning has been given, naming in all appropriate cases a reasonable time limit, and after such warning has remained unheeded [...]

Article 35 GC II

The following conditions shall not be considered as depriving hospital ships or sick-bays of vessels of the protection due to them: (1) The fact that the crews of ships or sick-bays are armed for the maintenance of order, for their own defence or that of the sick and wounded. (2) The presence on board of apparatus exclusively intended to facilitate navigation or communication. (3) The discovery on board hospital ships or in sick-bays of portable arms and ammunition taken from the wounded, sick and shipwrecked and not yet handed to the proper service. (4) The fact that the humanitarian activities of hospital ships and sick-bays of vessels or of the crews extend to the care of wounded, sick or shipwrecked civilians. (5) The transport of equipment and of personnel intended exclusively for medical duties, over and above the normal requirements.

Article 18 GC IV

Civilian hospitals organized to give care to the wounded and sick, the infirm and maternity cases, may in no circumstances be the object of

---

1633 Article 24–27 give similar protection to other types of hospital ships, their lifeboats and the coastal rescue craft.

attack but shall at all times be respected and protected by the Parties to the conflict. [1634]

Article 19 GC IV

The protection to which civilian hospitals are entitled shall not cease unless they are used to commit, outside their humanitarian duties, acts harmful to the enemy protection may, however, cease only after due warning has been given, naming, in all appropriate cases, a reasonable time limit and after such warning has remained unheeded.

The fact that sick or wounded members of the armed forces are nursed in these hospitals, or the presence of small arms and ammunition taken from such combatants and not yet been handed to the proper service, shall not be considered to be acts harmful to the enemy.

Article 12 AP I Protection of medical units[1635]

1. Medical units shall be respected and protected at all times and shall not be the object of attack.
2. Paragraph 1 shall apply to civilian medical units, provided that they:
   (a) belong to one of the Parties to the conflict;
   (b) are recognized and authorized by the competent authority of one of the Parties to the conflict; or
   (c) are authorized in conformity with (Article 9, paragraph 2 of this Protocol or Article 27 of the First Convention.
3. The Parties to the conflict are invited to notify each other of the location of their fixed medical units. The absence of such notification shall not exempt any of the Parties from the obligation to comply with the provisions of paragraph 1.

1634   See also Article 56 (2) GC VI.
1635   An. 8(e) AP I contains the following definition:
   'Medical units' means establishments and other units, whether military or civilian, organized for medical purposes, namely the search for, collection, transportation, diagnosis or treatment – including first-aid treatment – of the wounded, sick and shipwrecked, or for the prevention of disease. The term includes, for example, hospitals and other similar units, blood transfusion centres, preventive medicine centres and institutes, medical depots and the medical and pharmaceutical stores of such units. Medical units may be fixed or mobile, permanent or temporary.
   The principal aim of Article 12 AP I is to extend to all civilian medical units the protection which hitherto applied to all military medical units on the one hand (cf. Article 19 GC I), but only to civilian hospitals on the other (cf. An. 18 GC IV).

4. Under no circumstances shall medical units be used in an attempt to shield military objectives from attack. Whenever possible, the Parties to the conflict shall ensure that medical units are so sited that attacks against military objectives do not imperil their safety.

Article 13 AP I Discontinuance of protection of civilian medical units
The protection to which civilian medical units are entitled shall not cease unless they are used to commit, outside their humanitarian function, acts harmful to the enemy. Protection may, however, cease only after a warning has been given setting, whenever appropriate, a reasonable time-limit, and after such warning has remained unheeded.
The following shall not be considered as acts harmful to the enemy:
   (a) that the personnel of the unit are equipped with light individual weapons for their own defence or for that of the wounded and sick in their charge;
   (b) that the unit is guarded by a picket or by sentries or by an escort;
   (c) that small arms and ammunition taken from the wounded and sick, and not yet handed to the proper service, are found in the units;
   (d) that members of the armed forces or other combatants are in the unit for medical reasons.

Articles 24–31 AP I contain the modern law on the protection of medical aircraft. In one post-Second World War trial – the *Kurt Student* case – the accused was charged with bombing a hospital which was marked with a Red Cross.[1636] According to the commentator of the UNWCC (United Nations War Crimes Commission), the acts alleged by the charges were clear breaches of international law. Since the Tribunal never specifically quoted the precise provisions violated, the commentator set out the relevant articles of the 1929 Geneva Convention for the Amelioration of the Condition of the Wounded and Sick in Armies in the Field: Articles 6, 9, 19, 20, 22.[1637] Article 6 in particular describes the *actus reus:*

1636   UNWCC, *LRTWC*, Vol. IV, p. 118; 13 AD 296.
1637   UNWCC, *LRTWC*, Vol. IV, pp. 120 ff.

> Mobile medical formations, that is to say, those which are intended to accompany armies in the field, and the fixed establishments of the medical service shall be respected and protected by the belligerents.

Loss of protection

The above-mentioned objects are only protected provided they are not military objectives as defined in Article 52(2) AP I (see section Article 8(2)(b)(v)), subsection 'legal basis of the war crime').

Moreover, as provided in Art. 52(3) AP I,

> In case of doubt whether an object which is normally dedicated to civilian purposes, such as a place of worship, a house or other dwelling or a school, is being used to make an effective contribution to military action, it shall be presumed not to be so used.

However, it should be noted that in relation to medical and cultural objects, precise indications are given as to when those objects lose their protection,[1638] and further conditions are stipulated before they may be attacked.[1639]

Remarks concerning the mental element

The ICTY, in the *Blaskic* case, defined the mental element of the offence 'destruction or wilful damage done to institutions dedicated to religion, charity and education, the arts and sciences, historic monuments and works of art and science' as described in Article 3(d) of the ICTY Statute as follows:

> The damage or destruction must have been committed intentionally to institutions which may clearly be identified as dedicated to religion

---

1638 For cultural property see Article 4(2) of the 1954 Hague Convention in connection with Article 6(a) and (b) of the Second Protocol thereto and Article 13 of that Protocol; for hospitals and places where the sick and wounded are collected, see Ans. 21 first sentence, 22 GC I; 34 first sentence, 35 GC II; 19(1) first sentence and (2) GC IV; 13(1) first sentence and (2) AP I. With regard to hospital ships, see also Doswald-Beck (1995), no. 48, 49, pp. 136–39. With regard to medical aircraft, see also ibid., no. 54, 57, 58, pp. 143–46.

1639 For cultural property see Article 4(2) of the 1954 Hague Convention in connection with Article 6(c) and (d) of the Second Protocol thereto and Article 13 of that Protocol; for hospitals and places where the sick and wounded are collected, see Articles 21 second sentence GC I; 34 second sentence GC II; 19(1) second sentence GC IV; 13(I) second sentence AP I. With regard to hospital ships, see also Doswald-Beck (1995), nos. 50, 51, pp. 139–41.

or education and which were not being used for military purposes at the time of the acts[1640]

The ICTY did not indicate why it chose the term 'intentionally' instead of 'wilfully' as may be derived from the ICTY Statute.

In the *Kordic and Cerkez* case, it held

> The destruction or damage is committed wilfully and the accused intends by his acts to cause the destruction or damage of institutions dedicated to religion or education and not used for a military purpose.[1641]

The ICTY Prosecution defined the mental element of the offence 'destruction or willful[1642] damage to institutions dedicated to religion or education' in the following terms: 'The destruction or damage was committed willfully.'[1643]

Article 8(2)(e)(iv)

> Intentionally directing attacks against buildings dedicated to religion, education, art, science or charitable purposes, historic monuments, hospitals and places where the sick and wounded are collected, provided they are not military objectives.

Text adopted by the PrepCom

War crime of attacking protected objects[1644]

1. The perpetrator directed an attack.
2. The object of the attack was one or more buildings dedicated to religion, education, art, science or charitable purposes, historic

---

1640 ICTY Judgment, *Prosecutor v. Tihomir Blaskic*, IT-95-14-T, para. 185; 122 ILR 1 at 73.
1641 ICTY Judgment, *Prosecutor v. Dario Kordic and Mario Cerkez*, IT-95-14/2-T, para. 361.
1642 In the *Simic and Others* case the ICTY Prosecution defined the notion of 'wilful' as 'a form of intent which includes recklessness, but excludes ordinary negligence. "Wilful" means a positive intent to do something, which can be inferred if the consequences were foreseeable, while "recklessness" means wilful neglect that reaches the level of gross criminal negligence.' ICTY, Prosecutor's Pre-trial Brief, *Prosecutor v. Milan Simic and Others*, IT-95-9-PT, p. 35.
1643 ICTY, Prosecutor's Pre-trial Brief, *Prosecutor v. Dario Kordic and Mario Cerkez*, IT-95-14/2-PT, p. 49.
1644 The presence in the locality of persons specially protected under the Geneva Conventions of 1949 or of police forces retained for the sole purpose of maintaining law and order does not by itself render the locality a military objective.

monuments, hospitals or places where the sick and wounded are collected, which were not military objectives.

3. The perpetrator intended such building or buildings dedicated to religion, education, art, science or charitable purposes, historic monuments, hospitals or places where the sick and wounded are collected, which were not military objectives, to be the object of the attack.

4. The conduct took place in the context of and was associated with an armed conflict not of an international character.

5. The perpetrator was aware of factual circumstances that established the existence of an armed conflict.

Commentary[1645]

Travaux preparatoires/Understandings of the PrepCom

The PrepCom concluded that the elements of this war crime are identical to the elements of the corresponding war crime in an international armed conflict (Article 8(2)(b)(ix) ICC Statute).

Legal basis of the war crime

The term 'intentionally directing attacks against buildings dedicated to religion, education, art, science or charitable purposes, historic monuments, hospitals and places where the sick and wounded are collected, provided they are not military objectives' is derived to a large extent from Articles 27 and 56 of the 1907 Hague Regulations. It must be noted, however, that the Hague Regulations do not directly apply to non-international armed conflicts. An explicit treaty reference for this offence in internal armed conflicts does not exist. However, there are other provisions of relevance (for example, AP II, Hague Convention of 1954 for the Protection of Cultural Property), which are applicable in internal armed conflicts. These will be cited below.

1645   We reproduce the commentary from Dörmann et al. (2003), pp. 458–63.

Remarks concerning the elements

The conclusions stated under the section dealing with the corresponding offence in the context of international armed conflicts (Article 8(2)(b)(ix) ICC Statute) also apply to this offence when committed in the context of a non-international armed conflict. Given that both offences are formulated in exactly the same manner, there are no indications in the ICC Statute or other sources that this offence has different special constituent elements in an international or non-international armed conflict.

However, a number of rules which might be of relevance for the interpretation of the elements of this offence have developed, giving specific protection to specific objects in times of non-international armed conflicts.

Buildings dedicated to religion, education, art, science or charitable purposes, historic monuments

(1) General protection
The above-cited Article 56, which must be read in connection with Article 27 of the Hague Regulations, is still valid under customary international law and applies to non-international armed conflicts as well.

(2) Specific protections
Cultural or religious objects
The following provision of AP II contains specific rules on historic monuments, works of art or places of worship:

> Article 16
> Without prejudice to the provisions of the Hague Convention for the Protection of Cultural Property in the Event of Aimed Conflict of 14 May 1954, it is prohibited to commit any acts of hostility directed against historic monuments, works of art or places of worship which constitute the cultural or spiritual heritage of peoples, and to use them in support of the military effort.[1646]

1646 On the scope of the rule of protection, the ICRC Commentary on AP II states:
Protection of cultural objects and places of worship is achieved by means of two complementary rules, each involving a prohibition:
1) it is prohibited to commit 'any acts of hostility directed against'.
An act of hostility means any act related to the conflict which prejudices or may prejudice the physical integrity of protected objects. In fact, the article does not only prohibit the bringing about of deleterious effects as such, but any acts 'directed' against protected objects. Thus it is not necessary for there to be any damage for this provision to be violated.

As the ICRC Commentary on this provision points out, [the] expression 'without prejudice to' means that the conditions of application of the Convention are not modified by the Protocol, only of course as far as a Contracting Party is bound by the Convention. If it is not, only Article 16 applies.[1647]

Cultural property

The Hague Convention of 1954 for the Protection of Cultural Property, which defines cultural property in Article 1, applies also to non-international

---

2) it is prohibited to use protected objects in support of the military effort.
'Military effort' means any military activities undertaken for the conduct of hostilities. The second prohibition is the counterpart of the first, indispensable to ensure respect for this rule. If such objects were used in support of the military effort, they could become military objectives, assuming that their total or partial destruction offered the adversary – a specific military advantage, and as a result their protection would become illusory. In such a situation the question is if and exactly at what moment there is a right to attack such protected objects in the event that the second prohibition is not respected. Such a possibility should not be accepted without duly taking into account the fact that the objects concerned are of exceptional interest and universal value All possible measures should be taken to endeavour putting a stop to any use in support of the military effort (by giving due warnings, for example) in order to prevent the objects from being destroyed or damaged. In any case this is the spirit of the provision: it is an invitation to safeguard the heritage of mankind.
See Junod (1987), no. 4843 ff. (footnote omitted).
Concerning the second aspect, reference should be made also to the corresponding commentary on Article 53 AP I, which clarifies the conditions under which a protected object may be attacked when it is used to support the military effort:
If protected objects were used in support of the military effort, this would obviously constitute a violation of Article 53 of the Protocol, though it would not necessarily justify attacking them. To the extent that it is admitted that the right to do so does exist with regard to objects of exceptional value, such a right would depend on there being a military objective, or not, as defined in Article 52 paragraph 2. *A military objective is an object which makes 'an effective contribution to military action' for the adversary, and whose total or partial destruction, capture or neutralization 'in the circumstances ruling at the time, offers a definite military advantage' for the attacker. These conditions are therefore stricter than the simple condition that they must be 'in support of the military effort'.* For example, it is not permitted to destroy a cultural object whose use does not make any contribution to military action, nor a cultural object which has temporarily served as a refuge for combatants, but is no longer used as such. In addition, all preventive measures should be taken to terminate their use in support of the military effort (warnings, injunctions etc.) in order to prevent the destruction or damage of cultural objects. However, if it is decided to attack anyway the principle of proportionality should be respected, which means that the damage should not be excessive in relation to the concrete and direct military advantage anticipated, and all the precautions required by Article 57[...] should be taken. See Wenger (1987), no. 2079 (emphasis added, footnote omitted).

1647 Junod, Article 16 in ibid. no. 4832 (footnote omitted). It should be noted that, unlike Article 53 (Protection of cultural objects and of places of worship) of AP I. the Article under consideration here does not make reference to other applicable international instruments. In the absence of an explanation on this point in the Official Records, it may be recalled that the Hague Conventions of 1907 are not specifically applicable to non-international armed conflicts. However, this does not exclude the possibility that norms or customary international law might be of relevance.

armed conflicts.[1648] The specific protection of such cultural property is defined in particular in Article 4. For further details, see the discussion on the corresponding offence committed in international armed conflicts (section Article 8 (2)(b)(ix), subsection 'Legal basis of the war crime').

NB: The recently adopted Second Protocol to the Hague Convention of 1954 for the Protection of Cultural Property[1649] also applicable in non-international armed conflicts (Article 22), further develops Article 4(2) of the 1954 Convention in Article 6 (waiver of protection). A special case of enhanced protection is dealt with in Article 12. The Protocol contains specific criminality clauses in Article 15(1).

For further details, see the discussion on the corresponding offence committed in international armed conflicts (section Article8(2)(b)(ix), subsection 'Legal basis of the war crime').

RELIGIOUS OBJECTS

Religious objects may fall under the above-cited protections defined in AP II or the Hague Convention of 1954 on the Protection of Cultural Property if they *constitute the cultural or spiritual heritage of peoples* (AP II) or fulfil the conditions set forth in Article 1 of the 1954 Hague Convention. However, it should be noted that even without these additional qualifications they remain protected under customary international law to the same extent as civilian objects.

OBJECTS DEDICATED TO EDUCATION AND SCIENCE

These objects may also fall under the above-cited protections defined in AP II or the Hague Convention of 1954 on the Protection of Cultural Property if they *constitute the cultural or spiritual heritage of peoples* (AP II) or fulfil the conditions set forth in Article 1 of the 1954 Hague Convention. However, if they do not fall under those definitions, they are protected under customary international law to the same extent as civilian objects.

1648 Article 19:1. In the event of an armed conflict not of an international character occurring within the territory of one of the High Contracting Parties, each party to the conflict shall be bound to apply, as a minimum, the provisions of the present Convention which relate to respect for cultural property.

1649 Second Protocol to the Hague Convention of 1954 for the Protection of Cultural Property in the Event of Armed Conflict, adopted on 26 March 1999 (The Hague).

Hospitals and places where the sick and wounded are collected

Only one specific rule contained in a treaty of international humanitarian law, which accords protection for hospitals and places where the sick and wounded are collected, is applicable to non-international armed conflicts. Article 11 AP II reads as follows:

1. Medical units and transports shall be respected and protected at all times and shall not be the object of attack.
2. The protection to which medical units and transports are entitled shall not cease unless they are used to commit hostile acts, outside their humanitarian function. Protection may, however, cease only after a warning has been given setting, whenever appropriate, a reasonable time-limit, and after such warning has remained unheeded.

In addition, the protection may be inferred from common Article 3 GC which states that '[the] wounded and sick shall be collected and cared for'. The collection and care of wounded and sick maybe carried out only if the hospitals and places where sick and wounded are collected are protected against attacks.

Further rules under customary international law might be of relevance.

Loss of protection

The objects listed in Article 8(2)(e)(iv) of the ICC Statute are only protected provided they are not military objectives. Unlike provisions concerning international armed conflicts, there is no explicit definition of military objectives in existing treaties of international humanitarian law applicable in non-international armed conflicts (see in particular AP II). However, the definition found in Article 52(2) AP I is relevant to non-international armed conflicts too, as it was used for both international and non-international armed conflicts in Article 2(6) of the Protocol on Prohibitions or Restrictions on the use of Mines, Booby-Traps and Other Devices as amended on 3 May 1996 (Protocol II to the 1980 Convention as amended on 3 May 1996) and more recently in Article 1(6) of the Second Protocol to the Hague Convention of 1954 for the Protection of Cultural Property in the Event of Armed Conflict of 26 March 1999.

With respect to medical and cultural objects it should be noted that precise indications are given as to when those objects lose their protection (for cultural property, see Article 4(2) of the 1954 Hague Convention, together with Article 6(a) and (b) of the Second Protocol thereto and Article 13 of that Protocol; for hospitals and places where the sick and wounded are collected, see Article 11 first sentence AP II) and further conditions are stipulated that must be fulfilled before they may be attacked (for cultural property, see Article 4(2) of the 1954 Hague Convention, together with Article 6(c) and (d) of the Second Protocol thereto and Article 13 of that Protocol: for hospitals and places where the sick and wounded are collected, see Article 11 second sentence AP II).

Cambodian Law on the Establishment of Extraordinary Chambers in the Courts of Cambodia for the Prosecution of Crimes Committed During the Period of Democratic Kampuchea

ARTICLE 7 ON THE RESPONSIBILITY FOR DESTRUCTION OF CULTURAL PROPERTY DURING ARMED CONFLICT

The Khmer Rouge regime took power on 17 April 1975 and was overthrown on 7 January 1979. Perhaps up to 2 million people perished during this period of three years, eight months and twenty days. The end of the Khmer Rouge was followed by a civil war.[1650] That war finally ended in 1998, when the Khmer Rouge political and military structures were dismantled.[1651]

In 1997 the government requested that the UN assist in establishing a trial to prosecute the senior leaders of the Khmer Rouge. In 2001, the Cambodian National Assembly passed a law to create a court to try serious crimes committed during the Khmer Rouge regime 1975–79. This court is called the Extraordinary Chambers in the Courts of Cambodia for the Prosecution of Crimes Committed during the Period of Democratic Kampuchea (Extraordinary Chambers or ECCC). During negotiations with the UN, the Government of Cambodia insisted that, for the sake of the Cambodian people, the trial must be held in Cambodia and not in a distant and formal international environment, close to all witnesses, suspects and evidence

---

1650   The Khmer Rouge held power in Cambodia from 1975 to 1979 and aggressively pursued a policy of radical social reform that resulted in the deaths of hundreds of thousands of Cambodians through mass executions and physical privation. In January 1979, the government was overthrown by former Khmer Rouge functionaries, with substantial backing from the army of Viet Nam. In August of that year, a special court, the People's Revolutionary Tribunal, was constituted to try two of the Khmer Rouge government's most powerful leaders, Pol Pot and Ieng Sary. The charge against them was genocide as it was defined in the United Nation's 1948 Convention on Genocide. At the time, both men were in the Cambodian jungle leading the Khmer Rouge in a struggle to regain power; they were, therefore, tried in absentia. See De Nike, Quigley and Robinson (2000).

The trial of Pol Pot and Ieng Sary was the world's first genocide trial based on UN policy, as well as the first trial of a head of government on a human rights-related charge. The indictment and the judgment include several references to the destruction of museums, historical monuments, architectural treasures, damage to the temples of Angkor Thom and Angkor Wat (ibid., p. 475, document 2.4.08, pp. 529–30).

1651   Several books and articles deals with this tragic period of Cambodian history: Ramji and Van Schaack (2005); Cockayne (2005); Cohen (2007); Fawthrop (2004); Ciorciari (2006); Klein (2006); Lieberman (2005).

and using Cambodian staff and judges together with foreign personnel. It was also the most effective way to erode the 'culture of impunity'.[1652] Cambodia invited international participation because of the weakness of the Cambodian legal system and the international nature of the crimes, and to help in meeting international standards of justice. An agreement with the UN was ultimately reached in June 2003 detailing how the international community would assist and participate in the Extraordinary Chambers.[1653] The cooperation with the UN is based on the Agreement between the UN and Cambodia concerning the Prosecution under Cambodian Law of Crimes Committed during the Period of Democratic Kampuchea, signed in Phnom Penh on 6 June 2003.

ECCC Emblem: [1654]

The Extraordinary Chambers in the Courts of Cambodia for the Prosecution of Crimes Committed During the Period of Democratic Kampuchea (ECCC), also known under the name of Khmer Rouge Tribunal, is an autonomous 'mixed tribunal', which was established jointly by the Royal Government of Cambodia and the UN, but remains independent of both.

Trials, which begin in 2009, should bring to trial senior leaders of Democratic Kampuchea, and those most responsible for crimes committed

---

1652 Chhang (2000), p. 29.
1653 Extraordinary Chambers in the Courts of Cambodia for the Prosecution of Crimes Committed during the Period of Democratic Kampuchea (Extraordinary Chambers or ECCC): http://www. eccc.gov.kh/english/about_eccc.aspx. The process of the formation of the Extraordinary Chambers is very well described in Hammarberg (2001). See also Boyle (2002).
1654 The emblem represents the Extraordinary Chambers, combining a depiction of the administration of Cambodian justice during the ancient period of Angkor with the United Nations' wreath of olive branches symbolizing peace. The official colour is dark blue. The figure is seated on a dais and holds a sword, symbolizing the authority of the court. This also constiutes the central figure in the mural in the former Appeals Court in the Ministry of Justice in Phnom Penh, where it is flanked by two assistants referring to the law as inscribed on palm-leaf manuscripts. The official stamp shows the emblem surrounded by two circles in which is written in Khmer the full name of the Extraordinary Chambers in the Courts of Cambodia, together with the abbreviations ECCC for the English name and CETC for the French name (Chambres Extraordinaires au sein des Tribunaux Cambodgiens).

during the Khmer Rouge regime (17 April 1975–6 January 1979). The first introductory submission was finalized by the co-prosecutors on 18 July 2007. All five suspects were under provisional detention at the ECCC. The charged persons are: Kaing Guek Eav, alias Duch (former chief of S-21), charged with crimes against humanity, and Nuon Chea, Ieng Sary, Ieng Thirith and Khieu Samphan, charged with genocide, crimes against humanity, war crimes and crimes against religion.

Composition, procedure and decisions of the ECCC[1655]

The tribunal is set within the Cambodian court structure, consisting of a Trial Chamber and a Supreme Court Chamber (the latter serving as an appeal and final instance chamber). The Trial Chamber will be composed of five judges (three Cambodian and two International); the Supreme Court Chamber will consist of seven judges (four Cambodian and three International). Every decision requires a 'super-majority', meaning an affirmative vote of at least four out of five judges in the Trial Chamber, and at least five out of seven judges in the Supreme Court Chamber.

Two prosecutors were appointed, one Cambodian and the other international. Two co-investigating judges were also appointed, again one Cambodian and one international. The UN proposed the international judges and prosecutor for appointment, which were nominated by the Cambodian authorities.

Jurisdiction

The ECCC acts on the basis of Cambodian penal law, international humanitarian law and custom and international conventions recognized by Cambodia. It will try 'suspects'[1656] for the following crimes committed between 17 April 1975 and 6 January 1979. According to the Law on the Establishment of the Extraordinary Chambers, with the inclusion of amendments as promulgated on 27 October 2004, the Extraordinary

---

1655 Extensive documentation concerning the Khmer Rouge period of Cambodian history and the establishment and work of the Khmer Rouge Tribunal is available at the Documentation Centre of Cambodia, PO Box 1110, 66 Sihanouk Blvd., Phnom Penh, Cambodia, Tel.: +855 23 211 875, Fax: +855 23 210 358, e:dccam@online.com.kh; www.dccam.org; www.cambodiatribunal. org.

1656 Senior leaders of Democratic Kampuchea and those who were most responsible for the above acts are hereinafter designated as 'suspects' (Article 2, paragraph 2 of the Law on Establishment of ECCC).

Chambers shall have the power to bring to trial all suspects who committed the crimes set forth:

- Under the 1956 Penal Code of Cambodia: Homicide, Torture, Religious Persecution (Article 3 of the Law on Establishment of ECCC)
- Under international humanitarian law and custom, and international conventions recognized by Cambodia: Genocide, Crimes against humanity, Grave breaches of 1949 Geneva Conventions, Destructions of cultural property, Crime against internationally protected persons (Articles 4–8 of the Law on Establishment of ECCC).

What happened in Cambodia during the domination of the territory by so-called Democratic Kampuchea between 17 April 1975 and 6 January 1979 represents the most horrific criminal actions, comparable only with the crimes committed by Nazi Germany during the Second World War. Many books and documents described this inhuman period of human history.[1657]

Jurisdiction concerning cultural property

In the present context, our consideration is limited to the description of harm committed during the period 1975–1979 to the cultural property of Cambodia. Article 7 of the Law on the Establishment of the Extraordinary Chambers deals with this responsibility.

Article 7 of the *Law on the Establishment of the Extraordinary Chambers* states:

> The Extraordinary Chambers shall have the power to bring to trial all Suspects most responsible for the destruction of cultural property during armed conflict pursuant to the 1954 Hague Convention for Protection of Cultural Property in the Event of Armed Conflict during the period from 17 April 1975 to 6 January 1979.

The Article refers to the 1954 Hague Convention. It was pointed out that citing this Convention as the source of the crime of destruction of cultural property creates a problem, since the Convention does not set forth a crime and does not establish individual criminal responsibility for violations of its provision.[1658] The Hague Convention leaves to the States Parties 'to take,

---

1657   Kieran (2002); Meijer (2004); Jackson (1992); Taylor (2003).
1658   Ardema (2006), p. 68.

within the framework of their ordinary criminal jurisdiction, all necessary steps to prosecute and impose penal or disciplinary sanctions upon those persons, of whatever nationality, who commit or order to be committed a breach of the [...] Convention.'[1659] 'The Khmer Rouge Tribunal may be reluctant to infer a crime from a convention that neither establishes a crime nor mentions individual criminal responsibility.'[1660] Similar doubts were expressed by Steven R. Ratner and Jason S. Abrams, who consider that

> the Convention's nexus to armed conflict together with the absence of criminality under customary law for peacetime destruction means that only desecrations in connection with Cambodia's conflict with Vietnam or an internal conflict would trigger any criminal responsibility. Regarding interstate war, additional evidence would need to be gathered, though the usefulness of such an exercise is questionable due to the insignificance of this issue compared to other atrocities committed by Democratic Kampuchea. As for the internal conflict, assuming that the 1978 rebellion in the Eastern Zone meets the definition of non-international armed conflict from the Hague Convention, evidence would also need to be assembled regarding destruction of cultural property during these massacres.[1661]

On the other hand, the Khmer Rouge's destruction of cultural property is well documented.[1662] As part of their systematic attack upon Buddhism, the Khmer Rouge desecrated or destroyed most of the country's 3,000 pagodas, inflicting irreparable damage on statues, sacred literature and other religious items.[1663] Similar damage was inflicted on Muslim mosques of the Cham people. The regime also attacked Christian places of worship even disassembling the Catholic cathedral of Phnom Penh stone by stone until only a vacant lot remained.

Two authors from the Cambodia Documentation Centre, John D. Ciorciari and Youk Chhang, who published an article on cultural property, consider that 'war crimes and the destruction of cultural property could be

---

1659   Article 28 Sanctions of the 1954 Hague Convention.
1660   Ibid., p. 68.
1661   Ratner and Abrams (2001), p. 294.
1662   Ibid.
1663   See Harris (2007).

either difficult or easy to prove, depending on an adjudicator's ruling with respect to the existence of international armed conflict.'[1664]

Destruction of cultural property

Some of the documents most useful in proving war crimes will also be critical in establishing the liability of Communist Party of Kampuchea (CPK) leaders for the destruction of cultural property. The Khmer Rouge Tribunal Law defines the destruction of cultural property as a violation of the 1954 Hague Convention for the Protection of Cultural Property in the Event of Armed Conflict. The Hague Convention adopts a broad definition of cultural property, including monuments, archaeological sites, groups of buildings, works of art, books, archives, scientific collections, libraries, and a variety of other pieces of 'movable or immovable property of great importance to the cultural heritage of every people'.[1665] The offense of destroying cultural property could conceivably be subsumed under the umbrella of war crimes because it is generally understood to carry criminal sanctions only during a time of international or domestic armed conflict.[1666] Once the spatial and temporal parameters of armed conflict are set, the principal evidentiary challenge is simply to show that items of cultural property were destroyed with the requisite knowledge or intent of CPK leaders.

Documentary evidence, including interviews with survivors regarding the destruction of cultural property exists, although it is not as abundant as one might expect given the historical consensus that widespread attacks occurred on pagodas, mosques, churches, and various items of art and literature. One clear example of high-level intent to destroy cultural property appears in Item 6 of the 1976 Decisions, in which the CPK Center ordered that 'the Armed Forces demolish' the Christian Cathedral.[1667] A former *Santebal* cadre, Tern Moeng, has acknowledged his receipt of an order to destroy the Cathedral and his participation in its demolition.[1668] However, the Cathedral

---

1664 Ciorciari and Chhang (2005), p. 287.
1665 1954 Hague Convention for the Protection of Cultural Property in the Event of Armed Conflict, 14 May 1954, art. 4, 249 UNTS 215, 242–44.
1666 Ibid., art. 19.
1667 'Decisions of the Central Committee of a Variety of Questions' (30 March 1976) (Documentation Centre of Cambodia (DC-Cam) Catalogue No. 00693), in Chandler, Kiernan and Boua (1988), Item 6.
1668 Interview by Dara P. Vanthan et al., with Iem Moeng, Baribo district, Kampong Chhnang Province, Cambodia (10 July 2002). Transcript on file with the Documentation Centre of Cambodia (DC-Cam).

was located in Phnom Penh and destroyed early in the Pol Pot period. Thus, the act would be punishable only if an accountability forum adopts a very wide definition of international armed conflict in Democratic Kampuchea.

The Documentation Centre of Cambodia mapping reports[1669] identified many Buddhist pagodas, mosques, churches, and other religious buildings that were defaced and converted into prisons between 1975 and 1979.[1670] Interview transcripts provide evidence that CPK forces were engaged in the widespread destruction of mosques and pagodas.[1671] Documents from the 1979 Tribunal also include extensive reports of the destruction of cultural property.[1672] Numerous interviews and *Renakse* petitions offer further proof.[1673] For example, a surviving monk named Unn Tep asserts that CPK cadres destroyed Buddhist temples, religious schools and hospitals, and other attached facilities throughout Siem Riep.[1674]

Like many of the crimes discussed above, the destruction of cultural property appears to have been sufficiently widespread to put all members of the CPK Centre on notice and trigger a legal responsibility to investigate the offenses. Ultimately, however, 'the key determinant of CPK leaders' liability for most alleged destruction of cultural property will be a Democratic

---

1669 Documentation Centre of Cambodia, Mapping project, 1995–present. See http://www.dccam. org/Projects/Maps/Mapping.htm.

1670 Documentation Centre of Cambodia. *Forensic Pathology and Anthropology of Historical Mass Killing in Cambodia*. Final Report on Phase 2 of the Forensic Project, 14 January 2004. Includes – among many others – the discovery of the mass graves: Observations at Wat Kakoh by Local Witnesses: 'In late 1999, religious authorities at Wat Kakoh decided to construct a new structure on the grounds of the pagoda. A monk, the Venerable Keo Kosal, was assigned to dig the foundation for this new structure. In a grove of coconut trees approximately 30 metres south of the main pagoda building, the monk began to dig a hole for a corner post of the new structure. At a depth of approximately 1 metre, he struck a cache of bones that appeared to him to be human remains. The venerable ceased digging, and authorities soon notified the Documentation Centre of Cambodia. After Documentation Centre personnel had inspected the site in 2000, the monk subsequently refilled the hole, and temple authorities selected another location for the new structure. Thus far, the Project Team has been unable to locate any contemporaneous witnesses to events at Wat Kakoh during the Khmer Rouge regime. We have also been unable to recover any contemporaneous written documentation produced at this suspected execution site.'

1671 Interview by Dara P. Vanthan et al. with Chek Sam alias Saom Sam Ol, in Baribo District, Kampong Chhnang Province, Cambodia (12 July 2002). Transcript on file with DC-Cam. (Report of widespread CPK destruction of religious buildings in the Battambang area); interview by David Hawk with Him Mathot, Phnom Penh, Cambodia (April 1981). Transcript on file with DC-Cam.

1672 De Nike, Quigley and Robinson (2000), pp. 144–55.

1673 For a brief discussion of the CPK's destruction of cultural property, based on multiple interviews, see Becker (1986), pp. 264–65.

1674 'Petition of Unn Tep'. Renakse Collection, Siem Riep File. On file with DC-Cam.

Kampuchea accountability forum's determination regarding the scope of international armed conflict at the time of the alleged offenses.'[1675]

Dr. Youk Chhang, Director of the Documentation Centre of Cambodia, wrote recently:

> The Khmer Rouge trials are not only about justice; they are also about the Memory of Our Nation. . . . There may be no single answer to what really happened. However, we all have the obligation to participate in the search for truth. Together, we can build a better understanding of our common past.[1676]

1675   Ciorciari and Chhang (2005), p. 286.
1676   Chhang (2009).

PART IV
ANNEXES

1. Convention for the Protection of Cultural Property in the Event of Armed Conflict with Regulations for the Execution of the Convention. The Hague, 14 May 1954

2. Protocol to the Convention for the Protection of Cultural Property in the Event of Armed Conflict 1954, The Hague 14 May 1954

3. Second Protocol to the Hague Convention of 1954 for the Protection of Cultural Property in the Event of Armed Conflict, The Hague, 26 March 1999

1. CONVENTION FOR THE PROTECTION OF CULTURAL PROPERTY IN THE EVENT OF ARMED CONFLICT WITH REGULATIONS FOR THE EXECUTION OF THE CONVENTION

The Hague, 14 May 1954[1677]

The High Contracting Parties,

Recognizing that cultural property has suffered grave damage during recent armed conflicts and that, by reason of the developments in the technique of warfare, it is in increasing danger of destruction;

Being convinced that damage to cultural property belonging to any people whatsoever means damage to the cultural heritage of all mankind, since each people makes its contribution to the culture of the world;

Considering that the preservation of the cultural heritage is of great importance for all peoples of the world and that it is important that this heritage should receive international protection;

Guided by the principles concerning the protection of cultural property during armed conflict, as established in the Conventions of The Hague of 1899 and of 1907 and in the Washington Pact of 15 April, 1935;

Being of the opinion that such protection cannot be effective unless both national and international measures have been taken to organize it in time of peace;

Being determined to take all possible steps to protect cultural property;

Have agreed upon the following provisions:

Chapter I. General provisions regarding protection

Article 1. Definition of cultural property
For the purposes of the present Convention, the term 'cultural property' shall cover, irrespective of origin or ownership:

(a) movable or immovable property of great importance to the cultural heritage of every people, such as monuments of architecture, art or history, whether religious or secular; archaeological sites; groups of buildings which,

---

1677   For the table of signatures, ratifications and accesstions and the texts of the reservations and declarations, see the UNESCO web site: http://erc.unesco.org/cp/convention. asp?KO=13637&language=E

as a whole, are of historical or artistic interest; works of art; manuscripts, books and other objects of artistic, historical or archaeological interest; as well as scientific collections and important collections of books or archives or of reproductions of the property defined above;

(b) buildings whose main and effective purpose is to preserve or exhibit the movable cultural property defined in sub-paragraph (a) such as museums, large libraries and depositories of archives, and refuges intended to shelter, in the event of armed conflict, the movable cultural property defined in sub-paragraph (a);

(c) centers containing a large amount of cultural property as defined in sub-paragraphs (a) and (b), to be known as `centers containing monuments'.

Article 2. Protection of cultural property

For the purposes of the present Convention, the protection of cultural property shall comprise the safeguarding of and respect for such property.

Article 3. Safeguarding of cultural property

The High Contracting Parties undertake to prepare in time of peace for the safeguarding of cultural property situated within their own territory against the foreseeable effects of an armed conflict, by taking such measures as they consider appropriate.

Article 4. Respect for cultural property

1. The High Contracting Parties undertake to respect cultural property situated within their own territory as well as within the territory of other High Contracting Parties by refraining from any use of the property and its immediate surroundings or of the appliances in use for its protection for purposes which are likely to expose it to destruction or damage in the event of armed conflict; and by refraining from any act of hostility, directed against such property.

2. The obligations mentioned in paragraph 1 of the present Article may be waived only in cases where military necessity imperatively requires such a waiver.

3. The High Contracting Parties further undertake to prohibit, prevent and, if necessary, put a stop to any form of theft, pillage or misappropriation of, and any acts of vandalism directed against, cultural property. They shall refrain from requisitioning movable cultural property situated in the territory of another High Contracting Party.

4. They shall refrain from any act directed by way of reprisals against cultural property.

5. No High Contracting Party may evade the obligations incumbent upon it under the present Article, in respect of another High Contracting Party, by reason of the fact that the latter has not applied the measures of safeguard referred to in Article 3.

Article 5. Occupation
1. Any High Contracting Party in occupation of the whole or part of the territory of another High Contracting Party shall as far as possible support the competent national authorities of the occupied country in safeguarding and preserving its cultural property.
2. Should it prove necessary to take measures to preserve cultural property situated in occupied territory and damaged by military operations, and should the competent national authorities be unable to take such measures, the Occupying Power shall, as far as possible, and in close co-operation with such authorities, take the most necessary measures of preservation.
3. Any High Contracting Party whose government is considered their legitimate government by members of a resistance movement, shall, if possible, draw their attention to the obligation to comply with those provisions of the Convention dealing with respect for cultural property.

Article 6. Distinctive marking of cultural property
In accordance with the provisions of Article 16, cultural property may bear a distinctive emblem so as to facilitate its recognition.

Article 7. Military measures
1. The High Contracting Parties undertake to introduce in time of peace into their military regulations or instructions such provisions as may ensure observance of the present Convention, and to foster in the members of their armed forces a spirit of respect for the culture and cultural property of all peoples.
2. The High Contracting Parties undertake to plan or establish in peace-time, within their armed forces, services or specialist personnel whose purpose will be to secure respect for cultural property and to co-operate with the civilian authorities responsible for safeguarding it.

Chapter II. Special protection

Article 8. Granting of special protection
1. There may be placed under special protection a limited number of refuges intended to shelter movable cultural property in the event of armed conflict,

of centers containing monuments and other immovable cultural property of very great importance, provided that they:

(a) are situated at an adequate distance from any large industrial center or from any important military objective constituting a vulnerable point, such as, for example, an aerodrome, broadcasting station, establishment engaged upon work of national defense, a port or railway station of relative importance or a main line of communication;

(b) are not used for military purposes.

2. A refuge for movable cultural property may also be placed under special protection, whatever its location, if it is so constructed that, in all probability, it will not be damaged by bombs.

3. A center containing monuments shall be deemed to be used for military purposes whenever it is used for the movement of military personnel or material, even in transit. The same shall apply whenever activities directly connected with military operations, the stationing of military personnel, or the production of war material are carried on within the center.

4. The guarding of cultural property mentioned in paragraph 1 above by armed custodians specially empowered to do so, or the presence, in the vicinity of such cultural property, of police forces normally responsible for the maintenance of public order shall not be deemed to be used for military purposes.

5. If any cultural property mentioned in paragraph 1 of the present Article is situated near an important military objective as defined in the said paragraph, it may nevertheless be placed under special protection if the High Contracting Party asking for that protection undertakes, in the event of armed conflict, to make no use of the objective and particularly, in the case of a port, railway station or aerodrome, to divert all traffic there from. In that event, such diversion shall be prepared in time of peace.

6. Special protection is granted to cultural property by its entry in the 'Inter-national Register of Cultural Property under Special Protection'. This entry shall only be made, in accordance with the provisions of the present Convention and under the conditions provided for in the Regulations for the execution of the Convention.

Article 9. Immunity of cultural property under special protection
The High Contracting Parties undertake to ensure the immunity of cultural property under special protection by refraining, from the time of entry in the International Register, from any act of hostility directed against such property and, except for the cases provided for in paragraph 5 of Article 8, from any use of such property or its surroundings for military purposes.

Article 10. Identification and control

During an armed conflict, cultural property under special protection shall be marked with the distinctive emblem described in Article 16, and shall be open to international control as provided for in the Regulations for the execution of the Convention.

Article 11. Withdrawal of immunity

1. If one of the High Contracting Parties commits, in respect of any item of cultural property under special protection, a violation of the obligations under Article 9, the opposing Party shall, so long as this violation persists, be released from the obligation to ensure the immunity of the property concerned. Nevertheless, whenever possible, the latter Party shall first request the cessation of such violation within a reasonable time.

2. Apart from the case provided for in paragraph 1 of the present Article, immunity shall be withdrawn from cultural property under special protection only in exceptional cases of unavoidable military necessity, and only for such time as that necessity continues. Such necessity can be established only by the officer commanding a force the equivalent of a division in size or larger. Whenever circumstances permit, the opposing Party shall be notified, a reasonable time in advance, of the decision to withdraw immunity.

3. The Party withdrawing immunity shall, as soon as possible, so inform the Commissioner-General for cultural property provided for in the Regulations for the execution of the Convention, in writing, stating the reasons.

Chapter III. Transport of cultural property

Article 12. Transport under special protection

1. Transport exclusively engaged in the transfer of cultural property, whether within a territory or to another territory, may, at the request of the High Contracting Party concerned, take place under special protection in accordance with the conditions specified in the Regulations for the execution of the Convention.

2. Transport under special protection shall take place under the international supervision provided for in the aforesaid Regulations and shall display the distinctive emblem described in Article 16.

3. The High Contracting Parties shall refrain from any act of hostility directed against transport under special protection.

Article 13. Transport in urgent cases
1. If a High Contracting Party considers that the safety of certain cultural property requires its transfer and that the matter is of such urgency that the procedure laid down in Article 12 cannot be followed, especially at the beginning of an armed conflict, the transport may display the distinctive emblem described in Article 16, provided that an application for immunity referred to in Article 12 has not already been made and refused. As far as possible, notification of transfer should be made to the opposing' Parties. Nevertheless, transport conveying cultural property to the territory of another country may not display the distinctive' emblem unless immunity has been expressly granted to it.
2. The High Contracting Parties shall take, so far as possible, the necessary precautions to avoid acts of hostility directed against the transport described in paragraph 1 of the present Article and displaying the distinctive emblem.

Article 14. Immunity from seizure, capture and prize
1. Immunity from seizure, placing in prize, or capture shall be granted to:
(a) cultural property enjoying the protection provided for in Article 12 or that provided for in Article 13;
(b) the means of transport exclusively engaged in the transfer of such cultural property.
2. Nothing in the present Article shall limit the right of visit and search.

Chapter IV. Personnel

Article 15. Personnel
As far as is consistent with the interests of security, personnel engaged in the protection of cultural property shall, in the interests of such property, be re-spected and, if they fall into the hands of the opposing Party, shall be allowed to continue to carry out their duties whenever the cultural property for which they are responsible has also fallen into the hands of the opposing Party.

Chapter V. The distinctive emblem

Article 16. Emblem of the convention
1. The distinctive emblem of the Convention shall take the form of a shield, pointed below, persaltire blue and white (a shield consisting of a royal-blue square, one of the angles of which forms the point of the shield, and of a

royal-blue triangle above the square, the space on either side being taken up by a white triangle).

2. The emblem shall be used alone, or repeated three times in a triangular formation (one shield below), under the conditions provided for in Article 17.

Article 17. Use of the emblem

1. The distinctive emblem repeated three times may be used only as a means of identification of:

(a) immovable cultural property under special protection;

(b) the transport of cultural property under the conditions provided for in Articles 12 and 13;

(c) improvised refuges, under the conditions provided for in the Regulations for the execution of the Convention.

2. The distinctive emblem may be used alone only as a means of identification of:

(a) cultural property not under special protection;

(b) the persons responsible for the duties of control in accordance with the Regulations for the execution of the Convention;

(c) the personnel engaged in the protection of cultural property;

(d) the identity cards mentioned in the Regulations for the execution of the Convention.

3. During an armed conflict, the use of the distinctive emblem in any other cases than those mentioned in the preceding paragraphs of the present Article, and the use for any purpose whatever of a sign resembling the distinctive emblem, shall be forbidden.

4. The distinctive emblem may not be placed on any immovable cultural property unless at the same time there is displayed an authorization duly dated and signed by the competent authority of the High Contracting Party.

Chapter VI. Scope of application of the Convention

Article 18. Application of the Convention

1. Apart from the provisions which shall take effect in time of peace, the present Convention shall apply in the event of declared war or of any other armed conflict which may arise between two or more of the High Contracting Parties, even if the state of war is not recognized by, one or more of them.

2. The Convention shall also apply to all cases of partial or total occupation of the territory of a High Contracting Party, even if the said occupation meets with no armed resistance.

3. If one of the Powers in conflict is not a Party to the present Convention, the Powers which are Parties thereto shall nevertheless remain bound by it in their mutual relations. They shall furthermore be bound by the Convention, in relation to the said Power, if the latter has declared, that it accepts the provisions thereof and so long as it applies them.

Article 19. Conflicts not of an international character
1. In the event of an armed conflict not of an international character occurring within the territory of one of the High Contracting Parties, each party to the conflict shall be bound to apply, as, a minimum, the provisions of the present Convention which relate to respect for cultural property.
2. The parties to the conflict shall endeavour to bring into force, by means of special agreements, all or part of the other provisions of the present Convention.
3. The United Nations Educational, Scientific and Cultural Organization may offer its services to the parties to the conflict.
4. The application of the preceding provisions shall not affect the legal status of the parties to the conflict.

Chapter VII. Execution of the Convention

Article 20. Regulations for the execution of the Convention
The procedure by which the present Convention is to be applied is defined in the Regulations for its execution, which constitute an integral part thereof.

Article 21. Protecting powers
The present Convention and the Regulations for its execution shall be applied with the co-operation of the Protecting Powers responsible for safeguarding the interests of the Parties to the conflict.

Article 22. Conciliation procedure
1. The Protecting Powers shall lend their good offices in all cases where they may deem it useful in the interests of cultural property, particularly if there is disagreement between the Parties to the conflict as to the application or interpretation of the provisions of the present Convention or the Regulations for its execution.
2. For this purpose, each of the Protecting Powers may, either at the invitation of one Party, of the Director-General of the United Nations Educational, Scientific and Cultural Organization, or on its own initiative, propose to the

Parties to the conflict a meeting of their representatives, and in particular of the authorities responsible for the protection of cultural property, if considered appropriate on suitably chosen neutral territory. The Parties to the conflict shall be bound to give effect to the proposals for meeting made to them. The Protecting Powers shall propose for approval by the Parties to the conflict a person belonging to a neutral Power or a person presented by the Director General of the United Nations Educational, Scientific and Cultural Organization, which person shall be invited to take part in such a meeting in the capacity of Chairman.

Article 23. Assistance of UNESCO

1. The High Contracting Parties may call upon the United Nations Educational, Scientific and Cultural Organization for technical assistance in organizing the protection of their cultural property, or in connexion with any other problem arising out of the application of the present Convention or the Regulations for its execution. The Organization shall accord such assistance within the limits fixed by its programme and by its resources.
2. The Organization is authorized to make, on its own initiative, proposals on this matter to the High Contracting Parties.

Article 24. Special agreements

1. The High Contracting Parties may conclude special agreements for all matters concerning which they deem it suitable to make separate provision.
2. No special agreement may be concluded which would diminish the protection afforded by the present Convention to cultural property and to the personnel engaged in its protection.

Article 25. Dissemination of the Convention

The High Contracting Parties undertake, in time of peace as in time of armed conflict, to disseminate the text of the present Convention and the Regulations for its execution as widely as possible in their respective countries. They undertake, in particular, to include the study thereof in their programmes of military and, if possible, civilian training, so that its principles are made known to the whole population, especially the armed forces and personnel engaged in the protection of cultural property.

Article 26. Translations reports

1. The High Contracting Parties shall communicate to one another, through the Director-General of the United Nations Educational, Scientific and

Cultural Organization, the official translations of the present Convention and of the Regulations for its execution.

2. Furthermore, at least once every four years, they shall forward to the Director-General a report giving whatever information they think suitable concerning any measures being taken, prepared or contemplated by their respective administrations in fulfillment of the present Convention and of the Regulations for its execution.

Article 27. Meetings

1. The Director-General of the United Nations Educational, Scientific and Cultural Organization may, with the approval of the Executive Board, convene meetings of representatives of the High Contracting Parties. He must convene such a meeting if at least one-fifth of the High Contracting Parties so request.

2. Without prejudice to any other functions which have been conferred on it by the present Convention or the Regulations for its execution, the purpose of the meeting will be to study problems concerning the application of the Convention and of the Regulations for its execution, and to formulate recommendations in respect thereof.

3. The meeting may further undertake a revision of the Convention or the Regulations for its execution if the majority of the High Contracting Parties are represented, and in accordance with the provisions of Article 39.

Article 28. Sanctions

The High Contracting Parties undertake to take, within the framework of their ordinary criminal jurisdiction, all necessary steps to prosecute and impose penal or disciplinary sanctions upon those persons, of whatever nationality, who commit or order to be committed a breach of the present Convention. Final provisions

Article 29. Languages

1. The present Convention is drawn up in English, French, Russian and Spanish, the four texts being equally authoritative.

2. The United Nations Educational, Scientific and Cultural Organization shall arrange for translations of the Convention into the other official languages of its General Conference.

Article 30. Signature

The present Convention shall bear the date of 14 May, 1954 and, until the date of 31 December, 1954, shall remain open for signature by all States invited to the Conference which met at The Hague from 21 April, 1954 to 14 May, 1954.

Article 31. Ratification

1. The present Convention shall be subject to ratification by signatory States in accordance with their respective constitutional procedures.
2. The instruments of ratification shall be deposited with the Director-General of the United Nations Educational, Scientific and Cultural Organization.

Article 32. Accession

From the date of its entry into force, the present Convention shall be open for accession by all States mentioned in Article 30 which have not signed it, as well as any other State invited to accede by the Executive Board of the United Nations Educational, Scientific and Cultural Organization. Accession shall be effected by the deposit of an instrument of accession with the Director-General of the United Nations Educational, Scientific and Cultural Organization.

Article 33. Entry into force

1. The present Convention shall enter into force three months after five instruments of ratification have been deposited.
2. Thereafter, it shall enter into force, for each High Contracting Party, three months after the deposit of its instrument of ratification or accession.
3. The situations referred to in Articles 18 and 19 shall give immediate effect to ratifications or accessions deposited by the Parties to the conflict either before or after the beginning of hostilities or occupation. In such cases the Director-General of the United Nations Educational, Scientific and Cultural Organization shall transmit the communications referred to in Article 38 by the speediest method.

Article 34. Effective application

1. Each State Party to the Convention on the date of its entry into force shall take all necessary measures to ensure its effective application within a period of six months after such entry into force.
2. This period shall be six months from the date of deposit of the instruments of ratification or accession for any State which deposits its instrument of ratification or accession after the date of the entry into force of the Convention.

Article 35. Territorial extension of the Convention

Any High Contracting Party may, at the time of ratification or accession, or at any time thereafter, declare by notification addressed to the Director-General of the United Nations Educational, Scientific and Cultural Organization, that the present Convention shall extend to all or any of the territories for whose international relations it is responsible. The said notification shall take effect three months after the date of its receipt.

Article 36. Relation to previous conventions

1. In the relations between Powers which are bound by the Conventions of The Hague concerning the Laws and Customs of War on Land (IV) and concerning Naval Bombardment in Time of War (IX), whether those of 29 July, 1899 or those of 18 October, 1907, and which are Parties to the present Convention, this last Convention shall be supplementary to the aforementioned Convention (IX) and to the Regulations annexed to the aforementioned Convention (IV) and shall substitute for the emblem described in Article 5 of the aforementioned Convention (IX) the emblem described in Article 16 of the present Convention, in cases in which the present Convention and the Regulations for its execution provide for the use of this distinctive emblem.

2. In the relations between Powers which are bound by the Washington Pact of 15 April, 1935 for the Protection of Artistic and Scientific Institutions and of Historic Monuments (Roerich Pact) and which are Parties to the present Convention, the latter Convention shall be supplementary to the Roerich Pact and shall substitute for the distinguishing flag described in Article III of the Pact the emblem defined in Article 16 of the present Convention, in cases in which the present Convention and the Regulations for its execution provide for the use of this distinctive emblem.

Article 37. Denunciation

1. Each High Contracting Party may denounce the present Convention, on its own behalf, or on behalf of any territory for whose international relations it is responsible.

2. The denunciation shall be notified by an instrument in writing, deposited with the Director-General of the United Nations Educational, Scientific and Cultural Organization.

3. The denunciation shall take effect one year after the receipt of the instrument of denunciation. However, if, on the expiry of this period, the denouncing Party is involved in an armed conflict, the denunciation shall not take effect until the end of hostilities, or until the operations of repatriating cultural property are completed, whichever is the later.

Article 38. Notifications
The Director-General of the United Nations Educational, Scientific and Cultural Organization shall inform the States referred to in Articles 30 and 32, as well as the United Nations, of the deposit of all the instruments of ratification, accession or acceptance provided for in Articles 31, 32 and 39 and of the notifications and denunciations provided for respectively in Articles 35, 37 and 39.

Article 39. Revision of the Convention and of the Regulations for its execution
1. Any High Contracting Party may propose amendments to the present Convention or the Regulations for its execution. The text of any proposed amendment shall be communicated to the Director-General of the United Nations Educational, Scientific and Cultural Organization who shall transmit it to each High Contracting Party with the request that such Party reply within four months stating whether it:
(a) desires that a Conference be convened to consider the proposed amendment;
(b) favours the acceptance of the proposed amendment without a Conference; or
(c) favours the rejection of the proposed amendment without a Conference.
2. The Director-General shall transmit the replies, received under paragraph 1 of the present Article, to all High Contracting Parties.
3. If all the High Contracting Parties which have, within the prescribed time-limit, stated their views to the Director-General of the United Nations Educational, Scientific and Cultural Organization, pursuant to paragraph 1(b) of this Article, inform him that they favour acceptance of the amendment without a Conference, notification of their decision shall be made by the Director-General in accordance with Article 38. The amendment shall become effective for all the High Contracting Parties on the expiry of ninety days from the date of such notification.
4. The Director-General shall convene a Conference of the High Contracting Parties to consider the proposed amendment if requested to do so by more than one-third of the High Contracting Parties.
5. Amendments to the Convention or to the Regulations for its execution, dealt with under the provisions of the preceding paragraph, shall enter into force only after they have been unanimously adopted by the High Contracting Parties represented at the Conference and accepted by each of the High Con-tracting Parties.

6. Acceptance by the High Contracting Parties of amendments to, the Convention or to the Regulations for its execution, which have been adopted by the Conference mentioned in paragraphs 4 and 5, shall be effected by the deposit of a formal instrument with the Director-General of the United Nations Educational, Scientific and Cultural Organization.

7. After the entry into force of amendments to the present Convention or to the Regulations for its execution, only the text of the Convention or of the Regulations for its execution thus amended shall remain open for ratification or accession.

Article 40. Registration
In accordance with Article 102 of the Charter of the United Nations, the present Convention shall be registered with the Secretariat of the United Nations at the request of the Director-General of the United Nations Educational, Scientific and Cultural Organization.

IN FAITH WHEREOF the undersigned, duly authorized, have signed the present Convention.

Done at The Hague, this fourteenth day of May, 1954, in a single copy which shall be deposited in the archives of the United Nations Educational, Scientific and Cultural Organization, and certified true copies of which shall be delivered to all the States referred to in Articles 30 and 32 as well as to the United Nations.

Regulations for the Execution of the Convention for the Protection of Cultural Property in the Event of Armed Conflict

Chapter I. Control

Article 1. International list of persons
On the entry into force of the Convention, the Director-General of the United Nations Educational, Scientific and Cultural Organization shall compile an international list consisting of all persons nominated by the High Contracting Parties as qualified to carry out the functions of Commissioner-General for Cultural Property. On the initiative of the Director-General of the United Nations Educational, Scientific and Cultural Organization, this list shall be periodically revised on the basis of requests formulated by the High Contracting Parties.

Article 2. Organization of control

As soon as any High Contracting Party is engaged in an armed conflict to which Article 18 of the Convention applies:

(a) It shall appoint a representative for cultural property situated in its territory; if it is in occupation of another territory, it shall appoint a special representative for cultural property situated in that territory;

(b) The Protecting Power acting for each of the Parties in conflict with such High Contracting Party shall appoint delegates accredited to the latter in conformity with Article 3 below;

(c) A Commissioner-General for Cultural Property shall be appointed to such High Contracting Party in accordance with Article 4.

Article 3. Appointment of delegates of Protecting Powers

The Protecting Power shall appoint its delegates from among the members of its diplomatic or consular staff or, with the approval of the Party to which they will be accredited, from among other persons.

Article 4. Appointment of Commissioner-General

1. The Commissioner-General for Cultural Property shall be chosen from the international list of persons by joint agreement between the Party to which he will be accredited and the Protecting Powers acting on behalf of the opposing Parties.

2. Should the Parties fail to reach agreement within three weeks from the beginning of their discussions on this point, they shall request the President of the International Court of Justice to appoint the Commissioner-General, who shall not take up his duties until the Party to which he is accredited has approved his appointment.

Article 5. Functions of delegates

The delegates of the Protecting Powers shall take note of violations of the Convention, investigate, with the approval of the Party to which they are accredited, the circumstances in which they have occurred, make representations locally to secure their cessation and, if necessary, notify the Commissioner-General of such violations. They shall keep him informed of their activities.

Article 6. Functions of the Commissioner-General

1. The Commissioner-General for Cultural Property shall deal with all matters referred to him in connexion with the application of the Convention,

in conjunction with the representative of the Party to which he is accredited and with the delegates concerned.

2. He shall have powers of decision and appointment in the cases specified in the present Regulations.

3. With the agreement of the Party to which he is accredited, he shall have the right to order an investigation or to, conduct it himself.

4. He shall make any representations to the Parties to the conflict or to their Protecting Powers which he deems useful for the application of the Convention.

5. He shall draw up such reports as may be necessary on the application of the Convention and communicate them to the Parties concerned and to their Protecting Powers. He shall send copies to the Director-General of the United Nations Educational, Scientific and Cultural Organization, who may make use only of their technical contents.

6. If there is no Protecting Power, the Commissioner-General shall exercise the functions of the Protecting Power as laid down in Articles 21 and 22 of the Convention.

Article 7. Inspectors and experts

1. Whenever the Commissioner-General for Cultural Property considers it necessary, either at the request of the delegates concerned or after consultation with them, he shall propose, for the approval of the Party to which he is accredited, an inspector of cultural property to be charged with a specific mission. An inspector shall be responsible only to the Commissioner-General.

2. The Commissioner-General, delegates and inspectors may have recourse to the services of experts, who will also be proposed for the approval of the Party mentioned in the preceding paragraph.

Article 8. Discharge of the mission of control

The Commissioners-General for Cultural Property, delegates of the Protecting Powers, inspectors and experts shall in no case exceed their mandates. In particular, they shall take account of the security needs of the High Contracting Party to which they are accredited and shall in all circumstances act in accordance with the requirements of the military situation as communicated to them by that High Contracting Party.

Article 9. Substitutes for Protecting Powers

If a Party to the conflict does not benefit or ceases to benefit from the activities of a Protecting Power, a neutral State may be asked to undertake those functions of a Protecting Power which concern the appointment of a Commissioner-General for Cultural Property in accordance with the procedure laid down in Article 4 above. The Commissioner-General thus appointed shall, if need be, entrust to inspectors the functions of delegates of Protecting Powers as specified in the present Regulations.

Article 10. Expenses
The remuneration and expenses of the Commissioner-General for Cultural Property, inspectors and experts shall be met by the Party to which they are accredited. Remuneration and expenses of delegates of the Protecting Powers shall be subject to agreement between those Powers and the States whose interests they are safeguarding.

Chapter II. Special protection

Article 11. Improvised refuges
1. If, during an armed conflict, any High Contracting Party is induced by unforeseen circumstances to set up an improvised refuge and desires that it should be placed under special protection, it shall communicate this fact forthwith to the Commissioner-General accredited to that Party.
2. If the Commissioner-General considers that such a measure is justified by the circumstances and by the importance of the cultural property sheltered in' this improvised refuge, he may authorize the High Contracting Party to display on such refuge the distinctive emblem defined in Article 16 of the Convention. He shall communicate his decision without delay to the delegates of the Protecting Powers who are concerned, each of whom may, within a time limit of 30 days, order the immediate withdrawal of the emblem.
3. As soon as such delegates have signified their agreement or if the time limit of 30 days has passed without any of the delegates concerned having made an objection, and if, in the view of the Commissioner-General, the refuge fulfils the conditions laid down in Article 8 of the Convention, the Commissioner-General shall request the Director-General of the United Nations Educational, Scientific and Cultural Organization to enter the refuge in the Register of Cultural Property under Special Protection.

Article 12. International Register of Cultural Property under Special Protection
1. An 'International Register of Cultural Property under Special Protection' shall be prepared.

2. The Director-General of the United Nations Educational, Scientific and Cultural Organization shall maintain this Register. He shall furnish copies to the Secretary-General of the United Nations and to the High Contracting Parties.

3. The Register shall be divided into sections, each in the name of a High Contracting Party. Each section shall be subdivided into three paragraphs, headed: Refuges, Centers containing Monuments, Other Immovable Cultural Property. The Director-General shall determine what details each section shall contain.

Article 13. Requests for registration

1. Any High Contracting Party may submit to the Director-General of the United Nations Educational, Scientific and Cultural Organization an application for the entry in the Register of certain refuges, centers containing monuments or other immovable cultural property situated within its territory. Such application shall contain a description of the location of such property and shall certify that the property complies with the provisions of Article 8 of the Convention.

2. In the event of occupation, the Occupying Power shall be competent to make such application.

3. The Director-General of the United Nations Educational, Scientific and Cultural Organization shall, without delay, send copies of applications for registration to each of the High Contracting Parties.

Article 14. Objections

1. Any High Contracting Party may, by letter addressed to the Director-General of the United Nations Educational, Scientific and Cultural Organization, lodge an objection to the registration of cultural property. This letter must be received by him within four months of the day on which he sent a copy of the application for registration.

2. Such objection shall state the reasons giving rise to it, the only, valid grounds being that:

(a) the property is not cultural property;

(b) the property does not comply with the conditions mentioned in Article 8 of the Convention.

3. The Director-General shall send a copy of the letter of objection to the High Contracting Parties without delay. He shall, if necessary, seek the advice of the International Committee on Monuments, Artistic and Historical Sites and Archaeological Excavations and also, if he thinks fit, of any other competent organization or person.

4. The Director-General, or the High Contracting Party requesting registration, may make whatever representations they deem necessary to the High Contracting Parties which lodged the objection, with a view to causing the objection to 'be withdrawn.

5. If a High Contracting Party which has made an application for registration in time of peace becomes involved in an armed conflict before the entry has been made, the cultural property concerned shall at once be provisionally entered in the Register, by the Director-General, pending the confirmation, withdrawal or cancellation of any objection that may be, or may have been, made.

6. If, within a period of six months from the date of receipt of the letter of objection, the Director-General has not received from the High Contracting Party lodging the objection a communication stating that it has been withdrawn, the High Contracting Party applying for registration may request arbitration in accordance with the procedure in the following paragraph.

7. The request for •arbitration shall not be made more than one year after the date of receipt by the Director-General of the letter of objection. Each of the two Parties to the dispute shall appoint an arbitrator. When more than one objection has been lodged against an application for registration, the High Contracting Parties which have lodged the 'objections shall, by common consent, appoint a single arbitrator. These two arbitrators shall select a chief arbitrator from the international list mentioned in Article 1 of the present Regulations. If such arbitrators cannot agree upon their choice, they shall ask the President of the International Court of Justice to appoint a chief arbitrator who need not necessarily be chosen from the international list. The arbitral tribunal thus constituted shall fix its own procedure. There shall be no appeal from its decisions.

8. Each of the High Contracting Parties may declare, whenever a dispute to which it is a Party arises, that it does not wish to apply the arbitration procedure provided for in the preceding paragraph. In such cases, the objection to an application for registration shall be submitted by the Director-General to the High Contracting Parties. The objection will be confirmed only if the High Contracting Parties so decide by a two-third majority of the High Contracting Parties voting. The vote shall be taken by correspondence, unless the Directory-General of the United Nations Educational, Scientific and Cultural Organization deems it essential to convene a meeting under the powers conferred upon him by Article 27 of the Convention. If the Director-General decides to proceed with the vote by correspondence, he shall invite the High Contracting Parties to transmit their votes by sealed letter within six months from the day on which they were invited to do so.

Article 15. Registration

1. The Director-General of the United Nations Educational, Scientific and Cultural Organization shall cause to be entered in the Register, under a serial number, each item of property for which application for registration is made, provided that he has not received an objection within the time-limit prescribed in paragraph 1 of Article 14.

2. If an objection has been lodged, and without prejudice to the provision of paragraph 5 of Article 14, the Director-General shall enter property in the Register only if the objection has been withdrawn or has failed to be confirmed following the procedures laid down in either paragraph 7 or paragraph 8 of Article 14.

3. Whenever paragraph 3 of Article 11 applies, the Director-General shall enter property in the Register if so requested by the Commissioner-General for Cultural Property.

4. The Director-General shall send without delay to the Secretary-General of the United Nations, to the High Contracting Parties, and, at the request of the Party applying for registration, to all other States referred to in Articles 30 and 32 of the Convention, a certified copy of each entry in the Register. Entries shall become effective thirty days after despatch of such copies.

Article 16. Cancellation

1. The Director-General of the United Nations Educational, Scientific and Cultural Organization shall cause the registration of any property to be cancelled:

(a) at the request of the High Contracting Party within whose territory the cultural property is situated;

(b) if the High Contracting Party which requested registration has denounced the Convention, and when that denunciation has taken effect;

(c) in the special case provided for in Article 14, paragraph 5, when an objection has been confirmed following the procedures mentioned either in paragraph 7 or in paragraph 8 or Article 14.

2. The Director-General shall send without delay, to the Secretary-General of the United Nations and to all States which received a copy of the entry in the Register, a certified copy of its cancellation. Cancellation shall take effect thirty days after the despatch of such copies.

Chapter III. Transport of cultural property

Article 17. Procedure to obtain immunity

1. The request mentioned in paragraph I of Article 12 of the Convention shall be addressed to the Commissioner-General for Cultural Property. It shall mention the reasons on which it is based and specify the approximate number and the importance of the objects to be transferred, their present location, the location now envisaged, the means of transport to be used, the route to be followed, the date proposed for the transfer, and any other relevant information.

2. If the Commissioner-General, after taking such opinions as he deems fit, considers that such transfer is justified, he shall consult those delegates of the Protecting Powers who are concerned, on the measures proposed for carrying it out. Following such consultation, he shall notify the Parties to the conflict concerned of the transfer, including in such notification all useful information.

3. The Commissioner-General shall appoint one or more inspectors, who shall satisfy themselves that only the property stated in the request is to be transferred and that the transport is to be by the approved methods and bears the distinctive emblem. The inspector or inspectors shall accompany the property to its destination.

Article 18. Transport abroad

Where the transfer under special protection is to the territory of another country, it shall be governed not only by Article 12 of the Convention and by Article 17 of the present Regulations, but by the following further provisions:

(a) while the cultural property remains on the territory of another State, that State shall be its depositary and shall extend to it as great a measure of care as that which it bestows upon its own cultural property of comparable importance;

(b) the depositary State shall return the property only on the cessation of the conflict; such return shall be effected within six months from the date on which it was requested;

(c) during the various transfer operations, and while it remains on the territory of another State, the cultural property shall be exempt from confiscation and may not be disposed of either by the depositor or by the depositary. Nevertheless, when the safety of the property requires it, the depositary may, with the assent of the depositor, have the property transported to the territory of a third country, under the conditions laid down in the present article;

(d) the request for special protection shall indicate that the State to whose territory the property is to be transferred accepts the provisions of the present Article.

Article 19. Occupied territory

Whenever a High Contracting Party occupying territory of another High Contracting Party transfers cultural property to a refuge situated elsewhere in that territory, without being able to follow the procedure provided for in Article 17 of the Regulations, the transfer in question shall not be regarded as misappropriation within the meaning of Article 4 of the Convention, provided that the Commissioner-General for Cultural Property certifies in writing, after having consulted the usual custodians, that such transfer was rendered necessary by circumstances.

Chapter IV. The distinctive emblem

Article 20. Affixing of the emblem

1. The placing of the distinctive emblem and its degree of visibility shall be left to the discretion of the competent authorities of each High Contracting Party. It may be displayed on flags or armlets; it may be painted on an object or represented in any other appropriate form.

2. However, without prejudice to any possible fuller markings, the emblem shall, in the event of armed conflict and in the cases mentioned in Articles 12 and 13 of the Convention, be placed on the vehicles of transport so as to be clearly visible in daylight from the air as well as from the ground. The emblem shall be visible from the ground:

(a) at regular intervals sufficient to indicate clearly the perimeter of a centre containing monuments under special protection;

(b) at the entrance to other immovable cultural property under special protection.

Article 21. Identification of persons

1. The persons mentioned in Article 17, paragraph 2(b) and (c) of the Con-vention may wear an armlet bearing the distinctive emblem, issued and stamped by the competent authorities.

2. Such persons shall carry a special identity card bearing the distinctive emblem. This card shall mention at least the surname and first names, the

date of birth, the title or rank, and the function of the holder. The card shall bear the photograph of the holder as well as his signature or his fingerprints, or both. It shall bear the embossed stamp of the competent authorities.

3. Each High Contracting Party shall make out its own type of identity card, guided by the model annexed, by way of example, to the present Regulations. The High Contracting Parties shall transmit to each other a specimen of the model they are using. Identity cards shall be made out, if possible, at least in duplicate, one copy being kept by the issuing Power.

4. The said persons may not, without legitimate reason, be deprived of their identity card or of the right to wear the armlet.

2. PROTOCOL TO THE CONVENTION FOR THE PROTECTION OF CULTURAL PROPERTY IN THE EVENT OF ARMED CONFLICT 1954

The Hague 14 May 1954[1678]

The High Contracting Parties are agreed as follows :

I.

1. Each High Contracting Party undertakes to prevent the exportation, from a territory occupied by it during an armed conflict, of cultural property as defined in Article 1 of the Convention for the Protection of Cultural Property in the Event of Armed Conflict, signed at The Hague on 14 May, 1954.

2. Each High Contracting Party undertakes to take into its custody cultural property imported into its territory either directly or indirectly from any occupied territory. This shall either be effected automatically upon the importation of the property or, failing this, at the request of the authorities of that territory.

3. Each High Contracting Party undertakes to return, at the close of hostilities, to the competent authorities of the territory previously occupied, cultural property which is in its territory, if such property has been exported in contravention of the principle laid down in the first paragraph. Such property shall never be retained as war reparations.

4. The High Contracting Party whose obligation it was to prevent the exportation of cultural property from the territory occupied by it, shall pay an indemnity to the holders in good faith of any cultural property which has to be returned in accordance with the preceding paragraph.

1678 For the table of signatures, ratifications and accesstions and the texts of the reservations and declarations, see the UNESCO web site: http://erc.unesco.org/cp/convention. asp?KO=15391&language=E

II.

5. Cultural property coming from the territory of a High Contracting Party and deposited by it in the territory of another High Contracting Party for the purpose of protecting such property against the dangers of an armed conflict, shall be returned by the latter, at the end of hostilities, to the competent authorities of the territory from which it came.

III.

6. The present Protocol shall bear the date of 14 May, 1954 and, until the date of 31 December, 1954, shall remain open for signature by all States invited to the Conference which met at The Hague from 21 April, 1954 to 14 May, 1954.

7. (a) The present Protocol shall be subject to ratification by signatory States in accordance with their respective constitutional procedures.

(b) The instruments of ratification shall be deposited with the Director General of the United Nations Educational, Scientific and Cultural Organization.

8. From the date of its entry into force, the present Protocol shall be open for accession by all States mentioned in paragraph 6 which have not signed it as well as any other State invited to accede by the Executive Board of the United Nations Educational, Scientific and Cultural Organization. Accession shall be effected by the deposit of an instrument of accession with the Director-General of the United Nations Educational, Scientific and Cultural Organization.

9. The States referred to in paragraphs 6 and 8 may declare, at the time of signature, ratification or accession, that they will not be bound by the provisions of Section I or by those of Section II of the present Protocol.

10. (a) The present Protocol shall enter into force three months after five instruments of ratification have been deposited.

(b) Thereafter, it shall enter into force, for each High Contracting Party, three months after the deposit of its instrument of ratification or accession.

(c) The situations referred to in Articles 18 and 19 of the Convention for the Protection of Cultural Property in the Event of Armed Conflict, signed at The Hague on 14 May, 1954, shall give immediate effect to ratifications and accessions deposited by the Parties to the conflict either before or after the beginning of hostilities or occupation. In such cases, the Director-General of the United Nations Educational, Scientific and Cultural Organization shall transmit the communications' referred to in paragraph 14 by the speediest method.

11. (a) Each State Party to the Protocol on the date of its entry into force shall take all necessary measures to ensure its effective application within a period of six months after such entry into force.

(b) This period shall be six months from the date of deposit of the instruments of ratification or accession for any State which deposits its instrument of ratification or accession after the date of the entry into force of the Protocol.

12. Any High Contracting Party may, at the time of ratification or accession, or at any time thereafter, declare by notification addressed to the Director General of the United Nations Educational, Scientific and Cultural Organization, that the present Protocol shall extend to all or any of the territories for whose international relations it is responsible. The said notification shall take effect three months after the date of its receipt.

13. (a) Each High Contracting Party may denounce the present Protocol, on its own behalf, or on behalf of any territory for whose international relations it is responsible.

(b) The denunciation shall be notified by an instrument in writing, deposited with the Director-General of the United Nations Educational, Scientific and Cultural Organization.

(c) The denunciation shall take effect one year after receipt of the instrument of denunciation. However, if, on the expiry of this period, the denouncing Party is involved in an armed conflict, the denunciation shall not take effect until the end of hostilities, or until the operations of repatriating cultural property are completed, whichever is the later.

14. The Director-General of the United Nations Educational, Scientific and Cultural Organization shall inform the States referred to in paragraphs 6 and 8, as well as the United Nations, of the deposit of all the instruments of ratification, accession or acceptance provided for in paragraphs 7, 8 and 15 and the notifications and denunciations provided for respectively in paragraphs 12 and 13.

15. (a) The present Protocol may be revised if revision is requested by more than one-third of the High Contracting Parties.

(b) The Director-General of the United Nations Educational, Scientific and Cultural Organization shall convene a Conference for this purpose.

c) Amendments to the present Protocol shall enter into force only after they have been unanimously adopted by the High Contracting Parties represented at the Conference and accepted by each of the High Contracting Parties.

(d) Acceptance by the High Contracting Parties of amendments to the present Protocol, which have been adopted by the Conference mentioned in sub-paragraphs (b) and (c), shall be effected by the deposit of a formal instrument with the Director-General of the United Nations Educational, Scientific and Cultural Organization.

(e) After the entry into force of amendments to the present Protocol, only the text of the said Protocol thus amended shall remain open for ratification or accession.

In accordance with Article 102 of the Charter of the United Nations, the present Protocol shall be registered with the Secretariat of the United Nations at the request of the Director-General of the United Nations Educational, Scientific and Cultural Organization.

IN FAITH WHEREOF the undersigned, duly authorized, have signed the present Protocol.

Done at The Hague, this fourteenth day of May, 1954, in English, French, Russian and Spanish, the four texts being equally authoritative, in a single copy which shall be deposited in the archives of the United Nations Educational, Scientific and Cultural Organization, and certified true copies of which shall be delivered to all the States referred to in paragraphs 6 and 8 as well as to the United Nations.

3. SECOND PROTOCOL TO THE HAGUE CONVENTION OF 1954 FOR THE PROTECTION OF CULTURAL PROPERTY IN THE EVENT OF ARMED CONFLICT

The Hague, 26 March 1999[1679]

The Parties,

Conscious of the need to improve the protection of cultural property in the event of armed conflict and to establish an enhanced system of protection for specifically designated cultural property;

Reaffirming the importance of the provisions of the Convention for the Protection of Cultural Property in the Event of Armed Conflict, done at the Hague on 14 May 1954, and emphasizing the necessity to supplement these provisions through measures to reinforce their implementation;

Desiring to provide the High Contracting Parties to the Convention with a means of being more closely involved in the protection of cultural property in the event of armed conflict by establishing appropriate procedures therefor;

Considering that the rules governing the protection of cultural property in the event of armed conflict should reflect developments in international law;

Affirming that the rules of customary international law will continue to govern questions not regulated by the provisions of this Protocol;

Have agreed as follows:

Chapter 1 Introduction

Article 1 Definitions

For the purposes of this Protocol:

a) 'Party' means a State Party to this Protocol;

b) 'Cultural property' means cultural property as defined in Article 1 of the Convention;

c) 'Convention' means the Convention for the Protection of Cultural Property in the Event of Armed Conflict, done at The Hague on 14 May 1954;

1679 For the table of signatures, ratifications and accesstions and the texts of the reservations and declarations, see the UNESCO web site: http://erc.unesco.org/cp/convention. asp?KO=15207&language=E

d) 'High Contracting Party' means a State Party to the Convention;

e) 'Enhanced protection' means the system of enhanced protection established by Articles 10 and 11;

f) 'Military objective' means an object which by its nature, location, purpose, or use makes an effective contribution to military action and whose total or partial destruction, capture or neutralisation, in the circumstances ruling at the time, offers a definite military advantage;

g) 'Illicit' means under compulsion or otherwise in violation of the applicable rules of the domestic law of the occupied territory or of international law.

h) 'List' means the International List of Cultural Property under Enhanced Protection established in accordance with Article 27, sub-paragraph 1(b);

i) 'Director-General' means the Director-General of UNESCO;

j) 'UNESCO' means the United Nations Educational, Scientific and Cultural Organization;

k) 'First Protocol' means the Protocol for the Protection of Cultural Property in the Event of Armed Conflict done at The Hague on 14 May 1954;

Article 2 Relation to the Convention
This Protocol supplements the Convention in relations between the Parties.

Article 3 Scope of application
In addition to the provisions which shall apply in time of peace, this Protocol shall apply in situations referred to in Article 18 paragraphs 1 and 2 of the Convention and in Article 22 paragraph 1.

When one of the parties to an armed conflict is not bound by this Protocol, the Parties to this Protocol shall remain bound by it in their mutual relations. They shall furthermore be bound by this Protocol in relation to a State party to the conflict which is not bound by it, if the latter accepts the provisions of this Protocol and so long as it applies them.

Article 4 Relationship between Chapter 3 and other provisions of the Convention and this Protocol
The application of the provisions of Chapter 3 of this Protocol is without prejudice to:

a)   the application of the provisions of Chapter I of the Convention and of Chapter 2 of this Protocol;

b)   the application of the provisions of Chapter II of the Convention save that, as between Parties to this Protocol or as between a Party and a State which accepts and applies this Protocol in accordance with Article 3 paragraph 2, where cultural property has been granted both special protection and enhanced protection, only the provisions of enhanced protection shall apply.

Chapter 2 General provisions regarding protection

Article 5 Safeguarding of cultural property

Preparatory measures taken in time of peace for the safeguarding of cultural property against the foreseeable effects of an armed conflict pursuant to Article 3 of the Convention shall include, as appropriate, the preparation of inventories, the planning of emergency measures for protection against fire or structural collapse, the preparation for the removal of movable cultural property or the provision for adequate *in situ* protection of such property, and the designation of competent authorities responsible for the safeguarding of cultural property.

Article 6 Respect for cultural property

With the goal of ensuring respect for cultural property in accordance with Article 4 of the Convention:

a)   a waiver on the basis of imperative military necessity pursuant to Article 4 paragraph 2 of the Convention may only be invoked to direct an act of hostility against cultural property when and for as long as:

(i)   that cultural property has, by its function, been made into a military objective; and

(ii)   there is no feasible alternative available to obtain a similar military advantage to that offered by directing an act of hostility against that objective;

b)   a waiver on the basis of imperative military necessity pursuant to Article 4 paragraph 2 of the Convention may only be invoked to use cultural property for purposes which are likely to expose it to destruction or damage when and for as long as no choice is possible between such use of the cultural property and another feasible method for obtaining a similar military advantage;

c) the decision to invoke imperative military necessity shall only be taken by an officer commanding a force the equivalent of a battalion in size or larger, or a force smaller in size where circumstances do not permit otherwise;

d) in case of an attack based on a decision taken in accordance with sub-paragraph (a), an effective advance warning shall be given whenever circumstances permit.

Article 7 Precautions in attack

Without prejudice to other precautions required by international humanitarian law in the conduct of military operations, each Party to the conflict shall:

a) do everything feasible to verify that the objectives to be attacked are not cultural property protected under Article 4 of the Convention;

b) take all feasible precautions in the choice of means and methods of attack with a view to avoiding, and in any event to minimizing, incidental damage to cultural property protected under Article 4 of the Convention;

c) refrain from deciding to launch any attack which may be expected to cause incidental damage to cultural property protected under Article 4 of the Convention which would be excessive in relation to the concrete and direct military advantage anticipated; and

d) cancel or suspend an attack if it becomes apparent:

    (i)   that the objective is cultural property protected under Article 4 of the Convention;

    (ii)   that the attack may be expected to cause incidental damage to cultural property protected under Article 4 of the Convention which would be excessive in relation to the concrete and direct military advantage anticipated.

Article 8 Precautions against the effects of hostilities

The Parties to the conflict shall, to the maximum extent feasible:

a) remove movable cultural property from the vicinity of military objectives or provide for adequate *in situ* protection;

b) avoid locating military objectives near cultural property.

Article 9 Protection of cultural property in occupied territory

1. Without prejudice to the provisions of Articles 4 and 5 of the Convention, a Party in occupation of the whole or part of the territory of another Party shall prohibit and prevent in relation to the occupied territory:

a) any illicit export, other removal or transfer of ownership of cultural property;

b) any archaeological excavation, save where this is strictly required to safeguard, record or preserve cultural property;

c) any alteration to, or change of use of, cultural property which is intended to conceal or destroy cultural, historical or scientific evidence.

2. Any archaeological excavation of, alteration to, or change of use of, cultural property in occupied territory shall, unless circumstances do not permit, be carried out in close co-operation with the competent national authorities of the occupied territory.

Chapter 3 Enhanced Protection

Article 10 Enhanced protection

Cultural property may be placed under enhanced protection provided that it meets the following three conditions:

a) it is cultural heritage of the greatest importance for humanity;

b) it is protected by adequate domestic legal and administrative measures recognising its exceptional cultural and historic value and ensuring the highest level of protection;

c) it is not used for military purposes or to shield military sites and a declaration has been made by the Party which has control over the cultural property, confirming that it will not be so used.

Article 11 The granting of enhanced protection

1. Each Party should submit to the Committee a list of cultural property for which it intends to request the granting of enhanced protection.

2. The Party which has jurisdiction or control over the cultural property may request that it be included in the List to be established in accordance with Article 27 sub-paragraph 1(b). This request shall include all necessary information related to the criteria mentioned in Article 10. The Committee may invite a Party to request that cultural property be included in the List.

3. Other Parties, the International Committee of the Blue Shield and other non-governmental organizations with relevant expertise may recommend specific cultural property to the Committee. In such cases, the Committee may decide to invite a Party to request inclusion of that cultural property in the List.

4. Neither the request for inclusion of cultural property situated in a territory, sovereignty or jurisdiction over which is claimed by more than one State, nor its inclusion, shall in any way prejudice the rights of the parties to the dispute.

5. Upon receipt of a request for inclusion in the List, the Committee shall inform all Parties of the request. Parties may submit representations regarding such a request to the Committee within sixty days. These representations shall be made only on the basis of the criteria mentioned in Article 10. They shall be specific and related to facts. The Committee shall consider the representations, providing the Party requesting inclusion with a reasonable opportunity to respond before taking the decision. When such representations are before the Committee, decisions for inclusion in the List shall be taken, notwithstanding Article 26, by a majority of four-fifths of its members present and voting.

6. In deciding upon a request, the Committee should ask the advice of governmental and non-governmental organizations, as well as of individual experts.

7. A decision to grant or deny enhanced protection may only be made on the basis of the criteria mentioned in Article 10.

8. In exceptional cases, when the Committee has concluded that the Party requesting inclusion of cultural property in the List cannot fulfil the criteria of Article 10 sub-paragraph (b), the Committee may decide to grant enhanced protection, provided that the requesting Party submits a request for international assistance under Article 32.

9. Upon the outbreak of hostilities, a Party to the conflict may request, on an emergency basis, enhanced protection of cultural property under its jurisdiction or control by communicating this request to the Committee. The Committee shall transmit this request immediately to all Parties to the conflict. In such cases the Committee will consider representations from the Parties concerned on an expedited basis. The decision to grant provisional enhanced protection shall be taken as soon as possible and, notwithstanding Article 26, by a majority of four-fifths of its members present and voting. Provisional enhanced protection may be granted by the Committee pending the outcome of the regular procedure for the granting of enhanced protection, provided that the provisions of Article 10 sub-paragraphs (a) and (c) are met.

10. Enhanced protection shall be granted to cultural property by the Committee from the moment of its entry in the List.

11. The Director-General shall, without delay, send to the Secretary-General of the United Nations and to all Parties notification of any decision of the Committee to include cultural property on the List.

Article 12 Immunity of cultural property under enhanced protection
The Parties to a conflict shall ensure the immunity of cultural property under enhanced protection by refraining from making such property the object of attack or from any use of the property or its immediate surroundings in support of military action.

Article 13 Loss of enhanced protection
1. Cultural property under enhanced protection shall only lose such protection:
    a) if such protection is suspended or cancelled in accordance with Article 14; or
    b) if, and for as long as, the property has, by its use, become a military objective.
2. In the circumstances of sub-paragraph 1(b), such property may only be the object of attack if:
    a) the attack is the only feasible means of terminating the use of the property referred to in sub-paragraph 1(b);
    b) all feasible precautions are taken in the choice of means and methods of attack, with a view to terminating such use and avoiding, or in any event minimising, damage to the cultural property;
    c) unless circumstances do not permit, due to requirements of immediate self-defence:
        i.   the attack is ordered at the highest operational level of command;
        ii. effective advance warning is issued to the opposing forces requiring the termination of the use referred to in sub-paragraph 1(b); and
        iii. reasonable time is given to the opposing forces to redress the situation.

Article 14 Suspension and cancellation of enhanced protection
1. Where cultural property no longer meets any one of the criteria in Article 10 of this Protocol, the Committee may suspend its enhanced protection status or cancel that status by removing that cultural property from the List.

2. In the case of a serious violation of Article 12 in relation to cultural property under enhanced protection arising from its use in support of military action, the Committee may suspend its enhanced protection status. Where such violations are continuous, the Committee may exceptionally cancel the enhanced protection status by removing the cultural property from the List.

3. The Director-General shall, without delay, send to the Secretary-General of the United Nations and to all Parties to this Protocol notification of any decision of the Committee to suspend or cancel the enhanced protection of cultural property.

4. Before taking such a decision, the Committee shall afford an opportunity to the Parties to make their views known.

Chapter 4 Criminal responsibility and jurisdiction

Article 15 Serious violations of this Protocol

1. Any person commits an offence within the meaning of this Protocol if that person intentionally and in violation of the Convention or this Protocol commits any of the following acts:

    a) making cultural property under enhanced protection the object of attack;

    b) using cultural property under enhanced protection or its immediate surroundings in support of military action;

    c) extensive destruction or appropriation of cultural property protected under the Convention and this Protocol;

    d) making cultural property protected under the Convention and this Protocol the object of attack;

    e) theft, pillage or misappropriation of, or acts of vandalism directed against cultural property protected under the Convention.

2. Each Party shall adopt such measures as may be necessary to establish as criminal offences under its domestic law the offences set forth in this Article and to make such offences punishable by appropriate penalties. When doing so, Parties shall comply with general principles of law and international law, including the rules extending individual criminal responsibility to persons other than those who directly commit the act.

Article 16 Jurisdiction

1. Without prejudice to paragraph 2, each Party shall take the necessary legislative measures to establish its jurisdiction over offences set forth in Article 15 in the following cases:

    a) when such an offence is committed in the territory of that State;

    b) when the alleged offender is a national of that State;

    c) in the case of offences set forth in Article 15 sub-paragraphs (a) to (c), when the alleged offender is present in its territory.

2. With respect to the exercise of jurisdiction and without prejudice to Article 28 of the Convention:

    a) this Protocol does not preclude the incurring of individual criminal responsibility or the exercise of jurisdiction under national and international law that may be applicable, or affect the exercise of jurisdiction under customary international law;

    b) except in so far as a State which is not Party to this Protocol may accept and apply its provisions in accordance with Article 3 paragraph 2, members of the armed forces and nationals of a State which is not Party to this Protocol, except for those nationals serving in the armed forces of a State which is a Party to this Protocol, do not incur individual criminal responsibility by virtue of this Protocol, nor does this Protocol impose an obligation to establish jurisdiction over such persons or to extradite them.

Article 17 Prosecution

1. The Party in whose territory the alleged offender of an offence set forth in Article 15 sub-paragraphs 1(a) to (c) is found to be present shall, if it does not extradite that person, submit, without exception whatsoever and without undue delay, the case to its competent authorities, for the purpose of prosecution, through proceedings in accordance with its domestic law or with, if applicable, the relevant rules of international law.

2. Without prejudice to, if applicable, the relevant rules of international law, any person regarding whom proceedings are being carried out in connection with the Convention or this Protocol shall be guaranteed fair treatment and a fair trial in accordance with domestic law and international law at all stages of the proceedings, and in no cases shall be provided guarantees less favorable to such person than those provided by international law.

Article 18 Extradition

1.   The offences set forth in Article 15 sub-paragraphs 1(a) to (c) shall be deemed to be included as extraditable offences in any extradition treaty existing between any of the Parties before the entry into force of this Protocol. Parties undertake to include such offences in every extradition treaty to be subsequently concluded between them.
2.   When a Party which makes extradition conditional on the existence of a treaty receives a request for extradition from another Party with which it has no extradition treaty, the requested Party may, at its option, consider the present Protocol as the legal basis for extradition in respect of offences as set forth in Article 15 sub-paragraphs 1(a) to (c).
3.   Parties which do not make extradition conditional on the existence of a treaty shall recognise the offences set forth in Article 15 sub-paragraphs 1(a) to (c) as extraditable offences between them, subject to the conditions provided by the law of the requested Party.
4.   If necessary, offences set forth in Article 15 sub-paragraphs 1(a) to (c) shall be treated, for the purposes of extradition between Parties, as if they had been committed not only in the place in which they occurred but also in the territory of the Parties that have established jurisdiction in accordance with Article 16 paragraph 1.

Article 19 Mutual legal assistance

1.   Parties shall afford one another the greatest measure of assistance in connection with investigations or criminal or extradition proceedings brought in respect of the offences set forth in Article 15, including assistance in obtaining evidence at their disposal necessary for the proceedings.
2.   Parties shall carry out their obligations under paragraph 1 in conformity with any treaties or other arrangements on mutual legal assistance that may exist between them. In the absence of such treaties or arrangements, Parties shall afford one another assistance in accordance with their domestic law.

Article 20 Grounds for refusal

1.   For the purpose of extradition, offences set forth in Article 15 sub-paragraphs 1(a) to (c), and for the purpose of mutual legal assistance, offences set forth in Article 15 shall not be regarded as political offences nor as offences connected with political offences nor as offences inspired by political motives. Accordingly, a request for extradition or for mutual

legal assistance based on such offences may not be refused on the sole ground that it concerns a political offence or an offence connected with a political offence or an offence inspired by political motives.

2. Nothing in this Protocol shall be interpreted as imposing an obligation to extradite or to afford mutual legal assistance if the requested Party has substantial grounds for believing that the request for extradition for offences set forth in Article 15 sub-paragraphs 1(a) to (c) or for mutual legal assistance with respect to offences set forth in Article 15 has been made for the purpose of prosecuting or punishing a person on account of that person's race, religion, nationality, ethnic origin or political opinion or that compliance with the request would cause prejudice to that person's position for any of these reasons.

Article 21 Measures regarding other violations

1. Without prejudice to Article 28 of the Convention, each Party shall adopt such legislative, administrative or disciplinary measures as may be necessary to suppress the following acts when committed intentionally:
    a) any use of cultural property in violation of the Convention or this Protocol;
    b) any illicit export, other removal or transfer of ownership of cultural property from occupied territory in violation of the Convention or this Protocol.

Chapter 5 The protection of cultural property in armed conflicts not of an international character

Article 22 Armed conflicts not of an international character

1. This Protocol shall apply in the event of an armed conflict not of an international character, occurring within the territory of one of the Parties.

2. This Protocol shall not apply to situations of internal disturbances and tensions, such as riots, isolated and sporadic acts of violence and other acts of a similar nature.

3. Nothing in this Protocol shall be invoked for the purpose of affecting the sovereignty of a State or the responsibility of the government, by all legitimate means, to maintain or re-establish law and order in the State or to defend the national unity and territorial integrity of the State.

4. Nothing in this Protocol shall prejudice the primary jurisdiction of a Party in whose territory an armed conflict not of an international character occurs over the violations set forth in Article 15.
5. Nothing in this Protocol shall be invoked as a justification for intervening, directly or indirectly, for any reason whatever, in the armed conflict or in the internal or external affairs of the Party in the territory of which that conflict occurs.
6. The application of this Protocol to the situation referred to in paragraph 1 shall not affect the legal status of the parties to the conflict.
7. UNESCO may offer its services to the parties to the conflict.

Chapter 6 Institutional Issues

Article 23 Meeting of the Parties

1. The Meeting of the Parties shall be convened at the same time as the General Conference of UNESCO, and in co-ordination with the Meeting of the High Contracting Parties, if such a meeting has been called by the Director-General.
2. The Meeting of the Parties shall adopt its Rules of Procedure.
3. The Meeting of the Parties shall have the following functions:
    a) to elect the Members of the Committee, in accordance with Article 24 paragraph 1;
    b) to endorse the Guidelines developed by the Committee in accordance with Article 27 sub-paragraph 1(a);
    c) to provide guidelines for, and to supervise the use of the Fund by the Committee;
    d) to consider the report submitted by the Committee in accordance with Article 27 sub-paragraph 1(d);
    e) to discuss any problem related to the application of this Protocol, and to make recommendations, as appropriate.
4. At the request of at least one-fifth of the Parties, the Director-General shall convene an Extraordinary Meeting of the Parties.

Article 24 Committee for the Protection of Cultural Property in the Event of Armed Conflict

1. The Committee for the Protection of Cultural Property in the Event of Armed Conflict is hereby established. It shall be composed of twelve Parties which shall be elected by the Meeting of the Parties.

2. The Committee shall meet once a year in ordinary session and in extra-ordinary sessions whenever it deems necessary.
3. In determining membership of the Committee, Parties shall seek to ensure an equitable representation of the different regions and cultures of the world.
4. Parties members of the Committee shall choose as their representatives persons qualified in the fields of cultural heritage, defence or international law, and they shall endeavour, in consultation with one another, to ensure that the Committee as a whole contains adequate expertise in all these fields.

Article 25 Term of office
1. A Party shall be elected to the Committee for four years and shall be eligible for immediate re-election only once.
2. Notwithstanding the provisions of paragraph 1, the term of office of half of the members chosen at the time of the first election shall cease at the end of the first ordinary session of the Meeting of the Parties following that at which they were elected. These members shall be chosen by lot by the President of this Meeting after the first election.

Article 26 Rules of procedure
1. The Committee shall adopt its Rules of Procedure.
2. A majority of the members shall constitute a quorum. Decisions of the Committee shall be taken by a majority of two-thirds of its members voting.
3. Members shall not participate in the voting on any decisions relating to cultural property affected by an armed conflict to which they are parties.

Article 27 Functions
1. The Committee shall have the following functions:
a) to develop Guidelines for the implementation of this Protocol;
b) to grant, suspend or cancel enhanced protection for cultural property and to establish, maintain and promote the List of Cultural Property under Enhanced Protection;
c) to monitor and supervise the implementation of this Protocol and promote the identification of cultural property under enhanced protection;

d)   to consider and comment on reports of the Parties, to seek clarifications as required, and prepare its own report on the implementation of this Protocol for the Meeting of the Parties;

e)   to receive and consider requests for international assistance under Article 32;

f)   to determine the use of the Fund;

g)   to perform any other function which may be assigned to it by the Meeting of the Parties.

2.   The functions of the Committee shall be performed in co-operation with the Director-General.

3.   The Committee shall co-operate with international and national governmental and non-governmental organizations having objectives similar to those of the Convention, its First Protocol and this Protocol. To assist in the implementation of its functions, the Committee may invite to its meetings, in an advisory capacity, eminent professional organizations such as those which have formal relations with UNESCO, including the International Committee of the Blue Shield (ICBS) and its constituent bodies. Representatives of the International Centre for the Study of the Preservation and Restoration of Cultural Property (Rome Centre) (ICCROM) and of the International Committee of the Red Cross (ICRC) may also be invited to attend in an advisory capacity.

Article 28 Secretariat

The Committee shall be assisted by the Secretariat of UNESCO which shall prepare the Committee's documentation and the agenda for its meetings and shall have the responsibility for the implementation of its decisions.

Article 29 The Fund for the Protection of Cultural Property in the Event of Armed Conflict

1.   A Fund is hereby established for the following purposes:

a)   to provide financial or other assistance in support of preparatory or other measures to be taken in peacetime in accordance with, *inter alia*, Article 5, Article 10 sub-paragraph (b) and Article 30; and

b)   to provide financial or other assistance in relation to emergency, provisional or other measures to be taken in order to protect cultural property during periods of armed conflict or of immediate recovery after the end of hostilities in accordance with, *inter alia*, Article 8 sub-paragraph (a).

2.   The Fund shall constitute a trust fund, in conformity with the provisions of the financial regulations of UNESCO.

3.   Disbursements from the Fund shall be used only for such purposes as the Committee shall decide in accordance with the guidelines as defined in Article 23 sub-paragraph 3(c). The Committee may accept contributions to be used only for a certain programme or project, provided that the Committee shall have decided on the implementation of such programme or project.

4.   The resources of the Fund shall consist of:
  a)   voluntary contributions made by the Parties;
  b)   contributions, gifts or bequests made by:
      (i)   other States;
      (ii) UNESCO or other organizations of the United Nations system;
      (iii) other intergovernmental or non-governmental organizations; and
      (iv) public or private bodies or individuals;
  c)   any interest accruing on the Fund;
  d)   funds raised by collections and receipts from events organized for the benefit of the Fund; and
  e)   all other resources authorized by the guidelines applicable to the Fund.

Chapter 7 Dissemination of Information and International Assistance

Article 30 Dissemination

1.   The Parties shall endeavour by appropriate means, and in particular by educational and information programmes, to strengthen appreciation and respect for cultural property by their entire population.

2.   The Parties shall disseminate this Protocol as widely as possible, both in time of peace and in time of armed conflict.

3.   Any military or civilian authorities who, in time of armed conflict, assume responsibilities with respect to the application of this Protocol, shall be fully acquainted with the text thereof. To this end the Parties shall, as appropriate:
  a)   incorporate guidelines and instructions on the protection of cultural property in their military regulations;

b)   develop and implement, in cooperation with UNESCO and relevant governmental and non-governmental organizations, peacetime training and educational programmes;

c)   communicate to one another, through the Director-General, information on the laws, administrative provisions and measures taken under sub-paragraphs (a) and (b);

d)   communicate to one another, as soon as possible, through the Director-General, the laws and administrative provisions which they may adopt to ensure the application of this Protocol.

Article 31 International cooperation

In situations of serious violations of this Protocol, the Parties undertake to act, jointly through the Committee, or individually, in cooperation with UNESCO and the United Nations and in conformity with the Charter of the United Nations.

Article 32 International assistance

1.   A Party may request from the Committee international assistance for cultural property under enhanced protection as well as assistance with respect to the preparation, development or implementation of the laws, administrative provisions and measures referred to in Article 10.

2.   A party to the conflict, which is not a Party to this Protocol but which accepts and applies provisions in accordance with Article 3, paragraph 2, may request appropriate international assistance from the Committee.

3.   The Committee shall adopt rules for the submission of requests for international assistance and shall define the forms the international assistance may take.

4.   Parties are encouraged to give technical assistance of all kinds, through the Committee, to those Parties or parties to the conflict who request it.

Article 33 Assistance of UNESCO

1.   A Party may call upon UNESCO for technical assistance in organizing the protection of its cultural property, such as preparatory action to safeguard cultural property, preventive and organizational measures for emergency situations and compilation of national inventories of cultural property, or in connection with any other problem arising out of the application of this Protocol. UNESCO shall accord such assistance within the limits fixed by its programme and by its resources.

2. Parties are encouraged to provide technical assistance at bilateral or multilateral level.
3. UNESCO is authorized to make, on its own initiative, proposals on these matters to the Parties.

Chapter 8 Execution of this Protocol

Article 34 Protecting Powers
This Protocol shall be applied with the co-operation of the Protecting Powers responsible for safeguarding the interests of the Parties to the conflict.

Article 35 Conciliation procedure
1. The Protecting Powers shall lend their good offices in all cases where they may deem it useful in the interests of cultural property, particularly if there is disagreement between the Parties to the conflict as to the application or interpretation of the provisions of this Protocol.
2. For this purpose, each of the Protecting Powers may, either at the invitation of one Party, of the Director-General, or on its own initiative, propose to the Parties to the conflict a meeting of their representatives, and in particular of the authorities responsible for the protection of cultural property, if considered appropriate, on the territory of a State not party to the conflict. The Parties to the conflict shall be bound to give effect to the proposals for meeting made to them. The Protecting Powers shall propose for approval by the Parties to the conflict a person belonging to a State not party to the conflict or a person presented by the Director-General, which person shall be invited to take part in such a meeting in the capacity of Chairman.

Article 36 Conciliation in absence of Protecting Powers
1. In a conflict where no Protecting Powers are appointed the Director-General may lend good offices or act by any other form of conciliation or mediation, with a view to settling the disagreement.
2. At the invitation of one Party or of the Director-General, the Chairman of the Committee may propose to the Parties to the conflict a meeting of their representatives, and in particular of the authorities responsible for the protection of cultural property, if considered appropriate, on the territory of a State not party to the conflict.

Article 37 Translations and reports
1.   The Parties shall translate this Protocol into their official languages and shall communicate these official translations to the Director-General.
2.   The Parties shall submit to the Committee, every four years, a report on the implementation of this Protocol.

Article 38 State responsibility
No provision in this Protocol relating to individual criminal responsibility shall affect the responsibility of States under international law, including the duty to provide reparation.

Chapter 9 Final Clauses

Article 39 Languages
This Protocol is drawn up in Arabic, Chinese, English, French, Russian and Spanish, the six texts being equally authentic.

Article 40 Signature
This Protocol shall bear the date of 26 March 1999. It shall be opened for signature by all High Contracting Parties at The Hague from 17 May 1999 until 31 December 1999.

Article 41 Ratification, acceptance or approval
1.   This Protocol shall be subject to ratification, acceptance or approval by High Contracting Parties which have signed this Protocol, in accordance with their respective constitutional procedures.
2.   The instruments of ratification, acceptance or approval shall be deposited with the Director-General.

Article 42 Accession
1.   This Protocol shall be open for accession by other High Contracting Parties from 1 January 2000.
2.   Accession shall be effected by the deposit of an instrument of accession with the Director-General.

Article 43 Entry into force
1.   This Protocol shall enter into force three months after twenty instruments of ratification, acceptance, approval or accession have been deposited.

2.   Thereafter, it shall enter into force, for each Party, three months after the deposit of its instrument of ratification, acceptance, approval or accession.

Article 44 Entry into force in situations of armed conflict

The situations referred to in Articles 18 and 19 of the Convention shall give immediate effect to ratifications, acceptances or approvals of or accessions to this Protocol deposited by the parties to the conflict either before or after the beginning of hostilities or occupation. In such cases the Director-General shall transmit the communications referred to in Article 46 by the speediest method.

Article 45 Denunciation

1.   Each Party may denounce this Protocol.
2.   The denunciation shall be notified by an instrument in writing, deposited with the Director-General.
3.   The denunciation shall take effect one year after the receipt of the instrument of denunciation. However, if, on the expiry of this period, the denouncing Party is involved in an armed conflict, the denunciation shall not take effect until the end of hostilities, or until the operations of repatriating cultural property are completed, whichever is the later.

Article 46 Notifications

The Director-General shall inform all High Contracting Parties as well as the United Nations, of the deposit of all the instruments of ratification, acceptance, approval or accession provided for in Articles 41 and 42 and of denunciations provided for Article 45.

Article 47 Registration with the United Nations

In conformity with Article 102 of the Charter of the United Nations, this Protocol shall be registered with the Secretariat of the United Nations at the request of the Director-General.

IN FAITH WHEREOF the undersigned, duly authorized, have signed the present Protocol.

DONE at The Hague, this twenty-sixth day of March 1999, in a single copy which shall be deposited in the archives of the UNESCO, and certified true copies of which shall be delivered to all the High Contracting Parties.

SELECT BIBLIOGRAPHY

Abtahi, H. 2001. The protection of cultural property in times of armed conflict: the Practice of the International Criminal Tribunal for the former Yugoslavia. *Harvard Human Rights Journal*, Vol. 14, pp. 1–32.

Aldrich, G. H. 1998. *Analysis of the Preliminary Draft Second Protocol to the 1954 Hague Convention.* Mimeographed manuscript of 9 December.

Aleksandrov, E. 1979. *International Legal Protection of Cultural Property.* Sofia: Sofia Press.

——. 1978a. *La protection du patrimoine culturel en droit international public.* Sofia: Sofia Press, 1978.

——. 1978b. *Le Pacte Roerich et la protection internationale des institutions et des valeurs Culturelles.* Sofia: Sofia Press.

Aloisi, U. 1935. Protezione internazionale delle cose di pregio storico o artistico. *Giuistizia penale*, Vol. 41, pp. 577–600.

Alttunov, I. 1962. Problemata za zashtita na kulturnite tsennosti v sluchai na voina. *Izvestiia na Instituta za Pravni Nauki* (Sofia), Vol. 12, No. 2, pp. 31–70.

Ambos, K. 2002. Superior responsibility. A. Cassese, P. Gaeta and J. R. W. D. Jones (eds.), *The Rome Statute of the International Criminal Court: A Commentary.* Oxford: Oxford University Press, Vol. I, pp. 823–32.

American Society of International Law (ASIL). 1999. Restitution for historic wrongs: World War II's last chapter. *American Society of International Law. Proceedings of the Annual Meeting*, Vol. 93, p. 75 (panel summary).

——. 1977. The international protection of cultural property [Panel]. *American Society of International Law: Proceedings of the 71st Annual Meeting*, Vol. 71, pp. 196–207.

Anon. 1978. Der Schutz von Kulturgut in bewaffneten Konflikten. *Zivilschutz*, Vol. 25, No. 9, pp. 277–81.

Anon. 1964. Kriegsvölkerrecht: 'Der Schutz von Kulturgut bei bewaffneten Konflikten'. *Unterrichstblätter für die Bundeswehrverwaltung*, Vol. 3, pp. 174–76.

Anon. 1939. Guerre terrestre et aérienne. La protection des monuments et œuvres d'art au cours des conflits armés: projet de convention internationale et exposé des motifs. *Revue de droit international et de législation comparée*, Vol. 20, No. 3, pp. 608–24.

Anon. 1917. *Zerstörte Kunstdenkmäler an der Westfront. Das schonungslose Vorgehen der Engländer und Franzosen.* 2nd edn. Weimar: Kiepenheuer.

Arcioni, G. 1984. Protezione dei beni culturali: uno degli scopi della nostra difesa generale. *Rivista militare della svizzera italiana*, No. 5, pp. 365–74.

———. 1981. La protection des biens culturels – l'un des buts de notre défense générale. *Le mois économique et financier*, No. 9, pp. 23–25.

Ardema, A. 2006. The crimes to be judged by the Extraordinary Chambers. J. D. Ciorciari (ed.), *The Khmer Rouge Tribunal*. Phnom Penh, Cambodia: Documentation Center of Cambodia, , p. 55–79. http://www.dccam.org/Publication/Monographs/KR%20Trial.pdf

Armstead, J. H., Jr. 2008. The chain of command. L. Rothfield (ed.), *Antiquities under Siege: Cultural Heritage Protection after the Iraq War*. Lanham, Md.: AltaMira Press, pp. 117–24.

Arnoux de Fleury de l'Hermite, H. d'. 1934. *Objets et monuments d'art devant le droit des gens*. Ph.D. thesis, Université de Paris. Paris: L. Clerex.

Art and War: Special Edition. 2004. *DePaul Journal of Art and Entertainment Law*, Vol. 14, No. 1, pp. 1–169.

Art et archéologie: recueil de législation comparée et de droit international. 1939. No. 1, *La protection des collections nationales d'art et d'histoire: essai de réglementation internationale*. Paris: Office international des musées.

Auer, E. M. 1967a. Schutz der Kulturgüter bei bewaffneten Konflikten, IV: Erfahrungen mit Bergeräumen im zweiten Weltkrieg. *Mitteilungsblatt der Museen Österreichs*, Vol. 16, No. 9–10, pp. 159–62.

———. 1967b. Schutz der Kulturgüter bei bewaffneten Konflikten, V: Technische Richtlinie für Grundschutz in Gebäuden. *Mitteilungsblatt der Museen Österreichs*, Vol. 16, No. 11–12, pp. 191–92.

Aust, A. 2000. *Modern Treaty Law and Practice*. Cambridge: Cambridge University Press.

Bart, G. R. 2009. The ambiguous protection of schools under the law of war: time for parity with hospitals and religious buildings. *Georgetown Journal of International Law*, Vol. 40, No. 2, pp. 405–46.

Bassiouni, M. C. 1992. *Crimes against Humanity in International Criminal Law*. Dordrecht: Kluwer Law International.

———. 1983. Reflections on criminal jurisdiction in international protection of cultural property. *Syracuse Journal of International Law and Commerce*, Vol. 10, No. 2, pp. 218–322.

——— (ed.). 1986. *International Criminal Law*. 3 vols. Dobbs Ferry, N.Y.: Transnational Publishers.

Bassiouni, M. C. and Manikas, P. 1996. *The Law of the International Criminal Tribunal for the Former Yugoslavia.* Irvington-on-Hudson, N.Y.: Transnational Publishers.

Batouncov, G. 1955. *La protection des biens culturels, monuments historiques et oeuvres d'art en cas de conflit armé. Convention de La Haye, 14 mai 1954, sous les auspices de l'U.N.E.S.C.O.* Ph.D. thesis, Paris.

Becker, E. 1986. *When the War Was Over: Cambodia and Khmer Rouge Revolution.* New York: Simon and Schuster.

Belhumeur, J., Miatello, A. and Severino, R. 1996. Les atteintes aux biens culturels italiens pendant les conflits armés. M. Briat and J. A. Freedberg (eds.), *Legal Aspects of International Trade in Art.* International Sales of Works of Art, Vol. 5. The Hague: Kluwer Law International, pp. 185–208.

Berezowski, C. 1948. *Ochrona prawnomiedzynarodowa zabytkow i dziel sztuki w czasie wojny* [*International Legal Protection of Monuments and Works of Art in Wartime*]. Warsaw.

Berti, A. 1963. La convenzione per la protezione dei beni culturali in caso di conflitto armato. *Rassegna dell'arma dei carabinieri,* No. 2, pp. 301–10.

Bhat, P. I. 2001. Protection of cultural property under international humanitarian law: some emerging trends. *ISIL Year Book of International Humanitarian and Refugee Law,* Vol. 1, pp. 47–71.

Birov, V. A. 1998. Prize or plunder? The pillage of works of art and the international law of war. *New York University Journal of International Law and Politics,* Vol. 30, No. 1–2, pp. 201–49.

Bluntschli, J.-G. 1874. *Le droit international codifié.* Paris: Librairie de Guillaumin.

Bolla, G. 1975. Extension territoriale et application pratique de la Convention du 1954. S. Rosso-Mazzinghi (ed.), *Da Antonio Canova alla Convenzionè dell'Aja. Evoluzione della protezione della opera d'arte in caso di conflitto armatto.* Florence: Sansoni.

———. 1974. Protection of cultural property during armed conflicts. *Study Session: Collection of Lectures. International Institute of Human Rights,* Vol. 5, pp. 1–14.

Bories, C. 2005. *Les bombardements serbes sur la vieille ville de Dubrovnik: la protection internationale des biens culturels.* Paris: Pédone.

Bos, A. 2005. The importance of the 1899, 1907 and 1999 Hague Conferences for the Legal Protection of Cultural Property in the Event of Armed Conflict. *Museum International,* No. 228, pp. 32–40.

Bosly, H. 1986. La responsabilité des Etats et des individus quant à l'application de la Convention de La Haye sur la protection des biens culturels en cas de conflit armé. Istituto Internazionale di Diritto Umanitario (ed.), *La protezione internazionale dei beni culturali/The International Protection of Cultural Property/La protection internationale des biens culturels.* Rome: Foundazione Europa Dragan, pp. 81–86.

Bothe, M. War crimes. 2002. A. Cassese, P. Gaeta and J. R. W. D. Jones (eds.), *The Rome Statute of the International Criminal Court: A Commentary.* Oxford: Oxford University Press, Vol. I, pp. 379–426.

Bothe, M., Partsch, K. J. and Solf, W. A. 1982. *New Rules for Victims of Armed Conflicts: Commentary on the Two 1977 Protocols Additional to the Geneva Conventions of 1949.* The Hague: Martinus Nijhoff.

Bouchenaki, M. 2008. UNESCO and the Safeguarding of Cultural Heritage in Postconflict Situations: Efforts at UNESCO to Establish an Intergovernmental Fund for the Protection of Cultural Property in Times of Conflict. L. Rothfield (ed.), *Antiquities under Siege: Cultural Heritage Protection after the Iraq War.* Lanham, Md.: AltaMira Press, pp. 207–18.

Bowett, D. W. 1982. *The Law of International Institutions.* 4th edn. London: Stevens & Sons.

Boylan, P. J. 2002. The 1954 Hague Convention on the Protection of Cultural Property in the Event of Armed Conflict and Its 1954 and 1999 Protocols. F. Maniscalco (ed.), *La tutela del patrimonio culturale in caso di conflitto.* Naples: Massa, pp. 41–52.

———. 1993. *Review of the Convention for the Protection of Cultural Property in the Event of Armed Conflict (The Hague Convention of 1954).* Paris: UNESCO.

Boyle, D. 2002. Establishing the responsibility of the Khmer Rouge leadership for International Crimes. *Yearbook of International Humanitarian Law,* Vol. 5, pp. 167–218.

Breddels, J. 1986. The dissemination of the Hague Convention: armed forces, the civilian population and the academic circles. Istituto Internazionale di Diritto Umanitario (ed.), *La protezione internazionale dei beni culturali/The International Protection of Cultural Property/La protection internationale des biens culturels.* Rome: Foundazione Europa Dragan, pp. 101–5.

Breitenmoser, S. and Wilms, G. E. 1990. Human rights v. extradition: the Soering case. *Michigan Journal of International Law,* Vol. 11, pp. 845–86.

Breucker, J de. 1975a. La réserve des nécessités militaires dans la Convention de la Haye du 14 mai 1954 sur la protection des biens culturels. *Revue du droit pénal militaire et de droit de la guerre*, Vol. 14, pp. 255–69.

———. 1975b. Pour les vingt ans de la Convention de La Haye du 14 Mai 1954 pour la protection des biens culturels. *Revue belge de droit international*, Vol. 11, pp. 525–47.

Brüderlin, P. 1978. *Kulturgüterschutz in der Schweiz: gemäss internationalem Abkommen v. Den Haag 1954 über 'Kulturgüterschutz bei bewaffneten Konflikten'*. Zürich: Brüderlin.

Büchel, R. 2004. Mesures préventives prises en Suisse dans le cadre de la protection des biens culturels. *IRRC*, No. 854, pp. 325–36.

Büchel, R. and Hostettler, P. 2002. Protection of cultural property: reflections from a civilian and military point of view: what is cultural property, and how is it protected under international humanitarian law? E. R. Micewski and G. Sladek (eds.), *Protection of Cultural Property in the Event of Armed Conflict: A Challenge in Peace Support Operations*. Vienna: Armed Forces Printing Office, pp. 29–39. http://www.bmlv.gv.at/pdf_pool/publikationen/05_pcp.pdf

Bugnion, F. 2004. La genèse de la protection juridique des biens culturels en cas de conflit armé. *IRRC*, No. 854, pp. 313–24.

Buhse, K.-H. 1959. *Der Schutz von Kulturgut im Krieg. Unter besonderer Berücksichtigung der Konvention zum Schutze des Kulturguts im Falle eines bewaffneten Konfliktes vom 14 Mai 1954*. Hamburg: Hansischer Gildenver, Heitmann.

Buisman, C. 2003. IV. Defence and fair trial. R. Haveman, O. Kavran and J. Nicholls (eds.), *Supranational Criminal Law: A System Sui Generis*. Antwerp: Intersentia, pp. 167–237.

Bundesamt für zivilen Bevölkerungsschutz. 1966. *Der Schutz von Kulturgütern bei bewaffneten Konflikten: Haager Konvention vom 14. Mai 1954 für den Schutz von Kulturgütern bei bewaffneten Konflikten*. Bonn: Bundesamt für zivilen Bevölkerungsschutz.

Bundesministerium der Verteidigung. 1972. *Der Schutz von Kulturgut bei bewaffneten Konflikten in Bild und Wort*. Bonn: Bundesministerium der Verteidigung.

Burke, K. T. 1990. International transfers of stolen cultural property: should thieves continue to benefit from domestic laws favoring bona fide purchasers? *Loyola of Los Angeles International and Comparative Law Journal*, Vol. 13, No. 2, pp. 427–66.

Burr, N. R. 1952. *Safeguarding Our Cultural Heritage: A Bibliography on the Protection of Museums, Works of Art, Monuments, Archives and Libraries in Time of War.* Washington, DC: Library of Congress.

Bystrický, R. 1962. *Mezinarodní kulturní dohody a organizace [International Cultural Agreements and Organizations].* Prague: Orbis, pp. 178–84.

Calzada, M. de la. 1952. La protección juridica internacional del patrimonio cultural en caso de guerra. *Revista de estudios políticos,* Vol. 43, pp. 141–82.

Campagna, J. V. 2005. War or peace? It is time to ratify the 1954 Hague Convention for the Protection of Cultural Property in the Event of Armed Conflict. *Florida Journal of International Law,* Vol. 17, pp. 271–344.

Candrian, J. 2005. *L'immunité des États face aux droits de l'homme et à la protection des biens culturels: immunité de juridiction des États et droits de l'homme, immunité d'exécution des États et de leurs biens culturels.* Zurich: Schulthess.

Cardini, F. 1992. *La Culture de la Guerre.* Paris: Gallimard.

Carducci, G. 2008. The Implementation of International Treaties at the National Level: Law and Practice. L. Rothfield (ed.), *Antiquities under Siege: Cultural Heritage Protection after the Iraq War.* Lanham, Md.: AltaMira Press, pp. 89–100.

———. 2000a. Beni culturali in diritto internazionale pubblico e privato. *Enciclopedia giuridica italiana.* Rome: Treccani.

———. 2000b. L'obligation de restitution des biens culturels et des objets d'art en cas de conflit armé: droit coutumier et droit conventionnel avant et après la Convention de La Haye de 1954. L'importance du facteur temporel dans les rapports entre les traités et la coutume. *Revue générale de droit international public,* Vol. 104, No. 2, pp. 289–367.

———. 1997. *La Restitution internationale des biens culturels et des objets d'art volés ou illicitement exportés: droit commun, Directive CEE, Conventions de l'UNESCO et d'Unidroit.* Paris: LGDJ.

Casanovas y la Rosa, O. 1993. La protección internacional del patrimonio cultural. *Anuario Hispano-Luso-Americano de derecho internacional,* Vol. 10, pp. 45–113.

Cassese, A. 2003. *International Criminal Law.* Oxford: Oxford University Press.

———. 1996. The International Criminal Tribunal for the Former Yugoslavia and the implementation of international humanitarian law. Condorelli, L., La Rosa, A.-M. and Scherrer, S. (eds.), *Les Nations Unies et le droit international humanitaire.* Paris: Pédone, pp. 229–47.

Cassese, A., Gaeta, P. and Jones, J. R. W. D. (eds.). 2002. *The Rome Statute of the International Criminal Court: A Commentary.* 2 vols. Oxford: Oxford University Press.

Cassou, J. (ed.). 1947. *Le pillage par les Allemands des oeuvres d'art et des bibliothèques appartenant à des Juifs en France: Receuil de documents.* Paris: Éditions du centre.

Cavalli, F. 1960. La Santa Sede e la Convenzione dell'Aja per la protezione dei beni culturali in caso di conflitto armato. *Rivista di Studi Politici Internazionali*, Vol. 27, pp. 126–37.

Cera, R. 2005. La tutela del patrimonio culturale in Iraq. *Affari esteri*, Vol. 37, No. 147, pp. 635–43.

Chamberlain, K. 2004. *War and Cultural Heritage: An Analysis of the 1954 Convention for the Protection of Cultural Property in the Event of Armed Conflicts and Its Two Protocols.* Leicester: Institute of Art and Law.

——. 2003. The protection of cultural property in armed conflict. *Art, Antiquity and Law*, Vol. 8, No. 3, pp. 209–40.

Chandler, A. D., Jr. (ed.). 1970. *The Papers of Dwight David Eisenhower: The War Years.* 5 vols. Baltimore, Md.: Johns Hopkins University Press.

Chandler, D., Kiernan, B. and Boua, C. (eds.). 1988. *Pol Pot Plans the Future: Confidential Leadership Documents from Democratic Kampuchea, 1976-1977.* Translated by the editors. Southeast Asian Studies Monograph Series No. 33. New Haven, Conn.: Yale University Press.

Chhang, Y. 2009. Duch's hearing: a turning point for Cambodia. *Cambodia Tribunal Monitor*, 30 March. http://www.cambodiatribunal.org/index. php?option=com_myblog&show=test-68.html&Itemid=56

——. 2000. Universal Jurisdiction and the Problem of Impunity in Cambodia: The Khmer Rouge's Case. Report for Institute of International Council on Human Rights Policy International Conference, Geneva, 6–8 May 1999. *Searching for the Truth*, No.11, pp.27-29. http://dccam.org/ Projects/Magazines/Previous%20Englis/Issue11.pdf

Chklaver, G. 1938. La protection des monuments historiques et des oeuvres d'art en temps de guerre. *Premier Congrès d'Études Internationales: Paris, 30 septembre-7 octobre 1937.* Publication de l'Institut de hautes études internationales de l'Université de Paris, 1. Paris: Les Éditions Internationales, pp. 66–67.

——. 1933. Le mouvement en faveur du Pacte Roerich. *Revue de droit international*, Vol. 11, pp. 460–62.

————. 1930. Projet d'une Convention pour la protection des institutions et monuments consacrés aux arts et aux sciences. *Revue de droit international*, Vol. 6, pp. 52–81.

Ciorciari, J. D. (ed.). 2006. *The Khmer Rouge Tribunal*. Phnom Penh, Cambodia: Documentation Centre of Cambodia. http://www.dccam. org/Publication/Monographs/KR%20Trial.pdf

Ciorciari, J. D. and Chhang, Y. 2005. Documenting the crimes of Democratic Kampuchea. J. Ramji and B. Van Schaack (eds.), *Bringing the Khmer Rouge to Justice. Prosecuting Mass Violence before the Cambodian Courts*. Lewinston, N.Y.: Edwin Mellen Press, pp. 221–306. http://www.dccam. org/Archives/Documenting_the_Crimes_of_DK_by_John&Youk.pdf

Clemen, P. de. 1919. *Kunstschutz im Kriege. Berichte über den Zustand der Kunstdenkmäler auf den verschiedenen Kriegsschauplätzen und über die deutschen und österreichischen Massnahmen zu ihrer Erhaltung, Rettung, Erforschung*. 2 vols. Leipzig: E. A. Seemann.

————. 1916. *Der Zustand der Kunstdenkmäler auf dem westlichen Kriegschauplatz*. Leipzig: E. A. Seemann.

Clémens, R. 1937. *Le Projet de Monaco, le droit et la guerre: villes sanitaires et villes de sécurité, assistance sanitaire internationale*. Paris: Librairie du recueil Sirey.

Clément, E. 1996. UNESCO: Some specific cases of recovery of cultural property after an armed conflict. M. Briat and J. A. Freedberg (eds.), *Legal Aspects of International Trade in Art*. International Sales of Works of Art, Vol. 5. The Hague: Kluwer Law International, pp. 157–62.

————. 1995. Le réexamen de la Convention de La Haye de 1954 pour la protection des biens culturels en cas de conflit armé. N. Al-Naumi and R. Meese (eds.), *International Legal Issues Arising under the United Nations Decade of International Law*. The Hague: Martinus Nijhoff, pp. 133–50.

————. 1994. Some recent practical experience in the implementation of the 1954 Hague Convention. *International Journal of Cultural Property*, Vol. 3, No. 1, pp. 11–25.

————. 1993. Le concept de responsabilité collective de la communauté internationale pour la protection des biens culturels dans les conventions et recommendations de l'UNESCO. *Revue belge de droit international*, 26, No. 2, pp. 534–51.

Clément, E. and Quinio, F. 2004. La protection des biens culturels au Cambodge pendant la période des conflits armés, à travers l'application de la Convention de la Haye de 1954. *IRRC*, No. 854, pp. 389–97.

Clément, E. and Seguroal, A. 2004. Les instruments du droit international public pour la protection des biens culturels. N. Mezghani and M. Cornu (eds.), *Intérêt culturel et mondialisation*. Paris: L'Harmattan, pp. 77–116.

Cloşcă, I. 1980. New code for the protection of civilian population and property during armed conflict. *IRRC*, No. 219, pp. 287–315.

Cockayne, J. 2005. The fraying shoestring: rethinking hybrid war crimes tribunals. *Fordham International Law Journal*, Vol. 28, pp. 616–80.

Cohen, D. 2007. 'Hybrid' justice in East Timor, Sierra Leone and Cambodia: 'lessons learned' and prospects for the future. *Stanford Journal of International Law*, Vol. 43, pp. 1–38.

Colby, E. 1925. Aerial law and war targets. *American Journal of International Law*, Vol. 19, pp. 702–15.

Colloque d'experts européns sur la Convention de La Haye du 14 mai 1954 pour la protection des biens culturels en cas de conflit armé : Zurich (Suisse), les 29, 30 et 31 octobre 1969, [Zurich, SSPBC].

Colloque d'experts internationaux sur l'adaptation du droit international relatif à la protection de la propriété culturelle au développement technique des moyens de guerre. IIDH, Florence, 31 October 1.

Colwell-Chanthaphonh, C. and Piper, J. 2001. War and cultural property: the 1954 Hague Convention and the status of U.S. ratification. *International Journal of Cultural Property*, Vol. 10, No. 1, pp. 217–45.

Comitato del Patto internazionale Roerich. 1950. *Fonti bibliografiche del patto internazionale Roerich*. Bologna: Comitato del Patto Internazionale Roerich.

Coremans, P. B. 1946. *La protection scientifique des oeuvres d'art en temps de guerre; l'expérience européenne pendant les années 1939 à 1945*. Brussels: Laboratoire central des musées de Belgique.

Corn, G. S. 2005. Snipers in the minaret – what is the rule? The law of war and the protection of cultural property: a complex equation. *Army Lawyer*, July, pp. 28–40.

Crabb, J. 1986. International humanitarian law and the protection of cultural property. *Yearbook of the International Institute of Humanitarian Law*, pp. 267–69.

Crawford, J. 2003. The drafting of the Rome Statute. P. Sands (ed.), *From Nuremberg to The Hague: The Future of International Criminal Justice*. Cambridge: Cambridge University Press, pp. 109–56.

———. 2002. *The International Law Commission's Articles on State Responsibility: Introduction, Text and Commentaries*. Cambridge: Cambridge University Press.

Cuba, S. 1999. Stop the clock: the case to suspend the statute of limitations on claims for Nazi-looted art. *Cardozo Arts & Entertainment Law Journal*, Vol. 17, No. 2, pp. 447–89.

Cunning, A. 2003. The safeguarding of cultural property in times of war and peace. *Tulsa Journal of Comparative and International Law*, Vol. 11, pp. 211–38.

Czigler, S. V. 1938. *Schutz der Kunstwerke im Krieg*. Budapest.

Danse, M. 1963. Communication relative à la formation culturelle dans l'armée aérienne au regard des dispositions de l'article 7, 1er de la Convention du 14 mai 1954. *Recueil de la Société internationale de droit pénal militaire et de droit de la guerre*, Vol. 2, pp. 147–51.

David, E. 2008. *Principes de droit des conflits armés*. Brussels: Bruylant.

De Nike, H. J., Quigley, J. B. and Robinson, K. J. (eds.). 2000. *Genocide in Cambodia: Documents from the Trial of Pol Pot and Ieng Sary*. Philadelphia, Pa.: University of Pennsylvania Press.

Département fédéral de l'Interieur (Switzerland). 1963. *Protection des biens culturels en cas de conflit armé: Convention de La Haye du 14 mai 1954, Réglement d'exécution de la Convention, Protocole de La Haye du 14 mai 1954*. Bern: Département fédéral de l'Interieur.

Desch, T. 2002. Problems in the implementation of the Convention from the perspectives of international law. E. R. Micewski and G. Sladek (eds.), *Protection of Cultural Property in the Event of Armed Conflict: A Challenge in Peace Support Operations*. Vienna: Armed Forces Printing Office, pp. 13–27. http://www.bmlv.gv.at/pdf_pool/publikationen/05_pcp.pdf

———. 1999. The Second Protocol to the 1954 Hague Convention for the Protection of Cultural Property in the Event of Armed Conflict. *Yearbook of International Humanitarian Law*, Vol. 2, pp. 63–90.

———. 1998. The convention for the protection of cultural property in the event of armed conflict and its revision. *Humanitäres Völkerrecht*, Vol. 11, No. 2, pp. 103–9.

Dieng, A. 1986. Réflexions sur la protection de l'homme et du patrimoine culturel. Istituto Internazionale di Diritto Umanitario (ed.), *La protezione internazionale dei beni culturali/The International Protection of Cultural Property/La protection internationale des biens culturels*. Rome: Foundazione Europa Dragan, pp. 69–75.

Dinstein, Y. 2004a. *The Conduct of Hostilities under the Law of International Armed Conflict*. Cambridge: Cambridge University Press.

———. 2004b. The protection of cultural property and places of worship in international armed conflicts. *Studi di diritto internazionale in onore di*

Gaetano Arangio-Ruiz, Vol. 3. Naples: Editoriale Scientifica, pp. 1907–22.

———. 2001. Legitimate military objectives under the current jus in bello. *Israel Yearbook on Human Rights*, Vol. 31, pp. 1–34.

———. 1982. Military necessity. R. Bernhardt (ed.), *Encyclopedia of Public International Law*, Vol. 3. Amsterdam: North-Holland Publishing, pp. 274–76.

Dixit, R. K. 2004. Saving cultural property holocaust during armed conflicts. R. K. Dixit and C. Jayaraj (eds.), *Dynamics of International Law in the New Millenium*. New Delhi: Indian Society of International Law, pp. 183–96.

Dolzer, R. 1994. Die Kulturgüter im Friedensvölkerrecht. R. Dolzer, E. Jayme and R. Mussgnug (eds.), *Rechtsfragen des Internationalen Kulturgüterschutzes*. Symposium vom 22/23 Juni 1990 in Heidelberg. Heidelberg: C. F. Müller Juristischer Verlag, pp. 149–59.

Dolzer, R., Jayme, E. and Mussgnug, R. (eds.). 1994. *Rechtsfragen des Internationalen Kulturgüterschutzes*. Symposium vom 22/23 Juni 1990 in Heidelberg. Heidelberg: C. F. Müller Juristischer Verlag

Dörmann, K. 1993. The protection of cultural property as laid down in the Roerich-Pact of 15 April 1935. *Humanitäres Völkerrecht*, Vol. 6, pp. 230–31.

Dörmann, K., with contributions by L. Doswald-Beck and R. Kolb. 2003. *Elements of War Crimes under the Rome Statute of the International Criminal Court: Sources and Commentary*. Cambridge: Cambridge University Press, 2003.

Doswald-Beck, L. (ed.). 1995. *San Remo Manual on International Humanitarian Law Applicable to Armed Conflict at Sea*. Prepared by international lawyers and naval experts convened by the International Institute of Humanitarian Law. Cambridge: Cambridge University Press.

Driver, M. C. 2000. The protection of cultural property during wartime. *Review of European Community & International Environmental Law*, Vol. 9, pp. 1–12.

Duboff, L. D. (ed.). 1975. *Art Law: Domestic and International*. South Hackensack, N.J.: F. B. Rothman.

Dunbar, N. C. H. 1952. Military necessity in war crimes trials. *British Yearbook of International Law*, Vol. 29, pp. 442–52.

Dupuy, R. J. and Leonetti, A. 1979. La notion de conflit armé à caractère non international. A. Cassese (ed.), *The New Humanitarian Law of Armed Conflicts*. Naples: Editoriale Scientifica, pp. 272–74

Dutli, M.-T. 2002. *Protection of Cultural Property in the Event of Armed Conflict: Report on the Meeting of Experts (Geneva, 5–6 October 2000)*. Geneva, ICRC, Advisory Service on International Humanitarian Law.

Eirinberg, K. W. 1994. The United States reconsiders the 1954 Hague Convention. *International Journal of Cultural Property*, Vol. 3, No. 1, pp. 27–35.

Elbinger, L. K. 1992. The neutrality of art: the Roerich Pact's quest to protect art from the ignorance of man. *Foreign Service Journal*, April, pp. 16–20.

Engstler, L. 1969. Die Kennzeichnung von Kulturgut nach der Haager Konvention von 1954 zum Schutz von Kulturgut bei bewaffneten Konflikten. *Neue Juristische Wochenschrift*, Vol. 22, pp. 1514–18.

———. 1964. *Die territoriale Bindung von Kulturgütern im Rahmen des Völkerrechts*. Cologne: Heymann.

Eser, A. 2002. Individual criminal responsibility. A. Cassese, P. Gaeta and J. R. W. D. Jones (eds.), *The Rome Statute of the International Criminal Court: A Commentary*. 2 vols. Oxford: Oxford University Press, Vol. II, pp. 767–822.

Estreicher, K. (ed.). 1944. *Cultural Losses of Poland: Index of Polish cultural losses during the German occupation, 1939–1944*. London.

Eustathiades, C. T. 1960. La réserve des nécessités militaires et la Convention de La Haye pour la protection des biens culturels en cas de conflit armé. *Hommage d'une génération de juristes au Président Basdevant*. Paris: Pédone, pp. 183–209.

———. 1959. La protection des biens culturels en cas de conflit armé et la Convention de La Haye du 14 mai 1954. *Études de droit international, 1929–1959*, Vol. 3. Athens: Klissiounis, pp. 395–524.

Fabjan, K. 1971–1972. Kulturgüterschutz in der Praxis. Unter besonderer Berücksichtigung des Nahostkonfliktes. *Jahrbuch der Diplomatischen Akademie Wien 1971/1972*, pp. 90–99.

Fabrizio, M. 2006. *Le opere d'arte tra cooperazione internazionale e conflitti armati*. Padua: CEDAM.

Fauchille, P. 1915. Les attentats allemands contre les biens et les personnes en Belgique et en France d'après les rapports des Commissions d'enquête officielles. *Revue générale de droit international public*, Vol. 22, pp. 249–411.

Fawthrop, T. 2004. *Getting Away with Genocide? Elusive Justice and the Khmer Rouge Tribunal*. London: Pluto Press.

Feliciano, H. and Mullaney, T. M. 1998. Nazi-stolen art. *Whittier Law Review*, Vol. 20, No. 1, pp. 67–89.

Fernandez-Quintanilla, R. 1954. Un nuevo convenio de El Haya. *Cuadernos de política internacional*, Vol. 18, pp. 63–65.

Fischer, H. 1993. The protection of cultural property in armed conflicts: after the Hague Meeting of Experts. *Humanitäres Völkerrecht*, Vol. 6, No. 4, pp. 188–90.

Fischer, H., Kress, C. and Lüder, S. R. (eds.). 2001. *International and National Prosecution of Crimes under International Law: Current Developments*. Berlin: Berlin Verlag.

Fitschen, T. 1996. Licit international art trade in times of armed conflict? *International Journal of Cultural Property*, Vol. 5, No. 1, pp. 127–32.

Flanner, J. 1957. *Men and Monuments*. London: Hamish Hamilton.

Fleck, D. 1997. Military objectives and civilians: strategic bombing and the definition of military objectives. *Israel Yearbook on Human Rights*, Vol. 27, pp. 41–64.

Foramitti, H. 1971. Schutz der Kulturgüter bei bewaffneten Konflikten, XI. Teil 1 und 2: Einige Gesichtspunkte der Durchsetzbarkeit in modernen Kriegen. *Mitteilungsblatt der Museen Österreichs*, Vol. 20, No. 5–6, June, pp. 71–77; No. 7–8, pp. 107–14.

——. 1970. Schutz der Kulturgüter bei bewaffneten Konflikten, VIII. Teil A und B: Expertentagung Zürich. *Mitteilungsblatt der Museen Österreichs*, Vol. 19, No. 1–2, pp. 9–13; No. 3–4, pp. 41–52.

——. 1969. Schutz der Kulturgüter bei bewaffneten Konflikten, VII: Rückstellungsmöglichkeit von widerrechtlich entferntem Kulturgut nach bewaffneten Konflikten. *Mitteilungsblatt der Museen Österreichs*, Vol. 18, No. 3–4, pp. 53–59.

——. 1968. Schutz der Kulturgüter bei bewaffneten Konflikten, III: Der Fragebogen über Grundschutzbergungsräume. *Mitteilungsblatt der Museen Österreichs*, Vol. 17, No. 3–4, pp. 46–50.

Forsdyke, J. 1952. The museum in war-time. *British Museum Quarterly*, Vol. 15, pp. 1–9.

Forsyth, M. 2004. Casualties of war: the destruction of Iraq's cultural heritage as a result of U.S. action during and after the 1991 Gulf War. *DePaul Journal of Art and Entertainment Law*, Vol. 14, No. 1, pp. 73–107.

Foundoukidis, E. 1947. *La reconstruction sur le plan culturel*. Paris: International Museums Office.

————. 1936. L'office international des musées et la protection des monuments et œuvres d'art en temps de guerre. *Mouseion* (Paris), Vol. 35–36, pp. 187–200.

Francioni, F. 2008. Preamble. F. Francioni and F. Lenzerini (eds.), *The 1972 World Heritage Convention: A Commentary*. Oxford: Oxford University Press, pp. 11–22.

————. 1993. World Cultural Heritage List and national sovereignty. *Humanitäres Völkerrecht*, Vol. 6, No. 4, pp. 195–98.

Francioni, F. and Lenzerini, F. (eds.). 2008. *The 1972 World Heritage Convention: A Commentary*. Oxford: Oxford University Press.

Francioni, F. and Lenzerini, F. 2003. The destruction of the Buddhas of Bamiyan and international law. *European Journal of International Law*, Vol. 14, No. 4, pp. 619–51.

Frei, L. and Freschal, S. 1990. Origins and application of the United States-Switzerland Treaty on Mutual Assistance in Criminal Matters. *Harvard International Law Journal*, Vol. 31, pp. 77–79.

Fricke, A. 2005. Forever nearing the finish line: heritage policy and the problem of memory in postwar Beirut. *International Journal of Cultural Property*, Vol. 12, No. 2, pp. 163–81.

Friedman, L. (ed.). 1972. *The Law of War: A Documentary History*. 2 vols. New York: Random House.

Frigo, M. 2007. *La circolazione internazionale dei beni culturali: Diritto internazionale, diritto comunitario e diritto interno*. 2nd edn. Milan: Giuffrè Editore.

————. 2004. Biens culturels ou patrimoine culturel: un combat terminologique en droit international? *IRRC*, No. 854, pp. 367–78.

————. 1998. *La protezione dei Beni Culturali mobili e il Diritto Internazionale*. Milan: Giuffrè Editore.

Frulli, M. 2002. Le droit international et les obstacles à la mise en oeuvre de la responsabilité pénale pour crimes internationaux. A. Cassese and M. Delmas-Marty (eds.), *Crimes internationaux et juridictions internationales*. Paris: Presses Universitaires de France, pp. 215–25.

Gaagskaya Konventsiya 1954 goda o zashchite kulturnykh tsennostei v sluchae vooruzhennogo konflikta [*The 1954 Hague Convention for the Protection of Cultural Property in the Event of Armed Conflict*]. 1957. Moscow: Yurizdat.

Galenskaya, L. N. 1987. *Muzy i pravo. Pravovye voprosy mezhdunarodnogo sotrudnichestva v oblasti kul'tury* [*The Muses and the Law: Legal Questions*

Involved in International Cooperation in the Field of Culture]. Leningrad: Izdatel'stvo Leningradskogo universiteta.

———. 1986. International co-operation in cultural affairs. *Recueil des Cours Académie de Droit International*, Vol. 198, pp. 265–331.

Gardam, J. G. 1993. Proportionality and force in international law. *American Journal of International Law*, Vol. 87, pp. 391, 404–10.

Geiger, R. 1997. Legal assistance between states in criminal matters. R. Bernhardt (ed.), *Encyclopedia of Public International Law*, Vol. 9. Amsterdam: North-Holland Publishing, pp. 248–55.

Georgopoulos, T. 2001. Avez-vous bien dit 'crimes contre la culture'? La protection internationale des monuments historiques. *Revue Hellénique de droit international*, Vol. 54, pp. 459–82.

Gerstenblith, P. 2008. The 1954 Hague Convention on the Protection of Cultural Property in the Event of Armed Conflict: its background and prospects for ratification in the United States. L. Rothfield (ed.), *Antiquities under Siege: Cultural Heritage Protection after the Iraq War*. Lanham, Md.: AltaMira Press, pp. 79–88.

———. 2005. From Bamiyan to Baghdad: warfare and the preservation of cultural heritage at the beginning of the 21st century. *Georgetown Journal of International Law*, Vol. 37, No. 2, pp. 245–351.

Ghazali, E. 1977. *Contribution à l'étude des accords culturels vers un droit international de la culture*. Ph.D. thesis, Université de Paris I.

Gioia, A. 2003. The development of the international law relating to the protection of cultural property in the event of armed conflict: the Second Protocol to the 1954 Hague Convention. *Italian Yearbook of International Law*, Vol. 11, pp. 25–57.

Glaser, S. 1957. La protection internationale des valeurs humaines. *Revue générale de droit international public*, Vol. 60, pp. 211–41.

Gouttes, P. des. 1930. *La Convention de Genève pour l'amélioration du sort des blessés et des malades dans les armées en campagne du 27 juillet 1929. Commentaire*. Geneva: ICRC.

Goy, R. 2005. La destruction intentionnelle du patrimoine culturel en droit international. *Revue générale de droit international public*, Vol. 109, No. 2, pp. 273–304.

———. 1979. Le retour et la restitution des biens culturels à leur pays d'origine en cas d'appropriation illégale. *Revue générale de droit international public*, Vol. 83, pp. 962–85.

Graham, G. M. 1987. Protection and reversion of cultural property: issues of definition and justification. *International Lawyer*, Vol. 21, No. 3, pp. 755–93.

Greenfield, J. 2007. *The Return of Cultural Treasures*. Cambridge: Cambridge University Press.

Griffo, P. 1946. *La difesa del patrimonio archeologico agrigentino contro i pericoli della recente Guerra*. Agrigento: Soprintendenza alle antichità di Agrigento.

Grigore, I., Closca, I. and Badesc, C. 1994. *La protection des biens culturels en Roumanie*. Bucharest: Association roumaine de droit humanitaire.

Grimsted, P. K. 2002. Spoils of war returned: U.S. restitution of Nazi-looted cultural treasures to the USSR, 1945–1959. *PROLOGUE: Quarterly of the National Archives and Records Administration*, Vol. 34, No. 1, pp. 27–41. http://www.archives.gov.ua/Eng/NB/USRestitution.php

Grisolia, M. 1952. *La tutela delle cose d'arte*. Rome: Società Editrice del Foro Italiano.

Günther-Hornig, M. 1958. *Kunstschutz in den von Deutschland besetzten Gebieten 1939–1945*. Tübingen: Institut für Besatzungsfragen.

Habsburg-Lothringen, K. 2002. The destruction of cultural goods as a primary goal during war. E. R. Micewski and G. Sladek (eds.), *Protection of Cultural Property in the Event of Armed Conflict: A Challenge in Peace Support Operations*. Vienna, Austrian Military Printing Press, pp. 22–23. http://www.bmlv.gv.at/pdf_pool/publikationen/05_pcp.pdf

Hall, A. R. 1954. U.S. program for return of historic objects to countries of origin, 1944–1954. *The Department of State Bulletin*, Vol. 31, No. 797, pp. 493–98.

———. 1951. The recovery of cultural objects dispersed during World War II. *The Department of State Bulletin*, Vol. 25, No. 635, pp. 337–44.

Hammarberg, T. 2001. How the Khmer Rouge tribunal was agreed: Discussions between the Cambodian government and the UN. *Searching for the Truth*. Phnom Penh: Documentation Center of Cambodia. http://www.dccam.org/Tribunal/Analysis/How_Khmer_Rouge_Tribunal.htm

Harris, I. 2007. *Buddhism under Pol Pot*. Phnom Penh: Documentation Center of Cambodia.

Hartwig, B. 1967. Die Konvention zum Schutz von Kulturgut bei bewaffneten Konflikten. *Neue Zeitschrift für Wehrrecht*, Vol. 9, pp. 97–102; 145–51.

———. 1962. Welche militärisch bedeutsamen Änderungen bringt das Abkommen zum Schutz von Kulturgut bei bewaffneten Konflikten vom

14. Mai 1954? *Revue de Droit Pénal Militaire et de Droit de la Guerre,* Vol. 1, pp. 85–96.

———. 1961. Der Schutz von Kulturgut im Kriege. *Bundeswehrwaltung,* Vol. 5, pp. 33–36.

Haunton, M. 1995. Peacekeeping, occupation and cultural property. *University of British Columbia Law Review,* special issue, pp. 217–28.

Haveman, R., Kavran, O. and Nicholls, J. (eds.). 2003. *Supranational Criminal Law: A System Sui Generis.* Antwerp: Intersentia.

Held, C.-E. 2007. L'application aux conflits armés non internationaux du Deuxième Protocole relatif à la Convention de La Haye de 1954 pour la protection des biens culturels en cas de conflict armé. M. G. Kohen (ed.), *Promoting Justice, Human Rights and Conflict Resolution through International Law/La promotion de la justice, des droits de l'homme et du règlement des conflits par le droit international. Liber Amicorum Lucius Caflish.* Leiden: Martinus Nijhoff, pp. 255–66.

Henckaerts, J.-M. 2001. Nouvelles règles pour la protection des biens culturels en cas de conflit armé: la portée du deuxième protocole relatif à la Convention de La Haye de 1954 pour la protection des biens culturels en cas de conflit armé. M. T. Dutli, J. B. Martignoni and J. Gaudreau (eds.), *Protection des biens culturels en cas de conflit armé: rapport d'une réunion d'experts (Genève, 5–6 octobre 2000).* Geneva: ICRC, pp. 27–56.

———. 1999. New rules for the protection of cultural property in armed conflict: the significance of the Second Protocol to the 1954 Hague Convgention for the Protection of Cultural Property in the Event of Armed Conflict. *IRRC,* No. 835, pp. 593–620.

Henckaerts, J.-M. and Doswald-Back, L. 2005. *Customary International Humanitarian Law,* Vol. I: *Rules.* Cambridge: Cambridge University Press.

Herdegen, M. 1994. Der Kulturgüterschutz im Kriegsvölkerrecht. R. Dolzer, E. Jayme and R. Mussgnug (eds.), *Rechtsfragen des Internationalen Kulturgüterschutzes.* Symposium vom 22/23 Juni 1990 in Heidelberg. Heidelberg: C. F. Müller Juristischer Verlag, pp. 161–73.

Hertigan, R. S. 1983. *Lieber's Code and the Law of War.* Chicago: Precedent.

Hladík, J. 2008. Main activities of the UNESCO Secretariat related to the implementation of the Second Protocol to the Hague Convention of 1954 for the Protection of Cultural Objects in the Event of Armed Conflict. P. Meerts (ed.), *Culture and International Law.* The Hague: Hague Academic Press, pp. 155–66.

————. 2006. Protection of Cultural Property: The Legal Aspects. R. B. Jaques (ed.), Issues in International Law and Military Operations. *International Law Studies*, Vol. 80. Newport, R.I.: Naval War College, pp. 319–30.

————. 2005. La Convention de la Haye de 1954: quelques observations sur sa mise en oeuvre au niveau national. *Museum International*, No. 228, pp. 71–75.

————. 2004a. Fiftieth anniversary of the Hague Convention: commemorative symposium. *Art, Antiquity and Law*, Vol. 9, No. 4, pp. 413–17.

————. 2004b. Marking of cultural property with the distinctive emblem of the 1954 Hague Convention for the Protection of Cultural Property in the Event of Armed Conflict. *IRRC*, No. 854, pp. 379–87.

————. 2004c. The UNESCO Declaration concerning the Intentional Destruction of Cultural Heritage: a new instrument to protect cultural heritage. *Art, Antiquity and Law*, Vol. 9, No. 3, pp. 215–36.

————. 2002. UNESCO's ability to intervene in crisis and conflict. E. R. Micewski and G. Sladek (eds.), *Protection of Cultural Property in the Event of Armed Conflict: A Challenge in Peace Support Operations*. Vienna: Armed Forces Printing Office, pp. 41–47. http://www.bmlv.gv.at/pdf_pool/publikationen/05_pcp.pdf

————. 2001a. Activités de l'UNESCO en matière de mis en œuvre et de promotion de la Convention de la Haye de 1954 pour la protection des biens culturels en cas de conflit armé et de ses deux Protocoles. M. T. Dutli, J. B. Martignoni and J. Gaudreau (eds.), *Protection des biens culturels en cas de conflit armé: rapport d'une réunion d'experts (Genève, 5–6 octobre 2000)*. Geneva: ICRC, pp. 57–68.

————. 2001b. The control system under the Hague Convention for the Protection of Cultural Property in the Event of Armed Conflict 1954 and its Second Protocol. *Yearbook of International Humanitarian Law*, Vol. 4, pp. 419–31.

————. 2000. Reporting system under the 1954 Convention for the Protection of Cultural Property in the Event of Armed Conflict. *IRRC*, No. 840, pp. 1001–16.

————. 1999a. Diplomatic Conference on the Second Protocol to the Hague Convention for the Protection of Cultural Property in the Event of Armed Conflict, The Hague, Netherlands (March 15–26 1999). *International Journal of Cultural Property*, Vol. 8, No. 2, pp. 526–29.

————. 1999b. The 1954 Hague Convention for the Protection of Cultural Property in the Event of Armed Conflict and the Notion of Military

Necessity: the review of the 1954 Convention and the adoption of the Second Protocol thereto (26 March 1999). *IRRC*, No. 835, pp. 621–35.

————. 1998a. The review process of the 1954 Hague Convention for the Protection of Cultural Property in the Event of Armed Conflict and its impact on international humanitarian law. *Yearbook of International Humanitarian Law*, Vol. 1, pp. 313–22.

————. 1998b. The Third Meeting of the High Contracting Parties to the Hague Convention for the Protection of Cultural Property in the Event of Armed Conflict of 1954 (Paris, November 13, 1997). *International Journal of Cultural Property*, Vol. 7, No. 1, pp. 268–71.

————. 1996. Meeting of the High Contracting Parties to the Hague Convention for the Protection of Cultural Property in the Event of Armed Conflict of 1954. *International Journal of Cultural Property*, Vol. 5, No. 2, pp. 339–41.

Hollander, B. 1959. *The International Law of Art for Lawyers, Collectors and Artists*. London: Bowes & Bowes, pp. 17–55.

Holmes, J. T. 2002. Complementarity: national courts v. the ICC. A. Cassese, P. Gaeta and J. R. W. D. Jones (eds.), *The Rome Statute of the International Criminal Court*. Oxford: Oxford University Press, pp. 667–86.

Houdek, F. C. 1988. *Protection of Cultural Property and Archeological Resources: A Comprehensive Bibliography of Law-related Materials; International Law Bibliography*. New York: Oceana Publications.

Huppert, H.-H. 1968. *Die Vorbehaltsklausen der militarischen Notwendigkeit in den kriegsrechtlichen Konventionen, dargestellt am Kulturschutzabkommen vom 14. Mai 1954*. Würzburg: Schmitt & Mayer.

ICOMOS Sweden/Central Board of National Antiquities/Swedish National Commission for UNESCO. 1994. *Information as an Instrument for Protection against War Damages to the Cultural Heritage: Report from a Seminar, June 1994*. Stockholm, Svenska Unescoradets skriftserie, 4/1994. http://www.international.icomos.org/publications/war_damage_1994/stockholm1994.pdf

Institut suisse de cours administratifs. 1968. *La protection des biens culturels en cas de conflit armé: 126ᵉ cours organisé en accord avec le Département fédéral de l'Intérieur et la Société suisse pour la protection des biens culturels*. St. Gallen: Institut suisse de cours administratifs.

International Museums Office (OIM). 1939a. Conventions internationales en vigueur et autres déclarations de gouvernements concernant la protection des monuments et œuvres d'art au cours des conflits armés. *Mouseion* (Paris), supplement, September–October, pp. 5–12.

————. 1939b. Les Mesures de protection prises dans différents pays contre les dangers de la guerre. *Mouseion* (Paris), supplement, September–October, pp. 13–22.

————. 1939c. *La Protection des monuments et des oeuvres d'art en temps de guerre: Manuel technique et juridique.* Paris: Institut International de Coopération Intellectuelle.

International Union for the Conservation of Nature (ICEL). 1993. Protection of cultural and natural heritage sites in times of armed conflict: recommendations. *Environmental Policy and Law*, Vol. 23, No. 6, pp. 288–89.

Istituto Internazionale di Diritto Umanitario (ed.). 1986. *La protezione internazionale dei beni culturali/The International Protection of Cultural Property/La protection internationale des biens culturels.* Rome: Foundazione Europa Dragan.

Jackson, K. D. (ed.). 1992. *Cambodia, 1975–1978: Rendezvous with Death.* Princeton: Princeton University Press.

Jennings, R. and Watts, A. (eds.). 1996. *Oppenheim's International Law*, Vol. 1. 9th edn. London: Longman.

Jenschke, C. 2005. *Der völkerrechtliche Rückgabeanspruch auf in Kriegszeiten widerrechtlich verbrachte Kulturgüter.* Berlin: Duncker & Humblot.

Jevtich, M. 1975. Zastita muzejskih sbirki u slucaju rata [Protection of museum collections in the event of war]. Referenti VIII kongresu Saveza muzejskego drustava Jugoslavije. Pula, 26–28/5/1975, pt. 1. *Muzeologija* (Zagreb), Vol. 17, pp. 38–50.

Johnson, Major J. C. 2006–2007. Under new management: the obligation to protect cultural property during military occupation. *Military Law Review*, Vol. 190–191, pp. 111–52.

Kalshoven, F. 2005. The protection of cultural property in the event of armed conflict within the framework of international humanitarian law. *Museum International*, No. 228, pp. 61–70.

Kamenski, A. 1939. La Croix-Rouge des valeurs culturelles. *Journal de Genève*, 23 March.

Kaminski, T. 1979. Ochrona dobr kultury – najwyzsym moralnym-nakazem i obowieszkem [The protection of cultural property – an overriding moral obligation]. *Biuletyn informaacyjny Zarzadu muzéow i ochrony zabytkow* (Warsaw), No. 132, pp. 115–19.

Kastenberg, J. E. 1997. The legal regime for protecting cultural property during armed conflict. *Air Force Law Review*, Vol. 42, pp. 277–305.

Kaye, L. M. 1998a. Looted art: what can and should be done. *Cardozo Law Review*, Vol. 20, No. 3, pp. 657–70.

Kaye, L. M. 1998b. The recovery of stolen cultural property: a practitioner's view – war stories and morality tales. *Villanova Sports and Entertainment Law Journal*, Vol. 5, pp. 5–17.

Keane, D. 2004. The failure to protect cultural property in wartime. *DePaul Journal of Art and Entertainment Law*, Vol. 14, No. 1, pp. 1–38.

Kieran, B. 2002. *The Pol Pot Regime: Race, Power and Genocide in Cambodia under the Khmer Rouge, 1975–79*. New Haven, Conn. Yale University Press.

Kila, J. 2008. Utilizing military cultural experts in war and peace time: an introduction. P. Meerts (ed.), *Culture and International Law*. The Hague: Hague Academic Press, pp. 183–229.

Kilian, M. 1983. Kriegsvölkerrecht und Kulturgut. Die Bemühungen um den Schutz der Kulturgüter bei bewaffneten Auseinandersetzungen. *Neue Zeitschrift für Wehrrecht*, Vol. 25, pp. 41–57.

Kirsch, P. and Holmes, J. T. 2004. The birth of the International Criminal Court: the 1998 Rome Conference. O. Bekou and R. Cryer (eds.), *The International Criminal Court*. Aldershot: Ashgate/Dartmouth, 2004, pp. 3-39.

Kiss, A.-C. 1982. La Notion de patrimoine commun de l'humanité. *Recueil des Cours, Académie de Droit International*, Vol. 175, pp. 99–256.

Klein, K. M. 2006. Bringing the Khmer Rouge to justice: the challenges and risks facing the Joint Tribunal in Cambodia. *Northwestern Journal of International Human Rights*, Vol. 4, No. 3, pp. 549–66. http://www.law.northwestern.edu/journals/jihr/v4/n3/4/Klein.pdf

Knoops, G.-J. A. 2003. *An Introduction to the Law of International Criminal Tribunals*. Ardsley: Transnational Publishers.

Kossiakoff, M. 2004. The art of war: the protection of cultural property during the siege of Sarajevo (1992–95). *DePaul Journal of Art and Entertainment Law*, Vol. 14, No. 1, pp. 109–69.

Kowalski, W. W. 1998. *Art Treasures and War: A Study on the Restitution of Looted Cultural Property Pursuant to Public International Law*. Leicester: Institute of Art and Law.

Kraus, H. 1963. Das Haager Abkommen zum Schutz von Kulturgütern im Falle bewaffneter Zusammenstösse vom 14 Mai 1954. *Internationale Gegenwartsfragen: Völkerrecht, Staatenethik, Internationalpolitik. Ausgewählte kleine Schriften*. Würzburg: Holzner-Verlag, pp. 445–46.

————. 1956. Das Haager Abkommen zum Schutz von Kulturgutern im Falle bewaffneter Zusammenstösse vom 14 Mai 1954. W. Schätzel and H.-J. Schlochauer (eds.), *Rechtsfragen der internationalen Organisation. Festschrift für Hans Wehberg zu seinem 70. Geburtstag.* Frankfurt am Main: Vittorio Klostermann, pp. 211–25.

Kunick, J. C. 2003. World heritage in danger in the hotspots. *Indiana Law Journal*, Vol. 78, No. 2, pp. 619–58.

Kurtz, M. J. 2006. *America and the Return of Nazi Contraband: The Recovery of Europe's Cultural Treasures.* New York: Cambridge University Press.

Lambert, J. J. 1990. *Terrorism and Hostages in International Law: A Commentary on the Hostages Convention 1979.* Cambridge: Cambridge University Press.

Lapradelle, A. de. 1937. Le Pacte Roerich. *Nouvelles litteraires*, June.

Lapuente Garcia, A. 1941. *Appel aux intellectuels.* Buenos Aires.

Last, K. 2004. The resolution of cultural property disputes: some issues of definition. International Bureau of the Permanent Court of Arbitration (ed.), *Resolution of Cultural Property Disputes: Papers Emanating from the Seventh PCA International Law Seminar, May 23, 2003.* The Hague: Kluwer Law International, pp. 53–84.

Lattmann, E. 1974. *Schutz der Kulturgüter bei bewaffneten Konflikten. Die schweizerische Gesetzgebung und Praxis aufgrund des Haager Abkommens vom 14 Mai 1954 für den Schutz von Kulturgut bei bewaffneten Konflikten.* Züricher Studien zum internationalen Recht, Vol. 54. Zürich: Schulthess.

Lauterpacht, H. (ed.). 1953. *Annual Digest and Reports of Public International Law Cases: Being a Selection from the Decisions of International and National Courts and Tribunals Given during the Year 1948.* London, Butterworth and Co.

Lavachery, H. A. and Noblecourt, A. F. 1956. *Les Techniques de protection des biens culturels en cas de conflit armé.* Museums and Monuments No. VIII. Paris: UNESCO.

Lee, R. S. (ed.). 2001. *The International Criminal Court: Elements of Crimes and Rules of Procedure and Evidence.* Ardsley: Transnational Publishers.

Lehman, J. N. 1997. The continued struggle with stolen cultural property: the Hague Convention, and the UNIDROIT Draft Convention. *Arizona Journal of International and Comparative Law*, Vol. 14, No. 2, pp. 527–49.

Lenzerini, F. 2008. Articles 15–16, World Heritage Fund. F. Francioni and F. Lenzerini (eds.), *The 1972 World Heritage Convention: A Commentary*. Oxford: Oxford University Press, 2008, pp. 269–88.

Levie, H. S. 1980. *Protection of War Victims: Protocol 1 to the 1949 Geneva Conventions*, Vol. 3. Dobbs Ferry, N.Y.: Oceana Publications.

Lieberman, M. 2005. Salvaging the remains: the Khmer Rouge Tribunal on trial. *Military Law Journal*, No. 186, pp. 164–87. http://www.au.af.mil/au/awc/awcgate/law/khmer_tribunal_win05.pdf

Lippman, M. 1998. Art and ideology in the Third Reich: the protection of cultural property and the humanitarian law of war. *Dickinson Journal of International Law*, 17, No. 1, pp. 1–95.

Lorentz, S. 1966. Muzeum narodowe podozas powstania Warszawskiego [The National Museum during the Warsaw insurrection of 1944 – extracts from memoirs]. *Muzeanictwo* (Poznaň), No. 13, pp. 7–10, 205.

Maggiore, R. 1975. Jus in bello: il problema della protezione dei beni culturali nei conflitti armati. *Rassegna dell'arma dei carabinieri*, No. 5, pp. 879–908.

Mainetti, V. 2004. De nouvelles perspectives pour la protection des biens culturels en cas de conflit armé: l'entrée en vigueur du deuxième protocole relatif à la Convention de La Haye de 1954. *IRRC*, No. 854, pp. 337–66.

Makagiansar, M. 1986. The thirtieth anniversary of the Convention for the Protection of Cultural Property in the Event of Armed Conflict (The Hague, 1954): results and prospects. Istituto Internazionale di Diritto Umanitario (ed.), *La protezione internazionale dei beni culturali/The International Protection of Cultural Property/La protection internationale des biens culturels*. Rome: Foundazione Europa Dragan, pp. 27–40.

Malintoppi, A. 1966. *La protezione dei beni culturali in caso di conflitto armato*. Milan: Giuffrè Editore.

———. 1960. La protezione 'speciale' della Città del Vaticano in caso di conflitto armato. *Rivista di Diritto Internazionale*, Vol. 43, pp. 607–29.

Manhart, C. 2004. UNESCO's mandate and recent activities for the rehabilitation of Afghanistan's cultural heritage. *IRRC*, No. 854, pp. 401–14.

Maniscalco, F. 2007. *World heritage and war: linee guida per interventi a salvaguardia dei beni culturali nelle aree a rischio bellico*. Naples: Massa Editore.

Marguillier, A. 1919. *La destruction des monuments sur le front occidental: réponse aux plaidoyers allemands*. Brussels: G. Van Oest.

Marhic, G. 2001. Le Protocole de 1999 additionnel à la Convention de 1954 sur la protection des biens culturels en cas de conflit armé. P. Tavernier and L. Burgorgue-Larsen (eds.), *Un siècle de droit international humanitaire*. Brussels: Bruylant, pp. 44–54.

Matteucci, M. 1958. Su la convenzione per la protezione dei beni culturali in caso di conflitto armato. *Rivista di Diritto Internazionale*, Vol. 41, pp. 670–76.

Matyk, S. 2000. The restitution of cultural objects and the question of giving direct effect to the Protocol to the Hague Convention for the Protection of Cultural Property in the Event of Armed Conflict 1954. *International Journal of Cultural Property*, Vol. 9, No. 2, pp. 341–46.

Max-Planck-Institut für ausländisches öffentliches Recht und Völkerrecht. 1955. Dokumente zum Schutz der Kulturgüter bei bewaffneten Konflikten. *Zeitschrift für ausländisches öffentliches Recht und Völkerrecht*, Vol. 16, No. 1, pp. 76–102. http://www.hjil.de/16_1955_56/16_1955_1_b_76_102_1.pdf

McNair, A. D. [Lord McNair]. 1961. *The Law of Treaties*. Oxford: Clarendon Press.

Meerts, P. (ed.). 2008. *Culture and International Law*. The Hague: Hague Academic Press.

Meeting of Experts on the Application and Effectiveness of the Convention for the Protection of Cultural Property in the Event of Armed Conflict (The Hague, 14 May 1954). *Final Report*, The Hague, 5–7 July 1993. *Humanitäres Völkerrecht*, No. 4, pp. 232–34.

Meeting of Legal Experts on the Convention for the Protection of Cultural Property in the Event of Armed Conflict (The Hague, 1954), Vienna, 17–19 October 1983, *Final Report*. Paris, UNESCO (CLT-83/CONF.641/1).

Meijer, E. E. 2004. The Extraordinary Chambers in the Courts of Cambodia for Prosecuting Crimes Committed by the Khmer Rouge: jurisdiction, organization and procedure of an internationalized national tribunal. C. P. R. Romano, A. Nollkaemper and J. K. Kleffner (eds.), *Internationalized Criminal Courts and Tribunals: Sierra Leone, East Timor, Kosovo and Cambodia*. Oxford: Oxford University Press, pp. 207–32.

Meranghini, U. 1968. La difesa dei beni culturali dall'offesa bellica. *Revue de Droit Pénal Militaire et de Droit de la Guerre*, Vol. 7, pp. 133–46.

———. 1962. La protezione dei beni culturali nella guerra moderna. *Archivio di ricerche giuridiche*, Vol. 16, pp. 35–52.

Meron, T. 2005. The protection of cultural property in the event of armed conflict within the case-law of the International Criminal Tribunal for the Former Yugoslavia. *Museum International*, No. 228, pp. 41–60.

Merryman, J. H. 2006. *Imperialism, Art and Restitution*. Cambridge: Cambridge University Press.

———. 1989. The public interest in cultural property. *California Law Review*, Vol. 77, No. 2, pp. 339–64.

———. 1986. Two ways of thinking about cultural property. *American Journal of International Law*, Vol. 80, No. 4, pp. 831–53.

Merryman, J. H. and Elsen, A. E. 2002. *Law, Ethics and the Visual Arts*. 4th edn. The Hague: Kluwer Law International.

Mettraux, G. 2005. *International Crimes and the ad hoc Tribunals*. Oxford: Oxford University Press.

Meyer, D. A. 1993. The 1954 Hague Cultural Property Convention and its emergence into customary international law. *Boston University International Law Journal*, Vol. 11, pp. 349–89.

Meyrowitz, H. 1981. Le bombardement stratégique d'après le Protocole additionnel I aux Conventions de Genève. *Zeitschrift für ausländisches öffentliches Recht und Völkerrecht*, Vol. 41, pp. 1–68.

Micewski, E. R. and Sladek, G. (eds.). 2002. *Protection of Cultural Property in the Event of Armed Conflict: A Challenge in Peace Support Operations*. Vienna: Armed Forces Printing Office. http://www.bmlv.gv.at/pdf_pool/publikationen/05_pcp.pdf

Middle East Watch. 1991. *Needless Deaths in the Gulf War: Civilian Casualties during the Air Campaign and Violations of the Laws of War*. New York: Human Rights Watch. http://www.hrw.org/legacy/reports/1991/gulfwar

Mihan, G. 1944. *Looted Treasure: Germany's Raid on Art*. London: Alliance Press.

Miyazaki, S. 1984. The Martens Clause in international humanitarian law. C. Swinarski (ed.), *Etudes et essais sur le droit international humanitaire et sur les principes de la Croix-Rouge en l'honneur de Jean Pictet/Studies and Essays on International Humanitarian Law and Red Cross Principles in Honour of Jean Pictet*. Geneva: ICRC, pp. 433–44.

Monden, A. and Wils, G. 1986. Arts objects as common heritage of mankind. *Revue Belge du Droit International*, Vol. 19, pp. 327–38.

Moreillon, J. 1973. *Le Comité international de la Croix-Rouge et la protection des détenus politiques: les activités du CICR en faveur des personnes incarcérées dans leur propre pays à l'occasion de troubles ou de tensions internes.* Lausanne: Éditions L'Âge d'homme.

Mulinen, F. de. 1978. The law of war and the armed forces. *IRRC,* No. 202, pp. 20–45.

———. 1965. A propos de l'application en Suisse de la Convention de La Haye pour la protection des biens culturels. *Revue militaire suisse,* No. 4, pp. 181–88.

Müller, M. M. 1998. Cultural heritage protection: legitimacy, property and functionalism. *International Journal of Cultural Property,* Vol. 7, pp. 395–409.

Muranghini, U. 1961. Difesa dei Beni Culturali in caso di Guerra. *Recueil de la Société de Droit Pénal Militaire et Droit de la Guerre,* Vol. 2, p. 144–46.

Myerowitz, E. S. 1997. Protecting cultural property during a time of war: why Russia should return Nazi-looted art. *Fordham International Law Journal,* Vol. 20, pp. 1961–2002.

Nafziger, J. A. R. 1986. International penal aspects of crimes against cultural property and the protection of cultural property. M. C. Bassiouni (ed.), *International Criminal Law,* Vol. 1: *Crimes.* Dobbs Ferry, N.Y.: Transnational Publishers, pp. 525–39.

———. 1985. International penal aspects of protecting cultural property. *International Lawyer,* Vol. 19, No. 3, pp. 835–52.

———. 1976. UNESCO-centered management of international conflict over cultural property. *Hastings Law Journal,* Vol. 27, pp. 1051–67.

Nahlik, S. E. 1993. Zashchita kul'turnykh tsennostei. *Mezhdunarodnoe gumanitarnoe pravo.* Moscow: Institut problem gumanizma i meloserdiya, pp. 277–92.

———. 1990. Protección de los bienes culturales. UNESCO (ed.), *Las dimensiones internacionales del derecho humanitario.* Madrid: Tecnos-UNESCO, pp. 203–13.

———. 1988. Protection of cultural property. UNESCO (ed.), *International Dimensions of Humanitarian Law.* Paris: UNESCO, pp. 203–15.

———. 1986a. Convention for the Protection of Cultural Property in the Event of Armed Conflict, The Hague 1954: general and special protection. Istituto Internazionale di Diritto Umanitario (ed.), *La protezione internazionale dei beni culturali/The International Protection of Cultural Property/La protection internationale des biens culturels.* Rome: Fondazione Europa Dragan, pp. 87–100.

———. 1986b. Protection des biens culturels. UNESCO (ed.), *Les dimensions internationales du droit humanitaire.* Paris: UNESCO, pp. 237–49.

————. 1980. The case of displaced art treasures: history and appreciation of a Polish-Canadian strife. *German Yearbook of International Law*, Vol. 23, pp. 255–95.

————. 1976. International law and the protection of cultural property in armed conflicts. *Hastings Law Journal*, Vol. 27, No. 5, pp. 1069–87.

————. 1974. On some deficiencies of the Hague Convention of 1954 on the Protection of Cultural Property in the Event of Armed Conflict. *Annuaire de l'Association des Anciens Auditeurs de l'Académie de La Haye*, Vol. 44, pp. 100–8.

————. 1967. La protection internationale des biens culturels en cas de conflit armé. *Recueil des Cours Académie de Droit International*, Vol. 120, pp. 61–163.

————. 1962. Sprawa ochrony dobr kulturalnych w razie konfliktu zbrojnego [The protection of cultural property in the event of armed conflict]. *Newsletter of the Polish National Commission for UNESCO*, No. 9, pp. 19–21.

————. 1962. *Miedzynarodowa ochrona dobr kulturalnych: ochrona prawna w razie konfliktow zbrojnych* [*International Protection of Cultural Property: Legal Protection in the Event of Armed Conflict*]. Warsaw.

————. 1959–1960. Le cas des collections polonaises au Canada: considérations juridiques. *Annuaire polonais des affaires internationales 1959–1960*, pp. 172–90.

————. 1959. Des crimes contre les biens culturels. *Newsletter of the Association of Attenders and Alumni of the Hague Academy of International Law*, Vol. 29, pp. 14–27.

————. 1958. *Grabież dzieł sztuki: rodowód zbrodni międzynarodowej* [*The Plunder of Art objects: The Origin of Internatational Crime*]. Wrocław: Zakład narodowy im Ossolińskich, pp. 449–52.

NATO-Partnership for Peace (PfP) Conference. 1996. Final Communiqué on Cultural Heritage Protection in Wartime and in State of Emergency, Cracow, 21 June. http://www.icomos.org/blue_shield/krakowna.html

Neroni Slade, T. and Clark, R. S. 2002. Preamble and final clauses. R. S. Lee (ed.), *The International Criminal Court: The Making of the Rome Statute. Issues, Negotiations Results*. The Hague: Kluwer Law International, pp. 421–50.

Netherlands Archaeological Society. 1937. La Protection des monuments et objets historiques et artistiques contre les destructions de la guerre. Proposition de la Société néerlandaise d'archéologie. *Mouseion* (Paris), Vol. 39–40, pp. 81–89.

Nicholas, L. H. 1994. *The Rape of Europa: The Fate of Europe's Treasures in the Third Reich and the Second World War*. New York: Vintage Books.

Nieć, H. 1993. The 'human dimension' of the protection of cultural property in the event of armed conflict. *Humanitäres Völkerrecht*, Vol. 6, pp. 204–12.

Nieciówna, H. 1971. Sovereign rights to cultural property. *Polish Yearbook of International Law*, No. 4, pp. 239–53.

Noblecourt, A. 1958. *Protection of Cultural Property in the Event of Armed Conflicts*. Museums and Monuments No. VIII. Paris: UNESCO.

Nowlan, J. 1993. Cultural property and the Nuremberg War Crimes Trial. *Humanitäres Völkerrecht*, Vol. 6, No. 4, pp. 221–23.

Nunes y Dominguez, J. de J. 1938. La protection des monuments historiques et artistiques en temps de guerre et le droit international. *Premier Congrès d'Études I. Paris, 30 September–7 October 1937*. Publications de l'Institut des Hautes Études Internationales de l'Université de Paris. Paris: Éd. Internationales, pp. 68–83.

O'Connell, M. E. 2008. Beyond wealth: stories of art, war, and greed. *Alabama Law Review*, Vol. 59, pp. 1075–1105.

——. 2004. Occupation failures and the legality of armed conflict: the case of Iraqi cultural property. *Art, Antiquity and Law*, Vol. 9, No. 4, pp. 323–62.

O'Keefe, P. J. 2007. *Commentary on the 1970 UNESCO Convention*. 2nd edn. Leicester: Institute of Art and Law.

——. 2004. The First Protocol to the Hague Convention fifty years on. *Art, Antiquity and Law*, Vol. 9, No. 2, pp. 99–116.

O'Keefe, P. J. and Prott, L.V. 1985. Cultural property. R. Bernhardt (ed.), *Encyclopedia of Public International Law*, Vol. 9. Amsterdam: North-Holland Publishing, pp. 62–64.

O'Keefe, R. 2007. Protection of cultural property. D. Fleck (ed.), *The Handbook of International Humanitarian Law in Armed Conflicts*. 2nd edn. Oxford: Oxford University Press, pp. 433–74.

——. 2006. *The Protection of Cultural Property in Armed Conflict*. Cambridge: Cambridge University Press.

——. 2002. *National Implementation of the Penal Provisions of Chapter 4 of the Second Protocol of 26 March 1999 to the Hague Convention of 1954 for the Protection of Cultural Property in the Event of Armed Conflict*. 29 March (UNESCO document CLT/CIH/MCO/2002/PI/H/1). (A French version is also available: *Mise en oeuvre nationale des dispositions pénales du chapitre 4 du deuxième Protocole relatif à la Convention de La Haye de 1954 pour la protection des biens culturels en cas de conflit armé*. Report edited by R. O'Keefe, Cambridge University, 29 March 2002.)

———. The meaning of cultural property under the 1954 Hague Convention. *Netherlands International Law Review*, Vol. 46, No. 1, pp. 26–56.

Office fédéral de la protection civile. 1984–1985. *La protection des biens culturels*. Berne: Office fédéral de la protection civile.

Oppenheim, L. 1955. *International Law*, Vol. I. 8th edn. Edited by H. Lauterpacht. London: Longmans.

———. 1952. *International Law: A Treatise*, Vol. II. 7th edn. Edited by H. Lauterpacht. London: Longmans.

Oryslak, S. 1975. Ochrona zabytkow – obowiazkem panstwa i powinrroscia jego obywateli [The protection of historic monuments: the duty of the State and of its citizens]. *Biuletyn informacyjny Zarzadu muzéow i ochrony zabytkow* (Warsaw), No. 115, March–April, pp. 142–48.

Österreichische Gesellschaft für Kulturgüterschutz. 1995. *Der Kulturgüterschutz: Ein Aufruf zu transnationaler Aktion. Private Initiativen zwischen Interessen und Verantwortung*. Vienna: Österreichische Gesellschaft für Kulturgüterschutz.

———. 1983. *Vorsorge zum Schutz des kulturellen Erbes in Zeiten der Not und Gefahr. UNESCO-Konvention Den Haag 1954. Sonderausstellung Kulturgüterschutz*. Vienna: Österreichische Gesellschaft für Kulturgüterschutz.

Oxman, B. H. 1987 Jurisdiction of States. R. Bernhardt (ed.), *Encyclopedia of Public International Law*, Vol. 3. Amsterdam: North-Holland Publishing, pp. 45–69.

Oyer, H. E., III. 1999. The 1954 Hague Convention for the Protection of Cultural Property in the Event of Armed Conflict: is it working? A case study: the Persian Gulf War experience. *Columbia Journal of Law and the Arts*, Vol. 23, pp. 49–65.

Pabst, F. 2008. *Kulturgüterschutz in nicht-internationalen bewaffneten Konflikten*. Berlin: Duncker & Humblot.

Panzera, A. F. 1993. *La tutela internazionale dei beni culturali in tempo di guerra*. Turin: Giappichelli.

Parks, W. H. 1998. Protection of cultural property from the effects of war. M. Phelan (ed.), *The Law of Cultural Property and Natural Heritage: Protection, Transfer and Access*. Evanston, Ill.: Kalos Kapp Press, pp. 3/1–3/56.

———. 1997. The Protection of Civilians from Air Warfare. *Israel Yearbook on Human Rights*, Vol. 27, pp. 65–111.

————. 1995. 'Precision' and 'area' bombing: who did which, and when? *Journal of Strategic Studies*, Vol. 18, pp. 145–74.

————. 1990. Air war and the law of war. *Air Force Law Review*, Vol. 32, pp. 1–225.

Partsch, K. J. 1995. Protection of cultural property. D. Fleck. (ed.), *The Handbook of Humanitarian Law in Armed Conflicts*. Oxford: Oxford University Press, pp. 377–404.

Patchett, L. 2008. Articles 17–18, Activities to support World Heritage Fund. F. Francioni and F. Lenzerini (eds.), *The 1972 World Heritage Convention: A Commentary*. Oxford: Oxford University Press, pp. 289–304.

Pays-Bas. 1919. La protection des monuments et objets historiques et artistiques contre la destruction de la guerre. Proposition de la Société néerlandaise d'archéologie. *Revue générale de droit international public*, Vol. 26, p. 329.

Penna, L. R. 1986. State and individual responsibility for application of the Hague Convention. Istituto Internazionale di Diritto Umanitanio (ed.), *La protezione internazionale dei beni culturali/The International Protection of Cultural Property/La protection internationale des biens culturels*. Rome: Fondazione Europa Dragan, pp. 77–80.

Perow, A. 1936. *Roerich and his Banner of Peace*. Chicago: Rassvet.

Pfirter, D. 2001. Article 8(2)(b)(ix) – Attacking protected objects. R. S. Lee (ed.), *The International Criminal Court: Elements of Crimes and Rules of Procedure and Evidence*. Ardsley: Transnational Publishers, pp. 162–63.

Phuong, C. 2004. The protection of Iraqi cultural property. *International and Comparative Law Quarterly*, Vol. 53, pp. 985–98.

Pictet, J. S. 1985. *Une instituion unique en son genre: Le Comite International de la Croix-Rouge*. Geneva: Henry Dunant Institute.

————(ed.). 1952–60. *The Geneva Conventions of 12 August 1949: Commentary*. 4 vols. Geneva: ICRC.

Pignatelli y Meca, F. 2001. El Segundo Protocolo de la Convención de 1954 para la protección de los bienes culturales en caso de conflicto armado, hecho en La Haya el 26 de marzo de 1999. *Revista española de derecho militar*, Vol. 77, pp. 357–444.

Poncet, D. and Gully-Hart, P. 1986. Extradition: the European model. M. C. Bassiouni (ed.), *International Criminal Law*, Vol. II. Dobbs Ferry, N.Y.: Transnational Publishers, pp. 461–503.

Poulos, A. H. 2000. The Hague Convention for the Protection of Cultural Property in the Event of Armed Conflict: an historic analysis. *International Journal of Legal Information*, Vol. 28, No. 1, pp. 1–44.

Pradelle, G. de la. 2000. La compétence universelle. H. Ascensio, E. Decaux and A. Pellet (eds.), *Droit International Pénal*. Paris: Pédone, 2000, pp. 905–18.

Predome, G. 1950. Per una migliore protezione del patrimonio artistico monumentale in caso di guerra. *Rivista di studi politici internazionali*, Vol. 17, pp. 646–50.

Preux, J. de. 1986. La Convention de La Haye et le récent développement du droit des conflits armés. Istituto Internazionale di Dirtitto Umanitario (ed.), *La protezione internazionale dei beni culturali/The International Protection of Cultural Property/La protection internationale des biens culturels*. Rome: Fondazione Europa Dragan, pp. 107–17.

Prott, L. V. 2004. The prospects for the recovery of cultural heritage looted from Iraq: keynote address. International Bureau of the Permanent Court of Arbitration (ed.), *Resolution of Cultural Property Disputes: Papers Emanating from the Seventh PCA International Law Seminar, May 23, 2003*. The Hague: Kluwer Law International, pp. 23–29.

———. 1998. UNESCO and UNIDROIT: A partnership against trafficking in cultural objects. N. Palmer (ed.), *The Recovery of Stolen Art: A Collection of Essays*. London: Kluwer Law International, pp. 205–15.

———. 1996. The Protocol to the Convention for the Protection of Cultural Property in the Event of Armed Conflict (The Hague Convention), 1954. M. Briat and J. A. Freedberg (eds.), *Legal Aspects of International Trade in Art. International Sales of Works of Art*, Vol. 5. The Hague: Kluwer Law International, pp. 163–73.

———. 1988. Commentary: 1954 Hague Convention for the Protection of Cultural Property in the Event of Armed Conflict. N. Ronzitti (ed.), *The Law of Naval Warfare: A Collection of Agreements and Documents with Commentaries*. Dordrecht: Martinus Nijhoff, pp. 582–93.

———. 1983. International penal aspects of cultural protection. *Criminal Law Journal*, Vol. 7, pp. 207–17.

Prott, L. V. and O'Keefe, P. J. 1984. *Law and the Cultural Heritage*, Vol. I: *Discovery and Excavation*. Abingdon: Professional Books.

Przyborowska-Klimczak, A. 1989–1990. Les notions des 'biens culturels' et du 'patrimoine culturel mondial' dans le droit international. *Polish Yearbook of International Law*, Vol. 18, p. 51.

Quindry, F. E. 1931. Aerial bombardment of civil and military objectives. *Journal of Air Law*, Vol. 2, pp. 474–509.

Quynn, D. M. 1945. The art confiscation of the Napoleonic Wars. *The American Historical Review*, Vol. 50, pp. 437–60.

Ramji, J. and Van Schaack, B. (eds.). 2005. *Bringing the Khmer Rouge to Justice: Prosecuting Mass Violence before the Cambodian Courts*. Lewinston, N.Y.: Edwin Mellen Press.

Ratner, S. R. and Abrams, J. S. 2001. *Accountability for Human Rights Atrocities in International Law: Beyond the Nuremberg Legacy*. Oxford: Oxford University Press.

Redgwell, C. 2008. Article 2, Definition of natural heritage. F. Francioni and F. Lenzerini (eds.), *The 1972 World Heritage Convention: A Commentary*. Oxford: Oxford University Press, pp. 63–84.

Reichelt, G. 1985. La protection internationale des biens culturels. *Uniform Law Review*, Vol. 1, p. 42.

Renau, J. 1937. L'organisation de la défense du patrimoine artistique et historique espagnol pendant la guerre civile. *Mouseion* (Paris), 39–40, pp. 7–66.

Reuter, P. 1995. *Introduction to the Law of Treaties*. London: Kegan Paul International.

Riedel, E. H. 1982. Recognition of belligerency. R. Bernhardt (ed.), *Encyclopedia of Public International Law*, Vol. 4. Amsterdam: North-Holland Publishing, pp. 167–81.

Robertson A. H. and Merrills, J. G. 1996. *Human Rights in the World: An Introduction to the Study of the International Protection of Human Rights*. 4th edn. Manchester: Manchester University Press.

Rodgers, W. L. 1923. The laws of war concerning aviation and radio. *American Journal of International Law*, Vol. 17, pp. 629–40.

Rogers, A. P. V. 1996. *Law on the Battlefield*. 2nd edn. Manchester: Manchester University Press.

Rohn, P. H. 1997. *World Treaty Index*. 2nd edn. 5 vols. Buffalo: W. S. Hein (reprint of 1983 ed.).

Ronart, O. 1939. Le danger aérien et la sauvegarde des objets d'art aux Pays-Bas. *Revue générale de droit aérien*, Vol. 8, pp. 68–75.

Rothfield, L. (ed.). 2008. *Antiquities under Siege: Cultural Heritage Protection after the Iraq War*. Lanham, Md.: AltaMira Press.

Rousseau, C. 1983. *Le Droit des conflits armés*. Paris: Pédone.

Sabelli, D. 1997. La Convenzione sul patrimonio mondiale: limiti giuridico-politici. M. C. Ciciriello (ed.), *La protezione del patrimonio mondiale culturale e naturale a venticinque anni dalla Convenzione dell'UNESCO*. Naples: Editoriale Scientifica.

Sahovic, M. (ed.). 1972. *Principles of International Law Concerning Friendly Relations and Cooperation*. Dobbs Ferry, N.Y.: Oceana Publications.

Saint-Paul, G. 1938. *Le Lieu de Genève,* exposé général, Strasbourg: Imprimerie Arrault et Cie, Tours.

Salmon, J. (ed.). 2001. *Dictionnaire de droit international public.* Brussels: Bruylant.

Sandholtz, W. 2007. *Prohibiting Plunder: How Norms Change.* New York: Oxford University Press.

———. 2005. The Iraqi National Museum and international law: a duty to protect. *Columbia Journal of Transnational Law,* Vol. 44, No. 1, pp. 185–240.

Sandoz, Y. 2002. Competing priorities: placing cultural property on the humanitarian law agenda. M.-T. Dutli (ed.), *Protection of Cultural Property in the Event of Armed Conflict. Report on the Meeting of Experts (Geneva, 5–6 October 2000).* Geneva: ICRC, pp. 21–25.

———. 1995. *Implementing International Humanitarian Law.* Geneva: Henry Dunant Institute.

———. 1979. Le droit d'initiative du Comite international de la Croix-Rouge. *German Yearbook of International Law,* Vol. 22, pp. 352–72.

Sandoz, Y., Swiniarski, C. and Zimmermann, B. (eds.). 1987. *Commentary on the Additional Protocols of 8 June 1977 to the Geneva Conventions of 12 August 1949.* Geneva: ICRC, Martinus Nijhoff.

Sands, P. and Klein, P. (eds.). 2001. *Bowett's Law of International Institutions.* 5th edn. London: Sweet & Maxwell.

Sarholz, H. 1959. Der Schutz des Kulturguts im Kriege. Eine völkerrechtliche und sittliche Verpflichtung im Frieden. *Ziviler Luftschutz,* Vol. 23, pp. 343–49.

Sartori, V. 2006. *ARS in bello: Piccola storia dei beni culturali in Guerra.* Florence: Firenze Atheneum.

Schabas, W. A. 2007. *An Introduction to the International Criminal Court.* 3rd edn. Cambridge: Cambridge University Press.

———. 2002a. *The Abolition of the Death Penalty in International Law.* 3rd edn. Cambridge: Cambridge University Press.

———. 2002b. Penalties. A. Cassese, P. Gaeta and J. R. W. D. Jones (eds.), *The Rome Statute of the International Criminal Court: A Commentary.* 2 vols. Oxford: Oxford University Press, Vol. II, pp. 1497–1534.

———. 1997. Sentencing by international tribunals: a human rights approach. *Duke Journal of Comparative and International Law,* Vol. 7, pp. 461–517.

Scheer, B. D. 1973. *Schutz von Kulturgut bei bewaffneten Konflikten.* Bonn: Bundesamt für zivilen Bevölkerungsschutz.

Scheffer, D. J. 1998. America's stake in peace, security and justice. *ASIL Newsletter*, September-October. http://www.state.gov/www/policy_remarks/1998/980831_scheffer_icc.html

Schindler, D. and Toman, J. (eds.). 2004. *The Laws of Armed Conflicts: A Collection of Conventions, Resolutions and Other Documents.* 4th edn. Dordrecht: Martinus Nijhoff.

Schneider, J. T. 1935. *Report to the Secretary of the Interior on the Preservation of Historic Sites and Building.* Washington, DC: US Department of the Interior.

Schorlemer, S. von. 2004. Legal changes in the regime of the protection of cultural property in armed conflict. *Art, Antiquity and Law*, Vol. 9, No. 1, pp. 43–77.

Schweizerisches Institut für Verwaltungskurse an der Hochschule St. Gallen. 1967a. *Der Kulturgüterschutz bei bewaffneten Konflikten. Vortäge des Schweizerischen Verwaltungskurse an der Hochschule St. Gallen der 122. Kurs für Wirtschafts und Sozialwissenschaften am 10. und 11, April 1967 in St. Gallen.* St. Gallen: Schweizerisches Institut für Verwaltungskurse an der Hochschule St. Gallen.

———. 1967b. *Kurses der Schweizerischen Verwaltungskurse an der Hochschule St. Gallen fur Wirtschafts- und Sozialwissenschaftten am 10. und 11. April 1967, St. Gallen.* St. Gallen: Schweizerisches Institut für Verwaltungskurse an der Hochschule St. Gallen.

Scovazzi, T. 2008. Articles 8–11, World Heritage Committee and World Heritage List. F. Francioni and F. Lenzerini (eds.), *The 1972 World Heritage Convention: A Commentary.* Oxford: Oxford University Press, pp. 147–74.

Secrétariat général des 'Lieux de Genève' 'Zone Blanche', Association internationale pour la protection des populations civiles et des monuments historiques (ed.). 1943. *La guerre moderne et la protection des civils: Vers la solution de cet angoissant problème.* Geneva: Château Banquet.

Seidl-Hohenveldern, I. 1993. La protection internationale du patrimoine culturel national. *Revue générale de droit international public*, Vol. 97, p. 395.

———. 1992. Artefacts as national cultural heritage and as common heritage to mankind. E. G. Bello and B. A. Ajibola (eds.), *Essays in Honor of Judge Taslim Olawale Elias.* Dordrecht: Martinus Nijhoff, pp. 163–68.

Seršić, M. 1996. Protection of cultural property in time of armed conflict. *Netherlands Yearbook of International Law*, Vol. 27, pp. 3–38.

Shearer, I. A. 1971. *Extradition in International Law.* Manchester: Manchester University Press.

Shibayev, V. A. 1935. *Roerich Pact Signed by United States and All Latin American Governments.* Lahore: Lion Press.

Siegrist, M. 1928. *Nicholas Roerich, Apostle of World Unity.* New York: Roerich Museum.

Sieroszewski, W. 1974. *Ochrona prawna dobr kultury na forum miedzynarodowym w swietle legislacji UNESCO* [*The Legal Protection of Cultural Goods in the International Forum in the Light of UNESCO Legislation*]. Warsaw: Biblioteka muzealnictwa i ochrony zbytkow.

———. 1973. Konwencja haska z 1954 r. a konflikt na Bliskirn Wschodzie [The Hague Convention of 1954 and the Middle-East conflict]. *Ochrana zabytkow* (Warsaw), Vol. 26, No. 3, pp. 170–75.

Simpson, E. (ed.). 1997. *The Spoils of War: World War II and Its Aftermath; The Loss, Reappearance, and Recovery of Cultural Property.* New York: Abrams.

Sladek, G. (ed.). 1993. *Das kulturelle Erbe im Risiko der Modernität. Salzburger Symposium der Österreichischen Gesellschaft für Kulturgüterschutz.* Vienna: Österreichische Gesellschaft für Kulturgüterschutz.

Smirnoff, F. 1941. *Historische Baudenkmäler und deren Rechtsschutz in Kriegszeiten.* Zürich: Fretz und Wasmuth.

Sohn, L. B. (ed.). 1971–1974. Basic Documents on African Regional Organization. 4 Vols. Dobbs Ferry, N.Y.: Oceana Publications.

Solf, W. A. 1992. Cultural property, Protection in armed conflict. R. Bernhardt (ed.), *Encyclopedia of Public International Law,* Vol. 1. Amsterdam: North-Holland Publishing, pp. 892–97.

Solf, W. A. and Roach, J. A. (eds.). 1987. *Index of International Humanitarian Law.* Geneva: ICRC.

Spaigh, J. M. 1947. *Air Power and War Rights.* 3rd edn. London: Longmans, Green.

———. 1944. Legitimate objectives in air warfare. *British Yearbook of International Law,* Vol. 21, pp. 158–64.

Spieker, H. 2000. The protection of cultural property. V. Epping, H. Fischer and W. Heintschel von Heinegg (eds.), *Brücken nauen und begehen. Festschrift für Knut Ipsen zum 65. Geburtstag.* Munich: C. H. Beck, pp. 357–81.

Stavraki, E. 1996. *La Convention pour la protection des biens culturels en cas de conflit armé: une convention du droit international humanitaire.* Athens: Sakkoulas.

Stein, T. 1997. Extradition. R. Bernhardt (ed.), *Encyclopedia of Public International Law*, Vol. 2. Amsterdam: North-Holland Publishing, pp. 327–34.

Stone, P. G. and Farchakh Bajjaly, J. (eds.). 2008. *The Destruction of Cultural Heritage in Iraq*. Woodbridge, UK: Boydell Press.

Strahl, R. 1979. The retention and retrieval of art and antiquities through international and national means: the tug of war over cultural property. *Brooklyn Journal of International Law*, Vol. 5, No. 1, pp. 103–28.

Strebel, H. 1997. Martens Clause. R. Bernhardt (ed.), *Encyclopedia of Public International Law*, Vol. 3, pp. 326–27.

––––––. 1955–1956. Die Haager Konvention zum Schutze der Kulturgüter im Falle eines bewaffneten Konflikts vom 14 Mai 1954. *Zeitschrift für ausländisches öffentliches Recht und Völkerrecht*, Vol. 16, pp. 35–75.

Streiff, S. 1970a. Der Kulturgüterschild. Das Kennzeichen das Haager Abkommens für den Schutz von Kulturgut bei bewaffneten Konflikten. *Zivilschutz*, Vol. 17, pp. 161–64.

––––––. 1967. Das Personal des Kulturgüterschutzes. Der Kulturgüterschutz bei bewaffneten Konflikten. _, pp. 105–110.

––––––. 1965. Kulturgüterschutz als nationale Aufgabe und völkerrechtliche Verpflichtung. *Zivilschutz*, Vol. 12, pp. 44–49.

Sujanova, O. 1973. Ochrana pamiatok v pripade mimoriadnych okolností. *Muzeum* (Bratislava), Vol. 18, No. 4, pp. 212–19.

Svensma, T. P. 1954. The Intergovernmental Conference and Convention for the Protection of Cultural Property. *Library Review* (Copenhagen, Ejnar Munksgaard), pp. 76–83.

Symonides, J. 1997. Towards the amelioration of the protection of cultural property in times of armed conflict: recent UNESCO initiatives concerning the 1954 Hague Convention. *Human Person and International Law*, Vol. 2, pp. 1533–47.

Symposium organized on the occasion of the 30th Anniversary of the Hague Convention on the Protection of Cultural Property in the Event of Armed Conflict, in co-operation with UNESCO, ICRC, Facultà di Scienze Politiche, C. Alfieri, Centro studi turistici di Firenze under the auspices of the Italian Ministries of Cultural Property and Tourism, Florence, 22–24 November 1984. Istituto Internazionale di Diritto Umanitario (ed.), *La protezione internazionale dei beni culturali/The International Protection of Cultural Property/La protection internationale des biens culturels*. Rome: Foundazione Europa Dragan, 1986.

Tanja, G. J. 1994. Recent developments concerning the law for the protection of cultural property in the event of armed conflict. *Leiden Journal of International Law*, Vol. 7, No. 1, pp. 115–25.

Taudon, R. C. 1936. Roerich Pact Movement. *Allahbad Leader*, 17 October.

Taylor, F. H. 1948. *The Taste of Angels: A History of Art Collecting from Rameses to Napoleon*. Boston: Little, Brown & Co.

Taylor, R. S. 2003. Better later than never: Cambodia's Joint Tribunal. J. E. Stromseth (ed.), *Accountability for Atrocities: National and International Responses*. Ardsley: Transnational Publishers , pp. 237–79.

Taylor, T. 1992. *The Anatomy of the Nuremberg Trials*. New York: Alfred A. Knopf.

Terrier, F. 2002. Powers of the trial chamber. A. Cassese, P. Gaeta and J. R. W. D. Jones (eds.), *The Rome Statute of the International Criminal Court: A Commentary*. 2 vols. Oxford: Oxford University Press, Vol. II, pp. 1259–76.

Thurlow, M. D. 2005. Protecting cultural property in Iraq: how American military policy comports with international law. *Yale Human Rights and Development Law Journal*, Vol. 8, pp. 153–87.

Toman, J. 2008. The control system under the 1954 Hague Convention and its 1999 Second Protocol. P. Meerts (ed.), *Culture and International Law*. The Hague: Hague Academic Press, pp. 121–53.

——. 2005. The Hague Convention – A decisive step taken by the international community. *Museum International*, No. 228, pp. 7–31.

——. 1996. *The Protection of Cultural Property in the Event of Armed Conflict: Commentary on the Hague Convention of 14 May 1954*. Aldershot: Dartmouth/Paris: UNESCO.

——. 1984. La protection des biens culturels dans les conflits armés internationaux: cadre juridique et institutionnel. C. Swinarski (ed.), *Etudes et essais sur le droit international humanitaire et sur les principes de la Croix-Rouge en l'honneur de Jean Pictet/Studies and Essays on International Humanitarian Law and Red Cross Principles in Honour of Jean Pictet*. Geneva: ICRC, pp. 559–80.

——. 1983. *Le Mandat de l'UNESCO dans la mise en oeuvre de la Convention de La Haye pour la protection des biens culturels en cas de conflit armé*. Paris: UNESCO.

Treue, W. 1957. *Kunstraub: Über die Schicksale von Kunstwerken in Krieg, Revolution und Frieden*. Düsseldorf: Droste Verlag. English translation:

Art Plunder: The Fate of Works of Art in War, Revolution and Peace. London: Methuen, 1960.

Tulpinck, C. 1935. Les oeuvres de l'intelligence devant la guerre. *Revue de l'art ancien et moderne*, Vol. 68, pp. 326–30.

Tyler, B. J. 1999. The stolen museum: have United States art museums become inadvertent fences for stolen art works looted by the Nazis in World War II? *Rutgers Law Journal*, Vol. 30, No. 2, pp. 441–71.

UNESCO. 2004. *Basic Texts*. Paris: UNESCO. http://unesdoc.unesco.org/images/0013/001337/133729e.pdf

——. 1970. *Information on the Implementation of the Convention for the Protection of Cultural Property in Case of Armed Conflict, The Hague, 1954.* UNESCO/SHC/MD/6, 30 April. http://unesdoc.unesco.org/images/0012/001269/126960eb.pdf

——. 1967. *Protection of cultural property in case of armed conflict: Information on the Implementation of the Convention for the Protection of Cultural Property in Cases of Armed Conflict, The Hague, 1954.* Paris, UNESCO/SHC/MD/1.

——. 1956. *Final Act of the Intergovernmental Conference on the Protection of Cultural Property in the Event of Armed Conflict, The Hague, 1954.* Paris: UNESCO. http://unesdoc.unesco.org/images/0008/000824/082464mb.pdf

——. 1953. *Texts used as precedents for the Draft Convention for the Protection of Cultural Property in the Event of Armed Conflict.* UNESCO/ODG/2, 11 August.

UNESCO. *Report on the Implementation of the 1954 Hague Convention for the Protection of Cultural Property in the Event of Armed Conflict and its two 1954 and 1999 Protocols: Report on the Activities from 1995 to 2004.* UNESCO, Document Ref. CLT-2005/WS/6, Paris. http://unesdoc.unesco.org/images/0014/001407/140792e.pdf

United Nations (UN). 1996. *The Work of the International Law Commission.* 5th edn. New York: United Nations.

Unverhau, K. 1955. *Der Schutz von Kulturgütern bei bewaffneten Konflikten.* Göttingen University, Ph.D. thesis.

US Committee on Conservation of Cultural Resources. 1942. *The Protection of Cultural Resources Against the Hazards of War: A Preliminary Handbook.* Washington, DC: National Resources Planning Board. http://www.archive.org/stream/protectionofcult00uscorich#page/n1/mode/2up

Van den Wyngaert, C. and Dugard, J. 2002. Non-applicability of statute of limitations. A. Cassese, P. Gaeta and J. R. W. D. Jones (eds.), *The Rome*

Statute of the International Criminal Court: A Commentary. 2 vols. Oxford: Oxford University Press, Vol. I, pp. 873–88.

Varlamoff, M. T. 2004. The International Committee of the Blue Shield and the protection of cultural heritage in the event of armed conflict. *Revue de droit militaire et de droit de la guerre*, Vol. 43, No. 1–2, pp. 175–83.

Vedovato, G. 1961. La protezione del patrimonio storico artistico e culturale nella guerra moderna. *Recueils de la Société Internationale de Droit Pénal Militaire et Droit de la Guerre*, Vol. 2, pp. 117–39.

———. 1954. *Il patrimonio storico-artistico-culturale e la guerra aerea.* Prolusione inaugurale dell'Anno academico 1953–1954. Florence: Scuola di guerra aerea.

———. 1944. La protezione internazionale dei monumenti storici contro le offense aeree. *Rivista di studi politici internazionali*, Vol. 11, pp. 39–54. Reprinted in under the same title in: G. Vedovato, *Diritto internazionale bellico: tre studi.* Florence: Sansoni, pp. 173–217.

Venturini, G. 2001. War crimes in international armed conflicts. M. Politi and G. Nesi (eds.), *The Rome Statute of the International Criminal Court: A Challenge to Impunity.* Aldershot: Ashgate, pp. 95–105.

Vergier-Boimond, J. 1938. *Villes sanitaires et cités d'asile: contribution à l'étude des moyens de protection des formations sanitaires de l'armée et des populations civiles dans la guerre moderne.* Paris: Editions internationales.

Verri, P. 1992. *Dictionary of the International Law of Armed Conflict.* Geneva: ICRC.

———. 1985. The condition of cultural property in armed conflict: from antiquity to World War II. *IRRC*, No. 752, pp. 67–85; No. 753, 127–39.

Visscher, C. de. 1970. *Théories et réalités en droit international public.* 4th edn. Paris: Pédone.

———. 1957. *Theory and reality in public international law.* Translated from the French into English by E. Corbett. Princeton: Princeton University Press.

———. 1949. International protection of works of art and historic monuments. *International Information and Cultural Series*, Vol. 8, pp. 821–71.

———. 1935. La protection internationale des objets d'art et des monuments historiques. *Revue de droit international et de legislation comparée*, Vol. 16, pp. 32–7, 246–88.

Vrdoljak, A. F. 2008. Article 14, the Secretariat and support of the World Heritage Committee. F. Francioni and F. Lenzerini (eds.), *The 1972 World Heritage Convention: A Commentary.* Oxford: Oxford University Press, pp. 243–68.

Wachter, O. 1975. *Restaurierung und Erhaltung von Büchern, Archivalien und Graphiken. Mit Berücksichtigung des Kulturgüterschutzes laut Haager Konvention von 1954.* Vienna: H. Böhlaus.

Walton, K. D. 1999. Leave no stone unturned: the search for art stolen by the Nazis and the legal rules governing restitution of stolen art. *Fordham Intellectual Property Media & Entertainment Law Journal*, Vol. 9, No. 2, pp. 549–623.

Ward, B. 1994. War damage: the cultural heritage of Bosnia-Herzegovina. London Seminar 25, November 1993. *International Journal of Cultural Property*, Vol. 3, No. 2, pp. 355–57.

Wehberg, H. 1915. Der Schutz der Kunstwerke im Kriege. *Museumskunde*, Vol. 11, pp. 49–68.

Weidenbaum, P. 1939. Necessity in international law. *Transactions of Grotius Society*, Vol. 24, pp. 105–32.

Wenger, C. F. 1987. Article 53. Y. Sandoz, C. Swiniarski and B. Zimmermann (eds.), *Commentary on the Additional Protocols of 8 June 1977 to the Geneva Conventions of 12 August 1949.* Geneva: ICRC, Martinus Nijhoff, nos. 2064 ff.

Wilhelm, R.-J. 1955. The 'Red Cross of monuments': chronicle. *IRRC, English Supplement*, No. VIII, pp. 76–87, 118–23.

Wilkie, N. C. 2008. Governmental agencies and the protection of cultural property in times of war. L. Rothfield (ed.), *Antiquities under Siege: Cultural Heritage Protection after the Iraq War.* Lanham, Md.: AltaMira Press, pp. 237–48.

Williams, S. A. 1978. *The International and National Protection of Movable Cultural Property: A Comparative Study.* Dobbs Ferry, N.Y.: Oceana Publications.

Wilson, A. T. 1933. The laws of war in occupied territory. *Transactions of the Grotius Society*, Vol. 18, pp. 17–38.

Wissbroecker, D. 2004. Six Klimts, a Picasso, and a Schiele: recent litigation attempts to recover Nazi stolen art. *DePaul Journal of Art and Entertainment Law*, Vol. 14, No. 1, pp. 39–71.

Wolfrum, R. 2003. Protection of cultural property in armed conflict. *Israel Yearbook on Human Rights*, Vol. 32, pp. 305–38.

Woudenberg, N. van. 2008. Second Protocol to the 1954 Hague Convention for the Protection of Cultural Property in the Event of Armed Conflict: Dutch involvement. P. Meerts (ed.), *Culture and International Law.* The Hague: Hague Academic Press, pp. 167–82.

Wyss, M. P. 1992a. *Kultur als eine Dimension der Völkerrechtsordnung. Vom Kulturgüterschutz zur internationalen Kooperation.* Schweizer Studien zum internationalen Recht, No. 79. Zürich: Schulthess.

Wyss, M. P. 1992b. The protection of the cultural heritage and its legal dimensions. The Heidelberg Symposium 22–23 June 1990. *International Journal of Cultural Property*, Vol. 1, pp. 232–38.

Zargar, A. and Samadi, Y. 1993. Experiences of the Islamic Republic of Iran in the preservation of cultural property against war damages (The Hague Convention, 1954). *Humanitäres Völkerrecht*, Vol. 6, No. 4, pp. 213–16.

Zietelman, E. 1917. Der Krieg und die Denkmalpflege. *Zeitschrift für Völkerrecht*, Vol. 10, pp. 1–19.

NOTE:

For further bibliographical information, particularly on cultural property and international humanitarian law, see the following:

ICRC and Henry Dunant Institute. 1987. *Bibliography of International Humanitarian Law Applicable in Armed Conflicts.* 2nd edn. Geneva: ICRC and Henry Dunant Institute.

Fiedler, W. and Turner, S. 2003. *Bibliographie zum Recht des Internationalen Kulturgüterschutzes/Bibliography on the Law of the International Protection of Cultural Property.* Berlin: de Gruyter Recht.

INDEX

Achevé d'imprimer en décembre 2009
sur les presses de la Nouvelle Imprimerie Laballery
58500 Clamecy
Dépôt légal : décembre 2009
Numéro d'impression : 912013

Imprimé en France

La Nouvelle Imprimerie Laballery est titulaire de la marque Imprim'Vert®